THINK
PUBLIC RELATIONS

DENNIS L. WILCOX
San Jose State University

GLEN T. CAMERON
University of Missouri

BRYAN H. REBER
University of Georgia

JAE-HWA SHIN
University of Southern Mississippi

Allyn & Bacon

Boston Columbus Indianapolis New York San Francisco Upper Saddle River
Amsterdam Cape Town Dubai London Madrid Milan Munich Paris Montreal Toronto
Delhi Mexico City Sao Paulo Sydney Hong Kong Seoul Singapore Taipei Tokyo

Senior Acquisitions Editor: Jeanne Zalesky
Editorial Assistant: Stephanie Chaisson
Development Manager: Meg Botteon/David Kear
Development Editor: Erin Mulligan
Associate Development Editor: Angela Pickard
Marketing Manager: Wendy Gordon
Media Producer: Megan Higginbotham
Project Coordination, Text Design, and Electronic Page Makeup: Pre-Press PMG
Photo Researcher: Catherine Schnurr
Art Director, Cover: Anne Nieglos
Cover Designer: Anne DeMarinis
Cover Illustration/Photo: JGI/Jamie Grill/Blend Images/Alamy
Text Permissions: Sarah Bylund/Robyn Feller
Image Permissions: Zina Arabia/Catherine Schnurr
Manufacturing Buyer: Mary Ann Gloriande
Printer and Binder: Quebecor World/Dubuque
Cover Printer: Lehigh-Phoenix Color/Hagerstown

For permission to use copyrighted material, grateful acknowledgment is made to the copyright holders on pp. 390–391, which are hereby made part of this copyright page.

Library of Congress Cataloging-in-Publication Data
   Think public relations / Dennis L. Wilcox . . . [et al.].
      p. cm.
   ISBN-13: 978-0-205-78169-0
   ISBN-10: 0-205-78169-1
 1. Public relations. I. Wilcox, Dennis L.
   HM1221.T55 2010
   659.2—dc22

                              2010013003

1 2 3 4 5 6 7 8 9 10—QWD—13 12 11 10

**Allyn & Bacon
is an imprint of**

ISBN-13: 978-0-205-78169-0
ISBN-10:   0-205-78169-1

>brief CONTENTS

on the cover:

p. 76–79 Trends in Today's Practice of Public Relations
p. 80–81 A Growing Professional Practice
p. 81–83 Professionalism, Licensing, and Accreditation

p. 42–59 Managing Competition and Conflict

p. 226–243 The Internet and Social Media

p. 290–305 Global Public Relations

p. 268–285 Events and Promotions

>detailed
CONTENTS

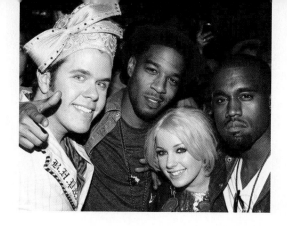

>acknowledgments

Many people have contributed to the production of this book. The authors wish to express our deep appreciation and admiration to development editor Erin Mulligan, in particular, who worked very closely with us on the manuscript and format. We also salute the outstanding support of Jeanne Zalesky, acquisitions editor, who had the vision and persistence to make it happen. Other individuals at Pearson/Allyn & Bacon who deserve our thanks include development manager David Kear, photo researcher Catherine Schnurr, and permission gurus Sarah Byland and Robyn Feller. We also wish to thank our respective spouses—Marianne, Marilyn, Sharon, and Tony—for their love and patience during the many nights and weekends we spent at our keyboards researching and writing this book.

DENNIS L. WILCOX

GLEN T. CAMERON

BRYAN H. REBER

JAE-HWA SHIN

>about the
AUTHORS

DENNIS L. WILCOX, Ph.D., is professor emeritus of public relations and past director of the School of Journalism and Mass Communications at San Jose State University, California. He is a Fellow and accredited (APR) member of the Public Relations Society of America (PRSA), former chair of the PRSA Educator's Academy, and past chair of the public relations division of Association for Education in Journalism and Mass Communication (AEJMC). Dr. Wilcox has written six books, including being the lead author of *Public Relations Strategies and Tactics* and *Public Relations Writing and Media Techniques*. His honors include PRSA's "Outstanding Educator," the Xifra-Award from the University of Girona (Spain), and an honorary doctorate from the University of Bucharest. He is active in the International Public Relations Association (IPRA) and a member of the Arthur W. Page Society, a group of senior communication executives. Dr. Wilcox regularly consults and gives lectures and workshops to students and professionals in a variety of nations. denniswilcox@msn.com

GLEN T. CAMERON, Ph.D., is Gregory Chair in Journalism Research and founder of the Health Communication Research Center at the University of Missouri. Dr. Cameron has authored more than 300 articles, chapters, award-winning conference papers, and books on public relations topics. A popular lecturer internationally, Dr. Cameron has received the Baskett-Mosse and Pathfinder awards for career achievement. The University of Missouri honored him in 2006 with the 21st Century Corps of Discovery Lectureship, which is given once each year by a globally recognized campus scholar. Dr. Cameron's ongoing public relations experience includes his management of more than $42 million in external funding of health public relations projects from sources such as the National Institutes of Health, the National Cancer Institute, Missouri Foundation for Health, the U.S. Department of Agriculture, the Centers for Disease Control and Prevention, the U.S Department of Defense, and Monsanto. Whenever he can, Dr. Cameron enjoys the rivers and mountains of his native Montana as well as wild spots around the world. camerong@missouri.edu

BRYAN H. REBER, Ph.D., is associate professor of public relations at the University of Georgia, Grady College of Journalism and Mass Communication. Dr. Reber teaches courses that offer an introduction to public relations, management, writing, and campaigns. On the graduate level, he teaches classes in topics including management, persuasion, campaign research, and public opinion. His research focuses on public relations theory, practice, pedagogy, and health communication and has been published in the *Journal of Public Relations Research, Journalism and Mass Communication Quarterly, Journal of Health Communication, Public Relations Review*, and *Journal of Broadcasting and Electronic Media*. Dr. Reber regularly presents his research at national and international academic conferences. He is the co-author of two books: *Gaining Influence in Public Relations* and *Public Relations Today: Managing Competition and Conflict*. Dr. Reber worked for 15 years in public relations at Bethel College, Kansas. He has conducted research for the Sierra Club, Ketchum, and the Georgia Hospital Association, among others. reber@uga.edu

JAE-HWA SHIN, Ph.D., Mph., is associate professor in the School of Mass Communication and Journalism at the University of Southern Mississippi. Dr. Shin is widely recognized as a prolific researcher in the field of public relations and has actively participated in the emerging development of public relations theory. She co-authored *Public Relations Today: Managing Conflict and Competition*, a text that incorporates her research, teaching, and professional experience. In addition, she has published her research in peer-reviewed journals such as *Public Relations Review, Journalism & Mass Communication Quarterly, Science Communication Journal*, and *Journal of Communication in Health Care*. Dr. Shin is an active presenter at national and international conferences such as those sponsored by the International Communication Association, National Communication Association, and Association for Education in Journalism and Mass Communication. Prior to her teaching at the University of Southern Mississippi, she worked as the Public Relations Director for the Korea Economic Research Institute of the Federation of Korean Industries. jaehwashin@yahoo.com

1 WHAT IS PUBLIC

A Busy Day

A day for Anne-Marie, an account executive in a St. Louis public relations firm, begins at 7 A.M. As she drinks her morning coffee, she checks RSS feeds on PR professional topics on her home computer, scanning blogs that cover industries she represents for her clients as well as her clients' websites. By 9 A.M., Anne-Marie is at her downtown office working on a news release about a client's new software product. She finishes the edits on the software product news release, gives it a once-over, and e-mails it to the client for approval. She attaches a note informing the client that an electronic news service can deliver the release to newspapers across the country later in the day. Two minutes later, Anne-Marie is managing a potentially serious issue brought to her attention by the firm's student intern, who has been collecting news clippings pertaining to another client so that the firm can take rapid, proactive responses to any emerging issues. She makes several high-priority e-mails and sets up a phone call meeting with her client to discuss next steps.

Anne-Marie's next activity is a brainstorming session with other staff members to generate creative ideas about a campaign to raise funds for the local AIDS foundation. Anne-Marie finds this client to be one of her most challenging because the nonprofit sector is so incredibly competitive. When she gets back to her office. She finds a number of telephone messages awaiting her attention. A reporter for a trade publication needs background information

RELATIONS?

on a story he is writing; a graphic designer has finished a rough draft of a brochure; a catering manager wants to finalize arrangements for a reception at an art gallery; and a video producer asks if she can attend the taping of a video news release next week.

Anne-Marie lunches with a client who wants her counsel on how to announce the closing of a plant in another state, a crisis communication challenge that is fraught with ethical quandaries. After lunch, Anne-Marie asks her assistant to check arrangements for a news conference next week in New York. She telephones a key editor to pitch a story about a client's new product. After that call is complete, she touches base with other members of her team, who are working on a 12-city media tour by an Olympic champion representing an athletic shoe company.

At 4 P.M., Anne-Marie checks several computer databases to gather information about a new client's industry. She also checks online news updates to determine if anything is occurring that involves or affects her clients. At 5 P.M., as she winds down from the day's hectic activities, she reviews news stories from a clipping service about one of her accounts, an association of strawberry producers. She is pleased to find that her feature story, which included recipes and color photos, appeared in 150 dailies.

1 Based on the description of Anne-Marie's day, how would you define public relations if a friend asked you what you were studying in this class?

2 Which components of public relations does Anne-Marie's workday involve?

3 How does Anne-Marie interact with journalists and use news coverage to inform her work throughout the day?

the challenge
OF PUBLIC
RELATIONS

think Which skills make PR professionals successful?

a s the chapter-opening scenario illustrates, the challenge of public relations (PR) is multifaceted. A public relations professional must have skills in written and interpersonal communication, research, negotiation, creativity, logistics, facilitation, and problem solving.

Indeed, those who seek a challenging career at the center of what's happening in modern organizations will find public relations to their liking. Owing to the variety of tasks—ranging from brochure layout to focus groups and polling data analysis—and the chance to work for clients and companies across the gamut of profit, nonprofit, and government sectors, more and more people like Anne-Marie are choosing the field of public relations every year.

CNN.com lists "public relations specialist" as one of the top fifty professions for job opportunity and salary potential. The 10-year job growth projection is a very healthy 24 percent, according to the U.S. Bureau of Labor Statistics.

global
SCOPE

public relations is a well-established academic subject that is taught throughout the world. Large numbers of students around the globe study public relations as a career field. In the United States, almost 200 universities have sequences or majors in public relations, and approximately 100 European universities offer studies in the subject. Many Asian universities—particularly those in Thailand, Singapore, and Malaysia—also offer major programs.

The public relations field is most extensively developed in the United States, where organizations spend almost $4.3 billion annually on public relations, according to estimates by Veronis Suhler Stevenson, a specialty banker in the communications industry.

Public relations in the United States is expected to become a $6.86 billion industry by 2012.

The Economist reports that the public relations market in China will amount to $1.8 billion in 2010, second only to Japan in the region.

China reports that more than **500,000 students** are studying aspects of public relations in its colleges and training institutions.

European companies spend approximately $3 billion each year on public relations. These expenditures continue to increase, reflecting the expansion of the European Union (EU) and the developing market economies of Russia and the now independent nations of the former Soviet Union.

Major growth is also occurring in the Asian public relations industry for several reasons. China is emerging as the "new frontier." Since opening it

to market capitalism, China's economy has been increasing at the rate of 8 percent annually. The public relations industry is sharing in this growth. The China International Public Relations Association (CIPRA) reports there are now 20,000 practitioners in the country.

Other nations, such as Malaysia, Korea, Thailand, Singapore, Indonesia, and India, are rapidly expanding their free-market economies as well, which creates a fertile environment for increased public relations activity. Latin America and Africa also present growth opportunities. A more detailed discussion of international public relations is found in Chapter 14.

A VARIETY OF definitions

People often define public relations by referring to some of its most visible techniques and tactics, such as coverage in a newspaper, a television interview with an organization's spokesperson, or the appearance of a celebrity at a special event. Knowing what professionals do every day can provide an important grounding about public relations, but it does not suffice as a definition.

Many people fail to understand that public relations is a process involving numerous subtle and far-reaching aspects beyond media coverage. It includes research and analysis, policy formation, programming, communication, and feedback from numerous publics. Its practitioners operate on two distinct levels—as advisers to their clients or to an organization's top management and as technicians who produce and disseminate messages in multiple media channels.

A number of definitions have been formulated over the years. In *Effective Public Relations*, Scott M. Cutlip, Allen H. Center, and Glen M. Broom state that "public relations is the management function that identifies, establishes, and maintains mutually beneficial relationships between an organization and the various publics on whom its success or failure depends." This approach represents the current belief that public

You can grasp the essential elements of effective public relations by remembering the following words and phrases: deliberate ... planned ... performance ... public interest ... two-way communication ... strategic ... that make up public relations activity.

DELIBERATE. Public relations activity is intentional. It is designed to influence, gain understanding, provide information, and obtain feedback.

PLANNED. Public relations activity is organized. Solutions to problems are discovered and logistics are thought out, with the activity taking place over a period of time. The activity is systematic, requiring research and analysis.

PERFORMANCE. Effective public relations is based on actual policies and performance. No amount of public relations will generate goodwill and support if an organization is unresponsive to community concerns.

PUBLIC INTEREST. Public relations activity should be mutually beneficial to the organization and the public; it provides for the alignment of the organization's self-interests with the public's concerns and interests.

TWO-WAY COMMUNICATION. Public relations is more than one-way dissemination of informational materials. It is equally important to solicit feedback.

STRATEGIC MANAGEMENT OF COMPETITION AND CONFLICT. Public relations is most effective when it is an integral part of decision making by top management. Public relations involves counseling and problem solving at high levels, not just the dissemination of information after a decision has been made by other leaders.

It isn't necessary to memorize any particular definition of public relations. It's more important to remember the key words used in the definitions that frame today's modern public relations.

think How can PR help to foster a mutually beneficial relationship between an organization and the public?

A Pacific Northwest timber company, despite a campaign with the theme "For Us, Every Day Is Earth Day," became known as the villain of Washington state because of its insistence on logging old-growth forests and bulldozing a logging road into a prime elk habitat.

Doritos PR Helps Steal the Super Bowl Away from Budweiser

IN 2009, **executives at Frito-Lay were frustrated; for two years Doritos ads had come in fourth in *USA Today*'s meter rankings of consumers' favorite Super Bowl ads. Budweiser had held the number one spot for a decade. To turn the tide, marketing and advertising executives at Frito-Lay partnered with pros at public relations firm Ketchum to develop a strategy to reach the target market of 16- to 24-year-olds.**

They encouraged their customers to develop consumer-created ads, aimed at knocking Budweiser out of the top ad meter spot. If a consumer could develop an ad that achieved that goal, he or she would be awarded $1 million by Frito-Lay. The role of the company's public relations representatives was to develop awareness of the campaign, drive consumers to enter the competition, and garner positive press before and after the Super Bowl.

Public relations practitioners researched Doritos consumer attitudes, monitored trends in consumer-generated content, "listened" to Doritos-related comments on the company's website as well as in the blogosphere, and identified trends in news cycles to determine opportunities in news coverage. Their research helped them understand that the most effective media to reach the primary target audience were blogs, social networking, and viral video websites. Of course, traditional media wouldn't be ignored because the secondary target audience—18- to 45-year-olds—would be reached by those media. Two public relations objectives were established: (1) drive consumers to submit and view entries on the company's contest website and (2) maintain news coverage of the contest for 6 months.

The PR team challenged Super Bowl and Doritos fans to create and submit ad entries and then to vote for their favorite

Advertisers paid an average of $3 million for a 30-second ad to be broadcast during the Super Bowl in 2009.

five entries. Frito-Lay targeted college newspapers, top film schools, and large universities as sources of potential entries; it employed Flickr and YouTube videos to raise awareness; and it encouraged grassroots supporters of entries to hold local events to drive online voting. Frito-Lay's PR partners also distributed audio news releases to more than 1,000 top-rated youth radio shows across the United States.

The public relations campaign met with great success, as described in *PRWeek*:

The Pittsburgh Steelers weren't the only winners on Super Bowl Sunday this year. Two brothers from Indiana, Joe and Dave Herbert, won Doritos' "Crash the Super Bowl" contest, and their "Free Doritos"

commercial aired during the game. But that wasn't all they won. When their ad hit number one in *USA Today*'s Super Bowl Ad Meter, the brothers scored again, pocketing a $1 million bonus. A media frenzy ensued. Within 48 hours, the brothers had done more than 50 interviews for outlets including *The Tonight Show with Jay Leno, Today,* CNN, and *USA Today.*

The public relations campaign exceeded expectations. It generated more than 1.4 billion media impressions, which were collectively worth more than $40 million. The contest website generated 2.5 million hits. The PR effort earned coverage in traditional and digital media—five stories in *USA Today,* three each in the *New York Times* and *Wall Street Journal,* and more than 360 online stories. The campaign succeeded in engaging enthusiasts on Facebook, YouTube, and Twitter as well.

Chris Kuechenmeister, director of PR at Frito-Lay, told *PRWeek,* "It's easily the best million dollars we ever spent.

1 Which public relations tactics did Frito-Lay and Ketchum use in this campaign?

2 How did public relations, marketing, and advertising intersect in this case? What was the role played by each?

3 Why is use of consumer-generated media an important tactic for public relations professionals to understand?

Source: Frito-Lay and Ketchum 2009 PRSA Silver Anvil winning entry.

relations is more than persuasion. Public relations should foster open, two-way communication and mutual understanding, while complying with the principle that an organization changes its attitudes and behaviors in the process. Change and accommodation occur for the organization—not just the target audience.

Although definitions of public relations have long emphasized the building of mutually beneficial relationships between the organization and its various publics, a more assertive definition has emerged over the past decade that forms the basis of this book. Glen T. Cameron, of the Missouri School of Journalism, defines public relations as the "strategic management of competition and conflict for the benefit of one's own organization—and when possible—also for the mutual benefit of the organization and its stakeholders or publics." This definition casts the public relations professional first and foremost as an advocate for the employer or client, but acknowledges the importance of mutual benefit when circumstances allow. It does *not* imply that the public relations professional acts only in the self-interest of the employer without due regard to honesty, integrity, and organizational transparency. Indeed, an ethical framework always guides the PR professional in his or her work.

> ❝The primary responsibility of the public relations counselor is to **provide** (management) **a thorough grasp of public sentiment.**❞
>
> Jim Osborne, former vice president of public affairs at Bell Canada

PUBLIC RELATIONS AS A **process**

Public relations is a process—that is, a series of actions, changes, or functions that bring about a result. Any number of attempts have been made to capture the public relations process, several of which are summarized here to provide a sense of how work in public relations unfolds. One way to describe the public relations process, and to remember its components, is to use the RACE acronym, which was first articulated by John Marston in his book *The Nature of Public Relations*.

think

How does research inform the actions that PR professionals take?

THE RACE ACRONYM

RESEARCH:
What is the problem or situation?

ACTION (program planning):
What is going to be done about it?

COMMUNICATION (execution):
How will the public be told?

EVALUATION:
Was the audience reached and what was the effect?

Diffusion-of-knowledge theorists call public relations people "linking agents." Sociologists refer to them as "boundary spanners," because they act to transfer information between two systems. As the concluding lines of the official statement on public relations by the Public Relations Society of America (PRSA) note: "The public relations practitioner utilizes a variety of professional communication skills and plays an integrative role both within the organization and between the organization and the external environment."

Official Statement on Public Relations

Public relations helps our complex, pluralistic society to reach decisions and function more effectively by contributing to mutual understanding among groups and institutions. It serves to bring private and public policies into harmony.

As a management function, public relations encompasses the following:

- Anticipating, analyzing, and interpreting public opinion, attitudes, and issues that might impact, for good or ill, the operations and plans of the organization.
- Counseling management at all levels in the organization with regard to policy decisions, courses of action, and communication, and taking into account their public ramifications and the organization's social or citizenship responsibilities.

- Researching, conducting, and evaluating, on a continuing basis, programs of action and communication to achieve informed public understanding necessary to the success of an organi-zation's aims. These may include marketing, financial, fund-raising, employee, community or government relations, and other programs.
- Planning and implementing the organization's efforts to influence or change public policy.
- Setting objectives, planning, budgeting, recruiting and training staff, and developing facilities—in short, managing the resources needed to perform all of the above.
- Examples of the knowledge that may be required in the professional practice of public relations include communication arts, psychology, social psychology, sociology, political science, economics, and the principles of management and ethics. Technical knowledge and skills are required for opinion research, public issues analysis, media relations, direct mail, institutional advertising, publications, film/video productions, special events, speeches, and presentations.

In helping to define and implement policy, the public relations practitioner utilizes a variety of professional communication skills and plays an integrative role both within the organization and between the organization and the external environment.

The public relations process also may be conceptualized in several steps. The PR Casebook example from page 7 is detailed in the steps outlined below.

In Step A, Frito-Lay used primary and secondary research to identify media trends and determine how to reach the 16- to 24-year-old target audience. During this process, the company essentially conducted a situation analysis— obtaining feedback from the target public, looking at what media were currently reporting on in its industry, examining past Super Bowl campaigns, and performing other forms of research.

In Step B, public relations personnel used the research results to establish objectives, which led to strategy development and recommendations to management. This is the adviser role of public relations.

In Step C, after management made its decisions, public relations personnel fully developed the "Crash the Super Bowl" campaign, including defining measurable objectives, strategies, and tactics; a timeline; a budget; and evaluation guidelines.

LEVEL ONE

A PR professionals at Frito-Lay used research and analysis to obtain insights into a problem from numerous sources, including comments posted on website forums and in blogs.

B The PR team analyzed these inputs and found that blogs, social networking, and viral video sites were essential media and recommended their inclusion in the campaign.

C Based on the company's policy, the PR team developed Doritos' "Crash the Super Bowl" contest campaign and secured approval from management.

Public relations is a cyclical process. Feedback leads to assessment of the program, an essential element of project refinement and development.

The PR team executed a program of action called the communication step. For the Doritos campaign, the communication step included inviting fans to vote online for ads and targeting college media.

In an effort to capture both informal and formal feedback about the communication process and its impact, Frito-Lay closely monitored entries about the process and its impact.

The PR campaign was evaluated in terms of media coverage, website hits, number of entries, and more to assess the effectiveness of the communication program and make any necessary adjustments.

D   **E**   **F**

LEVEL TWO

In Step D, the program was executed. Consumers were invited to create, submit, and vote on ads through the crashthesuperbowl.com website, distributing ANRs to youth radio programs, sending news releases to lifestyle reporters, developing social media networks, and more.

In Step E, the effectiveness of these actions was measured based on the number of entries, votes, and media coverage that the Doritos campaign garnered.

In Step F, the company undertook post-analysis and adjustment of the public relations program. The cycle was then repeated to solve related aspects of the problem that might require additional decision-making and action.

the components
OF PUBLIC RELATIONS

according to a monograph issued by the PRSA Foundation, public relations includes the following components:

- *Counseling*—Providing advice to management concerning policies, relationships, and communications.
- *Research*—Determining the attitudes and behaviors of groups to plan public relations strategies. Such research can be used to generate mutual understanding or influence and persuade publics.
- *Media Relations*—Working with mass media by seeking publicity or responding to their interests in the organization.
- *Publicity*—Disseminating planned messages through selected media to further an organization's interests.
- *Employee/Member Relations*—Responding to concerns, informing, and motivating an organization's employees or members.
- *Community Relations*—Undertaking activities with a community to maintain an environment that benefits both an organization and the community.
- *Public Affairs*—Developing effective involvement in public policy and helping an organization adapt to public expectations. The term "public affairs" is also used by government agencies to describe their public relations activities and by many corporations as an umbrella term to describe multiple public relations activities.
- *Government Affairs*—Relating directly with legislatures and regulatory agencies on behalf of an organization. Lobbying can be part of a government affairs program.
- *Issue Management*—Identifying and addressing issues of public concern that affect an organization.
- *Financial Relations*—Creating and maintaining investor confidence and building good relationships with the financial community. This aspect of public relations is also known as investor relations or shareholder relations.
- *Industry Relations*—Relating with other firms in the industry of an organization and with trade associations.
- *Development/Fund-Raising*—Demonstrating the need for and encouraging the public to support an organization, primarily through financial contributions.
- *Multicultural Relations/Workplace Diversity*—Relating with individuals and groups in various cultural groups.
- *Special Events*—Stimulating an interest in a person, product, or organization by means of a focused "happening" as well as activities designed to interact with publics and listen to them.
- *Marketing Communications*—Employing a combination of activities designed to sell a product, service, or idea, including advertising, collateral materials, publicity, promotion, direct mail, trade shows, and special events.

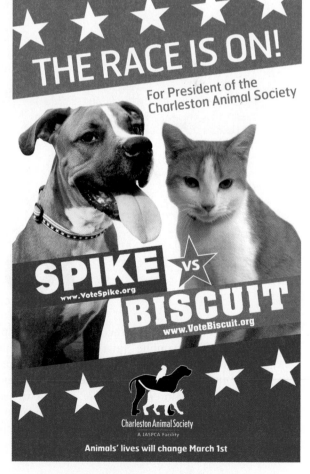

Working with a public relations firm, the Charleston (S.C.) Animal Society (CAS) organized a mock election campaign—Spike versus Biscuit—to raise awareness for the animal shelter. Spike the dog and Biscuit the cat announced platforms as they ran for president of the organization. The "candidates" produced posters, announced key endorsements, made campaign appearances, maintained Facebook diaries, and made YouTube commercials. The campaign raised awareness for a new $11 million adoption center and increased animal adoption rates in the Charleston area.

China has the fastest-growing public relations market in the world. The country, with more than 1.3 billion people, now has approximately 20,000 public relations practitioners and 3,000 public relations firms. Among them are a host of international public relations firms in residence, whose presence reflects China's emergence as a major economic power.

The China International Public Relations Association (CIPRA) estimated public relations revenues to be at least $300 million in 2002, and the industry continues to experience double-digit growth every year. In fact, it is estimated that China's public relations industry will accelerate this momentum, and the market could reach $1.8 billion in 2010. Currently, China's is the third-largest economy in the world.

The growth of Chinese public relations began to take off in the early 1990s as the country began to develop a market economy. Its gross domestic product (GDP) has rapidly expanded in recent years, and the central government has given a boost to the public relations industry by initiating significant mass media reforms, which in turn has led to a more friendly environment for business news and product publicity.

China also has joined the World Trade Organization (WTO), which has led to more public relations activity by international companies that are competing fiercely for customers around the globe. The biggest development, according to *The Economist,* is the soaring demand for public relations among Chinese companies

as they actively seek local consumers, foreign investment, and international outlets for their goods.

Undoubtedly, China's public relations practitioners will become leaders in the practice of digital public relations. There are an estimated 300 million Internet users and 650 million cell phone users in the country, a potentially receptive audience for digital, social media, and online public relations campaigns.

The 2008 Beijing Olympics and the promise of the 2010 Shanghai World Expo have only fueled expectations for the ongoing dynamic growth of public relations in China.

HOW PUBLIC RELATIONS DIFFERS FROM **journalism**

Writing is a common activity of both public relations professionals and journalists. Both also do their jobs in many of the same ways: They interview people, gather and synthesize large amounts of information, write in a journalistic style, and are trained to produce good copy on deadline. In fact, many reporters eventually change careers and become public relations practitioners.

This has led many people, including journalists, to draw the incorrect conclusion that little difference exists between public relations and journalism. For many people, public relations is simply being a "journalist-in-residence" for a nonmedia organization. In reality, despite sharing techniques, the two fields are fundamentally different in scope, objectives, audiences, and channels.

The channels that public relations professionals employ may combine mass media outlets—newspapers, magazines, radio, and television. They may also include direct mail, pamphlets, posters, newsletters, trade journals, special events, and messages shared via blogs, social media networks, or websites.

think Why is it important that journalists remain objective?

Scope

Public relations, as stated earlier, has many components, ranging from counseling to issues management and special events. Journalistic writing and media relations, although important, are only two of these elements. In addition, effective practice of public relations requires strategic thinking, problem-solving capability, and other management skills.

Objectives

Journalists gather and select information for the primary purpose of providing the public with news and information. Professors David Dozier and William Ehling state that in journalism, "communication activities are an end in themselves." Public relations personnel also gather facts and information for the purpose of informing the public, but their objective is different. Public relations communication activity is a means to the end—a way of manag-

ing competition and conflict in the best interests of the practitioner's employer. In other words, the objective is not only to inform, but also to change people's attitudes and behaviors so as to further an organization's goals and objectives.

Whereas journalists are objective observers, public relations personnel are advocates. Harold Burson, Chairman of the Burson-Marsteller public relations firm, makes the following point:

To be effective and credible, public relations messages must be based on facts. Nevertheless, we are advocates, and we need to remember that. We are advocates of a particular point of view—our client's or our employer's point of view. And while we recognize that serving the public interest best serves our client's interest, we are not journalists. That's not our job.

Audiences

Journalists write primarily for a mass audience—readers, listeners, or viewers of the medium for which they work. By definition, mass audiences are not well defined. A journalist on a daily newspaper, for

btw...

In its annual survey of marketing executives, *PRWeek* asked participants to rate the effectiveness of advertising, direct marketing, and public relations in terms of accomplishing certain marketing objectives. The respondents rated public relations as the "most effective" in the following categories:

> Premarket conditioning
> Strategy development
> Generating word of mouth
> Message development
> Building a brand's reputation
> Building corporate reputation
> Cultivating industry thought leaders
> Overcoming a crisis

Direct marketing was rated most effective in (1) launching a new product or service, (2) promoting a new product or service, (3) acquiring customers, (4) retaining customers, and (5) targeting niche audiences.

Advertising was rated most effective in only one category: building awareness.

Source: "Marketing Professionals Reveal the Role PR Plays in the Marketing Mix: Marketing Management Survey 2004." *PRWeek*, May 17, 2004, 1, 13–21.

HOW PUBLIC RELATIONS DIFFERS FROM advertising

Just as many people mistakenly equate publicity with public relations, so there is also some confusion about the distinction between publicity (one area of public relations) and advertising.

Although publicity and advertising both utilize mass media for dissemination of messages, the format and context are different. Publicity—information about an event, an individual or group, or a product—appears as a news item or feature story in the mass media. Material is prepared by public relations personnel and submitted to news departments for consideration. Reporters and editors, in their crucial role as gatekeepers, determine whether the material will be used or simply thrown away.

Advertising, in contrast, involves paid space and broadcast time. For example, organizations and individuals may contract with the advertising department of a mass media outlet for a full-page ad or a 60-second commercial. An organization writes the advertisement, decides which type style and graphics will be used, and controls where and when the advertisement runs. In other words, advertising involves renting space in a medium, where the advertiser has considerable control over the final message. The lion's share of revenues for all mass media comes from the sale of advertising space.

Other differences between public relations and advertising are summarized in the table below.

The major disadvantage of advertising, of course, is its cost. For example, a full-page color ad in the national edition of *Parade* magazine, which is distributed weekly in 470 newspapers to a circulation of 33 million, costs approximately $960,000. Costs for advertising campaigns that appear on network television can run into the millions of dollars. For this reason, companies are increasingly using a tool of public relations—product publicity—that is more cost-effective and often more credible because the message appears in a news context. One national study, for example, found that almost 70 percent of consumers place more weight on media coverage than advertising when determining their trust of companies and buying a product or service.

think — Is PR more cost-effective than advertising?

Advertising	Public Relations
Advertising works almost exclusively through mass media outlets.	Public relations relies on a number of communication tools—social media brochures, special events, speeches, news releases, feature stories, and so forth.
Advertising is addressed to external audiences—primarily consumers of goods and services	Public relations presents its message to specialized external audiences (stockholders, vendors, community leaders, environmental groups, and so on) and internal audiences (employees).
Advertising is readily identified as a specialized communication function.	Public relations is broader in scope, dealing with the policies and performance of the entire organization, from the morale of employees to the way telephone operators respond to calls.
Advertising is often used as a communication tool in public relations.	Public relations' activity often supports advertising campaigns.
Advertising's function is primarily to sell goods and services.	Public relations' function is to create a milieu in which an organization can thrive in complex, competitive environments. This goal calls for dealing with economic, social, and political factors that can affect the organization.

Public relations is the management process whose goal is to attain and maintain accord and positive behaviors among social groupings on which an organization depends to achieve its mission. Its fundamental responsibility is to build and maintain a hospitable environment for an organization.

VS

Marketing is the management process whose goal is to attract and satisfy customers (or clients) on a long-term basis to achieve an organization's economic objectives. Its fundamental responsibility is to build and maintain markets for an organization's products or services.

This difference between public relations and marketing is illustrated by the above descriptions of each field that a distinguished panel of educators and practitioners in public relations and marketing developed during a colloquium at San Diego State University.

HOW PUBLIC RELATIONS DIFFERS FROM marketing

Public relations is distinct from marketing in several ways, although their boundaries often overlap. Both deal with an organization's relationships and employ similar communication tools to reach the public. Both also have the ultimate purpose of ensuring an organization's success and economic survival. Public relations and marketing, however, approach this task from somewhat different perspectives.

Public relations is concerned with building relationships and generating goodwill for the organization; marketing is concerned with customers and selling products and services. Public relations does support sales, but additionally deals with a broad array of publics beyond customers. As James E. Grunig, editor of *Excellence in Public Relations*

and Communication Management, explains:

> [T]he marketing function should communicate with the markets for an organization's goods and services. Public relations should be concerned with all the publics of the organization. The major purpose of marketing is to make money for the organization by increasing the slope of the demand curve. The major purpose of public relations is to save money for the organization by building relationships with publics that constrain or enhance the ability of the organization to meet its mission.

Grunig also points out a fundamental difference between marketing and public relations in terms of how the public is described. Mar-

keting and advertising professionals tend to speak of "target markets," "consumers," and "customers." Public relations professionals tend to talk of "publics," "audiences," and "stakeholders"—that is, groups that are affected by or can affect an organization. According to Grunig, "Publics can arise within stakeholder categories—such as employees, communities, stockholders, governments, members, students, suppliers, and donors, as well as consumers."

How Public Relations Supports Marketing

Philip Kotler, professor of marketing at Northwestern University and the author of a leading marketing textbook, calls public relations the fifth "P" of marketing strategy,

which I call Marketing Public Relations (MPR) and the other public relations activities that define the corporation's relationships with its non-customer publics, which I label Corporate Public Relations (CPR).

Dennis L. Wilcox, in *Public Relations Writing and Media Techniques* (sixth edition), lists eight ways in which public relations activities contribute to fulfilling marketing objectives:

1 Developing new prospects for new markets, such as people who inquire after seeing or hearing a product release in the news media

2 Providing third-party endorsements—via newspapers, magazines, radio, and television—through news releases about a company's products or services, community involvement, inventions, and new plans

3 Generating sales leads, usually through articles in the trade press about new products and services

4 Paving the way for sales calls

5 Stretching an organization's advertising and promotional dollars through timely and supportive releases about it and its products

6 Providing inexpensive sales literature—articles about a company and its products can be reprinted as informative pieces for prospective customers

7 Establishing a corporation as an authoritative source of information on a given product

8 Helping to sell minor products that don't have large advertising budgets

> **In its market-support function, public relations is used to achieve a number of objectives. The most important of these are to raise awareness, to inform and educate, to gain understanding, to build trust, to make friends, to give people reasons to buy, and finally to create a climate of consumer acceptance.**
>
> Thomas Harris, *The Marketer's Guide to Public Relations*

which also includes the original four P's: product, price, place, and promotion. As he wrote in *Harvard Business Review*, "Public relations takes longer to cultivate, but when energized, it can help pull the company into the market."

When public relations is used to support directly an organization's marketing objectives, it is called marketing communications. This capacity was identified as a component of public relations earlier in the chapter.

A term, coined by Thomas Harris in his book *The Marketer's Guide to Public Relations*, is "marketing public relations." Harris says:

I make a clear distinction between those public relations functions [that] support marketing,

TOWARD AN INTEGRATED PERSPECTIVE: strategic COMMUNICATION

a lthough well-defined differences exist among the fields of advertising, marketing, and public relations, there is an increasing realization that an organization's goals and objectives can be best accomplished through an integrated approach, not just through marketing but through all communication functions. This understanding gave rise in the 1990s to such terms as *integrated marketing communications*, *convergent communications*, and *integrated communications*.

Several factors have fueled the trend toward integration:

1 The downsizing and reengineering of organizations have led to consolidated departments and reduced the number of staff members dedicated to various communication disciplines. As a result, one department, with fewer employees, is expected to do a greater variety of communication tasks.

2 Organizational marketing and communication departments are making do with tighter budgets. To avoid the high cost of advertising, many organizations are looking for alternative ways to deliver messages. These efforts may include building buzz by word of mouth, targeting influentials (i.e., "opinion leaders" or "trend setters"), web marketing, grassroots marketing, media relations and product publicity, and event sponsorship.

3 There is a growing realization that advertising, with its high costs, isn't the silver bullet that it used to be. Part of the problem is the increasing clutter of advertising (one estimate is that the average U.S. consumer is exposed to 237 ads each day, or about 86,000 each year) and advertising's general lack of credibility among consumers.

> **"We're beginning to see research that supports the superiority of PR over advertising to launch a brand. A recent study of 91 new product launches shows highly successful products are more likely to use PR-related activities than less successful ones... PR creates the brand. Advertising defends the brand."**
>
> Al and Laura Ries,
> *The Fall of Advertising and the Rise of PR*

Strategic communication requires grit and determination—but more specifically GRRIT—to successfully integrate advertising, marketing, and public relations:

G lobal/multicultural
R esearch based
R elationship focused
I nternet/new media oriented
T oolbox-driven tactics

GRRIT enables professionals to battle for success on behalf of an organization across a broad range of goals—from increased sales or better community relations, to brand loyalty or long-term donations for worthwhile causes.

The concept of integration reflects the increasing sophistication of organizations as they seek to use a variety of strategies and tactics to convey a consistent message. The metaphor might be the golfer with a variety of clubs in her bag. She may use one club (public relations) to launch a product, another club (advertising) to reinforce the message, and yet another club (Internet marketing) to actually sell the product or service to a well-defined audience.

APPLY YOUR KNOWLEDGE

WHAT WOULD YOU DO?

Managing Competition

Cold Stone Creamery is a relatively new ice cream company that faces stiff competition in the marketplace from established brands such as Ben & Jerry's, Baskin-Robbins, and Häagen-Dazs.

The first Cold Stone Creamery was founded in Tempe, Arizona, in 1998. Since then, the company has expanded to more than 500 stores (franchises) nationwide. In these stores, customers can personalize their servings by choosing a base flavor and a number of toppings. Employees mix the ice cream and the toppings by hand on a frozen granite stone (hence the company name and its market niche).

The challenge is to maximize store revenue and to increase market share. Research shows that the typical Cold Stone customer is a woman between the ages of 24 and 35, who brings her friends and family members with her.

The company has decided to do an integrated communications program for the next year that would involve public relations, advertising, and in-

store marketing promotions for some new products, such as ice cream cakes and non-fat flavors. The focus will be on enhancing the visibility of its stores at the local level and making Cold Stone a distinct brand among the clutter of other ice cream franchises in the community. Do some brainstorming. Which ideas and activities would you suggest? Remember—you need to be creative because you don't have a big budget.

4 It is now widely recognized that the marketing of products and services can be affected by public and social policy issues. For example, environmental legislation influences packaging and the content of products, a proposed luxury tax on expensive autos affects sales of those cars, and a company's support of Planned Parenthood or health benefits for same-sex partners may spur a product boycott.

The impact of such factors, which were not traditionally considered by marketing managers, has led many professionals to suggest that organizations should do a better job of integrating public relations and public affairs into their overall marketing considerations.

Jack Bergen, Senior Vice President of Corporate Affairs and Marketing for Siemens Corporation, agrees that organizations should do a better job of integrating public relations and public affairs into their overall marketing considerations. In an interview with *PRWeek*, he noted that public relations is the best place for leading strategy in marketing: "In developing strategy, you have multiple stakeholders. PR people understand the richness of the audiences that have an interest in the company; advertising just focuses on customers. Strategy is the development of options to accomplish an objective. PR people can develop these as they have the multiplicity of audiences and channels to use to reach them."

The concept of integration is less controversial than its implementation. It makes sense for an organization to coordinate its messages and communication strategies, but considerable discord arises on exactly how to accomplish this.

According to the consulting firm Osgood O'Donnell & Walsh, "The single biggest obstacle is company structure." In an article for *The Strategist*, the firm's principals wrote, "The communications functions—corporate communications, advertising, investor relations, and governmental affairs—are usually in different silos within companies, and interaction between their leaders is, for the most part voluntary (i.e., not required by senior management) and informal."

Nestlé raised awareness for its 80-year-old Butterfinger candy bar through an April Fools Day prank in which the company announced it was going to rename the candy bar "The Finger." The joke generated national buzz and a newfound consumer base for Butterfinger.

In some organizations, the marketing department has the dominant voice, and public relations is relegated to a support function in terms of techniques instead of playing a role in overall strategy development. This often means that public relations is responsible only for tactical work, such as creating product publicity, planning event promotions, and arranging media interviews at trade shows. Problems also arise in other organizations when advertising agencies attempt to do integrated programs. In many such cases, 90 percent of the communication budget is spent on advertising and 10 percent or less is spent on public relations.

Fortunately, such stories are becoming rarer as an increasing number of organizations have begun to emphasize the team approach to integrated communications. Experts in the various disciplines (advertising, public relations, direct promotion, marketing) now typically work as a team from the very beginning of a project. The role of public relations in the marketing mix is essentially defined by competition in the marketplace—competition between brands, competition for market share, and even competition for the loyalty of consumers. Chapter 3 looks at the role of public relations in managing conflict between organizations and groups—and even various publics—as a key component of the influence of public relations on the viability of companies and nonprofits alike.

9 Ways Public Relations Contributes to the Bottom Line

It is often said that public relations is a management process, not an event. Patrick Jackson, who has been active in the top leadership of the PRSA for many years and is one of the best-known public relations counselors in the United States, formulated this chart to show how public relations can contribute to the success of any organization.

PROCESS	PRINCIPAL ACTIVITIES	OUTCOMES
1 Awareness and information	Publicity, promotion, audience targeting	Pave the way for sales, fund-raising, stock offerings
2 Organizational motivation	Internal relations and communication	Build morale, teamwork, productivity, corporate culture
3 Issue anticipation	Research, liaison with audiences	Provide early warning on issues, constituency unrest, social/political anticipation
4 Opportunity identification	Interact with internal and external audiences	Discover new markets, products, audiences, methods, allies, issues
5 Crisis management	Respond to (or prevent) issues, coalition building	Protect position, retain allies and constituents, keep normal operations going despite battles
6 Overcoming executive isolation	Counsel senior managers	Encourage realistic, competitive, enlightened decisions
7 Change agent	Interact with internal and external audiences, research	Ease resistance to change, promote smooth transition
8 Social responsibility	Research, mount public interest projects and tie-ins, promote volunteerism/philanthropy	Create reputation, earn trust
9 Influencing public policy	Foster constituency relations, build coalitions, lobby, promote grassroots campaigns	Ensure public consent to activities, products, policies; remove political barriers

Summary

What Is Public Relations? p. 6

- Terms commonly incorporated into most definitions of public relations include *deliberate, planned, performance, public interest, two-way communication, strategic management of competition*, and *conflict management function.*

- Public relations is well established in the United States and throughout the world. Growth in this sector is currently strong in Europe and Asia, particularly China.

- The public relations process can be described with the RACE acronym: research, action, communication, evaluation.

What Are the Components of Public Relations? p. 11

- Public relations work includes counseling, media relations, publicity, community relations, governmental affairs, employee relations, investor relations, development/fund-raising, special events, and marketing communications.

How Does Public Relations Differ from Journalism? p. 12

- Although writing is an important activity in both public relations and journalism, the scope, objectives, and channels are different for each field.

How Does Public Relations Differ from Advertising? p. 14

- Publicity is just one area within public relations. It uses mass media to disseminate messages, as does advertising, although the format and context differ for PR and advertising.

- Publicity goes through media gatekeepers, who make the ultimate decision whether to use the material as part of a news story. Advertising involves paid space and time and is easily identified as being separate from news/editorial content.

How Does Public Relations Differ from Marketing? p. 15

- The functions of public relations often overlap with those of marketing. The primary purpose of public relations is to build relationships and generate goodwill with a variety of publics, however, whereas marketing focuses on customers and the sale of products and services.

- Public relations can be part of a marketing strategy. In such cases, it is often called marketing communications.

How Can an Integrated Approach to Public Relations Benefit an Organization? p. 17

- An organization's goals and objectives are best achieved by integrating the activities of advertising, marketing, and public relations to create a consistent message.

- Integration requires teamwork and the recognition that each field has strengths that complement and reinforce one another.

QUESTIONS

for *Review* and *Discussion*

1 What are the opportunities and obstacles for public relations practitioners?

2 There are many definitions of public relations. Of those found in this chapter, which do you think reflects reality best? Why?

3 Why is public relations so difficult to define? How would you define it based on what you know now?

4 Which of the steps in the public relations process do you think are most important to a successful campaign? Why?

5 Feedback is considered an important part of the public relations process. Why?

6 Many people think of public relations practitioners simply as "in-house journalists." What do you think are some of the major differences between public relations and journalism?

7 What do the authors of this book mean by the statement that public relations and journalism differ because of the "channels" they use?

8 What are the pros and cons of using public relations versus advertising to raise awareness about an organization's product or service?

9 It has been asserted that public relations creates brands, whereas advertising can only reinforce and defend a brand. Do you agree? Why or why not?

10 How does James Grunig differentiate between publics and stakeholders? How might this differentiation be useful in developing PR strategies?

11 How can PR fulfill marketing objectives?

12 Describe the concept of integrated communications (IC), which some people also call integrated marketing communications (IMC). Which four factors have led to the growth of integrated campaigns?

the THINK SPOT
www.thethinkspot.com

TACTICS

THE ECONOMIST

January 14, 2010 | NEW YORK From *The Economist* print edition

Other Firms' Suffering Has Bolstered the Public Relations Business

The past year or two has tested the idea that all publicity is good publicity, at least when it comes to business. Undeserved bonuses, plunging share prices, and government bail-outs, among other ills, have elicited the ire of the media and public—and created a bonanza for public relations firms. The recession has increased corporate demand for PR, analysts say, and enhanced the industry's status. "We used to be the tail n the dog," says Richard Edelman, the boss of Edelman, the world's biggest independent PR firm. But now, he continues, PR is "the organizing principle" behind many business decisions.

According to data from Veronis Suhler Stevenson (VSS), a private-equity firm, spending on public relations in America grew by more than 4% in 2008 and nearly 3% in 2009 to $3.7 billion. That is remarkable when compared with other forms of marketing. Spending on advertising contracted by nearly 3% in 2008 and by 8% in the past year. PR's position looks even rosier when word-of-mouth marketing, which includes services that PR firms often manage, such as outreach to bloggers, is included. Spending on such things increased by more than 10% in 2009.

Not all PR firms did as well as IPREX, a global consortium whose revenues increased by 14% last year. Many had to shed jobs, and some estimates show the industry's overall revenues declining, although not nearly as sharply as those of most of the businesses it serves. According to a survey by StevensGouldPincus, a consulting firm for the communications industry, nearly 64% of participating firms saw revenues slide in 2009 and only 23% saw revenues increase, perhaps because businesses put their faith only in the biggest and most established firms.

PR has done well in part because it is often cheaper than mass advertising campaigns. Its impact, in the form of favorable coverage in the media or online, can also be more easily measured. Moreover, PR firms are beginning to encroach on territory that used to be the domain of advertising firms, a sign of their increasing clout. They used chiefly to pitch story ideas to media outlets and try to get their clients mentioned in newspapers. Now they also

---

PR professionals assert that they have the most influence with executives in times of crisis. A PR professional's strategic communication and media relations skills are absolutely essential to an organization when there is a problem. And a crisis can, in turn, create new opportunities for increased public relations activity and influence.

Public relations as a profession is expanding, based on the growth in spending. According to the U.S. Bureau of Labor Statistics, public relations is expected to grow by 24 percent between 2008 and 2018, while advertising is predicted to show little or no change during the same time frame.

Chapter 1 notes that public relations is hard to define in part because its communications reach is so vast. When you think of PR, it is important to consider of all the ways it is used to reach its key publics—media relations, customer relations, social media, events, research, and so much more.

dream up and orchestrate live events, web launches, and the like. "When you look at advertising versus public relations, it's not going to be those clearly defined silos," says Christopher Graes, the boss of Ogilvy Public Relations Worldwide. "It may be indistinguishable at some point where one ends and the other begins."

PR has also benefited from the changing media landscape. The withering of many traditional media outlets has left fewer journalists from fewer firms covering business. That makes PR doubly important, both for attracting journalists' attention and for helping firms bypass old routes altogether and disseminate news by posting press releases on their websites, for example.

The rise of the Internet and social media has given PR a big boost. Many big firms have a presence on social networking sites, such as Facebook and Twitter, overseen by PR staff. PR firms are increasingly called on to track what consumers are saying about their clients online and to respond directly to any negative commentary. When two employees of Domino's, a pizza chain, uploaded a video of themselves apparently sticking ingredients for dishes they ere preparing up their noses, the firm responded by posting a video of its own online, of a senior executive apologizing for the incident.

Blow-dried blogs

That sort of content is proliferating. A PR firm called Ketchum helped IBM start a blog about sustainability, complete with posts written by the technology firm's executives. It also created cartoons on the subject that it uploaded to YouTube. Edelman recently worked with eBay on the launch of a web-only magazine, "The Inside

Source," which provides articles on shopping and tells readers what is selling well on the online retail giant's website.

VSS forecasts that spending on PR in America will surpass $8 billion by 2013, with much of the growth coming from online projects such as these. According to Miles Nadal, chief executive of MDC Partners, a media holding company, investment in digital PR accelerated during the recession "and will go forward in perpetuity" because clients became more focused on measuring the impact of their effort. The Internet offers various yardsticks, from traffic to cheerleading websites to numbers of Facebook fans, whereas the number of people who see a conventional advertisement is much harder to gauge.

Perhaps the best indication of PR's growing importance is the attention it is attracting from regulators. They are worried that PR firms do not make it clear enough that they are behind much seemingly independent commentary on blogs and social networks. In October America's Federal Trade Commission published new guidelines for bloggers, requiring them to disclose whether they ad been paid by companies or received free merchandise. Further regulation is likely. But that will not hamper PR's growth, says Jim Rutherfurd of VSS. After all, companies that fall foul of the rules will need the help of a PR firm.

Perpetuity is synonymous with "eternity." That's a pretty long time—and good news for PR if Miles Nadal is correct!

Research and meaningful measurement of message reach and effectiveness are key to any public relations campaign.

Transparency is important no matter through what the medium of the message is. It is always imperative that public relations makes the source of the message known. Not only does hiding a source invite increased regulation, it erodes trust within publics.

It is easier to bypass media gatekeepers now, but it may not always be the best path. Posting company news only on the corporate website can result in missed opportunities for third-party endorsements and the credibility that is associated with a story that appears in the mainstream media.

A substantial part of public relations' growth and stability throughout the recession has been linked to PR expertise in social media. By monitoring social media sites, PR pros are effectively and quickly able to counter negative messages and identify potential future problems.

2 CAREERS IN

Be Prepared

Jordan knew before he went to college that he wanted to be a public relations practitioner, so he began immediately to seek out and take advantage of opportunities. He was the PR chairman for his fraternity, the director of the student not-for-profit PR firm, and president of the university's Public Relations Student Society of America (PRSSA) chapter. Jordan vied for and received a highly competitive internship with Coca-Cola in Atlanta. He also interned at a couple of local PR firms—one had national and regional clients, the other had primarily local community clients. When Jordan graduated with a degree in public relations from the journalism school and a certificate in business leadership from the business school, he was in demand by prospective employers.

Because he had internship experience in both corporate and agency settings, Jordan was able to make an informed decision about his career track. He decided the variety and pace of the agency world was most appealing to him, but he didn't feel the need to be part of a huge agency. Jordan applied to and received offers from several agencies. He ended up picking a regional agency because of its reputation as a good place to work—it had been named one of the top ten places in the state to work. Furthermore, in his interview, Jordan had learned that he would be able to apply both his research and social media skills in this job.

Jordan accepted the job and was offered an above-average entry-level salary of $40,000 because of his exceptional background and diverse experience. Like most entry-level PR agency employees, Jordan started as an assistant account executive, but he

PUBLIC RELATIONS

quickly climbed the ladder. He was hired, in part, for his technical and strategic skills in social media, and Jordan soon became the go-to guy in the agency for any social media questions. Most of his colleagues had been out of college for a while, so his youth and understanding of the potential for using social media as part of PR campaigns earned him roles in building online strategies for many clients. He even began giving social media workshops to his colleagues. Jordan almost instantly moved from a primarily technician role to a more managerial role in his agency. He sees only bright possibilities in his future and for the future of his chosen profession.

❶ Based on Jordan's experience, how do you think you should prepare for a career in public relations?

❷ Do you think you would like to be in a primarily technician or managerial role? Why?

❸ What are the differences between corporate and agency public relations practice?

A CHANGING focus IN PUBLIC RELATIONS

a person entering the field of public relations has the opportunity to develop a career that encompasses numerous areas of this increasingly diverse profession. Similarly, a wide variety of personal traits and skills contribute to success in this arena. Certain abilities, such as writing well, are necessary for all areas, but many public relations practitioners also go on to develop specialized skills in particular practice areas, such as investor relations, governmental affairs, or brand management.

Competition and conflict management are more essential than ever to organizations in a complex world where public acceptance and support are key to a company's or a nonprofit group's success. Now more than ever, this competition takes place on the global stage. Certainly, the daily news coverage of conflicts arising from heated competition or from clashing ideologies and worldviews showcases the importance of public relations skills.

Traditionally, it was widely believed that public relations practitioners should begin their careers as newspaper reporters or wire service correspondents to polish their writing skills and to learn firsthand how the media function. In an earlier era, a large percentage of public relations people did, indeed, have newspaper or broadcast experience.

UPS, with its fleet of 99,000 vehicles logging 2 billion miles annually, needed to make consumers and activists aware of what it was doing to offset its carbon footprint. In a "Brown Goes Green" media relations campaign, UPS highlighted its environmental responsibility programs and let consumers know how it was striving to reduce emissions from its ubiquitous brown vehicles.

Many of the leading pioneers in public relations were originally journalists. This, however, is no longer true, for several reasons. First, the field of public relations has broadened far beyond the concept of

think

What sort of experiences and coursework are the best training for success in public relations?

btw...

The growth of public relations as a career field distinctly separate from journalism has spawned any number of public relations courses, sequences, and majors. Increasingly, universities have established joint public relations/advertising programs, in part because of the growing trend toward integrated marketing communications, as discussed in Chapter 1. The Public Relations Student Society of America (PRSSA) now has 304 chapters and a membership of 10,000 students. The Commission on Public Relations Education, which includes public relations educators and representatives from all of the major professional organizations, has set the standard for an ideal curriculum. In its updated 2006 report, the commission recommended seven basic courses:
(1) introduction to public relations; (2) case studies in public relations; (3) public relations research, measurement, and evaluation; (4) public relations law and ethics; (5) public relations writing and production; (6) public relations planning and management; and (7) a supervised public relations internship.

"media relations" and placing publicity in the mass media. Today, much writing in public relations is done for controlled media, such as company publications, direct mail campaigns to key audiences, speech writing, brochures, and material posted on an organization's website. With this approach, no media savvy or contacts are necessary. Writing skill and knowledge of the media are still vital, but so is training in management, logistics, event management, coalition building, budgeting, and supervision of personnel. A *PRWeek* survey found that less than one-third of current PR practitioners are former journalists.

Journalists still go into public relations, primarily for salary gains and the opportunity to have a greater variety of job duties, but the ones who make a successful transition have the ability to adapt and are quick learners. Peter Himler, Executive Vice President of Burson-Marsteller, told *PRWeek* that many journalists fail to make the switch to public relations. He said, "They may not come into the PR field knowing how to create consensus among clients and PR teams and, while they may know how to write, they may lack an understanding of how to use PR tools appropriately—when to use a press release, when to have a press conference, or when to use a video news release, for example."

Fortunately, the number of public relations jobs continues to increase as the field expands. The Bureau of Labor Statistics, as noted in Chapter 1, predicts an 24 percent increase in employment through 2018.

The Range of Public Relations Work

According to the experts, some specialty areas of public relations will be particularly "job-rich" over the next five years. The industry group most often cited as an area of growth for PR professionals is the pharmaceutical/biotechnology industry. The spotlight also is on financial services, media companies, health care, and security segments of the technology industry.

Another expanding area of public relations practice is crisis communication counseling. This key role strengthens the influence of public relations in organizations, but is an area that requires considerable professional experience. Crisis management, which takes place within the larger context of strategic management of conflict, is where many practitioners find their greatest satisfaction as professionals who have an impact on their organization and add enormous value to the viability of their department.

Women and men entering public relations find employment in a variety of settings, including public relations firms; corporations; nonprofit organizations; entertainment, sports, and travel; government and politics; education; and international public relations. The largest single employer group is public relations firms, which handle a variety of tasks for any number of clients.

Where the Jobs Are

The major areas and the percentage of practitioners who work in each area, according to a 2006 survey of practitioners by *PRWeek*.

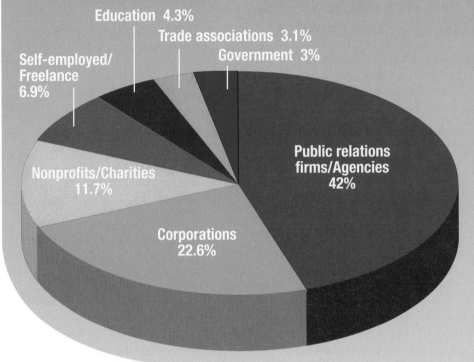

Education 4.3%
Trade associations 3.1%
Government 3%
Self-employed/Freelance 6.9%
Nonprofits/Charities 11.7%
Public relations firms/Agencies 42%
Corporations 22.6%

> **❝ Knowing government protocols and procedures can provide an edge to both biotech and financial PR practitioners as Enron-era scrutiny of public companies and their accounting practices has created a demand for such expertise. ❞**
>
> Belinda Hulin, writing in *Tactics*

personal
QUALIFICATIONS AND
ATTITUDES

any attempt to define a single public relations type of personality is pointless, because the field is so diverse that it needs people of differing personalities. Some practitioners deal with clients and the public in person on a frequent basis; others work primarily at their desks, planning, writing, and researching. Many do both. Whether in a creative position, in a resident journalist slot pitching stories to the media, in a job requiring lots of people skills and socializing, or in a top executive post shaping policy and direction for an employer in the external communication environment, the focus is always on helping meet the organization's goals and objectives—that is, on managing competition and conflict.

Five Essential Abilities

Individuals who plan careers in public relations should develop knowledge and ability in five basic areas, no matter which type of work they ultimately engage in.

1 Writing Skills The ability to convey information and ideas in written documents clearly and concisely is essential. Good grammar and good spelling are vital.

2 Research Ability Arguments must be supported by facts rather than generalities. A person must have the persistence and ability to gather information from a variety of sources, as well as be able to conduct original research by designing and implementing opinion polls or audits. Skillful use of the Internet and computer databases is an important element of research work. Reading newspapers and magazines is also important.

3 Planning Expertise Communication tools and activities must be carefully developed and coordinated. A person needs to be a good planner to make certain that materials are distributed in a timely manner, events occur without problems, and budgets are not exceeded. Public relations people must be highly organized and detail oriented, yet still able to see the "big picture."

4 Problem-Solving Ability Innovative ideas and fresh approaches solve complex problems and make a public relations program unique and memorable. Higher salaries and more frequent promotions go to those individuals who show top management they can solve problems creatively.

5 Business/Economics Competence The increasing emphasis on public relations as a management function calls for public relations students to learn the "nuts and bolts" of business and economics. Students preparing for careers in public relations should obtain a solid grounding by taking elective courses in economics, marketing, and especially management.

Of course, every job in public relations doesn't require all five essential abilities in equal proportion. The right mix often depends on your specific job responsibilities and assignments.

> **think**
> Why is a solid business background essential to success in public relations?

> **"The greatest need PR people have is understanding how a business and, more importantly, how a public company operates."**
>
> Joel Curren, Senior Vice President of CKPR in Chicago

Social scientific research skills are increasingly more valuable in the workplace as research ability takes on greater importance, accounting for significantly higher salaries for master's-trained professionals.

WHAT EMPLOYERS WANT: 10 QUALITIES

PR Tactics, the monthly publication of the Public Relations Society of America (PRSA), asked job-placement experts which set of skills and experience was needed in today's employment market. Belinda Hulin compiled the following list based on the top responses:

Good Writing

Excellent writing skills are more necessary now than ever before.

Intelligence

Although the descriptions vary ("bright," "clever," and "quick-witted"), placement executives agree that modern public relations isn't a refuge for people with mediocre minds and lackluster personalities.

Cultural Literacy

Employers want individuals who are well rounded and well educated about the arts, humanities, and current events. According to *PR Tactics*, "You can't expect management to take your advice if you have no shared frame of reference."

The Ability to Recognize a Good Story When You See One

The ability to manage your organization's image—in both large and small ways—starts with the identification and management of good stories that give the organization visibility, build brand recognition, and enhance the organization's reputation.

Media Savvy

Media convergence means that there are now multiple platforms for disseminating the organization's message—social media, print media, webcasts, Internet news sites, radio and television, and so on. Each platform has different deadlines, formats, and needs. Understanding their unique characteristics and being able to work with editors in each domain is essential.

Contacts

Cordial relationships with people in media, government, industry groups, and nonprofit organizations, as well as with colleagues in other companies, will serve you well. The ability to pick up the phone and get crucial information or make things happen is essential.

Good Business Sense

The best companies weave public relations into their overall business strategy. To work at that level, however, public relations practitioners need to have a firm understanding of how the business operates in general and how an employer's industry works in particular.

Broad Communications Experience

To succeed, a PR professional must be familiar with all aspects of communications, from in-house newsletters to media and investor relations documents.

Specialized Experience

After getting some general experience, individuals should consider developing a specialty. Health care, finance, and technology are some of the most promising areas today.

Avoid Career Clichés

If your only reason for getting into the PR business is because you "like people" and enjoy organizing events, you should think about another field. Employers are looking for broad-based individuals with multiple communication and problem-solving skills.

Pepsi Creates Social Media Buzz with Amp App

TODAY'S PUBLIC RELATIONS PRACTITIONER needs a toolbox filled with diverse skills—writing, research, planning, problem solving, and business competence among them. When Pepsi entered the popular iPhone application (app) arena with an app meant to promote its Amp energy drink to its target demographic of young men, all of these skills were needed, in addition to conflict management capabilities.

The "Amp up before you score" app was released in October 2009 to a chorus of both cheers and boos. The app takes what the company claimed was a tongue-in-cheek approach to reaching its target public. *PRWeek* described the app in an October 16, 2009 editorial:

> If you haven't seen it, the app purports to help guys "score" with the ladies—ladies [who] appear in the app in a couple of dozen curvaceous stereotypes including "nerd," "sorority girl," "military chick," "princess," and lo-and-behold, "business woman." That would have been bad

enough, but the app also encourages users to take notes on said conquests, share the bragging via Facebook, and even provides tips on how to better "score" with these women.

Pepsi and Amp apologized via Twitter and Amp's Facebook page. In Twitter shorthand, the post went as follows: "Our app tried 2 show the humorous lengths guys go2 get women, We apologize if it's in bad taste and appreciate ur feedback." But, Pepsi didn't immediately pull the app, which some critics said nullified the apology. "The app hasn't been pulled so the apology is disingenuous, is it not?" Lynne Johnson, Senior Vice President of Social Media for the Advertising Research Foundation told *AdWeek*.

Social networking blog Mashable criticized the app with a headline that parodied an iPhone slogan: "Alienate your female customers? Pepsi has an app for that." Mashable reported in its blog entry, "Amp has actually built features into its application that make it seem one can systematically score by exploiting women's naivety. Beyond that, they actively encourage users to promote such conquests through social media." While noting that the app is aimed at "dudes," it's the women who had a problem with the app, according to Mashable.

Others gave Pepsi credit for creating the PR furor. In the same *AdWeek* article, Bill Sipper, senior partner at Cascada Consulting, was quoted as saying, "The bottom line is this is just another edgy

way to advertise Amp. Kudos to them for having the Associated Press and everyone talking about it. It's a good way to break out of a cluttered category. After all, we're talking about a soft drink, not nuclear waste." Even Mashable acknowledged that the app was being quite successful in creating "buzz."

Pepsi spokeswoman Nicole Bradley told the Associated Press that the application was available only to people 17 and older who "choose to opt in to the experience." "The application was designed to entertain and appeal to Amp's target. We'll continue to monitor the feedback from all parties and act accordingly," she said.

But after a week of controversy, PepsiCo decided pull the app. "We have decided to discontinue the Amp iPhone application," a Pepsi spokesman said in a statement. "We've listened to a variety of audiences and determined this was the most appropriate course of action."

Public relations practitioners, advertising execs, and marketers may continue to debate whether the Amp app was savvy or stupid. But several things are clear: Pepsi was targeting its key public based on research and social media expertise, it laid low and didn't do more than acknowledge the controversy and promise to monitor the situation, and it created publicity for a brand that was then a distant fourth among energy drinks. But the company may have also alienated, for a brief period of time, a key constituency for other Pepsi products—women.

1 Did Pepsi and Amp manage this controversy appropriately?

2 How could Pepsi have addressed concerns short of pulling the app?

3 Do you think the app was simply a publicity stunt? Why or why not?

ORGANIZATIONAL
roles

Systematic research has shown that there is a hierarchy of roles in public relations practice. Professors Glen Broom and David Dozier of San Diego State University were among the first researchers to identify organizational roles ranging from the communication technician to the communication manager.

Practitioners in the technician role, for example, are primarily responsible for producing communication products and implementing decisions made by others. They take photographs, write brochures, prepare news releases, and organize events. These individuals function primarily at the "tactical" level of public relations work; they do not participate in policy decision making, nor are they responsible for outcomes. Many entry-level positions in public relations are at the technician level, but there are also many experienced practitioners whose specialty is tactical duties such as writing and editing newsletters, maintaining information on the company's intranet or website, or even working primarily with the media in the placement of publicity.

At the other end of the employment spectrum is the communication manager. Practitioners playing this role are perceived by others as the organization's public relations experts. They make communication policy decisions and are held accountable by others and themselves

Job Levels in Public Relations

EXECUTIVE
Organizational leadership and management, including developing the organizational vision, corporate mission, strategic objectives, annual goals, businesses, broad strategies, policies, and systems

DIRECTOR
Constituency and issue-trend analysis; communication and operational planning at departmental level, including planning, organizing, leading, controlling, evaluating, and problem solving

MANAGER
Constituency and issue-trend analysis; departmental management, including organizing, budgeting, leading, controlling, evaluating, and problem solving

SUPERVISOR
Project supervision, including planning, scheduling, budgeting, organizing, leading, controlling, and problem solving

ENTRY-LEVEL TECHNICIAN
Use of technical "craft" skills to disseminate information, persuade, gather data, or solicit feedback

Source: Adapted from the *Public Relations Professional Career Guide.* Public Relations Society of America, 33 Maiden Lane, New York, NY 10038.

for the success or failure of communication programs. Managers counsel senior management, oversee multiple communication strategies, and supervise a number of employees who are responsible for tactical implementation.

Other research conducted since Broom and Dozier's study indicates that the differences between managers and technicians aren't that clear-cut. In smaller operations, a public relations professional may perform daily activities at both manager and technician levels.

The Value of Internships

Internships are extremely popular in the communications industry, and a student whose résumé includes practical work experience along with a good academic record has an important advantage when seeking permanent employment. The Commission on Public Relations Education believes the internship is so important that it is one of the seven basic courses it recommends for any quality college or university public relations curriculum.

An internship is a win-win situation for both the student and the organization. The student, in most cases, not only receives academic credit but also gets firsthand knowledge of work in the professional world. This gives the student an advantage in getting that all-important first job after graduation. In many cases, employers often hire recent graduates who worked as interns in their offices. As *PRWeek* reporter Sara Calabro says:

> Agencies and corporate communications departments are beginning to see interns as the

think Why would an organization be more likely to favor a job candidate with internship experience?

btw...

Although national and international firms routinely pay interns, this is often not the case at the local level. Many smaller companies claim that they cannot afford to pay an intern or that the opportunity to gain training and experience should be more than adequate compensation. Dave DeVries, a senior PR manager for the PCS Division of Sprint, disagrees. He wrote in PRSA's *Tactics,* "Unpaid internships severely limit the field of potential candidates" because, as he points out, the best and brightest students will always gravitate to employers who pay. Former *Fortune* 500 executive Tom Hagley also argued in *Tactics* that paying interns enables the students to focus effort and maintain high performance standards, resulting in an excellent return on any salary investment by the company.

Indeed, there seems to be a strong correlation between paid internships and starting salaries in the field. On the one hand, most public relations firms and departments provide some level of paid internships, and entry-level salaries are comparatively high. On the other hand, television stations are notorious for not paying interns, and entry-level salaries in that arena ($24,000) are the lowest in the communications field. Salaries are discussed in the next section.

In sum, students should make a concentrated effort to negotiate paid internships. In general, these internships provide more meaningful experience and the employers have higher expectations.

future of their companies. While a few years ago, it was typical for an intern to work for nothing, it is almost unheard of for an internship to be unpaid these days. Examples of the essential work now entrusted to interns include tasks such as media monitoring, writing press releases, financial estimating, and compiling status reports. In many cases, interns are being included in all team and client meetings, as well as brainstorming sessions.

Many major public relations firms have formal internship programs. At Edelman Worldwide, for example, students enroll in "Edel-U," an internal training program that exposes them to all aspects of agency work. The summer internship program at Weber Shandwick in Boston is called "Weber University." Calabro cites Jane Dolan, a senior account executive, who says that upper management is always impressed with the work that interns do for their final projects. "It is amazing to see them go from zero to 100 in a matter of months," says Dolan.

Hill & Knowlton also has an extensive internship training program in its New York office, taking about 40 interns each year from an applicant pool of 600 to 700 students. In its view, the internship program is "the cheapest and most effective recruiting tool available." Ketchum also places great emphasis on finding outstanding interns and making sure they are actively involved in account work rather than spending most of their time running the photocopier or stuffing media kits.

Of course, it's not always possible for a student to do an internship in Chicago or New York. Even so, many opportunities are available at local public relations firms, businesses, and nonprofit agencies. It is important, however, that the organization have at least one experienced public relations professional who can mentor a student and ensure that he or she gets an opportunity to do a variety of tasks to maximize the learning experience.

salaries
IN PUBLIC
RELATIONS

public relations work pays relatively well compared to other communication professions. Many practitioners say they like the income and opportunities for steady advancement, and they also enjoy the variety and fast pace that the field provides.

Entry-Level Salaries

Several surveys have attempted to pinpoint the national average salary for recent graduates in their first full-time job in the public relations field. Probably the most definitive survey is the one conducted by Lee Becker and his associates at the University of Georgia. They work with journalism and mass communications programs throughout the nation to compile a list of recent graduates who are then surveyed (www.grady.uga.edu/annualsurveys/).

The latest data available (published in 2008 and based on previous-year data) show that the median annual salary for recent graduates working in public relations was $31,000. This is slightly higher than the median national average for all communication fields, which is $30,000.

Another survey, conducted by *PRWeek*, provided a more optimistic view on starting salaries in public relations. The 2009 survey of salaries, for example, found that the median salary for entry-level professionals with less than 2 years of experience was $36,000. The median salary for professionals with 3 to 4 years of experience was $50,000. The results of this survey certainly suggest that strong performers in the first 4 years of work enjoy very good pay prospects.

think **Why do you think people starting out in PR earn more than their peers working in other communication fields?**

Salaries for Experienced Professionals

While the national median salary for practitioners with 7 to 10 years of experience is approximately $85,000, the median salary for practitioners with more than 20 years of experience is considerably higher— $138,500.

Salaries, of course, depend on a number of factors, including geographic location, job title, the industry, and even the public relations specialty. Major metropolitan areas, for example, generally have higher salaries, but there are also some regional differences.

An Overview of Salaries in the Public Relations Field

PRWeek conducts an annual survey of salaries. The following tables are excerpted from its 2009 survey, which polled 1,160 practitioners in the field.

Practitioners by Gender

Male 37 %
Female 63 %

Salary by Gender

5 or more years experience	Men	$120,000
	Women	$91,000
Less than 5 years experience	Men	$50,000
	Women	$44,000

Median Salary by Years of Experience

1–2 yrs	$36,000
3–4 yrs	$50,000
5–6 yrs	$62,000
7–10 yrs	$85,000
11–15	$107,700
16–20 yrs	$120,000
21+ yrs	$138,500

Median Salary by Work Setting

Agency	$90,000
Corporation	$103,000
Government	$81,000
Nonprofit	$66,200
Self-employed	$94,000
Trade association	$82,000
Education	$63,500

Median Salary by Job Title

Chairman/President/CEO	$150,000
Director/Managing Director/Partner	$116,000
Executive Vice President	$203,000
Senior Vice President	$180,000
Vice President	$125,000
Communications Director	$100,000
Communications Manager	$75,000
Acct Supervisor	$75,000
Acct Manager	$58,000
Senior Acct Executive	$54,500
Acct Executive	$42,000
Acct Coord	$35,000

Source: "Salary Survey 2009." *PRWeek*, Special Report, February 23, 2009, 11–18.

The Gender Gap

$120,000

$50,000

$91,000

$44,000

| years of experience | 1–5 | > 5 | 1–5 | > 5 |

Job title also means a lot when it comes to determining salary. A senior vice president (SVP) receives a median of $180,000, whereas an account executive at a public relations firm gets $42,000. In terms of setting, individuals who work for a corporation make a median salary of $103,000, whereas those who work for a nonprofit net only $66,200 per year.

In terms of the senior ranks, *PRWeek* notes a survey by Korn/Kerry consultants that profiled the chief communication officers of *Fortune* 200 companies. The average base salary for these individuals was $335,000, and the total cash package (with bonuses and stock) was almost $600,000.

You should be aware, however, that the *PRWeek* salary figures are based on a poll of 1,160 respondents. The salaries reported in this survey may or may not be indicative of the entire field. In the absence of more complete salary data, however, surveys by publications such as *PRWeek* have become the standard reference in the industry.

A good source for checking current salaries for public relations in major cities throughout the United States and around the world is PRSA's website: www.prsa.org/jobcenter. It posts current openings and provides the salary ranges for various job classifications. For example, PRSA listed the national median salary for an SVP in 2009 as $164,000; however, in the largest markets (New York, Atlanta, Chicago, and Los Angeles), the average SVP earned $179,600. The median for a public relations specialist in those cities, by comparison, was $80,000.

Salaries for Women: The Gender Gap

The *PRWeek* survey clearly shows an across-the-board gender gap in salaries.

The salary advantage that men enjoy over women is not unique to public relations. It is widespread in most of U.S. business—indeed, throughout the world. The American Federation of Labor–Congress of Industrial Organizations (AFL-CIO) reports that women are paid about 75 cents for every dollar in salary men receive, a figure that has changed little over the past 10 years.

A number of studies have probed the pay differential between men and women in public relations. The first studies, starting in the 1980s, simply noted the gap without taking into consideration the multiple factors that could lead to discrepancies. Some of these factors include

(1) the number of years in the field, (2) technician duties versus managerial responsibilities, (3) the nature of the industry, (4) the size of the organization, and (5) women's attempts to balance work and family.

Some studies, for example, concluded that women were relatively new to the field and didn't have the experience yet to compete with men who had been in the field for some years. Inherent in this finding was the fact that women traditionally are assigned low-paying "technician" roles.

Others have tried to explain the salary differential in other ways. *PRWeek* points out that male respondents to its annual survey have been in the business for an average of 15 years, while the women respondents average only 11.7 years in the business. Others have noted that women have a tendency to work in areas of public relations that traditionally have low salaries, such as community relations, employee communications, or nonprofits. In contrast, a large percentage of practitioners in finance and investor relations—which pay well—are men.

Professors Linda Aldoory and Elizabeth Toth of the University of Maryland also explored discrepancies in salaries in an article for the *Journal of Public Relations Research* (2002). They presented a number of factors, but essentially concluded:

> The difference in the average salary of male respondents compared to female respondents was statistically significant. Regression analysis revealed that years of public relations experience accounted for much of the variance, but that gender and job interruptions also accounted for the salary difference. Age and education level were not found to be a significant influence on salary.

The role of women in public relations, and the increased feminization of the field (70 percent of the practitioners in the United States are now women), will be discussed as a major trend line in Chapter 4.

❝ Women are segregated into the lower-level technician role, spending time on routine activities such as writing, editing, and handling media relations. Conversely, more men are promoted into the more powerful managerial role, engaging in such activities as counseling senior management, and making key policy decisions. ❞

Julie O'Neil, professor at Texas Christian University, summarizes the conclusion of several studies in the *Journal of Public Relations Research*.

Median Salaries for Communication Majors

Average median yearly salaries reported by recent graduates for communication fields.

$24K	$26K	$28K	$29.1K	$30K	$30.5K	$30.5K	$31K	$33K	$33.8K
Television	Weeklies	Consumer magazines	Daily newspapers	Advertising	Radio	Newsletters/trades	Public relations	World Wide Web	Cable television

Source: 2008 Annual Survey of Journalism and Mass Communication Enrollments, Grady College of Mass Communication and Journalism, University of Georgia.

the value of
PUBLIC RELATIONS

today more than ever, the world needs not just more information, but also savvy communicators and facilitators who can explain the goals and aspirations of individuals, organizations, and governments to others in a socially responsive manner.

Public relations provides businesses and society with a vital service. On a practical level, Laurence Moskowitz, chairman and CEO of Medialink, says that public relations is "informative. It's part of the news,

"Clear and consistent communication helps organizations achieve their goals, employees to work to their potential, customers to make informed choices, investors to make an accurate assessment of an organization, and society to form fair judgments of industries, organizations, and issues."

Tom Glover, writing in *Profile*, the magazine of the Institute of Public Relations in the United Kingdom

the program, the article, the stuff readers and viewers want. It's relevant. Positive messaging through the news lifts other forms of marketing, too. Good PR increases the effectiveness of ads, direct mail, sponsorship, and all other forms of 'permission' marketing."

But the latest developments in public relations push the field beyond information dissemination. Today's practitioner must understand what effect information and communication efforts will have on the competitive position of the employer, whether that employer operates in the for-profit or nonprofit sector of the economy. By helping the modern organization manage competition and conflict, public relations professionals in this century are bringing added value to their employers, thereby earning them a chance to exert greater influence over the destiny of the organizations where they practice public relations. That earned influence leads to greater respect and better rewards in everything from salary to personal satisfaction.

> **think** Which vital service does public relations provide to modern organizations?

APPLY YOUR KNOWLEDGE

WHAT WOULD YOU DO?

A typical entry-level job posting at the PRSA.org job center is exemplified by this one from Phoenix-based Rose & Allyn Public Relations:

Job Description: Task master. The one who keeps the trains running on time. Jack of all trades. Rose & Allyn seeks a pro to be responsible for supporting the public relations, marketing, and promotional activities of Rose & Allyn Public Relations and its executives. Must be able to manage a large multitask workload and contribute ideas and skills to benefit our clients as well as the firm. Strong writing, grammatical, accounting, and organizational skills are essential. Experience in social networking sites, graphic design, video production, and editing a plus. Must understand that "9–5" is relative.

Rose & Allyn was looking for someone who had a bachelor's degree in communications, journalism, or a related field. The firm also expressed a desire for someone with "experience in Quickbooks, graphic design, video production and editing, and social networking sites," calling such experience "a strong plus."

Viewing job postings like this one can help students plan for their future job searches. As new graduates, many students are concerned that they might not have what it takes to land an entry-level position. Perhaps they haven't taken what they perceive as the right combination of communications and business classes. Perhaps they haven't had any internships or they haven't had the "right" internships. Clay Agee, a 2007 graduate of the University of Alabama, wrote in the April 2008 issue of *Public Relations Tactics* about his experience as a recent, job-seeking, PR graduate. He experienced what he described as a "roller-coaster ride" in his job search.

How will you land your first job? What skill set do you believe you already have that will help you be successful in the profession? It is never too soon to be thinking along these lines. Create or update your own résumé and then draft an inquiry letter to this employer about yourself. Share the letter with a classmate and discuss ways you can make sure you are considered for an interview.

Summary

How Is the Field of Public Relations Changing? p. 26

- In the past, individuals entering the field of public relations were often former journalists, but that is no longer the case because public relations has evolved beyond publicity and media relations.

- Public relations is now widely recognized as its own distinct academic discipline in colleges and universities throughout the world.

- Competition and conflict management are more essential than ever to organizations in a complex world where public acceptance and support are key to a company's or a nonprofit group's success.

Which Personal Qualifications, Attitudes, and Abilities Help Professionals Succeed in Public Relations? p. 28

- Those who plan careers in public relations should have the following abilities: writing skills, research ability, planning expertise, problem-solving ability, and business/economic competence.

Which Types of Careers Are Available in Public Relations? p. 32

- Public relations professionals are employed in a variety of fields: corporations, nonprofits, entertainment and sports, politics and government, education, and international organizations and businesses.

How Much Do Public Relations Professionals Earn? p. 34

- Entry-level salaries are higher in public relations than in many other communications fields.

- A person with 1 or 2 years of experience can earn a salary of approximately $36,000, whereas a more experienced professional can earn a six-figure salary.

- Although the gender gap has somewhat narrowed, in general women working in PR earn less than men.

QUESTIONS for *Review* and *Discussion*

1. The text says that former journalists often don't always make a good transition to public relations work. Explain why this is so.

2. Public relations people work for a variety of organizations. Which type of organization would you prefer if you were to pursue work in public relations?

3. The text mentions five essential qualities for working in public relations. On a scale of 1 to 10, how would you rate yourself on each ability? How can you improve on the qualities in which you rank yourself lowest?

4. Why is it important for a student to complete an internship in college? Do you think interns should be paid?

5. In the text, it states that job-placement directors agree that employers typically look for ten key qualities in applicants. Can you name at least five of the ten qualities?

6. Discuss entry-level salaries in public relations. Do you think they are low, high, or about what you expected? What about the salaries for experienced professionals?

7. Is there still a gender gap in salaries in public relations? If so, do you think that it is caused by discrimination or do other factors explain the salary discrepancy?

the THINK SPOT
www.thethinkspot.com

3 MANAGING COMPETITION

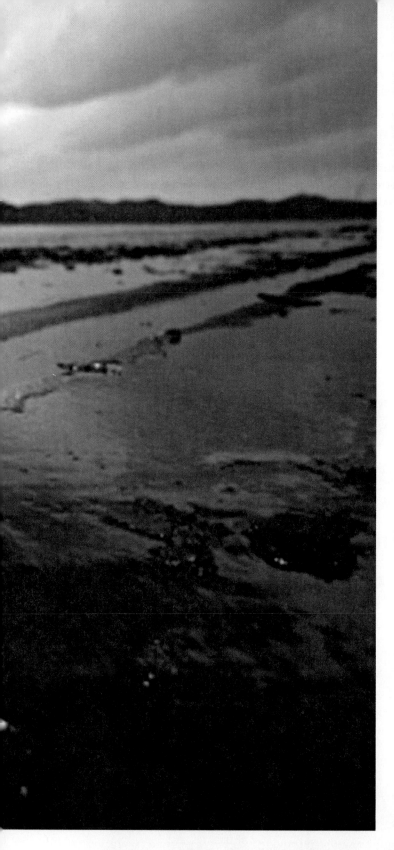

Ask Yourself

> What Role Do Competition and Conflict Play in Public Relations? p. 44

> What Are the Phases of the Conflict Management Life Cycle? p. 48

> How Can Public Relations Professionals Best Manage the Conflict Management Life Cycle? p. 50

A Classic Case in Crisis Management

Exxon is still identified with the major oil spill that occurred in Prince William Sound, Alaska, in 1989. The company adopted a defensive strategy when one of its ships, the *Exxon Valdez*, hit a reef and spilled nearly 240,000 barrels of oil into the surrounding—and previously pristine—environment. The disaster, which qualifies as one of history's worst environmental accidents, was badly mismanaged from the beginning.

Exxon management commenced its crisis communication strategy by making excuses. Management claimed that Exxon, as a corporation, wasn't at fault because (1) the weather wasn't ideal, (2) the charts provided by the U.S. Coast Guard were out-of-date, and (3) the captain of the ship was derelict in his duties because he was drinking while on duty. As cleanup efforts began, Exxon also tried to shift the blame by maintaining that government bureaucracy and prohibitions against the use of certain chemicals were hampering the company's best efforts.

Exxon also used the strategy of justification to minimize the damage, saying that environmentalists in the government were exaggerating the ill effects of the spill on bird and animal life. Meanwhile, negative press coverage was intense, and public outrage continued to escalate. William J. Small of Fordham University, who researched the press coverage, wrote, "Probably no other company ever got a more damaging portrayal in the mass media." More than 18,000 customers cut up their Exxon credit cards, late-night talk show hosts ridiculed the company, and Congressional committees started hearings. Exxon dropped from number 8 to number 110 on *Fortune*'s list of most-admired companies.

Exxon's response to all of these developments was again somewhat ineffective. It did try the strategy of ingratiation by running

AND CONFLICT

full-page advertisements stating that the company was sorry for the oil spill—but still did not take responsibility for the incident. Instead of calming the storm, that approach further enraged the public. Exxon also took corrective action and cleaned up the oil spill, spending approximately $3 billion on its efforts. The company received little credit for this action, however, because most of the public believed it was done only under government pressure. By the time the cleanup was finished, public attitudes about Exxon had already been formed.

❶ Do you think that Exxon performed as well as could be expected or could the company have done a better job of dealing with the crisis situation?

❷ Does dealing with critical media coverage on the scale of the *Exxon Valdez* oil spill crisis appeal to you as a career challenge?

❸ Once the crisis was over, do you think that the members of Exxon's public relations department would be well advised to put the oil spill behind them or was their work just beginning as managers of conflict?

A NEW WAY OF THINKING:
conflict & competition

P ublic relations (PR) can be defined as the *strategic management of conflict and competition in the best interests of an organization and, when possible, also in the interests of key publics.* Successful public relations professionals believe in their employers and work in the employers' interests to compete against others and to handle any conflict that might arise. The paramount concern of professionals is managing communication in the interests of their employers and clients to enhance their competitive position and handle conflict effectively, provided the objectives of their employers are worthy and ethical.

This definition is more assertive than definitions that emphasize building mutually beneficial relationships between an organization and its various stakeholders. Building relationships is a key objective, but it is only part of the larger role that public relations plays in ensuring an organization's success.

Public relations enables both for-profit and nonprofit organizations to compete for limited resources

When Target decided to ban the Salvation Army from collecting donations at its store entrances during the holiday season, the store immediately found itself in conflict with various community groups that charged the store with being a "Grinch" and not supporting the needs of the poor and homeless. Target had to manage the attacks on the company's charitable reputation and deal with a possible consumer boycott and threats to its revenues.

COMPETITION and CONFLICT

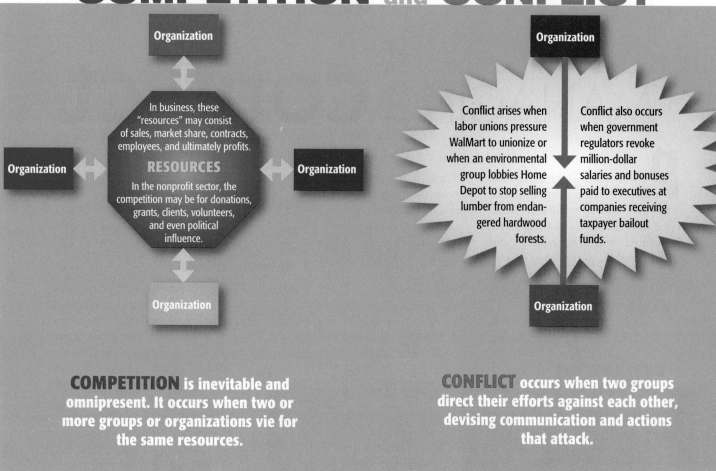

In business, these "resources" may consist of sales, market share, contracts, employees, and ultimately profits.

RESOURCES

In the nonprofit sector, the competition may be for donations, grants, clients, volunteers, and even political influence.

Conflict arises when labor unions pressure WalMart to unionize or when an environmental group lobbies Home Depot to stop selling lumber from endangered hardwood forests.

Conflict also occurs when government regulators revoke million-dollar salaries and bonuses paid to executives at companies receiving taxpayer bailout funds.

COMPETITION is inevitable and omnipresent. It occurs when two or more groups or organizations vie for the same resources.

CONFLICT occurs when two groups direct their efforts against each other, devising communication and actions that attack.

(e.g., customers, volunteers, employees, donations, grants) and to engage in healthy, honest conflict with those who hold different views of what is best and right for society. Achieving these sorts of objectives increases the value of public relations to an organization. It is also how public relations professionals earn the influence that leads to greater recognition by top management, increased respect in the field, and, ultimately, better-paying, more secure positions for public relations professionals in general.

Although competition and conflict are closely related, this book makes a distinction between the two. Most public relations activities and programs deal with competition between organizations for sales and customers. Conflict, in contrast, usually involves confrontations and attacks between

organizations and various stakeholders or publics.

Admittedly, the distinction between competition and conflict is partly a matter of degree, but it is also a matter of focus. In competition, everyone's eyes are on the prize—such as sales or political support, for example. With conflict, the eyes are on the opposition—that is, on dealing with or initiating threats of some sort or another. In either case, striving for mutual benefit is extremely important. It involves balancing the interests of an employer or client with those of a number of stakeholders. Often, professionals can accommodate the interests of both the organization and its various publics. But sometimes organizations may not be able to please all of their publics because there are differences in worldviews. Wal-Mart may please labor unions

by paying more employee benefits, but consumers who like low prices may object to that policy if it means that the company will charge more for its goods. Environmentalists may want to close a steel plant, but the company's employees and the local community may be avid supporters of keeping the plant open despite any environmental concerns. Given competing agendas and issues, public relations professionals must look first to the needs of the organization, and then manage the inevitable conflicts that arise.

think To whom does a PR professional owe primary allegiance?

THE ROLE OF PUBLIC RELATIONS IN MANAGING **conflict**

public relations professionals must develop communication strategies and processes to influence the course of conflicts to the benefit of their organizations and, when possible, to the benefit of the organizations' many constituents. This deliberate influence is called *strategic conflict management*.

Public relations can involve reducing conflict, as is frequently the case in crisis management. At some times, conflict is escalated for activist purposes, such as when anti-abortion advocates picket health clinics and assault clients, doctors, and nurses. Other strategies are less dramatic, such as when industry advocates lobby to open parts of the Alaskan wilderness to exploration for oil, striving to win approval

think — Is conflict always bad for organizations?

from the public—and ultimately, from Congress.

Conflict management often occurs when a business or industry contends with government regulators or activist groups that seem determined to curtail operations through what the industry considers excessive safety or environmental standards. Industries will often organize as coalitions or trade groups to fight back. For example, the American Coalition for Clean Coal Electricity (cleancoalusa.org) has a $60 million budget to run advocacy ads on television claiming that industry innovations have turned coal into a clean, abundant source of energy. Speeches and news releases from this organization also warn against excessive regulation that would curtail the role of coal in America's energy future. On the other side, environmental groups such as the Sierra Club lobby Congress and regulatory agencies for restrictions in coal burning, claiming that the concept of "clean" coal is a myth. Solar energy enthusiasts, in an effort to capitalize on the clean coal controversy, have employed an interesting approach. One such group hosts a website that uses the words "clean coal" in its URL; only when they reach the website do visitors learn that the site actually touts solar technology. This guerrilla tactic is called an anti-site.

STRATEGIC
Conflict Management in the Real World

These scenarios share a common theme: the strategic management of conflict. Conflict management is one of the most interesting, vibrant, and essential functions of public relations.

- A public relations professional takes charge of the temporary press briefing room that was built near the site of a plant explosion, funneling all press and family inquiries to this location, and offering fax, phone, and Internet access to a flock of reporters.

- Recognizing the need for domestic fuel sources in an uncertain world, a Washington, D.C., lobbyist works with his PR firm to bolster arguments for federal subsidies to ethanol producers in the U.S. Corn Belt.

- As American waistlines bulge, the National Institutes of Health calls for the creation of centers to prevent obesity and related diseases.

- After news leaks about an instance of sexual harassment in the workplace, a spokesperson expresses mortification about the ethical performance of her company and pledges to change the company culture.

Moral Conflicts Pose Special Challenges

When organizations clash over a heated issue or a moral conflict such as embryonic stem cell research or capital punishment, charges leveled at the opposition often aim at impugning the ethics of the opponent. Often, such charges can be paraphrased as "*We* are just trying to tell the truth, but *they* are lying and twisting facts." Sometimes this "truth telling" is contrasted with the "spin" practiced by the other side—even though both sides use the same tactics in addition to a full range of persuasive public relations strategies. When proponents embrace absolute moral values in this way, they fail to reach out to, or understand, the other side.

Most news conferences begin with an opening statement by the organization holding the news conference. Write an opening statement for a press conference on a current moral conflict some-

where in the world. You might write the opening script for the Obama administration regarding deployment of additional Army battalions to Afghanistan or for a peace advocacy group disappointed that the President is escalating the conflict. Write your statement for the side that you support most strongly. Then try to understand the worldview of the other side and compose an opening statement for that group.

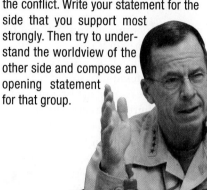

Does this exercise prove that it is foolish for public relations people to stand for something they believe in when there is no absolute right or wrong? Or does the classic adage "You've got to stand for something, or you'll fall for anything" ring more true in your ears?

Sometimes an organization is able to catch a conflict at an early stage and reduce damage to the organization by employing a strategy that crisis management experts term "stealing thunder." In other cases, an issue may smolder for some time before turning into a major fire. For example, lavish executive salary packages had periodically emerged as a point of contention over the past decade. Nevertheless, it wasn't until the 2009 economic collapse in the United States, which was precipitated largely by rampant speculation perpetrated by high-salaried managers in banking and insurance, that a groundswell of resentment encouraged the Obama administration to impose salary caps and start criminal investigations into the practices of these firms. Proactive policies by corporate boards to limit compensation packages would have forestalled the issue.

Unfortunately, most conflict situations are not clear-cut in terms of an ideal solution. In many cases, public relations professionals will not be able to accommodate the concerns of an activist group or a particular public because of many factors, including those related to the continued viability of the organization. In such cases, public relations professionals must make tough calls and advocate on behalf of their organizations.

KFC is not going out of the chicken business just because People for the Ethical Treatment of Animals (PETA) pickets stores about the inhumane slaughter of chickens. KFC, however, has accommodated activist concerns by taking additional steps to ensure that its suppliers employ humane slaughtering methods.

it depends:
FACTORS THAT AFFECT CONFLICT MANAGEMENT

Working with management, a public relations professional or team must determine the stance the organization will take toward each stakeholder involved in a conflict situation. This stance then determines the strategy employed—what will be done and why. The stance-driven approach to public relations began with the discovery that virtually all practitioners share an unstated, informal approach to managing conflict and competition: "It depends." In essence, the stance taken "depends" on many factors, and it changes in response to changing circumstances.

The Threat Appraisal Model

A good public relations practitioner monitors for threats, assesses them, arrives at a stance for the organization, and begins communication efforts from that stance. Practitioners face a complex set of forces to monitor and consider. One approach is the *threat appraisal model.* A threat to an organization requires an assessment of the demands that the threat makes on the organization as well as an assessment of the resources available to address the threat. An identified threat forces the public relations professional to consider a variety of factors. Are the knowledge, time, finances, and management commitment available to combat the threat? On another level, what is the best method to assess the severity of the danger? Is it a difficult situation with the potential to have a long duration, or is it a

relatively simple matter that can be resolved fairly quickly?

After carefully assessing the threat, professionals sometimes decide to ignore an issue or a pressure group, thereby saving themselves and their clients time, energy, and trouble. For example, the director of communications for the Atlanta Olympic Games learned through the grapevine that some local citizens planned to protest the use of a conservative talk radio station as distributor of audio news releases about the Games. C. Richard Yarbrough, director of communication, had the protest group checked out by a staffer, who found that only a handful of local people—who were neither well organized nor very well connected to the media or power brokers in Atlanta—were involved.

Armed with this information, Yarbrough considered a number of factors, which are part of the threat

think

Which factors determine how a public relations professional reacts to conflict?

appraisal model. What was the real danger to the image and reputation of Atlanta? Could this movement gain coverage and support, resulting in embarrassment? Once under way, would a protest take a great deal of time and money to address? In this case, his concern was reduced by learning that the group was not likely to get better organized or reach a critical mass. Consequently, his threat appraisal resulted in a stance-based decision to ignore the group. It turned out to be the right decision; the "movement" quietly went away.

Contingency Theory

Two fundamental principles underlie the definition of public relations as strategic management of competition and conflict. The first principle is that many factors determine the stance or position of an organization

---

btw...

Glen Cameron and his colleagues at the University of MIssouri identified at least 86 contingency variables divided into 11 groups that on two levels caused organizations to adopt a particular stance on a conflict. Five groups of variables were external: (1) external threats, (2) industry-specific environment, (3) general political/social environment, (4) external public characteristics, and (5) the issue under consideration. Six groups of variables were internal: (1) general corporate/organizational characteristics, (2) characteristics of the public relations department, (3) top management characteristics, (4) internal threats, (5) personality characteristics of involved organization members, and (6) relationship characteristics.

PR professionals will change stance as events and factors emerge as is indicated in the real life examples.

Competing
Litigation
Public Relations
Arguing
Competition
Contending
Compromising
Avoiding
Cooperation
Collaborating
Negotiation
Compromise
Capitulation
Apology and Restitution

CONTINGENCY CONTINUUM

PURE ADVOCACY

PURE ACCOMMODATION

When it was claimed that used syringes were found in cans of Pepsi, the company took the stance that such claims were a hoax and stood 100 percent behind its product, resisting suggestions that a product recall was needed.

After the Odwalla beverage company found that a problem in production was linked to food poisoning it immediately issued a product recall. Odwalla also offered to pay all medical expenses of the victims and made a full apology to the public.

when it comes to dealing with conflict and perceived threats. The second principle is that the public relations stance for dealing with a particular audience or public must be dynamic. The stance must change as events unfold; there is a continuum of stances ranging from pure advocacy to pure accommodation. These two principles form the basis of *contingency theory*.

Contingency factors. The public relations approach that is used is "contingent" on many factors that professionals must take into account.

In a survey of 1,000 members of the Public Relations Society of America (PRSA), most practitioners reported that the expertise and experience of the public relations

professional play a major role in formulating the proper strategy for dealing with a conflict or issue. Organizational-level variables, however, are also important. Likewise, the values and attitudes of top management clearly have a great influence on how an organization responds to conflict and threats.

The contingency continuum. Depending on circumstances, factors such as the attitudes of top management, and the judgment of public relations professionals, may move the organization either toward or away from accommodation of a public. Thus the range of response forms a continuum from pure advocacy to pure accommodation.

Pure advocacy is a hard-nosed stance of completely disagreeing with or refuting the arguments, claims, or threats of a competitor or a group concerned about an issue. The other extreme on this continuum is pure accommodation. In this case, the orga-nization agrees with its critics, changes its policies, makes restitution, and even makes a full public apology for its actions. Of course, there are other stances in between these two extremes that an organization can take. In this sense, the continuum shows the dynamism of strategic conflict management. In many cases, an organization initially adopts a pure advocacy stance, but as the situation changes, new information comes to light, and public opinion shifts, the stance changes toward more accommodation, provided such a move does not violate deeply held principles.

> ❝What appears to us as rational and real is determined by the organizational culture we exist within and the economic and political reality that structures that culture … In times of uncertainty and danger, the organization reverts to denial, ritual, and rigidity and invokes its own version of reality as a basic defense against external evidence or attack.❞

Astrid Kersten, LaRoche College

it depends: factors that affect conflict management **49**

THE CONFLICT MANAGEMENT
life cycle

Successful public relations professionals serve as more than communication technicians carrying out the tactics of organizing events, writing news releases, handling news conferences, and pitching stories to journalists. They also take on the responsibility within the organization for managing conflict and weathering the crisis situations inevitably faced by all organizations at one time or another.

The conflict management life cycle illustrates the "big picture" of how to manage a conflict. Strategic conflict management can be divided into four general phases, but bear in mind that the lines between the phases are not absolute and that some techniques overlap in actual practice. Furthermore, in the exciting world of public relations, busy practitioners may be actively managing different competitive situations as well as conflicts in each of the four phases simultaneously.

Proactive Phase

The proactive phase of the conflict management life cycle includes activities and thought processes that can prevent a conflict from arising or from getting out of hand. The first step in the phase is environmental scanning—the constant reading, listening, and watching of current affairs with an eye toward the organization's interests. As new issues emerge, tracking becomes more focused and systematic through processes such as blog monitoring and daily news story scanning. Issues management occurs when the organization makes behavioral changes or creates strategic plans for ways to address emerging issues. In the proactive phase, well-run organizations also develop a general crisis plan as a first step in preparing for the worst—an issue or an event that escalates to crisis proportions.

Strategic Phase

In the strategic phase, an emerging conflict is identified as meriting concerted action by the public relations professional. Three broad strategies are undertaken in this phase. Through risk communication, dangers or threats to people or organizations are conveyed to forestall personal injury, health problems, and environmental damage. Conflict-positioning strategies enable the organization to position itself favorably in anticipation of actions such as litigation, boycott, adverse legislation, elections, or similar events that will play out in "the court of public opinion." To be prepared for the worst outcome—that is, an issue that resists risk communication efforts and becomes a conflict of crisis proportions—a specific crisis management plan is developed.

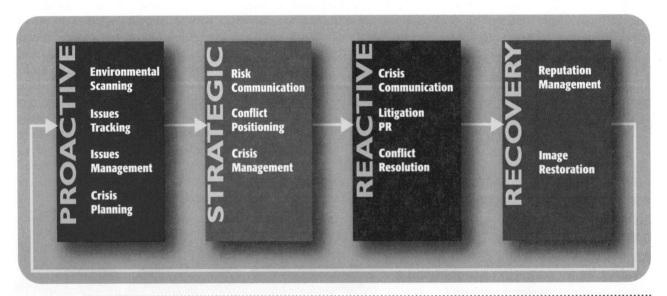

This figure shows the four phases of the conflict management life cycle and numerous techniques that public relations people use to deal with conflict. Typically, events move through time from left to right along the life cycle. At the end of the cycle, the process begins all over again on the left side of the cycle.

Water Purveyors Face Conflict and Competition

THE BOTTLED WATER INDUSTRY faces the challenge of dealing with both competition and conflict in the marketplace. Some of the competition comes from companies (such as Brita) that promote the attachment of a water filter on a faucet for tap water. Other competition comes from companies (such as Nalgene or SIGG) that promote the use of their reusable water containers. Tappening, one company that manufactures reusable containers, has placed ads directly attacking bottled water. One ad even made the claim that "Bottled water makes acid rain fall on playgrounds." Brita, not to be outdone, has used photos in its ads of oil running out of people's mouths above the caption, "Last year, 16 million gallons of oil were consumed to make plastic water bottles."

Conflict comes from various environmental groups that state that drinking bottled water is environmentally unfriendly. These groups explain that plastic bottles generate greenhouse gasses, fill landfills, and contribute to large carbon footprints because they are shipped from such exotic places as Fiji and Iceland.

The $12 billion bottled water industry is clearly under attack from its competition and environmental groups. In fact, partially as a result of the economic recession in 2009 and campaigns such as those mounted by Brita and Tappening, sales of bottled water declined almost 10 percent in that year. The main question, of course, is whether the industry can change consumer's perceptions and reverse the sales curves.

The bottled water industry, which is represented by trade groups such as the International Bottled Water Association and the Natural Hydration Council, insists that its critics are being unfair. Jeremy Clarke, director of the Natural Hydration Council, counters their claims by saying, "Bottled water is the cheapest, greenest, healthiest drink on the shelf. It's a packaged product and must be understood in that context." Joseph Doss, the chief executive of the International Bottled Water Association, chimes in, "In the marketplace, bottled water considers its competition to be soft drinks, soda, juices, and teas. Pitting bottled water versus tap water just doesn't seem like a useful exercise."

1 Do you think the bottled water industry is being unjustly criticized?

2 If you were public relations counsel for Aquafina or Dasani, what conflict management strategy would you propose?

Reactive Phase

Once the issue or imminent conflict reaches a critical level of impact on the organization, the public relations professional must react to events as they unfold in the external communication environment. Crisis communication includes the implementation of the crisis management plan as well as 24/7 efforts to meet the needs of publics such as disaster victims, employees, government officials, and the media. When conflict has emerged but is not careening out of control, conflict resolution techniques are used to bring a heated conflict—such as collapsed salary negotiations—to a favorable resolution. Often, the most intractable conflicts end up in the courts. Litigation public relations employs communication strategies and publicity efforts in support of legal actions or trials.

think Is the job of public relations finished once a conflict has been resolved?

Recovery Phase

In the aftermath of a crisis or a high-profile, heated conflict with a public, an organization employs strategies to bolster or repair its reputation. Reputation management includes conducting systematic research to learn the state of the organization's reputation and then taking steps to improve it. When the damage is extreme, image restoration strategies can help, provided the organization is willing to undergo genuine change.

MANAGING THE life cycle OF A CONFLICT

although challenging, conflict management is not impossible. Four systematic processes provide guidance and structure for this highly rewarding role played by public relations professionals in managing competition and conflict: (1) issues management, (2) strategic positioning and risk communication, (3) crisis management, (4) and reputation management.

Issues Management

Identifying and dealing with issues in a timely manner is one of the more important functions of the proactive phase of the conflict management life cycle. Issues manage-

ment is a systematic approach to predicting problems, anticipating threats, minimizing surprises, resolving issues, and preventing crises.

Issues management is proactive planning. Writing in *Public Relations Review*, Philip Gaunt and Jeff Ollenburger say, "Issues management is proactive in that it tries to identify issues and influence decisions regarding them before they have a detrimental effect on a corporation." Gaunt and Ollenburger contrast the issues management approach with crisis management, which is essentially reactive in nature. They note, "Crisis management tends to be more reactive,

dealing with an issue after it becomes public knowledge and affects the company." Active planning and prevention through issues management often mean the difference between a

> **❝Effective issues management requires two-way communications, formal environmental scanning, and active sense-making strategies.❞**
> **Martha Lauzen,**
> **San Diego State University**

Public relations counselors W. Howard Chase and Barrie L. Jones were among the first practitioners to specialize in **issues management.** They defined the process as consisting of five basic steps: (1) issue identification, (2) issue analysis, (3) strategy options, (4) an action plan, and (5) the evaluation of results.

Step ❶ Issue Identification.
Organizations should track the alternative press, mainstream media, online chat groups, and the newsletters of activist groups to learn which issues and concerns are being discussed. Of particular importance is establishing a trend line of coverage.

Step ❷ Issue Analysis.
Once an emerging issue has been identified, the next step is to assess its potential impact on and threat to the organization. Another consideration is to determine whether the organization is vulnerable on the issue.

Step ❸ Strategy Options.
If the company decides that the emerging issue is potentially damaging, it must then consider what to do about it. The pros and cons of each option are weighed against what is most practical and economical for the company.

Step ❹ Action Plan.
Once a specific policy (stance) has been decided on, the fourth step is to communicate it to all interested publics.

Step ❺ Evaluation.
With the new policy in place and communicated, the final step is to evaluate the results. Has news coverage been positive? Is the company being positioned as an industry leader? Have public perceptions of the company and the industry improved? If the company has acted soon enough, perhaps the greatest measurement of success is avoiding the media coverage that occurs when a problem becomes a crisis.

think How can early issue identification help prevent a crisis?

noncrisis and a crisis—or, as one practitioner put it, the difference between little or no news coverage and a front-page headline. This point is particularly relevant because studies have shown that the majority of organizational crises are self-inflicted, in that management ignored early warning signs.

With appropriate handling, issues and situations can be managed or even forestalled by public relations professionals before they become crises, or before they lead to significant losses for the organization, such as a diminished reputation, alienation of key stakeholders, and financial damage to the organization.

Strategic Positioning and Risk Communication

Strategic positioning is any verbal or written exchange that attempts to communicate information to position the organization favorably regarding competition or an anticipated conflict. Ideally, the public relations professional communicates in a way that not only positions the organization favorably in the face of competition and imminent conflict, but also favorably influences the actual behavior of the organization. For example, facing enormous financial losses and the need to lay off thousands of employees, General Motors announced that it was freezing executive salaries. This measure reduced the level of criticism directed toward the employee layoffs that followed.

Often, public relations professionals can communicate in ways that reduce risks for affected publics and for their employers. Communicating about risks to public health and safety and the environment is a

SUGGESTIONS
FOR COMMUNICATORS

Suzanne Zoda, writing on risk communication in *Communication World*, gives the following suggestions to communicators:

- **Begin early and initiate a dialogue.**

  Do not wait until the opposition marshals its forces. Early contact with anyone who may be concerned or affected is vital to establishing trust.

- **Actively solicit and identify concerns.**

  Informal discussions, surveys, interviews, and focus groups are effective in evaluating issues and identifying outrage factors.

- **Recognize the public as a legitimate partner in the process.**

  Engage interested groups in two-way communication and involve key opinion leaders.

- **Address issues of concern,**

  even if they do not directly pertain to the situation.

- **Anticipate and prepare for hostility.**

  To defuse a situation, use a conflict resolution approach. Identify areas of agreement and work toward common ground.

- **Understand the needs of the news media.**

  Provide accurate, timely information and respond promptly to requests.

- **Always be honest, even when it hurts.**

particularly important role for public relations professionals.

Organizations, including large corporations, are increasingly engaging in risk communication to inform the public of risks such as those associated with food products, chemical spills, radioactive waste disposal, or the placement of drug abuse treatment centers or halfway houses in neighborhoods. These issues deserve public notice in fairness to the general populace. In addition, expensive lawsuits, restrictive legislation, consumer boycotts, and public debate may result if organizations fail to disclose potential hazards. As is often the case, doing the right thing in conflict management often proves the least disruptive tactic in the long run. When risk communication fails, however, an organization may face a true crisis.

Crisis Management

In public relations, high-profile events such as accidents, terrorist attacks, disease pandemics, and natural disasters can dwarf the effectiveness of even the best strategic positioning and risk management strategies. This is when crisis management takes over. The conflict management process, which includes ongoing issues management and risk communication efforts, is severely tested during crisis situations when a high degree of uncertainty exists. Unfortunately, even the most thoughtfully designed conflict management process cannot prepare an organization to deal with certain crises, such as planes flying into the World Trade Center. And sometimes, even when risk communication is employed to prevent an issue from evolving into a major problem, that issue will grow into a crisis. At such times, verifiable information about what is happening or has happened may be lacking.

Uncertainty causes people to become more active

Some risks may occur naturally, such as beach undertows and riptides that require warning signs and flyers in hotel rooms, or they may be associated with a product, such as an air bag or a lawn mower.

DANGEROUS SHOREBREAK

STRONG CURRENT

think Why are the first 24 hours after a crisis so crucial in public relations?

seekers of information and, research suggests, more dependent on the media for information to satisfy the human desire for closure. A crisis situation, in other words, puts a great deal of pressure on organizations to respond with complete and accurate information as quickly as possible. How an organization responds in the first 24 hours, experts say, often determines whether the situation remains an "incident" or becomes a full-blown crisis.

Crises are not always unexpected. One study by the Institute for Crisis Management found that only 14 percent of business crises were unexpected. The remaining 86 percent were

what the institute called "smoldering crises," in which an organization was aware of a potential business disruption long before the public found out about it. The study also found that management—or in some cases, mismanagement—caused 78 percent of the crises.

"Most organizations have a crisis plan to deal with sudden crises, like accidents," says Robert B. Irvine, president of the Institute. "However, our data indicates many businesses are denying or ducking serious problems that eventually will ignite and cost them millions of dollars and lost management time."

Echoing Irvine's thought, another study by Steven Fink found that 89 percent of the chief executive officers of *Fortune* 500 companies

What is a Crisis?

Kathleen Fearn-Banks, in her book *Crisis Communications: A Casebook Approach,* defines a crisis as a "major occurrence with a potentially negative outcome affecting the organization, company, or industry, as well as its publics, products, services, or good name." In other words, an organizational crisis can constitute any number of situations. A *PRWeek* article included "a product recall; a plane crash; a very public sexual harassment suit; a gunman holding hostages in your office; an *E. coli* bacteria contamination scare; a market crash, along with the worth of your company stock; a labor union strike; [and] a hospital malpractice suit" in its list of crisis scenarios.

Many professionals offer advice on what to do during a crisis. Here's a compilation of good suggestions:

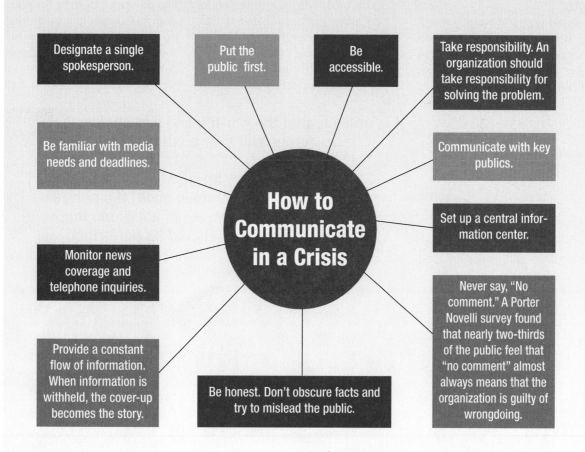

Designate a single spokesperson.

Put the public first.

Be accessible.

Take responsibility. An organization should take responsibility for solving the problem.

Be familiar with media needs and deadlines.

Communicate with key publics.

How to Communicate in a Crisis

Set up a central information center.

Monitor news coverage and telephone inquiries.

Never say, "No comment." A Porter Novelli survey found that nearly two-thirds of the public feel that "no comment" almost always means that the organization is guilty of wrongdoing.

Provide a constant flow of information. When information is withheld, the cover-up becomes the story.

Be honest. Don't obscure facts and try to mislead the public.

With proper issues management and conflict planning many smoldering crises could potentially be prevented from bursting into flames.

reported that a business crisis was almost inevitable; however, 50 percent admitted that they did not have a crisis management plan. This situation has prompted crisis consultant Kenneth Myers to write, "If economics is the dismal science, then contingency planning is the abysmal science." As academics Donald Chisholm and Martin Landry have noted, "When people believe that because nothing has gone wrong, nothing will go wrong, they court disaster. There is noise in every system and every design. If this fact is ignored, nature soon reminds us of our folly."

How various organizations respond to crises. Recent research has shown that organizations don't all respond to crises in the same way. Indeed, W. Timothy Coombs of Eastern Illinois University postulates that an organization's response may vary on a continuum from defensive to accommodative. Here is a list of crisis communication strategies that an organization may use:

- *Attack the Accuser*—The party that claims a crisis exists is confronted and its logic and facts are faulted; sometimes the organization threatens a lawsuit.
- *Denial*—The organization explains that there is no crisis.
- *Excuse*—The organization minimizes its responsibility for the crisis by denying any intention to do harm and saying that it had no control over the events that led to the crisis. This strategy is often used when a natural disaster or product tampering occurs.

- *Justification*—The crisis is minimized with a statement that no serious damage or injuries resulted. Sometimes, the blame is shifted to the victims. This is often done when a consumer misuses a product or when an industrial accident occurs.
- *Ingratiation*—The organization acts to appease the public involved. Consumers who complain are given coupons or the organization makes a donation to a charitable organization.
- *Corrective Action*—The organization takes steps to repair the damage from the crisis and to prevent it from happening again.
- *Full Apology*—The organization takes responsibility and asks forgiveness. Some compensation of money or aid is often included.

The Coombs typology gives options for crisis communication management depending on the situation and the stance taken by the organization. As Coombs notes, organizations do have to consider more accommodative strategies (ingratiation, corrective action, full apology) if defensive strategies (attack accuser,

It is unlikely that the pro-life and pro-choice forces will ever achieve mutual understanding and accommodation, much less arrive at a substantive compromise about the nature or number of abortions that should be performed each year.

denial, excuse) are not effective. The more accommodative strategies not only meet immediate crisis communication demands but can also help to subsequently repair an organization's reputation or restore previous sales levels.

Often, however, an organization doesn't adopt an accommodative strategy because of corporate culture and other constraints included in the contingency theory of conflict management matrix. Organizations do not, and sometimes cannot, engage in two-way communication and accommodative strategies when confronted with a crisis or conflict with a given public. In some cases, the contingency theory contends that the ideal of mutual understanding and accommodation doesn't

CLASSIC CRISIS
MANAGEMENT CAMPAIGNS

The crisis communication strategies outlined by Coombs (see p. 54) are useful in evaluating how an organization handles a crisis. Intel, for example, first denied in 1994 that there was a problem with its new Pentium chip. As the crisis deepened and was covered extensively in the mainstream press, Intel tried the strategy of justification, saying that the problem wasn't serious enough to warrant replacing the chips. It minimized the concerns of end users such as engineers and computer programmers. Only after considerable damage had been done to Intel's reputation and IBM had suspended orders for the chip did Intel take corrective action to replace the chips, and Andy Grove, Intel's president, issue a full apology.

Of course, not all crisis communication strategies need to be accommodative to be successful. Pepsi-Cola was able to mount an effective defensive crisis communication strategy and avoid a recall when a hoax of nationwide proportions created an intense but short-lived crisis for the soft-drink company.

The crisis began when the media reported that a man in Tacoma, Washington, claimed that he had found a syringe inside a can of Diet Pepsi. As the news spread, men and women across the country made similar claims of finding a broken sewing needle, a screw, a bullet, and even a narcotics vial in their Pepsi cans. As a consequence, some people demanded a recall of all Pepsi products—an action that would have had major economic consequences for the company.

Company officials were confident that insertion of foreign objects into cans on high-speed, closely controlled bottling lines was virtually impossible, so they chose to defend their product. The urgent problem, then, was to convince the public that the product was safe, and that any foreign objects found had been inserted after the cans had been opened.

Pepsi officials and their public relations staff employed several strategies. One approach was to attack the accuser. Company officials said the foreign objects probably got into the cans after they were opened, and even explained that many people make such claims just to collect compensation from the company. The company also announced that it would pursue legal action against anyone making false claims about the integrity of the company's products.

Pepsi also adopted the strategy of denial, saying that there was no crisis. Pepsi president Craig E. Weatherup immediately made appearances on national television programs and gave newspaper interviews to state the company's case that its bottling lines were secure. Helping to convince the public was U.S. Food and Drug Administration Commissioner David Kessler, who said that a recall was not necessary.

These quick actions deflated the public's concern, and polls showed considerable acceptance of Pepsi's contention that the problem was a hoax. A week after the scare began, Pepsi ran full-page advertisements with the headline, "Pepsi is pleased to announce . . . Nothing." It stated, "As America now knows, those stories about Diet Pepsi were a hoax. . . ."

The classic cases highlighted here illustrate one emphasis of contingency theory: No single crisis communication strategy is appropriate for all situations. Indeed, as Coombs indicates, "It is only by understanding the crisis situation that the crisis manager can select the appropriate response for the crisis."

occur because both sides have staked out highly rigid positions and are not willing to compromise their strong moral positions. Taking such an inflexible stance can be a foolish strategy and a sign of lack of professionalism.

At other times, conflict is a natural state between competing interests, such as oil interests seeking to open Alaskan wildlife refuges to oil exploration and environmental groups seeking to block that exploration. Frequently, one's stance and strategies for conflict management entail assessment and balancing of many factors.

Reputation Management

Reputation is the collective representation of an organization's past performance that describes the firm's ability to deliver valued outcomes to multiple stakeholders. Put in plain terms, reputation is the track record of an organization in the public's mind.

The three foundations of reputation. Reputation scholars describe reputation as having three foundations: (1) economic performance, (2) social responsiveness, and (3) the ability to deliver valuable outcomes to stakeholders. Public relations plays a role in all three foundations of reputation, but professionals who manage conflict effectively will especially enhance the latter two. The social responsiveness of an organization results from careful issues tracking and effective positioning of the organization. It is further enhanced when risk communication is compelling and persuasive. The ability to make valuable contributions to stakeholders who depend on the organization results in part from the organization's ability to fend off threats that might impair its mission.

In addition to tracking and dealing proactively with issues, convey-

Public relations scholar Lisa Lyon makes the point that reputation, unlike corporate image, is owned by the public. Reputation isn't formed by packaging or slogans. A good reputation is created and destroyed by everything an organization does, from the way it manages employees to the way it handles conflicts with outside constituents.

ing risks to publics, and managing crises as they arise, public relations practitioners are faced with the need to apologize at those times when all efforts to manage conflict have fallen short. The future trust and credibility of the organization are at stake, based on how well this recovery phase of conflict management is handled.

The frequent platitude in post-crisis communication is that practitioners should acknowledge failings, apologize, and then put the events in the past as quickly as possible. In reality, Lyon (see quote above) has found that apology is not always effective because of the hypocrisy factor. When an organization has a questionable track record (i.e., a bad reputation), the apology may be viewed as insincere and hypocritical. Coombs suggests a relational approach, which assumes that crises are episodes within a larger stakeholder–organizational relationship.

Applying the contingency theory, considering how stakeholders perceive the situation can help communicators determine which strategy is best to rebuild the stakeholder–organization relationship and restore the organization's reputation.

Image restoration. Reputation repair and maintenance is a long-term process, but one of the first steps in the process is the final one in the conflict management life cycle. The image restoration strategy that an organization chooses depends a great deal on the situation, or what has already been described as the "it depends" concept. If an organization is truly innocent, a simple denial is a good strategy. Not many situations are that clear-cut, however. Consequently, a more common strategy is acknowledging the issue, but making it clear that the situation was an accident or the result of a decision with unintentional consequences. Professor William Benoit of Ohio State University calls this approach the strategy of "evading" responsibility.

Another strategy for restoring an organization's reputation relies

think **Which factors determine how effective an apology is?**

on reducing offensiveness. Ultimately, the most accommodative response is a profuse apology by the organization to the public and its various stakeholders.

Despite the public relations practitioner's best efforts, a strategy or combination of strategies may not necessarily restore the organization's reputation. A great deal depends on the perceptions of the public and other stakeholders. Do they find the explanation credible? Do they believe the organization is telling the truth? Do they think the organization is acting in the public interest? In many cases, an organization may start out with a defensive strategy only to find that the situation ultimately demands corrective action or an apology to restore its reputation.

Déjà Vu–All Over Again

To paraphrase Yogi Berra, conflict management is like déjà vu all over again. The best organizations, led by the best public relations professionals, will strive to improve performance by starting once again along the left side of the conflict management life cycle, with tasks such as environmental scanning and issues tracking. Issues that are deemed important receive attention for crisis planning and risk communication. When preventive measures fail, the crisis must be handled with the best interests of all parties held in a delicate balance. Then restoration and burnishing of the organization's reputation must be given due attention. At all times, the goal is to change organizational behavior in ways that minimize damaging conflict, not only for the sake of the organization, but also for its many stakeholders.

WHAT WOULD YOU DO?

This chapter points out that public relations professionals can influence the larger goals of an organization through litigation public relations by addressing the marketplace of ideas that revolves around lawsuits and court proceedings. Sometimes the litigation hinges on momentous questions facing society. For example, recent controversies have sprung up about the legal rights surrounding the patenting of life forms developed in labs. These life forms can be specialized plants or biopharmaceuticals—or potentially in the future, nano-creatures that will carry out medical procedures inside the human body.

The *Fortune* 500 company Monsanto is alternately demonized or glorified for its agricultural breakthroughs in patenting plant seeds that increase production, tolerate drought, or resist herbicides. For example, Monsanto has invested enormous amounts in developing a soybean plant that enables farmers to spray pernicious weeds (using a pesticide from Monsanto called Roundup) without harming the food plant itself. Less tilling is required and harvests are higher—but of course, there is a catch.

Traditionally, farmers have kept some of their crop to serve as seed for the coming year. This practice is a violation of Monsanto's patent requiring new seed to be purchased each season. To protect its patent, the company has filed suit against small farmers and businesses that reseed with its Roundup-Ready soybeans. (The fascinating documentary film *Food Inc.* puts a very human face on this litigation.)

Monsanto's decision to sue—undoubtedly a difficult one for a corporate

giant that operates globally and claims to be a key player in the battle to end worldwide hunger—has served as a lightning rod for media coverage and contentious discussion. The company is taking an advocacy stance in the courts in defense of its right to protect its (expensively developed) intellectual property. Naturally, the publisher of this textbook would not want a small bookstore to buy one copy, photocopy it, and sell the copies to hundreds of students each semester. But does the same hold for copying (growing) a plant?

In what ways does the adversarial stance taken by Monsanto shape its communication strategies? Draft a proposal for a campaign to address the issues that the company's stance necessitates. Discuss with your classmates how a movement on the continuum toward a more accommodative stance might cause you to revise your campaign.

Summary

What Role Do Competition and Conflict Play in Public Relations? p. 44

- Public relations can be defined as strategic management of competition and conflict.

- Some of the most crucial roles played by public relations professionals involve the strategic management of conflict.

- The outstanding practitioner monitors for threats, assesses those threats, arrives at a desirable stance for the organization, and then begins communication efforts from that stance. One approach is the *threat appraisal model*.

- *Contingency theory* argues for a dynamic and multifaceted approach to dealing with conflict in the field.

What Are the Phases of the Conflict Management Life Cycle? p. 48

- Strategic conflict management can be broadly divided into four phases, with specific techniques and functions being part of each phase: the proactive phase, the strategic phase, the reactive phase, and the recovery phase.

- The life cycle emphasizes that conflict management is ongoing and cyclical in nature.

How Can Public Relations Professionals Best Manage the Conflict Management Life Cycle? p. 50

- Issues management is a proactive and systematic approach to predicting problems, anticipating threats, minimizing surprises, resolving issues, and preventing crises.

- The five steps in the issues management process are issue identification, issue analysis, strategy options, an action plan, and evaluation of results.

- Risk communication attempts to convey information regarding risks to public health and safety and the environment.

- The communication process is severely tested in crisis situations, which can take many forms. A common problem is the lack of crisis management plans. Organizations' responses vary from defensive to accommodative.

- One of an organization's most valuable assets is its reputation, which is influenced by how the organization deals with conflict, and particularly crises that generate significant media attention.

QUESTIONS
for *Review* and *Discussion*

1. Do you accept the proposition that conflict management is one of the most important functions of public relations? Why or why not?

2. What are the five steps in the issues management process?

3. How can effective issues management prevent organizational crises?

4. Both Exxon and Pepsi used defensive crisis communication strategies. One succeeded, while the other failed. Which factors do you think made the difference?

5. What is risk communication?

6. How would you use the contingency theory of conflict management (the continuum from accommodation to advocacy) in advising management on a rising conflict situation?

7. Do you think that image restoration is merely a superficial fix or a substantive solution to adverse events? Support your view with some examples from current news stories.

8. Why would lawyers benefit from working closely with public relations counsel? For litigation? For dispute resolution through effective negotiation?

9. Do you think it is ethical for legal counsel to be assisted by public relations expertise?

the
THINK SPOT
www.thethinkspot.com

TACTICS

NEW YORK MAGAZINE

Maybe Tiger Woods Knows Exactly What He Is Doing

This editorial defies the formulaic, simplistic advice: acknowledge wrong-doing, apologize, and move on.

Tiger's screwing this all up, the thinking goes. He's blown it from the start—from going into hiding, to the half-assed mea culpas he posted on his website ("I'm not perfect"), to his announcement that he's taking a leave of absence from his career. In a year in which another serial womanizer, David Letterman, laid out a nearly perfect road map for damage control in similarly trying circumstances—disclose early and cleanly so that, for God's sake, you don't create a vacuum for the tabloid press to fill!—well, why is Tiger doing pretty much the exact opposite? Is one of the world's great one-man brands actually one of the world's most clueless brand managers?

Maybe not. Maybe Tiger knows exactly what he's doing. Let's consider his four-point game plan so far—which, yeah, might actually amount to a strategy:

1. Let the bit players take the stage.

Research indicates that one strategy that is often effective when a PR crisis hits is for the subject of controversy—in this case, Tiger Woods—to "steal the thunder" by announcing a problem before the media breaks the story. Conventional wisdom indicates this minimizes the thunderous news coverage and forces journalists to scramble to share the limelight with the perpetrator and to fill up gaping 24-hour news holes with little or no advance notice. By "stealing the media's thunder," the subject gets to call the shots and determine the pacing of the story rather than letting the media do so.

Journalists sometimes overestimate the power of public relations attempts to shape a situation or to "spin" a message in some way that magically defies the reality of the situation. Discuss this question with classmates or visiting professionals: Does spin work?

The Letterman tactic of early, clean disclosure only works if you know exactly what you're disclosing. Dave's extramarital excursions occurred within his own tightly controlled environment—in the office of the show (and corporation, Worldwide Pants) that he runs. He hooked up with, apparently, trusted (and discreet) coworkers. He was able to take charge of the narrative only because his lovers (and his wife) allowed him to. Tiger's entanglements, on the other hand, involved a sprawling, worldwide network of obviously indiscreet and deeply unpredictable characters. There was no way he could even partially address all the rumors without begging a million new questions. You can't control chaos, you can't spin the unspinnable—Tiger must have realized that as soon as the first of his flirty text messages leaked to the tabloid press. So he just waited to see what would come next—knowing there'd be a lot of nexts. What's happening now, to Tiger's benefit, is that the members of his harem are essentially beginning to cancel each other out. Nobody can keep the club promoter apart from the cocktail waitress, apart from the other cocktail waitress, apart from the supposed prostitute, apart from . . .

2. Go on an "indefinite break."

Brilliant! Especially since leaving his sabbatical open-ended creates a whole new narrative of anticipation—or, actually, desperation. Because clearly the entire golf-industrial complex is seriously screwed by Tiger's disappearing act—from Nike, which basically built its entire golf business around Tiger, to the PGA tour, as lampooned on *Saturday Night Live* last weekend.

Everybody expected Tiger to skip some golf events—he's still in bunker mode—but announcing it as "indefinite" flips the script and puts Tiger back in control. Essentially, he's all like, *Okay, you all hate me so much? Fine! Go ahead and live without me!* In a split second he went from being golf's albatross to golf's future savior (the second coming of Tiger).

3. With apologies to Nike, Just **** it!

Yesterday came word that Elin is set to divorce Tiger. Yeah, Tiger has made noises about working to save his marriage, but does anybody doubt that a split isn't the best thing for everybody—especially Tiger? (Particularly if we believe TMZ's report [TMZ is a celebrity news website] that Elin is physically abusive?) Frankly, when you think about it, Tiger's history with his harem is so wide-ranging and reckless that you almost have to conclude that he was engineering his own downfall. It's a cliché, but he probably wanted to get caught. From the earliest days of his career, as Charles P. Pierce recently wrote for *Esquire*, he "was something of a hound." ("Everybody knew. Everybody had a story.") Golden handcuffs—all those insanely lucrative endorsement deals—forced Tiger to play-act the Happily Married Family Man, but clearly his bliss lay and lies elsewhere. Woods, poor bastard, just wanted to live the George Clooney lifestyle! He chose to continue to live that life even after he got married, knowing full well that sooner or later the house of cards of his carefully constructed image would come crashing down. Like Michael Jackson, Tiger Woods may have been a guy who just couldn't say no—was told he couldn't afford to say no—to his handlers. So he found another way to say no—indirectly, but much more forcefully.

4. Stew in your own mess—it's a form of penance.

Is it possible to begin to feel pity for a guy so under siege because of his own reckless actions? Yeah, definitely. In fact, a key turning point in the eventual Redemption of Tiger Woods came with Monday's *Post* cover, with its "TIGER'S AGONY" headline, and the bits about how he's only "barely hanging on." See? It's happening already! Tiger has been waterboarded for weeks by the media, and now the media (even the Murdochian press!) is actually beginning to ascribe qualities of stoicism and sufferance to their torturee. It's like Stockholm Syndrome in reverse.

The real beauty of Tiger's strategy is that he doesn't have to worry about playing his cards right—because he's not technically in the game. When you decline to follow the usual damage-control script, there's no danger of falling off-script. Media pile-ons always reverse themselves in due time, and by then, Tiger, perversely ennobled by his ordeal, will be ready to play golf again.

Without even breaking a sweat, he could come out of this as a whole new sort of athlete: the Media Gauntlet Iron Man.

By: Simon Dumenco

4 THE GROWTH OF

Ask Yourself

> Which Key Events and Individuals Shaped the History of Public Relations? p. 66

> What Are the Trends in Today's Practice of Public Relations? p. 76

> In What Ways Is Public Relations Evolving and Growing as a Professional Practice? p. 80

> What Are the Major Professional Public Relations Organizations and What Do They Do? p. 81

Like all history, the history of public relations is constantly being examined, interpreted, and reinterpreted. In September 2006, *Business Wire*—a leading news wire source for press releases, photos, multimedia and regulatory filings—hosted events celebrating the 100th anniversary of public relations pioneer Ivy Lee's first press release. Lee has been widely hailed as one of the fathers of modern public relations. But in his blog "A PR Guy's Musings," industry observer Stuart Bruce wrote: "I can accept that Ivy Lee ... put out his first press release in 1906 but it is a bit of a stretch to claim it as the 100th anniversary of the press release." Public relations historian Karen Miller Russell, who was a panelist at one of *Business Wire's* celebratory events, noted "the news release isn't really 100 years old." She asserted that politicians used news releases at least 10 years before Lee's 1906 piece and newspaper editors in the 1800s were already complaining about publicists "stealing space." Russell assured her audience, however, that Lee was one of the first to begin issuing what he called "handouts" in a large-scale way beginning around 1906.

Nothing changes more constantly than the past! To quote yet another cliché, the past is also prelude to the future. In the mid-twentieth century, after he had coaxed women to smoke Lucky Strike cigarettes and children to carve animals out of Ivory soap, Edward Bernays—another key figure in the history of public relations—began promoting the idea of licensure for public relations professionals. Today, with no licensing standards yet adopted by the profession, the debate still continues about the value of licensing. While professional associations have programs through which practitioners can be "accredited," proponents of licensing say it's not the same.

A PROFESSION

The personalities, issues, and debates from public relations' past continue to be foundational to today's practice. What we learn from history informs us and ultimately makes us better public relations professionals.

❶ In addition to the press release, which tactics of public relations have become commonplace in our modern world? How is the Internet changing some of these old standards and the ways in which they are employed?

❷ If you were hiring a public relations professional for your business or nonprofit organization, would it matter to you whether he or she was licensed or accredited? Why or why not?

a brief history
OF PUBLIC RELATIONS

the practice of public relations is not new. Even in ancient epochs, practitioners used public relations tactics to manage conflict and to gain a competitive advantage over rival individuals or points of view.

Ancient Beginnings
The roots of public relations stretch back to the civilizations of Babylonia, Greece, and Rome. Ancient civilizations used persuasion to promote the authority of governments and religions. Of course, these efforts were not known as "public relations," but the techniques would certainly be familiar to public relations practitioners today: interpersonal communication with opinion leaders, public speeches, written and visual communication, staged events, publicity, and other tactics.

It has often been said that the Rosetta Stone, which provided a key for modern translation and understanding of ancient Egyptian hieroglyphics, was basically a publicity release touting the pharaoh's accomplishments. Similarly, the ancient Olympic Games organizers used promotional techniques to enhance the perception of athletes as heroes in much the same way as they do in the modern Olympic Games. Then, as now, athletes competed on and off the field for the hearts and minds of sports fans, employing public relations tactics such as public appearances and media interviews.

Politician Julius Caesar had ambitions to become emperor of the Roman Empire. He organized elaborate parades whenever he returned from winning a battle to burnish

think Can you think of a modern instance of a religious or political organization using public relations to promote a position to the public?

his image as an outstanding commander and leader. After Caesar became a consul of Rome in 59 BCE, he had clerks make a record of senatorial and other public proceedings and post them on walls throughout the city. These *acta diurna*, or "daily doings," were among the world's first newspapers.

The concept of conflict, discussed in Chapter 3, is also not a new theme in the practice of public relations. Pope Urban II persuaded thousands of followers to serve God and gain forgiveness for their sins by engaging in the Holy Crusades against the Muslims. Six centuries later, the Church was among the first to use the word *propaganda*,

It has often been said that the Rosetta Stone, which provided a key for modern understanding of ancient Egyptian hieroglyphics, was basically a publicity release touting the pharaoh's accomplishments.

Press agents succeeded in glorifying Davy Crockett as a frontier hero to draw political support from Andrew Jackson and made a legend out of frontiersman Daniel Boone. John Burke was the press agent who made Buffalo Bill's Wild West Show a household name throughout the United States. Buffalo Bill and Annie Oakley were the rock stars of their age.

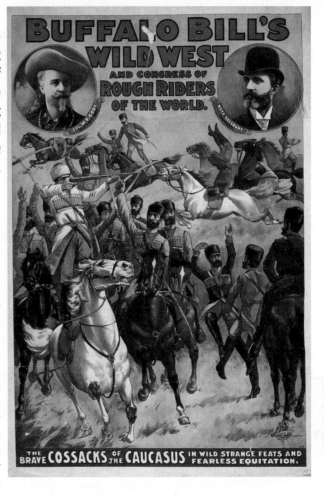

when Pope Gregory XV established the College of Propaganda, which was created to supervise foreign missions and train priests to propagate the faith.

During the Renaissance, Venetian bankers in the fifteenth and sixteenth centuries practiced the fine art of investor relations. They were probably the first, along with local Catholic bishops, to adopt the concept of corporate philanthropy by sponsoring such artists as Michelangelo.

Public Relations in Colonial America

To promote immigration to America, in 1584, Sir Walter Raleigh sent back to England glowing accounts of what was actually a swamp-filled Roanoke Island. (Eric the Red took the same persuasive stance, circa 985 CE when he discovered a land of ice and rock and named it Greenland.) Spanish explorers publicized the never-discovered Seven Cities of Gold and the fabled Fountain of Youth to lure prospective adventurers and colonists to the New World.

Public relations played an active role in building support for the conflict that led to American independence—engaging in what modern public relations practitioners term *conflict positioning*. The Boston Tea Party, which *PRWeek* has called the "the greatest and best-known publicity stunt of all time," was the inspiration of Samuel Adams, a man who understood that symbolism can sway public opinion, and that American colonists would have to advocate for only one acceptable solution—the rejection of British rule. The colonists threw crates of tea leaves from a British trade ship into Boston

harbor to protest excessive British taxation on items such as tea, and the rest is history.

Thomas Paine's persuasive writing was also instrumental in bringing lukewarm citizens into the Revolutionary movement. His pamphlet titled "Common Sense" sold more than 120,000 copies in three months. Influencing the makeup of the new political system were the *Federalist Papers*, 85 letters written by Alexander Hamilton, James Madison, and John Jay.

The Age of the Press Agent

The 1800s was a period of growth and expansion in the United States, an era that featured growing competition for consumers' attention and loyalty. It also was the golden age of the press agent—a publicist who works for recognition of an organization or individual. The period was the age of hype, in which organizations employed the media and various tactics to promote individuals, causes, or even products or services.

These old-time press agents and the people they represented played on the gullibility of the public and its desire to be entertained. Advertisements and press releases were exaggerated to the point of being outright lies. Doing advance work for an attraction, press agents would drop tickets on the desk of a newspaper editor, along with the announcements. Generous publicity generally followed on the heels of

these gifts, and the journalists and their families flocked to the free entertainment with little regard for the ethical considerations that largely prohibits such practices today.

It is no surprise, then, that today's public relations practitioner, exercising the highly sophisticated skills of evaluation, counseling, communications, and influencing management policies, shudders at the suggestion that public relations grew out of press agentry. And yet some aspects of modern public relations have their roots in the practice.

Public Relation Grows as America Grows

Just as they were used to lure colonists to seventeenth-century America, publicity and promotion were employed in the nineteenth century to populate the western United States. Land speculators distributed pamphlets and publicity

btw...

Phineas T. Barnum, the great American showman of the nineteenth century, was the master of what historian Daniel Boorstin calls the *pseudoevent*—a planned happening that occurs primarily for the purpose of being reported. Barnum used flowery language and exaggeration to promote his various attractions in an age when the public was hungry for any form of entertainment.

Through Barnum's press agentry, Tom Thumb became one of the sensations of the century. Standing just over 30 inches tall, Thumb was exceptional at singing, dancing, and performing comedy monologues. Barnum even made Thumb a

European phenomenon by introducing him to society leaders in London. An invitation to Buckingham Palace followed, and from then on Thumb played to packed houses every night. Barnum certainly knew the value of opinion leaders and third-party endorsement.

Another Barnum success was the promotion of Jenny Lind, the "Swedish Nightingale." Barnum promoted her and her beautiful singing on a national tour in the United States, making her a pop icon even before the Civil War. Barnum filled auditoriums on opening nights by donating part of the proceeds to charity. As a civic activity, the event attracted many of the town's opinion

leaders, whereupon the general public flocked to attend succeeding performances. This tactic is still employed today by entertainment publicists.

---

that described almost every community as "the garden spot of the West," which one critic of the time called "downright puffery, full of exaggerated statements, and high-wrought and false-colored descriptions." One brochure about Nebraska, for example, described the territory as the "Gulf stream of migration ... bounded on the north by the 'Aurora Borealis' and on the south by the Day of Judgment." Other brochures were more down-to-earth, describing the fertile land and abundant water, and touting the opportunity to build a fortune.

American railroads, in particular, used extensive public relations and press agentry to attract settlers and expand their operations. People and communities were necessary throughout the western United States to provide a business opportunity for rail companies. Consequently, such companies as the Burlington and Missouri Railroad took it upon themselves to promote western settlement from England and other places. For example, the Burlington and Missouri Railroad set up an information office in Liv-

erpool that distributed fact sheets and maps and placed stories in the local press. In addition, the railroad promoted lectures about migrating to the American West.

Near the end of the nineteenth century, the Atchison, Topeka and Santa Fe Railway launched a campaign to entice tourists to the Southwest. It commissioned dozens of painters and photographers to depict the dramatic landscape and show romanticized American Indians weaving, grinding corn, and dancing.

A wave of industrialization and urbanization swept the nation after the Civil War. New concentrations of wealth led to concerns about business practices. In 1888, the Mutual Life Insurance Company hired a journalist to write news releases designed to stave off criticism and improve its image. In 1889, Westinghouse Corporation established what is thought to be the first in-house publicity department. In 1897, the term *public relations* was first used by the Association of American Railroads in a company listing.

The Rise of Politics and Activism

The nineteenth century also saw the development and use of public relations tactics on the political and activist front. Amos Kendall, a former Kentucky newspaper editor, became an intimate member of President Andrew Jackson's "Kitchen Cabinet"; he could be considered the first presidential press secretary.

Kendall sampled public opinion on issues, advised Jackson, and skillfully interpreted the president's rough-hewn ideas, molding them into powerful speeches and news releases. He also served as Jackson's advance agent on trips, wrote glowing articles that he sent to supportive newspapers, and is believed to be the first person to use newspaper reprints in public relations campaigns; almost every complimentary story or editorial about Jackson was reprinted and widely circulated. Article reprints are still a standard tactic in today's PR practice.

Supporters and leaders of causes such as abolition, suffrage, and prohibition of alcohol employed

GIVE MOTHER THE VOTE
WE NEED IT

VOTES FOR OUR MOTHERS

OUR FOOD   OUR HEALTH   OUR PLAY
OUR HOMES   OUR SCHOOLS   OUR WORK
ARE RULED BY MEN'S VOTES

Isn't it a funny thing
That Father cannot see
Why Mother ought to have a vote
On how these things should be?

THINK IT OVER

Printed by National Woman Suffrage Publishing Company, Inc., 505 Fifth Avenue, New York

publicity to maximum effect throughout the nineteenth century. One of the most influential publicity ventures for the abolition movement was the publication of Harriet Beecher Stowe's *Uncle Tom's Cabin*.

Amelia Bloomer, a women's rights advocate, garnered plenty of media publicity by wearing loose-fitting trousers in protest of the corset. Noted temperance crusader Carrie Nation became nationally known by invading saloons and destroying the liquor bottles and bars with an axe.

Activists have been using public relations tactics throughout history. In the 1860s, naturalist John Muir wrote in the *New York Times* and other publications about the importance of protecting the Yosemite Valley in California. In 1889, he worked with the editor of *Century Magazine*, Robert Underwood Johnson, to promote a campaign requesting Congressional support for Yosemite National Park. The activist public relations campaign succeeded—and generations of people have enjoyed the benefits of a protected Yosemite.

Modern Public Relations Comes of Age

As the use of publicity gained acceptance, the first publicity agency, known as the Publicity Bureau, was established in Boston in 1900 with Harvard College as its most presti-

gious client. George F. Parker and Ivy Ledbetter Lee opened a publicity office in New York City in 1904. Public relations practice continued to evolve in the 1900s, as business leaders and politicians increasingly employed public relations tactics. This growth also provided an opportunity for the rise of the independent counselor.

Although public relations practitioners through the ages have been thoughtful about their communication approaches, the idea of public relations as a strategic endeavor really took hold in the early twentieth century. The Georgia-born and Princeton-educated Ivy Ledbetter Lee was the first public relations counselor. He began as a journalist, became a publicist, and soon expanded that role to become the first public relations counsel.

When Lee opened his public relations firm, he issued a declaration of principles that signaled a new practice model: public information. His emphasis was on the dissemination of truthful, accurate information rather than the distortions, hype, and exaggerations that characterized press agentry. Lee's declaration, which

Henry Ford was the first major industrialist in the United States, and he was among **the first to use two basic public relations concepts**. The first was the notion of **positioning**—the idea that credit and publicity always go to those who do something first. The second idea was the importance of being **accessible** to the press.

In 1900, Ford obtained press coverage of the prototype Model T by demonstrating it to a reporter from the Detroit Tribune. By 1903, Ford was receiving **widespread publicity** by racing his cars—a practice still used by today's auto makers ("Win on Sunday; sell on Monday"). Ford hired Barney Oldfield, a champion bicycle racer and a popular personality, to drive a Model T at a record speed of about 60 miles per hour. The publicity from these speed runs gave Ford financial backing and **a ready market**.

Ford became a **household name** because he was willing to be interviewed by the press on almost any subject, including the gold standard, evolution, alcohol, foreign affairs, and even capital punishment.

President Theodore Roosevelt was a master at generating publicity. He was the first president to make extensive use of **news conferences and interviews** to build support for his favorite projects. On a trip to Yosemite National Park, Roosevelt was accompanied by a large group of reporters and photographers who wrote glowing articles about Roosevelt's pet project—the need to preserve areas for public recreational use. The toy **teddy bear** had its origins on a hunting trip taken by Roosevelt, who was once again accompanied by reporters. During the trip he spared the life of a small bear, an incident that impressed the journalists enough to inspire them **to write about it**. A toymaker saw the stories and began to make and market "Teddy" bears in recognition of the president's humane gesture.

stemmed from his journalistic orientation, read, in part:

> This is not a secret press bureau. All our work is done in the open. We aim to supply news.... In brief, our plan is, frankly and openly, in behalf of business concerns and public institutions, to supply to the press and the public of the United States prompt and accurate information concerning subjects which is of value and interest to the public.

Lee began handling media relations for the Pennsylvania Railroad, but is best known for his work for John D. Rockefeller, Jr. Lee was hired to provide strategic counsel in the wake of the vicious strike-breaking activities known as the Ludlow Massacre at the Rockefeller family's Colorado Fuel and Iron (CF&I) company plant.

To do so, Lee employed strategies central to the conflict management life cycle (see Chapter 3). In the proactive phase, he did environmental scanning by going to Colorado for fact finding (research) and talking to both sides. He found that labor leaders were effectively getting their views out by freely talking to the media, but that the company's executives were tight-lipped and inaccessible. The result was a barrage of negative publicity and public criticism directed at CF&I and the Rockefeller family. Lee also researched the miners' grievances and their conflict methods.

In the strategic phase, he proposed disseminating a series of informational bulletins to get the

Rockefeller side of the story out to opinion leaders in Colorado and beyond. In the reactive phase, Lee convinced the governor of Colorado to write an article supporting the position taken by CF&I. He also convinced Rockefeller to visit the plant and talk with miners and their families, making sure the press was there to record Rockefeller eating in the workers' hall, swinging a pickaxe in the mine, and having a beer with workers after hours. The press loved it, which led to the recovery phase of the conflict management life cycle.

Through a *muscular approach* to public relations—that is, by employing careful strategy and a broad array of tactics—Lee prevented the United Mine Workers from gaining a foothold in the Rockefeller mines. Through strategic counsel, Lee provided both his client and the miners with some level of success and satisfaction and put their conflict to rest.

Lee continued as a counselor to the Rockefeller family and its various companies, but he also counseled a number of other clients, too. For example, he advised the American Tobacco Company to initiate a profit-sharing plan, the Pennsylvania Railroad to beautify its stations, and the movie industry to stop inflated advertising and develop a voluntary code of censorship. See the PR Casebook box in this chapter to learn about Lee's work with New York's first subway.

Ivy Lee is remembered today for four important contributions to public relations:

- Advancing the concept that business and industry should align themselves with the public interest
- Dealing with top executives and carrying out no program unless it has the active support of management
- Maintaining open communication with the news media
- Emphasizing the necessity of humanizing business and bringing its public relations down to the community level of employees, customers, and neighbors

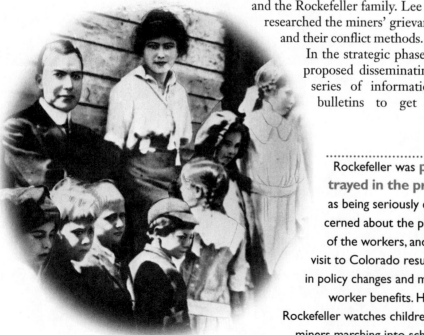

Rockefeller was **portrayed in the press** as being seriously concerned about the plight of the workers, and his visit to Colorado resulted in policy changes and more worker benefits. Here, Rockefeller watches children of miners marching into school.

Constructive Public Relations for the New York Subway

IVY LEE was retained by the New York subway system in 1916 to foster public understanding and support.

The Interborough Rapid Transit Company (IRT) faced many new challenges as it began its second decade of operation. It was completing construction and expanding service, but it also faced competition from a rival system, the Brooklyn Rapid Transit Company (later known as BMT).

Under Ivy Lee's direction, the IRT took an innovative approach, communicating directly with its passengers through pamphlets, brochures, and posters "to establish a close understanding of its work and policies." The most famous and influential products of Lee's campaign were two concurrently appearing poster series: *The Subway Sun* and *The Elevated Express.*

Between 1918, when the first posters appeared, and 1932, when the series ended, these posters became New York institutions. They entertained and informed millions of subway commuters during World War I and through the Great Depression. Lee's posters announced the introduction of coin-operated turnstiles, describing the turnstiles as "a change which revolutionized the daily habits of millions of people." Posters also explained the need for fare increases in the 1920s, extolled the fast direct train service to baseball games at Yankee Stadium and the Polo Grounds, and supplied information on how to get to other city institutions (such as the one shown here). Designed to resemble the front page of a newspaper, *The Subway Sun* and *The Elevated Express* announced the opening of the 42nd Street shuttle between Grand Central Station and Times Square; asked riders to not block the doors; and urged them to visit the city's free swimming pools. As the subways became more crowded, the IRT used the posters to promote its "open air" elevated lines as a more comfortable alternative.

Today, more than 90 years later, Lee's idea of communicating directly to passengers through posters, pamphlets, and brochures is still being used by public transit systems around the world. Many of the themes are the same as those evident in Lee's day—public safety, system improvements, travel advisories, subway etiquette, and public service announcements.

1 Imagine you are representing a mass transit company today. What would you do to increase ridership? Which themes might be appealing?

2 Where do you see posters used to promote products, issues, or services directly to consumers? How could they have been more effective in your opinion?

3 Have you ever ridden on mass transit? If so, what struck you about the experience? Imagine you are participating in a focus group with other riders. Which pros and cons would you share with the researchers conducting the focus group? How could such information help inform a communications campaign with current or prospective riders?

IT'S GREAT TO BE A NEW YORKER

Our Men KNOW Their Jobs

Elevated Express
Published now and then by the Interborough Rapid Transit Company

Always Dependable

VOLUME VI — OCTOBER — NUMBER 27

Your Children and you will enjoy seeing the thousand and one wonders in the Museum of Natural History

Take the West Side Elevated to 81st Street

The Subway Station at 79th Street is only 2½ Blocks away

Interborough Rapid Transit Co.

Another PR innovator was George Creel, also a former newspaper reporter. Creel was asked by President Woodrow Wilson to organize a massive public relations effort to unite the nation and to influence world opinion during World War I. Wilson accepted Creel's advice that hatred of the Germans should be downplayed and that loyalty and confidence in the government should be emphasized. The Committee on Public Information also publicized the war aims and Wilson's ideals—to make the world safe for democracy and to make World War I "the war to end all wars."

This massive publicity effort had a profound effect on the development of public relations by demonstrating the success of these techniques. It also awakened awareness in Americans of the power of mediated information in changing public attitudes and behavior. This realization, coupled with postwar analysis of British propaganda devices, resulted in a number of scholarly books and college courses on the subject. Among these books was Walter Lippmann's classic *Public Opinion* (1922), in which he pointed out how people are moved to action by "the pictures in our heads."

Edward B. Bernays was one of several individuals who served on the Creel Committee and went on to become a successful and widely known public relations counselor. Bernays, through brilliant campaigns and extensive self-promotion, became known as the "father of modern public relations" by the time of his death in 1995 at the age of 103.

Bernays, the nephew of Sigmund Freud, conceptualized a model of public relations that emphasized the application of social science research and behavioral psychology to formulate campaigns and messages that could change people's perceptions and encourage certain behaviors. Unlike Lee's public information model, which emphasized the distribution of accurate news, Bernays'

think

What are the key differences between the approaches advocated by Lee and Bernays?

model essentially focused on advocacy and scientific persuasion. It included listening to the audience, but the purpose of feedback was to formulate a better persuasive message.

Bernays became a major spokesperson for the "new" public relations with the publication of his 1923 book, *Crystallizing Public Opinion.* His first sentence announced:

"In writing this book I have tried to set down the broad principles that govern the new profession of public relations counsel." In the pages that followed, Bernays outlined the scope, function, methods, techniques, and social responsibilities of a *public relations counsel*—a term that was to become the core of public relations practice.

Journalist Larry Tye credits Bernays, who was named by *Life* magazine in 1990 as one of the 100 most important Americans of the

Edward Bernays, over the course of his long career, had many successful campaigns (some controversial) that have become classics.

Lucky Strike Cigarettes.
Bernays found that, while smoking was seen primarily as a man's activity, women smoked cigarettes as an expression of liberation and power. Based on his research, he labeled cigarettes women's "Torches of Freedom" and planted the idea with some socialites that they should be seen smoking cigarettes when they strutted their fashion in New York's 1929 Easter Parade. Journalists reported on the event and smoking became a more acceptable—even fashionable—activity among women.

Procter & Gamble's Ivory Soap. Procter & Gamble sold its Ivory Soap bars by the millions after Bernays came up with the idea of sponsoring soap sculpture contests for school-age children. In the first year alone, 22 million schoolchildren participated in the contest, which eventually ran for 35 years.

Light's Golden Jubilee. To celebrate the fiftieth anniversary of Thomas Edison's invention of the electric light bulb, Bernays arranged the attention-getting Light's Golden Jubilee in 1929. It was his idea that the world's utilities would all shut off their power at one time, for one minute, to honor Edison. President Herbert Hoover and many dignitaries were on hand for the event, and the U.S. Post Office issued a commemorative two-cent postage stamp.

twentieth century, with developing a unique approach to solving problems. Instead of thinking first about tactics, Bernays would always think about the "big idea" on how to motivate people. The bacon industry, for example, wanted to promote its product, so Bernays came up with the idea of having doctors across the land endorse a hearty breakfast. No mention was made of bacon, but sales soared anyway as people took the advice and started eating the traditional breakfast of bacon and eggs.

One historian described Bernays as "the first and doubtless the leading ideologist of public relations."

Bernays had a powerful partner in his wife, Doris E. Fleischman, who was a talented writer, an ardent feminist, and, at one time, the Sunday editor of the *New York Tribune*. Fleischman was an equal partner in the work of Bernays' firm, interviewing clients, writing news releases, editing the company's newsletter, and writing and editing books and magazine articles.

Public Relations Expands in Postwar America

During the second half of the twentieth century, the practice of public relations became firmly established as an indispensable part of America's economic, political, and social development.

The booming economy after World War II produced rapid growth in all areas of public relations. Companies opened public relations departments or expanded existing ones. Government staffs increased in size, as did the PR staffs of nonprofits such as educational institutions and health and welfare agencies. Television emerged in the early 1950s as a national medium and as a new challenge for public relations professionals. New counseling firms sprang up nationwide.

btw...

Typical of the public relations programs of large corporations at midcentury was that employed by the Aluminum Company of America (ALCOA). Heading the operation was a vice president for public relations–advertising, who was aided by an assistant public relations director and advertising manager. Departments included community relations, product publicity, motion pictures and exhibits, employee publications, the news bureau, and speech writing. The *Alcoa News* magazine was published for all employees, and separate publications were published for each of the company's 20 plants throughout the United States. The company's main broadcast effort was sponsorship of Edward R. Murrow's *See It Now* television program.

The growth of the economy was one reason for the expansion of public relations. Other factors also played key roles:

- Dramatic increases in urban and suburban populations
- The advent of "big business," "big labor," and "big government"
- Scientific and technological advances, including automation and computerization
- The communications revolution and proliferation of mass media
- The dawn of a new bottom-line financial consideration approach to decision making, which replaced the more personalized deliberations of previous, more genteel, times

Many people felt bewildered by rapid change, cut off from the sense of community that characterized previous generations. They sought power through innumerable pressure groups, focusing on causes such as environmentalism, working conditions, and civil rights. Public opinion, registered through new, more sophisticated methods of polling, became increasingly powerful in both opposing and effecting change.

As their physical and psychological separation from their publics grew, American business and industry turned increasingly to public relations specialists for audience analysis, strategic planning, issues management, and even the creation of supportive environments for the selling of products and services. Mass media also became more complex and sophisticated, and demand for specialists in media relations grew in tandem.

By 1950, an estimated 17,000 men and 2,000 women were employed as practitioners in public relations and publicity. In 1960, the U.S. Census counted 23,870 men and 7,271 women in public relations, although some observers put the figure at approximately 35,000. Since 1960, the number of public relations practitioners has increased dramatically; it now stands at approximately 300,000 nationwide. The latest estimate from the U.S. Department of Labor predicts that public relations jobs will grow faster than jobs in most fields, with a projected 24 percent increase in the number of public relations specialists and 13 percent increase in the number of public relations managers occurring from 2008 to 2018.

Evolving Practice and Philosophy

Thanks to breakthroughs in social science research, the focus of public relations had shifted during the first half of the twentieth century from press agentry and a journalistic approach, to the psychological and sociological effects of persuasive communication on target audiences. The 1960s saw Vietnam War protests, the civil rights movement, the environmental movement, interest in women's rights, and a host of other issues come to the fore of American consciousness. Antibusiness sentiment was high, and corporations adjusted their policies in an effort to generate public goodwill and understanding. Thus the idea of issues management was added to the job description of the public relations manager. It marked the first expression of the idea that public relations should do more than persuade people that corporate policy was correct.

During this period, the idea emerged among business managers that perhaps it would be beneficial to have a dialogue with various publics and adapt corporate policy to suit their particular concerns. James Grunig, in his interpretation of the evolutionary models of public relations (see the box below), labeled this approach *two-way symmetric communication* because it involves balance between the organization and its various publics; that is, the organization and the public influence each other.

4 CLASSIC MODELS of Public Relations

James Grunig and Todd Hunt presented a typology of public relations practice in their 1984 book *Managing Public Relations*. Although all four models are practiced today in varying degrees, the "ideal" mode of practice is the two-way symmetric model.

Press Agentry/Publicity

Press agentry/publicity entails one-way communication, primarily through the mass media, to distribute information that may be exaggerated, distorted, or even incomplete to "hype" a cause, product, or service. Its purpose is advocacy, and little or no research is required. P. T. Barnum was the leading historical figure during this model's heyday. Sports, theater, music, and film—think of the classic Hollywood publicist—are the main fields in which this model is used today.

Public Information

One-way distribution of information, not necessarily with a persuasive intent, is the purpose of the public information model, which is based on the journalistic ideal of accuracy and completeness. The mass media serve as the primary channel for dissemination of the information. There is fact finding for content, but little audience research regarding attitudes and dispositions. Ivy Lee, a former journalist, is the leading historical figure who promoted this model's development. Government, nonprofit groups, and other public institutions use this practice model today.

Two-Way Asymmetric

Scientific persuasion is the purpose, and communication is two-way in this model, albeit with imbalanced effects. The model has a feedback loop, but its primary purpose is to help the communicator better understand the audience and discover how to persuade it to accept the practitioner's message. Research is used to plan activities and establish objectives as well as to learn whether objectives have been met. Edward Bernays was the leading historical figure during the two-way asymmetric model's beginnings. Marketing and advertising departments in competitive businesses and public relations firms are the primary places in which this practice model is found today.

Two-Way Symmetric

Gaining mutual understanding is the purpose of the two-way symmetric model, in which communication is two-way, with balanced effects. Formative research is used mainly to learn how the public perceives an organization and to determine which consequences organizational actions/ policy might have on the public. Evaluative research is used to measure whether public relations efforts have improved public understanding. The goal of this "relationship building" is to identify policies and actions that are mutually beneficial to both parties. Edward B. Bernays, later in his life, supported this model. Today educators and professional leaders are the main proponents of this model, which is practiced in organizations that engage in issue identification, crisis and risk management, and long-range strategic planning.

The 1970s was an era of reform in the stock market. The field of investor relations boomed. By the 1980s, the concept that public relations was a management function was in full bloom. The practice was actively moving toward the strategic approach. Public relations practitioners endorsed the concept of management by objective (MBO) as they sought to convince higher management that public relations did, indeed, contribute to the bottom line.

think How do the different models of public relations reflect the times in which they were developed?

An awareness of reputation, or perception, management began to dominate in the 1990s. Burson-Marsteller, one of the largest public relations firms, decided that its business was not public relations, but rather "perception management." Other firms declared that their business was "reputation management." The idea of "public relations as conflict management" is directly linked to the notion of reputation management. Public relations people work to maintain credibility, to build solid internal and external relationships, and to manage issues. Inherent in this conceptualization is the idea that public relations personnel should enhance corporate social responsibility (CSR) by employing research to do (1) environmental monitoring, (2) public relations audits, (3) communication audits, and (4) social audits.

By 2000, a number of scholars and practitioners were beginning to view the practice of public relations as "relationship management," the basic idea being that public relations practitioners are in the business of building and fostering relationships with an organization's various publics. Relationship management builds on James Grunig's idea of

CLASSIC CAMPAIGNS
Show the Power of Public Relations

During the last half of the twentieth century, a number of organizations and causes used effective public relations to accomplish highly visible results. *PRWeek* convened a panel of public relations experts and came up with some of the "greatest campaigns ever" during this time period.

- **THE CIVIL RIGHTS CAMPAIGN.** Martin Luther King, Jr., was an outstanding civil rights advocate and a great communicator. He organized the 1963 civil rights campaign and used such techniques as well-written, well-delivered speeches; letter writing; lobbying; and staged events (nonviolent protests) to turn a powerful idea into reality.

- **SEAT BELT CAMPAIGN.** In the 1980s, the U.S. automotive industry got the nation to "buckle up" by engaging in an extensive public relations campaign. Tactics included winning the support of news media across the country, interactive displays, celebrity endorsements, letter-writing campaigns, and several publicity events, such as buckling a 600-foot-wide safety belt around a Hollywood sign.

- **STARKIST TUNA.** When negative media coverage threatened the tuna industry because dolphins were getting caught in fishermen's nets, StarKist led the industry in changing fishing practices with conferences, videos, and an Earth Day coali-

tion. Approximately 90 percent of the U.S. public heard about the company's efforts, and StarKist was praised as an environmental leader.

- **TYLENOL CRISIS.** Johnson & Johnson's handling of what could have been a disastrous event for the company has become the classic model for a product recall. When several people had died from taking cyanide-laced Tylenol capsules, a national panic erupted. Many thought the company would never recover from the damage caused by the tampering. However, the company issued a complete recall, redesigned the packaging so that it was tamperproof, and launched a media campaign to keep the public fully informed. The result was that Tylenol survived the crisis and again became a best seller.

- **UNDERSTANDING AIDS.** This successful health education campaign changed the way that AIDS was perceived by Americans. In addition to a national mailing of a brochure titled Understanding AIDS, grassroots activities that specifically targeted African Americans and Hispanics were undertaken.

- **MACY'S THANKSGIVING DAY PARADE.** For more than 80 years, the Macy's department store has sponsored the Macy's Thanksgiving Day Parade. Viewing the parade has become a holiday tradition for many American families. In addition, it was the centerpiece of the 1947 film *Miracle on 34th Street* (which has been remade four times and was turned into a Broadway musical as well).

Michael Kent and Maureen Taylor of the University of Oklahoma wrote in a *Public Relations Review* article that a "theoretical shift, from public relations reflecting an emphasis on managing communication, to an emphasis on communication as a tool of negotiating relationships, has been taking place for some time."

two-way symmetric communication, but goes beyond it by recognizing that an organization's publics are, as Stephen Bruning of Capital University notes, "active, interactive, and equal participants of an ongoing communication process."

The dialogic (dialogue) model of public relations that has emerged

since 2000 is an extension of relationship management. Although the authors of this textbook value healthy long-term relationships with various publics, moral obligations and other forces within an organization sometimes require professionals to make difficult decisions. Considerations of investors, employees, citizens, and activists inevitably come into conflict on occasion. Public relations professionals should have their fingers on the pulse of their various publics so that they can help executives make decisions—decisions that are often difficult because they are intended to deal with conflict. For example, when faced with contractual obligations to pay bonuses to top-performing executives while simultaneously laying off assembly-line workers because product demand is down, how does one balance moral and business obligations and manage the public and media reaction?

The concept of dialogue places less emphasis on mass media distribution of messages and more on interpersonal channels. Kent and Taylor, for example, say that the Internet and World Wide Web are excellent vehicles for dialogue if websites are interactive.

Although there has been a somewhat linear progression in public relations practice and philosophy as the field has expanded, today's practice represents a mixture of the various public relations models. The Hollywood publicist/press agent and the public information officer for the government agency are still with us. Likewise, marketing communications, which almost exclusively uses the concept of scientific persuasion, and two-way asymmetric communication persist. However, when it comes to issues management and relationship building, the two-way symmetric and dialogue models are generally considered to be the most appropriate.

trends IN TODAY'S PRACTICE OF PUBLIC RELATIONS

technological and social changes have continued to transform aspects of public relations practice during the first decade of the twenty-first century. The feminization of the field, the search for more ethnic and cultural diversity, and other trends will shape the practice in the years to come.

Feminization of the Field
In terms of personnel, the most dramatic change has been the transformation of public relations from a male-dominated field to one in which women now constitute approximately 70 percent of practitioners. The shift has been going on for several decades. In 1979, women made up 41 percent of the public re-

lations workforce; by 1983, they had become the majority (50.1 percent). A decade later, the figure stood at 66.3 percent. By 2000, the proportion of jobs held by women had leveled off at about 70 percent, where it remains today. In contrast, women accounted for approximately 60 percent of the U.S. workforce in 2009, according to the U.S. Bureau of Labor Statistics. The national organizations also reflect this feminization trend. About 75 percent of the membership in the International Association of Business Communicators (IABC) is female, and the Public Relations Society of America

(PRSA) says that more than 50 percent of its members are women. However, the Arthur W. Page Society, whose membership is made up of senior-level communication executives, remains majority male.

Approximately 64 percent of all majors in journalism and mass communications programs are now women, and 70 to 75 percent of public relations majors are female. It's worth noting that women also constitute the majority of students in law school, veterinary programs, and a number of other academic disciplines. By comparison, according to a 2009 article in *Time* magazine,

women now constitute 32 percent of lawyers and 28 percent of medical doctors in the United States.

Despite this trend toward feminization of the public relations profession, salary and job description disparities between men and women persist in the field (See Chapter 2). A number of studies have shown that the majority of women in public relations earn less money than their male counterparts and are usually found at the tactical level of public relations practice rather than the management/counseling role. Writing in the *Journal of Public Relations Research*, University of Maryland professors Linda Aldoory and Elizabeth Toth say, "Surveys and focus groups continue to [show] ... that, although the public relations profession is almost 70 percent women today, men are often favored for hiring, higher salaries, and promotions to management positions."

Some women in public relations have become the top communications officers of their corporations. In spite of their success, Professor Emeritus Larissa Grunig of the University of Maryland is concerned about highlighting women who have made it to the top, calling it "compensatory feminism." According to Grunig, the success of a few individuals can give the false idea that across-the-board progress is being achieved.

These arguments and concerns have somewhat dissipated over the years. That public relations is a high-status profession may still be debated, but the power and influence of women in the PR management suite are clearly stronger today than they have ever been. Also, salaries remain fairly high compared to those found in other female-dominated fields.

think In addition to the benefits inherent in pursuing a culture of fairness, what might be another reason it would be in the best interest of a public relations firm to have a diverse staff?

Statistics and surveys note the persistence of a gender gap in salaries and reveal that there continue to be fewer women than men in senior management. A number of reasons for these stubborn trends have been offered, but recent research seems to indicate that the biggest factor is years of experience in the field. Youjin Choi and Linda Childers Hon of the University of Florida found that "[t]he number of years of respondents' professional experience was the single significant predictor of income." Aldoory and Toth found years of experience to be a significant factor in income inequity, but cited evidence that gender and interrupting a career also have an effect on salaries and job advancement.

The organizational environment may affect a woman's rise to top management as well—a theory called the *structionalist perspective.* Toth argues that more women than men fulfill the technician role—a less powerful role than the managerial role—because of different on-the-job experiences. Choi and Hon also point to organizational structure as a problem, noting that women in many organizations are excluded from influential networks, have a paucity of role models, and must work in male-dominated environments.

Choi and Hon, however, did find that organizations (such as many public relations firms) where women occupied 40 to 60 percent of the managerial positions are "gender integrated" and more friendly environments for the advancement of women than male-dominated organizational structures. In other words, those organizations committed to gender equity are the organizations that practiced the most excellent public relations.

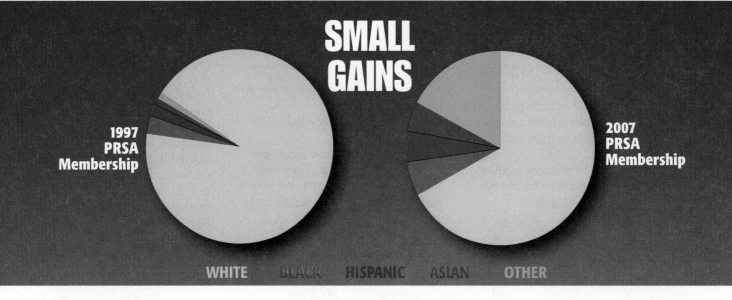

SMALL GAINS

1997 PRSA Membership

2007 PRSA Membership

WHITE   BLACK   HISPANIC   ASIAN   OTHER

The Importance of Diversity

According to the U.S. Census Bureau, minorities now constitute 34 percent of the 304 million people in the United States. The fastest-growing, and now largest, minority group in this country is Hispanics. Hispanics account for 15 percent of the U.S. population, compared with 13 percent for Blacks/African Americans. Asian/Pacific Islanders make up 4 percent, and Native Americans constitute 1 percent of the population.

The number of minorities in public relations falls considerably short of equaling the percentage in the general population. One major goal is to somehow make the field of public relations more representative of the population as a whole.

Many public relations employers express the desire to hire more minority candidates, but they have difficulty doing so because they receive so few applications. One thorny problem that has yet to be overcome in this regard is the education pipeline. In a 2008 *PRWeek* survey, 54 percent of respondents strongly agreed that their organizations had a hard time recruiting ethnic minorities, while 37 percent strongly agreed that their organization had a hard time retaining them once they were successfully recruited. When asked what kept them from recruiting and retaining

minorities, a majority of respondents indicated there were not enough minority role models (58 percent) and that their organization was not active enough in recruiting minorities (54 percent).

The percentage of ethnic group members in public relations has improved over the past decade, and many companies are now making a concerted effort to attract more minorities. Hispanics, in particular, constitute a major audience for marketers and source of public relations specialists because of their spending power. Reaching major ethnic audiences requires specialized knowledge and messages tailored to their particular cultures and values.

As part of their efforts to attract more minority members to the

public relations profession, the PRSA (www.diversity.prsa.org) and other major public relations organizations are increasing minority scholarships, organizing career fairs, and giving awards to local chapters that institute diversity programs. PRSA informs members of diversity issues by including news from the Hispanic PR wire and Black PR wire on its website home page (www.prsa.org).

In addition, groups such as the National Black Public Relations Society (BPRS), the Hispanic Public Relations Association (HPRA), and the Asian American Advertising and Public Relations Association (AAAPRA) are being asked to help public relations firms and companies identify qualified job applicants.

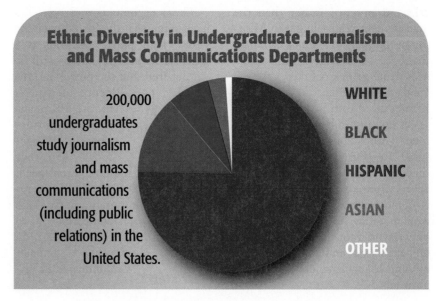

Ethnic Diversity in Undergraduate Journalism and Mass Communications Departments

200,000 undergraduates study journalism and mass communications (including public relations) in the United States.

WHITE

BLACK

HISPANIC

ASIAN

OTHER

Leaders of these minority associations, however, say that employers must make a greater effort to recruit minorities to public relations by going to traditionally black colleges, participating in more college career fairs, enlisting the aid of college professors to identify good candidates, and even placing job ads in publications that reach a variety of ethnic groups.

The globalization of public relations has also created a strong need for employees from diverse cultural backgrounds. Firms need staff who possess multiple-language skills, personal knowledge of other nations, and sensitivity to the customs and attitudes of others. Knowledge of Spanish and Asian languages, such as Chinese, will be especially valuable in coming years.

Other Major Trends in Public Relations

A number of issues will likely influence the practice of public relations in the coming years.

Transparency. Instant global communications, corporate finance scandals, government regulation, and the increased public demand for accountability have made it necessary for all society's institutions, including

The Hispanic population in the United States is expected to increase by 188 percent between 2000 and 2050. The Hispanic consumer market is now worth about $926 billion in this country, according to the American Marketing Association.

business and industry, to be more transparent in their operations.

An ever-broadening social media toolbox. The social media boom began with the advent of weblogs or "blogs" in the late 1990s. MySpace and Facebook emerged shortly thereafter and nearly simultaneously (August 2003 and February 2004, respectively). Facebook became the largest worldwide social network in mid-2008; it now has 300 million users worldwide compared to MySpace's 125 million users. The development of YouTube provided an easy platform for video blogs or "vlogs," while Flickr allowed for easy photo

sharing. Twitter, a microblogging platform, was founded in March 2006 as a means of allowing friends, celebrities, causes, and companies to inform one another about what they are doing in real time.

This expanding social media toolbox provides both opportunities and challenges for public relations practitioners. Opportunities include the ability to communicate directly with stakeholders, unfettered by gatekeepers; challenges include keeping up with messages and critics in real time.

Increased emphasis on evaluation. Public relations professionals will continue to improve measurement techniques for showing management how their activities actually contribute to the bottom line.

Managing the 24/7 news cycle. The flow of news and information is now a global activity that occurs 24 hours a day, 7 days a week. As a consequence, public relations personnel must constantly update information, answer journalists' inquiries at all hours of the day, and be aware that any and all information is readily available to a worldwide audience. New media and technology make it possible to disseminate news and information all day long, but the effect is often one of overwhelming information overload. A major challenge to today's practitioners is figuring out how to cope with the cascade of information and how to give it shape and purpose so it has relevance to multiple audiences.

New directions in mass media. The power of the traditional media isn't what it used to be. In the United States, circulation of daily newspapers dropped 10 percent in the first nine months of 2009. In a 2009 survey co-sponsored by Ketchum and the University of Southern California, 65 percent of consumers said they use major network television news as a source of information. The Pew Project for Excellence in Journalism, however, reported that the network evening news ratings for ABC, CBS, and NBC fell from

btw...

Nestlé attempted to tap into the Hispanic market in 2009 with its introduction of its Delicias line. Both the products and the campaign were developed with Hispanic consumers in mind. The product line includes *tres leches* and mango flavors, and the promotion includes a partnership with Major League Soccer (MLS). "From a media standpoint, we did an awareness campaign. We targeted food editors in general, for publications that are Spanish-based," Jessica Vasisht, brand manager for Nestlé ice cream, told *PRWeek*. "From a PR standpoint, we went more grassroots and have been involved in festivals and events in key markets such as Los Angeles, New York, and Chicago." Nestlé also had a celebrity chef demonstrate recipes made with the new products and sponsored a weekly segment on Univision.

Source: "Nestlé builds relationship with Hispanics on Delicias." *PRWeek,* August 17, 2009.

a combined 52.1 million viewers per night in 1980 to 22.8 million viewers per night in 2008. In short, there have been 1 million fewer viewers of these broadcasts each year, even though the U.S. population is growing by about 2.8 million people each year. Primetime cable news viewership, by comparison, jumped from 2.7 million viewers in 2007 to 4.2 million viewers in 2008, according to the Pew report.

Public relations personnel are expanding their communication tools to account for the fact that no single mass medium is now a proven vehicle for reaching key publics. One resulting change is the shift to electronic preparation of media materials. The printed news release and media kit have become somewhat antiquated. In fact, an International Association of Business Communicators (IABC) study found that electronic newsletters, e-mail notices, websites, and CDs or DVDs have largely replaced print materials in this realm.

Outsourcing to public relations firms. The outsourcing trend developed some years ago in the public relations field, but now it's almost universal. This is not to say that corporate public relations departments are disappearing, but increasingly such tasks as media relations, annual reports, and sponsored events are being outsourced to independent public relations firms.

The importance of lifelong learning. Given the rapid additions to knowledge in today's society, public relations personnel will need to continually update their knowledge base just to stay current. New findings in a variety of fields are emerging that can be applied to public relations practice. These fields include behavioral genetics, evolutionary social psychology, economics, the physics of information, social network analysis, and semiotic game theory. In addition, the need to specialize in a particular field or area of public relations will likely intensify because it's becoming almost impossible for a generalist to master the detailed knowledge required for such areas as health care and financial relations.

a growing PROFESSIONAL PRACTICE

Public relations as a profession faces several criticisms—practitioners are sometimes accused of being unethical, spinmeisters, or worse. One way that the profession has chosen to address such criticism is through the education of practitioners about issues related to professional practice. By "professional" practice, we mean that public relations practitioners should have a common set of ideals and expectations for what is acceptable in practice. For public relations to be considered a respected importance of profession, many practitioners argue, it must have guiding standards like those that govern lawyers, doctors, teachers, nurses, accountants, and other professions.

think What are the advantages of joining a professional organization—to the individual and to the profession as a whole?

The Public Relations Society of America

The largest national public relations organization in the world is the Public Relations Society of America; the group's website can be found at www.prsa.org. PRSA is headquartered in New York City. It has more than 21,000 members and more than 100 chapters nationwide. It also has 17 professional interest sections that represent such areas as business and industry, counseling firms, independent practitioners, the military, government agencies, associations, hospitals, schools, nonprofit organizations, and even educators.

PRSA has an extensive professional development program that offers short courses, seminars, teleconferences, and webcasts throughout the year. In addition to workshops and seminars, PRSA holds an annual meeting and publishes *Tactics*, a monthly tabloid of current news and professional tips, and the *Strategist*, a quarterly magazine with in-depth articles about the profession and issues related to practice. The organization also sponsors the Silver Anvil and Bronze Anvil awards to recognize outstanding public relations campaigns.

PRSA is also the parent organization of the Public Relations Student Society of America (PRSSA), whose website can be found at www.prssa. org. The student groups offer career-related programs at the local chapter level and provide mentoring and networking with the local professional PRSA chapter. PRSSA makes available a national publication, *Forum*, and sponsors a national case study competition to encourage students to exercise the analytical skills and mature judgment required for public relations problem solving. After graduation, PRSSA members are eligible to become associate members of PRSA.

> **PRSSA is the world's largest preprofessional public relations organization, with almost 300 campus chapters and more than 10,000 student members.**

The International Association of Business Communicators

The second-largest organization of communication and public relations professionals, with more than 16,000 members in 80 nations, is the International Association of Business Communicators. Its website can be accessed at www.iabc. com. Most members of this group live in the United States, but the IABC also has many members in Canada, the United Kingdom, and Hong Kong.

IABC, headquartered in San Francisco, has similar objectives as the PRSA. It holds year-round seminars and workshops and an annual meeting. The organization also has an awards program, known as the Gold Quill, that honors excellence in business communication.

The IABC's publication is *Communication World*, which fea-

tures professional tips and articles on current issues. IABC also sponsors campus student chapters, but these groups are not comparable to PRSSA in size or organizational structure.

The International Public Relations Association

A third organization, which is global in scope, is the International Public Relations Association (IPRA), based in London. The group's website is www.ipra.org. IPRA has 1000 members in 96 nations. Its membership is primarily senior international public relations executives, and its mission is "to provide intellectual leadership in the practice of international public relations by making available to our members the services and information that will help them to meet their professional responsibilities and to succeed in their careers."

IPRA organizes regional and international conferences to discuss issues in global public relations. It also reaches its widespread membership through its website and *Frontline*, its premier publication, which is available online. IPRA issues Gold Papers on public relations practice and conducts an annual awards competition (Golden World Awards).

professionalism, LICENSING, AND ACCREDITATION

is public relations a profession? Should its practitioners be licensed? Does the accreditation of practitioners constitute a sufficient guarantee of their talents and integrity? These and related questions remain the topic of ongoing discussion within the public relations profession.

Professionalism

Among public relations practitioners, there are considerable differences of opinion about whether public relations is a craft, a skill, or a developing profession. Certainly, at its present level, public relations

does not qualify as a profession in the same sense that medicine and law do. Public relations does not have prescribed standards of educational preparation, a mandatory period of apprenticeship, or state laws that govern admission to the

> ## "We act as publicists, yet we talk of counseling. We perform as technologists in communication, but we aspire to be decision-makers dealing in policy."

profession. Adding to the confusion about professionalism is the difficulty of ascertaining what constitutes public relations practice.

At the same time, there is a rapidly expanding body of literature about public relations—including this text and many others in the field. The two major scholarly publications serving the field are *Public Relations Review* and *Journal of Public Relations Research*. Substantial progress also is being made in developing theories of public relations, conducting research, and publishing scholarly journals.

The Institute for Public Relations (www.instituteforpr.org) and the University of Southern California's Annenberg Center Strategic Public Relations Center (www.annenberg.usc.edu/sprc) are commonly regarded as the two major "think tanks" in the public relations field. Other research centers in public relations are the Plank Center for Leadership in Public Relations at the University of Alabama (www.plankcenter.ua.edu) and the Arthur W. Page Center for Integrity in Public Communication at Penn State University (www.pagecenter.comm.psu.edu)

Licensing

Proposals that public relations practitioners be licensed were discussed even before PRSA was founded 60 years ago. One proponent, Edward B. Bernays, believed that licensing would protect the profession and the public from incompetent, shoddy opportunists who do not have the knowledge, talent, or ethics required of public relations professionals.

Under the licensing approach, only those individuals who pass rigid examinations and tests of personal integrity could call themselves "public relations" counselors. Those not licensed would have to call themselves "publicists" or adopt some other designation. So far, the opponents of licensing seem to have carried the day. Today, there is no particular interest on the part of the public relations industry, the consumer movement,

think How might licensing change how public relations professionals do business?

There is also the idea, advanced by many professionals and PRSA itself, that the most important thing is for the individual to act like a professional in the field. This means that a practitioner should have the following qualities:

- A sense of independence
- A sense of responsibility to society and the public interest
- Concern for the competence and honor of the profession as a whole
- A higher loyalty to the standards of the profession and fellow professionals than to the employer of the moment

Unfortunately, a major barrier to professionalism is the attitude that many practitioners themselves have toward their work. As James Grunig and Todd Hunt note in their book *Managing Public Relations,* practitioners tend to hold more "careerist" values than professional values. In other words, they place higher importance on job security, prestige in the organization, salary level, and recognition from superiors than on the values just listed. For example, 47 percent of the respondents in a survey of IABC members gave a neutral or highly negative answer when asked if they would quit their jobs rather than act against their ethical values. In addition, 55 percent considered it "somewhat ethical" to present oneself misleadingly as the only means of achieving an objective. Almost all agreed, however, that ethics is an important matter, worthy of further study.

On another level, many practitioners are limited in their professionalism by what might be termed a "technician mentality." These people narrowly define professionalism as the ability to do a competent job of executing the mechanics of communicating (preparing news releases, brochures, newsletters, and so on) even if the information provided by management or a client is in bad taste, is misleading, lacks documentation, or is just plain wrong.

Some practitioners defend the technician mentality, arguing that public relations people are like lawyers in the court of public opinion. Everyone is entitled to his or her viewpoint, these practitioners argue, and whether the public relations person agrees or not, the client or employer has a right to be heard. Thus, they say, a public relations representative is a paid advocate, just as a lawyer is. The flaw in this argument is that public relations people are not lawyers, who operate in a court of law where judicial standards are applied. In addition, lawyers have been known to turn down clients or resign from a case because they doubted the client's story.

Finally, courts are increasingly holding public relations firms accountable for information disseminated on behalf of a client. Clearly, it is no longer acceptable to say, "The client told me to do it."

ethics in ACTION

Arguments for Licensing Advocates say licensing would be beneficial to the profession because it would:	**Arguments Against Licensing** Opponents of licensing say that it won't work because:
• Define public relations • Establish uniform educational criteria • Set uniform professional standards • Protect clients and employers from imposters • Protect qualified practitioners from unethical or unqualified competition • Raise practitioners' overall credibility.	• Any licensing in the communications field would violate the First Amendment; civil and criminal laws exist to deal with malpractice • Licensing is a function of state governments, but public relations people often work on national and international levels • Licensing ensures only minimum competence and professional standards, not high ethical behavior • The credibility and status of an occupation are not necessarily ensured through licensing • Setting up the machinery for licensing and policing would be very expensive to taxpayers

or even state governments to initiate any form of legislated licensing. An alternative to licensing is accreditation.

Accreditation

The major effort to improve standards and professionalism in public relations around the world has entailed the establishment of accreditation programs. This means that practitioners voluntarily go through a process by which a national organization "certifies" that they are competent, qualified professionals.

PRSA began its accreditation program more than 40 years ago. A testing process for members provides the opportunity to earn Accredited in Public Relations (APR) status. Other groups have also established accreditation programs.

The approach used by most national groups is to administer written and oral exams and require candidates to submit a portfolio of work samples to a committee of professional peers. Approximately 10 percent of

IABC's 15,500 members have earned the ABC designation.

Most groups also have guidelines stating how many years of experience are required before a person can apply for accredited or membership status. Some groups are beginning to require continuing education as a prerequisite for professional certification.

The PRSA approach. When it developed a program for its members in 1965, PRSA was one of the first public relations organizations to offer accreditation. Candidates are required to take a preview course (available online), complete a "readiness" questionnaire, and show a portfolio of work to a panel of professional peers before taking the written exam, which is available at test centers throughout the United States. In addition, the member must have 5 years of professional experience.

To date, approximately 5,000 practitioners have earned APR status, or 18 percent of the PRSA's membership.

Topics covered in PRSA Accreditation Exam

History and current issues in public relations 2%

Information technology 2%

Media relations 5%

Crisis communication management 10%

Management skills 10%

Business literacy 10%

Communication models and theories 15%

Advanced communication skills 1%

Research, planning, execution, and evaluation of programs 30%

Ethics and law 15%

Which Key Events and Individuals Shaped the History of Public Relations? p. 66

- Although *public relations* is a twentieth-century term, the roots of this practice go back to ancient Egyptian, Greek, and Roman times.

- The American Revolution, in part, was the result of such staged events as the Boston Tea Party, and the publication of the *Federalist Papers* help cement the federal system of the new government.

- The 1800s were the golden age of the press agent. P. T. Barnum used many techniques that are still employed today. In addition, the settlement of the American West was driven in large part by promotions created by land developers and U.S. railroads.

- From 1900 to 1950, the practice of public relations was transformed by individuals such as Henry Ford, Ivy Lee, George Creel, and Edward B. Bernays. The concept moved from press agentry to the more journalistic approach of distributing accurate public information.

- In the period from 1950 to 2000, organizations found it necessary to employ public relations specialists to effectively communicate with the mass media and a variety of publics. This was the age of scientific persuasion, management by objective, and strategic thinking.

What Are the Trends in Today's Practice of Public Relations? p. 76

- A major trend in public relations has been the influx of women into the field. Women now account for roughly 70 percent of public relations practitioners in the United States.

- The public relations workforce is still overwhelmingly white. Efforts are being made to diversify the workforce to better represent ethnic/minority groups.

In What Ways Is Public Relations Evolving and Growing as a Professional Practice? p. 80

- Four classic models of public relations are the press agentry/publicity, public information, two-way asymmetric, and two-way symmetric models. Although all four models are practiced today in varying degrees, the "ideal" one is the two-way symmetric model.

What Are the Major Professional Public Relations Organizations and What Do They Do? p. 81

- Professional organizations such as PRSA, IABC, and IPRA play an important role in setting standards and providing education and networking opportunities for public relations professionals.

- Freedom of speech concerns severely limit the concept of licensing in the communication fields, including public relations. Accreditation programs for practitioners, with continuing education, is an attractive alternative.

QUESTIONS for *Review* and *Discussion*

1. Which concepts of publicity and public relations practiced by P. T. Barnum should modern practitioners use? Which should they reject?

2. What four important contributions did Ivy Lee make to public relations?

3. The Boston Tea Party has been described as the "greatest and best-known publicity stunt of all time." Would you agree? Do you believe that staged events are a legitimate way to publicize a cause and motivate people?

4. Describe briefly the publicity strategies employed by Henry Ford.

5. What is your assessment of Ivy Lee's work for the Rockefeller family in the Colorado Fuel & Iron Company labor strife? Do you think his approach was sound? What would you have done differently?

6. Summarize the major developments in the philosophy and practice of public relations from the 1920s to 2010.

7. James Grunig outlined four models of public relations practice. Name and describe each one. Do these models help explain the evolution of public relations theory?

8. Modern public relations is described as "relationship management." How would you describe this concept to a friend? A newer concept suggests that the purpose of public relations is to establish a "dialogue" with individuals and various publics. Is this a worthy concept?

9. Females now constitute the majority of public relations personnel. How do you personally feel about this trend toward feminization of the field? Does it make the field of public relations more attractive or less attractive to you?

10. Should public relations practitioners be licensed? What are the pros and cons of licensing?

11. How do "careerism" and the "technician mentality" undermine efforts to establish professional standards in public relations?

the THINKSPOT

www.thethinkspot.com

TODAY'S PRACTICE:

5 DEPARTMENTS

Have you ever picked up the phone and ordered a pizza? Papa John's Pizza recognized that by encouraging this simple act over the years, the pizza industry had developed a proven record of engaging technology successfully. In light of that successful track record, the organization decided it would now be a good idea to encourage customers to use the telephone in a different way. To that end, it began to encourage customers to text their orders in from their cell phones.

Papa John's was already a technology leader; it was among the first members of the pizza delivery industry to allow customers to order their pizzas from its website. Now the company was poised to become the first national pizza chain to allow ordering via text. To help promote this new policy, it engaged public relations firm Fleishman-Hillard.

Fleishman-Hillard's research revealed that, at that time, 74 percent of Americans ages 18 to 34 regularly used their mobile phones for more than talking. Sixty-five percent of mobile phone users ages 18 to 29 said they habitually texted friends, family members, and others. Papa John's developed a strategy meant to attract texters and reap the benefits of providing extra convenience to this vital market segment.

The first step was to reach investors and industry leaders. Fleishman-Hillard managed to place an exclusive article on Papa John's new business model in the *Wall Street Journal*. It followed up the business announcement with an event at the Mall of America in Bloomington, Minnesota. Fran Capo, the World's Fastest Talker, and Morgan Pozgar, the World's Fastest Texter, were invited to the event and pitted against each other in a

AND FIRMS

pizza ordering contest. Predictably, Pozgar won, texting her pizza order faster than even fast-talking Capo. The event received coverage in *USA Today* and Associated Press distribution. More than 450 television segments resulted from national feeds of the event. Eighty-four blogs and web forums mentioned the contest. A YouTube video of the event received thousands of hits. Most importantly, more than 114,000 people registered their mobile phone numbers with Papa John's and opted to receive special offers via text.

❶ Do you think Fleishman-Hillard's strategy and tactics were effective for reaching young adults? Why or why not? What would you have done differently?

❷ Which other businesses successfully use texting as part of their customer relations? Do you think texting is an important public relations tactic? Why or why not?

PUBLIC RELATIONS
departments

f or more than a century, public relations departments have served companies and organizations. Today, public relations is expanding from its traditional functions to exercise influence in the highest levels of management. In a changing environment, and faced with the variety of pressures, executives increasingly see public relations not as simply public-ity and one-way communication, but rather as a complex and dynamic process of negotiation and compromise with a number of key publics. James Grunig, head of a six-year IABC (International Association of Business Communicators) Foundation research study on Excellence in Public Relations and Communications Management, calls the new approach "building good relationships with strategic publics," which requires public relations executives to be "strategic communication managers rather than communication technicians."

Grunig continues:

When public relations helps that organization build relationships, it saves the organization money by reducing the costs of litigation, regulation, legislation, pressure campaign boycotts, or lost revenue that result from bad relationships with publics— publics that become activist groups when relationships are bad. It also helps the organization make money by cultivating relationships with donors, customers, shareholders, and legislators.

The results of the IABC study seem to indicate that chief executive officers (CEOs) consider public relations to be a good investment. A survey of 200 organizations showed that CEOs considered public relations operations to provide a 184 percent return on investment (ROI), a figure just below what the respondents awarded to customer service and sales/marketing.

Ideally, professional public relations people assist top management in developing policy and communicating with various groups. Indeed, the IABC study emphasizes that CEOs want communication that is strategic, is based on research, and involves two-way communication with key publics.

WEEKLY.   VOLUME XXXL, NO. 1581.

THE
ALTERNATING
SYSTEM.

Incandescent Electric Lighting from Central Stations made Universal, Economical, and Profitable, irrespective of distance.

The Westinghouse Electric Co.,
PITTSBURGH, PA.
Eastern Office, 17 CORTLANDT STREET, NEW YORK.

George Westinghouse reportedly created the first corporate public relations department in 1889 when he hired two men to publicize his pet project, alternating current (AC) electricity. Eventually Westinghouse's approach won out over Thomas A. Edison's direct current (DC) system, and AC electricity became the standard in the United States. Westinghouse's public relations department concept has grown into a fundamental part of today's electronic world.

Organizational Factors Determine the Role of Public Relations

Research indicates that the role of public relations in an organization often depends on the type of organization, the perceptions of top management, and even the capabilities of the public relations executive. Studies conducted by Professor Larissa Grunig at the University of Maryland and Mark McElreath at Towson State University, among others, show that large, complex organizations have a greater tendency than do smaller firms to include public relations in the policy-making process.

Companies such as IBM and General Motors, which operate in a highly competitive environment, are more sensitive than many other firms to policy issues and public attitudes and have a vested interest in establishing a solid corporate identity. Consequently, they place greater emphasis on news conferences, formal contact with the media, writing executive speeches, and counseling management about issues that could potentially affect the corporate bottom line. In such organizations—which management theorists classify as mixed organic/mechanical—the authority and power of the public relations department are quite high; public relations is part of what is called the "dominant coalition" and has a great deal of autonomy.

In contrast, a small-scale organization that offers a standardized product or service feels few public pressures and faces little governmental regulatory interest. It has nominal public relations activity, and staff members are relegated to technician roles such as producing the company newsletter and issuing routine news releases. Public relations in such traditional organizations has little or no input into management decisions and policy formation.

Research also indicates that the type of organization involved may be less significant in predicting the role of its public relations department than are the perceptions and

expectations of its top management. In many organizations, top-level management perceives public relations as primarily a journalistic and technical function—that is, as media relations and publicity. In large-scale mechanical organizations of low complexity, there is also a tendency to think of public relations as merely a support function of the marketing department.

Such perceptions severely limit the role of the public relations department as well as its power to take part in management decision making. In these types of organizations, public relations is relegated to a tactical function—preparing messages without input on what should be communicated. In many cases, however, public relations personnel self-select technician roles because they lack a knowledge base in research, environmental scanning, problem solving, and managing total communication strategies or because they are more personally

think Why is it important for organizational health that public relations be part of the managerial subsystem and contribute to the company's overall strategy?

fulfilled by working tactically rather than strategically.

The most reputable *Fortune* 500 corporations tend to think of public relations as a strategic management tool. A study by the University of Southern California (USC) Annenberg Strategic Public Relations Center and the Council of Public Relations Firms found that these companies dedicated a larger percentage of their gross revenues to public relations activities, extensively used outside public relations firms to supplement their own large staffs, and did not have their public relations staff report to the marketing department.

The primary indicator of a department's influence and power, however, is whether the top communication officer has a seat at the management table. In fact, to gain and maintain a seat at the management table should be an ongoing goal of public relations practitioners. Experts indicate that it is increasingly common for the top public relations practitioner in an organization to report to the CEO. But these PR pros must know how to contribute to maintain their place at the table, according to Tom Martin, former Senior Vice President of Corporate Relations for ITT Industries. In its 2007 survey of 520 senior-level practitioners, the Annenberg Strategic Public Relations Center found that 64 percent of all respondents and a clear majority of nonprofit respondents reported to the "C-Suite" (CEO, COO [chief operating officer], or chairperson). According to the report, these practitioners asserted that "their CEOs believed that PR contributed to financial success and market share, and that reputation contributed to the overall success of the organization."

What Public Relations Departments Are Called

A public relations department in an organization goes by many names—and often it is not simply "public relations." In the largest corporations (the *Fortune* 500), the terms *corporate communications* and *communications* outnumber *public relations* as the title of this department by almost four to one.

O'Dwyer's PR Services Report, in a survey of the *Fortune* 500 companies, found 200 such communication departments and only 48 public relations departments. Among those companies switching from "public relations" to "corporate communications" in recent years are Procter & Gamble and Hershey Candies. In both cases, the companies said that the relabeling occurred because the department had expanded beyond "public relations" to include such activities as employee communications, shareholder communications, annual reports, consumer relations, and corporate philanthropy.

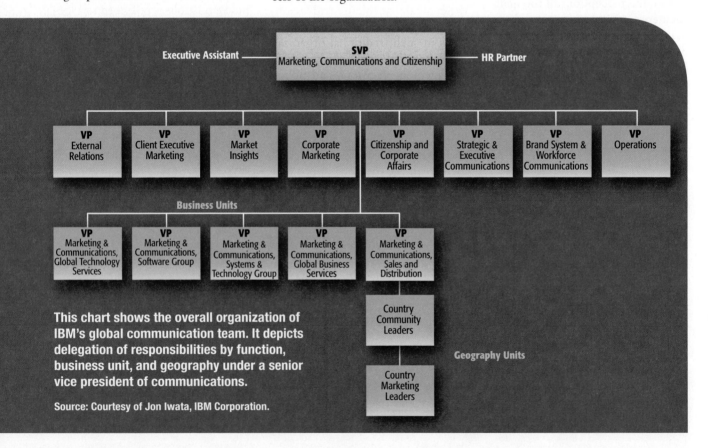

This chart shows the overall organization of IBM's global communication team. It depicts delegation of responsibilities by function, business unit, and geography under a senior vice president of communications.

Source: Courtesy of Jon Iwata, IBM Corporation.

Consultant Alfred Geduldig has offered another reason. He told *O'Dwyer's PR Services Report* that the term "public relations" had suffered from repeated derogatory usage, causing companies to move away from it. He also thought that the increasing use of the term "corporate communications" signaled that public relations people were doing many more things in a company now than they had in the past, reflecting an integration of communications services.

Other names used for public relations departments in the corporate world include *corporate relations, investor relations, public affairs, marketing communications, global communications, public and community relations,* and *external affairs.* Government agencies, educational institutions, and charitable organizations typically use such terms as *public affairs, community relations, public information,* and even *market services.*

How Public Relations Departments Are Organized

The head executive of a public relations or similarly named department usually has one of three titles: manager, director, or vice president. A vice president of corporate communications may have direct responsibility for the additional activities of advertising and marketing communications.

A department usually is divided into specialized sections that have a coordinator or manager. Common divisions found in large corporations include media relations, investor relations, consumer affairs, governmental relations, community relations, marketing communications, and employee communications.

One of the world's largest corporations, General Electric, has communication managers in 29 divisions and 18 global regions in addition to 6 corporate communication executives and 9 communication executives who specialize in

issues such as financial communications, labor issues, and the Olympic Games. The range of job titles runs from Executive Vice President for Corporate Communications at NBC Universal to Communication Director in the GE Energy division. Worldwide, General Electric has hundreds of persons in various public relations functions.

Companies like GE are the exceptions, however. The USC study found that between 2005 and 2007, there was a near universal growth in public relations staff size from an average of 40 to 60 employees among the largest companies. Another study by the Conference Board of other large U.S. corporations found that the typical public relations department had nine professionals. The USC study found that the average annual budget across all categories, from corporate to nonprofit, increased by 7 percent between surveys to $4.4 million. Of course, thousands of even smaller companies employ only one or two public relations practitioners.

Public relations personnel may be dispersed throughout an organization in such a manner that an observer can have difficulty ascertaining the true extent of public relations activity. Some staff may focus on marketing communications in the marketing department. Others may be assigned to the personnel department as communication specialists producing newsletters and brochures. Still others may be in marketing, working exclusively on product publicity. Decentralization of the public relations function, and the frictions it causes, will be discussed later in this chapter.

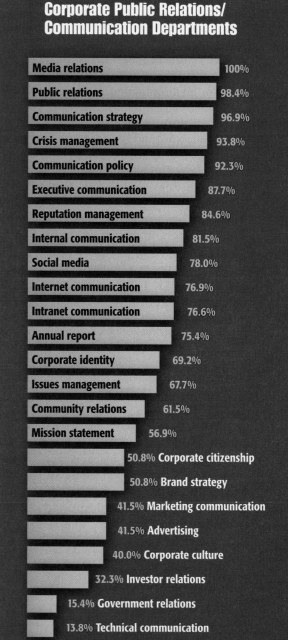

WHO IS DOING WHAT?

The Functions of Corporate Public Relations/ Communication Departments

Media relations	100%
Public relations	98.4%
Communication strategy	96.9%
Crisis management	93.8%
Communication policy	92.3%
Executive communication	87.7%
Reputation management	84.6%
Internal communication	81.5%
Social media	78.0%
Internet communication	76.9%
Intranet communication	76.6%
Annual report	75.4%
Corporate identity	69.2%
Issues management	67.7%
Community relations	61.5%
Mission statement	56.9%
50.8% Corporate citizenship	
50.8% Brand strategy	
41.5% Marketing communication	
41.5% Advertising	
40.0% Corporate culture	
32.3% Investor relations	
15.4% Government relations	
13.8% Technical communication	
9.2% Ethics	
7.7% Training and development	

The percentages of corporate departments that participate in various activities as indicated in response to a 2009 survey by Corporate Communication International (CCI).

Source: Corporate Communication International, 2009 Corporate Communication Practices and Trends Survey, www.corporatecomm.org.

Line and Staff Functions

Traditional management theory divides an organization into line and staff functions. A line manager, such as a vice president of manufacturing, can delegate authority, set production goals, hire employees, and directly influence the work of others. Staff people, in contrast, have little or no direct authority. Instead, they indirectly influence the work of others through suggestions, recommendations, and advice.

According to accepted management theory, public relations is a staff function. Public relations professionals are experts in communication; line managers, including the CEO, rely on them to use their skills in preparing and processing data, making recommendations, and executing communication programs to meet organizational objectives.

Public relations staff members, for example, may find through a community survey that people have only a vague understanding of what their company manufactures. To improve community comprehension and create greater rapport, the public relations department may recommend to top management that a community open house be held, featuring product demonstrations, tours, and entertainment.

Notice that the PR department simply recommends this action. It has no direct authority to decide on its own to hold an open house or to order various departments within the company to cooperate. If top management approves the proposal, the department may take responsibility for organizing the event. Top management, as line managers, has the authority to direct all departments to cooperate in the activity. Although public relations departments can function only with the approval of top management, they may exert varying levels of influence over the organization and its direction. These levels will be discussed shortly.

The power and influence of a public relations department usually result from access to top management, which uses advice and recommendations from the remainder of the organization to formulate policy. That is why public relations, as well as other staff functions, is located high in the organizational chart and is called on by top management to make reports and recommendations on issues affecting the entire company. In today's environment, public acceptance or nonacceptance of a proposed policy is an important factor in decision making.

> **think**
>
> How do line and staff functions and influence differ?

Levels of Influence

Management experts state that staff functions in an organization operate at various levels of influence and authority. At the lowest level, the staff function may be simply advisory: Line management has no obligation to take recommendations or even request them.

When the public relations department serves in a purely *advisory* role, it often is not effective. A cautionary tale about this approach can be found in the recent scandal involving American International Group (AIG). One of the reasons that the insurance giant generated a great deal of public, legislative, and media criticism in 2009 was because public relations was apparently relegated to such a low level within the company. In fact, it seemed to be, for all practical purposes, nonexistent. AIG was paying Burson-Marsteller, Hill and Knowlton, and Levick Strategic Communications for their advice—yet executives still made the questionable decisions to fund a $440,000 posh retreat in California and an $86,000 partridge-hunting trip in the English countryside. All of this activity occurred in the wake of the company accepting billions of dollars from the federal government to stave off financial ruin.

Johnson & Johnson, in contrast, accords its public relations staff function higher status. The Tylenol crisis in the 1980s, in which seven persons died after taking capsules that had been tampered with and contained cyanide, is a classic case that clearly shows how the company based much of its reaction and quick recall of the product on the advice of public relations staff. In this case, public relations occupied a *compulsory-advisory* position. Under a *compulsory-advisory* setup,

> **The former president of RJR Nabisco, F. Ross Johnson, told the *Wall Street Journal* in an interview that his senior public relations aide was "Numero Uno" and quipped, "He is the only one who has an unlimited budget and exceeds it every year."**

organizational policy requires that line managers (top management) at least listen to the appropriate staff experts before deciding on a strategy.

Another level of advisory relationship within an organization is *concurring authority*. For instance, an operating division wishing to publish a brochure cannot do so unless the public relations department approves the copy and layout. If differences arise, the parties must agree before work can proceed. Many firms use this mode to prevent departments and divisions from disseminating materials that do not conform with company standards.

Concurring authority may limit the freedom of the public relations department. For example, some companies have a policy that all employee-created magazine articles and external news releases must be reviewed by the legal staff before publication. The material cannot be disseminated until legal and public relations personnel have agreed on what will be said. The situation is even more restrictive for public relations when the legal department has command authority to change a news release with or without the consent of public relations. This is one reason that newspaper editors find some news releases so filled with "legalese" as to be almost unreadable.

Sometimes legal counsel and public relations practitioners work collaboratively. When Norfolk Southern railroad embarked on a bid to buy Conrail, Norfolk Southern's public relations executive Robert Fort recalled that in-house representatives of public relations and law met daily. "We had to be very careful what we said and how we said it and also to get it reported to the Securities and Exchange Commission on a daily basis," said one of Norfolk Southern's in-house lawyers. Fort noted that legal and public relations personnel were on equal footing. "In the past . . . eventually, if there is a point of contention between PR and law, law usually wins," he explained. "In this case, the law department was actually asking us, and not only asking us for our advice, but then used it

The Challenge of Being a Spokesperson

One duty of a public relations practitioner is to serve as an organization's official spokesperson. What a spokesperson tells the media is not considered a personal opinion, but rather management's official response or stance to a situation or event. Lauren Fernandez, a public relations professional and blogger, says, "As PR professionals, we represent a client, brand, and organization."

The challenge comes when a spokesperson may personally disagree with what he or she is asked to say on behalf of the organization. Or, in some cases, a public relations professional may be asked to give information to the media that he or she knows is untrue or deliberately misleading. Consider these examples:

- A public relations spokesperson for Apple Computer told the media that Steve Jobs was taking a six-month leave of absence to correct a "hormonal imbalance." In actuality, Jobs secretly flew to a medical center in Memphis to get a liver transplant.
- The press secretary for South Carolina Governor Mark Sanford told the media that the governor was hiking on the Appalachian Trail when, in fact, he was in Argentina having an extramarital affair. When reporters asked about reports that the governor was seen

ethics in ACTION

boarding a plane at the Atlanta airport, the press secretary flatly denied it.

- The public relations spokesperson for insurance giant AIG was criticized by columnists and bloggers for justifying company actions such as financing large executive bonuses and spending $150,000 for a three-day retreat at a five-star resort for its sales representatives while the company was also petitioning Congress for a $85 billion bailout.

These examples raise important ethical issues. Should a spokesperson just tell the media what the organization wants communicated, or should the individual also be guided by what he or she thinks is truthful and accurate? If you were a spokesperson for an organization, and management wanted you to make statements that you knew were misleading or even a lie,

what would you do?

when we gave it to them. I think they recognized that this was an historic event about to take place here and that as it unfolded it was going to have to be won on the basis of public opinion."

Logic dictates that an organization needs a coordinated and integrated approach to communications strategy. Indeed, one survey found that 65 percent of corporate managers are now spending more time on developing integrated communication programs than they had in the past.

Sources of Friction

Ideally, public relations is part of the managerial subsystem and contributes to organizational strategy. Public relations is, say professors James and Larissa Grunig, "the management of communication between an organization and its publics." Of course, other staff functions are also involved in the communication process with internal and external publics. In addition, internal friction can occur. Internal friction often involves the relationship between public relations and legal, human resources, advertising, and marketing departments.

Legal. Legal staff members are always concerned about the possible effect of any public statement on current or potential litigation. Consequently, lawyers often frustrate public relations personnel by taking the attitude that any public statement can potentially be used against the organization in a lawsuit. Conflicts over which information to release and when often have a paralyzing effect on decision making, causing the organization to seem unresponsive to public concerns. This is particularly true in a crisis, when the public demands immediate release of information.

Human Resources. Turf battles often erupt between human resources and public relations over who is responsible for employee communications. Human resources personnel believe that they should

control the flow of information; public relations administrators counter that satisfactory external communications cannot be achieved unless effective employee relations are conducted simultaneously. Layoffs, for example, affect not only employees but also the community and investors.

Advertising. Advertising and public relations departments often collide because they compete for funds to communicate with external audiences. Philosophical differences may also arise. Advertising's approach to communications may be, "Will it increase sales?"; public relations might ask, "Will it make friends?" These different orientations can cause breakdowns in coordination of overall strategy.

Marketing. Marketing personnel, like advertising staff members, tend to think exclusively of customers or potential buyers as key publics. In contrast, public relations practitioners define *publics* in a broader sense—as any group that can affect the operations of the organization. These publics include governmental agencies, environmental groups, neighborhood

"We believe, then, that public relations must emerge as a discipline DISTINCT FROM MARKETING and that it must be practiced separately from marketing in the organization."
James Grunig

groups, and a host of other publics that marketing would not consider customers.

The Trend Toward Outsourcing

A major trend among U.S. corporations has been the outsourcing of services, whether those services comprise telecommunications, accounting, customer service, software engineering, or even legal services. Similarly, more organizations have sought to outsource their communication activities to public relations firms and outside contractors. Indeed, the USC and Council of Public Relations Firms study found that *Fortune* 500 companies

Achieving the Goal of Developing INTEGRATED Communication Programs

- Representatives of departments should serve together on key committees to exchange information on how various programs can complement one another so as to achieve the overall organizational objectives. If representatives from human resources, public relations, legal, and investor relations present a united front to senior managers, their influence can increase exponentially.

- Collaboration or coalition building among departments with shared interests in communication issues can help achieve organization-wide business goals.

- Heads of departments should be equals in job title so that the autonomy of one department is not subverted by another.

- All department heads should report to the same superior, so that all viewpoints are considered before an appropriate strategy is formulated.

- Informal, regular contacts with representatives of other departments help dispel mind-sets and create understanding and respect for one another's viewpoints.

- Written policies should be established to spell out the responsibilities of each department. Such policies are helpful in settling disputes over which department has authority to communicate with employees or alter a news release.

now spend 25 percent of their public relations budgets on outside firms. Almost 90 percent of the companies use outside public relations counsel to varying degrees.

A national survey by *PRWeek* found that companies of all sizes spent, on average, more than 40 percent of their public relations budget on the services of outside firms. In high-technology fields, the percentage was even higher—a whopping 66 percent of the corporate budget. In contrast, nonprofits allocated an average of 38 percent of their budgets for external public relations services. A study by USC found that 30 percent of the average public relations budget went to agencies.

The most frequent reason given for outsourcing is to obtain expertise and resources to the organization that cannot be found internally. A second reason cited is the need to supplement internal staffs during peak periods of activity.

The trend toward outsourcing of the public relations function, say many experts, follows what has occurred in advertising. Today, approximately 90 percent of corporate and institutional advertising is handled by agencies rather than by in-house departments. It currently appears that public relations firms will be the major beneficiaries of this trend. The traditional "agency of record" concept, however, seems to be in decline. Today's major corporations, instead of using just one firm, now use multiple firms for various projects.

Most Frequently Outsourced Activities

1. Writing and communications
2. Media relations
3. Publicity
4. Strategy and planning
5. Event planning.

Source: Bisbee & Co. and Leone Marketing Research.

This chart depicts three examples of corporate management organization, showing the important position of public relations.

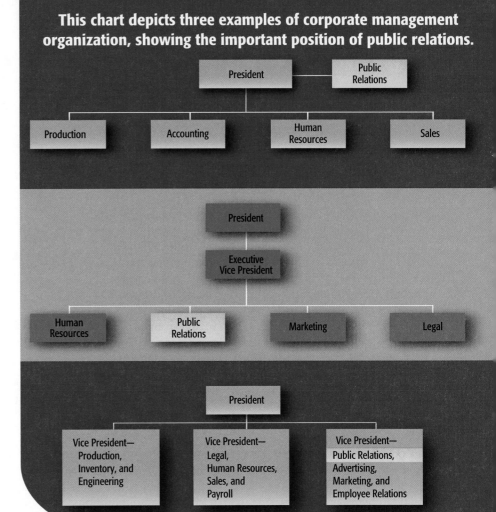

An Annenberg study found that *Fortune* 500 companies now typically work with three or four different agencies to "cherry-pick" the best agency for a particular situation.

Since 2002, the University of Southern California Annenberg Strategic Public Relations Center has conducted a biennial survey of senior-level public relations practitioners. The survey, named the GAP (Generally Accepted Practices) Study, examines everything from percentage of gross revenue spent on public relations to the profession's reporting structure. In 2007, the GAP V results included the following findings:

- PR budgets increased 7 percent and were anticipated to increase another 5 percent in 2008.
- CEOs believe public relations contributes to positive corporate reputation, market share, financial success, and sales.
- Only 6 percent of the average public relations budget is allocated to evaluation or measuring success.
- The public relations function reports to the CEO, COO, or chairperson in 64 percent of organizations; it reports to marketing in 23 percent of organizations.
- Some 56 percent of GAP respondents said their companies used outside agencies in 2007; 93 percent of the very largest public organizations used outside agencies.
- Companies with revenues of more than $1.6 billion, public (57%) and private (65%), tend to work with multiple agencies.

PUBLIC RELATIONS firms

Public relations firms are found in every industrialized nation and most of the developing world. They range in size from one- or two-person operations to global giants such as Edelman, which employs almost 3,200 professionals in 16 U.S. offices and 58 offices around the world. The scope of services they provide to clients varies, although some common denominators do exist. Large or small, each firm gives counsel and performs technical services required to carry out an agreed-upon program. The firm may operate as an adjunct to an organization's public relations department or, if no department exists, conduct the entire effort.

The United States, because of its large population and economic base, is home to most of the world's public relations firms (about 9,000, according to one count) and generates the most fee income. In fact, the international committee of the Public Relations Consultancies Association reported in a worldwide study that the fee income of U.S. firms "plainly dwarfs those in all other regions."

In 2008, the five largest independent firms (Edelman, Waggener Ed-strom Worldwide, Ruder Finn, APCO Worldwide, and Qorvis Communication) generated $570,254,661 in revenues in the United States alone. (The largest firms, such as Burson-Marsteller and Ketchum, are part of conglomerate holding companies that don't release separate financial data for each of their companies.)

American public relations firms have proliferated in proportion to the growth of the global economy. As U.S. companies expanded after World War II into booming domestic and worldwide markets, many corporations felt a need for public relations firms that could provide them with professional expertise in communications.

Increased urbanization, expansion of government bureaucracy and regulation, more sophisticated mass media systems, the rise of consumerism, international trade, and the demand for more information have also stimulated the growth of public relations firms. Executives of

think Why does the United States have more public relations firms than all the other nations combined?

public relations firms predict healthy future growth for the industry as more countries adopt free-market economies and more international media outlets such as CNN are established. In addition, the skyrocketing use of the Internet has expanded the global reach of public relations firms. In a 2008 survey, *PRWeek* reported that 75.4 percent of marketing practitioners said they expected spending to increase in digital and online media. More than half (51.2 percent) said they considered traditional online media tactics to be their top priority in the coming 12 months.

Public relations firms are beginning to discard the term *public relations* as part of their official names. Thus it's "Burson-Marsteller," not "Burson-Marsteller Public Relations." Other firms use the term *communications* to describe their business. For example, Fenton Communications describes itself as a "public interest communications firm."

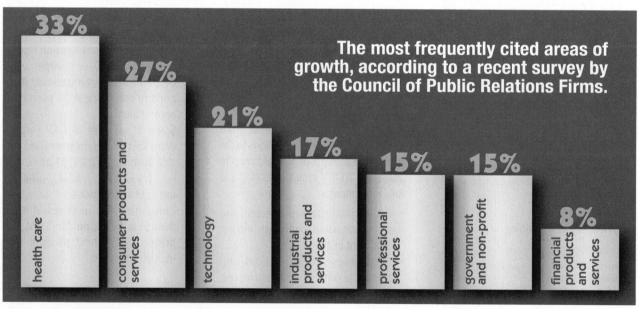

33% health care

27% consumer products and services

21% technology

17% industrial products and services

15% professional services

15% government and non-profit

8% financial products and services

The most frequently cited areas of growth, according to a recent survey by the Council of Public Relations Firms.

A public relations firm was retained to publicize and organize the grand opening of the Smithsonian's National Museum of the American Indian. The ceremonies, which generated extensive media coverage, featured representatives from various tribes in full regalia.

Increasingly, public relations firms are emphasizing the counseling aspect of their services, although most of their revenues come from implementing tactical aspects, such as writing news releases and organizing special events or media tours. The transition to counseling is best expressed by Harold Burson, chairman of Burson-Marsteller, who once told an audience, "In the beginning, top management used to say to us, 'Here's the message; deliver it.' Then it became, 'What should we say?' Now, in smart organizations, it's 'What should we do?'"

Because of the counseling function, we use the phrase "public relations *firm*" instead of "public relations *agency*" throughout this book. Advertising firms, in contrast, are properly called agencies because they serve as agents, buying time or space on behalf of a client.

A good source of information about public relations counseling is the Council of Public Relations Firms, which has approximately 100 member firms. This group provides information on its website (www.prfirms.org) about trends in the industry and offers advice on how to select a public relations firm, as well as a variety of other materials. It also offers the popular publication *Careers in Public Relations: Opportunities in a Dynamic Industry*. The Council of Public Relations Firms also operates a career center and posts résumés on its website of individuals looking for employment with a public relations firm.

Services Provided by Public Relations Firms

Public relations firms provide a variety of services:

- **Marketing Communications.** Promote products and services through such tools as news releases, feature stories, special events, brochures, and media tours.
- **Executive Speech Training.** Coach top executives on public affairs activities, including personal appearances.
- **Research and Evaluation.** Conduct scientific surveys to measure public attitudes and perceptions.
- **Crisis Communication.** Counsel management on what to say and do in an emergency such as an oil spill or a product recall.
- **Media Analysis.** Examine appropriate media for targeting specific messages to key audiences.
- **Community Relations.** Counsel management on ways to achieve official and public support for such projects as building or expanding a factory.
- **Events Management.** Plan and conduct news conferences, anniversary celebrations, rallies, symposia, and national conferences.
- **Public Affairs.** Prepare materials and testimony for government hearings and regulatory bodies, and prepare background briefings as well.
- **Branding and Corporate Reputation.** Provide advice on programs that establish a company brand and its reputation for quality.
- **Financial Relations.** Counsel management on ways to avoid takeover by another firm and effectively communicate with stockholders, security analysts, and institutional investors.

Public relations firms also offer specialty services. Ketchum and Edelman have formed "digital media" practices that concentrate on the Internet and social media. Burson-Marsteller set up a specialty area in environmental communications. After the terrorist attacks of September 11, 2001, Fleishman-Hillard set up a practice in homeland security. Other firms offer specialty services in such areas as litigation public relations to help organizations give their side of the story when major lawsuits are filed.

Global Reach

Public relations firms, large and small, usually are in metropolitan areas. On an international level, firms and their offices or affiliates can be found in most of the world's major cities and capitals. Fleishman-Hillard, for example, has employees in 46 countries. Ogilvy Public Relations has 1,700 employees in 9 U.S. offices and 65 offices worldwide.

The importance of international operations is reflected in the fact that most of the major public relations firms generate substantial revenues from international operations. Edelman, for example, had $450 million in revenues in 2008, but one-third of this revenue came from its international offices. Burson-Marsteller, with 71 offices abroad, generates about half of its revenues from its international operations.

International work is not reserved only for large firms. Small- and medium-sized firms around the world have formed working partnerships with one another so that they can more effectively serve their clients' needs. One prominent group in this regard is Worldcom Public Relations Group, with 110 firms in 91 cities on 5 continents. Other groups include Pinnacle Worldwide, with 34 firms in 10 nations, and Iprex, with 68 firms with 90 offices in 30 nations.

When working as part of an affiliation, firms cooperate with one another to service clients with international public relations needs. For example, a firm in India may call its affiliate in Los Angeles to handle the details of news coverage for a visiting trade delegation from India. Bob Oltmanns, head of Iprex, told *PRWeek*, "One of the reasons we started in the first place was to provide clients with a need for reach beyond their own markets with a viable alternative to the large multinational agencies."

Firms Win Golden World Awards

Public relations firms around the world handle a variety of assignments. Here are some that have received a Golden World award from the International Public Relations Association (IPRA):

- *Weber Shandwick* (Hong Kong). Conducted a cervical cancer awareness campaign. In Asia, three women die every minute from cervical cancer. The company's campaign for a cervical cancer vaccine, Cervarix, led to increased vaccination rates.
- *InHouse* (Turkey). Turk Telecom embarked on a project to move customers from paper bills to e-bills with its "Save a Tree, Plant a Tree" program. As part of this campaign, 1 million Turkish households switched to e-bills, saving 50,000 trees, and Turk Telecom planted an additional 100,000 trees.
- *Horizon Communication Group* (Australia). The group coordinated a campaign to position New Caledonia "as one of the best gourmet experiences outside France." Its efforts were instrumental in increasing visitation to New Caledonia by Australians by 10 percent and elevating "gourmet dining" to the number 1 reason for Australians to visit New Caledonia.
- *Solid Relations* (Greece). The firm educated journalists on the health and beauty benefits of "catechins"—antioxidants found in green tea—with tea times, dinners, and symposia featuring selected health and beauty journalists. Lipton thus paved the way for acceptance by journalists and Greek women of its Lipton Linea green tea as a "drinking cosmetic."
- *Prime* (Sweden). During a six-week healthcare strike in Stockholm, crisis communicators used websites, mass media, advertisements, phone banks, and local transports to ensure that Stockholmers were able to find health care as emergency rooms were shut down on a rolling basis.

The Rise of Communication Conglomerates

Until the 1970s, the largest public relations firms were independently owned by their founders or, in some cases, by employee stockholders. A significant change began in 1973, when Carl Byoir & Associates, then the largest U.S. public relations firm, was purchased by the advertising firm of Foote, Cone & Belding. In short order, other large public relations firms were purchased by major advertising agencies.

Today, both public relations firms and advertising agencies have become part of large, diversified holding companies with global reach. Interpublic Group (IPG) not only owns Foote, Cone & Belding (now called Draftfcb) and other advertising agencies, but also 14 public relations firms. These firms include Weber Shandwick, GolinHarris,

Carmichael Lynch Spong, DeVries Public Relations, MWW Group, and Tierney Communications.

IPG, despite total 2008 revenues of $6.9 billion, is only the third-largest holding company. Omnicom, the largest with $13.4 billion in revenues, generates almost 60 percent of its revenues outside of advertising. Like the other communication conglomerates, it owns a host of companies specializing in such areas as advertising, marketing, billboards, direct mail, special event promotion, graphic design, survey research, and public relations. For example, Omnicom owns seven major public relations firms, including Brodeur Partners, Porter Novelli, Fleishman-Hillard, Cone, Ketchum, Gavin Anderson, and Clark & Weinstock. London-based WPP is the second-largest holding company, with revenues of $10.6 billion. Among its holdings are six leading public relations firms, including Burson-Marsteller, Hill & Knowlton, and Cohn & Wolfe.

> **think**
>
> **What advantages can a global conglomerate offer a corporate client? What are the disadvantages of going with a large conglomerate?**

Large conglomerates may acquire public relations firms for several reasons. One is the natural evolutionary step of integrating various communication disciplines into "total communication networks." Supporters of integration say that no single-function agency or firm is equipped with the personnel or resources to handle complex, often global, integrated marketing functions efficiently for a client. In addition, joint efforts by public relations and advertising professionals can offer prospective clients greater communications impact, generate more business, and expand the number of geographical locations served around the world.

A second reason is purely economic. Holding companies find public relations firms to be attractive investments. According to *PRWeek*, revenues from advertising clients have remained somewhat static over the years, whereas revenues of public relations firms often experience double-digit growth.

Although earlier efforts to create total communication networks for clients often met with limited success, an increasing body of evidence indicates that the strategy may now be working. Considerable new business is also generated when units of the same conglomerate refer customers to each other. As communication campaigns become more integrated, even more synergy will become commonplace.

Holding companies originally started out primarily as a stable of advertising agencies under one umbrella, but they have evolved considerably beyond that with the acquisition of public relations firms and other specialty communication companies. London-based WPP, for example, now employs 69,000 people in more than 100 nations. Martin Sorrell, chairman of WPP (London), told a *Wall Street Journal* interviewer, "If you want to upset me, call me an advertising agency. The strategic objective is for two-thirds of our revenue to come from nontraditional advertising in 5 to 10 years. Because of fragmentation, TiVo, and Sky Plus, clients and ourselves have to look at everything. Instead of focusing on network television, we have to look at public relations and radio and outdoor and mobile messaging and satellite. Media planning becomes more important."

Sorrell also makes the point that "one size doesn't fit all" when it comes to global communications strategies and campaigns. Campaigns still have to be tailored to local customs, ethnic groups, and religious preferences. For example, Muslims now constitute 26 percent of the world's population, and by 2014 they will account for 30 percent. By the same year, two-thirds of the world's population will be Asian.

Structure of a Counseling Firm

A small public relations firm may consist only of the owner (president) and an assistant (vice president) who are supported by an administrative assistant. As you might expect, larger firms generally have a more extended hierarchy.

The organization of Ketchum in San Francisco is fairly typical. The president is based in Ketchum's New York office, so the executive vice president is the on-site director in San Francisco. A senior vice president is associate director of operations. Next in line are several vice presidents who primarily do account supervision or special projects.

Each account supervisor is in charge of one major account or several smaller ones. Each account executive, who reports to an account supervisor, is in direct contact with the client and handles most of the day-to-day activity involving that account. At the bottom of the pecking order are the assistant account executives, who do routine maintenance work by compiling media lists, gathering information, and writing rough drafts of news releases.

Recent college graduates usually start as assistant account executives. Once they learn the firm's procedures and show ability, promotion to account executive may occur within 6 to 18 months. After two or three years, it is not uncommon for an account executive to become an account supervisor.

Executives at the vice presidential level and above are typically heavily involved in selling their firm's services. To prosper, a firm must continually seek new business and sell additional services to current clients. To that end, the upper management of the firm calls on prospective clients, prepares proposals, and makes new business presentations. In this very competitive field, a firm that is not adept at selling itself does not succeed and prosper.

Firms frequently organize account teams, especially to serve a client whose program is multifaceted. One member of the team may set up a nationwide media tour in which an organization representative is booked on television talk shows. Another may supervise all materials for the print media, including news stories, feature articles, background kits, and artwork. A

third may concentrate on the trade press or arrange special events.

Pros and Cons of Using a Public Relations Firm

Because public relations is a service industry, a firm's major asset is its people. Potential clients thinking about hiring a public relations firm usually base their decisions on the quality of the staff at the public relations firm, according to a survey of *Fortune* 500 corporate communication vice presidents.

Thomas L. Harris, a consultant who conducted a survey of corporate communication directors, found that clients believe that meeting deadlines and keeping promises are the most important criteria for evaluating firms. Other important considerations were, in descending order, client services; honest, accurate billing; creativity; and knowledge of the client's industry.

Advantages. Public relations firms offer several advantages for the organizations that hire them when compared to doing the work in an in-house basis:

- *Objectivity.* The firm can analyze a client's needs or problems from a

---

Major Public Relations Firms Are Owned by CONGLOMERATES

An estimated 60 percent of the global business in public relations is conducted by firms that are owned by communication conglomerates that also own advertising agencies, marketing firms, billboard companies, direct mail firms, and special event specialty shops. The following list identifies the major holding companies based on their 2008 total revenues, including the percentage of their revenues that came from nonadvertising sources:

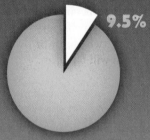

9.5% 10.2% 16% 36% 60%

OMNICOM
Total revenues: $13.4 billion
Percentage of revenues from public relations: 9.5 percent, or about $1.27 billion
Public relations firms owned: Brodeur, Porter Novelli, Fleishman-Hillard, Cone, Ketchum, Gavin Anderson, and Clark & Weinstock

WPP
Total revenues: $10.6 billion
Percentage of revenues from public relations: 10.2 percent, or about $1.08 billion
Public relations firms owned: Hill & Knowlton; Cohn & Wolfe; Burson-Marsteller; Ogilvy Public Relations; Robinson Lerer & Montgomery; and the GCI Group

INTERPUBLIC GROUP
Total revenues: $6.96 billion
Percentage of revenues from public relations: 16 percent, or about $1.1 billion
Public relations firms owned: MWW Group, Weber Shandwick, GolinHarris, DeVries Public Relations, Carmichael Lynch Spong, BNC, Slay PR, Rogers & Cowan, Tierney Communications, and PMK/HBH

PUBLICIS GROUPE
Total revenues: $6.1 billion
Percentage of revenues from public relations: 36 percent, or about $2.19 billion
Public relations firms owned: Publicis Dialog, Publicis Consultants, and MS&L

HAVAS
Total revenues: $2.19 billion
Percentage of revenues from public relations: 60 percent, or about $1.3 billion
Public relations firms owned: Euro RSCG Magnet and Abernathy MacGregor

Source: "Agency Business Report 2009." *PRWeek*, April 27, 2009, 46–47.

Taking SXSW to the Next Level

AUSTIN, TEXAS, has been the home for the South by Southwest musical festival since 1986.

In 1993, the South by Southwest Music Conference (SXSW) was joined by the SXSW Film Conference and SXSW Interactive Festival (SXSWi). SXSWi is a series of presentations; networking opportunities; a venue for the sharing of new websites, video games, and start-up ideas; and an important trade show. At first, the interactive festival did not have the high profile and broad appeal of the music and film festivals, but SXSWi public relations staffers, together with members of the Austin office of the Porter Novelli public relations firm, were determined to change that situation. Press attendance at SXSWi had grown from 75 media members in 2007 to more than 200 in 2008 when they decided they were ready to take it to the next level.

Media relations at SXSWi was already renowned for the VIP treatment lavished on media influentials at the festival. The SXSWi PR staff, together with Porter Novelli's Austin staff, began looking for new ways to build on their past successes and improve their promotion of the industry trends and technology luminaries at the event. One step in the right direction was an August 2008 news release announcing the launch of the "Panel Picker" online voting application process, which generated early buzz for the mid-March 2009 event.

Porter Novelli also developed an array of first-class press materials. The comprehensive press kit included an at-a-glance schedule, hot picks for panel and evening activities, industry contact information, and personalized event information. The company also developed toolkits for participating businesses that included press release templates, wire distribution options, and PR tips and hints for the conference.

More than 300 interactive press representatives attended the conference. *Advertising Age* noted, "Often dubbed the Sundance of new media, SXSWi is the bellwether for what lies ahead for digital culture." *The Guardian* of London reported, "SXSW Interactive spans gaming, web content, web design, development, academia, social media, mobile . . . but what it does more than any other event is a special mix of the arts and digital culture with technology. There are no suits, no boring product pitches—SXSWi is about ideas and trends in new digital tools and technologies."

1 How would you measure the success of Porter Novelli and the SXSWi PR staff in improving press coverage in 2009?

2 If you were on the staff at Porter Novelli, how would you reach journalists who are interested in digital media and online trends?

3 Think of a local arts festival or trade show event in your community. How would you promote the event? How could the staff of a public relations firm help you?

new perspective and offer fresh insights.

- *A Variety of Skills and Expertise.* The firm has specialists, whether in speech writing, trade magazine placement, or helping with investor relations.
- *Extensive Resources.* The firm has abundant media contacts and works regularly with numerous suppliers of products and services. It has research materials, including data information banks. International jobs, such as handling the corporate sponsorship issues that arise in conjunction with the Olympics, benefit from the extensive resources of a firm.
- *Offices Throughout the Country.* A national public relations program requires coordination in major cities. Large firms have on-site staffs or affiliate firms in many cities and even around the world.
- *Special Problem-Solving Skills.* A firm may have extensive experience and a solid reputation in desired areas. For example, Burson-Marsteller is well known for its expertise in crisis communications, health and medical issues, and international coordination of special projects. Hill & Knowlton is known for its expertise in public affairs, and Ketchum is the leader in consumer marketing.
- *Credibility.* A successful public relations firm has a solid reputation for professional, ethical work. When it is represented by such a firm, a client is likely to get more attention among opinion leaders in mass media, government, and the financial community.

Disadvantages. There are also drawbacks to using public relations firms:

- *Superficial Grasp of the Client's Unique Problems.* Although objectivity is gained from an outsider's perspective, there is often a disadvantage in that the public relations firm may not thoroughly understand the client's business or needs.
- *Lack of Full-Time Commitment.* A public relations firm has many clients. Therefore, no single client can monopolize its personnel and other resources.
- *Need for Prolonged Briefing Period.* Some companies become frustrated because time and money are needed for a public relations firm to research the organization and make recommendations. Consequently, the actual launch of a public relations program may take weeks or months.
- *Resentment by Internal Staff.* The public relations staff members of a client organization may resent the use of outside counsel because they think it implies that they lack the ability to do the job.
- *Need for Strong Direction by Top Management.* High-level executives must take the time to brief outside counsel on the specific objectives to be fulfilled.
- *Need for Full Information and Confidence.* A client must be willing to share its information—including the skeletons in its closet—with outside counsel. See the Ethics in Action box earlier in this chapter for an illustration of why cooperation between the public relations firm and the client is essential.
- *Costs.* Outside counsel is expensive. In many situations, routine public relations work can be handled at lower cost by internal staff.

Fees and Charges

The three most common methods of charging clients used by public relations firms, which are also used by law firms and management consultants, are (1) basic hourly fee, plus out-of-pocket expenses; (2) retainer fee; and (3) fixed project fee. A fourth strategy—pay for placement—is used less often.

- *Basic Hourly Fee, Plus Out-of-Pocket Expenses.* The number of hours spent on a client's account is tabulated each month and billed to the client. Work by personnel in the counseling firm is billed at various hourly rates. Out-of-pocket expenses, such as cab fares, car rentals, airline tickets, and meals, are also billed to the client. In a typical $100,000 campaign, approximately 70 percent of the budget is spent on staff salaries.
- *Retainer Fee.* A basic monthly charge billed to the client covers ordinary administrative and overhead expenses for maintaining the account and being "on call" for advice and strategic counseling. This approach might be the preferred choice of clients who have in-house capabilities for executing communication campaigns but who still need the advice of experts during the planning phase.

A Job at a Corporation or a PR Firm?

Recent college graduates often ponder the pros and cons of joining a corporate department or going to work for a public relations firm.

Corporate PR: Depth of Experience	PR Firm: Breadth of Experience
Jobs more difficult to find without experience; duties more narrowly focused.	Experience gained quickly. (Tip: Find a mentor you can learn from.)
Sometimes little variety at entry level.	Variety. Usually work with several clients and on several projects at same time. Opportunity for rapid advancement.
Growth sometimes limited unless you are willing to switch employers.	
Can be slower paced.	Fast-paced, exciting.
Heavy involvement with executive staff; see impact almost instantly. You are an important component in the "big picture."	Seldom see the impact of your work for a client; removed from "action."
	Abilities get honed and polished. (This is where a mentor really helps.)
Strength in all areas expected. Not a lot of time for coaching by peers.	Networking with other professionals leads to better job opportunities.
Sometimes so involved in your work that you don't have time for networking.	Learn other skills, such as how to do presentations and budgets and establish deadlines.
Same "client" all the time. Advantage: Get to know organization really well. Disadvantage: Can become boring.	Intense daily pressure on billable hours, high productivity. Some firms are real "sweatshops."
Less intense daily pressure; more emphasis on accomplishing longer-term results.	Somewhat high employment turnover.
Less turnover.	Budgets and resources can be limited.
More resources usually available.	Salary traditionally low at entry level.
Salaries tend to be higher.	Insurance, medical benefits can be minimal.
Benefits usually good, sometimes excellent.	Little opportunity for profit sharing, stock options.
More opportunities available.	High emphasis on tactical skills, production of materials.
Can be more managerial and involved in strategic planning.	

Many retainer fees specify the number of hours that the firm will spend on an account each month. Any additional work is billed at normal hourly rates. Out-of-pocket expenses are usually billed separately.

- *Fixed Project Fee.* The public relations firm agrees to do a specific project, such as an annual report, a newsletter, or a special event, for a fixed fee. For example, a counseling firm may write and produce a quarterly newsletter for $30,000 annually. The fixed fee is the least popular payment option among public relations firms because it is difficult to predict all work and expenses in advance. Many clients, however, like fixed fees for a specific project because it is easier to budget and there are no "surprises."
- *Pay for Placement.* With this payment method, which is not widely used, clients don't pay for hours worked but rather for actual placements of articles in the print media and broadcast mentions. Placement fees for a major story can range anywhere from $1,500 to $15,000 depending on the prestige, circulation, or audience size of the media outlet that uses a story proposed by a pay-for-placement firm. The vast majority of public relations firms don't use this business model for several reasons: It reduces public relations to media relations and media placement, when it is in reality a much broader field; it presents cash-flow problems because payment isn't made until a placement is made; and media gatekeepers ultimately decide what to use and what not to use, so placement is never guaranteed despite the number of hours firm staff members devote to "pitching" a story.

The primary basis of the most common methods that a public relations firm charges for its services—the basic hourly fee, the retainer fee, and the fixed project fee—is to estimate the number of hours that a particular project will take to plan, execute, and evaluate. The first method—the basic hourly fee—is the most flexible and most widely used among large firms. It is preferred by public relations people because they are paid for the exact number of hours spent on a project. In contrast, the retainer fee and the fixed project fee are based on an estimate of how many hours it will take to service a client.

A number of variables are considered when a public relations firm estimates the cost of a program. These factors include the size and duration of the project, the geographical locations involved, the number of personnel assigned to the project, and the type of client. A major variable, of course, is billing for the use of the firm's personnel to a client at the proper hourly rate.

An account executive may earn approximately $65,000 per year. Benefits (health insurance, pension plan, and so on) may cost the firm an additional $23,000. Thus the annual cost of the employee to the firm totals $88,000. Assuming there are 1,600 billable hours in a year (after deducting vacation time and holidays), the account executive makes $55 per hour.

The standard industry practice is to bill clients at least three times a person's salary. This multiple allows the firm to pay for office space, equipment, insurance, and supplies, and try to operate at a profit level of 10 to 20 percent before taxes. Thus the billing rate of the account executive (3 × $55) is rounded to $165 per hour. One survey by consultants StevensGouldPincus (SGP) found that account managers billed an average of $198 per hour. Senior vice presidents of PR firms billed at $287 per hour, and the average CEO of a PR firm billed at $343 per hour. The CEO of a large firm with $25 million or more in revenues averaged $505 per hour.

The primary income of a public relations firm comes from the sale of staff time, but some additional income results from markups on photocopying, telephone, fax, and artwork the firm supervises. The standard markup in the trade is between 15 and 20 percent.

APPLY YOUR KNOWLEDGE

WHAT WOULD YOU DO? THE JOB OFFER

You will graduate from college in several months and are planning a career in public relations. After several interviews, you receive two job offers.

One offer is with a high-technology company that makes inkjet printers and scanners for the consumer market. The corporate communications department has approximately 20 professionals, and it is customary for beginners to start in employee publications or product publicity. Later, with more experience, you might be assigned to do marketing communications for a product group or work in a specialized area such as investor relations, governmental affairs, or even community relations.

The second job offer is from a local office of a large, national public relations firm. You would begin as an assistant account executive and work on several accounts, including a chain of fast-food restaurants and an insurance company. The jobs pay about the same, but the corporation offers better insurance and medical plans.

Taking into consideration the pros and cons of working for public relations firms versus corporations, decide what job would best fit your abilities and preferences. Explain your reasons to a classmate.

Summary

Which Factors Determine the Roles and Status of Public Relations Departments in an Organization? p. 89

- Organizations, depending on their culture and the wishes of top management, structure the public relations function in various ways.

- The role of public relations in an organization depends on the type of organization, the perceptions of top management, and the capabilities of the public relations executive and staff.

Which Levels of Influences Can Public Relations Departments Exercise in an Organization? p. 92

- Public relations is a staff function rather than a line function.

- Public relations professionals often serve at the tactical and technician levels, but others are counselors to the top executive and have a role in policy making.

- Public relations is expanding from its traditional functions to exercise influence in the highest levels of management.

Which Services Do Public Relations Firms Provide? p. 97

- Public relations firms come in all sizes and are found worldwide, providing myriad services. The scope of services they provide to clients varies, but there are common denominators.

- In recent decades, many public relations firms have either merged with advertising agencies or become subsidiaries of diversified holding companies.

What Are the Pros and Cons of Employing a Public Relations Firm? p. 100

- Advantages of using outside firms include versatility and extensive resources, among other considerations.

- Disadvantages associated with outside public relations firms is that they may lack the full-time commitment of an in-house department, need a lot of direction, and are often more expensive.

QUESTIONS
for *Review* and *Discussion*

1. How have the role and function of public relations departments changed in recent years?

2. In what ways do the structure and culture of an organization affect the role and influence of the public relations department?

3. Which kinds of knowledge does a manager of a public relations department need today?

4. The names of many departments now include the term "corporate communications" instead of "public relations." Do you think the first term is more appropriate? Why or why not?

5. What is the difference between a line function and a staff function? To which function does public relations belong, and why?

6. Why is a compulsory-advisory role within an organization a good one for a public relations department to have?

7. Which four areas of an organization are the most likely to develop friction with public relations? Explain.

8. Name at least seven services that a public relations firm offers clients.

9. How important is international business to U.S. public relations firms?

10. What are the standard methods used by a public relations firm to charge for its services?

the THINK SPOT

www.thethinkspot.com

TACTICS

PRWeek

Kimberly Maul, January 15, 2010, *PRWeek*

Census Campaign Focuses on Messaging, Minority Communities

A trend in public relations is the increased integration of PR with advertising and marketing. The synergy of these strategic communication fields is a feature of many modern successful campaigns.

Because this campaign is for the U.S. Census, the target public is huge and diverse. It's important to reach young people and old people; poor people and rich people; whites, African Americans, Hispanic Americans, and other minority groups; city dwellers and rural residents.

How will these different tactics help organizers reach different publics?

Research is essential to develop pithy campaign messages such as this one.

WASHINGTON: The Census Bureau unveiled its four-month marketing campaign for its 2010 Census this week, integrating advertising, social media, experiential marketing, and more. A focus this time is on minority communities, encouraging them to participate and be properly counted, which would have benefits down the line.

Overall, the Census Bureau and its team of agencies have one main goal: "to increase the proportion of American households that fill out the questionnaire and mail it back," said Robert Groves, director of the US Census Bureau. "The strategy is to get the word out in every medium, every market that we can." The campaign kicks off first with a spot during the Golden Globes on January 17 and then more officially on January 18.

Advertisements will appear during major events including the Super Bowl and the 2010 Olympics. Online, the 2010 Census has its website, a blog written by Groves, and a presence on social media such as Twitter and Facebook. The Portrait of America Road Tour kicked off on January 4, an educational element of the campaign.

"At this phase, all guns are blasting away at once because the basic level of knowledge of the country about the 2010 Census is at its lowest point," Groves told *PRWeek*. He added that the message is all about the fact that participating in the Census is important, easy, and safe.

That messaging is especially critical as the Census reaches out to multicultural groups, targeting those that may have traditionally been underrepresented due to distrust of government or lack of knowledge of the Census. In order to combat that, the Census Bureau is partnering with national, local, and community-based organizations to build trust in those communities. Ads will be produced in 28 different languages, and several firms are helping with multicultural outreach, including IW Group and GlobalHue.

Whether you're promoting the U.S. Census or a product recall, having a local partner is a real asset in building credibility and encouraging trust.

The budget for the entire integrated marketing campaign is $340 million, with around $133 million set aside for paid advertising. The Census Bureau is working with Draftfcb for advertising, Weber Shandwick for PR, Jack Morton for experiential marketing, IW Group for Asian American outreach, and GlobalHue for African American and GlobalHue Latino for Hispanic work.

Director Groves said the money spent on this marketing campaign will save the taxpayers money in the end, which is another message point.

"We know that for every one percentage point of the household population that does not return the form, we're going to send out people to call on those households and we'll spend about $85 million doing that," he explained. "So if I can save that $85 million by increasing the response rate by 1% through advertising, it's a good deal for the taxpayer."

Weber Shandwick will help promote this and other messages, as part of its responsibilities, explained Brooke Worden, VP at Weber Shandwick. Other responsibilities include earned media, issues management, social media, and some work with ethnic media.

"It's an integrated campaign, so all companies are working together and in tandem," Worden added. The PR plan is to have a national strategy of building awareness, and regionally, equipping Census employees with tools and training.

The 2010 Census will have an impact on the country in many ways, and in communications, the expected increase in multicultural consumers, especially in areas like Texas and Arizona, will alter the way they reach out.

"I expect the Census results to highlight the demographic shifts, such as U.S.-born Hispanics now surpassing immigrants as the biggest source of Hispanic growth," said Sonia Sroka, VP of Hispanic marketing for Porter Novelli. "We'll see an increase in specialty marketing, product development, and personalized communications."

"There is no question that the minority population is going to be the big story for 2010 and 2011, just as it was for 2000," added Armando Azarloza, the president of the Axis Agency. He suggested that the Road Tour and partnerships with community leaders will be most effective to reach the Hispanic population. "There's a little bit of an education process and I think the government has a really good story to tell. [The partners] are steadfast advocates in their communities and getting them on board can be a strong tool."

Mary Crawford, MD of public affairs at Burson-Marsteller's Washington office, agrees that the partnership element and having a credible voice in the community is necessary. This grassroots outreach, she said, is about "getting into their lives, rather than expecting them to come to you."

A campaign that is so large, with target publics so diverse, demands that organizers tap the specialties of several public relations firms.

No doubt, research coupled with experience in working with the Hispanic community contributed to this strategy and these conclusions.

With any communication campaign, it's essential to provide evidence of the value it provides to the organization or client.

The elements of this campaign offer evidence of the diverse expertise that PR professionals bring to the integrated communication table.

6 RESEARCH AND

Mobile cell telephones and smart phones are causing concern for public health advocates, who cite driver cell phone use as a source of increased automobile accidents, injury, and death. Nationwide Insurance has a vested interest in keeping auto accidents to a minimum, so it developed a campaign, in conjunction with public relations firm Fleishman-Hillard, aimed at educating people about the dangers of "driving while distracted" (DWD).

Nationwide founded its campaign on data collected in a national survey of more than 1,500 drivers. The data "provided great insight into the American public's perception of DWD, as well as the actions and habits that contribute to the national DWD issue," according to Nationwide's award-winning PRSA Silver Anvil entry.

After gathering survey responses directly from drivers, Nationwide searched for news coverage of this issue in the Factiva and LexisNexis databases. This content analysis allowed the company to identify and target journalists who had covered the issue.

One of the primary objectives of Nationwide and Fleishman-Hillard was to "influence Americans' behaviors and reduce dangers of DWD through the use of technology and education, and by encouraging enforcement of the issue." Nationwide targeted drivers and key decision makers, such as legislators and parents of young drivers. The company used information gathered in the survey to garner media coverage. It hosted educational events at high schools and sponsored a Washington, D.C., symposium on DWD focused on lawmakers. In addition, the insurance firm partnered with technology company Aegis Mobility in promoting DriveAssist, a product that "detects when a cell phone is in a moving vehicle," alerting a driver when others are DWD.

CAMPAIGN PLANNING

News coverage of Nationwide's survey generated 134 million impressions, or $2.1 million in advertising equivalency. Media coverage included pieces done by the *CBS Early Show*, the *New York Times*, and CNN. The Washington, D.C., symposium resulted in the National Safety Council calling for a complete ban on cell phone use while driving.

Developing a complete campaign that is informed by research and can be evaluated for its contribution to the organization's bottom line should be every public relations practitioner's goal. Nationwide and Fleishman-Hillard provided a good example of these elements in this PRSA Silver Anvil Award–winning campaign.

❶ Despite Nationwide's attempts to curtail DWD, this behavior remains a problem. How could college students be further persuaded to limit their cell phone use while driving?

❷ Which medium and messages are most effective for reaching and informing teenagers and young adults about the dangers of DWD?

THE
four essential
steps OF EFFECTIVE
PUBLIC RELATIONS

effective public relations is a process with four essential steps: (1) research, (2) planning, (3) communication, and (4) measurement. *Research* provides the information required to understand the needs of publics and to develop powerful messages. *Planning* is referred to as the central function of management; it is the process of setting goals and objectives and determining ways to meet them.

Communication is related to message strategy—making a message more appealing and persuasive to the public. *Measurement* (or evaluation) is becoming increasingly important in our profession. Executives justifiably demand accountability from public relations practitioners. Measurement techniques provide a means for demonstrating to management that public relations is achieving objectives and contribut-

ing in a meaningful way to the organization.

This chapter describes the first two of these steps—research and planning—and examines the role they play in an effective public relations program. The third and fourth steps in the process—communication and measurement—are addressed in the following chapter.

> **"Research is the controlled, objective, and systematic gathering of information for the purpose of describing and understanding."**
>
> **Glen Broom and David Dozier**
> **in *Using Research in Public Relations***

research:
THE FIRST STEP

the crucial first step in the public relations process is research. Research is an integral part of the planning, program development, and measurement process. In basic terms, research is a form of listening.

Before public relations professionals can develop a program, they must gather collect and inter-

pret data. Research is essential. It informs top managers as they make policy decisions and map out strategies for effective communication programs. Research also provides a way to evaluate and measure a program once it has been completed. Meaningful measurement can lead to greater

- ▶ **What is the problem?**

- ▶ **Which kind of information is needed?**

- ▶ **How will the research results be used?**

- ▶ **Which specific public (or publics) should be researched?**

- ▶ **Should the organization do the research in-house or hire an outside consultant?**

- ▶ **How will research data be analyzed, reported, or applied?**

- ▶ **How soon are the results needed?**

- ▶ **How much will the research cost?**

accountability and credibility with upper management.

Different types of research can accomplish an organization's objectives and meet its information needs. The choice of research type really depends on the particular subject and situation. As always, time and budget are major considerations, as is the perceived importance of the situation.

Many questions should be asked before formulating a research design:

Asking key questions helps public relations professionals determine the extent and nature of the research needed. Sometimes, only informal research is required, because of budget concerns or the need for immediate information. At other times, a random scientific survey is appropriate, despite its high cost and time investment, because more precise data are needed. The pros and cons of various research methods are discussed later in this chapter.

Using Research

Research is a key part of virtually every phase of a communications program. Studies show that public relations departments typically spend 3 to 5 percent of their budgets on research—and some experts argue that this share should be as much as 10 percent. Public relations professionals use research in a number of ways.

Achieving Credibility with Management. Executives want facts, not guesses and hunches. One criticism of public relations practitioners is that they too often don't link communications issues to business outcomes. Research paves the way for such linkages.

Defining Audiences and Segmenting Publics. Detailed information about demographics, lifestyles, characteristics, and consumption patterns helps to ensure that mes-

think How does research help determine what to say and whom to say it to in a public relations campaign?

sages reach the proper audiences. A successful children's immunization information campaign in California, for example, was based on State Health Department statistics showing that past immunization programs had not reached rural children and that Hispanic and Vietnamese children were not being immunized at the same rates as children in other ethnic groups.

Formulating Strategy. Too much money can be spent pursuing the wrong strategies. Consider what happened when officials of the New Hampshire paper industry, given bad press about logging and waterway pollution, thought a campaign was needed to tell the public what it

> The inclusion of public relations personnel in an organization's policy and decision-making structure is *strongly correlated* with their ability to do research and link findings to organizational objectives.

Top management in many organizations is increasingly isolated from the concerns of employees, customers, and other important publics. Research helps bridge the gap by periodically surveying key publics about problems and concerns. This feedback serves as a "reality check" for executives and often leads to better policies and communication strategies.

RESEARCH CAN INFLUENCE PUBLIC OPINION

Facts and figures, compiled from a variety of primary and secondary sources, can change public opinion. A coalition called Ohioans for Responsible Health Information, which opposed a ballot measure to require cancer warnings on thousands of products from plywood to peanut butter, commissioned universities and other credible outside sources to research the economic impact of such legislation on consumers and major industries. The research, which was used as the basis of the grassroots campaign, led to the defeat of the ballot measure.

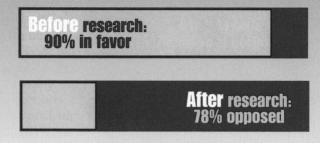

Before research: 90% in favor

After research: 78% opposed

Fate of Ohio state ballot measure to require cancer warning labels

was doing to reduce pollution. An opinion survey of 800 state residents by a public relations firm, however, indicated that the public was already generally satisfied with the industry's efforts. Consequently, the new strategy focused on reinforcing positive themes such as worker safety, employment, and environmental responsibility. Research was extremely critical in appraising whether a threat existed and served to inform the paper industry's strategy, and it helped officials focus communication resources where they would do the organization the most good.

Testing Messages. Research can determine which particular message is most salient to a target audience. According to one focus group study for a campaign to encourage carpooling, the message that resonated the most with commuters was saving time and money, not improving air quality or saving the environment. As a result, the campaign emphasized how many minutes could be cut from an average commute by using carpool lanes and the annual savings to be had by reducing gasoline, insurance, and car maintenance expenditures.

Preventing Crises. An estimated 90 percent of organizational crises are caused by internal operational problems rather than by unexpected natural disasters or external issues. Research can often uncover trouble spots and public concerns before they become news. Analyzing complaints made to a toll-free number or

monitoring chat rooms on the Internet, for example, might tip off an organization that it should act before a problem attracts media attention. Professionals can prevent a conflict or crisis through environmental scanning and other research tactics.

Monitoring the Competition. Savvy organizations keep track of what the competition is doing. Competition monitoring can be done by using surveys that ask consumers to comment on competing products, content analysis of the competition's media coverage, and reviews of industry reports in trade journals. Monitoring can be made much easier by setting up alerts that are fed directly to an e-mail inbox. Google Alerts, for example, allows a user to choose a list of search terms; once it is set up, news information that mentions the selected terms is delivered via e-mail. Google Alerts is promoted as being useful in "monitoring a developing news story" or "keeping current on a competitor or industry." Similarly, RSS feeds can be set up from key websites. For more sophisticated and targeted monitoring, commercial Internet monitoring services are also available. Such research helps an organization shape its marketing and communication strategies to counter a competitor's strengths and capitalize on its weaknesses.

Generating Publicity. Polls and surveys can generate publicity for an organization. Indeed, many surveys seem to be designed with publicity in mind. Norelco Phillips,

when it introduced a new shaver for men called Bodygroom, drew publicity for the new product by citing a telephone survey that found more than half of the male respondents preferred a hairless back to any other body part. Another 72 percent said they used a razor to remove hair in even the most sensitive places. Similarly, Simmons Bedding Company once got publicity when it polled people to find out if they slept in the nude.

Measuring Success. The bottom line of any public relations program is whether the time and money spent accomplished the stated objective. Measurement—the last step of the public relations process—is discussed in Chapter 7. In this chapter we will focus on various ways of doing research.

Research Techniques

When the term *research* is used, people tend to think only of scientific surveys and complex statistics. In public relations, however, research techniques are used to gather data and information as well.

In fact, a survey of practitioners by Walter K. Lindenmann, former senior vice president and director of research for Ketchum, found that three-fourths of the respondents described their research techniques as casual and informal rather than scientific and precise. The technique cited most often was literature searches/database information retrieval. This technique is called secondary research, because it uses existing information in books, magazine articles, electronic databases, and so on. In contrast, with primary research, new and original information is generated through research designed to answer a specific question. Examples of primary research include in-depth interviews, focus groups, surveys, and polls.

Another way to categorize research is by distinguishing between qualitative and quantitative research. In general, qualitative research affords researchers rich insights and understanding of situations or target publics. It also provides "red flags," or warnings, when strong or adverse responses occur. These responses may not be easy to extrapolate to a larger population and, therefore, are often referred to as "soft" data, but they provide practitioners with early warnings of potential problems. In contrast, quantitative research is often more expensive and complicated, but it allows for greater extrapolation to large populations. For this reason, its findings are sometimes known as "hard" data. If enormous amounts of money are

Qualitative Research VS Quantitative Research	
"Soft" data	"Hard" data
Usually uses open-ended questions, unstructured	Usually uses close-ended questions, requires forced choices, highly structured
Exploratory in nature; probing, "fishing expedition" type of research	Descriptive or explanatory type of research
Usually valid, but not reliable	Usually valid and reliable
Rarely projectable to larger audiences	Usually projectable to larger audiences
Generally uses nonrandom samples	Generally uses random samples
Examples: Focus groups; one-on-one, in-depth interviews; observation; participation; role-playing studies; convenience polling	Examples: Telephone polls; mail surveys; mall-intercept studies; face-to-face interviews; shared cost, or omnibus, studies; panel studies

to be spent on a national campaign, it may be best to make an investment in quantitative research.

Organizational Materials. Robert Kendall, in his book *Public Relations Campaign Strategies*, terms the process of researching organizational materials *archival research.* Such materials may include an organization's policy statements, speeches by key executives, past issues of employee newsletters and magazines, reports on past public relations and marketing efforts, and news clippings. Marketing statistics, in particular, often provide baseline data for public relations firms that are hired to launch a new product or boost awareness and sales of an existing product or service. Archival research also is a major component in audits that are intended to determine how an organization communicates to its internal and external publics.

Library and Online Database Methods. Reference books, academic journals, and trade publications can be found in every library. Online databases such as Proquest, Factiva, and LexisNexis contain abstracts or full-text of thousands— or even millions—of articles.

As one of its many programs to boost brand awareness, Miller Genuine Draft sponsored a "reunion ride" on Harley-Davidson Motor Company's ninetieth anniversary. Ketchum generated extensive media publicity about the "ride" and Miller's sponsorship that was 98 percent positive. Perhaps more importantly, sales increased in all but two of the cities included in the event.

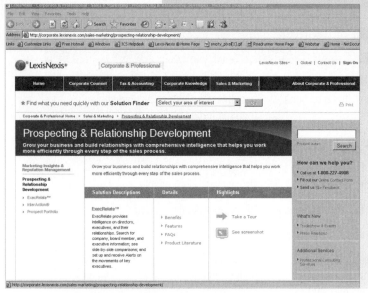

- *Burrelle's Broadcast Database* contains the full-text transcripts of radio and television programs within 24 hours after they are transmitted. Sources include ABC, NBC, CBS, CNN, National Public Radio, and selected syndicated programs.

- *Dow Jones Factiva News/Retrieval* electronically transmits up-to-the-second global coverage of business news, economic indicators, and industry and market data.

- *LexisNexis* includes millions of full-text articles from magazines, newspapers, and news services including the full text of the *New York Times* and *The Washington Post.*

Some common reference sources used by public relations professionals include the *Statistical Abstract of the United States* (http://www.census.gov/statab), which summarizes census information; the Gallup Poll (http://poll.gallup.com/), which provides an index of public opinion on a variety of issues; and *Simmons Study Media and Markets*, an extensive annual survey of households on product usage by brand and exposure to various media.

Online databases are available on a subscription basis and usually

Literature searches—the most often used informal research method in public relations—can tap an estimated 1,500 electronic databases that store an enormous amount of current and historical information.

charge by how many minutes the service is in use.

Public relations practitioners need to follow current events and public affairs issues so that they can provide thoughtful counsel in their organizations. Reading newspapers and watching television news programs is a habit that young professionals should embrace.

Information delivery systems now seem to be virtually limitless in number and form. Web-based magazines (zinio.com) or newspapers (pressdisplay.com and newsstand.com) provide products that are formatted like their print counterparts, but also include online links and video. Smart phones feature free or moderately priced applications that allow access to quality news sources, such as the *New York Times*, *USA Today*, CNN Mobile, World News Feed, and many others. These services make the work of monitoring news and trends easier for on-the-go professionals. Services such as Audible.com deliver audio to MP3 players, including content from newspapers, books, television, and radio broadcasts, and podcasts, thereby

enabling commuters to multitask. Some newspapers also provide interactive versions of their daily editions that are read to car commuters through satellite radio; users can then save or forward stories to colleagues. Listeners of National Public Radio (NPR) can also forward stories or order transcripts or broadcasts.

This wide array of information resources enables public relations practitioners to stay current and be knowledgeable about their own organization and its place in the larger world.

The Internet and World Wide Web. The Internet is a powerful research tool for the public relations practitioner. Any number of corporations, nonprofit organizations, trade groups, special-interest groups, foundations, universities, think tanks, and government agencies post reams of data on the Internet, usually in the form of home pages on the World Wide Web.

Online search engines are essential for finding information on the Internet. With literally millions of possible websites, search engines make it possible for a researcher to

---

Public relations departments and firms use online databases for the following purposes:

- Research facts to support a proposed project or campaign that requires top management approval
- Keep up-to-date with news about clients and their competitors
- Track an organization's media campaigns and competitors' press announcements
- Locate a special quote or impressive statistic for a speech or report
- Track press and business reaction to an organization's latest actions
- Locate an expert who can provide advice on an issue or a possible strategy
- Keep top management apprised of current business trends and issues
- Learn about the demographics and attitudes of target publics

simply type in a key word or two, click "Go," and in a few seconds receive all of the links that the search engine has found that relate to a given topic. Search engines such as Google also have become locations for sharing expertise and problem-solving skills regarding a wide array of topics. In the Google Groups section of the Google Web site (www.groups.google.com), helpful information can be found on everything from recreation to business to the arts.

Researchers can use specialized search engines or search tools to locate audio and video content or content of topical interest, such as sports or business news. Reviews and directories of search engines are available at searchenginewatch.com. Public relations professionals should visit such sites frequently to stay current on search capabilities as well as to monitor changes in search engines' policies, such as fees required for high placement in search results.

Researchers can use profession-specific social media such as PROpenMic.org and newsgroups such as PRFORUM, a newsgroup dedicated to public relations topics, to request information from others. Discussion groups and blogs are increasingly common sources of information for public relations practitioners. There are several Yahoo!-based PR discussion groups—NYC-PublicRelations Group, SmallPRAgencyPros, PR-Bytes, PRMindshare, PRQuorum, and Young-PRPros are examples. Pro-

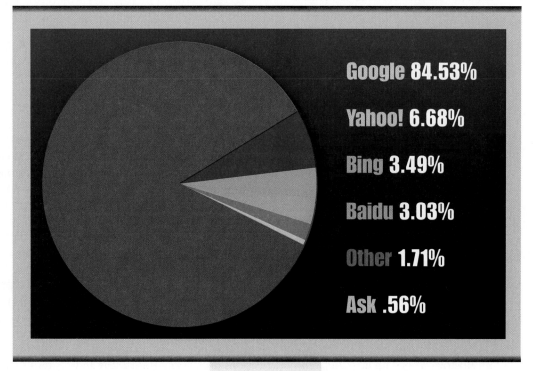

think

How can Internet search engines help inform public relations campaign development?

fessional organizations such as the Public Relations Society of America and the International Association of Business Communicators support members-only discussion groups, known as PRCOnline and Member-Speak, respectively. Blogs, including briansolis.com, examine PR business trends. IABC has blogs addressing branding, employee communications, measurement, and media relations compiled in the IABC Exchange (http://x.iabc.com/available-exchange-sites/).

Content Analysis. Content analysis is the systematic and objective counting or categorizing of content. In public relations, content often is selected from media coverage of a topic or organization. This research method can be relatively informal or quite scientific in terms of random sampling and establishing specific subject categories. It is often applied to news stories about an organization.

Surfing the Internet: HELPFUL SITES for Public Relations Professionals

- *Statistical Abstract of the United States*: www.census.gov/compendia/statab/
- The PR Survey Observer: www.clientize.com/home.asp
- Bureau of Labor Statistics: www.bls.gov
- Environmental News Network: www.enn.com
- A list of home pages of various public relations firms: www.prfirms.org
- International Association of Business Communicators (IABC): www.iabc.com
- Public Relations Society of America (PRSA): www.prsa.org
- Business Wire (hyperlinks to corporate home pages): www.businesswire.com/portal/site/home/
- Zinio Magazine Reader: www.zinio.com
- NewsStand, Inc.: www.home.newsstand.com
- Vanderbilt Television News Archive: tvnews.vanderbilt.edu/

Google was by far the most popular search engine worldwide in late 2009, with 84.53 percent of the global market, according to www.marketshare.hitslink.com.

Google 84.53%

Yahoo! 6.68%

Bing 3.49%

Baidu 3.03%

Other 1.71%

Ask .56%

Surveys of public opinion, which are often conducted by researchers on the street or in shopping malls, help public relations practitioners target audiences they wish to reach and to shape their messages.

At a basic level, a researcher can assemble news clips in a scrapbook and count the number of column inches. Don Stacks, University of Miami professor and author of *Primer of Public Relations Research*, writes that content analysis "is particularly appropriate for the analysis of documents, speeches, media releases, video content and scripts, interviews, and focus groups. The key to content analysis is that it is done objectively ..., content is treated systematically ..., [and] messages are transformed from qualitative statements to numbers, data that can be quantified and compared against other data."

A good example of content analysis is the way one company evaluated press coverage of its publicity campaign to celebrate its one-hundredth anniversary. The campaign's success was measured by a low-budget content analysis of 427 references to the client and its product in newspapers, magazines, radio, and television. The content analysis revealed that the client's themes and copy points were included in the media coverage.

Content analysis can also help determine if a need exists for additional public relations efforts. For instance, Faneuil Hall Marketplace in Boston stepped up its public relations activities after it discovered that the number of travel articles published about it had decreased.

An anniversary celebration of the marketplace helped to generate increased coverage.

Content analysis also can be applied to letters and phone calls, which often provide good feedback about problems with an organization's policies and services. A pattern of letters and phone calls pointing out a problem is evidence that something should be done.

Interviews. As with content analysis, interviews can be conducted in several different ways. Almost everyone talks to colleagues on a daily basis and calls other organizations to gather information. In fact, public relations personnel faced with solving a particular problem often "interview" other public relations professionals for ideas and suggestions.

If information is needed on public opinion and attitudes, many public relations firms will conduct short interviews with people in a shopping mall or other public place. This kind of interview is called an intercept interview, because people are literally intercepted in public places and asked their opinions.

Although the intercept interview does not use a generalizable sampling method (i.e., the results cannot be applied to the general population), it does give an organization a sense of current thinking or exposure to certain messages. Intercept interviews last only two to five minutes.

Sometimes, the best approach is to conduct more in-depth interviews in an effort to obtain more comprehensive information. A major fund-raising project by charitable groups, for example, may require in-depth interviews of community and business opinion leaders to ascertain support levels for the campaign. The success of any major fund drive depends on the support of key leaders and wealthy individuals. This more in-depth approach is called purposive interviewing, because the interviewees are carefully selected based on their expertise, influence, or leadership in the community.

Focus Groups. A good alternative to individual interviews is the focus group. The focus group technique is widely used in advertising, marketing, and public relations to help identify the attitudes and motivations of important publics. Another purpose of focus groups is to formulate or pretest message themes and communication strategies before launching a full campaign. Focus groups usually consist of 8 to 12 people who possess the characteristics of the larger target audience, such as employees, consumers, or community residents.

During a focus group, a trained facilitator uses nondirective interviewing techniques that encourage group members to talk freely about a topic or give candid reactions to suggested message themes. The setting is usually a conference room, and the discussion is informal. A focus group may last one or two hours, depending on the subject matter.

A focus group, by definition, is an informal research procedure that develops qualitative information rather than hard data. Results obtained through this research technique cannot be summarized by percentages or even projected to an entire population. Nevertheless, focus groups are useful in identifying the range of attitudes and opinions among participants. Such insights can help an organization structure its messages or, on another level, formulate hypotheses and questions to be covered by a quantitative research survey.

Increasingly, focus groups are being conducted online. With this approach, the technique can be as simple as posing a question to an online chat or interest group. Re-

A brochure about employee medical benefits or pension plans, for example, should be pretested with rank-and-file employees for *readability* and *comprehension*.

searchers also are using more formal selection processes to invite far-flung participants to meet in a prearranged virtual space. In the coming years, techniques and services will be further developed for cost-effective, online focus group research.

Copy Testing. All too often, organizations fail to communicate effectively because they produce and distribute materials that a target audience can't understand. In many cases, the material is written above the educational level of the audience. To avoid this problem, representatives of the target audience should be asked to read or view the material in draft form before it is mass-produced and distributed. This type of copy testing can be done on a one-on-one basis or in a small-group setting.

In some cases, executives and lawyers who must approve the copy may understand the material, but a worker with a high school educa-

tion might find the material difficult to follow.

Another approach to determine the degree of difficulty of material is to apply a readability formula to the draft copy. Fog, Flesch, and similar techniques relate the number of words and syllables per sentence or passage with reading level. Highly complex sentences and multisyllabic words are typically best suited to a college-educated audience.

Two ways to test copy using Internet sources are via web surveys and wikis. Web survey systems such as Survey Artisan (www.surveyartisan.com) allow attachment of video or photo files that can be critiqued by a target audience across many locations. A less sophisticated, but equally effective way to test copy is simply to attach the copy to an e-mail and provide a link to an online survey. Similarly, photos or videos can be tested through secure Flickr or YouTube sharing

In another adaptation of digital media, it has become increasingly common practice to conduct and record focus groups at various points around the country or the globe and then upload these recordings to a secure server to be webcast to the client. The focus group files can remain available for review via password on the web. Time and location are becoming less relevant to conducting focus groups, increasing the potential applications of this research method.

communities. A wiki is a website that allows users to easily edit content; these sites provide a way for clients or audience members to critique and correct copy, essentially turning audience members into copy collaborators.

Scientific Sampling Methods. The research techniques discussed in the previous section can provide public relations personnel with good insights and help them formulate effective programs. Increasingly, however, public relations professionals need to conduct polls and surveys, as well as more rigorous content analyses, using highly precise scientific sampling methods. Such sampling is based on two important factors: randomness and a large number of respondents.

think

Why is it important to use a random sample if possible when conducting research?

Random Sampling

Effective polls and surveys require a random sample. In statistics, this means that everyone in the targeted audience (as defined by the researcher) has an equal or known chance of being selected for the survey. The group selected in this manner is also called a probability sample. In contrast, a nonprobability sample is not randomly selected at all—an important consideration because improper sampling can lead to misleading results.

The most precise random sample is generated from lists that contain the name of every person in the target audience. Selection of such a sample is a simple matter if you're conducting a random survey of an organization's employees or members, because the researcher can randomly select, for example, every twenty-fifth name on a list. However, care must be taken to avoid patterns in the lists based on rank or employee category. It is always advisable to choose large

intervals between selected names so that the researcher makes numerous passes through the list. Computerized lists often allow for random selection of names.

Another method commonly used to ensure appropriate representation is to draw a random sample that matches the statistical characteristics of the audience. This practice is called quota sampling. Human resources departments usually have breakdowns of employees by job classification, and it is relatively easy to proportion a sample accordingly. For example, if 42 percent of the employees work on the assembly line, then 42 percent of the sample should consist of assembly-line workers. A quota sample can be drawn based on any number of demographic factors—age, sex, religion, race, income—depending on the purpose of the survey.

Random sampling becomes more difficult when comprehensive lists are not available. In those cases, researchers surveying the general population often use telephone directories or customer lists to select respondents at random. A more rigorous technique employs random computerized generation of telephone numbers; this process ensures that new and unlisted numbers are included in the sample.

Sample Size

In any probability study, sample size is an important factor. In public relations, the primary purpose of poll data is to get indications of attitudes and opinions, not to predict elections. Therefore, it is not usually necessary or practical to do a scientific sampling of 1,500 people.

A 10 percent error would be acceptable if a public relations person, for example, asked employees what they want to read in the company magazine. Sixty percent may indicate that they would like to see more news about opportunities for promotion. If only 100 employees were properly surveyed, it really doesn't

A number of factors can influence who is interviewed using the mall-intercept method, such as the time of day or location of the intercept interviews.

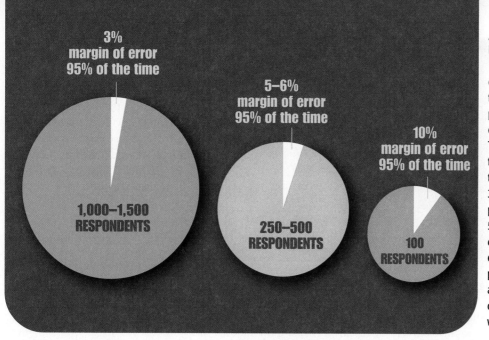

3%
margin of error
95% of the time

1,000–1,500
RESPONDENTS

5–6%
margin of error
95% of the time

250–500
RESPONDENTS

10%
margin of error
95% of the time

100
RESPONDENTS

National polling firms usually sample 1,000 to 1,500 people and get a highly accurate idea of what the U.S. adult population is thinking. A sample of 1,500 people provides a margin of error within 3 percentage points 95 percent of the time. That means that 19 out of 20 times when the same questionnaire is administered, the results should be within the same 3 percentage points and reflect the whole population accurately. A sample of 250 to 500 people provides relatively accurate data—with a 5 or 6 percent margin of error—that will help to determine general public attitudes and opinions. A sample of approximately 100 people, accurately drawn according to probability guidelines, will have a 10 percent margin of error.

matter if the actual percentage is 50 or 70 percent. Such a percentage, in either case, would be sufficient to justify an increase in news stories about advancement opportunities.

Reaching Respondents

Once a sample has been identified and a questionnaire has been developed, it must be delivered to prospective respondents. There are pros and cons to each method of delivery—(1) mail questionnaires; (2) telephone surveys; (3) personal interviews; (4) piggyback, or omnibus, surveys; and (5) web and e-mail surveys.

Mail Questionnaires. Questionnaires may be used in a variety of settings. For different reasons, most survey questionnaires are mailed to respondents. However, mail questionnaires do have some disadvantages—most notably, a low response rate. The more closely people identify with the organization and the questions, the better the response.

The response rate to a mail questionnaire can be increased, say experts, if all the guidelines of questionnaire construction are followed. In addition, researchers should keep the following suggestions in mind:

- Include a stamped, self-addressed return envelope and a personally signed letter explaining the

Questionnaire Guidelines

Steps to take when preparing and administering a questionnaire:

- [ ] Determine the type of information that is needed and in what detail.

- [ ] State the objectives of the survey in writing.

- [ ] Decide which group(s) will receive the questionnaire.

- [ ] Determine the optimal sample size.

- [ ] State the purpose of the survey and guarantee anonymity to respondents.

- [ ] Use closed-ended (multiple-choice) answers as often as possible. Respondents find it easier and less time-consuming to select answers than to compose their own.

- [ ] Design the questionnaire in such a way that answers can be easily coded for statistical analysis.

- [ ] Strive to make the questionnaire contain no more than 25 questions. Long questionnaires put people off and reduce the number of responses, particularly in print questionnaires, because it is easy to see how long the survey will take to complete.

- [ ] Use categories when asking questions about education, age, and income. People are more willing to answer when a category or range is used. For example, what category best describes your age: (a) younger than 25; (b) 26 to 40; and so on.

- [ ] Use simple, familiar words. Readability should be appropriate for the group being sampled. At the same time, don't talk down to respondents. Avoid ambiguous words and phrases that may confuse respondents.

- [ ] Edit out leading questions that suggest a specific correct response or bias an answer.

- [ ] Remember to consider the context and placement of questions. Keep in mind that questions can influence responses to subsequent questions.

- [ ] Provide space at the end of the questionnaire for respondents' comments and observations. This area allows them to provide additional information or elaboration that may not have been covered in the main body of the questionnaire.

- [ ] Pretest the questions for understanding and possible bias. Arrange for representatives of the proposed sampling group to read the questionnaire and provide feedback as to how it can be improved.

importance of participating in the survey.

- Provide an incentive. Commercial firms often encourage people to fill out questionnaires by including a token amount of money or a discount coupon. Other researchers promise to share the results of the survey with the respondents.

- Mail questionnaires by first-class mail. Some research shows that placing special-issue stamps on the envelope attracts greater interest than simply using a postage meter.

- Mail a reminder postcard three or four days after the questionnaire has been sent.

- Do a second mailing (either to nonrespondents or to the entire sample) two or three weeks after the first mailing. Again, enclose a stamped, self-addressed return envelope and a cover letter explaining the crucial need for the recipient's participation.

Telephone Surveys. Surveys by telephone, particularly those that are locally based, are used extensively by research firms. The major disadvantage of telephone surveys is the difficulty in getting access to telephone numbers. In many urban areas, as many as one-third to one-half of all numbers are unlisted. Although researchers can let a computer program pick numbers through random dialing, this method is not as effective as actually knowing who is being called. The dominance of cellular telephones whose numbers are not listed is another increasingly difficult hurdle for telephone surveys. Because cell phone numbers are portable, it is difficult to know whether the 212 prefix you dialed belongs to a current or former resident of New York City or someone who simply wants to appear to be from New York. Another barrier is convincing

respondents that a legitimate poll or survey is being taken. Far too many salespeople attempt to sell goods by posing as researchers.

Personal Interviews. The personal interview is the most expensive form of research because it requires trained staff and travel. If travel within a city is involved, a trained interviewer may be able to interview only 8 or 10 people per day, and salaries and transportation costs make this technique quite expensive. Considerable advance work is required to arrange interviews and appointments and, as previously noted, residents are reluctant to admit strangers into their homes.

Nevertheless, in some instances personal interviews can be cost-effective. Most notably, they can generate a wealth of information if the setting is controlled. Many research firms conduct personal interviews at national conventions or trade shows, where there is a concentration of people with similar interests.

Piggyback Surveys. An alternative method of reaching respondents is the piggyback survey, also known as the omnibus survey. In basic terms, an organization "buys" a question in a national survey conducted by a survey organization such as Gallup or Harris. For example, General Mills may place one or two questions in a national poll that ask respondents which professional athletes they most admire as a way to find new endorsers for its breakfast foods. In the same survey, the American Cancer Society may place a question asking how the public feels about new government guidelines regarding cancer screening examination frequency.

This research method is attractive to public relations people for two reasons. The first reason is cost: An organization pays much less to participate in a piggyback poll than to conduct its own survey. A second reason is expertise: Firms such as Gallup or

Reasons most survey questionnaires are mailed to respondents:

1. Because the researchers have better control as to who receives the questionnaire, they can make sure that the survey is representative.
2. Large geographic areas can be covered economically.
3. It is less expensive to administer paper-based questionnaires than to hire interviewers to conduct personal interviews.
4. Large numbers of people can be included at minimal cost.

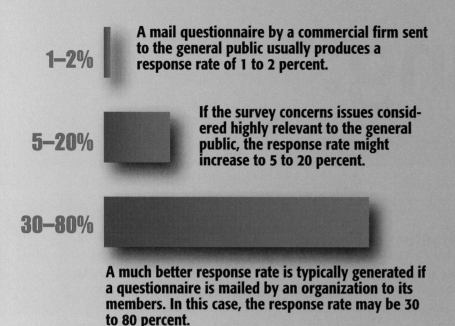

1–2% A mail questionnaire by a commercial firm sent to the general public usually produces a response rate of 1 to 2 percent.

5–20% If the survey concerns issues considered highly relevant to the general public, the response rate might increase to 5 to 20 percent.

30–80% A much better response rate is typically generated if a questionnaire is mailed by an organization to its members. In this case, the response rate may be 30 to 80 percent.

Harris have the skill and organization to conduct surveys properly and efficiently.

Piggyback surveys, however, do have limitations. An organization can get only a small snapshot of public opinion with one or two questions, and the subject matter must be relevant to the general public.

Web and E-Mail Surveys. The newest way to reach respondents is through electronic communications. One such method is to post a questionnaire on an organization's website and ask visitors to complete it online. The advantage of this approach is that responses are immediately available and results are added to the running tabulation. For example, an undergraduate campaign team sought to test messages about the National Wildlife Foundation's travel program, which was targeted at persons older than age 50. The students sampled from an e-mail list of university alumni by year of graduation so that they reached the appropriate age group. They invited the alumni to visit a website and rate several of the travel program's message strategies.

Researchers use several methods to attract respondents to a website, including (1) banner ads announcing the survey on other websites or online networks, (2) sending e-mail invitations to members of the target audience, (3) telephoning individuals with an invitation to participate, and (4) sending a postcard.

The major disadvantage of web surveys is that it is difficult to control the exact characteristics of the respondents, because a website is accessible to virtually anyone with a computer and an Internet connection. It is also very important to prevent repeated participation by the same respondent by identifying the unique identifying number of the computer (called the IP address) and allowing only one submission from that address. One of the biggest problems for online surveys is the low response rate due to the impersonal nature of the survey and the ease of exiting the survey's website with a single mouse click. For this reason, many online surveys begin with the most crucial questions.

If reaching a specific audience is important, an e-mail survey may be sent to a list of known respondents. Organizations can compile e-mail lists of clients or customers or purchase e-mail address lists from a variety of sources. Full-service web survey companies target populations, collect responses, and deliver data to the client. The costs of such surveys can be low if an online survey service such as freeonlinesurveys.com—more of a do-it-yourself service—is used. Zoomerang (info.zoomerang.com) and Harris Interactive recruit and maintain pools of respondents to fit profiles that clients want to survey. Gender, income, and political persuasion are examples of characteristics that can be selected for web survey purposes.

The telephone survey has several advantages:

>The response (or non-response) is immediate. A researcher doesn't have to wait several weeks for responses to arrive (or not arrive) by mail.

>A telephone call is personal. It is effective communication, and it is much less expensive than a personal interview.

>A telephone call is less intrusive than going door-to-door and interviewing people. Surveys have found that many people are willing to talk on the phone for as long as 45 minutes, but they will not stand at a door for more than 5 or 10 minutes and are unwilling to admit strangers to their homes.

>The response rate, if the survey is properly composed and the phone interviewers trained, can reach 80 to 90 percent.

planning:
THE SECOND STEP

the second step of the public relations process, following the research step, is program planning. Before professionals implement any public relations activity, they must give considerable thought to which steps should be taken in which order to accomplish an organization's objectives.

> ## "No longer are we simply in the business of putting press releases out; we're in the business of solving business problems through communications."
>
> Larry Werner, senior consultant

A good public relations program should support an organization's business, marketing, and communications objectives and be strategic. A practitioner must think about a situation, analyze what can be done about it, creatively conceptualize the appropriate strategies and tactics, and determine how the results will be measured. Planning also involves the coordination of multiple methods—news releases, special events, webpages, social media sites, press kits, CD-ROM distribution, news conferences, media interviews, brochures, newsletters, speeches, and so on—to achieve specific results.

Systematic planning prevents haphazard, ineffective communication. Having a blueprint of what is to be done and how it will be executed makes programs more effective and public relations more valuable to the organization.

Approaches to Planning

Planning is like putting together a jigsaw puzzle. Research provides the various pieces. Next, it is necessary to arrange the pieces so that a coherent design, or picture, emerges. The best planning is systematic—gathering information, analyzing it, and creatively applying it for the specific purpose of attaining an objective.

In the two approaches to planning discussed here, the emphasis is on asking and answering questions to generate a road map for success. One popular approach to planning is a process called "management by objective" (MBO). MBO provides focus and direction to strategy formulation and allows organizations to achieve specific objectives.

In their book *Public Relations Management by Objectives*, Norman R. Nager and T. Harrell Allen discuss nine basic MBO steps that can help a practitioner conceptualize everything from a simple news release to a multifaceted communications program. The steps serve as a planning checklist that provides the basis for strategic planning.

By working through the checklist adapted from Nager and Allen's book, a practitioner has in place the general building blocks for assembling a public relations plan. These building blocks serve as background to create a specific plan. Ketchum, a global public relations firm, offers more pointed questions in its "Strategic Planning Model for Public Relations." Ketchum's organizational model makes sense to professionals and clients alike,

think — How is asking the right questions key to strategic planning?

moving both parties toward a clear situation analysis needed to make planning relevant to the client's overall objectives.

These two approaches to planning, MBO and Ketchum's model, lead to the next important step—writing a strategic public relations plan. The elements of such a plan are explained in the following section.

The Eight Elements of a Program Plan

A public relations program plan identifies what is to be done, why, and how to accomplish it. By preparing such a plan, either as a brief outline or as a more extensive document, the practitioner can make certain that all elements have been properly considered and that everyone involved understands the "big picture."

It is common practice for public relations firms to prepare a program plan for client approval and possible modification before implementing a public relations campaign. At that time, both the public relations firm and the client reach a mutual understanding of the campaign's objectives and the means to be used to accomplish them. Public relations departments of organizations also map out particular campaigns or show the departments' plans for the coming year.

The 9 Basic MBO Steps

1. Client/Employer Objectives. What is the purpose of the communication, and how does it promote or achieve the objectives of the organization? Specific objectives such as "to make consumers aware of the product's high quality" are more meaningful than "to make people aware of the product."

2. Audience/Publics. Who exactly should be reached with the message, and how can that audience help achieve the organization's objectives? What are the characteristics of the audience, and how can demographic information be used to structure the message? For example, the primary audience for a campaign to encourage carpooling consists of people who regularly drive to work, not the general public.

3. Audience Objectives. What is it that the audience wants to know, and how can the message be tailored to audience self-interest? Consumers are more interested in the color and clarity of a flat-screen television than in the technological differences among plasma, LCD, and LED models.

4. Media Channels. What is the appropriate channel for reaching the audience, and how can multiple channels (e.g., news media, blogs, brochures) reinforce the message? An ad may be best for making consumers aware of a new product, but a news release may be better for conveying consumer information about the product.

5. Media Channel Objectives. What is the media gatekeeper looking for in a news angle, and why would a particular publication be interested in the information?

6. Sources and Questions. Which primary and secondary sources of information are required to provide a factual base for the message? Which experts should be interviewed? Which databases should be used to conduct research? For instance, a quote from a project engineer about a new technology is better than a quote from the marketing vice president.

7. Communication Strategies. Which factors will affect the dissemination and acceptance of the message? Are there other events or pieces of information that negate or reinforce the message? A campaign to conserve water is more salient if there has been a recent drought.

8. Essence of the Message. What is the planned communication impact on the audience? Is the message designed merely to inform, or is it designed to change attitudes and behavior? Informing people about the values of physical fitness is different from instructing them about how to achieve it.

9. Nonverbal Support. How can photographs, graphs, films, and artwork clarify and visually enhance the written message? Bar graphs or pie charts are easier to understand than columns of numbers.

Ketchum's Strategic Planning Model

encourages professionals to ask and determine answers to key questions about facts, goals, and audiences when planning public relations efforts.

FACTS

- *Category Facts.* What are recent industry trends?
- *Product/Service Issues.* What are the significant characteristics of the product, service, or issue?
- *Competitive Facts.* Who are the competitors, and what are their competitive strengths, similarities, and differences?
- *Customer Facts.* Who uses the product and why?

GOALS

- *Business Objectives.* What are the company's business objectives? What is the time frame?
- *Role of Public Relations.* How does public relations fit into the marketing mix?
- *Sources of New Business.* Which sectors will produce growth?

AUDIENCE

- *Target Audiences.* Who are the target audiences? What are their "hot buttons"?
- *Current Mind-Set.* How do audiences feel about the product, service, or issue?
- *Desired Mind-Set.* How do we want them to feel?

KEY MESSAGE

- *Main Point.* What one key message must be conveyed to change or reinforce mind-sets?

Although there can be some variation, public relations plans include eight basic elements:

1. Situation
2. Objectives
3. Audience
4. Strategy
5. Tactics
6. Calendar/timetable
7. Budget
8. Measurement

1 SITUATION. Public relations professionals cannot set valid objectives without a clear understanding of the situation that led to the conclusion that there was a need for a public relations program. Three situations often prompt a public relations program: the organization must conduct a remedial program to overcome a problem or negative situation; the organization needs to conduct a specific one-time project; or the organization wants

to reinforce an ongoing effort to preserve its reputation and public support.

• Loss of market share and declining sales often require a remedial program. For example, Ford Motor Company developed an extensive public relations campaign in 2009 and saw its retail market share increase for 10 out of 11 months for the first time since 1995, according to *PRWeek*. Other organizations may launch such campaigns to change public perceptions.

• Specific one-time events often lead to public relations programs. The introduction of Microsoft's Windows 7 operating system was a one-time event; it required a program plan that covered many months of prelaunch activities.

• Program plans are also initiated to preserve and develop customer or public support. Department 56, a leading designer and manufacturer of miniature lighted village collectibles, already had a successful business, but it wanted new customers. Its public relations program to accomplish this goal included distribution of brochures on home decoration for the Christmas holidays and participation by its dealers in local efforts to decorate Ronald McDonald houses.

• It is a good idea to include relevant research as part of the situation in a program plan. In the case of Department 56, consumer market analysis revealed a strong link between consumers interested in home decorating and those involved in collecting. Such research provides the foundation for setting program objectives and shaping other elements of the program plan.

• The program plan is informed by proactive research. The proactive phase of the conflict management life cycle involves tracking issues to assess potential competition or threats. When an imminent threat looms, the threat appraisal model helps determine how much of a threat the situation poses to the organization. The greater the threat, the more important the strategizing, planning, and development of objectives.

2 OBJECTIVES. Once the situation or problem is understood, the next step is to establish objectives for the program. A proposed objective should be evaluated by asking three questions: Does it really address the situation? Is it realistic and achievable? Can success be measured in meaningful terms?

• Professionals usually state an objective in terms of program outcomes rather than inputs. Objectives should not be the "means" but the "end." A poor objective, for example, is to "generate publicity for a new product." Publicity is not an "end" in itself; the actual objective is to "create consumer awareness about a new product."

• It is particularly important that public relations objectives complement and reinforce the organization's objectives. Basically, objectives are either informational or motivational.

• Many public relations plans are designed primarily to expose audiences to information and to increase awareness of an issue, an event, or a product; these are referred to as informational objectives. Many communication and marketing professionals believe that the major criteria for public relations

For the relaunch of Coca-Cola's "Full Throttle Fury" power drink in 2009, the company used research to identify the drink's target audience—African American males. The tag line, "Go Full Throttle or Go Home," and the spokesman, hip-hop artist Big Boi, were chosen with this target audience in mind.

What did Fleishman-Hillard do for Brown?

WHETHER A PUBLIC RELATIONS campaign is community-wide or global, it should include eight steps. Consider how the award-winning campaign developed by Fleishman-Hillard for United Parcel Service (UPS) met these criteria.

1 *Situation.* UPS delivers 15.5 million packages worldwide every day. To do so, the company operates approximately 99,000 vehicles and logs 2 billion miles per year. Because of the huge carbon footprint left by such a fleet, shipping customers often ask for data about emissions linked to package delivery. UPS tracks such data and wanted to communicate its commitment to doing all it can to limit its environmental impact.

2 *Objectives.* Research found that customer requests for data about UPS's carbon footprint had increased 243 percent in a single quarter, which led to the following objectives:

Position UPS as a company committed to environmental responsibility by showcasing initiatives with positive environmental impacts that are measurable.

Highlight the technologies UPS employs to be more efficient and reduce its environmental impact.

3 *Target Audience.* Current and prospective customers, investors, and public officials were among UPS's target publics.

4 *Strategies.* UPS and Fleishman-Hillard decided the strategy would be to identify "proof points" about UPS's efforts to minimize its environmental impact and to develop stories around these points that were remarkable enough to trump other corporate "green stories."

5 *Tactics.* On Earth Day, the pair pitched a story about UPS's high-tech routing system, which helps avoid left turns to reduce emissions. In its PRSA Silver Anvil summary, UPS reported, "The key is minimizing left turns, which require drivers to idle at intersections to wait for traffic to pass, burning excess fuel and generating excess emissions." The press materials noted that this policy reduces emissions by 32,000 metric tons of CO_2 (equal to the annual output of 5,200 automobiles).

When UPS placed the world's largest order for hybrid vehicles, press coverage was actively pursued. Similarly, UPS announced a new paperless invoice system to save paper and make global invoicing easier. Many other activities were aggressively pitched to the media in this media relations campaign.

6 *Calendar.* The program consisted of nine major announcements to the press over the course of one year.

7 *Budget.* The budget for the campaign was undisclosed.

8 *Measurement.* Evaluation consisted of counting impressions (the potential number of people who saw or heard the stories) and identifying prestige media placements. The "left turn" story generated 76.9 million impressions, appearing twice in *Parade* magazine, on the *CBS Early Show*, and in *USA Today*. The "hybrid vehicle order" story was printed in *The Wall Street Journal* and in *USA Today*, and was picked up by the Associated Press, earning 7.8 million impressions. The paperless invoice story was distributed by Reuters and the AP. It garnered 3.7 million impressions.

---

effectiveness are an increase in public awareness and delivery of key messages. The following are examples of informational objectives:

- Travelocity: "Increase consumers' overall awareness and excitement for the brand."
- National Association of Manufacturers (NAM): "Educate target audiences on the fundamental importance of manufacturing to our nation's current competitiveness and future prosperity."

• One difficulty with informational objectives is measuring how well a particular objective has been achieved. Public awareness and the extent to which education takes place are somewhat abstract and difficult to quantify. Survey research can be informative but many organizations infer "awareness" by counting the number of media placements. In reality, however, message exposure doesn't necessarily mean increased public awareness.

• Although changing attitudes and influencing behavior are difficult to accomplish in a public relations campaign, motivational objectives are easier to measure. That's because they are bottom-line oriented and are based on clearly measurable results that can be quantified. This is true whether the goal is an increase in product sales, a sellout crowd for a theatrical performance, or more donations to a charitable agency. The following are examples of motivational objectives:

- Duracell Batteries: "Distribute all of the branded 'guidebooks' [Together We Can Become Safe Families] and coupons to consumers in the major metropolitan cities."
- AT&T U-verse (TV, high-speed Internet, and digital home phone service): "Double the number of U-verse media stories in the second half of 2008 versus the first half."
- Doritos: "Drive consumer engagement in the contest via submissions and video views on the program website."

• A public relations program will often have both informational and motivational objectives. A good example is the Fighting Hunger in Wisconsin campaign. Its objectives were to increase public awareness of hunger in Wisconsin, enlist additional volunteers, and raise more money than in the previous year to support hunger relief programs around the state.

3 AUDIENCE. Public relations programs should be directed toward specific and defined audiences or publics. Although some campaigns are directed to the general public, such instances are the exception. Even the M&M's Candy national "election" campaign to select a new color (blue) for its famous mix was designed to reach consumers 24 years of age or younger.

• Public relations practitioners typically target specific publics within the general public through market research that identifies key publics based on such demographic factors as age, income, social strata, education, existing ownership or consumption of specific products, and residence. For example, market research told M&M's Candy that young people were the primary consumers of its product. On a more basic level, a water conservation campaign defines its target audience by geography—people living in a particular city or area.

• In many cases, common sense is all that is needed to adequately define a specific public. Take, for example, the Ohio vaccination program for children younger than the age of two. The primary audience for the message is parents with young children. Other audiences are pregnant women and medical professionals who treat young children. Perhaps a more complex situation involves a company that wants to increase the sale of a CD program on home improvement for do-it-yourselfers. Again, the primary audience is not the general public, but rather those persons who actually have computers with CD-ROM drives and enjoy working around the house. Such criteria would exclude a large percentage of the U.S. population.

• The following are examples of how some of the organizations already mentioned have defined target audiences:

- Duracell: "Women, ages 25–54 with children, who are the primary shoppers for their households"
- AT&T U-verse: "Existing and potential customers"; "national, local, industry, and online media"; "internal audiences"
- Doritos: "Core: 16- to 24-year-olds; broader: 18- to 45-year-olds"

• Some organizations identify the media as a "public." On occasion, in

In a Turkish tourism campaign, the strategy of combating "negative stereotypes and lack of knowledge about Turkey" included key messages designed to reinforce the country's assets: historical/cultural sites, natural beauty, upscale accommodations, great shopping, excellent cuisine, ideal weather, and friendly people. In an effort to position Turkey as part of Europe instead of the Middle East, the themes "Center of World History" and "Where Europe Becomes Exotic" were used.

programs that seek media endorsements or that try to change how the media report on an organization or an issue, editors and reporters can become a legitimate "public." In general, however, mass media outlets fall in the category of a "means to an end." In other words, they represent channels to reach defined audiences that need to be informed, persuaded, and motivated.

• A thorough understanding of the primary and secondary publics is key to accomplishing a program's objectives. Such knowledge also provides guidance on the selection of appropriate strategies and tactics to reach defined audiences.

4 STRATEGY. A strategy statement describes how, in concept, a campaign will achieve objectives; it provides guidelines and themes for the overall program. Strategy statements provide a rationale for planned actions and program components. Professionals can outline one general strategy or several strategies, depending on the objectives and the audience.

• In the Doritos campaign mentioned previously in this section, strategies were to: "Invite America to develop Doritos' Super Bowl ads"; "Award the winning creator with $1 million if he or she can beat the professionally produced spots and place No. 1 in *USA Today*'s ad meter"; and "Implement a two-pronged media outreach approach to simultaneously reach Doritos' core target audience and likely entrants while maintaining ongoing coverage in mainstream news outlets."

• The strategy element of a program plan should determine key themes and messages to reiterate throughout the campaign on all publicity materials. The Ohio juvenile immunization program "was based on the concept that parents love their children and want them to be healthy." The theme of the campaign was "Project L.O.V.E.," with the subhead "Love Our Kids Vaccination Project."

5 TACTICS. Tactics are the nuts-and-bolts part of the plan. They describe, in sequence, the specific activities that put strategies into operation and achieve the stated objectives. Tactics use the tools of communication to reach primary and secondary audiences with key messages.

6 CALENDAR/TIMETABLE. The three aspects of timing in a program plan are deciding when a campaign should be conducted, determining the proper sequence of activities, and compiling a list of steps that must be completed to produce a finished product. All three aspects are important to achieving maximum effectiveness.

7 BUDGET. No program plan is complete without a budget. Both clients and employers inevitably ask, "How much will this program cost?" In many cases, the reverse approach is taken. That is, organizations may establish an amount they can afford and then ask the public relations staff or firm to write a program plan that fits the budget.

Cost is a driving factor; spending large sums to reach members of the general public on matters in which they have no stake or interest is nonproductive and a WASTE OF MONEY.

• A budget can be divided into two categories: staff time and out-of-pocket (OOP) expenses. Staff and administrative time usually consumes the lion's share of any public relations budget. In a $100,000 campaign done by a public relations firm, for example, it is not unusual for 70 percent of the program cost to consist of salaries and administrative fees.

• One method of budgeting is to use two columns. The left column lists the staff cost for writing a pamphlet or compiling a press kit. The right column lists the actual OOP

btw...

IKEA, the Swedish home furnishing superstore, had three primary campaign goals: (1) increasing sales, (2) increasing traffic to IKEA-USA.com, and (3) reinforcing brand messages, such as "IKEA has everything you need to live and make a home" and "Home is the most important place in the world." IKEA allowed comedian Mark Malkoff to live in a New Jersey IKEA for a week in early 2008. The tactic was a calculated risk for the company because it allowed Malkoff creative freedom while he lived in the store 24/7. This tactic took advantage of a publicity stunt, a comic treatment, and social media:

> Malkoff posted 25 web-i-sodes on MarkLivesInIKEA.com during his week living in the store. These humorous postings included interactions with security guards and disbelieving customers.
> IKEA hosted a farewell party for Malkoff, generating publicity at the completion of his week.
> IKEA arranged interviews with corporate executives and store personnel regarding Malkoff's IKEA residency.
> The $13,500 campaign earned a lot of bang for the buck, according to *PRWeek*, which selected the campaign as the 2009 campaign of the year.
> Malkoff's website received 15 million hits, IKEA blog coverage increased 356 percent over the course of the year following the stunt, and 382 million positive impressions came from coverage on programs such as *Today* and *Good Morning America*, and on CNN.

TIMING. Program planning should take into account the environmental context of the situation and the time when key messages are most meaningful to the intended audience. A campaign to encourage carpooling, for example, might be more successful if it follows on the heels of a major price increase in gasoline or a government report that traffic congestion has reached gridlock proportions.

Some subjects are seasonal. Department 56, the designer and manufacturer of miniature lighted village collectibles and other holiday giftware, timed the bulk of its campaign for November to take advantage of the Christmas holidays, when interest in its product lines peaked. Charitable agencies, such as the Wisconsin hunger project, also gear their campaigns toward the Christmas season.

By the same token, strawberry producers increase public relations efforts in May and June, when a crop comes to market and stores have large supplies of the fruit. Similarly, a software program on income tax preparation attracts the most audience interest in February and March, just before the April 15 filing deadline.

SCHEDULING. Another aspect of timing is the scheduling and sequencing of various tactics or activities. A typical pattern is to concentrate the most effort at the beginning of a campaign, when a number of tactics are implemented. The launch phase of a campaign, much like that of a rocket, requires a burst of activity just to break the awareness barrier. By comparison, after the campaign has achieved orbit, less energy and fewer activities are required to maintain momentum. Public relations campaigns often are the first stage of an integrated marketing communications program. Once public relations has created awareness and customer anticipation of a new product, the second stage may be an advertising and direct mail campaign.

COMPILING A CALENDAR. An integral part of timing is advance planning. A video news release, a press kit, or a brochure often takes weeks or months to prepare. Arrangements for special events also take considerable time. Practitioners must take into account the deadlines of publications. Monthly periodicals, for example, frequently need to receive information at least six to eight weeks before publication. A popular talk show may book guests three or four months in advance. The public relations professional must think ahead to make things happen in the right sequence, at the right time. One way to achieve this goal is to compile timelines and charts that list the necessary steps and their required completion dates.

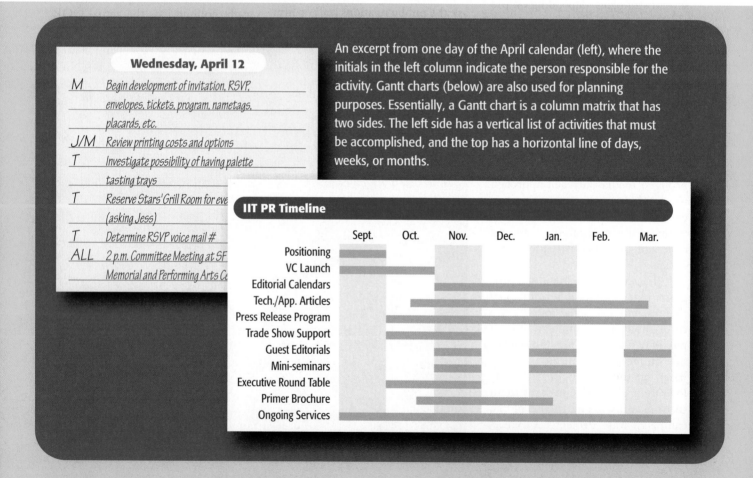

Wednesday, April 12

M	Begin development of invitation, RSVP, envelopes, tickets, program, nametags, placards, etc.
J/M	Review printing costs and options
T	Investigate possibility of having palette tasting trays
T	Reserve Stars' Grill Room for eve (asking Jess)
T	Determine RSVP voice mail #
ALL	2 p.m. Committee Meeting at SF Memorial and Performing Arts Ce

An excerpt from one day of the April calendar (left), where the initials in the left column indicate the person responsible for the activity. Gantt charts (below) are also used for planning purposes. Essentially, a Gantt chart is a column matrix that has two sides. The left side has a vertical list of activities that must be accomplished, and the top has a horizontal line of days, weeks, or months.

IIT PR Timeline

Sept. | Oct. | Nov. | Dec. | Jan. | Feb. | Mar.

- Positioning
- VC Launch
- Editorial Calendars
- Tech./App. Articles
- Press Release Program
- Trade Show Support
- Guest Editorials
- Mini-seminars
- Executive Round Table
- Primer Brochure
- Ongoing Services

BUDGETS FOR THREE CAMPAIGNS

Duracell Campaign

$600,000 including both the agency fee and OOP expenses. Program budget skewed heavily toward OOP expenses, because it accounted for production of 150,000 guidebooks and 300,000 coupons, website development, market research, a ten-city preparedness survey, a $250,000 donation to the American Red Cross, and all other miscellaneous expenses related to the program.

Turkish Tourism Campaign

$650,000 for 15-month program: $450,000 in public relations firm fees and $200,000 in expenses.

Doritos Campaign

$450,000 for the campaign to generate entries into its Super Bowl advertisement contest, plus $1 million OOP expenses for prize money for the award-winning entry and the additional costs of the Super Bowl advertising spot.

---

expense for having the pamphlet or press kit designed, printed, and delivered. Internal public relations staffs, whose members are on the payroll, often complete only the OOP expenses budget. It is good practice to allocate approximately 10 percent of the budget for contingencies or unexpected costs.

• In a program plan, professionals usually estimate budgets on the basis of experience and requests from vendors for estimates. After the program is completed, the measurement process involves assessment of estimated expenses versus actual expenses.

8 MEASUREMENT. The evaluation element of a plan relates directly back to the stated objectives of the program. Objectives must be measurable in some way to show clients and employers that the program accomplished its purpose. Evaluation criteria should be realistic, credible, specific, and in line with client or employer expectations. The measurement section of a program plan should restate the objectives and list the measurement methods to be used.

• Measurement of an informational objective often entails a compilation of news clips and an analysis of key message point appearance. Other methods include determining the number of

brochures distributed or the estimated number of viewers who saw a video news release. Sales or market share increases often are used to measure and evaluate motivational objectives, as are the number of people who called a toll-free number for more information, or benchmark surveys that measure

people's perceptions before and after a campaign.

• We have now covered the first two essential steps in effective public relations: research and planning. In Chapter 7, we address the last two steps: communication and measurement.

APPLY YOUR KNOWLEDGE

WHAT WOULD YOU DO?

Sunshine Cafe, a chain of coffee houses, conducted market research and found that college students would be an excellent audience for its product and services. To this end, Sunshine Cafe has contacted your public relations firm and asked that you develop a comprehensive plan to do two things: (1) create brand awareness among college students and (2) increase walk-in business at its local stores in college towns.

Using the eight-point planning outline described in this chapter, write a public relations program for Sunshine Cafe. You should consider a variety of communication tools, including campus events. No money has been allocated for advertising.

Summary

What Are the Four Essential Steps of Effective Public Relations? p. 110

- Effective public relations is a process with four essential steps: (1) research, (2) planning, (3) communication, and (4) measurement.

How Is Research Conducted and Used in Public Relations? p. 111

- Research is the basic groundwork of any public relations program; it involves the gathering and interpretation of information and is used in every phase of a communications program.

- Secondary research uses information from library sources and, increasingly, from online and Internet sources. Primary research involves gathering new information through interviews or sampling procedures.

- The sampling method constrains the extent to which the findings can be analyzed in detail and extrapolated to a larger population. Probability samples generate the best results, particularly when doing quantitative research.

- Survey respondents may be reached by mail, e-mail, telephone, the Internet, personal interviews, or piggyback (omnibus) surveys.

What Role Does Planning Play in Effective Public Relations? p. 122

- After research, the next step is strategic program planning

- Two approaches to planning are management by objective (MBO) and Ketchum's strategic Planning Model. Both involve asking and answering many questions.

What Are the Eight Elements of a Program Plan? p. 122

- A program plan is either a brief outline or an extensive document prepared for client approval that identifies what is to be done and how.

- Program plans usually include eight elements: situation, objectives, audience, strategy, tactics, a calendar or timetable, budget, and measurement.

WATER RESTRICTIONS

The City of Melbourne has closed this water feature in order to conserve water in support of water restrictions

For further information please contact the Hotline on 9658 9658

QUESTIONS for *Review* and *Discussion*

1. Which questions should a public relations professional ask before formulating a research design?

2. Identify at least five ways that research is used in public relations.

3. How can survey research be used as a publicity tool?

4. What is the procedure for organizing and conducting a focus group?

5. What are the pros and cons of using focus groups?

6. Which guidelines should be followed when releasing the results of a survey to the media and the public?

7. Name the eight elements of a program plan.

8. Explain the difference between an informational objective and a motivational objective.

9. What is the difference between a strategy and an objective?

the
THINK SPOT
www.thethinkspot.com

7 COMMUNICATION

Who Turned Out the Lights?

Earth Hour is a worldwide event organized by the World Wildlife Fund (WWF) that is held each year on the last Saturday in March. From formative research for the Earth Hour campaign, WWF found that although 73 percent of those surveyed had an interest in environmental issues, only 22 percent had heard of Earth Hour and even fewer were planning on participating.

WWF developed a number of objectives related to Earth Hour, such as "Highlight solutions and encourage involvement across all levels of society—from government to business to individuals—to address the issue of climate change in an engaging and accessible manner." Once they had their objectives in place, WWF executives engaged public relations firms in four U.S. cities to help develop a nationwide strategy for a public relations campaign.

WWF and its partner public relations firms identified iconic landmarks in each U.S. time zone. The idea was that events relating to these landmarks would serve as local news hooks. The activity that WWF was asking people, governments, and businesses to engage in was simple—and it became the theme of the campaign—"Those who see the light . . . turn it off!" This turn of phrase suggested that people enlightened about climate change would take the lead in limiting unnecessary energy use. To drive this point home and raise awareness, during the 8 to 9 P.M. Earth Hour in each time zone, the lights that illuminated the chosen

AND MEASUREMENT

iconic landmarks were turned off. Pre-event activities included distributing 20,000 bumper stickers to students that read "I'm not afraid of the dark" and providing media kits to journalists.

When the day arrived, 97 percent of Atlanta's downtown skyline went dark, as did Wrigley Field and the Sears Tower in Chicago, and Ghirardelli Square and the Golden Gate Bridge in San Francisco. The effectiveness of the campaign was measured not only by the willingness on the part of these landmarks to participate, but also by the media coverage of Earth Hour and public awareness. Earth Hour was covered by every major U.S. medium, and a post-campaign survey found a 56 percent increase in public awareness of Earth Hour.

❶ Describe how you might develop an Earth Hour campaign on your campus. What would you need to know about existing student, faculty, and university administrator attitudes? Which groups might you partner with to develop a campaign?

❷ What would your campaign objectives be? How would you reach target publics with your messages?

❸ How would you measure the success of your campaign?

communication:
THE THIRD STEP

as you will recall from Chapter 6, the four essential steps of effective public relations are research, planning, communication, and measurement. In this chapter, we discuss the third and fourth steps of this process—communication and measurement.

The third step in the public relations process, after research and planning, is communication. Communication is sometimes referred to as execution. In a public relations program, communication is the process and the means by which objectives are achieved. A program's strategies and tactics may take the form of news releases, news conferences, special events, brochures, viral marketing, speeches, bumper stickers, newsletters, webcasts, rallies, posters, and the like.

THE **goals** OF COMMUNICATION

the goals of communication are to inform, persuade, motivate, or achieve mutual understanding.

Kirk Hallahan of Colorado State University makes the point that today's communication revolution has given public relations professionals a full range of communication tools and media, and the traditional approach of simply obtaining publicity through the mass media—newspapers, magazines, radio, and television—is no longer sufficient, if it ever was:

PR program planners need to reexamine their traditional approaches to the practice and think about media broadly and strategically. PR media planners must now address some of the same questions that confront advertisers. What media best meet a program's objectives? How can media be combined to enhance program effectiveness? What media are most efficient to reach key audience?

An Integrated Public Relations Media Model

The variety and scope of media and communication tools available to public relations professionals runs the gamut from mass media (public media) to one-on-one communication (interpersonal communication). Here, in chart form, is a concept developed by Professor Kirk Hallahan at Colorado State University.

MASS COMMUNICATION
High tech
Perceptually Based
Low Social Presence
Asynchronous

PERSONALIZED COMMUNICATION
Low tech
Experientially Based
High Social Presence
Synchronous

Public Media	Controlled Media	Interactive Media	Events	One-on-One
Key Uses in a Communication Program				
Build awareness; Enhance credibility	Promotion; Provide detailed information	Respond to queries; Exchange information; Engage users	Motivate participants; Reinforce existing beliefs, attitudes	Obtain commitments; Negotiation, resolution of problems.
Principal Examples of Media				
Publicity/advertising/ advertorials/product placements in Newspapers Magazines Radio Television *Paid advertising* Transit media Out-of-home media (Billboards, posters, electronic displays) Directories Venue signage Movie theater trailers, advertising	Brochures Newsletters Sponsored magazines Annual reports Books Direct mail Exhibits and displays Point-of-purchase support DVDs/Video brochures Statement inserts Other collateral or printed ephemera Advertising specialties	E-mail, instant, text and microblog messages E-newsletters, e-zines Automated telephone call systems Web sites, Blogs Vodcasts/podcasts Games Web conferences, Webinars, webcasts Information kiosks Internets and Extranets Social networking sites Forums (chats, groups) Media sharing sites Paid text/display click-through advertising	Meetings/conferences Speeches/presentations Government or judicial testimony Trade shows, exhibitions Demonstrations/rallies Sponsored events Observances/anniversaries Contests/sweepstakes Recognition award programs (Often supported with multi-media presentations)	Personal visits/lobbying Correspondence Telephone calls

To be an effective communicator, you must understand three factors:

1 WHAT constitutes communication and how people receive messages

2 HOW people process information and change their perceptions

3 WHICH kinds of media and communication tools are most appropriate for a particular message.

When planning a message on behalf of an employer or client, public relations professionals must consider a number of variables. In addition to examining proposed content, a successful communicator determines exactly which objective is being targeted through the communication. James Grunig, emeritus professor of public relations at the University of Maryland, cites five key objectives:

1 Message Exposure. Public relations personnel provide materials to the mass media and disseminate other messages through controlled media such as newsletters and brochures. Intended audiences are exposed to the message in various forms.

2 Accurate Dissemination of the Message. The basic information, often filtered by media gatekeepers, remains intact as it is transmitted through various media.

3 Acceptance of the Message. Based on its view of reality, the audience not only retains the message, but also accepts it as valid.

4 **Attitude Change.** The audience not only believes the message, but also makes a verbal or mental commitment to change behavior as a result of the message.

5 **Change in Overt Behavior.** Members of the audience actually change their current behavior or purchase the product and use it.

Most public relations experts usually aim to achieve the first two objectives: exposure to the message and accurate dissemination of that message. Achieving the last three objectives depends in large part on a mix of variables—predisposition to the message, peer reinforcement, feasibility of the suggested action, and environmental context, to name a few.

The first two objectives are easier to accomplish than attitude change. Although the communicator cannot always control the outcome of a message, effective dissemination is the beginning of a process that leads to opinion change and adoption of products or services. For these reasons, it is important to review all components of the communication process.

think **What are the five primary objectives of an effective public relations campaign?**

Making Sure the Audience Receives the Message

Several communication models explain how a message moves from sender to recipient. Some are quite complex, attempting to incorporate an almost infinite number of events, ideas, objects, and people that interact among the message, channel, and receiver. Most communication models, however, focus on only four basic elements. David K. Berlo's classic model is an example. It features a sender/source (encoder), a message, a channel, and a receiver (decoder).

> **"To be successful, a message must be received by the intended individual or audience. It must get the audience's attention. It must be understood. It must be believed. It must be remembered. And ultimately, in some fashion, it must be acted upon. Failure to accomplish any of these tasks means the entire message fails."**
>
> David Therkelsen, Executive Director of Crisis Connection in St. Paul, Minnesota

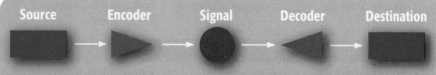

Mass media researcher Wilbur Schramm started with a simple communication model, but he later expanded the process to include the concept of shared fields of experience.

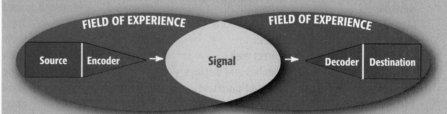

Shared experience refers to the concept that little or no communication is achieved unless the sender and the receiver share a common language and even an overlapping cultural or educational background. The importance of shared experience is apparent if a highly technical news release about a new computer system causes a local business editor to shake his or her head in bewilderment. Effective communication takes place within a sphere of "shared experience."

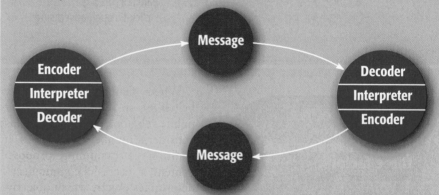

Schramm's third model incorporates the idea of continuous feedback. Both the sender and the receiver continually encode, interpret, decode, transmit, and receive information. This looping process is integral to models that show the public relations process of research, planning, communication, and measurement as cyclical. Communication to internal and external audiences produces feedback that is taken into consideration during research (the first step of the public relations process) and measurement (the fourth step). In this way, the structure and dissemination of messages are continuously refined.

A fifth element—feedback from the receiver to the sender—is incorporated into modern models of communication.

Feedback can also be thought of as two-way communication. One-way communication, from sender to receiver, simply disseminates information. This kind of monologue is less effective than two-way communication, which establishes a dialogue between the sender and the receiver. Grunig postulates that the ideal public relations model consists of two-way symmetric communication. In other words, communication should be balanced between the sender and the receiver. In reality, research shows that most organizations have mixed motives when they engage in two-way communication with audiences.

The practice of public relations is dynamic. During any campaign, motives and strategic goals may change depending on a variety of factors. For example, as a public relations practitioner you may advocate providing a new benefit for employees. In doing so, your motives are mixed: Employees will be pleased with the new benefit, but your real objective is to save the organization money by limiting employee turnover.

> **❝In the symmetric model, understanding is the principal objective of public relations, rather than persuasion.❞**
> **James Grunig**

The most effective type of two-way communication, of course, is interpersonal or face-to-face communication between two people. Likewise, small-group discussion is very effective. In both forms, the message is fortified by gestures, facial expressions, intimacy, tone of voice, and immediate feedback. If a listener asks a question or appears puzzled, the speaker has an instant cue and can rephrase the information or amplify a point.

Barriers to communication multiply in large-group meetings and, ultimately, in the mass media. Via mass media outlets, organizational materials can reach thousands and even millions of people, but the psychological and physical distance between sender and receiver in these types of campaigns is considerable. Communication is less effective because the audience is no longer involved with the source. No immediate feedback is possible, and the message may become distorted as it passes through the various mass media gatekeepers.

Models of communication emphasize the importance of feedback as an integral component of the process. As they implement communication strategies, successful public relations personnel pay careful and constant attention to feedback.

Making the Audience Pay Attention to the Message

Although in public relations much emphasis is given to the formation and dissemination of messages, this effort is wasted if the audience pays no attention. It is important to remember the axiom of Walt Seifert, a pioneer public relations educator at Ohio State University: "Dissemination does not equal publication, and publication does not equal absorption and action." In other words, "All who receive your message won't publish it, and all who read or hear your message won't understand or act upon it."

Strategy should be based on more than common sense or rote routines. The management of competition and conflict requires a sophisticated understanding of the climate in which an organization operates and the dispositions of its publics on a variety of matters. Social psychologists recognize that, at any given time, the majority of an audience is not particularly interested in a message or in adopting an idea. This doesn't mean, however, that audiences are merely passive receivers of information.

People use mass media for a variety of purposes:

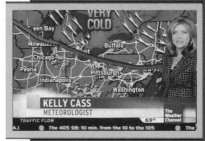

Surveillance of the environment to find out what is happening, locally or even globally, that has some impact on them

Entertainment and diversion

Reinforcement of their opinions and predispositions

Decision making about buying a product or service

Sociologist Harold Lasswell defined the act of communication as "Who says what, in which channel, to whom, with what effect?"

The basic premise of media uses and gratification theory of communication is that the communication process is interactive. The communicator wants to inform and even persuade; the recipient wants to be entertained, informed, or alerted to opportunities that can fulfill individual needs. This theory assumes that people make highly intelligent choices about which messages require their attention and fulfill their needs. If this is true—and research indicates it is—the public relations communicator must tailor messages that focus on grabbing the audience's attention.

One approach for achieving this goal is to understand the mental state of the intended audience. In *Managing Public Relations*, James Grunig and Todd Hunt suggest that communication strategies be designed to attract the attention of two kinds of audiences: those who actively seek information and those who passively process information.

Passive audiences may initially pay attention to a message only because it is entertaining and offers a diversion. They can be made aware of the message through brief encounters: a billboard glimpsed on the way to work, a radio announcement heard in the car, a television advertisement broadcast before a show begins, or an informational flyer picked up in a doctor's waiting room. In other words, passive audiences use communication channels that can be accessed while they are doing something else.

For this reason, passive audiences need messages that are stylish and creative. Photos, illustrations, and catchy slogans lure this type of audience into processing the information. Press agentry, dramatic images, celebrity pitches, radio and television announcements, and events featuring entertainment can make passive audiences aware of a message. The objectives of communications are simply exposure to, and accurate dissemination of, messages. In most public relations campaigns, communications are designed to reach primarily passive audiences.

In contrast, a communicator employs a different approach with audiences that actively seek information. These people are already interested in the message and are typically seeking more sophisticated supplemental information. Effective tools for delivering this content may include links to more detailed information on an organization's website, brochures, in-depth newspaper and magazine articles, slide presentations, video presentations, symposiums and conferences, major speeches before key groups, and demonstrations at trade shows.

More efficient communication can be achieved if the intended audience is segmented as much as possible. After dividing an audience into segments, a practitioner can select the appropriate communication tools for each group. Even within a public category, demands may be different. For example, factory-line workers don't have the same concerns as senior vice presidents, but they're all employees and should be addressed by employee communications. A good public relations campaign always takes into account the needs of diverse categories within a public.

Making Sure the Message Is Understood

Communication is the act of transmitting information, ideas, and attitudes from one person to another. In any situation, communication can take place only if the sender and the receiver have a common understanding of the symbols being used.

The degree to which two people understand each other depends heavily on their common comprehension of words. Anyone who has traveled abroad can readily attest that very little communication can occur between two people who speak different languages. Even if the sender and the receiver speak the same language and live in the same country, the effectiveness of their communication depends on a variety of key factors, such as education, social economic class, regional differences, nationality, and cultural background.

Employee communication specialists are keenly aware of these differences, as multicultural workforces have become the norm for

At any given time, an intended audience contains both passive and active information seekers. For this reason, multiple messages and a variety of communication tools should be used in a full-fledged information campaign.

btw...

The most widely known readability formula was developed by Rudolph Flesch. It assesses average sentence length and the number of one-syllable words per 100 words. If a randomly selected sample of 100 words contains 4.2 sentences and 142 syllables, it is ranked at about the ninth-grade level. This is the level for which most news releases and daily newspapers strive. Long, complex sentences (more than 19 words) and multisyllabic words ("compensation" instead of "pay") reduce comprehension for the average reader.

The Cloze procedure, developed by William Taylor, also tests comprehension. The concept underlying this method comes from the idea of closure—the human tendency to complete a familiar but incomplete pattern. In the Cloze procedure, copy is tested for comprehension and redundancy by having test subjects read passages in which every fifth or ninth word is removed. Their ability to fill in the missing words determines whether the pattern of words is familiar and people can understand the message.

most organizations. The globalization of the economy has resulted in organizations with operations and employees in many countries as well as the increasingly diverse composition of the American workforce. In light of these trends, communicators need to be informed about cultural differences and conflicting values so that they can establish common ground and build bridges among various groups.

Audience background and literacy level are important considerations for any communicator. The key is to produce messages that appeal, in content and structure, to the characteristics of the audience.

One approach is to copy-test all public relations materials on a target audience. This step can help convince management— and communicators— that what they like isn't necessarily what the audience wants, needs, or understands. Another strategy is to apply readability and comprehension formulas to materials before they are produced and disseminated. Learning theory makes the case that the simpler the piece of writing, the easier it will be for audiences to understand the message.

Making the Message Credible

Credibility is one key variable in the communication process. Members of the audience must perceive a source as knowledgeable and expert on the subject as well as honest and objective. Audiences, for example, ascribe lower credibility to statements in an advertisement than to the same information contained in a news article, because news articles are selected by media gatekeepers and are perceived as more objective.

Source credibility is a problem for any organizational spokesperson, because the public already has a bias based on the person's relationship to the organization. The problem of source credibility is the main reason that organizations, whenever possible, use respected outside experts or celebrities as representatives to convey their messages.

Another variable is the context of the message. Action (performance) speaks louder than a stack of news releases. A bank may spend thousands of dollars on a promotion campaign with the slogan, "Your Friendly Bank—Where Service Counts," but the effort is wasted if employees are not trained to be friendly and courteous. Incompatible rhetoric and actions can even be amusing at times. At a press briefing about the importance of "buying American," the U.S. Chamber of Commerce passed out commemorative coffee mugs marked in small print on the bottom, "Made in China."

think

Why is it important for a communicator to understand the cultural background of an audience?

In a study conducted for the GCI Group,

Opinion Research Corporation found that **MORE THAN HALF** of those surveyed were likely to believe that a large company is probably guilty of wrongdoing if it is being investigated by a government agency or if a major lawsuit is filed against the company.

Over **1/2** believe a large company that is being sued or under investigation is probably guilty.

Only **1/3** would trust the statements of a large company.

Increase Audience Understanding & Comprehension

Use Symbols, Acronyms, and Slogans

Message clarity and simplicity are enhanced by the use of symbols, acronyms, and slogans. These forms of shorthand conceptualize an idea so it can travel through extended lines of communication.

Avoid Jargon

One source of blocked communication is technical and bureaucratic jargon. Social scientists call it semantic noise when such language is delivered to a general audience. Jargon interferes with the message and impedes the receiver's ability to understand it. A news release may be perfectly appropriate for an engineering publication serving a particular industry, but the same information must be written in simpler terms for the readers of a daily newspaper.

Corporate symbols such as the Mercedes Benz star, the Nike swoosh, and the apple of Apple Computer are known throughout the world. Corporations invest time and money to make their names and logos synonymous with quality and service—a process referred to as *branding*. A corporate symbol should be unique, memorable, widely recognized, and appropriate. Organizations seek unique symbols that convey the essence of what they are or what they hope to be.

Avoid Clichés and Hype Words

Highly charged words with connotative meanings can pose problems, and overuse of clichés and hype words can seriously undermine the credibility of a message. Author and viral marketing specialist David Meerman Scott analyzed more than 700,000 news releases in 2008 to determine the most commonly overused words and phrases; the top 15, in descending order, were innovate, pleased to, unique, focused on, leading provider, commitment, partnership, new and improved, leverage, 120 percent, cost-effective, next generation, 110 percent, flexible, and world class.

Avoid Euphemisms

Public relations personnel should use positive, favorable words to convey a message, but they have an ethical responsibility not to use euphemisms—that is, words that hide information or mislead readers. Probably little danger exists in substituting positive words, such as saying a person has a disability rather than using the word handicapped. More dangerous are euphemisms that actually alter the meaning or impact of a word or concept. Writers call this practice doublespeak—words that pretend to communicate but really do not. Corporations often use euphemisms and doublespeak to hide unfavorable news. Reducing the number of employees, for example, may be called "right-sizing."

Avoid Discriminatory Language

In today's world, effective communication also means nondiscriminatory communication. Public relations personnel should double-check every message to eliminate undesirable gender, racial, and ethnic connotations. More information about reaching diverse audiences can be found in Chapter 10.

....

Advertising Age listed the top five slogans of the twentieth century as "Diamonds Are Forever" (De Beers), "Just Do It" (Nike), "The Pause That Refreshes" (Coca-Cola), "Tastes Great, Less Filling" (Miller Lite), and "We Try Harder" (Avis).

think

Is it unusual for members of an audience to change their mind about source credibility?

Involvement is another important predisposition that influences how messages are processed by audience members. Involvement can be described in simple terms as interest in or concern about an issue or a product. Those with higher involvement often process persuasive messages with greater attention to detail and to logical argument (central processing), whereas those with low involvement in a topic are impressed more by incidental cues, such as an attractive spokesperson, humor, or the sheer number of arguments given. The public relations professional can capitalize on the involvement concept by devising messages that focus more on "what is said" for high-involvement audiences and that pay more attention to "who says it" for low-involvement audiences.

Making the Message Memorable

For several reasons, many messages prepared by public relations personnel are repeated extensively. Consequently, communicators often build repetition into a message. Key points are mentioned at the beginning and then summarized at the end. If the source is asking the receiver to call for more information or write for a brochure, the telephone number or address is repeated several times. Such precautions also fight entropy, which is the information disintegration that occurs as media channels and people process the message and pass it on to others.

The key to effective communication and message retention is conveying information in a variety of ways via multiple communication channels. This "shotgun approach" helps people remember the message as they receive it through different media and extends the message to both passive and active audiences.

Making Sure the Audience Acts on the Message

The ultimate purpose of any message is to affect the recipient. Public relations personnel communicate messages on behalf of organizations

REPETITION
REPETITION
REPETITION
REPETITION
REPETITION
REPETITION
REPETITION
REPETITION
REPETITION
REPETITION
REPETITION
REPETITION
REPETITION
REPETITION
REPETITION

- Is NECESSARY because all members of a target audience don't see or hear the message at the same time. Not everyone reads the newspaper on a particular day or watches the same television news program.
- REMINDS the audience, so there is less chance of failure to remember the message. If a source has high credibility, repetition prevents erosion of opinion change.
- Helps the audience REMEMBER the message itself. Studies have shown that advertising is quickly forgotten if not repeated constantly.
- Can lead to IMPROVED LEARNING and increase the chance of penetrating audience indifference or resistance.
- OFFSETS THE "NOISE" surrounding a message. People often hear or see messages in an environment filled with distractions—a baby crying, the conversations of family members or office staff, a barking dog—or even while daydreaming or thinking of other things.
- Contributes to CREDIBILITY. A study funded by public relations firm Edelman Worldwide found that 60 percent of the respondents had to hear a message about a company three to five times before they believed it.

to change perceptions, attitudes, opinions, or behavior in some way. **Factors Influencing Adoption.** The communicator should be aware of the various factors that affect the persuasion stage of the adoption process and attempt to implement communication strategies that will overcome as many objections as possible. Repeating a message in various ways, reducing its complexity, taking into account competing

One study about employee communications found that rank-and-file workers got only **20% of a message** that had -passed through four levels of managers.

Marketing communications has the objective of convincing people to buy goods and services.

THE FIVE-STAGE ADOPTION PROCESS

Getting people to act on a message is not a simple process. Research shows that it can be a somewhat lengthy and complex procedure that depends on a number of intervening influences. One key to understanding how people accept new ideas or products is to analyze the adoption process.

1. **AWARENESS.** A person becomes aware of an idea or a new product, often by means of an advertisement or a news story.

2. **INTEREST.** The individual seeks more information about the idea or the product, perhaps by ordering a brochure, picking up a pamphlet, or reading an in-depth article in a newspaper or magazine.

3. **EVALUATION.** The potential consumer evaluates the idea or the product on the basis of how it meets specific needs and wants. Feedback from friends and family is part of this process.

4. **TRIAL.** The person tries the product or the idea on an experimental basis, by using a sample, witnessing a demonstration, or making qualifying statements such as "I read . . ."

5. **ADOPTION.** The individual begins to use the product on a regular basis or integrates the idea into his or her belief system. "I read . . ." becomes "I think . . . ."

A person does not necessarily go through all five stages with any given idea or product. The process may end after any step. In fact, the process is like a large funnel; although many people are made aware of an idea or a product, only a few will ultimately adopt it.

messages, and structuring the message to meet the needs of the audience are ways to achieve this goal.

Another aspect to consider is the amount of time needed to adopt a new idea or product. Depending on the individual and situation, the entire adoption process may take place almost instantly if it is of minor consequence or requires low-level commitment. Buying a new brand of soft drink or a bar of soap is relatively inexpensive and often done on impulse. In contrast, deciding to buy a new car or vote for a particular candidate may involve an adoption process that takes several weeks or months.

Everett Rogers's research shows that people approach innovation in different ways, depending on their personality traits and the risk involved. "Innovators" are venturesome individuals who are eager to try new ideas, whereas "laggards" are traditionalists who are the last to adopt anything. Between the two extremes are "early adopters," who are opinion leaders; "early majority" members, who take the deliberate approach; and "late majority" members, who are often skeptical but bow to peer pressure. Communicators often segment audiences and target their messages toward those who have "innovator" or "early adopter" characteristics and would be predisposed to adopting new ideas.

Of particular interest to public relations practitioners is the primary source of information at each step in the adoption process. Mass media vehicles such as advertising, short news articles, feature stories, and radio and television news announcements are most influential at the awareness stage of the adoption process. For example, a news article or a television announcement makes people aware of an idea, event, or new product. They may also first become aware of the message through such vehicles as direct mail, office memos, and simple brochures.

Individuals at the interest stage also rely on mass media vehicles, but at this point are actively seeking information and pay attention to longer, in-depth articles. They rely more on detailed brochures, specialized publications, and reviews posted by consumers on the Internet to provide details.

At the evaluation, trial, and adoption stages, group norms and opinions are the most influential. Feedback—negative or positive—from friends and peers may determine the likelihood of adoption. If a person's friends generally disap-

prove of a candidate, a movie, or an automobile brand, it is unlikely that the individual will complete the adoption process even if he or she is highly sold on the idea. If a person does make a commitment, mass media vehicles become reinforcing mechanisms.

The complexities of the adoption process show that public relations communicators need to think about the entire communication process—from the formulation of the message to the ways in which receivers ultimately process the information and make decisions. By doing so, communicators can form more effective message strategies and develop realistic objectives for what can actually be accomplished.

A number of factors affect the persuasion stage of the adoption process. Everett Rogers, author of *Diffusion of Innovation,* lists at least five.

1. **Relative Advantage**— the degree to which an innovation is perceived as better than the idea it replaces

2. **Compatibility**— the degree to which an innovation is perceived as being consistent with the existing values, experiences, and needs of potential adopters

3. **Complexity**— the degree to which an innovation is perceived as difficult to understand and use

4. **Trialability**— the degree to which an innovation may be experienced on a limited basis

5. **Observability**— the degree to which the results of an innovation are visible to others

measurement:
THE FOURTH STEP

The fourth step of the public relations process is measurement—the evaluation of results against agreed-upon objectives established during planning. Professor James Bissland, formerly of Bowling Green State University, defines evaluation as "the systematic assessment of a program and its results. It is a means

for practitioners to offer accountability to clients—and to themselves."

The desire to do a better job next time is a major reason for evaluating public relations efforts, but another, equally important driving force is the widespread adoption of the "management by objectives" system by clients and employers. They

> **"Your program is intended to cause observable impact—to change or maintain something about a situation. So, after the program, you use research to measure and document program effects.**
>
> Professors Glen Broom and David Dozier of San Diego State University

think — How does evaluation improve the public relations process?

want to know if the money, time, and effort expended on public relations are well spent and how they contribute to the realization of an organizational objective. Furthermore, evaluation or monitoring throughout a campaign may suggest that tactics or organizational stances should change. Measurement helps practitioners make appropriate adjustments in the dynamic, ever-changing reality that is public relations practice.

Objectives: A Prerequisite for Measurement

Before any public relations program can be properly evaluated, it is important to have a clearly established set of measurable objectives. These should be part of the program plan.

Public relations personnel and management should agree on the criteria that will be used to measure success. One Ketchum monograph simply states, "Write the most precise, most results-oriented objectives you can that are realistic, credible, measurable, and compatible with the client's demands on public relations."

Also, don't wait until the end of the public relations program to determine how it will be evaluated. Albert L. Schweitzer of Fleishman-Hillard makes the point that "evaluating impact/results starts in the planning stage. You break down the problem into measurable goals and objectives; then after implementing the program, you measure the results against goals."

If an objective is informational, measurement techniques must show how successfully information was communicated to target audiences. Such techniques fall under the rubrics of "message dissemination"

Although objectives may vary, every practitioner should ask the following **BASIC MEASUREMENT QUESTIONS:**

- Was the activity or program adequately planned?
- Did the recipients of the message understand it?
- How could the program strategy have been more effective?
- Were all primary and secondary audiences reached?
- Was the desired organizational objective achieved?
- Did any unforeseen circumstances affect the success of the program or activity?
- Did the program or activity fall within its budget?
- Which steps might be taken to improve the success of similar future activities?

and "audience exposure," but they do not measure the effect on attitudes or overt behavior and action. Motivational objectives are more difficult to accomplish. If the objective is to increase sales or market share, it is important to show that the public relations efforts caused the increase, rather than advertising or marketing strategies. Or, if the objective is to change attitudes or opinions, research should be done both before and after the public re-

lations activity to measure the percentage of change.

Measurement and Evaluation Status

In the last decade, public relations professionals have made considerable progress in evaluation research, resulting in an improved ability to tell clients and employers exactly what has been accomplished. Sophisticated techniques are used, including computerized news clip analysis, survey sampling, quasi-experimental designs in which the audience is divided into groups that see different aspects of a public relations campaign, and attempts to correlate efforts directly with sales.

Today, the trend toward more systematic measurement is well established. One reason for this emphasis on measurement: There is increasing pressure on all parts of the organization—including public relations—to prove their value to the "bottom line."

Walter K. Lindenmann, a former senior vice president and director of research at Ketchum, in *Public Relations Quarterly* suggests that public relations personnel use a mix of measurement techniques, many borrowed from advertising and marketing, to provide more complete evaluation. In addition, he notes that at least three levels of

Katherine Delahaye Paine, founder of public relations measurement firm KDPaine & Partners, recommends that 10 percent of a public relations budget should be devoted to measurement and evaluation.

measurement and evaluation exist. On the most basic level are compilations of message distribution and media placement. The second level, which requires more sophisticated techniques, deals with the measurement of audience awareness, comprehension, and retention of the message. The most advanced level is the measurement of changes in attitudes, opinions, and behavior.

> ❝First, it is possible to measure public relations effectiveness. . . . Second, measuring public relations effectiveness does not have to be either unbelievably expensive or laboriously time-consuming.❞
>
> Walter K. Lindenmann

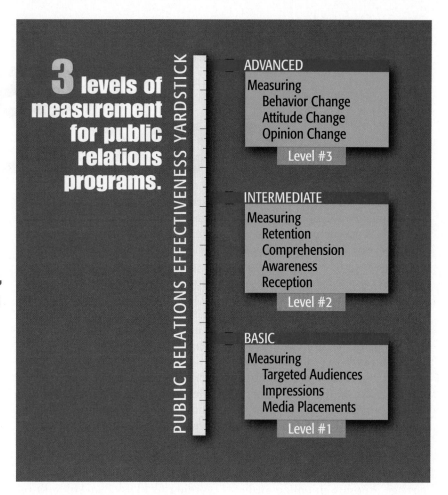

3 levels of measurement for public relations programs.

PUBLIC RELATIONS EFFECTIVENESS YARDSTICK

ADVANCED
Measuring
  Behavior Change
  Attitude Change
  Opinion Change
    Level #3

INTERMEDIATE
Measuring
  Retention
  Comprehension
  Awareness
  Reception
    Level #2

BASIC
Measuring
  Targeted Audiences
  Impressions
  Media Placements
    Level #1

MEASUREMENT OF
production

One elementary form of evaluation is simply counting how many news releases, feature stories, photos, letters, and the like are produced in a given period of time. This kind of evaluation is intended to give management an idea of a staff's productivity and output. Public relations professionals, however, do not believe that this kind of evaluation is very meaningful because it emphasizes quantity instead of quality. It may actually be more cost-effective to write fewer news releases and spend more time on the few that really are newsworthy and are more likely to be picked up by leading publications.

Another production measurement approach involves specifying what the public relations person should accomplish from media coverage. Perhaps a client wants to evaluate a campaign based on the number of feature stories that run in the top newspapers in the region or the number of news releases picked up by local media outlets. Such evaluation criteria not only are unrealistic, but are al-

think Why is measurement of production *not* the most meaningful way to evaluate communication efforts?

most impossible to guarantee, because media gatekeepers—not the public relations person—make these decisions.

MEASUREMENT OF message exposure

the most widely practiced form of public relations program evaluation is the compilation of press clippings and radio or television mentions. Local public relations firms and company departments often have a staff member scan and clip area newspapers for relevant articles. Large companies with regional, national, or even international outreach typically hire clipping services to scan large numbers of publications. Electronic clipping services can monitor and tape major radio and television programs on a contractual basis. Burrelle's, for example, monitors nearly 400 local TV stations in 150 cities. To track message exposure in online media, public relations practitioners may simply count hits on a website or visits to a blog; they may also count posted comments on a blog, which would suggest a higher level of exposure and involvement. Social media such as Facebook can be plat-

forms for messaging as well. Exposure might be measured by the number of "fans" an organization or cause accumulates. Web tracking systems and firms are discussed in more detail in Chapter 11.

Strategic research by Hallmark Cards and its public relations firm, Fleishman-Hillard, identified the need for a reinvigoration and reintroduction of its 18-year-old Shoebox card line. Customers expressed affection for the humorous line, but said it had grown stale and even offensive. In response, the line was revamped and relaunched. Hallmark used media clips as one measure of its Shoebox relaunch campaign. According to Fleishman-Hillard's report, which was the basis for the firm's receipt of a Silver Anvil award from PRSA:

> PR strategies and tactics generated nearly 141 million trackable impressions. Radio outreach resulted in more than 100 million impressions. . . . Television outreach resulted in 17 million impressions nationwide, including WB's "The Daily Buzz," (seen in 134 markets), "ABC World News Weekend," The Weather Channel, WE cable network, CNN, and more than 80 local stations.

Similar analysis was provided for print coverage. Such a compilation, which measures media acceptance of the story, revealed that Hallmark received massive coverage for the reintroduction of its Shoebox line.

Media Impressions

In addition to the number of media placements, public relations departments and firms report how many people may have been exposed to the message. These numbers are described as *media impressions*, or the potential audience reached by a periodical or a broadcast program.

A regional or national news story can generate millions of impressions by simple multiplication of each placement by the circulation or audience of each medium. Consider these examples:

- United Health Foundation (UHF) and Fleishman-Hillard developed a branding campaign to position UHF's annual edition of "America's Health Rankings" as the definitive source for state-by-state health information. The public relations campaign generated more than 1,600 stories, including 486 mentions in online sources, and 314 million media

X circulation of 130,000 = 130,000 media impressions

If a story about an organization appears in a local daily newspaper that has a circulation of 130,000, the number of media impressions is 130,000. If another story is published the next day, it counts for 130,000 more impressions. Estimated audiences for radio and television programs, certified by auditing organizations, also are used to compile media impressions.

Effectiveness of Measurement Tools

BenchPoint, a measurement firm, conducted a global survey of public relations and communications professionals for the First European Measurement Summit in Berlin, which was held in June 2009. Respondents, primarily Europeans and Americans, ranked the effectiveness of measurement tools.

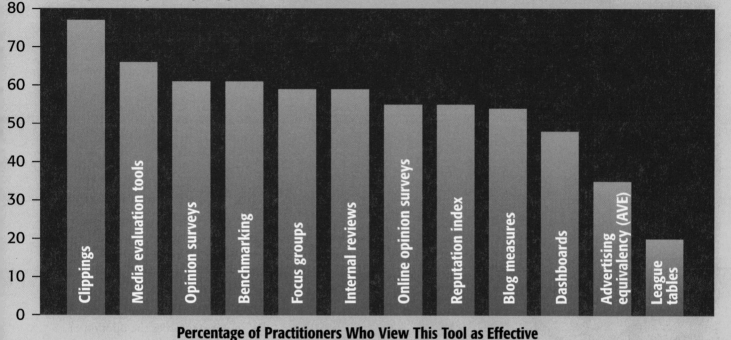

Percentage of Practitioners Who View This Tool as Effective

impressions, 108.8 million of which were online impressions.

• M&M's Candy conducted a national contest to choose a new color for its bite-size treats. Public relations activities generated 1.06 billion impressions from 10,000 television, radio, and print placements, which included 36,000 print column inches, 12 hours of television news coverage, and 74 hours of radio broadcast time.

Media impressions are commonly used in advertising to document the breadth of penetration of a particular message. Such figures give a rough estimate of how many people are exposed to a message. Unfortunately, they do not disclose how many people actually read or heard the stories or, more important, how many absorbed or acted on the information. Other techniques are needed for this kind of evaluation.

Internet Hits

A cyberspace version of media impressions involves counting the number of people reached via an organization's website or through social media posts. Each instance of a person accessing a site is regarded as a hit or a visit.

The Smithsonian Institution promoted the grand opening of its new National Museum of the American Indian (NMAI) in Washington, D.C. The museum's website was mentioned in media relations material. Hill & Knowlton, the museum's public relations firm, noted, "25% of print coverage referenced the NMAI Web site, contributing to 1.2 million hits (17,025 visits) per day (prior average was 233,000 hits)."

Advertising Equivalency

Another evaluation approach involves calculation of the value of message exposure, referred to as advertising equivalency (AVE). This methodology involves converting the value of stories in the regular news columns or on the air into their equivalent advertising costs. For example, a five-inch arti-

cle in a trade magazine that charges $100 per column inch for advertising would be worth $500 in publicity value.

Hampton Hotels' "Save a Landmark" campaign to restore Memphis's National Civil Rights Museum was evaluated by using advertising equivalency. As Hampton Hotels and its public relations firm Cohn & Wolfe reported, the program "generated more than 220 media placements, 394,233,117 gross impressions, an estimated $6,075,122 in advertising equivalency." They estimated that the program generated a return on investment of 17 to 1.

Some practitioners may even take the approach of calculating the cost of advertising for the

think Is advertising equivalency an exact science?

same amount of space devoted to a news story and then multiplying that total three to six times, reflecting the results of research showing that a news story has greater credibility than an advertisement. For example, if Hampton Hotels multiplied the equivalent advertising space by three, it could say that the editorial space was worth $18 million in publicity for the "Save a Landmark" campaign.

Although such dollar amounts may impress top management, the technique of calculating advertising equivalency is really comparing apples with oranges. One reason why the two can't be compared is the

fundamental difference between advertising and publicity. Advertising copy is directly controlled by the organization and can be oriented to specific objectives. The organization dictates the content, size, placement and timing of the message. News mentions, by comparison, are determined by media gatekeepers and can be negative, neutral, or positive. In addition, a news release can be edited to the point that key corporate messages are deleted. In other words, the organization can't control the size, placement, timing or content of such items.

Ultimately, the utility of the AVE approach becomes a question of what is being measured. Should an article be counted as equivalent to advertising space if it is negative? Is a 15-inch article that mentions the organization only once among six other organizations comparable to 15 column inches of advertising space? Also, the numbers game doesn't take into account that a 4-inch article in the *Wall Street Journal* may be more valuable in reaching key publics than a 20-inch article in a local daily.

In short, the dollar-value approach to measuring publicity effectiveness is somewhat suspect. The Institute for Public Relations (IPR) Measurement Commission voted in 2009 to "reject AVEs, the concept and the practice." The practice of equating publicity with advertising rates for comparable space also does not engender good media relations, because it reinforces the opinion of many media gatekeepers that all news releases are just attempts to get free advertising.

Systematic Tracking

As noted earlier, message exposure traditionally has been measured by sheer volume of mentions. Technological advances, however, now make it possible to track media placements in a more sophisticated way.

Computer databases can be used to analyze the content of media placements based on such variables as market penetration, type of publication, tone of coverage, sources quoted, and mention of key copy points. Ketchum, for example, can build as many as 40 variables into its computer program, including the tracking of reporter bylines to determine if a journalist is predisposed negatively or positively toward the client's key messages. Other firms, such as Carma International and Delahaye Medialink, do extensive analysis for clients using databases such as LexisNexis.

The value of systematic tracking is manifold. Continuing, regular feedback during a campaign can

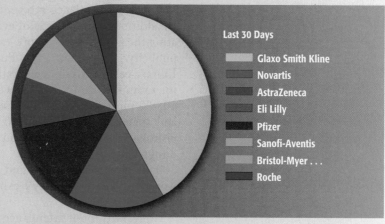

Corporate Share of Voice

Last 30 Days

- Glaxo Smith Kline
- Novartis
- AstraZeneca
- Eli Lilly
- Pfizer
- Sanofi-Aventis
- Bristol-Myer . . .
- Roche

Media analysis by Factiva Insight from Dow Jones uses text mining and visualization technologies to present a graphical view of third-party data in the Factiva database and on the web. The chart above shows the amount of coverage various pharmaceutical companies received in a one-month period.

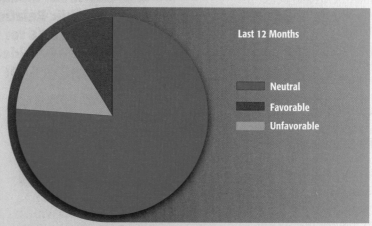

GSK Favorability

Last 12 Months

- Neutral
- Favorable
- Unfavorable

This chart shows an analysis of media coverage for a company in terms of what percentage of stories were neutral, favorable, and unfavorable. Such data help organizations assess the effectiveness of their media relations efforts.

> ❝ **The world doesn't need more data. What it needs is analyzed data.** ❞

Katharine Paine, former president of Delahaye Medialink

identify whether an organization's publicity efforts are paying off in terms of placements and mention of key messages. Tracking coverage and comparing it over a period of time is called *benchmarking*.

An example of benchmarking is the campaign that Capitoline/MS&L public relations conducted on behalf of the Turkish government to make Americans more aware of Turkey as a travel destination. By comparing the number of stories before and after the campaign was launched, Carma International found that articles with Turkey as the primary destination increased 400 percent. Favorable articles on Turkey increased 90 percent from the previous year.

Another form of analysis is comparing the number of news releases sent with the number actually published and in which kinds of periodicals. Such analysis often helps a public relations department determine which kinds of publicity are most effective and earn the most return on investment (ROI).

Information Requests

Counting the number of requests for more information generated by a public relations effort is yet another form of media exposure evaluation. A story in a newspaper or an appearance by a company spokesperson on a broadcast often provides information about where people can get more information about a subject. In many cases, a toll-free number is provided.

An information program by the U.S. Centers for Disease Control and Prevention on H1N1 infection ("swine flu") earned the CDC 45,000 followers on one of its Twit-

ter accounts, CDCemergency. The CDC developed dozens of podcasts, video public service announcements (PSAs), brochures, flyers, and FAQs and made them available in PDF format for download. During the beginning days of the H1N1 outbreak, the CDC received 300 media requests for information from its website each day.

Cost per Person

Message exposure can also be monitored by determining the cost of reaching each member of the

audience. This technique is commonly used in advertising to place costs in perspective. Although a 30-second commercial during the 2010 Super Bowl telecast cost $3 million, advertisers believed it was well worth the price because an audience of more than 106 million would be reached for less than three cents each. This was a relative bargain, even if several million viewers visited the refrigerator while the commercial played.

Cost-effectiveness, as this technique is known, is often used to evaluate public relations campaigns. Specifically, cost per thousand (CPM) is calculated by taking the cost of the publicity program and dividing it by the total number of media impressions.

Brita water filtering systems are owned by The Clorox Company. In 2008, Brita developed a "Filter for Good" environmental sustainability program that promoted filtered water over bottled water. Clorox developed a program that linked media impressions to CPM and return on investment (ROI). *PRWeek* reported, "The focus on impressions means the company analyzes how many times a person comes in contact with brand messaging through editorial placements and other efforts. The more impressions per dollar spent, the lower the cost per thousand (CPM) and better the ROI."

David Kellis, Senior Group PR Manager for Clorox, told *PRWeek*, "Looking at impressions per market over the course of the year, we were able to correlate sales per market and the assumption held up—the better CPM was leading to really strong ROI." Clorox found that it didn't have to spend a lot of money to have a good return on investment. In short, effective public relations helped Clorox reach a large number of people with only a relatively small investment.

Audience Attendance

Measuring attendance at events is an additional, simple way of evaluating the effectiveness of pre-event publicity. The New York Public Library centennial day celebration, for example, attracted a crowd of 10,000 for a sound and laser show and speeches. In addition, 20,000 visitors came to the library on the designated day and more than 200,000 people from around the world visited the library's exhibitions during the year.

Conversely, poor attendance at a meeting or event can indicate inadequate publicity and promotion. Another major cause of lackluster attendance is apathy (lack of public interest), even when people are aware that a meeting or event is taking place. Low attendance usually results in considerable finger-pointing; thus an objective evaluation of exactly what happened—or didn't happen—is a good policy.

Cost per Click

Public relations practitioners also measure cost per click (CPC) in online and social media. In 2009, Page One Public Relations estimated that CPC was $0.56 for Twitter and $0.32 for YouTube videos. That compares to a CPC of $1.91 for Internet advertising.

YOUTUBE VIDEOS   TWEETS   INTERNET ADS

MEASUREMENT OF
audience
awareness

think What can survey research tools tell public relations professionals about the effectiveness of public relations campaigns?

measuring message dissemination and audience exposure is one thing. An even higher level of evaluation is involved in determining whether the audience actually became aware of the message and understood it. PR measurement expert Walter Lindenmann calls this the second level of public relations evaluation. He notes:

> At this level, public relations practitioners measure whether target audience groups actually received the messages directed at

them: whether they paid attention to those messages, whether they understood the messages, and whether they have retained those messages in any shape or form.

The tools of survey research answer such questions. Members of the target audience are asked about the message and what they remember about it. Public awareness of which organization sponsors an event also is important. BayBank found that only 59 percent of the spectators recognized the bank as sponsor of the Head of the Charles Regatta, a series of boat races on the Charles River in Massachusetts. Through various innovations, increased publicity efforts, and more signage at the following year's regatta, BayBank (which has since been absorbed by another bank) raised public awareness to 90 percent.

Another way of measuring audience awareness and comprehension is day-after recall. With this method, participants are asked to view a specific television program or read a particular news story. The next day they are interviewed to learn which messages they remembered.

MEASUREMENT OF audience attitudes

> **The only way to determine if communications are making an impact is by pre- and post-test research. The first survey measures the status quo. The second one will demonstrate any change and the direction of that change.**
>
> Frank R. Stansberry, former Manager of Guest Affairs for Coca-Cola

Closely related to audience awareness and understanding of a message are changes in an audience's perceptions and attitudes that result from internalization of the message. A major technique to determine such changes is the *baseline study*, which entails measurements of audience attitudes and opinions before, during, and after a public relations campaign. Baseline studies, also called benchmark studies, measure the percentage difference in attitudes and opinions as a result of increased information and publicity. A number of intervening variables may account for changes in attitude, of course, but statistical analysis of variance can help pinpoint how much of the change is attributable to public relations efforts.

The insurance company Prudential Financial regularly conducts baseline studies. When it implemented a corporate social responsibility (CSR) program that provided matching grants to volunteer medical service squads so they could purchase portable cardiac arrest equipment to treat heart attack victims before they reach the hospital, baseline research found that its favorable corporate reputation rating among survey respondents increased from 48 percent to 77 percent over a two-year period.

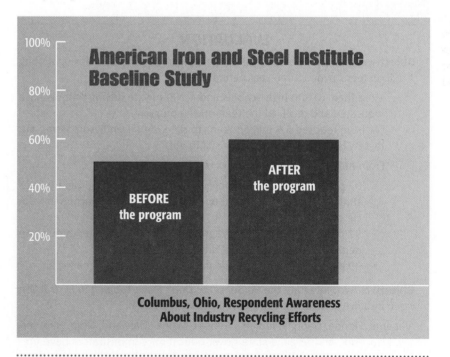

The American Iron and Steel Institute conducted a baseline study to determine the effectiveness of its campaign to inform the public about the industry's recycling efforts. Before the program, only 52 percent of the respondents in Columbus, Ohio, were aware that steel cans are recyclable. After the campaign, that percentage rose to 64 percent.

MEASUREMENT OF
audience
action

think What is the ultimate goal of any public relations activity?

he ultimate objective of any public relations effort, as has been pointed out repeatedly, is to accomplish organizational objectives. The objective of an amateur theater group is not to get media publicity; the objective is to sell tickets. The objective of an environmental organization such as Greenpeace is not to get editorials written in favor of whales, but rather to motivate the public (1) to write elected officials, (2) to send donations to fund its preservation efforts, and (3) to get protective legislation passed. The objective of a company is to sell its products and services, not get 200 million media impressions. In all cases, the tools and activities of public relations are a means, not an end. Thus public relations efforts ultimately are evaluated on how well they help an organization achieve its objectives.

Cingular Wireless (now AT&T) and its public relations firm, Ketchum, employed a variety of primary and secondary research methods when developing a campaign aimed at curtailing the practice of teenagers "driving while distracted." These methods included data analysis of highway traffic safety statistics

> **The outcome of a successful public relations program is not a hefty stack of news stories. . . . Communication is important only in the effects it achieves among publics.**
>
> David Dozier,
> San Diego State University

Cingular Wireless Campaign Analysis

EVALUATION

Objective One: Create awareness of the dangers of distracted driving among 3 million teens over a three-year period:

- More than 10,000 high schools and 4,200 private driving schools have requested and received the teen-driving program.
- We have reached 5.6 million teens to date, significantly surpassing our three-year goal with 11 months still to go!

From the 1,000 educator surveys received to date:

- 93 percent of teachers strongly agree/agree that this program gives students a new perspective on the role of driver distraction in vehicle collisions.
- 92 percent strongly agree/agree that the program generated student interest in the topic of driver distraction.
- 99 percent of instructors said they would use the program again.

Objective Two: Integrate the *Be Sensible: Don't Drive Yourself to Distraction* video into five state driver education programs by 2004:

Alabama, Florida, Georgia, Indiana, Kansas, Maine, Maryland, Ohio, New Jersey, New York, and Virginia state driver education administrators have embraced the "Be Sensible" teen program by distributing the program to all driver education teachers statewide.

Cingular's "Be Sensible: Don't Drive Yourself to Distraction" program received several awards, including the CINE Golden Eagle and U.S. International Film and Video Festival Silver Screen.

that showed teens are four times more likely to be in distraction-related accidents and focus groups with educators to better understand how to communicate with teens. In its PRSA Silver Anvil award–winning application, Ketchum recounted how measurable objectives were addressed:

Employers and clients increasingly have their eyes on the bottom line of public relations campaigns. This scrutiny and attention to accountability shape the emphasis on measurement in public relations. As both this chapter and Chapter 6 illustrate, the public relations process is driven by the interaction among research, strategic planning and measurable objectives, creative tactics and messaging, and credible measurement techniques.

Media Reality Check

COUNTING CLIPPINGS is still the most common PR evaluation technique (see the BenchPoint survey data on page 147). More sophisticated measurements also exist, however. Each year the Institute for Public Relations awards a "Golden Ruler Award" in recognition of innovation in PR measurement. In 2009, the winning entry was from MetLife and Echo Research Inc.

MetLife wanted to ensure not only that its information was appearing in the media—the clipping count method—but also that the information was accurate when it appeared in these outlets. Content analysis is not an unusual metric in public relations, but MetLife and Echo Research took matters a step further. They developed "Media Reality Check," which analyzes message accuracy by focusing on basic facts, misstatements, and omissions.

This research method was used to achieve two objectives:

- "Determine the degree to which correct, incorrect, and only partially correct information is included in news and other stories"

- "Determine the extent to which key information is omitted or misreported from coverage"

The method was applied to all articles on life insurance appearing in 26 major daily newspapers, leading personal finance magazines and websites, newswire services, and selected general consumer magazines over the course of one year. MetLife and Echo Research found that 94 percent of these articles contained at least one factual error or serious omission, and on average each had three omissions and one misstatement of basic facts related to life insurance.

In their winning entry, the companies reported, "The research revealed that the most frequent writers on life insurance were not always the most accurate, indi-cating the need for strong media education programs even among experienced personal finance writers." These findings not only allowed MetLife to sharpen its messages, but also highlighted a need to develop a proactive media relations campaign targeted at key business journalists.

In later qualitative research focused on members of the media and "influencers," MetLife found that its content analysis-driven strategy was on target. Focus group participants said, "The company that makes insurance products clear and easy to understand will win."

1. What are some ways that your favorite retail store might use research and measurement to develop better public relations campaigns?

2. Which of the four public relations steps—research, planning, communication, or measurement—are most important in your estimation? Justify your choice.

APPLY YOUR KNOWLEDGE
WHAT WOULD YOU DO?

Your student public relations agency has received a $2,000 grant from the U.S. Census Bureau to conduct a campaign on your campus to inform students about the importance of participating in the national census, which is conducted every 10 years.

One feature of the 2010 census is a short count form; it contains only ten questions that will take individuals about 10 minutes to complete. Information collected in the census is used to apportion the seats in the U.S. House of Representatives and to distribute more than $400 billion in federal funds each year, including financial aid to students.

Your agency needs to develop an information campaign on campus that will use a variety of communication tactics to reach all students and encourage them to participate in the census. You should think about ways to effectively use campus media, conduct outreach to various student groups, and stage activities (events) that would attract student attention. What would you suggest? Prepare a memo that (1) states the objective of your information campaign, (2) lists your primary and secondary audiences on campus, (3) outlines your key strategy, (4) gives specific details about which tactics will be used, and (5) describes how your team will measure (evaluate) the success of your campaign.

Summary

What Are the Goals of Public Relations Communication? p. 134

- Five possible objectives of communication are message exposure, accurate dissemination of the message, acceptance of the message, attitude change, and change in overt behavior.

Which Factors Influence Message Reception, Comprehension, Retention, and Credibility, and Adoption? p. 135

- Successful communication involves interaction, or shared experience, because the message must be not only sent but also received. The larger the audience, the greater the number of barriers to communication.

- Communicators must tailor messages to get recipients' attention. Messages for passive audiences must demonstrate style and creativity, whereas messages for an audience actively seeking information must contain more sophisticated content; an effective message describes an obvious benefit.

- The most basic element necessary for understanding between communicator and audience is a common language. Public relations practitioners must consider their audiences and style their language appropriately, taking into consideration literacy levels, clarity and simplicity of language, and avoidance of discriminatory language.

- Key variables in message believability include source credibility, context, and the audience's predispositions, especially members' level of involvement.

- Messages are often repeated extensively in several ways, through a variety of channels, to reach all members of the target audience, help them remember the message, and enhance their learning.

- Five steps in acceptance of new ideas or products are awareness, interest, evaluation, trial, and adoption.

- The adoption process is affected by relative advantage, compatibility, complexity, trialability, and observability.

Why Is Measurement of Public Relations Program Effectiveness Important? p. 143

- Evaluation is the measurement of results against objectives; it can enhance future performance and establish whether the goals of management by objective have been met.

- Criteria must be set to evaluate the level of success in attaining the established objectives.

Which Methods Are Used to Measure the Effectiveness of Public Relations Programs? p. 145

- On the most basic level, practitioners can measure message distribution and media placements. A second level would entail measurement of audience awareness, comprehension, and retention. The most advanced level is the measurement of changes in attitudes, opinions, and behaviors.

- Several criteria can be used to measure message exposure, including the compilation of press clippings and radio/television mentions; media impressions, or the potential audience reached; number of hits on a website; advertising equivalency; systematic tracking by use of computer databases; requests for additional information; and audience attendance at special events.

- Changes in audience attitudes can be evaluated through a baseline or benchmark study, which focuses on measuring awareness and opinions before, during, and after a public relations campaign.

- Ultimately, public relations campaigns are evaluated based on how they help an organization achieve its objectives through changing audience behavior, whether it involves sales, fund-raising, or the election of a candidate.

QUESTIONS for *Review* and *Discussion*

1. Kirk Hallahan lists five categories of media and communication tools. What are they?

2. Why is two-way communication (feedback) an important aspect of effective communication?

3. Which kinds of messages and communication channels would you use for a passive audience? For an active information-seeking audience?

4. Why is it necessary to use a variety of messages and communication channels in a public relations program?

5. Explain the five steps of the adoption process. What are some of the factors that affect the adoption of an idea or product?

6. What is the role of stated objectives in evaluating public relations programs?

7. List four ways that publicity activity is evaluated. What, if any, are the drawbacks of each evaluation method?

8. How does measurement of message exposure differ from measurement of audience comprehension of the message?

9. Which methods can be used to evaluate the effectiveness of a company newsletter or magazine?

the THINK SPOT
www.thethinkspot.com

TACTICS

GALLUP

Jeffrey M. Jones | *Gallup*, December 4, 2009

Public opinion is often divided, as these poll results clearly indicate.

Public relations professionals use polls to identify key audiences and assess public opinion.

Gauging the dimensions of public opinion can help interest groups move people to action. Converting a hostile opinion into a positive one is one of the most challenging tasks faced by public relations practitioners.

Very few issues lead to unanimity of public opinion. The breakdown of how opinion splits is often highly complex; it may even seem that groups hold contradictory opinions on similar issues.

George Gallup was one of the pioneers of scientific polling in the United States. Polling has become almost synonymous with his name. The American Institute of Public Opinion has continued this work since Gallup's death in 1984. The questions asked in the polls often require simple answers, such as "yes" or "no." The polls now address a myriad of diverse topics.

Americans Split on Whether Goals in Afghanistan Will Be Met

Forty-eight percent say the U.S. is certain or likely to meet its goals

PRINCETON, NJ—The unveiling of President Obama's new military strategy for Afghanistan has not left Americans overly confident that it will succeed—48 percent say the United States is certain or likely to achieve its goals in the war, while 45 percent say the United States is unlikely to do so or is certain not to achieve its aims.

These results are based on a one-night reaction poll of 1,000 Americans conducted December 2, the night after Obama's nationally televised address to unveil the new war strategy. The poll found Americans more likely to favor (51 percent) than oppose (40 percent) the new strategy.

There are a significant number of doubters even among those who support the new war policy. Among this group, 61 percent believe the United States is likely to achieve its goals, but 35 percent are pessimistic. Likewise, though the majority of the new policy's opponents do not expect the United States to achieve its goals in Afghanistan, that is far from a unanimous position.

There are modest differences in expectations for success by party, with 56 percent of Republicans, 47 percent of independents, and 45 percent of Democrats believing the United States will achieve its goals.

Cost and Security Concerns

Some opponents of escalating the United States' involvement in Afghanistan are questioning the increasing costs to the United States of the war effort. And many Americans share this concern, at least to some degree. The poll finds 73 percent saying they are worried about the war's costs making it more difficult for the United States to address domestic problems, including 32 percent who are very worried.

Some Democratic members of Congress have called for a new income tax to help fund the increased cost of U.S. military operations in Afghanistan brought about by the decision to send an additional

30,000 service men and women there. However, the top two Democrats in Congress, Speaker of the House Nancy Pelosi and House Majority Leader Steny Hoyer, have come out in opposition to such a tax, making its passage highly unlikely. It would appear Pelosi and Hoyer are in tune with American public opinion; the poll shows that Americans overwhelmingly oppose a war surtax, by 68 percent to 24 percent.

While much of the Democratic criticism of the new Afghanistan policy has centered on cost, Republicans have expressed concern about setting a timetable for withdrawal. The poll finds 55 percent of Americans saying they are concerned that withdrawing troops from Afghanistan would make the United States more vulnerable to terrorist attacks, including 19 percent who are very concerned.

In line with the concerns of their party leaders, rank-and-file Democrats are more concerned about the war's costs limiting the United States' ability to address domestic problems, while rank-and-file Republicans are more concerned that withdrawing troops could affect U.S. security from terrorism.

Even if a substantial proportion of Americans doubt the United States' ability to succeed in Afghanistan or express concern about possible outcomes of the new war policy, the public generally does not second-guess the initial decision to enter the war. The poll finds 62 percent saying that, looking back, sending troops to Afghanistan was the right thing to do, while 32 percent say it was the wrong thing. This is similar to what Gallup has found on its primary "mistake" trend question that measures support for the war.

Results are based on telephone interviews with 1,005 national adults, aged 18 and older, conducted December 2, 2009. For results based on the total sample of national adults, one can say with 95 percent confidence that the maximum margin of sampling error is ±4 percentage points.

Interviews are conducted with respondents on land-line telephones and cellular phones.

In addition to sampling error, question wording and practical difficulties in conducting surveys can introduce error or bias into the findings of public opinion polls.

Polls conducted entirely in one day, such as this one, are subject to additional error or bias not found in polls conducted over several days.

Despite an initial tendency to support wars, public opinion on a war's progress is typically highly malleable. It is very difficult to predict the direction of public opinion due to the number of variables that may affect it—time, the economy, media coverage, and so on.

Pollsters often use telephone interviews to gather data. Because an increasing number of people are using cellular phones in lieu of land-line phones, poll results are considered more valid if the people sampled include individuals who use land-lines as well as people who use cellular phones.

Polls provide a "snapshot" of public opinion at a given time. Public opinion depends on issues and is constantly evolving. An issue that elicits a lukewarm response one day might draw heated reactions the next.

8 PUBLIC OPINION

A Heated Battle Over Healthcare Reform

On March 23, 2010, after a battle that had lasted more than a year, President Barack Obama's healthcare reform legislation became law. Reform legislation was favored by more than half of the country when it was announced in early 2009 by President Obama and Democrats in Congress. But by the spring, support had eroded following a series of town hall meetings dominated by conservative constituents. Critics garnered headlines, railing about government takeover of health care, reduced freedom of choice, and the specter of government "death panels."

Public opinion was divided sharply; individuals who were polled sometimes even appeared to be divided against themselves. An ABC/*Washington Post* poll found in July 2009 that 57 percent of U.S. adults were unhappy with the current healthcare system, but 83 percent were satisfied with the care that they themselves received. More strikingly, according to a *New York Times*/CBS News poll, 72 percent favored a public option, but 63 percent had serious reservations about the negative effects of government intervention in the healthcare system.

Obama's plan narrowly escaped the fate of then President Bill Clinton's 1993 plan to provide universal health insurance coverage for all Americans. Clinton's proposal had astonishing public support initially. But its chances were crushed after a relentless and highly successful public relations campaign was waged by insurance and pharmaceutical companies. Similarly, Obama's plan had appeared doomed when deceased Massachusetts Senator Ted Kennedy's seat went to Republican Scott Brown, leaving Democrats without a filibuster-proof majority.

AND PERSUASION

Part of the problem for the president and his allies was that the proposed 2009 healthcare legislation was enormously complex and proponents initially failed to offer a clear message for why it should be adopted. Oppositions groups such as FreedomWorks and Americans for Prosperity dominated news coverage by offering a few simple messages, appealing to fear, and encouraging public demonstrations. Like Bill Clinton, President Obama tends to shift messages and become caught up in details. Not until July 2009 did Obama make a strong, direct, and emotional appeal in his message for passage of healthcare reform legislation.

Yet important differences have emerged between 1994 and 2010. President Obama managed to win the support of groups representing the pharmaceutical industry (Pharmaceutical Research and Manufacturers of America [PhRMA] and Pharmaceutical Industry Labor–Management Association [PILMA]) that were opposed to reform 15 years earlier. While opposition groups dominated the debate in 1994, this time around pro-reform groups (such as the Center for Economic and Social Rights and Physicians for a National Health Program) spent nearly as much on public relations as did their opponents. Grassroots initiatives, supported by social media formats

such as Facebook and Twitter, also introduced an important facet to the debate, serving to multiply the effect of traditional news platforms.

❶ **How was public opinion in the case of healthcare reform informed by interest groups and mass media coverage?**

❷ **What persuasion techniques did proponents and opponents of health care reform use to present their messages in 1993/94 and in 2009/2010?**

❸ **Now that the bill has passed, how has public opinion about healthcare reform changed?**

what is
PUBLIC OPINION?

editorial cartoonists humanize public opinion in the form of John or Jane Q. Public, characters who have come to symbolize the way people think about any given issue. The reality is that public opinion is somewhat elusive and extremely difficult to measure at any given moment.

People constantly form and revise their opinions about public figures, like David Beckham or Michele Obama or Tiger Woods, often in response to recent television appearances or Internet gossip. The court of public opinion is fickle and variable. Yesterday's superstars may be tomorrow's has-beens, until they release a ghostwritten tell-all biography and are again thrust into the public spotlight. Accurately predicting the future direction of public opinion is extremely difficult because of the number of contingent variables involved.

In fact, few issues inspire unanimity of thought, and public opinion is usually split in several directions that may be in conflict with one an-

By permission of Mike Luckovich and Creators Syndicate, Inc.

other. Even when members of an identifiable group share common beliefs and interests, the opinions of individuals or subgroups within the larger group may vary widely. For example, the issue of Israeli–Palestinian relations in the United States arouses a variety of responses among Christian groups.

Fundamentalists tend to support Israeli policy unequivocally, linking current events to biblical prophecy, whereas liberal Christians are likely to express some sympathy for the concept of Palestinian sovereignty. Likewise, there will always be various conflicting public opinions about hot-button issues such as abortion, same-sex marriage, euthanasia, and war.

Typically only a small number of people at any given time participate in public opinion formation on specific issues. However, once people and the press begin to refer to public opinion on an issue as an accomplished fact, it can take on its own momentum. According to Irving Crespi, a prolific public opinion researcher, public opinion can be an almost tangible force that affects all kinds of people, altering their beliefs or attitudes about controversial issues.

Three reasons explain the profound influence of vocal segments of society and public opinion momentum:

1. Psychologists have found that the public by and large tends to be passive.

2. One issue may engage the attention of a part of the population with a particular vested interest, whereas another issue arouses the interest of another segment.

3. People have some opinions that may conflict or compete with the opinions of others regarding the same issue. People also sometimes hold contradictory opinions or attitudes.

Understanding and assessing the dynamics of competing or conflicting opinions is a crucial dimension of public relations work. The formation of public opinion is a constantly evolving process, and should not be regarded as static by public relations professionals. The public is often noncommittal about an issue, but once motivated to address it, they form attitudes and beliefs and take action to achieve their interests throughout the life cycle of the issue. Public relations professionals need to identify and track identifiable public opinions, and even strive to create or boost these opinions, to affect public relations outcomes.

Public opinion plays a role in moving a group of people to action in relation to an issue. Awareness and discussion leads to crystallization of opinions and consensus building among the public. As awareness grows, the issue becomes a matter of public discussion and debate, often garnering extensive media coverage. Through media coverage, the issue is placed on the public agenda and even more people become aware of it.

Suppose, for example, activist and special-interest groups organize a protest against scenic areas being threatened by logging or strip mining. Although these groups may have no formal power, they could serve as "agenda stimuli" for the media, which crave controversy and conflict. Opportunities for vivid television coverage would arise when activists stage rallies and demonstrations. As is often the case, the issue may become simplified by the media into an us-versus-them stance. Opinion leaders might then begin to discuss the issue, perhaps viewing it as being symbolic of broader environmental and societal issues.

Public relations professionals often identify key audiences or publics through analysis of public opinion, thereby resolving the issue from their standpoint. For example, news in February 2006 that the U.S. government would contract with DP World, a company owned by the state of Dubai in the United Arab Emirates, to operate 21 U.S. ports swiftly led to a massive public outcry. Public opinion was further aroused when it was learned that President George W. Bush's administration had not informed Congress of the deal until a short time before it was to be finalized. In March 2006, a CNN/USA Today/Gallup poll revealed that 66 percent of respondents were opposed to the deal and only 17 percent were in favor of it. Even though port security was to remain under U.S. control, it struck many Americans as highly suspect that a corporation owned by an Arab country would be in charge of operations. Because of the outcry from the public, which was an important audience, the deal soon fell victim to Congressional opposition and the pressure of overwhelming negative public opinion.

Public Opinion Evolves

78% favor a ban on smoking in restaurants.

76% favor a ban on smoking in the workplace.

26% favor a ban on smoking in licensed pubs.

Results of Public Opinion Polls in Cardiff, Wales in 2004

Aware that public opinion varies, the Welsh government responded accordingly when they imposed a selective smoking ban. "I want to [set policy], as much as possible, in partnership—listening and learning from others." Health Minister Jane Hutt stated, implying that if public opinion on the issue changed, her ministry would reflect the evolving viewpoints.

OPINION LEADERS AS
catalysts

SaveDarfur.org

According to research in *Roper Reports*, 10 to 12 percent of the population, identified by the magazine as "influentials," drive public opinion and consumer trends. Knowledgeable experts who articulate opinions about specific issues in public discussion are called *opinion leaders*.

Sociologists Elihu Katz and Paul Lazarsfeld define opinion leaders as people who, because of their interest in and knowledge of a subject, become experts and inform others either formally as spokespeople or informally through daily interaction with family members, colleagues, and peers. Opinion leaders are not necessarily highly visible in the community, nor are they always leaders in other regards—it is as common to find an opinion leader among a group of coal miners or housewives as it is among a group of politicians or *Fortune* 500 company executives. Opinion leaders are evenly distributed among the social, economic, and educational strata within their community. They help frame and define issues that often have their roots in individuals' self-interests. It is through the influence of opinion leaders that public opinion often crystallizes into a measurable entity. Public relations professionals attempt to influence these leaders just as they seek to influence the public at large.

The Flow of Opinion

Many public relations campaigns, and particularly those in the public affairs arena, concentrate on identifying and reaching key opinion leaders who are pivotal to the success or failure of an idea or project. In 1948, sociologists Paul Lazarsfeld, Bernard Berelson, and Hazel Gaudet published a paper entitled "The People's Choice" that analyzed how people choose candidates in an election. They found that the mass media had minimal influence on electoral choices, but voters did rely on person-to-person communication with formal and informal opinion leaders.

These findings, refined by Lazarsfeld and Katz, became known as the two-step flow theory of communication. Although later research confirmed that multiple steps were involved, the basic concept remains valid. Public opinion is generally formed around the views

Informal opinion leaders have clout with peers because of some special characteristic. In general, informal opinion leaders exert considerable influence on their peer groups by being highly informed, articulate, and credible on particular issues. For example, actor George Clooney has emerged as opinion leader on a wide range of issues. Although many Americans find his ideas about the political process controversial, Clooney's advocacy to end genocide in the Darfur region of western Sudan in Africa is generally admired.

of people who have taken the time to sift information, evaluate it, and form an opinion that is expressed to others. Information is disseminated through the media (print, radio, and television) to opinion leaders, who then interact with other less informed members of the public. It is through the filter of face-to-face interactions between opinion leaders and others, rather than directly from the media itself, that public opinion is formed.

The multiple-step flow model, *N*-step theory, and diffusion theory can be graphically illustrated.

think

Who influences your opinions?

People seldom make a decision on their own. We are influenced by friends, parents, educators, supervisors, church leaders, physicians, public officials, celebrities, and the media in general when deciding to vote for a president or city mayor, or to purchase a car or even toothpaste.

Multiple-Step Flow

OPINION MAKERS derive large amounts of information from the mass media and other sources and share that information with people.

The **ATTENTIVE PUBLIC** is interested in the issue but rely on opinion leaders to synthesize and interpret information.

The **INATTENTIVE PUBLIC** are unaware of or uninterested in the issue and remain outside the opinion-formation process.

N-step Theory

N-step theory states that individuals are seldom influenced by only one opinion leader but actually interact with different leaders.

Diffusion Theory

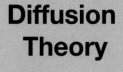

Individuals adopt new ideas or products in five stages: awareness, interest, trial, evaluation, and adoption. Individuals are influenced by media in the first two steps and by friends and family members in the third and fourth steps. Each individual is a decision maker who adopts a new idea or product when they reach the final step.

Step 1
AWARENESS

Step 2
INTEREST

Step 3
TRIAL

Step 4
EVALUATION

Step 5
ADOPTION

THE ROLE OF
mass media

Public relations personnel can reach opinion leaders to influence key publics. They can also reach targeted publics directly via the mass media such as radio, television, newspapers, blogs, and magazines. *Mass media*, as the term implies, means that information from a source can be efficiently and rapidly disseminated to masses of people, sometimes literally millions. The mass media inform and influence people daily. Thus it is important to understand who controls the media and sets the media agenda.

Oscar H. Gandy, Jr., of the University of Pennsylvania, and other theorists have concluded that public relations professionals are major players in forming public opinion because they are often the first to provide mass media with information. Although journalists argue that they rarely use public relations materials, one simply has to look at the daily newspaper to see this type of material—for example,

comes from public relations sources in the form of "information subsidies."

To better understand how public relations practitioners inform the public and shape public opinion via the mass media, let's review briefly some theories about mass media effects.

Agenda Setting

One early theory, pioneered by mass communications researchers Max McCombs and Don Shaw, contends that media content sets the agenda for public discussion. People tend to talk about what they see or hear on the television news programs or read on the front pages of newspapers. According to this theory, the media, by selecting stories and headlines, tell the public what to think about, albeit not necessarily what to think. The war on terrorism, for example, ranked high on the media agenda for several years, but public opinion polls indicated a variety of viewpoints on the subject. Social scientist Joseph Klapper calls this the limited-effects model of mass media. He postulates, "Mass media ordinarily does not serve as a necessary and sufficient cause for audience effects, but rather functions among and through a nexus of mediating factors and influence." Such factors include the way that opinion leaders analyze and interpret the information provided by the mass media.

More recently, Wayne Wanta of Oklahoma State University and other scholars of agenda-setting theory have found evidence that the

Tourists Beware?

A number of news stories about the 2005 disappearance of Alabama high school student Natalee Holloway focused on the potential danger for tourists in Aruba. The island actually has a relatively low crime rate compared to other countries in the region. Nevertheless, the attention devoted to the Holloway case led to the public perception in the United States that travel to Aruba might be ill advised.

media not only set agendas but also convey a set of attributes about the various subjects in the news. These positive or negative attributes are internalized and, in turn, color public opinion. Research is ongoing regarding how public relations efforts can build the media agenda, and thus affect public opinion.

From a public relations standpoint, even getting a subject on the media agenda is an accomplishment that advances organizational goals. In a striking example, sales of Apple's iPhone rose as the media reported on its success and the public became increasingly aware of this "hot" item.

Framing

Media content is influenced by a broad array of forces, ranging from the professionalism of individual journalists to corporate ownership

a quote from the press officer at the sheriff's department, an article on a new computer product, statistics from the local real estate board, or even a postgame interview with the winning quarterback. In almost all cases, a public relations source provided the information or arranged the interview. Indeed, Gandy estimates that as much as 50 percent of what the media carry

of media outlets to cultural and ideological factors, according to Pamela J. Shoemaker at Syracuse University and Steve Reeves at the University of Texas–Austin. Traditionally, framing theory was related to how journalists selected certain facts, themes, treatments, and even words to "frame," or shape, a story. This effort goes beyond journalists' simple selection of potential news stories in their role as gatekeepers and involves their interpretation of issues or creation of subtle nuances. For example, how media frame the debate over health care and the role of health maintenance organizations often plays a major role in public

> **Mass media scholars have long argued that it is important to understand the ways in which journalistic framing of issues occurs because such framing impacts public understanding and, consequently, policy formation.**
>
> Julie L. Andsager, University of Iowa and Angela Powers, Kansas State University.

perceptions of the issues involved.

Increasingly, scholars and professionals apply framing theory to public relations efforts. In a paper titled "PR Goes to War: The Effects of Public Relations Campaigns on Media Framing of the Kuwait and Bosnian Crises," James Tankard and Bill Israel noted that the governments involved in these conflicts used public relations professionals to help frame the issues involved. The issues, as framed by public relations professionals, were then reflected in press coverage and, in turn, influenced the public's opinion about the crises. Tankard and Israel point out that the media dependency of most Americans—who often have little direct knowledge of such faraway places or the complex issues involved in international conflicts—means that they accept the media's version of reality, which originally came from what the two researchers describe as "special interest groups or other groups with particular causes."

Dietram Scheufele at the University of Wisconsin–Madison suggests that two types of framing exist: media framing and audience framing. He argues that framing is a continuous process and that the behavioral, attitudinal, cognitive, and affective statuses of individuals influence how they interpret issues. For example, voters in Florida may be less likely to respond favorably to a story about increased school funding, because a large number of Floridians are older than the age of 65 (16.7 percent) and have already raised their children. Conversely, voters in Georgia, a state with fewer people older than age 65 (9.2 percent), might react more favorably to school funding increases. However, a range of variables, beliefs, and attitudes simultaneously affect how individuals interpret an issue.

think — What role does the media play in forming the public opinion of you and your peers?

Political science professors Shanto Iyengar and Donald Kinder focus on the media's power to prime people in a more subtle but significant form of persuasive effect. They note how public relations professionals working for political campaigns seek to emphasize considerations that will help voters decide in their favor, often enlisting the expertise of a popular leader in service of this objective, and to downplay those considerations that will hurt their cause or candidate. Ultimately, the goal is to encourage voters to change the basis on which they make decisions about voting rather than simply change their choices about a given candidate or issue.

btw...

Most public relations personnel rarely find themselves framing the issues of an international conflict, but they do exercise framing or positioning strategies for any number of products and services. For example, when Edelman was considering the best strategy for the launch of Apple's iMac computer, one of the strong themes (or frames) it developed was that Apple was on the way back to prosperity after several years of massive losses and erosion of customer support. Indeed, one headline in a daily newspaper proclaimed, "Apple Regains Its Stride." Such framing obviously bolstered investor and consumer confidence in the company.

Censorship & Google China

Entry into a global market poses public relations opportunities and challenges for diverse kinds of companies because of the different and often conflicting cultures, values, norms, rules, and laws they inevitably encounter when venturing outside their domestic market. Companies can hardly succeed in a foreign market unless they can win the court of public opinion at home.

The market for Internet service in China holds enormous profit potential for U.S.

computer software and support corporations. With an estimated 400 million current Internet users (a number close to, or exceeding, the number of users in the United States) and a total population estimated at more than 1.5 billion as of July 2009, the potential for growth in China is staggering. Thus it is comes as little surprise that Google, together with rivals Yahoo!, Microsoft, and local Chinese company Baidu and Alibaba, were eager to sign deals with the Chinese government to provide Internet service and support. However, that decision has come at a notable cost.

At the crux of the issue is the Chinese government's insistence that all online activity be subject to scrutiny by the Golden Shield Project, which is thought to employ approximately 30,000 "Internet police." The Golden Shield (also known as "The Great Firewall of China") censors content it considers obscene or offensive. It has also restricted political speech, blocking search terms related to such topics as Falun Gong, Tiananmen Square, Tibet and the Dalai Lama, freedom of the press, and the Taiwanese government. Strangely enough, the Golden Shield also blocks search terms related to Karl Marx and communism. Google initially agreed to abide by this censorship practice in order to do business in China and faced widespread criticism for doing so.

Although Kai-Fu Lee, CEO of Google China, resigned in September 2009 amid the heated debate over censorship issues, Google remained adamant about its decision to enter the Chinese market. The company defended its actions by arguing that Internet service with restrictions is better than no Internet service at all. In March 2010 Google suddenly reversed course. They stopped censoring Internet searches, closed google.cn and began routing traffic through Hong Kong. The decision to abandon the Chinese market may have a significant impact on the company's bottom line, costing as much as $30 billion in revenue over time. However, the company's stand on principal may pay dividends across the globe. According to financial analyst Andrew Whit, the company now has "irreproachable proof of its editorial objectivity."

What would you do? Do you think Chinese "Netizens" will suffer or benefit from Google's decision to withdraw to Hong Kong?

How does Google's decision to pull out of China affect public perception about the company?

What strategies could Google use to manage public relations if it were to return to China?

THE ROLE OF conflict

the process of public discourse is often rooted in conflict. Social scientists and legal scholars define conflict as any situation in which two or more individuals, groups, organizations, or communities perceive a divergence of interests. Conflict theory offers insight into differences among individuals or groups and explains conflicting interests, goals, values, or desires. Public opinion often reflects such

different, or even conflicting, views, attitudes, and behaviors.

According to conflict resolution scholars Morton Deutsch and Peter Colman, conflict in the public arena does not necessarily yield negative outcomes, but rather creates a constructive process that builds toward consensus. Indeed, conflict or consensus is an actual theme of court opinions, which regulate and help ensure social stability and peaceful

change within a democratic society. Conflict itself is an inherent constraint within social structures.

Controversies often serve to shape public opinion intensively and extensively. Public relations professionals frequently have the challenging role of trying to minimize or resolve controversy in conflict situations.

At other times public relations practitioners may generate or promote controversy to engender positive or supportive public opinion. The Western Fuels Association, for example, hired Jack Bonner to manufacture a "grassroots" public relations campaign between 1997 and 2001. The website www.globalwarmingcost.org posed as an informational site, but surreptitiously

Conflict, as a component of news, ranges from wars to philosophical differences of opinion. Daily news stories and op-ed pieces include people criticizing government agencies or policies, a company's fraud, or celebrity scandals. Given the public's penchant for pleasure in the tribulations of others and voyeurism, it is little wonder that the daily news is filled with stories of conflict and turmoil.

generated e-mails signed by those who answered questions about their heating costs to Congressional representatives who supported the Western Fuels Association's views.

Mass media play a role in the unfolding of a conflict and serve to promote public debate by engaging widespread public involvement, a process known as *escalation*. They may also mediate among parties and de-escalate the conflict. Often, increasing direct communication between parties does more harm than good, as the same arguments tend to repeated in a destructive way and non-negotiable positions are confirmed and hardened. Mediated communication and shuttle diplomacy can be an effective means of resolving conflict, particularly at the early stages of a dispute. The role of the media is to interpret the issue, deliver the position of the opposing party, and even suggest avenues for resolution. George Will's "The Last Word" columns and Fareed Zakaria's editorials in *Newsweek* provide excel-

lent examples of the media's ability to interpret competing positions and offer avenues for resolution. Not infrequently, well-reasoned counterpoints are printed in the same issue.

Conflict is inherent in how a reporter frames an issue, because the reporter's story on a conflict can be the sole information available to an audience. For example, a news story by an investigative reporter with special access to information about a controversial secret program at the Pentagon may represent the only perspective seen by the public. How that reporter frames the conflict can bias the public in favor of one party, or one solution, over another. Because the media are so crucial not only to presenting and explaining conflicts but also to keeping them from escalating, it is necessary for the parties involved in the conflict and public relations practitioners involved to know how to work effec-

tively with the media. Similarly, the media play a central role when public relations professionals want a conflict to escalate, thereby bringing the issue to the fore.

All too often conflict is regarded as more newsworthy than its resolution. Details about a volatile political election or corporate malfeasance are far more interesting to the public than the reporting of an amicable settlement or an acquittal.

The media's inclination to focus on tribulation posing as human interest often creates a dilemma for their sources. To maintain their credibility as objective judges of information, journalists are primed for conflict as part of their strategic approach to dealing with sources, whereas public relations practitioners, as advocates for favorable coverage, have a tendency to be

think Why do mass media news broadcasts emphasize conflict?

accommodative or cooperative with reporters, according to researchers Jae-Hwa Shin and Glen T. Cameron. The relationships between public relations professionals and journalists exist along a continuum ranging from conflict to cooperation. Public relations professionals should understand journalists' orientation to escalate conflict as a means of maintaining balance and independence. These practitioners should also try to transform conflicts in constructive ways. Rather than reporting only from the perspective of a dominant power such as governments and delivering the ideology of media conglomerates, the public interest can best be served by healthy competition among public relations sources and the media. From this perspective, public relations serves as a social force in the ongoing creation of news and news trends or agendas.

The PR Casebook box on page 169 looks at how Wal-Mart has negotiated a stream of negative publicity through crisis management public relations.

btw...

A radio-frequency transmitting ID-tag system for consumer goods, introduced in 2003, enabled products that consumers purchase to be identified and tracked along the supply chain. The nonprofit group Consumers Against Supermarket Privacy Invasion and Numbering raised concerns about potential for abuse that could result from companies collecting and storing personal information about individual consumer habits. Massachusetts Institute of Technology (MIT), which developed the tags, hired PR firm Fleishman-Hillard to "neutralize opposition," according to an article in *PRWeek*. Part of the strategy used was "conveying the inevitability of technology."

persuasion
IN PUBLIC OPINION

Persuasion has been around since the dawn of human history. More than 2,500 years ago, the Greeks formalized the concept of persuasion by instituting rhetoric, the art of using language effectively and persuasively, as a central part of their educational system. Aristotle was the first to set down the ideas of ethos, logos, and pathos, which roughly translate to "source credibility," "logical argument," and "emotional appeal," respectively. Richard Perloff, author of *The Dynamics of Persuasion*, offers an updated definition of persuasion: "Persuasion is an activity or process in which a communicator attempts to induce a change in the belief, attitude, or behavior of another person or group of persons through the transmission of a message in a context in which the persuadee has some degree of free choice."

Most public relations efforts are persuasive communication management and ultimately seek to change the attitudes and behavior of people. For example, public relations professionals disseminate information about their products or services to potential customers in an effort to persuade them to recognize or buy those products or services. They also try to persuade legislators and other politicians in seeking favorable tax or regulatory actions. Politicians, for their part, use public relations to attract votes or raise money. Nonprofit organizations such as Greenpeace or the Red Cross persuade people to become aware of social or environmental issues, take actions, and donate money.

The dominant view of public relations is one of persuasive communication actions performed on behalf of clients, according to Professors Dean Kruckeberg at the University of North Carolina–Charlotte and Ken Starck at the University of Iowa. Oscar Gandy, Jr., adds that "the primary role of public relations is one of purposeful, self-interested

> **[P]ublic relations professionals are influential rhetors. They design, place, and repeat messages on behalf of sponsors on an array of topics that shape views of government, charitable organizations, institutions of public education, products and consumerism, capitalism, labor, health, and leisure. These professionals speak, write, and use visual images to discuss topics and take stances on public policies at the local, state, and federal levels.**
>
> Robert Heath, University of Houston

communications." Edward Bernays called public relations the "engineering" of consent to create "a favorable and positive climate of opinion toward the individual, product, institution, or idea which is represented."

The Uses of Persuasion

Persuasion is used to (1) change or neutralize hostile opinions, (2) crystallize latent opinions and positive attitudes, and (3) maintain favorable opinions.

The most difficult persuasive task is to turn hostile opinions into favorable ones. There is much truth to the old adage, "Don't confuse me with the facts; my mind is made up." Once people have decided, for instance, that oil companies are making excessive profits, they tend to ignore or disbelieve any information that contradicts this view. The

public may overlook information pointing to geopolitical factors or increased demand from countries such as China and India as affecting the price of oil, and instead believe that executives at Exxon-Mobil and the Shell Group are conspiring to gouge consumers. Each of us, as Walter Lippmann has described, has pictures in his or her head based

on an individual perception of reality. People generalize from personal experience, what they read in the newspaper or see on television, and what peers tell them. For example, if a person has an encounter with a rude clerk, the inclination is to generalize that the entire department store chain is not very good.

Persuasion becomes much easier when the message is compatible with a person's general disposition toward a subject. For example, if a person tends to identify Toyota as a company with a good reputation, he or she may express this feeling by purchasing one of its cars. A recall can adversely affect consumer opinion quickly, however. Nonprofit agencies usually crystallize the public's inherent inclination to aid the less fortunate by asking for donations. Both examples illustrate the reason why organizations strive to have a good reputation—it translates into sales and donations.

War over Wal-Mart: Retail Giant Fights Back

FOR MORE THAN A DECADE, the retail giant Wal-Mart has been under fire from critics who claim the company exploits its workers by paying low wages and paltry benefits, contributes to the trade deficit by encouraging overseas sweatshops in places such as China, and destroys neighborhood businesses through uncompetitive pricing. The negative publicity directed at the company was exacerbated by a series of lawsuits calling attention to the alleged poor treatment of its employees, a dramatic 2005 documentary entitled *Wal-Mart: The High Cost of Low Price*, and pressure from activist groups including Wal-Mart Watch and Wake-Up Wal-Mart. Wal-Mart has made strides to improve its image and has redressed many of the charges of unfair treatment of their workers.

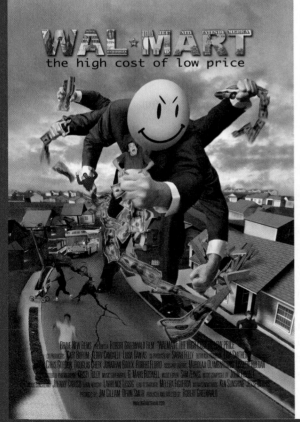

Despite these gains, Wal-Mart continues to draw fire for its labor practices. Wal-Mart Watch, for example, is highly critical of the company for its strident opposition of the Employee Free Choice Act. The act would allow employees the right to negotiate wages and other benefits through collective bargaining and unions.

Wal-Mart has also been criticized for being slow to offer affordable health insurance to its employees. Wal-Mart Watch has estimated that a worker could pay as much as $12,000 to insure his or her family with the company's plan—a particularly burdensome figure considering that the average employee salary in 2009 was approximately $20,000 per year.

On its behalf, the company has pointed out that opinion polls show that working families support Wal-Mart. Polls conducted by Quinnipiac University and the Pew Charitable Trusts (PCT) reported that 69 to 70 percent of American families had a favorable opinion of the retailer in 2004. However, the PCT poll also revealed that 31 percent of respondents had a negative opinion of the retailer. More recently, Wal-Mart ranked at the bottom when respondents were asked which company came to mind when they thought of "the most socially responsible company" as part of the Corporate Citizenship Study conducted in June 2009 by Landor, Burson-Marsteller, and Penn, Scheon & Berland (a company that has recently won part of Wal-Mart's PR contract, previously administered exclusively by Edelman).

In 2005, the Wal-Mart PR team attempted to counter negative publicity by promoting *Why Wal-Mart Works & Why That Drives Some People C-r-a-z-y*, a film that casts the retailer in a more favorable light. The company has also made some significant recent strides to improve its public image. First, in spite of the fact Wal-Mart had earned a reputation as one of the strongest opponent of employer mandates, and currently provides health insurance to only 50 percent of its employees, the company announced in June 2009 that it supported the employer-mandated healthcare plan endorsed by President Barack Obama. Wal-Mart has also taken an aggressive stance on energy, partnering with the Alliance to Save Energy to educate consumers about ways to save money on gasoline, and the with National Association of Counties to promote energy efficiency in the home. The company made corresponding adjustments to its own energy use, earning a respectable fifty-ninth position among the 500 largest U.S. companies as ranked by *Newsweek,* with leading environmental researchers KLD Research & Analytics, Trucost, and Corporate Register.com, for its "green" practices.

1 What efforts did Wal-Mart make to counter negative public opinion?

2 What do public opinion polls now indicate about the reputation of Wal-Mart?

3 Do poll results show that Wal-Mart has improved its reputation?

A Major Persuasion Concept:
EVERYONE IS DOING IT

President Obama has tapped leading behavioral scientists to advise his administration on how to sell his ideas and policies to the American public. Research by behaviorists, for example, points out that the messages should remain simple (like Obama's mantras of "change" and "hope" as presidential campaign themes) and relay the impression that "everyone is doing it."

Robert Cialdini, author of the popular book *Influence*, told Michael Grunwald of *Time* magazine, "People want to do what they think others will do." Cialdini and other behaviorists say getting people to alter their behavior is difficult, but they suggest the following strategies may be effective.

Make It Clear

Better information and more lucid material, from sources such as websites that explain the situation, can help people make better choices. "Public outreach and celebrity spokespersons can help; strict rules requiring disclosure can clarity can help more."

Make It Easy

Individuals are lazy. Enrolling people for a service or program is better than asking them to sign up themselves. That's why magazines automatically extend subscriptions, and a person has to take action to opt out. In most cases, people don't opt out because it takes more effort. "We'll do almost anything—even things that are good for us—to avoid extra paperwork."

Make It Popular

According to Grunwald, "Nothing drives behavior more than the power of conformity. Research shows that homeowners are most likely to save energy, weatherize, or recycle when they think everyone else is doing it."

Persuasion and Negotiation

Persuasion is comparable to negotiation. Negotiation is the process by which two or more parties attempt to settle disputes, reach agreement about courses of action, and bargain for individual or collective advantage. Negotiation is sometimes used in lieu of bringing a lawsuit in the courts as a means of alternative dispute resolution (ADR), whereas persuasion conspicuously occurs in the marketplace as a form of communicative action, according to professor Jae-Hwa Shin at the University of Southern Mississippi. In nearly all cases, some degree of conflict exists between parties, both in persuasion and in negotiation. Like negotiators, a persuader and the persuadee intentionally or unconsciously bargain according to their interests, values, or needs and, ideally, are willing to compromise on the differences. There is always some degree of resistance on the part of the persuadee based on his or her inclination to accept or reject the persuader's message and terms.

How parties position themselves before negotiations begin can be crucial to how the give-and-take unfolds. Public relations can play a major role in this positioning. As a consequence, persuasion is an integral component of the public relations effort to bring parties into ultimate agreement. For example, using persuasion to put your organization on an equal footing with a competitor could lead to the realization that the two parties need to talk. In other words, public relations can be used as a tool leading to the ADR process. ADR takes place outside the traditional courtroom and has gained acceptance among public relations professionals, the legal profession, and the public at large. It is typically much less expensive, and often much more efficient, than a traditional lawsuit.

"Public relations, based on the contingency theory, can be viewed as a constructive creator of antecedent conditions for alternative dispute resolution," note researchers Bryan Reber, Fritz Cropp, and Glen Cameron. They illustrate this idea with a case in which public relations and legal professionals worked cooperatively to negotiate the hostile takeover bid of Conrail by Norfolk Southern railroad in the mid-1990s. Conrail resisted Norfolk Southern's bid to buy the company, favoring a deal tendered by CSX that was less favorable to Conrail's stockholders.

With the help of a public relations campaign coordinated by Fleishman-Hilliard, Norfolk Southern effectively persuaded its target audiences that the company's offer was more fiscally sound, preserved competition, and best served shipping clients. The public relations campaign, which helped sway public opinion in Norfolk Southern's favor, facilitated the negotiation process. The three companies ultimately reached a mutually beneficial agreement: CSX would purchase Conrail and immediately sell 58 percent of the rail routes and assets to Norfolk Southern.

think What might the financial advantage of having a good reputation be to an organization?

factors IN PERSUASIVE COMMUNICATION

a number of factors are involved in persuasive communication, and public relations practitioners should be knowledgeable about each component embedded in the communication process: sender, message, channel, and receiver. The following section is a brief discussion of ten factors related to these components: (1) audience analysis, (2) appeals to self-interest, (3) audience participation, (4) suggestions for action, (5) source credibility, (6) clarity of message, (7) content and structure of messages, (8) channels, (9) timing and context, and (10) reinforcement.

Audience Analysis

Knowledge of audience characteristics such as beliefs, attitudes, values, concerns, and lifestyles is an essential part of persuasion. It helps communicators tailor messages that are salient, answer a felt need, and provide a logical course of action. Because demographic information cannot be changed and psychographic factors are not easily affected by a public relations campaign, understanding such predisposing characteristics is critical to creating messages that do not conflict with those characteristics.

Basic *demographic* information, which is readily available through census data, can help determine an audience's age, gender, ethnicity, income, education, and geographic residence groupings. Other data that are often gathered by marketing departments include information on a group's buying habits, disposable income, and ways of spending leisure time. Polls and surveys may tap a target audience's attitudes, opinions, and concerns. Such research can reveal much about the public's resistance to some ideas, as well as its predisposition to support others.

Another audience-analysis tool is *psychographics*. This method attempts to classify people based on their lifestyle, attitudes, values, and beliefs. The Values and Lifestyle Program, known as VALS, was developed by SRI International, a research organization in Menlo Park, California. VALS is routinely used in public relations to help communicators structure persuasive messages to different elements of the population. A good illustration is the way Burson-Marsteller used VALS in preparing a public relations campaign for the National Turkey Foundation. The client's problem was simple: how to encourage turkey consumption throughout the year, not just at Thanksgiving and Christmas.

PROPAGANDA

No discussion of persuasion would be complete without mentioning propaganda and the techniques associated with it. Its roots stretch back to the seventeenth century, when the Roman Catholic Church set up the Congregatio de Propaganda Fide ("congregation for propagating the faith"). Today, propaganda connotes falsehood, lies, deceit, disinformation, and duplicity—practices that opposing groups and governments accuse one another of employing. Advertising and public relations messages for commercial purposes often use several techniques commonly associated with propaganda:

- **Plain Folks**. An approach often used by individuals to show humble beginnings and empathy with the average citizen. Political candidates, in particular, are quite fond of recounting their "humble" beginnings.
- **Testimonial**. A frequently used device to achieve source credibility. A well-known expert, popular celebrity, or average citizen gives testimony about the value of a product or the wisdom of a decision.
- **Bandwagon**. The implication or direct statement that everyone wants the product or that the idea has overwhelming support encourages people to agree with the idea—for example, "Now it's easier than ever to learn why more people choose AT&T."
- **Card Stacking**. The selection of facts and data to build an overwhelming case on one side of the issue, while concealing the other side. This technique is particularly effective because what is presented is often factually accurate, but misleads by omitting crucial aspects that allow the audience to make an informed decision.
- **Transfer**. The technique of associating the person, product, or organization with something that has high status, visibility, or credibility. This approach is often used in advertising and political campaigns. For example, many car dealerships display enormous American flags, an unsubtle attempt to suggest that buying a new car is a patriotic act.
- **Glittering Generalities**. The technique of linking a cause, product, or idea with favorable abstractions such as freedom, justice, democracy, and the American way. Groups such as Hezbollah in the Middle East have sometimes linked acts of terrorism with the aim of achieving political freedom or social justice.

Public relations professionals should be aware of these techniques and make certain that they don't intentionally use them to deceive and mislead the public. Ethical responsibilities exist in every form of persuasive communication.

One element of the public was called "sustainers and survivors"; VALS identified members of this group as low-income, poorly educated, often elderly people who ate at erratic hours, consumed inexpensive foods, and seldom ate out. Another element was known as the "belongers," who were highly family oriented and served foods in traditional ways. The "achievers" were those who were more innovative and willing to try new foods.

Burson-Marsteller tailored a strategy for each group. This segmentation of the consumer market into various VALS lifestyles enabled the company to select appropriate media for pitching specific story ideas. An article placed in *True Experience*, a publication reaching a population with the demographic characteristics of survivors and sustainers, was headlined "A Terrific Budget-Stretching Meal." Articles in *Better Homes and Gardens* with such titles as "Streamlined Summer Classics" and stories about barbecued turkey on the Fourth of July were used to reach belongers. Articles for achievers in *Food and Wine* and *Gourmet* magazines included recipes for turkey salad and turkey tetrazzini.

Appeals to Self-Interest

People become involved in issues or pay attention to messages that appeal to their psychological, economic, or situational needs. For example, if a cosmetics company wants to emphasize the antiaging effects of a new face cream, its messages might include testimonials from a well-known actress who may appeal to an older demographic group, such as Meryl Streep. If it wishes to market the product to younger women, it may seek to employ Kristen Stewart of *Twilight* movie fame.

Appeals to self-interest are also used by charitable organizations to increase donations. While charities don't sell products, they do need volunteers and donations. Charities can increase the effectiveness of their appeals by carefully structuring their messages to highlight what volunteers or donors might receive in return. This is not to say that altruism is dead. Thousands of people give freely of their time and money to

Demographics for Key Groups

Baby Boomers:

- Born between the 1946 and 1964
- Have established their careers and are planning for impending retirement
- Primary concerns include their health status and financial security
- Politically active and heavy consumers of print media and television

Generation X:

- Born between the mid-1960s and the early 1980s
- Heavy users of new media
- Tend to make purchases based on technological appeal

Millenials:

- Born between 1981 and 2000
- Under intense pressure from parents and peers to achieve
- Tend to follow structure, be team-oriented, and accept social mores

Because of their predisposition to novel, technological innovation, Generation Xers may be more likely to be interested in purchasing a revolutionary automobile during the first model year than boomers or millenials

charitable organizations, but they do receive something in return. The "something in return" may be self-esteem, ego gratification, recognition from peers and the community, a sense of belonging, the opportunity to make a contribution to society, or even a tax deduction. Public relations people understand these psychological needs and rewards, which explains why there is always recognition of volunteers in newsletters and at award banquets.

Twentieth-century American sociologist Harold Lasswell asserted that people are motivated by eight basic appeals: to power, respect, well-being, affection, wealth, skill, enlightenment, and physical and mental vitality. Psychologist Abraham Maslow, in his renowned psychological theory, asserted that any appeal to self-interest must be based on a five-level hierarchy of needs:

- The first (and lowest) level involves basic needs such as food, water, shelter, and even such things as transportation to and from work.
- The second level involves "security" needs; people need to feel secure in their jobs, safe in their homes, and confident about their retirement.
- The third level includes "belonging" needs—people seek association with others. This need explains why individuals join organizations or communities.
- The fourth level consists of "love" needs; humans have a need to be wanted and loved.
- At the fifth and highest level in Maslow's hierarchy are "self-actualization" needs.

Once the needs in the first four levels have been met, Maslow says that people are free to achieve maximum personal potential—for example, through traveling extensively or becoming a recognized expert on orchids.

Maslow's hierarchy helps to explain why some public information campaigns have difficulty getting their messages across to people classified in the VALS categories as "survivors" and "sustainers." Efforts to inform low-income groups about AIDS provide an example of this problem. For these groups, the potential danger of AIDS may be less arresting in comparison to the day-to-day problems of poverty and their pursuit of basic needs such as daily food and shelter.

The challenge for public relations personnel, as creators of persuasive messages, is to tailor information to create, fill, or reduce a need. According to social scientists, success in persuasion largely depends on accurate assessment of audience needs and their self-interests.

Why is it important for public relations people to understand people's basic needs?

Audience Participation

Attitude or beliefs are changed or enhanced by audience involvement and participation. Nineteenth-century showman P. T. Barnum clearly recognized the power of audience participation. He observed that many people were willing to pay admission to see obvious hoaxes, such as the "Feejee mermaid" (a stuffed monkey sewn to the tail of a fish), because they enjoyed the process of exposing the "humbuggery" to their presumably less sophisticated companions.

Today, audience participation can take many forms. For example, an organization may have employees discuss productivity in a quality-control circle. Management may already have figured out what is needed, but if workers are involved in the problem solving, they are more committed to making the solution work because they participated in the decision-making process. Participation may also be encouraged by distribution of samples, whereby companies let consumers try a product without expense.

Activist groups use participation as a way of helping people actualize their beliefs. Not only do rallies and demonstrations give people a sense of belonging, but the act of participation also reinforces their beliefs. Asking people to do something, such as conserve energy, collect donations, or picket, activates a form of self-actualization and commitment.

Suggestions for Action

A key principle of persuasion is that people endorse ideas and take actions only if they are accompanied by a proposed action from the sponsor. Recommendations for action must be clear to follow. Public relations practitioners not only must ask people to conserve energy, for instance, but must also furnish detailed data and ideas about how to do it.

Source Credibility

A message is more believable to an intended audience if the source has credibility with that audience. Source credibility is based on three factors.

The first factor is *expertise*. Does the audience perceive the person as an expert on the subject? The California Strawberry Advisory Board, for example, arranged for a home economist to appear on television talk shows to discuss nutrition and to demonstrate easy-to-follow strawberry recipes. The viewers, primarily homemakers, identified with the representative and found her highly credible. By the same token, a manufacturer of sunscreen lotion used a professor of pharmacology and a past president of the State Pharmacy Board to discuss the scientific merits of its sunscreen versus other suntan lotions.

The second component is *sincerity*. Does the person come across as believing what he or she is saying? Christopher Kennedy Lawford's book *Symptoms of Withdrawal* has been widely hailed as an honest portrayal of drug and alcohol addiction. Conversely, author James Frey's memoir on a similar subject, *A Million Little Pieces*, was exposed as containing fabrications. Nevertheless, the apparent sincerity of his descriptions of his struggle with drug addiction made the book a best seller before Frey was unmasked as a fraud.

The third component, which is even more elusive, is *charisma*. Is the individual attractive, self-assured, and articulate, projecting an image of competence and leadership? President Barack Obama is an excellent example. His polished, inspiring public speaking have made him a

PR CAMPAIGN PROVIDES REAL-WORLD SUGGESTIONS FOR ACTION

A campaign conducted by Pacific Gas & Electric Company provides an example of suggestions for action. The utility inaugurated a Zero Interest Program (ZIP) to offer customers a way to implement energy-saving ideas. The program involved several components:

- *Energy Kit.* A telephone hotline was established and widely publicized so interested customers could order an energy kit detailing what the average homeowner could do to reduce energy use.
- *Service Bureau.* The company, at no charge, sent representatives to homes to check the efficiency of water heaters and furnaces, measure the amount of insulation, and check doors and windows for drafts.
- *ZIP.* The cost of making a home more energy efficient was funded by zero-interest loans to qualified customers.

A Friend's Recommendation Is MOST Trusted

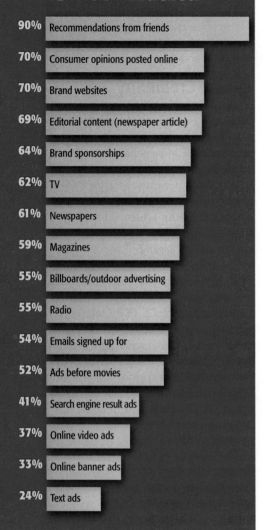

90%	Recommendations from friends
70%	Consumer opinions posted online
70%	Brand websites
69%	Editorial content (newspaper article)
64%	Brand sponsorships
62%	TV
61%	Newspapers
59%	Magazines
55%	Billboards/outdoor advertising
55%	Radio
54%	Emails signed up for
52%	Ads before movies
41%	Search engine result ads
37%	Online video ads
33%	Online banner ads
24%	Text ads

The Nielsen Global Online Consumer Survey of more than 25,000 Internet consumers in 50 nations found that recommendations from personal friends or opinions posted by consumers online are the most trusted form of source credibility. Advertisers and public relations personnel should be encouraged to learn that company websites are also trusted by 70 percent of consumers.

Source: Nielsen Global Online Consumer Survey, April 2009.

August 2007, football player Michael Vick was suspended from the NFL. When the conviction was announced, companies such as Nike, Kraft Foods, AirTran, and Coca-Cola suspended or failed to renew endorsement deals with Vick. He was subsequently released from the Atlanta Falcons, and his role as a spokesperson was complicated further by his prison sentence. Vick has recently signed with the Philadelphia Eagles—whether he can recover his prominence remains to be seen. Likewise, Tiger Woods, the most desired product spokesperson, has placed his career in jeopardy with alleged indiscretions.

"Anytime an advertiser pins its image to a star, whether an athlete or an actor, it takes a chance that reality won't live up to the storyboard," says Christina White, a reporter for the *Wall Street Journal*.

Studies show that the impact of a persuasive message will generally tend to decrease over time. The "sleeper effect" predicts that a message from a low-credibility source will actually increase in persuasiveness under the right circumstances. Low credibility may be caused by a "discounting cued", such as when a government official predicts improving economic conditions, because he or she is presumed to be biased. However, the message may gain credibility when dissociated from its source.

Clarity of Message

Many messages fail because the audience finds them unnecessarily complex in content or language. The most persuasive messages are direct, are simply expressed, and contain only one primary idea.

Public relations personnel should always ask two questions: (1) Will the audience understand the message? and (2) What do I want the audience to do with the message? Although persuasion theory says that people retain information better and form stronger opinions when they are asked to draw their own conclusions, this factor doesn't negate the importance of explicitly stating which action an audience should take. Is it to buy the product, visit a showroom, write a member of Congress, or make a $10 donation? If an explicit request for action is not part of the message, members of the audience may not understand what is expected of them.

> **think** What are the pros and cons of using celebrities for product endorsements?

charismatic figure. Obama has the aura of a person possessed of high intellect and is able to empathize with a broad range of people.

Using celebrities has its problems, however. One is sheer number of celebrity endorsements, to the point that the public sometimes can't remember who endorses what. A second problem can be overexposure of a celebrity, such as Anna Kournikova, who earns millions of dollars annually from endorsing several products.

The third problem occurs when an endorser's actions undercut the product or service. For example, after pleading guilty to animal cruelty in connection with dog fighting in

> **Management expert Peter Drucker once said, "An innovation, to be effective, has to be simple and it has to be focused. It should do only one thing, otherwise it confuses."**

Channels

Different media with different features can be used for diverse public relations purposes. Television is visual, sensational, and entertaining. Newspapers offer a lot of in-depth information and discuss conflicting views. Radio is flexible or adaptable in format and content, and is accessible to people at almost any place and at any time. Radio also reaches target audiences quickly, making it an effective means of communication in crisis situations. New forms of communication, such as Twitter, provide companies and organizations with the ability to reach thousands or millions of followers with instant, targeted messages. Likewise, social networking sites such as Facebook and

think Which channels would be most effective if you were promoting a new public recreation facility in your city?

MySpace are immediate channels of communication about an emerging event or crisis.

Ultimately, however, face-to-face communication is often more effective than mass media broadcasts. According to communication scholar Steve H. Chaffee, people seek information from available sources, and interpersonal sources often are effective ways to reach people, even through word of mouth. For exam-

ple, a company president speaking with employees who are threatening to strike may encourage a compromise through a personal appeal, whereas a mass-media message could make the employees angrier via interrupted messages, confused interpretation, or the impersonal nature of the statements.

Timing and Context

A message tends to be more persuasive if environmental factors support the message or if the message is received within the context of other messages and situations with which the individual is familiar. These factors are called *timing* and *context*, respectively. For example, information from a utility on how to conserve energy will be more salient if the consumer has just received a January

Content and Structure of Messages

A number of techniques can make a message more persuasive. Expert communicators employ many different devices for this purpose, including drama, surveys and polls, statistics, examples, mass media endorsements, and emotional appeals.

DRAMA AND STORIES The first task of a communicator is to get the audience's attention. This objective is often accomplished by graphically illustrating an event or situation. For instance, newspapers often dramatize a story to generate reader interest in an issue. Drama also is used in public relations. Relief organizations, in particular, attempt to galvanize public concern and donations through stark black-and-white photographs and emotionally charged descriptions of suffering and disease.

SURVEYS AND POLLS Airlines and auto manufacturers use the results of surveys and polls to show that they are first in "customer satisfaction," "service," and even "leg room" or "cargo space."

STATISTICS Numbers convey objectivity, size, and importance in a credible way that can influence public opinion. Caterpillar, for example, got considerable media publicity for its new 797 mining dump truck by combining statistics and some humor. In the news release for the largest truck in the world, the company announced that the bed of the truck was so large that it could haul the following payloads: 4 blue whales, 217 taxicabs, 1,200 grand pianos, or 23,490 Furby dolls.

EXAMPLES A statement of opinion is often more persuasive if some examples are given.

For instance, a school board may solicit support for a bond issue by citing examples of how present facilities are inadequate for student needs.

ENDORSEMENTS In addition to endorsements by paid celebrities, products and services may benefit from favorable statements by experts in the form of a third-party endorsement. A well-known medical specialist may publicly state that a particular brand of exercise equipment is best for general conditioning. The media also produce news stories about new products and services that, because of the media's perceived

objectivity, are considered a form of third-party endorsement.

CAUSES AND RATIONALES People tend to accept social ideas, norms, or practices engaged in by a group or society, thereby forging a psychological connection to the community. Public relations professionals must assess and understand the social norms of a target audience to provide messages that emphasize tangible social benefits. By advocating a cause that taps into social norms and one that an audience is passionate about, public relations personnel effectively reach the audience and generate goodwill. For example, an athletic footwear company, by sponsoring a breast cancer awareness event such as a walkathon, builds good faith with potential consumers whose norms support better health.

EMOTIONAL APPEALS Fund-raising letters from nonprofit groups, in particular, often use emotional appeals as a persuasive device. Such pleas can do much to galvanize the public into action—but they also can backfire. A description of suffering makes many people uncomfortable. As a result, they may tune out the message rather than take action. Research indicates, however, that moderate fear appeal, accompanied by a relatively easy solution, is effective. Allstate Insurance, for example, has run print ads warning about the dangers of texting while driving. The ad leads with the statistic that 5,000 teenagers will die as a result of texting at the wheel. Humor appeals are also effective at enhancing attention, message comprehension, and recall.

heating bill. A pamphlet on a new stock offering will be more effective if it accompanies an investor's dividend check. A citizens' group lobbying for a stoplight will receive more attention if a major accident has just occurred at the intersection in question.

Political candidates are aware of public concerns and avidly read polls to learn which issues are most important to voters. For example, if polls indicate that crime and unemployment are key issues, the candidate will refer to these issues—and offer his or her proposals to resolve them—in the campaign.

Timing and context also play an important role in achieving publicity in the mass media. Public relations personnel should read newspapers and watch television news programs to find out which topics the media gatekeepers consider newsworthy. A manufacturer of a locking device for computer files got extensive media coverage about its product simply because its release followed a rash of news stories about thieves' gaining access to bank accounts through computers. Public relations professionals aim to disseminate information at the time when it is most highly valued.

Reinforcement

People tend to ignore or react negatively to messages that conflict

with their value or belief systems. A public relations campaign that is out of sync with an audience's core beliefs is unlikely to be successful. For this reason, it is important for public relations professionals to have a firm understanding of the public's core values so they can be taken into consideration when designing a message aimed at that particular audience. Opponents to healthcare reform, for example, capitalized on the core values of many citizens who believed that the government should not be involved in administering healthcare plans.

People seek and support messages that support their currently held beliefs and avoid those that challenge these attitudes. Beliefs and attitudes that are not fully formed can be affected by persuasive messages; in contrast, long-established values are highly resistant to change. In addition, attitudes that have been tested are more resistant to change. Public relations professionals can use such inoculated attitudes to create resistance to potentially opposing arguments or negative publicity. In a crisis situation, inoculation accompanied by tested beliefs can help a public figure or a company get through a crisis and maintain its prior reputation.

the limits
OF PERSUASION

In reality, the effectiveness of persuasive techniques is greatly exaggerated. Persuasion is not an exact science, and no surefire way exists to predict that people or media gatekeepers will be persuaded to believe a message or act on it. If persuasive techniques were as refined as the critics say, all people

would be driving the same make of automobile, using the same soap, and voting for the same political candidate. In practice, the ability to persuade is contingent on a complex set of factors as opposed to persuasive messages that translate directly into behavior. Conflicting and competing messages frequently interrupt or cancel one another through a course of ongoing communication, given the freedom of receivers to be selective or even apathetic regarding particular messages.

For purposes of discussion, the limitations on effective persuasive messages can be listed as lack of message penetration, competing messages, self-selection, and self-perception.

Lack of Message Penetration

Despite modern communication technologies, the diffusion of messages is not pervasive. Not everyone, of course, watches the same television programs or reads the same newspapers and magazines. Not everyone views the same websites or reads the same blogs. Not everyone receives the same mail or attends the same meetings. Not everyone the communicator wants to reach will be in the eventual audience. Despite advances in audience-segmentation techniques, communicators cannot ensure that 100 percent of their intended audiences will be reached.

There is also the problem of message distortion as messages pass through media gatekeepers such as reporters and editors. Key message points often are left out, buried among less relevant information or placed in ineffective contexts, or even delivered in an unintended or negative way.

Competing or Conflicting Messages

Today, communication experts realize that no message is received in a vacuum. Messages are filtered through social structures and belief systems. Nationality, race, religion, gender, cultural patterns, family, and friends are among the variables that screen out and dilute persuasive messages. According to social scientists, a person usually conforms to the standards of his or her family and friends; most people do not believe or act on messages that are contrary to the norms of their peer group. In addition, people receive countless competing and conflicting messages daily, which often diffuses the persuasiveness of the message.

Self-Selection

The people most wanted in an audience are often the least likely to be there. Vehement supporters or loyalists frequently ignore information from the other side. They do so by being selective about messages that they listen to, reading books, newspaper editorials, blogs, and magazine articles and viewing television programs that support their predispositions. This tendency explains why social scientists say that the media are more effective in reinforcing existing attitudes than in changing them.

think

How might a PR campaign reach a person who does not watch TV or listen to radio?

Self-Perception

Self-perception is the channel through which messages are interpreted. Different people will perceive the same information differently, depending on their predispositions and preexisting opinions.

Depending on a person's views, an action by an organization may be considered a "great contribution to the community" or a "self-serving gimmick." Social judgment theory suggests that internal factors such as beliefs, attitudes, and values will limit the extent to which an individual accepts or rejects a persuasive message.

Persuasion DON'TS

Public relations professionals, by definition, are advocates for their clients and employers. Not surprisingly, then, they emphasize use of persuasive communication that presents a selective message so as to influence a particular public in some way. At the same time, public relations practitioners must conduct their activities in an ethical manner.

Persuasive messages require truth, honesty, and candor for two practical reasons. First, as noted by Robert Heath, a professor at the University of Texas–Houston, a message is already suspect because it is advanced on behalf of a client or organization. Second, half-truths and misleading information do not serve the best interests of the public or the organization.

The use of persuasive techniques, therefore, calls for some additional guidelines. Professor Richard L. Johannesen of Northern Illinois University, writing in Persuasion: Reception and Responsibility, a text by Charles Larson, lists the following ethical criteria for using persuasive devices that should be kept in mind by every public relations professional:

- **DON'T** use false, fabricated, misrepresented, distorted, or irrelevant evidence to support arguments or claims.
- **DON'T** intentionally use specious, unsupported, or illogical reasoning.
- **DON'T** represent yourself as informed or as an "expert" on a subject when you are not.
- **DON'T** use irrelevant appeals to divert attention or scrutiny from the issue at hand. Among the appeals that commonly serve such a purpose are smear attacks on an opponent's character and appeals to hatred and bigotry or innuendo.
- **DON'T** ask your audience to link your idea or proposal to emotion-laden values, motives, or goals to which it actually is not related.
- **DON'T** deceive your audience by concealing your real purpose, your self-interest, the group you represent, or your position as an advocate of a viewpoint.
- **DON'T** distort, hide, or misrepresent the number, scope, intensity, or undesirable features of consequences.
- **DON'T** use emotional appeals that lack a supporting basis of evidence or reasoning or that would not be accepted if the audience had time and opportunity to examine the subject itself.
- **DON'T** oversimplify complex situations into simplistic, two-valued, either–or, polar views or choices.
- **DON'T** pretend certainty when tentativeness and degrees of probability would be more accurate.
- **DON'T** advocate something in which you do not believe yourself.

Summary

What Is Public Opinion? p. 160

- Public opinion can be difficult to measure; there are few, if any, issues on which the public (which is, in fact, many publics) can be said to have a unanimous opinion. In reality, only a small number of people will have opinions on any given issue.

- Engaging the interest of a public involves affecting its self-interest.

Who Are Opinion Leaders? p. 162

- People who are knowledgeable and articulate on specific issues can be either formal opinion leaders (power leaders) or informal opinion leaders (role models).

- Opinion "flows" from these leaders to the public, often through the mass media.

What Role Do the Mass Media Play in Shaping Public Opinion? p. 164

- Information from public relations sources often reaches the public through mass media, defined as radio, television, newspaper, magazines, and electronic media.

- The mass media frame issues insofar as journalists select certain facts and disregard others.

- Journalists and public relations professionals frequently use the agenda-setting process in public discourse and act as gatekeepers, subtly affecting how the public interprets issues through selectiveness and nuance.

How Does Conflict Affect Public Discourse? p. 166

- Conflict has been defined as a situation in which two or more factions perceive a divergence of interests. In public relations, conflict theory offers insight into the differences among individuals and groups and analyzes conflicts of interest, goals, desires, and values.

- The media play a role in unfolding conflicts and can promote public debate regarding the issue. The media also mediate or resolve conflicts in the court of public opinion by offering directions for conflict resolution.

What Makes Communication Persuasive? p. 171

- The dominant view of public relations is that its practitioners engage in persuasive communications on behalf of their clients.

- Persuasion can be used to change or neutralize hostile opinions, crystallize latent opinions and positive attitudes, and reinforce favorable opinions.

- Factors involved in persuasion include audience analysis, audience participation, suggestions for action, source credibility, appeal to self-interest, message clarity, content and structure of messages, timing and context, and channels.

What Are the Limitations of Persuasion? p. 176

- The limitations on effective persuasive messages include lack of message penetration, competing messages, self-selection, and self-perception.

QUESTIONS
for *Review* and *Discussion*

1. Public opinion is highly influenced by self-interest and events. Define and explain these concepts.

2. What is the role of opinion leaders in the formation of public opinion?

3. What is the role of media in the formation of public opinion?

4. Which theories about mass media effect are relevant to the formation of public opinion?

5. Name the three objectives of persuasion in public relations work. Which objective is the most difficult to accomplish?

6. Name and describe the nine factors involved in persuasive communication.

7. List the three factors involved in source credibility.

8. List the five levels of Maslow's hierarchy of needs. Why is it important for public relations people to understand people's basic needs?

9. Which techniques can be used to write persuasive messages?

10. Name several propaganda techniques and list ways they might be employed by public relations practitioners.

the
THINK SPOT
www.thethinkspot.com

9 ETHICS AND

Ask Yourself

> Why Is Ethics a Relevant Issue for Public Relations Practitioners? p. 182

> What Do Public Relations Professionals Need to Know About Defamation, Employee and Privacy Rights, Copyright, and Trademark Laws? p. 186

> Which Guidelines and Government Agencies Govern the Commercial Speech Used by Public Relations Professionals? p. 196

> How Can Public Relations Professionals Facilitate Good Working Relationships with Lawyers? p. 199

Turkeys and Eagles

In 2008, Scott McClellan, press secretary for the George W. Bush administration, wrote a "tell-all" critical book in which he admitted that he lied to Americans, albeit inadvertently. The admission led to a firestorm of criticism of McClellan as well as the public relations profession. In its defense, the Public Relations Society of American (PRSA) condemned McClellan, asserting, "The McClellan book raises critical issues about the role of public relations professionals and ethical obligations." The statement, issued by Jeffrey Julin, chair and CEO of the PRSA, went on to list sections from the organization's Code of Ethics that urge practitioners to engage in truthful communication.

Legal news analyst Andrew Cohen reacted in a commentary aired on *CBS Sunday Morning*, stating, "Apparently an industry—the very essence of which is to try to convince people that a turkey is really an eagle—has a rule that condemns lying." He went on to aggressively critique the PRSA reaction: "The Public Relations Society of America states, 'We adhere to the highest standards of accuracy and truth in advancing the interests of those we represent.' This clause strikes me as if the Burglar's Association of America had as its creed, 'Thou shalt not steal.'

Cohen continued, "Show me a PR person who is accurate and truthful, and I'll show you a PR person who is unemployed. The reason companies or governments hire oodles of PR people is because PR people are trained to be slickly untruthful, or half truthful ..."

THE LAW

In an open letter to Cohen, Julin responded: "Contrary to baseless assertions, truth and accuracy are the bread and butter of the public relations profession. In a business where success hinges on critical relationships built over many years with clients, journalists, and a Web 2.0–empowered public, one's credibility is the singular badge of viability."

Cohen wrote his own open letter: "I am sure there are honest and accurate public relations people out there." But he didn't back down from his earlier thesis: "I am sorry if it offended some of you. But consider it a wake-up call. For a profession that lives or dies on public perceptions, you folks in public relations have as much work to do as the legal profession and the journalism profession (and the political profession) in changing the negative attitudes of your now-cynical audiences."

❶ Do you think Cohen's assertions are correct? Explain your answer.

❷ Is the public relations profession inherently unethical because it advocates for its organizations or clients? Why or why not?

❸ How can public relations improve its image as an ethical profession?

WHAT IS ethics?

today's public relations practitioners are faced with myriad ethical dilemmas and legal issues. A well-prepared professional is ready to deal effectively with these issues. In this chapter, we examine some of the ethical concerns and legal issues facing public relations practitioners.

A person's conduct is measured not only against his or her conscience, but also against some norm of acceptability that is determined by society, professional groups, or even a person's employer. The difficulty in ascertaining whether an act is ethical lies in the fact that individuals have different standards and perceptions of what is "right" or "wrong." Most ethical conflicts are not black-or–white issues, but rather fall into a gray area.

The Ethical Advocate

Because public relations practitioners serve as advocates for their organizations or clients and yet also must strive to represent the interests of various stakeholders in their organizations, difficult ethical issues are bound to arise. Students, as well as public relations critics, are often concerned about whether a public relations practitioner can ethically communicate at the same time he or she is serving as an advocate for a particular client or organization. To some, traditional ethics prohibits a person from assuming an advocacy role because in that role a person is "biased" and trying to "manipulate" people.

David L. Martinson of Florida International University makes the point, however, that the concept of role differentiation is important. Society, in general, expects public relations people to be advocates, just as they expect advertising copywriters to make a product sound attractive, journalists to be objective,

> **Ethics is concerned with how we should live our lives. It focuses on questions about what is right or wrong, fair or unfair, caring or uncaring, good or bad, responsible or irresponsible, and the like.**
>
> James Jaksa and Michael Pritchard
> in *Communication Ethics: Methods of Analysis*

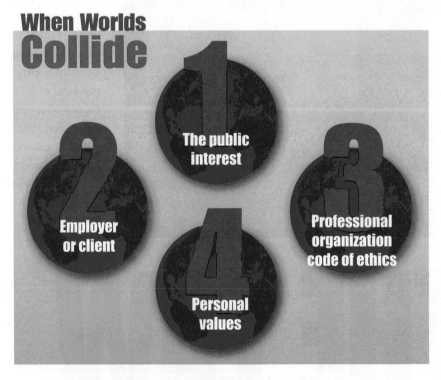

When Worlds Collide

1. The public interest
2. Employer or client
3. Professional organization code of ethics
4. Personal values

and attorneys to defend someone in court. Because of such expectations, Martinson believes that "Public relations practitioners are justified in disseminating persuasive information so long as objective and reasonable persons would view those persuasive efforts as truthful." Some public relations theorists have argued that pure advocacy—that is, unwavering support for the organization's or client's position—is unethical. They suggest that the most ethical way to practice public relations is to consider accommodating the needs of both organizations and their publics.

Contingency theory takes a more nuanced view. From this perspective, public relations practitioners sometimes face a categorical imperative, or moral obligation, to advocate purely for the organization's position. For example, what would the ethical advocate representing the cattle industry do when faced with demands from People for the Ethical Treatment of Animals (PETA) to stop producing beef products? Would the ethical advocate—a person who works for the cattle industry because he or she believes in modern agriculture's role in feeding the world—attempt to find ways to accommodate PETA's demands? Or would he or she continue to purely advocate for cattle-raising clients? Instances frequently arise when conflict between an organization and its publics is unavoidable due to a clash of worldviews. To accommodate the demands of a public, such as PETA, would be unethical when a categorical moral imperative to advocate for your organization or client drives your professional decisions.

think When is it the moral obligation of a public relations professional to advocate purely for a client's position, even in the face of opposition?

WHAT WOULD YOU DO if you were asked to keep news about a planned layoff from your coworkers?

WHAT IF YOUR SUPERVISOR asked you to defend your company's questionable environmental practices?

WHAT IF YOUR CLIENT asked you to make positive, but unsubstantiated, claims about a new product?

professional
GUIDELINES

Professional organizations such as the Public Relations Society of America and the International Association of Business Communicators (IABC) have developed standards for ethical, professional public relations practice and worked to help society understand the role of public relations. Practitioners and public relations scholars alike suggest that professional organizations can play a key and powerful role in advancing ethical practice.

Codes of Conduct

Nearly every national public relations organization has developed a code of ethics, and the codes of such organizations as the Canadian Public Relations Society (CPRS), the Public Relations Institute of Southern Africa (PRISA), and the Public Relations Institute of Australia (PRIA) are very similar to the PRSA code. Most national organizations place heavy emphasis on educating their members on professional standards rather than having a highly structured grievance process in place. They do exercise the right, however,

PRSA CODE OF ETHICS

The Public Relations Society of America (PRSA) has a fairly comprehensive code of ethics for its members. The group believes that "professional values are vital to the integrity of the profession as a whole."

Its six core values are as follows:

1 ADVOCACY: Serving the public interest by acting as responsible advocates for clients or employers.

2 HONESTY: Adhering to the highest standards of accuracy and truth in advancing the interests of clients and employers.

3 EXPERTISE: Advancing the profession through continued professional development, research, and education.

4 INDEPENDENCE: Providing objective counsel and being accountable for individual actions.

5 LOYALTY: Being faithful to clients and employers, but also honoring an obligation to serve the public interest.

6 FAIRNESS: Respecting all opinions and supporting the right of free expression.

The following is a summary of the major provisions and the kinds of activities that would constitute improper conduct.

Free Flow of Information

The free flow of accurate and truthful information is essential to serving the public interest in a democratic society. You should not give an expensive gift to a journalist as a bribe so that he or she will write favorable stories about the organization or its products.

Competition

Healthy and fair competition among professionals should take place within an ethical framework. An employee of an organization should not share information with a public relations firm that is in competition with other firms for the organization's business. You should not disparage your competitors or spread malicious rumors about them to recruit business or to hire their employees.

Disclosure of Information

Open communication is essential to informed decision making in a democratic society. You should not conduct grassroots and letter-writing campaigns on behalf of undisclosed interest groups. In addition, you should not deceive the public by employing people to pose as "volunteers" at a public meeting. Intentionally leaving out essential information or giving a false impression of a company's financial performance is considered "lying by omission." If you do discover that inaccurate information has been disseminated, you have a responsibility to correct it immediately.

Safeguarding Confidences

Client trust requires appropriate protection of confidential and private information. You should not leak proprietary information that could adversely affect some other party. If you change jobs, you should not use confidential information from your previous employer to increase the competitive advantage of your new employer.

Conflicts of Interest

Avoid real, potential, or perceived conflicts of interest among clients, employers, and the public. A public relations firm should inform a prospective client that it already represents a competitor or has a conflicting interest.

Enhancing the Profession

Public relations professionals should work constantly to strengthen the public's trust in the profession. If a product is unsafe under certain usage or conditions, you have an obligation to disclose this information.

to censure or expel members who violate the organization's code or who are convicted of a crime in a court of law.

The IABC's code is based on the principle that professional communication should be not only legal and ethical, but also in good taste and sensitive to cultural values and beliefs. Members are encouraged to be truthful, accurate, and fair in all of their communications. The code is published in several languages, and IABC bylaws require that articles on ethics and professional conduct be published in the organization's monthly publication, *Communication World*. In addition, the organization includes sessions on ethics at its annual meeting, conducts workshops on ethics, and encourages chapters to include discussions of ethics in their local programs.

Critics often complain that such codes of ethics "have no teeth" because there's really no punishment for being unethical and unprofessional. Even if a practitioner is expelled from the organization, he or she can continue to work in the public relations field.

Problems with code enforcement are not unique to public relations groups, of course. Professional organizations, including the Society for Professional Journalists, are voluntary organizations, and they lack the legal authority to ban members from the field because no license is required to practice. Such organizations run a high risk of being sued for defamation or restricting the First Amendment

think If a profession does not license its members, can it enforce ethical standards?

guarantee of free speech if they try to expel members or restrict their occupations.

Consequently, most professional groups believe that the primary purpose of establishing codes of ethics is not enforcement, but rather education and information.

PRSA CONDEMNS Deceptive Practices

The Public Relations Society of America (PRSA) issued a statement in mid-2009 that condemned instances of malpractice in public relations work. It reads: "PRSA states categorically that misrepresenting the nature of editorial content or intentionally failing to clearly reveal the source of message contents is unethical."

The statement condemned practices such as the following:

► A public relations firm allegedly asked its interns to write positive product reviews for online message boards.

► A lobbying firm sent out letters using letterheads taken from other organizations.

► Bloggers posted favorable reviews about products but failed to disclose that they were paid for their postings.

► Special-interest groups created and funded "citizen" front groups to disseminate information without disclosing the actual source.

They seek to enunciate standards of conduct that will guide members in their professional lives. This approach seems to work. Several studies have shown that the members of PRSA and other organizations have a much higher awareness of ethics and professional standards than nonmembers.

Ethics in Individual Practice

Even in light of codes of professional practice and formalized accreditation, ethics in public relations can boil down to deeply troubling questions for the individual practitioner: Would I lie for my employer? Would I rig a doorprize drawing so that a favorite client can win? Would I deceive someone to gain information about another agency's clients? Would I cover up a hazardous condition? Would I issue a news release presenting only half the truth? Would I quit my job rather than cooperate in a questionable activity? In other words, to what extent, if

any, would I compromise my personal beliefs?

These and similar questions plague the lives of many public relations professionals. If employers make a suggestion that involves questionable ethics, the public relations person often can talk them out of the idea by citing the possible consequences of such an action—adverse media publicity, for example.

Adherence to professional standards of conduct—being truly independent—is the chief measure of a public relations professional. Faced with such personal demands as mortgages to pay and children to educate, practitioners may be strongly tempted to become sycophants and decline to express their views forcefully to an employer, or to resign. But ethics in public relations really begins with the individual—and is directly related to his or her own value system as well as to the good of society. Although it is important to show loyalty to an employer, practitioners must never allow a client or an employer to rob them of their self-esteem.

DEALING WITH THE news media

t he most practical consideration facing a public relations specialist in his or her dealings with the news media is that anything less than total honesty will destroy credibility and, with it, the practitioner's usefulness to an employer.

Achieving trust is the aim of all practitioners, and it can be earned only through highly professional and ethical behavior. Public relations practitioners should not undermine their relationship with members of the media by providing junkets of questionable merit, invitations to extravagant parties, expensive gifts, or personal favors to media representatives. Gifts of any kind, according to PRSA, can contaminate the free flow of accurate and truthful information to the public.

Although it may be presumed that public relations representatives would benefit from being able to influence journalists with gifts or offers of paid advertising, this is not the case. A major selling point of

....

In the AIG example, transparency of communication was important, and the perceived lack of it ultimately damaged the organization that public relations was meant to help.

public relations work is the third-party credibility of reporters and editors. The public trusts journalists to be objective and to be basically impartial in the dissemination of information. If the public loses that trust because they believe the media can be "bought," the information provided by public relations sources also becomes less trusted.

Transparency is another issue. Should a celebrity who mentions a product on a television talk show reveal that he or she is being paid by the company to endorse its product? Should tax dollars be spent on public relations? These questions often lie at the heart of real-world situations.

For example, when the insurance giant American International Group (AIG) faced potential financial collapse in 2008 and 2009, the U.S. government provided $180 billion in "bailout" support to ensure the company's ongoing viability. In exchange, U.S. taxpayers were awarded an 80 percent stake in the company. As AIG tried to emerge from its financial morass, it hired several outside public relations firms. The disclosure of AIG's retention of these outside pub-

think How can gift giving undermine the credibility of a public relations professional?

lic relations firms led to loud objections on Capitol Hill and elsewhere.

AIG company spokesman Nick Ashooh told *Time* magazine that the public relations firms had specific assignments: "Sard Verbinnen & Co. helps to structure statements on the bailout, Kekst & Co. focuses on sales of assets to pay back federal loans, Burson-Marsteller handles controversial issues, and Hill & Knowlton fields inquiries from Capitol Hill and prepares Congressional testimony for company officials. . . . If the criticism was we were running image-advertising or doing sponsorships to make ourselves look better, I could see that. But we're doing a lot of information processing. It's really been just responding to inquiries [from Congress and the press]."

Ashooh told *Time* that precisely what was being paid to the firms could not be disclosed because of the proprietary nature of contracts. Congressman Peter Welch (Democrat–Vermont) responded in *Time*, "That's the whole culture of concealment that's helped some of our bigger financial enterprises get away with murder." He argued that taxpayers are "entitled to know how company money is being spent" without the information being "dressed up with the benefit of high-priced media folks."

Liberal news commentator Rachel Maddow also took on AIG and its public relations firms, especially Burson-Marsteller. She said, "We're paying the bill for PR firms to spin us about how awesome AIG secretly is." After reciting a list of the firm's past and current clients, Maddow opined, "When evil needs public relations, evil has Burson-Marsteller on speed dial."

Following the broadcast of Maddow's critique, *PRWeek* reported that Burson-Marsteller CEO Mark Penn distributed an internal memo stating that Burson-Marsteller was "proud to work for AIG—work that has nothing to do with 'burnishing [its] image' but is all about helping this company handle the massive volume of media, government, and employee interest in [its] situation."

PUBLIC RELATIONS AND the law

just as public relations practitioners deal with ethical quandaries on a regular basis, so, too, do they face issues that can get themselves or their clients into legal trouble. Depending on the field of practice, regulatory and legal demands can be a part of everyday life for a public relations professional. Globalization adds to the complexity of dealing with these demands. And in all fields of practice, public relations professionals often find themselves dealing with legal questions regarding copyright, privacy, liability, and other related issues.

On more than one occasion, the courts have ruled that public relations firms cannot hide behind the defense of "The client told me to do it." Public relations firms have a legal responsibility to practice "due diligence" in the type of information and documentation supplied by a client. Regulatory agencies such as the Federal Trade Commission have power under the Lanham Act to file charges against public relations firms that distribute false and misleading information.

Legal HOT Water

The law and its many ramifications can be somewhat abstract to the average person. Many people may have difficulty imagining exactly how public relations personnel can run afoul of the law or generate a lawsuit simply by communicating information. What follows is a sampling of recent government regulatory agency cases and lawsuits that involved public relations materials and the work of practitioners:

- Cosmetic surgery company Lifestyle Lift paid a $300,000 settlement to the New York State Attorney General's office after being accused of having employees post fake consumer reviews online.
- The Securities and Exchange Commission (SEC) filed suit against MitoPharm Corporation and its public relations firm for hyping the benefits of MitoPharm's anti-aging and nutritional supplements. The lawsuit alleged that the PR firm "embarked on an aggressive public relations campaign that centered on the misleading promotion" of products.
- The Federal Trade Commission (FTC) ruled that two video news releases from King Pharmaceuticals were "false and misleading" because they omitted mention of the risks associated with a painkiller drug and presented misleading claims.

- American Apparel paid a $5 million settlement to film director Woody Allen for using his image in an advertising campaign and other promotional literature without his permission.
- Westwood One sued TransMedia and its client Pompano Helicopter for $42 million, alleging that they attempted to injure the radio network's stock prices and reputation through a series of defamatory news releases.
- A former employee filed a libel suit against office supply company Staples after the firm e-mailed a memo to 1,500 division employees stating that the employee was fired for violating company travel and expense reimbursements policies.
- A Chicago man sued for invasion of privacy after he appeared in a video news release for a cholesterol-lowering drug because the company and video producer didn't tell him the actual purpose of the taping.
- A San Francisco public relations practitioner who was fired by his employer for refusing to write misleading news releases won a lawsuit against his former employer for "unlawful dismissal."

Many of these charges were eventually dismissed or settled out of court, but the organizations paid dearly for the adverse publicity and the expense of defending themselves.

Defamation

Public relations professionals should make a point of becoming thoroughly familiar with the concepts of libel and slander. Such knowledge is crucial if an organization's internal and external communications are to meet legal and regulatory standards with a minimum of legal complications.

> **think**
>
> **Why are corporations considered "public figures" by the courts in cases involving defamation?**

Traditionally, *libel* was the term used for a printed falsehood and *slander* was the term used for an oral statement that was false. Today, as a practical matter, there is little difference in the two, and the courts often use *defamation* as a collective term for these types of offenses. Essentially, defamation is making a false statement about a person (or organization) that creates public hatred, contempt, or ridicule, or inflicts injury on reputation.

Private citizens usually have more success winning defamation suits than do public figures or corporations. With public figures—government officials, entertainers, political candidates, and other newsworthy personalities—there is the extra test of whether the libelous statements were made with actual malice (*New York Times v. Sullivan*). *Actual malice* was defined by the U.S. Supreme Court as making the libelous statement while knowing the information was false or publishing the information with

"reckless disregard" as to whether it was false.

Corporations, to some degree, also are considered "public figures" by the courts for three reasons:

1. They engage in advertising and promotion offering products and services to the public.

2. They are often involved in matters of public controversy and public policy.

3. They have some degree of access to the media—through regular advertising and news releases—that enables them to respond and rebut defamatory charges made against them.

This is not to say that corporations cannot win lawsuits regarding defamation. For example, General Motors (GM) filed a multimillion-dollar defamation suit against NBC after the network's *Dateline* news program carried a story about gas tanks on GM pickup trucks exploding in side-impact collisions. In a news conference, GM's general counsel meticulously provided evidence that NBC had inserted toy rocket "igniters" in the gas tanks, understated the

vehicle speed at the moment of impact, and wrongly claimed that the fuel tanks could be easily ruptured. Within 24 hours after the suit was filed, NBC caved in. It agreed to air a nine-minute apology on the news program and pay GM $2 million to cover the cost of its investigation.

Increasingly, corporations are also filing defamation suits against bloggers and even individuals who tweet about their businesses. A woman in Chicago, for example, was slapped with a $50,000 defamation suit after tweeting that a real estate company didn't do anything about her moldy apartment. The company claimed that the tweet "maliciously and wrongfully published the false and defamatory tweet on Twitter, thereby allowing the tweet to be distributed throughout the world."

Avoiding Libel Suits

Libel suits can be filed against organizational officials who make libelous accusations during a media interview, send out news releases that make false statements, or injure someone's reputation. For example, some executives have lived to regret that they lost control during a news conference and called the leaders of a labor union "a bunch of crooks and compulsive liars" and a news reporter "a pimp for all environmental groups." Such language, although highly quotable and

Mark Cuban, the owner of the Dallas Mavericks basketball team, was fined $25,000 for criticizing a referee in a tweet after a game.

Prove It!

A person filing a libel suit usually must prove four things:

1. The false statement was communicated to others through print, broadcast, or electronic means.

2. The person claiming to be libeled was identified or is identifiable.

3. There is actual injury in the form of money losses, loss of reputation, or mental suffering.

4. The person making the statement was malicious or negligent.

Make It Work, People

THE REALITY SHOW *PROJECT RUNWAY* ran into legal problems when its producers wanted to move the program from Bravo to Lifetime. Bravo is owned by NBC Universal, whose lawyers said the Weinstein Company (which owns and produces the show) violated its contract in taking *Project Runway* to Lifetime.

PR CASEBOOK

After a decision by the New York Supreme Court that NBC Universal still had rights to *Project Runway*, a legal and public relations battle ensued. In a press release, NBC Universal said, "The overwhelming evidence demonstrated that the Weinstein Company violated NBC Universal's right of first refusal to future cycles of 'Project Runway.' After hearing all of the evidence, the court issued an order prohibiting the Weinstein Company from taking the show or any spinoff to Lifetime."

The Weinstein Company also released a statement, "We are glad that the court held that NBC Universal cannot exhibit the program on Bravo and that the court required NBC Universal to post a minimum $20 million bond. Obviously we will be appealing and remain committed to our partners." Lifetime said simply it was "disappointed" with the court's finding.

At New York's Fashion Week in February 2009, supermodel and *Project Runway* host Heidi Klum filmed the season six finale in Bryant Park, even though it was uncertain there would ever even be a season six.

The legal and public relations battle went on for nearly a year before it was settled out of court in mid-2009 for "tons of millions of dollars," according to deadlinehollywooddaily.com. Harvey Weinstein of the Weinstein Company said, "I want to personally congratulate [NBC Universal's] Jeff Zucker and NBC Universal on their success in the litigation and thank Jeff for resolving this in a professional manner. We look forward to working together on our ongoing projects." At last, Klum and design coach Tim Gunn were able to see their sixth season aired on *Project Runway's* new home network.

The back-and-forth public statements are aimed at forming public opinion in favor of each side and at the same time, putting pressure on the other side. This is standard public relations behavior in the midst of a legal battle.

1 Do you think it is appropriate for public relations practitioners to try to move public opinion in a favorable direction during a legal battle?

2 Should public relations practitioners have a strong voice during a legal action, or should they defer to the lawyers involved?

3 Think about a high-profile legal case and then try to dissect the communication you see or hear related to the case. Where do you see the hand of public relations at work?

colorful, can provoke legal retaliation. Accurate information, and a delicate choice of words, must be used in all news releases. That's why it's common for a news release to state that an executive has left the company for "personal reasons" even if he or she may have been fired for incompetence or violation of company policies.

Another potentially dangerous practice is making unflattering comments about the competition's products. Although comparative advertising is the norm in the United

States, companies walk a narrow line between comparison and "trade libel," or "product disparagement." Statements should be truthful, with factual evidence and scientific data available to substantiate them. Companies often charge competitors with overstepping the boundary between "puffery" and "factual representation."

employee
COMMUNICATIONS

Public relations staff must be particularly sensitive to the issue of employee privacy and have a good understanding of employee rights and responsibilities as these topics relate to a number of legal and ethical issues.

For example, it is no longer true, if it ever was, that an organization has an unlimited right to publicize the activities of its employees in employee newsletters. In fact, according to Morton J. Simon, a Philadelphia lawyer and author of *Public Relations Law*, "It should not be assumed that a person's status as an employee waives his right to privacy." Simon correctly points out that a company newsletter or magazine does not enjoy the same First Amendment protection as the news media enjoy when they claim "newsworthiness" and "public interest." A number of court cases, he says, show that company newsletters are considered commercial tools of trade. This distinction does not impede the effectiveness of newsletters, but it does indicate editors should try to keep employee stories organization oriented.

Product Publicity and Advertising

An organization must have a signed release on file if it wants to use photographs or comments of its employees and other individuals in product publicity, sales brochures, and advertising. An added precaution is to give some financial compensation to make a more binding contract.

Chemical Bank of New York unfortunately learned this lesson the hard way. The bank used pictures of 39 employees in various advertisements designed to "humanize" the bank's image, but the employees maintained that no one had requested permission to use their photos in advertisements. Another problem was that the pictures had been taken as long as five years before they began appearing in the series of advertisements.

An attorney for the employees, who sued for $600,000 in damages, said, "The bank took the individuality of these employees and used that individuality to make a profit." The judge agreed, ruling that the bank

had violated New York's privacy law. The action is called misappropriation of personality, discussed later in this chapter.

Employee Free Speech

A modern, progressive organization encourages employee comments and even criticisms. Indeed, many employee newspapers carry letters to the editor because they breed a healthy atmosphere of two-way communication and make company publications more credible.

At the same time, recent developments have indicated that not all is well for employee freedom of expression. An employee of Google, for example, was fired for using a Google-sponsored blog (a website open to public access) to post a chronicle of his first week on the job for friends and family on a personal blog. In another case, an employee of a software firm in Los Angeles was fired for posting complaints about her boss and obnoxious coworkers on her personal blog.

Although employee privacy remains an important consideration,

Written permission for use of the image should be obtained if the employee's photograph will appear in sales brochures or even in the corporate annual report. The same rule applies to other situations. A graduate of Lafayette College **sued the college** for using a photo of his mother and him at graduation ceremonies, **without their permission,** in a financial aid brochure.

the trend is toward increased monitoring of employee e-mail by employers. Employers are concerned about being held liable if an employee posts a racial slur, engages in sexual harassment online, and even transmits sexually explicit jokes that might cause another employee to perceive the workplace as a "hostile" environment. In other words, everyone should assume that any

e-mails they write at work are subject to monitoring and that they can be fired if they violate company policy. Further complicating this issue is the fact that government employees may have their e-mails made public if some interested party files a Freedom of Information Act (FOIA) request. E-mails produced by a public employee on a government-owned computer are considered requestable documents under the FOIA.

Other important—and sometimes controversial—aspects of employee free speech include whistle-blowing and protection of an organization's trade secrets. State and federal laws generally protect the right of employees to "blow the whistle" if an organization is guilty of illegal activity. Whistle-blowing can occur in corporate, nonprofit, and government organizations. For example, an employee might blow the whistle on his or her organization by reporting to the Environmental Protection Agency the illegal release of a toxic substance from a manufacturing plant.

copyright LAW

Should a news release be copyrighted? How about a corporate annual report? Can a *New Yorker* cartoon be used in the company magazine without permission? What about reprinting an article from *Fortune* magazine and distributing it to the company's sales staff? Are government reports copyrighted? What constitutes copyright infringement?

These are questions that a public relations professional should be able to answer. Knowledge of copyright law is important from two perspectives: (1) which organizational materials should be copyrighted and (2) how the copyrighted materials of others may be used correctly. In

very simple terms, *copyright* means protection of a creative work from unauthorized use.

The shield of copyright protection was weakened somewhat in 1991, when the U.S. Supreme Court ruled unanimously that directories, computer databases, and other compilations of facts may be copied and republished unless they display "some minimum degree of creativity." The court stated, "Raw facts may be copied at will."

Thus a copyright does not protect ideas, but only the specific ways in which those ideas are expressed. An idea for promoting a product, for example, cannot be copyrighted—but brochures, drawings, news fea-

tures, animated cartoons, display booths, photographs, recordings, videotapes, corporate symbols, slogans, and the like that express a particular idea can be copyrighted.

Because much money, effort, time, and creative talent are spent on developing organizational materials, obtaining copyright protection for them is important. By copyrighting materials, a company can prevent its competitors from capitalizing on its creative work or producing a facsimile brochure that may mislead the public.

The law presumes that material produced in some tangible form is copyrighted from the moment it is created. This presumption of copyright is often sufficient to discourage unauthorized use, and the writer or creator of the material has some legal protection if he or she can prove that the material was created before another person claims it.

A more formal step, providing full legal protection, is official registration of the copyrighted work within three months after its creation. This process consists of depositing two copies of the manuscript (it is not necessary that it has been published), recording, or artwork with the Copyright Office of the Library of Congress. Registration is not a condition of copyright protection, but it is a prerequisite to an infringement action against unauthorized use by others. The Copyright Term Extension Act, passed in 1998 and reaffirmed by the U.S. Supreme Court (*Eldred v. Ashcroft*) in 2003, protects original material for the life of the creator plus 70 years for individual works and 95 years from publication for copyrights held by corporations.

fair use VERSUS Infringement

Public relations people are in the business of gathering information from a variety of sources, so it is important to know where fair use ends and infringement begins. *Fair use* means that part of a copyrighted article may be quoted directly, but the quoted material must be brief in relation to the length of the original work. It may be, for example, only one paragraph in a 750-word article, but as long as a 300-word passage in a long article or book chapter. Complete attribution of the source must be given regardless of the length of the quotation. If the passage is quoted verbatim, quote marks must be used to signal this fact.

The concept of fair use has distinct limitations if part of the copyrighted material is to be used in advertisements and promotional brochures. In this case, permission from the copyright holder to reuse the original material is required. It also is important for the original source to approve the context in which the quote is used. A quote taken out of context often runs into legal trouble if it implies endorsement of a product or service.

Photography and Artwork

The copyright law makes it clear that freelance and commercial photographers retain ownership of their work. In other words, a customer who buys a copyrighted photo owns the item itself, but not the right to make additional copies. That right remains with the photographer, unless it is explicitly transferred in writing to someone else.

In a further extension of this right, the duplication of copyrighted photos is also illegal. This interpretation was established in a 1990 U.S. Federal District Court case in which the Professional Photographers of America (PP of A) sued a nationwide photofinishing firm for ignoring copyright notices on pictures sent for additional copies. Computer manipulation of original artwork can also violate copyright provisions.

Freelance photographers generally charge for a picture on the basis of its use. If it is used only once, perhaps for an employee newsletter, the fee is low. In contrast, if the company wants to use the picture in the corporate annual report or on the company calendar, the fee may be considerably higher. Arrangements and fees then can be determined for one-time use, unlimited use, or the payment of royalties every time the picture is used.

Slightly changing a copyrighted photo or a piece of artwork can also be considered a violation of copyright if the intent is to capitalize on widespread recognition of the original art. This was the case when the estate of the children's author Dr. Seuss (Theodor Geisel) won a $1.5 million judgment against a Los Angeles T-shirt maker for infringement of copyright. The manufacturer had portrayed a parody of Dr. Seuss's Cat in the Hat character smoking marijuana and giving the peace sign. Similarly, sports logos are registered trademarks, and a licensing fee must be paid before anyone can use logos for commercial products and promotions. Teams in

think Why is the concept of fair use applied differently when it comes to advertising and promotional materials?

The penalty for not paying a licensing fee is steep. During Super Bowl week, the NFL typically confiscates roughly $1 million in bogus goods and files criminal charges against the offending vendors.

the National Football League and the National Basketball Association earn more than $3 billion annually selling licensed merchandise, and the sale of college and university trademarked goods is rapidly approaching that mark.

The Rights of Freelance Writers

Although the rights of freelance photographers have been established for some years, it was only recently that freelance writers gained more control over the ownership of their work. In the case of *Community for Creative Non-violence v. Reid*, the U.S. Supreme Court in 1989 ruled that writers retained ownership of their work and that purchasers of it simply gained a "license" to reproduce the copyrighted work. Under this interpretation of the copyright law, ownership of a writer's work is subject to negotiation and contractual agreement. Writers may agree to assign all copyright rights to the work they have been hired to do or they may give permission only for a specific one-time use. In a related matter, freelance writers won a major victory in 2001 when the Supreme Court (*New York Times v. Tasini*) ruled that publishers, by making articles accessible through electronic databases, infringed on the copyrights of freelance contributors.

Public relations firms and corporate public relations departments are responsible for ensuring compliance with the copyright law. This means that all agreements with a freelance writer must be documented in writing, and the use of the material must be clearly stated. Ideally, public relations personnel should negotiate multiple rights and even complete ownership of the copyright.

Copyright Issues on the Internet

The Internet has raised new issues about the protection of intellectual property.

DOWNLOADING MATERIAL. In general, the same rules apply to cyberspace as to more long-standing methods of disseminating ideas. Original materials in digital form are still protected by copyright. The fair use limits for materials found on the Internet are essentially the same as those for materials disseminated by any other means.

Related to this issue is the use of news articles and features that are sent via e-mail or the web to the clients of clipping services. An organization may use such clips to track its publicity efforts, but it cannot distribute the article on its own website or intranet without obtaining permission and paying a royalty to the publication in which the article appeared. One national clipping service, Burrelle's, has already reached agreements with more than 300 newspapers to have its customers pay a small royalty fee in exchange for being able to make photocopies of clippings and make greater use of them.

UPLOADING MATERIAL. In many cases, owners of copyrighted material have uploaded various kinds of information with the intention of making it freely available. Examples of these items include software, games, and even the entire text of *The Hitchhiker's Guide to the Galaxy*. The problem comes, however, when third parties upload copyrighted material without permission. Consequently, copyright holders are increasingly patrolling the Internet to stop the unauthorized use of material.

trademark LAW ™

What do the names Coca-Cola, Marlboro, and IBM; the Olympic rings; and the logo of the Dallas Cowboys have in common? They are all registered trademarks protected by law.

A *trademark* is a word, symbol, or slogan, used singly or in combination, that identifies a product's origin. According to Susan L. Cohen, writing in *Editor & Publisher*'s annual trademark supplement, "It also serves as an indicator of quality, a kind of shorthand for consumers to use in recognizing goods in a complex marketplace." Research indicates, for example, that 53 percent of Americans say brand quality takes precedence over price considerations. Consequently, branding is important to companies and organizations.

The Protection of Trademarks

Trademarks are always capitalized and are never used as nouns. They are always used as adjectives modifying nouns. For example, the proper terms are "Kleenex tissues," "Xerox copies," and "Rollerblade skates." A person who "uses a Kleenex," "makes a Xerox," or "goes Rollerblading" is violating trademark law.

Organizations adamantly insist on the proper use of trademarks to avoid the problem of having a name or slogan become generic. Put another way, a brand name becomes a common noun through general public use. Some trade names that have become generic include *aspirin, thermos, cornflakes, nylon, cellophane*, and *yo-yo*. This means that any company can now use these names to describe a product.

Trademark Infringement

Today, in a marketplace populated with thousands of businesses and organizations, finding a trademark

сё будет Coca-Cola Присоединяйся!

There has been a proliferation of trademarks and service marks in modern society. Coca-Cola may be the world's most recognized trademark, according to some studies, but it is only one of almost 1 million active trademarks registered with the federal Patent and Trademark Office.

In 2007, Shanghai Xingbake Cafe was fined 500,000 yuan (64,000 U.S. dollars) for infringing on Starbuck's trademark and was ordered to change its name and make a public apology to Starbucks.

not already in use is extremely difficult. The task becomes even more frustrating when competing organizations claim similar slogans or trademarks. The complexity of finding a new name, coupled with the attempts of many to capitalize on an already known trade name, has spawned a number of lawsuits claiming trademark infringement. Consider the following examples:

- *Entrepreneur* magazine was awarded $337,000 in court damages after filing a trademark infringement lawsuit against a public relations firm that changed its name to "EntrepreneurPR."
- *Fox News* filed a suit against satirist and author Al Franken because the title of his book was *Lies and the Lying Liars Who Tell Them: A Fair and Balanced Look at the Right*. Fox claimed that the phrase "fair and balanced" was trademarked.
- The widow of the man who said, "Let's roll," when he and others tried to overpower the hijackers of Flight 93 over Pennsylvania on September 11, 2001, petitioned the federal government to trademark the phrase. She wanted to license the phrase to fund a foundation to assist children who had lost a parent.
- Phi Beta Kappa, the academic honor society, filed a $5 million trademark infringement suit against Compaq Computer Corp. after the company launched a "Phi Beta Compaq" promotion targeted at college students.
- MADD (Mothers Against Drunk Driving) filed a trademark suit against DAMMADD, a nonprofit group established to spread antidrug messages. MADD said the similar name would confuse the public.

In these cases and many others, organizations claimed that their registered trademarks were being improperly exploited for commercial or organizational purposes.

Misappropriation of Personality

A form of trademark infringement also can result from the unauthorized use of well-known entertainers, professional athletes, and other public figures in an organization's publicity and advertising materials. A photo of Robert Pattinson may make a company's advertising campaign more interesting, but the courts would call it "misappropriation of personality" if permission and licensing fees have not been negotiated.

Deceased celebrities are also protected from exploitation by others. To use a likeness or actual photo of a personality such as Elvis Presley, Marilyn Monroe, or Michael Jackson, the user must pay a licensing

think What is the downside for a corporation whose trademark becomes too commonly used?

fee to an agent representing the family, studio, or estate of the deceased. The estate of Peanuts comic strip creator Charles Schulz collects licensing fees amounting to approximately $30 million annually. The estates of NASCAR icon Dale Earnhardt and Beatle John Lennon each garner about $20 million per year in fees.

The legal doctrine is the right of publicity, which gives entertainers, athletes, and other celebrities the sole ability to cash in on their fame. This legal right is loosely akin to a trademark or copyright, and many states have made it a commercial asset that can be inherited by a celebrity's descendents.

regulations by
GOVERNMENT AGENCIES

the promotion of products and services, whether through advertising, product publicity, or other techniques, is not protected by the First Amendment. Instead, the courts have traditionally ruled that such activities fall under the doctrine of commercial speech. As a consequence, messages can be regulated by the state in the interest of public health, safety, and consumer protection.

Both the states and the federal government have passed legislation that regulates commercial speech and even restricts it if standards of disclosure, truth, and accuracy are violated. One result of such legislation was the banning of cigarette advertising on television in the 1960s. Public relations personnel involved in product publicity and the distribution of financial information should be aware of any applicable guidelines established by government agencies.

The Federal Trade Commission

The Federal Trade Commission (FTC) has jurisdiction to determine if advertisements are deceptive or misleading. Public relations personnel should also know that the commission has jurisdiction over product news releases and other forms of product publicity, such as videos and brochures. In the eyes of the FTC, both advertisements and product publicity materials are vehicles of commercial trade—and, therefore,

think How do government regulations on advertising protect consumers?

subject to regulation. In fact, Section 43(a) of the Lanham Act makes it clear that anyone, including public relations personnel, may be subject to liability claims if that person participates in the making or dissemination of a false and misleading representation in any advertising or promotional material. This legislation applies to advertising and public relations firms, which also can be held liable for writing, producing, and distributing product publicity materials on behalf of their clients.

An example of an FTC complaint is one filed against Campbell Soup Company for claiming that its soups were low in fat and cholesterol and, therefore, helpful in fighting heart disease. The FTC charged that the claim was deceptive because publicity and advertisements failed to disclose that the soups had a high sodium content, which increases the risk of heart disease.

The Campbell's case raises an important aspect of FTC guidelines. Although a publicized fact may be accurate in itself, FTC staff also consider the context or "net impression received by the consumers." In this case, advertising copywriters and publicists ignored the information about the high sodium level, which created an entirely new perspective on the health benefits of Campbell's soup.

Hollywood's abuse of endorsements and testimonials to publicize its films also has attracted the scrutiny of the FTC. Sony Pictures, for example, was found to have concocted quotes from a fictitious movie critic to publicize four of its films. Twentieth Century Fox admitted that it had hired actors to appear in "man in the street" commercials to portray unpaid moviegoers.

FTC investigators are always on the lookout for unsubstantiated claims and various forms of misleading or deceptive information. Some of the terms in promotional materials that trigger FTC interest are *authentic*, *certified*, *cure*, *custom-made*, *germ-free*, *natural*, *unbreakable*, *perfect*, *first-class*, *exclusive*, and *reliable*. In recent years, the FTC also has established guidelines for "green" marketing and the use of the terms *low-carb* and *organic* in advertisements and publicity materials for food products.

In 2009, the FTC ruled that anyone who endorses a product, including celebrities and bloggers, must make explicit the compensation received from companies. The FTC guidelines also state that businesses and reviewers (including bloggers) may be held liable for any false statements about a product.

Companies found in violation of FTC guidelines are usually given the opportunity to sign a consent decree. Under such an agreement, the company admits no wrongdoing but agrees to change its advertising and publicity claims. Companies may also be fined by the FTC or ordered to engage in corrective advertising and publicity.

The Securities and Exchange Commission

The trend of megamergers and the publicity-grabbing initial public offerings (IPOs) of many new companies that began in the 1990s and continues today has made the Securities and Exchange Commission (SEC) a household name in the business world. Such deals have also made the practice of investor relations increasingly important. The SEC closely monitors the financial affairs of publicly traded companies and protects the interests of stockholders.

The SEC guidelines on public disclosure and insider trading are particularly relevant to corporate public relations staff members who must meet these requirements. The distribution of misleading information or failure to make a timely disclosure of material information may be the basis of liability under the SEC code. A company may even be liable if, despite satisfying regulations by getting information out, it conveys crucial information in a vague way or buries it deep within the news release.

A good example of how companies may run afoul of SEC rules is Enron, the now-defunct Houston-based energy company that became the largest corporate failure in U.S. history. The company was charged with a number of SEC violations, including the distribution of misleading news releases about its finances. According to Congressional testimony, the company issued a quarterly earnings news release that falsely led investors to believe that the company was "on track" to meet strong earnings growth in 2002. Three months later, the company was bankrupt.

The SEC has volumes of regulations, but the three concepts most pertinent to public relations personnel are as follows:

1. Full information must be given on anything that might materially affect the company's stock.
2. Timely disclosure is essential.
3. Insider trading is illegal.

A court may examine all information released by a company, including news releases, to determine whether, taken as a whole, they create an "overall misleading" impression.

In 2000, the SEC issued another regulation related to fair disclosure, known as Reg FD. Although regulations already existed regarding "material disclosure" of information that could affect the price of

---

The SEC's booklet on "plain English" gives helpful writing hints such as
(1) make sentences short;
(2) use *we* and *our*, *you* and *your*; and
(3) say it with an active verb.
More information about SEC guidelines can be accessed at its website:

www.sec.gov

stock, the new regulation expanded the concept by requiring publicly traded companies to broadly disseminate "material" information via a news release, webcast, or SEC filing. According to the SEC, Reg FD is intended to ensure that *all* investors—not just brokerage firms and analysts—receive financial information from a company at the same time.

Other Regulatory Agencies

Although the FTC and the SEC are the major federal agencies concerned with the content of advertising and publicity materials, other agencies have also established guidelines that can affect practitioners in these fields.

The Food and Drug Administration. The Food and Drug Administration (FDA) oversees the advertising and promotion of prescription drugs, over-the-counter medicines, cosmetics, and food. Under the federal Food, Drug, and Cosmetic Act, any "person" (which includes advertising and public relations firms) who "causes the misbranding" of products through the dissemination of false and misleading information may be held liable under provisions of the law.

The FDA has established specific guidelines for video, audio, and print news releases on healthcare topics.

First, the release must provide "fair balance" by telling consumers about both the risks and the benefits of the drug or treatment. Second, the writer must be clear about the limitations of a particular drug or treatment—for example, that it may not help people with certain conditions. Third, a news release or media kit should be accompanied by supplementary product sheets or brochures that give full prescribing information.

Other federal agencies that occasionally get involved in distribution of public relations materials includes the Bureau of Alcohol, Tobacco and Firearms, and the Federal Communications Commission.

liability for
SPONSORED EVENTS

public relations personnel often focus on the planning and logistics of events. Consequently, they must also take steps to protect their organizations from liability and possible lawsuits associated with those activities.

Plant tours, open houses and other events should not be undertaken lightly. They require detailed planning by the public relations staff to guarantee the safety and comfort of visitors. Consideration must be given to such factors as possible work disruptions as groups pass through the plant, safety, and amount of staffing required.

A well-marked tour route is essential; it is equally important to have trained escort staff and tour guides. Guides should be well versed in company history and operations, and their comments should be somewhat standardized to make sure that key facts are conveyed. In addition, guides should be trained in first aid

and thoroughly briefed on what to do in case of an accident. At the beginning of the tour, the guide should outline to the visitors what they will see, the amount of walking involved, the time required, and the number of stairs. This warning tells visitors what they can expect.

Many of the points about plant tours are also applicable to open houses. The added problem with open houses is having the presence of large numbers of people on the plant site at the same time. Such an event calls for special logistical planning by the public relations staff. Such precautions will generate goodwill and limit the company's liability. It should be noted, however, that a plaintiff can still collect if negligence on the part of the company can be proved.

Promotional events are planned primarily to promote product sales, increase organizational visibility, or raise money for charitable causes.

Events that attract crowds require the same kind of planning as open houses. Public relations personnel should be concerned about traffic flow, adequate restroom facilities, signage, and security.

Liability insurance is a necessity when any such events are planned. Any public event sponsored by an organization should be insured against accidents that might result in lawsuits charging negligence. Organizations can purchase comprehensive insurance to cover a variety of events or a specific event. The need for liability insurance also applies to charitable organizations if they sponsor a 10-K run, a bicycle race, or a hot-air balloon race. Participants should sign a release form that protects the organization against liability in case of an accident. Promotional events that use public streets and parks also need permits from the appropriate city departments.

WORKING WITH lawyers

this chapter has outlined a number of areas in which the release of information (or the lack of release) raises legal issues for an organization. Public relations personnel must be aware of legal pitfalls, but they are not lawyers. By the same token, lawyers aren't experts in public relations and often lack sufficient understanding of how important the court of public opinion is in determining the reputation and credibility of an organization.

In today's business environment, with its high potential for litigation, it is essential for public relations professionals and lawyers to have cooperative relationships. The relationship between lawyers and public relations practitioners is such an important issue that both professions regularly deal with it in publications and seminars. In the public relations arena, *PR News* has an online newsletter, *Crisis and Legal PR Bulletin*, and provides publications and programming that address the intersection of law and public relations. On the other side, the University of Georgia School of Law has provided practicing lawyers with a daylong continuing education program titled "Winning in the Court of Public Opinion."

Keys to WINNING in the Court of Law— and in the Court of Public Opinion

PRSA's monthly tabloid *Tactics* offers these tips:

1. Make carefully planned public comments in the earliest stages of a crisis or legal issue.

2. Understand the perspective of lawyers and allow them to review statements when an organization is facing or involved in litigation.

3. Public relations practitioners need to guard against providing information to the opposing side in a legal case.

4. Public relations professionals should counsel and coach the legal team.

5. Build support from other interested parties, such as industry associations or chambers of commerce.

6. Develop a litigation communication team before you need it.

APPLY YOUR KNOWLEDGE

WHAT WOULD YOU DO? TO ACCEPT OR REJECT A CLIENT

A well-known professional baseball player is suspected of having used steroids and other performance-enhancing drugs. He has not been charged with any crime. His agent asks you to advise and assist him in handling the intense media interest in the case. The agent wants you to try to place favorable stories about the baseball star in the media and create a positive environment for him. If the athlete is formally accused, it could mean irreparable damage to his baseball career.

You are not asked to do anything unethical. The money is quite good, and you know the publicity from working on the case will probably help your public relations consulting career, especially if the athlete is exonerated. Would you take the account?

The agent tells you confidentially that the athlete has admitted that he took some substance that was unknown to him, but may have been steroids. Does this information affect your decision? What are the ethics of the situation as you see them? Write a brief essay defending your choice.

Summary

Why Is Ethics a Relevant Issue for Public Relations Practitioners? p. 182

- Ethics refers to a person's value system and the means by which he or she determines right and wrong.

- Even if a person is an advocate for a particular organization or cause, the individual can always behave in an ethical manner. Because of the concept of role differentiation, society understands that the advocate is operating within an assigned role, much like a defense lawyer or prosecuting attorney in court.

- Groups such as PRSA, IABC, and IPRA play an important role in setting the standards and ethical behavior of the public relations profession. Most professional organizations have published codes of conduct and educational programs.

What Do Public Relations Professionals Need to Know About Defamation, Employee and Privacy Rights, Copyright, and Trademark Laws? p. 186

- There is now little practical difference between libel and slander; the two are often collectively referred to as defamation. The concept of defamation involves a false and malicious (or at least negligent) communication with an identifiable subject who is injured either financially or by loss of reputation or mental suffering.

- It is important to get written permission to publish photos or use employees in advertising materials, and to be cautious in releasing personal information about employees to the media.

- Employees are limited in expressing opinions within the corporate environment. E-mail sent from company-owned computers, for example, is company property and subject to monitoring. Employees can be fired (or former employees sued) for revealing trade secrets. Whistle-blowers, however, have protection against retaliation.

- Copyright is the protection of creative work from unauthorized use. It is assumed that published works are copyrighted, and permission must be obtained to reprint such material. The doctrine of fair use allows limited quotation, as in a book review.

- Unless a company has a specific contract with a freelance writer, photographer, or artist to produce work that will be exclusively owned by that company, the freelancer owns his or her work.

- New copyright issues have been raised by the popularity of the Internet and the ease of downloading, uploading, and disseminating images and information.

- A trademark is a word, symbol, or slogan that identifies a product's origin. It can be registered with the U.S. Patent and Trademark Office. Companies vigorously protect trademarks to prevent them from becoming common nouns.

Which Guidelines and Government Agencies Govern the Commercial Speech Used by Public Relations Professionals? p. 196

- Commercial speech is regulated by the government in the interest of public health, safety, and consumer protection.

- The agencies involved in this regulation include the Federal Trade Commission, the Securities and Exchange Commission, the Food and Drug Administration, and the Bureau of Alcohol, Tobacco, and Firearms.

How Can Public Relations Professionals Facilitate Good Working Relationships with Lawyers? p. 199

- To effectively manage all the issues discussed in this chapter, a cooperative relationship must exist between public relations personnel and legal counsel.

- Public relations practitioners should be aware of legal concepts and regulatory guidelines and receive briefings from the legal staff on impending developments.

QUESTIONS for Review and Discussion

1. Define ethics in your own words. Why might two individuals disagree about what constitutes an ethical dilemma or concern?

2. Some critics say voluntary codes of ethics "have no teeth" because they cannot be enforced. Are there other reasons for having codes of ethics?

3. How can a public relations professional play the role of an "ethical advocate"?

4. Public relations practitioners often have conflicting loyalties. In your opinion, do they owe their first allegiance to their client or employer or to the standards of their professional organization, such as PRSA?

5. Why are gifts to the media considered unprofessional and, at times, unethical?

6. Why do public relations staff and firms need to know the legal aspects of creating and distributing messages?

7. Which steps can a public relations person take to avoid libel suits?

8. What is the concept of fair comment and criticism?

9. Which precautions can a public relations person take to avoid invasion of privacy lawsuits?

10. If an organization wants to use the photo or comments of an employee or a customer in an advertisement, which precautions should be taken?

11. Which basic guidelines of copyright law should public relations professionals know about?

12. How do public relations people help an organization protect its trademarks?

the THINK SPOT
www.thethinkspot.com

TACTICS

PRWeek

Nicole Zerillo, *PRWeek*, January 26, 2009

Financial Sector Targets Diverse Audiences

Public relations professionals need to consider and employ multiple approaches to reach diverse audiences. Effective public relations campaigns research the interests and characteristics of the audience and then develop strategies and tools to reach them effectively.

Audiences in the United States are characterized by their diversity, and multiculturalism and regional difference are often key considerations in PR campaign development in this country. Audience diversity is not an issue only in the United States, of course: Public relations professionals must develop strategies to target ethnically and culturally diverse groups all over the globe as well.

Effective community engagement frequently takes place on a grassroots level. Technology has enabled stakeholders to engage a wide variety of constituents much more easily so as to build support for a position.

Financial services companies are using a variety of tactics to reach diverse audiences. In today's competitive financial services industry, creating effective communications platforms targeting different multicultural markets is viewed as an important investment for the future.

For that reason, several companies in the sector are becoming increasingly fluent in creating PR programs that are sensitive to different cultural values.

In building communications' strategies, "[we] look at the different communities," says Alfredo Padilla, VP of corporate communications for Comerica Bank. "Some [groups] are . . . sophisticated in terms of financial products, and some . . . are not."

At Comerica, a company with branches across North America, the team targets multicultural groups through regional outreach teams, says Janice Tessier, VP and manager of diversity initiatives at Comerica."We need dedicated groups in each market," she adds. "We may have an overarching communications strategy [for specific targets]. A lot of outreach is grassroots level. It's about building relationships within those specific communities."

Working solely with its in-house PR team, Comerica promotes its programs to key multicultural markets, including Arab Americans, by connecting via local grassroots efforts, such as sponsorships and programs at centers of influence within key communities. For example, in Michigan, the company has targeted this community by establishing relationships with organizations such as the American Arab Chamber of Commerce (AACC).Through the AACC, the company reaches out to Arab American entrepreneurs and provides them with advice and information in finance seminars, Tessier says.

Also, Comerica publicizes financial education information through targeted outreach to local publications geared to specific communities. "From a media and corporate communications standpoint . . . we look carefully at what the need is," Padilla says. "And, we . . . tailor those communications [and] press releases that make sense for the community."

Community Influence

Another way that the bank seeks to create a connection is by having branch locations that "mirror" the community, he adds. For example, the

Gauging the values, lifestyle, and interests of specific audience segments is becoming increasingly important as the diversity of the U.S. population increases.

The Hispanic population is growing in the U.S. market—and so is the Hispanic presence in the public relations industry.

Viral campaigns, which generally take place online through social media such as Facebook or Twitter, have emerged in recent years as part of PR professionals' arsenal of tactics. These channels can be astonishingly fast and effective. For example, more than $20 million for victims of the January 12, 2010, earthquake in Haiti was raised through text messaging in just the first few days following the natural disaster.

One of the most salient aspects of American history is immigration. Although immigrants may become assimilated over time, many retain distinctive cultural and religious interests. Public relations professionals should be attuned to the diverse interests within these subgroups.

Although Twitter, Facebook, MySpace, YouTube, and other online media are replacing many traditional means of communicating with audiences, human interaction and personalization remain important in public relations activities.

In many cultures, face-to-face interactions are more effective than media channels. Some demographics are more inclined to respond positively to nonmedia channels, because these channels are perceived to have greater credibility and to provide more accessibility.

Branding has become an increasingly important asset for organizations. Being able to readily identify a product, service, or position allows stakeholders to maintain loyalty and become an identifiable part of a community.

---

newly opened Cerritos Banking Center in Los Angeles' Koreatown was built according to the principles of Feng Shui, Padilla says.

"We're very careful about understanding the culture, as well as providing the services and the products that make sense [for] the community," he adds. "We want to be the eyes and the ears of the community as we open new branches."

Authentic involvement in the community has also been a focus of the regional bank National Penn. With the support of Hispanic AOR Bauza & Associates, it has sought to strengthen its outreach to the Hispanic community by directly addressing cultural values that might make customers hesitant about using financial services. For example, the bank addressed the distrust many Hispanics have with financial organizations and releasing personal information with a "Shred Day" in September. For the event, the company provided a shredding truck outside one of its community offices in Wyomissing, Pennsylvania, a suburb of Reading, Pennsylvania, according to Wilson Camelo, principal and VP of PR for Bauza. Scott Fainor, National Penn's president and CEO, says, "I was out there picking up boxes . . . and other bankers were out there . . . getting the word out that we're committed."

The bank also promotes its interest and understanding of the community through participation in local Hispanic community celebrations and holidays, like Three Kings Day. Also, the company is working on increasing the number of employees able to speak Spanish, as Hispanic customers have a "high level of value preference [for] more face-to-face interactions," Fainor says.

National Bank has found it effective to promote programs beyond traditional channels, such as placing features on financial programs in local newspapers, having Latino employees hand out flyers, or including information in church bulletins, says Cathy Bower, SVP of corporate communications. "You can't just use a traditional channel; [to be successful] you have to work within the network of the community," she adds.

Trust and incentive to use brand financial products can also come from promotions that tie into multicultural consumers' countries of origin, where family might still live. Western Union promoted its "Cash, the perfect gift" campaign to highlight money as the ideal gift for the 2008 holiday season. The effort was directed at general consumer and multicultural segments, says Dan Diaz, Western Union's VP of communications for the Americas. The effort included targeted media outreach and spokespeople.

To reach the Asian community, the company partnered with YouTube celebrity HappySlip, aka Christine Gambito, to create a viral campaign highlighting the Western Union experience. In its outreach to the Hispanic market, the company partnered with Univision's *Despierta América* co-host Ana Maria Canseco for appearances.

Celebrity Factor

It was important for celebrities to have contact with the consumers and convey their connection with the brand. For example, Canseco relayed how she used to pick up money at Western Union sent from her uncle in the United States when she was a child living in Mexico, Diaz says. "Our consumer base is primarily living in a country other than their own . . . It's all about the . . . family and the individual who is thinking [about] supporting their loved one back home," Diaz says.

In consumer outreach, he says, the company seeks to align [itself] with different cultural and religious holidays. "[It's about] honoring their culture and celebrating with them [their] festivities," he explains.

Tips for Targeting Multicultural Audiences

One size does not fit all. While banks and other financial services companies might not offer products specifically created for different multicultural communities, outreach is best when it's tailored and targeted to regional initiatives and local centers of influence, which can help direct programs and messaging

Speaking the language is not enough. Though bilingual services and outreach are valuable commodities when tapping new multicultural demos, making sure that cultural values and meanings do not get lost in the translation can pose a challenge

Corporate sponsorship requires a personal touch. Simply having a name on the banner for cultural events might not be effective in courting new multicultural groups, especially if representatives are not present and directly interacting with the community

10 REACHING

Nike Negotiates the Cultural Landscape

In June 2007, Arab American groups called for a boycott of the new Nike Air Bakin basketball shoes. The groups contended that a logo on the back of the shoes too closely resembled the Arabic word for Allah. Writing the name of God in secular contexts is prohibited in the religion of Islam. As a result, Nike recalled 38,000 pairs of shoes and covered the offending logo with a patch. The company also diverted an additional 30,000 pairs from shipping to Saudi Arabia, Kuwait, Malaysia, Indonesia, and Turkey. In the end, it was forced to destroy thousands of pairs of shoes. A company vice president issued an apology to Muslims in general, and the Council of American–Islamic Relations agreed to call off the boycott.

It seems clear that Nike had not intentionally tried to offend the Muslim community. At the same time, the very expensive gaffe could have been avoided by paying greater attention to cultural mores and conducting more market research, such as focus groups. The company has made a commitment to supporting cultural diversity. In addition, in light of claims about unfair labor practices in the developing countries where its shoes are primarily manufactured, Nike has made recent efforts to bolster its corporate responsibility.

In fact, Nike was far more successful in reaching European audiences with the Stand Up Speak Up campaign, also launched in 2007. The campaign targeted violence, abuse, and racial bigotry. Nike produced commercials featuring well-known soccer players, such as Atto Addo and Roberto Carlos, holding placards in five languages expressing their concern about abuse. Black-and-white wristbands given to fans at soccer games reinforced the message in a participatory manner. The campaign

DIVERSE AUDIENCES

was well received and reinforced the message of racial harmony in a way that undercut the suggestion that Nike was attacking Muslims. Taken together, however, these two cases of campaigns carried out by the same company in the same year illustrate the challenges and opportunities that face public relations professionals.

❶ Which characteristics of the Muslim audience did Nike fail to take into account?

❷ Which steps did Nike take to respond to the crisis with its Muslim audience? What could additional response might the company have made?

❸ How can the perception that a company is socially responsible enhance its image and reputation and promote brand loyalty?

THE nature OF THE PUBLIC RELATIONS audience

If the audience for public relations messages was a monolithic whole, the work of practitioners would be far easier—and far less stimulating. In reality, an audience is a complex intermingling of groups with diverse cultural, ethnic, religious, and socioeconomic attributes, whose interests coincide at times and conflict in other situations.

A successful public relations campaign takes into account the shifting dynamics of audiences and targets those segments of an audience that are most desirable for its particular purpose. It also employs traditional and digital media that would be most effective in reaching those segments.

Diversity is the most significant aspect of the mass audience, or general public, in the United States. Differences in geography, history, culture, and economy among the regions of this sprawling country are striking; ranchers in Montana have different attitudes than residents in heavily populated Eastern Seaboard cities. Yet people in the two areas often share national interests. Ethnicity, generational differences, and socioeconomic status also shape the audience segments that public relations practitioners address. For example, the American Heart Association (AHA) provides specific resources aimed at African American and Hispanic populations. In particular, the Power to End

Stroke movement is an AHA initiative targeted to African Americans. *Soul Food Recipes*, a publication subsidized by the AHA, encourages healthy eating habits as part of the effort to prevent the likelihood of stroke in this group.

The international audience for public relations has expanded swiftly. Growth of global corporations and expanded foreign marketing by smaller firms creates new public relations challenges, however, as does increased foreign ownership of U.S. companies. International audiences are a diverse and significant target for public relations campaigns. For example, McDonald's has 31,000 restaurants in 119 countries. This company successfully tailors public relations campaigns along with its menus and décor to match the culture and values of each nation. For example, because eating beef is prohibited by the Hindu religion in India,

Some audience segments are easily identifiable and reachable as "prepackaged publics." For example, advocacy, civic, educational, and charitable organizations are generally well-organized groups whose members are bound by common interests; thus they constitute ready-made targets for public relations practitioners.

McDonald's offers the Maharaja Mac made from chicken or lamb.

Technology can be used to segment a mass audience and compile valuable demographic information. Public relations professionals can employ search engines and digital databases to conduct both primary and secondary research to narrow in on desirable target audiences. Geographic and social statistics from Census Bureau reports provide a rich foundation, which can be broken down by census tract and ZIP code. Data on automobile registrations, voter registrations, sales figures, mailing lists, and church and organization memberships also can be merged into computer databases.

The Internet and World Wide Web also provide an efficient and effective way to move beyond geographical limits in public relations messages, but they require quicker responses to their swiftly changing audiences. In the twenty-first century, people are becoming more visually oriented and seem to have shorter attention spans. The enormous impact of television has increased visual orientation, with many people now obtaining virtually all of their news from their TVs. Television news and entertainment programs increasingly are presented as discrete and quickly shifting images. At computer screens, consumers are exposed to dynamic multimedia content, including websites with streaming videos, regularly updated blogs, instant messaging, and web forums.

The swift pace of presentation may lead to viewers' shortened attention spans. In recognition of this trend, political leaders now reach the public largely in 10-second "sound bites." Television and the Internet also serve as a potent communicator of manners, mores, and aspirations.

American Idol and reality shows, for example, have made the dream of becoming famous seem tangible—if only, as artist Andy Warhol predicted in 1968, for 15 minutes.

Audiences sometimes coalesce around single issues. Some individ-

One marketing research organization, Claritas, has divided the Chicago metropolitan area into **62 lifestyle clusters** and assigned a name to each cluster. For example, the buying habits of "Boomers & Babies," Claritas says, include "rent more than five videos a month, buy children frozen dinners, read parenting magazines."

uals become so zealously involved in promoting or opposing a single issue that they lose the social and political balance so necessary to support a democracy. Animal rights and right-to-life activists frequently have been accused of going too far. For example, in 2008, seven member of the animal rights group Stop Huntingdon Animal Cruelty were convicted of blackmail in the United Kingdom for actions against managers of the Huntingdon Life Sciences research organization. Tactics of the group included physical assaults on workers, firebombing of cars, harassing communications, and bomb threats.

Society places a heavy emphasis on personality and celebrity. Sports stars, television and movie actors, and musical performers are virtually worshipped. When stars embrace causes, people often take note of those causes. Increasingly, celebrities are used as spokespersons and fund-raisers, even though their expertise as performers does not necessarily qualify them as experts or opinion leaders.

Another modern development with implications for public relations practice is the strong distrust of authority and suspicion of conspiracy that have arisen from sensationalistic investigative reporting. For example, the unethical business practices of executives at Enron, Tyco, WorldCom, Arthur Andersen, and other large corporations have generated a recent atmosphere of general distrust toward corporations. Legal (but highly suspect) practices such as unregulated dealing in credit default swaps and the slicing-and-dicing of derivatives by banks and insurance companies such as JP Morgan and AIG were largely responsible for the 2008 economic recession. Adding to this sense of unease, the highly publicized—and highly illegal—Ponzi schemes perpetuated by Bernie Madoff and Allen Stanford have made

think — How has television shaped the characteristics of modern American audiences?

investors and people in general skeptical about the motives and honesty of financial managers and Wall Street as a whole. People are so bombarded with exaggerated political promises, see so much financial chicanery, and are exposed to

Actors **Angelina Jolie**, **Brad Pitt**, **George Clooney**, **Alec Baldwin**, and **Susan Sarandon**, and musicians **Bono of U2** and **Chris Martin of Coldplay** have all been outspoken advocates of political causes; other celebrities such as **Robert Redford** and **Don Henley** have worked for causes more quietly behind the scenes. Actors **Ronald Reagan**, **Arnold Schwarzenegger**, and **Clint Eastwood**; singer **Sonny Bono**; and professional wrestler **Jesse Ventura** all capitalized on their fame to rise to political office.

so much misleading or even contradictory information that many of them now distrust what they read and hear in the news. Many consumers suspect evil motives of anyone trying to sell them anything, and tend to enjoy gossip and believe rumors. The need for public relations programs to develop an atmosphere of justifiable, rational trust is obvious.

Public relations has, by necessity, become more strategic in practice; audiences are targeted very precisely and in some instances messages are even customized at the individual level. In healthcare settings, for example, e-mail messages can be tailored to the individual patient based on his or her most recent examination. Not only can the public relations professional target a precise public, but in many cases the

practitioner can actually bypass the mass media and communicate directly with the preselected audience through customized mailings or other direct means such as personalized e-mails or broadcast faxes. The use of communication channels that directly reach an audience is called controlled media. Examples of controlled media include sponsored films or videos and events, which are discussed later in this chapter.

As the demographic makeup of the United States continues to change dramatically, some major target audiences have emerged that deserve special attention. One is senior citizens, also known simply as seniors. This group frequently is defined as men and women 65 years or older, although some sociologists, marketing experts, and organizations such as AARP (formerly

the American Association of Retired Persons) include everyone older than age 50. Comparable groups include the so-called tween market, which consists of youths age 7 to 12; the well-defined teenage demographic group; and baby boomers, defined as people born between 1946 and 1964.

Other emerging audiences with unique profiles include gender and lifestyle groups such as those made up of women, members of religious groups, or the gay community, as well as groups formed by racial and ethnic minorities, particularly audiences of African American and Hispanic descent. Beyond the diversity of ethnic markets in the United States, similar trends have become evident in an international context as the power of global markets has obviously risen.

age group
AUDIENCES

Youth

Public relations professionals have long recognized the importance of the youth market. Children and teenagers are an important demographic to marketers because they influence their parents' buying decisions, have their own purchasing power, and will mature into adult consumers. According to consumer market research company Packaged Facts, today's youth market (15- to 24-year-olds) has more than $500 billion of purchasing power.

Trends toward smaller families, started later, and dual incomes have led to greater disposable income for many U.S. families. Likewise, an unprecedented emphasis has been placed on the importance of child rearing. Television talk shows, websites targeted to parents, parenting books, and magazine articles, combined with advertising messages associating brand loyalty with good parenting, have led to increased spending by parents on children. Guilt can play a role as well. Parents pressed for time may provide material goods for children and teenagers in lieu of attention.

Today's children have greater autonomy and decision-making power within the family than their predecessors in previous generations. Children often pester or nag their parents into purchasing items they would not otherwise buy. *Kidfluence*, a marketing publication, notes that pestering can be divided into two categories—"persistence" and "importance." Persistence nagging (a plea that is repeated over and over again) is less sophisticated than importance nagging, which appeals to parents' desire to provide the best

for their children. Like every new generation before them, this generation of children causes adults to fret about their character but shows signs that they, too, will rise to the challenges that come with maturity.

The current youth market has been labeled as *Generation Y* (Gen Y), a term used for those born between 1981 and 2003. They succeed *Generation X* (Gen X), which was born between 1965 and 1980—a demographic group that is fre-

quently defined as independent, tech savvy, and resourceful.

Because they are such voracious consumers of electronic media, some pundits have labeled Generation Y "the E-Generation." The Fortino Group (Pittsburgh) projects that the typical member of Generation Y will spend 23 years online during his or her lifetime.

Some General Characteristics of YOUTH

Generation Y values relationships and trust. In a survey of 1,200 teens worldwide, Ketchum's Global Brand Marketing Practice found:

- Parents still rule when it comes to advice about careers and drugs, and even for product decisions.
- Trust in information is derived from relationships.
- The top five sources of advice are parents, doctors, clergy, friends, and teachers.
- As avid and skilled Internet users, Gen Y is savvy about unfiltered and unpoliced content.
- Teens recognize the credibility of editorial content compared to ads and even public service announcements, with television being the most trusted medium for them.
- Publicity for products and issues will influence members of Gen Y, whether those messages are directed at them or at those to whom they look for advice.

Spending one-third of their lives online will have interesting effects on Gen Y members:

- They will spend as much time interacting with friends online as in person.
- Initial interaction online will precede most dating and marriages.
- They will spend ten times more time online than in interaction with parents.
- They will be more reserved in social skills.
- They will be savvy and skeptical about online identities such as chat participants.
- They will not tolerate print forms, slow application processes, and archaic systems.

Some General Characteristics of BABY BOOMERS

- Baby boomers tend to define themselves according to their profession.
- Baby boomers are, as a group, well educated and take pride in accomplishment.
- Baby boomers often question authority and are likely to take a strong position on social issues.
- Baby boomers are competitive, particularly when it comes to their careers.
- Baby boomers have great appreciation for leisure time, which they believe is well earned.

think How is the youth market of today distinct from the audiences made up of their parents and grandparents?

Baby Boomers

The term *baby boomer* refers to people born between 1946 and 1964. This period was characterized by a high birth rate and general prosperity in the United States following World War II. Unlike their parents, baby boomers did not suffer through prolonged economic depression and enjoyed many advantages as the international stature of the United States grew. As a consequence, they are less reluctant to spend disposable income on consumer goods and luxury items. However, the outlook of baby boomers varies widely depending on when they were born during the 1946–1964 span. Those born in the late 1940s and early 1950s faced the turmoil of the Vietnam era. Those born later, who did not experience the war as directly, share many of the characteristics of Generation X. People born between 1956 and 1964 are sometimes referred to as "shadow baby boomers."

Baby boomers represent the first generation to come of age during the advent of television. As such, their buying habits and lifestyle are heavily influenced by visual advertising. As the same time, they tend as a group to be more skeptical and discerning than their parents' generation. Messages about health, responsible parenting and child care, and active lifestyles tend to resonate with baby boomers.

The first baby boomers will turn 65 in 2011. By 2030, approximately one-fifth of the U.S. population, or 71.5 million people, will be 65 or older. Advances in medical science and a concern for health among baby boomers mean that they will certainly be the longest-lived generation. Their buying power is esti-

mated at $50 billion, making them the largest and most economically advantaged group in the United States. The aging of the baby boomers will bolster the ranks of the already powerful AARP, which lobbies for legislation on health care and other political issues

Seniors

Medical advances and better living conditions have improved life expectancy to the point that today 37.8 million Americans, or 12.8 percent of the U.S. population, are age 65 or

older, according to the 2008 U.S. Census data. According to Census Bureau projections, 21 percent of the U.S. population will be 65 or older by 2050. The heavy upsurge in the senior population will peak at 50 million by 2025, when a critical mass of the post–World War II baby boomers will pass age 65.

Older citizens form an important opinion group and a consumer market with special interests. As is the case with other demographic groups, they are not a monolithic audience, but rather display many

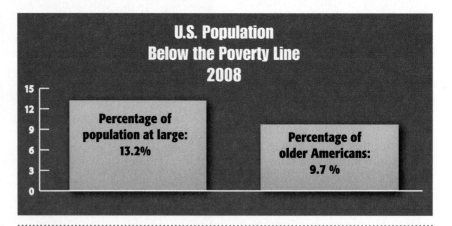

U.S. Population Below the Poverty Line 2008

Percentage of population at large: 13.2%

Percentage of older Americans: 9.7 %

Seniors are financially better off than the stereotypes suggest. The Census Bureau reports that people age 65 to 74 have more discretionary income than any other group. The median annual income of U.S. seniors was $18,208 in 2008, and they own approximately 70 percent of the country's assets. In many instances, seniors' homes are completely paid for.

variations in personality, interest, financial status, health concerns, and lifestyles. Nevertheless, public relations professionals should not overlook the general characteristics of the senior audience.

According to Neilson/NetRating, seniors older than the age of 65 were the fastest-growing segment of the U.S. population using the Internet in 2003, increasing at a rate of about 25 percent per year. In 2000, seniors accounted for 5.6 percent of Internet users. In 2004, 22 percent of seniors used the Internet. By 2008, according to a Pew Research Study, that number had more than doubled, to 45 percent. Notably Facebook, in 2009, reported that its fastest-growing demographic was individuals older than the age of 50. In general, however, seniors lag behind younger age groups in their use of social media. Unsurprisingly, seniors are also among the largest consumers of television, magazines, books, and newspapers.

Some General Characteristics of SENIORS

- With the perspective of long experience, seniors often are less easily convinced than young adults, demand value in the things they buy, and pay little attention to fads.
- They vote in greater numbers than their juniors and are more intense readers of newspapers and magazines. Retirees also watch television more frequently than younger persons.
- Seniors represent an excellent source of volunteers for social, health, and cultural organizations because they have time and often are looking for something to do.
- They are extremely health conscious, out of self-interest, and want to know about medical developments. A Census Bureau study showed that most people older than age 65 say they are in good health; not until their mid-80s do they frequently need assistance in daily living.
- Although they are poor customers for household goods, seniors eat out frequently and do a lot of gift buying. They also travel frequently, accounting for approximately 80 percent of commercial vacation travel.

gender/lifestyle
AUDIENCES

emerging audiences, such as women, members of religious groups, and the gay community, have characteristics that public relations professionals should make themselves more aware of, so that they may communicate effectively with these growing demographic groups.

Women

Women constitute an enormous and diverse demographic group that has always been an important and distinct target audience from marketing and public relations standpoints. Women account for more than half of the world's population and express varied interests and perspectives. In many global settings, women are beginning to exercise the kind of political and social power that they attained in the United States, Europe, and parts of Asia during the last century.

In addition to their impressive purchasing power, women are more than men likely to exercise influence as opinion leaders. Research suggests that women have a larger network of friends and tend to maintain more regular contact with the circle of friends and acquaintances than men. They tend to value the opinions of friends, experts, and media as opposed to

"Today's women hold an overwhelming share of consumer purchasing influence, making more than 80% of household purchase decisions, and spending over $3.3 trillion annually."

Kelley Skoloda, Director of Global Brand Marketing, Ketchum

marketing messages. Public relations giant Ketchum has established a division named Women 25 to 54 to meet the needs of companies and organizations seeking to reach this demographic group. The company coined the term "multiminded" to describe how women negotiate their various roles as professionals, mothers, wives, caregivers, and so forth. Because of time pressures and competition for their attention, women are thought to receive and absorb information in smaller chunks.

Women as a Special Audience: Breast Cancer Awareness in Pakistan

The Women's Empowerment Group, a nongovernmental organization (NGO) in Pakistan, had a major public relations challenge. Statistics showed that the country has the highest rate of breast cancer of any Asian nation. However, Pakistan's conservative Muslim society made public discussion of anything related to women's bodies a very sensitive topic. Indeed, the majority of Pakistani women are reluctant to be examined by doctors because of shyness and social customs.

Given this situation, the Women's Empowerment Group sought to break the taboos by enlisting the support of the then–First Lady, Begum Sehba Musharraf, to launch the first-ever nationwide Breast Cancer Awareness Campaign. Its primary objectives were to make breast cancer an acceptable topic for discussion in the public domain of Pakistan, to create widespread awareness about breast cancer among urban and rural women, and to promote breast self-examination.

The tactics used included the following measures: (1) distribution of easy-to-read brochures through utility bills, health clinics, and women's colleges; (2) news releases, articles, and interviews in the press; (3) establishment of a bilingual, interactive website for women to get information and exchange information; (4) live discussion programs on FM radio and national television; (5) establishment of support groups; and (6) seminars and workshops for women's groups in various cities.

Because of the prominent spokespersons and the distribution of culturally sensitive promotional materials, the campaign was able to overcome the constraints of a conservative Islamic society and make breast cancer part of the national health agenda. Several governmental ministries became partners in the campaign for breast cancer awareness, and the Ministry of Health in Punjab even started a pilot project to train 3,700 local health volunteers to teach breast self-examination to women. Extensive coverage about the campaign and breast cancer appeared in local print, broadcast, and electronic media. International news outlets, such as BBC, also covered the story.

Source: International Public Relations Association (IPRA), Golden World Awards 2005.

Gays and Lesbians

The gay community shows impressive growth as an emerging demographic. According to a yearly census conducted by OpusComm Group, the S. I. Newhouse School of Public Communications at Syracuse University, and Scarborough Research, between 22 and 30 million gay, lesbian, bisexual, and transgendered (GLBT) people live in the United States.

Like members of the evangelical Christian demographic group (discussed later in this chapter), GLBT consumers tend to support companies and brands that reflect and support their views. To that end, Human Rights Campaign launched the "Buying for Equality 2010" initiative to help identify companies sympathetic to GLBT issues.

According to Garber, the gay community has high brand loyalty, purchasing products that target advertisements to gay consumers and support gay issues. Subaru pioneered "gay-specific" advertising in 1996 with a campaign specifically targeting lesbian consumers using gay tennis star Martina Navratilova as a spokesperson. The Internet travel site Orbitz, Absolut Vodka, Campbell's, Disney, Ford, and BMW have also made efforts to appeal directly to gay audiences.

Although emerging GLBT audiences have a great deal of appeal to marketers, public relations professionals should be careful about the messages they release. The GLBT community may be offended by conventional or normative principles

How can public relations professionals leverage the informal opinion leadership role played by various community members?

Gay households have a median income of $65,000 per year and typically are highly educated. Witeck-Combs/Harris Interactive and MarketResearch.com estimate that GLBT individuals spend between $712 billion per year.

that conflict with their values and lifestyles. As with any target audience, public relations professionals need to consider the identities of these audience members when undertaking public relations efforts.

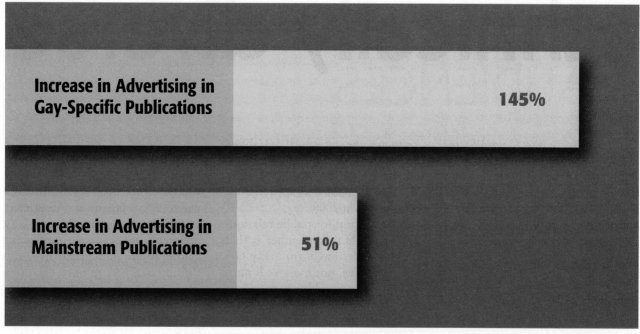

Increase in Advertising in Gay-Specific Publications — 145%

Increase in Advertising in Mainstream Publications — 51%

Gay Press Report noted that advertising in media with gay-specific content represented a $181.9 million market in 2007, up 148 percent from the value in 1996. This compares to a 51 percent rise in value for mainstream publication advertising over the same period.

Religious Groups

As society changes, new audiences continually emerge. Public relations professionals must be aware of this dynamic and pay attention to such audiences. For example, Catholic and evangelical Christian religious groups are growing in size and sometimes bonding together in new constellations. Movies such as *The Passion of Christ* (2004) and *The Da Vinci Code* (2006) have served as a focal point around which such groups have shown their influence and expressed their values and concerns, both positive and negative.

According to Packaged Facts, the U.S. religious publishing and products (RPP) market amounted to $6 billion in 2008. From a marketing/ public relations point of view, it is clear that products and services structured around religious themes sell. The RPP market has achieved mainstream status and continues to grow a steady rate. In a global setting, it competes with other religious traditions.

Sales of books with Christian themes, excluding Bibles, has increased fourfold since 1980, and Christian music now accounts for approximately 5 percent of all CD sales.

ethnically diverse
AUDIENCES

historically, the United States has welcomed millions of immigrants and assimilated them into the cultural mainstream. Immigrants have given the United States an eclectic mixture of personal values, habits, lifestyles, and perceptions that have been absorbed slowly, sometimes reluctantly.

Recently, ethnic groups—primarily Hispanics, African Americans, Asian Americans, and Native Americans—as a whole have been growing five times faster than the general population. Nonwhite ethnic groups now account for the ma-

jority in some states such as California. The U.S. Census Bureau announced that 34 percent of the population claimed minority ethnic background in 2008.

A basic point for public relations professionals to remember is that these populations form many target audiences, not massive homogeneous groups whose members have identical interests. Hispanics in Miami may have different cultures and concerns than Hispanics living in Texas or Arizona. To be more precise, even the common terms for minority groups, such as

Asian American, misrepresent the cultural diversity among racial groups. For example, the lifestyles, values, and interests of fourth-generation Japanese Americans in Los Angeles are dramatically different from those prevalent among recent immigrants from the Philippines. A public relations professional must identify and define an audience with particular care and sensitivity, not only taking race into account but also considering the cultural and ethnic self-identity of target audience segments.

Getting the Word Out on Gay Tourism

ACCORDING THE INTERNATIONAL GAY AND LESBIAN ASSOCIATION (IGLTA), the value of the gay tourism market exceeds $64.5 billion per year in the United States. More than cities and several states sponsor public relations efforts to encourage gay, lesbian, bisexual, and transgendered (GLBT) tourists to visit. New York City, for example, created "The Rainbow Pilgrimage" campaign to promote GLBT travel by commemorating the fortieth anniversary of the Stonewall Riots, the seminal event in the history of the fight for gay rights in New York City.

The IGLTA promoted GLBT Pride events in more than a dozen cities between August and November 2009. Pride events, according to the Human Right Campaign, provide community members with a "unique opportunity to celebrate and mobilize around key issues." In 2008–2009, one key issue was same-sex marriage. Although voters in California defeated Proposition 8, which would have legalized

the ... turesque ... honeymoon," but even the older generations don't bat an eyelid at queer couples walking hand in hand into local shops and restaurants."

Of course, not all residents or politicians are equally eager to have their states known as favorite destinations for GLBT couples. When a poster announcing "South Carolina is so Gay!" appeared in Underground stations during London's Gay Pride Week, the "low-level" staffer in the South Carolina Department of Parks, Recreations, and Tourism who had signed off on the initiative was promptly fired. South Carolina State Representative David Thomas worried that taxpayers would be "irate" to learn that tax dollars where used to promote homosexuality. "We're so gay?" Charleston resident Ventphis Stafford asked rhetorically. "Nah. Wrong state. Go to California." Given the size of the market, one wonders whether Thomas, Stafford, or the head of the Department of Tourism are wise to so quickly turn away the influx of cash GLBT couples can add to state coffers.

1 How can organizations benefit from paying attention to niche markets such as the GLBT community?

2 How can messages that target a niche market avoid spurring a backlash or contributing to reinforcement of stereotypes?

3 What would be some public relations strategies to effectively reach emerging gender and lifestyle audiences?

Freedom started here.

In addition to our famous historical sites, Philadelphia and Its Countryside has scores of gay-friendly restaurants, clubs, theaters and shops where you will feel warmly welcomed. We invite you to have a great time in the place where all people were given the freedom to live life as they choose. To plan your next trip, reserve a hotel package, or download a brochure, visit gophila.com/gay.

PHiLADELPHiA
★Get your history straight and your nightlife gay.

Bucks • Chester • Delaware • Montgomery • Philadelphia Counties

 PENNSYLVANIA www.visitPA.com

 Philadelphia Gay Tourism Caucus

 GREATER PHILADELPHIA TOURISM MARKETING CORPORATION LOVE

 PHILLY'S MORE FUN WHEN YOU SLEEP OVER

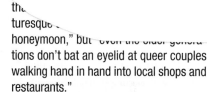

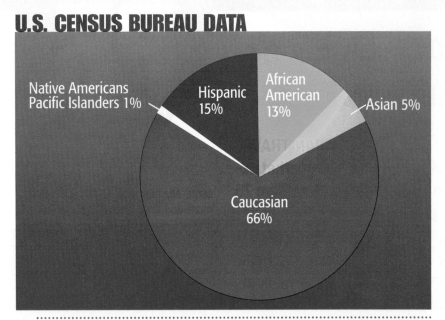

Native Americans Pacific Islanders 1%

Hispanic 15%

African American 13%

Asian 5%

Caucasian 66%

Caucasians accounted for 66 percent of Americans in 2007, down from 77 percent in 2000. According to the Census Bureau, even greater changes will occur by 2050. Notably, Hispanics will account for nearly one-fourth of the U.S. population in that year.

Diversity Media

The number and reach of the minority media through which messages can be delivered has increased, just as the number of their constituents has expanded. While the number of general market newspapers declined between 2008 and 2009, nearly 200 new Hispanic newspapers were founded during the same period. Spanish-language and African American radio stations also have increased in number. According to Arbitron, 872 radio stations across the United States broadcast in Spanish in 2008. Also according to Arbitron, more than 90 percent of Hispanics in every demographic group tune in to the radio each week. Two Spanish-language TV networks, Univision and Telemundo, serve millions of viewers. The Black Entertainment Television Network (BET) has a large national audience—peaking at about 350,000 daily viewers in 2007. Newscasts on KTSF reach 91,000

think **Why is it never safe to assume that all native Spanish speakers share similar values?**

Cantonese speakers each night in the area around San Francisco, where Asians make up approximately 20 percent of the regional population. Many cable and satellite providers offer special packages in a variety of native languages. A substantial number of outlets exist for public relations messages, provided news releases and story pitches are translated and culturally appropriate.

Business Wire, a major distributor of public relations messages, recognizes this diversity of interest among racial and ethnic minority groups and operates separate Hispanic, African American, and Asian American media circuits within the United States.

Public relations practitioners also should be aware of mixed-race individuals whose representation in the media is perhaps more complex. Barack Obama, the first U.S. president of acknowledged mixed race, is often portrayed simply as an African American in media

representations—celebrated as the first "black president." For example, Peggy Noonan wrote in the *Wall Street Journal* that Obama was "the brilliant young black man" prior to his election. Similarly, Tiger Woods's Thai heritage is not noted as often as his African ancestry. To describe or represent a complex ancestry, it would seem, requires a great deal of effort and finesse, and it is difficult to find a clear consensus on just how to do it successfully yet sensitively.

Hispanics

The expansion of the Hispanic population represents a challenge for public relations practitioners. Merely translating messages into Spanish is not sufficient for ensuring that they reach this population in the intended fashion. Instead, public relations practitioners must proactively shape communications to be responsive to Hispanic culture. According to New America Strategies Group and DemoGraph Corporation, Hispanic culture traditionally places great emphasis on family and children and spends three times more on health care and entertainment than comparable non-Hispanic households. Hispanic spending on consumer goods has so far outpaced that of other ethnic groups in the United States.

Radio is an especially important way to reach this ethnic group. Surveys show that the average Hispanic person listens to the radio 26 to 30 hours per week, about 13 percent more than the general population. Hispanic station KLVE-FM has the largest audience in Los Angeles, more than any English-language station.

Television also has a large, rapidly expanding Hispanic audience. According to the Nielsen rating service, the number of Hispanic households with televsions rose by an estimated 4.3 percent in the 2008–2009 span. This rate of increase outpaces that of other ethnic groups at a rate of 3 to 1. Univision, the predominant Spanish-language

Reaching Out to Hispanics

In the United States, Hispanic populations are estimated to include approximately 46 million persons (approximately 15 percent of the total U.S. population), having increased at a rate of 3.2 percent between 2007 and 2008. Despite a slightly lower immigration rate for Hispanics in recent years, the U.S. Hispanic market has continued to expand at a pace that surpasses the growth rates for other demographic groups in the country. Given these numbers, it is no surprise that many organizations and corporations have made efforts to target Hispanic constituents and consumers.

Public relations campaigns have tended to focus on cultural factors such as the perceived Hispanic emphasis on traditional values and ethnic pride. For example, Colgate targeted mothers in its "El Mes de la Salud Bucal" campaign to promote oral health because it recognized the importance of maternal influence in Hispanic culture. Heineken's recent "Demuestra Quein Eres" ("Give Yourself a Good Name") Mural Arts Series tapped into cultural pride and traditional Hispanic male concern with reputation. However, Mike Valdes-Fauli, managing director of U.S. Hispanic practice at The Jeffrey Group, envisions public relations targeting evolving "less blatant and transparent hooks."

Hispanic consumers have been prime consumers of media, but the recent economic downturn has taken its toll on Hispanic print outlets. Several magazines targeting Latino audiences have suspended publication, including two (*Hoy* and *Sport Illustrated Latino*) of the four major sports magazines. Bilingual and English-language publications have been especially hard hit, as Hispanic advertising dollars gravitated more exclusively toward Spanish-language publications. "We were going to have to be extra crafty, creative, and strategic if we were going to continue to secure quality Hispanic media coverage for our clients," said Melissa Karp Smith, executive vice president of RL Public Relations/Sportivo.

One result of the crisis in the Hispanic print media has been that consumers have been increasingly turning to online sources for information. Latino audiences have trailed other demographic groups in terms of Internet use, but the gulf is narrowing rapidly. As a result, the use of social marketing and networks among Latinos has expanded. For example, American Airlines used Twitter and Facebook to promote its AA Advantage program to Hispanic audiences. Fleishman-Hilliard is working with the Boy Scouts of America to create bilingual social media components on Scouting.org in an effort to "reintroduce Scouting to America."

TV network, claims to reach three-fourths of Hispanic viewers. Univision consistently has ranked fourth or fifth among all broadcast networks in the 18- to 34-year-old demographic, according to Nielsen's National Television Index. The Spanish-language TV network Telemundo is also making impressive market share gains.

African Americans

Historically the most readily identifiable racial group in the United States, African Americans are far from a monolithic group sharing a common heritage or goals. African American households wield about $700 billion in buying power. In recent years, affluent members of the African American community have been responsible for many of these purchases. Specialized magazines, such as *Uptown*, and websites catering to affluent African American professionals have seen a marked increase in readership. "The world is now a different place for the affluent African American demographic," said Len Burnett, co-founder of *Uptown*. "Luxury brands understand the importance of niche shoppers with disposable income and *Uptown* delivers them efficiently." Business Wire's "Black PR Wire" includes listings for more than 1,000 black-owned publications, including both newspapers and magazines.

The urban market is often associated with African Americans, although it is not necessarily exclusively urban or restricted to people of African descent. Although 40 percent of African Americans do live in the ten largest U.S. cities, the urban market is defined by fashion trends set by hip-hop music stars, and it extends principally to member of Generation X and Y of all ethic backgrounds.

Like all Americans, African Americans have faced harsh economic times in recent years. In one survey, the Pew Research Center found that 44 percent of African American respondents did not believe that their situation would improve in 2007,

CAVEAT EMPTOR

Promoting Financial Literacy in Minority Communities

In tough economic times, money management is at the top of nearly everyone's list of concerns. But financial literacy has long been identified among the top concerns of many minority groups. According to a Harris Interactive Poll conducted for the National Foundation for Credit Counseling, 50 percent of African Americans and 45 percent of Hispanic adults grade their own financial acumen as a C, D, or F, compared to 38 percent of Caucasians who do so. Kim Hunter, president of Lagrant Communications, notes that messages about economic development, home ownership, and financial literacy have particular resonance among African American audiences.

New Initiatives

Many organizations, including NGOs, grassroots associations, corporations, and government agencies, have sought to address this concern through initiatives to increase financial literacy among African Americans and other minority groups. For example, Jump$tart has supported financial education programs in public schools since 1995. In 2008, the United States Conference of Mayors sponsored the National Dollar Wi$e Campaign in four cities to promote financial education programs. The same year, the U.S. Treasury Department sponsored the National Financial Literacy Challenge for high school students. Some of these initiatives, such as Budgetball, the National Academy of Public

Administration's adaptation of basketball to a financial setting, have been designed specifically to reach urban and minority populations.

Harmful or Helpful

The objectivity of some of these financial advice programs has come under scrutiny question. The Dollar Wi$e Campaign was underwritten by Countrywide Mortgage, a company that sold many of the subprime mortgages now blamed in part for the financial crisis of 2008.

Other initiatives skate dangerously close to doing more harm than good. CompuCredit launched a financial literacy initiative in 2004 in partnership with historically black universities. The Community Financial Services Association (CFSA) developed a program for inner-city children entitled "Youth Learn & Save." Although the goals of these programs are laudable, commentators such as Stephanie Jones, writing in Mother Jones, have questioned the rationale of inviting a payday loan company (CompuCredit) and its lobbying group (CFSA) to offer financial advice. Complicating matters even further, some leaders of the Southern Christian Leadership Conference (SCLC), an organization founded by Dr. Martin Luther King, Jr., came to the defense of CompuCredit. SCLC president Charles Steele argued that payday loans are often the only source of credit available in financially underserved neighborhoods.

compared to 57 percent of those surveyed ten years earlier. Perhaps more troubling, more than two-thirds of survey participants believed

that there was a significant difference in values between economically disadvantaged and more affluent African Americans.

global
AUDIENCES

audiences in places such as Russia, China, India, Latin America, and Europe are drawing the attention of public relations professionals as trade (and, correspondingly, public relations) expands globally. Public relations professionals must overcome language barriers and consider social differences if they are to practice culturally appropriate and locally acceptable public relations. Differences in lifestyles, customs, values, and cultures are not the only challenges. Unique aspects of the local political, economic, and industrial structures also affect the strategic planning and execution of public relations campaigns.

China is one growing market undergoing revolutionary political, social, and industrial changes. Since it reopened to Western markets in 1978, the growth of business opportunities in China has been phenomenal. Despite the dark shadow of corruption and government regulation as ongoing concerns, American and European companies have embraced the Chinese market. Awareness of local customs and business practices is critical in pursuing these opportunities, however. "There are cultural differences that you have to become attuned to," said Cynthia He, an investment relations manager with the search engine company Baidu in China during an interview with *Time* magazine Asia edition reporter Bill Powell. "I've been at meetings when I've been very blunt in pointing something out, and there will be an awkward second or two of silence, and then someone will politely say, 'Well, that's a very American way of looking at it,' which is another way of saying, 'Hey, will you tone it down a bit!'" In China, personal influence is important in every aspect of the business, social, and media systems. For example, if public relations practitioners want to send out news releases, they may need to get to know the reporters personally as part of the process.

think — What are some of the challenges to reaching global audiences with cultural, social, economic, and political differences?

Companies occasionally make missteps when entering international markets. Sony Entertainment, for example, drew fierce criticism in 2007 when it used a decapitated goat to promote the videogame *God of War II* in Athens, Greece. After the fact, Sony issued a statement apologizing for the campaign: "We recognize that the use of a dead goat was in poor taste and fell below the high standards of conduct we set for ourselves." Sony also drew fire for allowing a subsidiary company, Insomniac Games, to use Manchester Cathedral as a setting in *Resistance: Fall of Man*. In the game, players fought gun battles in the sacred historical building.

btw...

When McDonald's opened its first restaurant in Russia immediately after the breakup of the Soviet Union in 1991, the press embraced the fast-food restaurant as a symbol of all that was positive about Western culture in contrast to Soviet culture. As the novelty of Western-style capitalism wore thin, however, public relations in Russia reincorporated old-style Soviet propaganda tools. Corruption became common, as so-called public relations "technologists" funneled millions of dollars into journalists' hands in exchange for favorable press coverage. Overloading the press with rumor and hearsay about rival politicians or corporations—a technique known as "black public relations"—was also a frequent strategy.

With the dawn of the new millennium, Russian public relations professionals began to recognize the benefit of modern public relations approaches. They assisted the German manufacturer Bosch, for example, in launching a major campaign to convince Russians of the advantage of owning a dishwasher. By enlisting artists and musicians as advocates, Bosch increased its sales by 70 percent in a brief period. An art installation entitled "A Monument to the Amount of Time Wasted on Washing Up" was particularly successful at helping define public need for a dishwasher. An art installation in the United States or Canada would probably be ineffective in convincing consumers to buy such a product; because of cultural differences, however, it was successful in Russia.

MATCHING THE
audience
WITH THE media

given the broad array of print, audio, visual, and new media outlets available, public relations practitioners must make wise choices to use their time and budgets efficiently and effectively to produce desired outcomes. Some general guidelines can be given for matching audiences with the media. In this section, we quickly introduce the different types of media; in Chapters 11 and 12, we go into more details about each key media type, the way in which materials are prepared for media, and the most effective use of each form in public relations efforts.

Print

Print media are the most effective choice for delivering a message that requires absorption of details and contemplation by receivers. Printed matter can be read repeatedly and kept for reference. Newspapers are comparatively fast to disseminate information and have the most widespread impact of the print outlets. Magazines, although slower to disseminate topical information, are better for reaching special-interest audiences. Books take even longer to publish and subsequently digest, but can generate strong impact over time. Increasingly, traditional media primarily appeal to older or more highly educated audiences.

Newspapers are aimed at an audience of varying educational and economic levels and are designed for family reading. They attempt to include something of interest to men, women, and children. Newspaper editors cast a wide net to cap-

ture the reading interests of as many people as possible. Newspapers have a broad appeal among adults and are effective at handling complex or in-depth material that television cannot adequately cover. While hard copies of newspapers such as the *New York Times*, *Washington Post*, or *Wall Street Journal* reach older public opinion leaders, young people tend to turn to print newspapers less often, favoring online media instead.

Magazines differ markedly from newspapers in terms of content, time frame, and methods of operation. Thus they present different opportunities and problems to public relations practitioners. In contrast to daily newspapers, which have tight deadlines, magazines may be published weekly, monthly, or sometimes quarterly. Because these publications usually deal with sub-

jects in greater depth than newspapers do, magazine editors may allot months for the development of an article. Public relations professionals who seek to supply subject ideas or ready-to-publish material to magazines must plan much further ahead than is necessary with newspapers.

Because their writing and publication is a time-consuming process, often involving years from the conception of an idea until the appear-

> A public relations practitioner has four principal approaches for getting material into magazines and trade publications:
>
> **1.** Submit a story idea that would promote the practitioner's cause, either directly or subtly, and urge the editor to have a writer (either a freelancer or a staff member), develop the story on assignment.
>
> **2.** Query the editor by telephone or e-mail, and outline the article idea to get tentative approval.
>
> **3.** Submit a completed article, written either by the practitioner or by an independent writer under contract, and hope that the editor will accept it for publication. In this and the two previously mentioned instances, the editor should be made fully aware of the source of the suggestion or article.
>
> **4.** For trade journals and other periodicals that use such material, submit a feature or news story via e-mail or through a digital distribution firm such as Business Wire.

ance of the printed volume, books are not popularly recognized as public relations tools. Yet they can be. A book, especially a hardcover one, has stature in the minds of readers. Books promulgate ideas—usually complex concepts that require greater detail and analysis than news stories or magazine pieces. As channels of communication, books reach thoughtful audiences, including opinion leaders, who are willing to devote time to their study. Publication of a book often starts a trend or focuses national discussion on an issue. In addition, e-books represent an emerging market.

Radio and Video

Radio's greatest advantages are its flexibility and ability to reach specific target audiences. Messages can be prepared for and broadcast on radio more rapidly than on television, and at a much lower cost. Because there are nine times as many radio stations as TV stations in the United States, audience exposure is easier to obtain. The downside is that the audiences reached by radio are smaller than their television-watching counterparts.

Speed and mobility are the special attributes that make radio unique among the major media, although Internet communications such as blogs and podcasting are threatening to unseat radio from this unique position. If urgency justifies such action, messages can be placed on the air almost instantly upon their receipt at a radio station. Because radio programming is more loosely structured than television programming, interruption of a program for an urgent announcement can be done with less internal decision making.

Television

Television has the strongest emotional impact of any type of mass media. The vividness and personality of the TV communicator creates

99 percent of U.S. households owned one or more television sets in 2009.

The average American family watches television for 7 hours each day.

According to estimates provided by the A. C. Nielsen Company, the average American family watches television about 7 hours per day despite the advent of the Internet. Little wonder that public relations specialists look upon television as an enormous arena in which to tell their stories.

an influence that print media cannot match. Television currently has the largest and broadest audience.

The fundamental factor that differentiates television from other media and gives it such pervasive impact is its visual element. Producers of entertainment shows, newscasts, and commercials regard movement on the screen as essential. Something must happen to hold the viewer's attention. The single "talking head" set against a simple backdrop once common to television news programs has given way in recent years to bold graphics, running headlines, sports scores, and stock quotes—sometimes to the detriment of the central message.

Video is another important public relations tool. Both corporations and nonprofit organizations use films

think How is the Internet changing the role that radio plays in public relations campaigns?

and videos for internal purposes as part of audiovisual programs to train and inform their employees or for external purposes to inform and influence the public, the financial community, or visitors touring their facilities. For example, when Levi Strauss & Co. needed to explain to its employees a new personnel management program called Teamwork, it prepared a video for them. Like some other corporations, San Diego Gas & Electric Company produces a periodic *Employee Video News Magazine*. The topics covered range from the company's annual meeting to an employee's campaign against graffiti.

Online Media

Online media were once thought of as just a supplemental method of reaching a generally well-educated, relatively affluent audience. In recent years, however, their role has expanded exponentially. Currently, 80 percent of U.S. households own a computer and 92 percent of those who own a computer have Internet

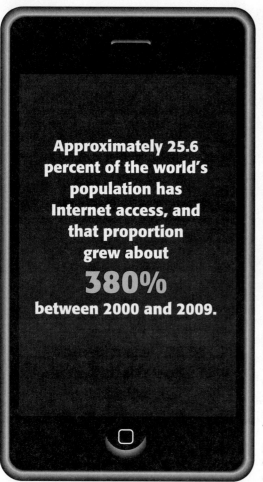

Approximately 25.6 percent of the world's population has Internet access, and that proportion grew about 380% between 2000 and 2009.

access. In the foreseeable future, it is likely that electronic media delivery systems, such as Internet and wireless communications, will overtake print media and even television as the primary source of information.

The personal computer represents a significant and swiftly expanding tool for public relations practitioners. E-mail and the Internet's ability to deliver information about clients' projects, to establish contacts with reporters, and to exchange ideas has drastically altered the intellectual and entertainment landscape in the brief span of 15 years: It is surprising to recall that e-mail was not widely used before the early 1990s and that the first World Wide Web page appeared in 1991.

The Internet and World Wide Web offer unusual opportunities to reach audiences with messages in the exact form that public relations practitioners conceive them.

Millions of companies, nonprofit organizations, and individuals maintain sites on the World Wide Web, from which they explain their companies and brands, promote their products and services, and often sell merchandise directly to consumers. They post text, audio, and video news releases and other company materials on their websites so that anyone can easily access them. Although most sites are readily accessible to the public, some require access codes or have other access limitations. By participating in online discussion groups, chat rooms, and similar online interchanges, public relations people often reach opinion leaders in specific fields with facts and opinions favorable to their cause. They even directly reach target consumers, investors, community members, and employees without having to pass through any media gatekeepers. Using e-mails and listservs, public relations practitioners can deliver specially tailored messages to precisely targeted audiences.

Public relations professionals especially depend on online media for communicating with Generations X and Y. Members of Gen X and Gen Y spend a lot of time in front of computers, searching the web, chatting with their friends, playing videogames, or shopping online. The virtual environment allows them opportunities to multitask, perhaps doing research for a paper while also making friends whom they may never meet face-to-face, and in the most extreme instances, even dating and marrying someone from the other side of the world.

Social Media

Increased use of social media by public relations practitioners is a relatively recent trend. Social media tools offer opportunities and challenges to reach diverse audiences in new ways. Facebook, YouTube, MySpace, and similar sites provide forums for people to exchange ideas, make virtual friends, and pursue romantic relationships. The downside, of course, is the potential for abuse. As with the Internet in general, it is often difficult to ascertain the accuracy of sources and disclosure of personal information poses potentially dangerous consequences.

As the realization of all-digital public relations initiatives looms on the horizon, professionals would do well to remember that multicultural audiences are among the most enthusiastic and voracious consumers of social media. A survey conducted

According to the Florida State University Center for Hispanic Marketing Communications, 36 percent of English-preferring Hispanics, 34 percent of Asians, 37 percent of Spanish-preferring Hispanics, and 26 percent of African Americans use social networks at least once a week.

Muestra Tu Herencia was Kodak's first all-digital marketing effort targeting a multicultural group.

by MEE Productions found that 96 percent of urban youth access the Internet and that Hispanics represent the fastest-growing demographic group online today. Eleven percent of Internet users are African American, and more than 90 percent of Asian Americans are connected online.

Clearly, social media represent an emerging venue for public relations communication. A few companies and organizations have made strides in exploiting this channel. For example, Kodak recently developed an interactive website that encourages Hispanic consumers to participate by posting photographs on a virtual scrapbook called *Mutestra Tu Herencia* (Show Your Heritage). Honda has enlisted MySpace to promote the famous Battle of the Bands that takes place each year at historical black colleges.

Of course, many challenges must be overcome when using social media for public relations applications. Chief among them is the need to develop tactics to ensure cultural relevancy, avoid clichés, and move beyond standardized approaches.

> "Social media for many companies is still very much a young endeavor. When you combine taking baby steps in social media with equal baby steps you might be taking in multicultural (media), it means you are being even more cautious as you go in."
>
> Manny Ruiz, president of PR Newswire Multicultural Services

APPLY YOUR KNOWLEDGE

WHAT WOULD YOU DO?

The latest innovation in sun care is spray-on sunscreen canisters, which emit a clear mist that completely coats the skin without damaging the ozone layer. Dermatologists claim that spray-on sunscreens offer the same protection as lotions. They also have the advantage of being easy to apply, which means that individuals will be more likely to coat every part of the body rather than just dabbing a little lotion on their arms, nose, or shoulders.

Banana Boat brand is currently marketing its UltraMist sunblock to compete with other major brand offerings such as Coppertone Continuous Spray and Neutrogena Fresh Cooling Body Mist Sunblock. In addition, Target and Wal-Mart plan to market their own brands of spray-on sunscreens.

Market research indicates that a major demographic group for spray-on sunscreens is college students, who, whenever they can, spend time sun tanning and going to the beach. Indeed, spring break finds thousands of college students crowding the beaches of Florida, Texas, California, and Mexico.

Banana Boat has retained your public relations firm to develop a product publicity program for UltraMist sunblock aimed directly at the college audience. One suggestion for making Banana Boat the market leader is to position the company as the leading authority on sunscreens and ways to use them effectively, including educating the public about SPF ratings, among other things.

Plan a public relations campaign that would reach college students through traditional media (i.e., newspapers, magazines, radio, television) as well as online media and social media. Don't forget to explain which kinds of special events or promotions you would plan to effectively reach the target audience.

Summary

How Does the Diverse Nature of Audiences Affect Public Relations Practice? p. 206

- The public relations practitioner must reach a diverse and constantly changing audience. One of the most important aspects of this job is identifying the target audience so as to appropriately and effectively customize communications and public relations efforts.

- Current trends affecting the public relations field include an increase in the public's diversity, use of technology, visual orientation, fervent support for single issues, emphasis on personality and celebrity, a strong distrust of authority, and expanding international audiences.

How Can Information About the General Characteristics of Key Demographic Groups Inform Effective Public Relations Efforts? p. 209

- The senior group has grown in number—and in affluence—as

life span has increased. Young people represent another growing audience with a changing face. Their values, lifestyle, interests, and consumption patterns are conspicuously different from those of other demographic groups. In the United States, baby boomers are an economically advantaged group with great purchasing power.

- Women have significant purchasing power and exercise great influence as opinion leaders in general. The gay, lesbian, bisexual and transgender (GLBT) community has been defined as an emerging demographic and lifestyle group that travels, consumes luxury goods, and tends to support companies that are sympathetic to gay and lesbian issues. Religious groups such as Catholic and evangelical religious groups are growing in market and political power.

- The ethnic-minority population is increasing at five times the rate of the general population in the United States, though such groups comprise many different target audiences. When addressing these publics, the public relations practitioner must be sensitive to the special issues, con-

cerns, or interests of specific national and ethnic audiences.

- Hispanics are the fastest-growing ethnic group in the United States. They are increasingly regular users of social media. The rise of affluent African Americans is an important aspect of public relations.

- Sensitively addressing language and cultural differences is the primary challenge in reaching global audiences.

Why Is It Important to Match Media Type to Audience? p. 220

- Each type of media has different strengths when serving as a channel for different types of communication.

- Public relations practitioners should consider the appropriate media (or, sometimes, a single medium) for each public relations campaign so as to speak effectively to target audiences.

QUESTIONS for *Review* and *Discussion*

1. Which key characteristics of the youth market have been identified as relevant to public relations practice? What are the media-use habits of this public?

2. Why is the senior audience so important to public relations practice in the United States? What are some of the characteristics of this audience?

3. How can women's roles as opinion leaders be leveraged from a public relations standpoint?

4. How can public relations professionals effectively reach different gender and lifestyle audiences, such as GLBT and religious groups?

5. What are some of the opportunities for public relations professionals regarding emerging audiences?

6. How do you think the various changes in the racial and ethnic makeup of the United States will affect the practice of public relations in the future?

7. What are some challenges facing public relations professionals in dealing with global audiences?

8. Describe three ways in which public relations practitioners can effectively use online media.

9. What are some attractive features of social media in terms of reaching audiences? What are some possibilities for the public relations specialist to take advantage of the growth of sites like Facebook and Twitter?

the THINKSPOT
www.thethinkspot.com

11 THE INTERNET

You Can't Get Too Close to the Suns

The Phoenix Suns basketball team is one of several NBA teams that has embraced social media as a way of building team visibility and reaching out to fans.

The Suns already had an award-winning website when, based on its rampant popularity, team executives decided to incorporate social media into their overall communications strategy. The team started a proprietary social network, Planet Orange, in 2007 and then added fan pages on Facebook and Twitter. By the end of 2009, the Suns' Facebook page had approximately 60,000 fans and its tweets had some 20,000 followers.

The Suns realized the potential of Twitter (@SunsWebmaster) when one of its star players, Shaquille O'Neal (THE REAL.SHAQ), joined Twitter in 2008 to counter an imposter and his tweets quickly drew more than 2.5 million followers. Jeramie McPeek, a Suns vice president, told Lindsey Miller of Ragan.com, "We all fell in love with it for connecting to our fan base. Our fans were not necessarily coming to Suns.com, but they were pulling up Facebook, MySpace, and YouTube. We need to be in those places; we need to be where the fans are."

Twitter, in particular, has been successful in building communications, interaction, and building the fan base. The Suns have a main organization Twitter feed, one run by players and staff, another run by the Suns Dancers, and yet another run by the team's "gorilla" mascot. To facilitate interaction, the Suns ask fans such questions as which music to play at games. In addition, managers and players may answer fan questions live during a Twitter chat. According to Miller of Ragan.com, this information may be "a live game tweet, short, funny anecdotes, direct quotes

AND SOCIAL MEDIA

from practice, 'This Date in Suns History' trivia, and even birthday wishes to players and former players."

Most importantly, of course, its use of social media helps the team build and maintain its fan base. The team makes sure the Twitter feed is full of exclusive knowledge. In general, it posts practically anything that's interesting or funny on Twitter, where the team-generated messages are short and prolific; the team's Facebook updates are more limited in number and only very important items are posted.

❶ If an organization has a good website, does it also need to have a presence on social networking sites?

❷ How do social media such as Twitter and Facebook build customer or fan loyalty for a brand or a team?

❸ What, if any, are potential problems when employees or players tweet about their company or team?

THE internet IS everywhere

today's students have grown up with the Internet, so much so that it is difficult for them to imagine life without it. Even many of their parents fail to understand that the Internet is a revolutionary concept that has transformed a media system dating back to Gutenberg's invention of the printing press in the 1400s.

For 500 years, a form of mass media dominated the world's landscape that was characterized by being (1) centralized/top-down, (2) costly to publish, (3) controlled by professional gatekeepers known as editors and publishers, and (4) mostly one-way communication with limited feedback channels. Thanks to the Internet, that situation has changed dramatically, so that now there are now two spheres of influence that are constantly interacting with each other. CooperKatz

World Domination

Source: Internet World Stats (www.internetworldstats.com), November 2009.

Percentage of population who use the Internet.

and Company, the New York–based public relations firm, refers to these areas as the mediasphere and the blogosphere.

The new media system, in a noted departure from traditional media, features (1) widespread broadband; (2) cheap or free, easy-to-use online publishing tools; (3) new distribution channels; (4) mobile devices, such as camera phones; and (5) new advertising paradigms. The

think

How has the Internet made media more democratic?

Internet has literally compelled the democratization of information around the world for the first time in history.

The Internet, which was originally created as a tool for academic researchers in the 1960s, came into widespread public use in the 1990s—and the rest is history. Indeed, the worldwide adoption of the Internet has taken less time than the growth of any other mass medium. The growth

The Gutenberg Bible, one of the first printed books in Europe, was created by Johannes Gutenberg in Germany in the 1450s. It has iconic status as the book that marks the start of the "Gutenberg Revolution" and the age of the printed book.

of the Internet and the World Wide Web continues at an astounding rate, and any figures given today are out of date almost before they are published.

> *Whereas it took nearly 40 years before there were 50 million listeners of radio and 13 years until television reached an audience of 50 million, a mere 4 years passed (after it became widely available) before 50 million users were logging on to the Internet.*
>
> **Marc Newman,**
> **General Manager of Medialink Dallas**

Number of days in an average year that Americans spend communicating with others, broken down by communication method

210 days	Person-to-person contact
195 days	Mobile phone
125 days	Land-line phone
125 days	Text messaging
72 days	E-mail
55 days	Instant messaging:
39 days	Social networking websites
8 days	Letters or cards

Social Interaction in the Internet Age

Source: Pew Research Center, Survey on Social Isolation and New Technology, 2009.

LEVERAGING THE power OF THE web

the exponential growth of the World Wide Web is due, in large part, to browsers such as Internet Explorer and search engines such as Google that have made the web accessible to literally billions of people. The web has some highly attractive characteristics that enable public relations people to do a better job of distributing a variety of messages:

- Users can update information quickly, without having to reprint brochures and other materials. This is an important consideration when it comes to major news events and dealing with a crisis.
- The web allows for interactivity; viewers can ask questions about products or services, download information of value to them, and let an organization know what they think.
- Online readers can dig deeper into subjects that interest them by linking to information provided on other sites, other articles, and sources.

- A great amount of material can be posted. There is no space or time limitation.
- The web is a cost-effective method of disseminating information on a global basis to the public and journalists.
- Organizations can reach niche markets and audiences on a direct basis without messages being filtered through traditional mass media gatekeepers (editors).
- The media and other users can access details about an organization on a 24/7 basis from anywhere in the world.

A website, from a public relations standpoint, is literally a distribution system in cyberspace. Organizations can use their websites to market products and services as well as to post news releases, corporate backgrounders, product information, position papers, and even photos of key executives or plant locations. Members of the public, as well as media personnel, can access this in-

think Why is the Internet referred to as a two-way form of communication?

formation and download selected materials into their computers and print out hard copies. Websites have also become more interactive in recent years, and can provide public relations professionals with valuable feedback from consumers and the general public.

In many cases, an organization's website is hyperlinked to other webpages and information sources. A user can jump immediately to a related website by hovering the cursor over various icons and clicking a mouse. Business Wire's website, for example, is linked to the home pages of various organizations that use its distribution services.

Numerous surveys indicate that journalists also extensively use

Virtual Public Relations

Organizations leverage their websites in different ways:

- Federal Express (FedEx) uses its website for investor relations, making stock prices, analyses of company performance, the company's annual report, and other financial information readily available.
- Rutherford Hill Winery in California offers an online video tour of the winery.
- L.L. Bean's website presents a history of the company, featuring details on how it crafts its famous hand-sewn shoes, and provides visitors with a list of attractions at 900 state and national parks.
- IBM, a global corporation, has areas of its website devoted to its activities on various continents. One series on Africa, for example, provides PDFs of case studies and short video clips.
- Starbucks, in an effort to revive its brand, launched a website on which customers can offer the company suggestions about products and its stores. The site was modeled on social networking sites and allows users to post comments in response to other respondents' ideas.

Westchester Medical Center, which posts a virtual encyclopedia of disease and healthcare information, is available to the public for free. The site also establishes the medical center as a premier medical facility by describing its multiple clinics and medical services.

---

websites to retrieve current news releases and other materials. According to NetMarketing, companies today are sending out fewer media kits and getting fewer phone inquiries in favor of putting more material on websites. As Rick Rudman, president of Capital Hill Software, told *PR Tactics*, "The days of just posting press releases on your website are gone. Today, journalists, investors, all audiences expect to find media kits, photos, annual reports, and multimedia presentations about your organization at your press center." Indeed, one might even begin to wonder, in this Internet era, is there any reason to provide printed materials at all?

One common objective for organizational websites is marketing communication. Organizations ranging from mom-and-pop businesses to multinational corporations have portals to sell products and services directly to the public. Other marketing approaches might include page links through which potential customers can learn about the organization and its approach to producing environmentally friendly "green" products.

A preliminary step that all users should complete before creating a webpage is to identify the potential audience and its particular needs. Focus groups, personal interviews, and surveys often help organizations design a user-friendly site.

Paying attention to the needs of the audience also helps organizations decide exactly which links to list on the home page. Intel's home page, for example, has a short list of just three categories: Work, Play, and About Intel. Under each category, there are index tabs linking to specific areas. The Work area, for example, includes tabs for products,

support, downloads, online communities, and technology. Under the About Intel area, tabs quickly link users to more information on corporate history, executive biographies, the press room, and the sign-up process for RSS feeds and Intel newsletters. Indeed, being able to navigate a website with ease is the key to an effective site.

Interactivity

A unique characteristic of the Internet and the World Wide Web, which traditional mass media do not offer, is interactivity between the sender and the receiver. One key aspect of interactivity is the "pull" concept. On the web, users actively search for ("pull") sites that can answer specific questions. At the website itself, visitor also actively "pull" information from the various links that are provided. In other words, consumers are constantly interacting with a site and "pulling" the information most

A 2009 survey by *PRWeek* found that 90% of journalists regularly use corporate websites to get information about organizations.

KEEP THEM COMING BACK FOR MORE

1. High-quality content
2. Ease of use
3. Quick to download
4. Frequently updated

Four main reasons why visitors return to a website according to Forrester Research.

relevant to them. Users have total control over which information they call up and how deep they want to delve into a subject. In contrast, under the "push" concept, information is delivered to the consumer without active participation. Traditional mass media—radio, TV, newspapers, magazines—are illustrative of the "push" concept, as are news releases that are automatically sent to media.

Another aspect of interactivity is the ability of a person to engage in a dialogue with an organization. Many websites, for example, encourage questions and feedback by providing an e-mail address that the user can click to send a message.

Unfortunately, the idea of "interactivity" and encouraging feedback is more buzzword than reality on many websites. According to reporter Thomas E. Weber of *The Wall Street Journal*, "Many big companies invite a dialogue with consumers at their Internet outposts but are ill-prepared to keep up their end of the conversation." He continues, *The Wall Street Journal* zapped e-mail inquiries to two dozen major corporate Web sites with e-mail capabilities and found many of them decidedly speechless. Nine never responded. Two took three weeks to transmit a reply, while others sent stock responses that failed to address the query. Only three companies adequately answered within a day."

A delayed response to an e-mail query, or no response at all, damages an organization's reputation and credibility. Ideally, an e-mail query should be answered by an organization within 24 hours after its receipt. Although it is good public relations to solicit feedback from the public, an organization should

think twice about providing e-mail response forms on its website if its infrastructure isn't capable of handling the queries.

Cost-Effectiveness

Websites require staffing and budget. One good way to convince management that a website is well worth the investment and contributes to the "bottom line" is to calculate its return on investment (ROI). In this kind of analysis, you compare the cost of the website to the cost of accomplishing similar goals by other means. Hewlett-Packard, for example, says its saves $8 million per month by allowing customers to download printer drivers instead of mailing them out to customers on disks. Cisco Systems says news release distribution via its website, NEWS@

Cisco, saves it about $125,000 annually in distribution wire costs. Substantial savings can also be realized by minimizing or completely eliminating the need for brochures and other printed materials.

Terry Colgan, Senior Account Manager at Oki Business Digital, told *Interactive Public Relations*, "Since I know the cost of printing/warehousing and distributing data sheets, catalogs, and other pre-sales materials, I can calculate ROI based on documents downloaded or ordered via fax. In fact, Oki earned a 285 percent ROI in its very first year on the Web." Amy Jackson, Director of Interactive Communications at Middleberg Associates, says calculating ROI on your website is one of the best ways to evaluate your online success: "Companies [that] invest in developing comprehensive, well-managed online media rooms can save thousands of dollars on printing and faxing costs if the media can readily find what they are looking for on the Web."

btw...

The Broward County Public Schools in Fort Lauderdale, Florida, successfully leveraged the web's interactivity when the school board was working on two new policies, and it realized that not everyone could attend meetings to discuss the proposed policies. Board members decided to post the policy drafts on the school system's website and allow the public to e-mail their comments and views to the district. Dozens of e-mail messages were received, and website visitor suggestions helped shape policy revisions. The Public Relations Society of America awarded the school district a Bronze Anvil for its website, commenting, "For Broward County Public Schools, interactive is much more than a buzzword; it is a working program to make a school district function better."

webcasts:
REAL-TIME INTERACTION

a website may often be enhanced and supplemented with webcasts. Webcasting has become more common as bandwidth has increased and technology has evolved. In fact, one survey found that more than 90 percent of public companies use webcasts for everything from employee training to briefings for financial analysts and news conferences launching a new product. One big advantage associated with webcasts is that they save time and money by eliminating the need for participants to travel.

Thomson Financial defines a webcast as "any event, live or archived, which involves the transmission of information from a person or organization to a larger audience over the Internet. Webcasts can be as simple as an audio-only address from a CEO or as elaborate as an audio/video Webcast with a PowerPoint slide show presented from multiple locations with follow-up questions from the audience."

In one notable example demonstrating the power of this approach, the U.S. Bureau of Engraving and Printing (BEP) used a webcast news conference to launch the redesigned $5 bill. The webcast featured U.S. Treasury, BEP, Federal Reserve, and U.S. Secret Service officials, who explained the bill's new counterfeit prevention security features to 250 reporters from around the world. The webcast also helped drive traffic to BEP's website; subsequently the site experienced a 1,000 percent

A good media-oriented webcast was hosted by the Chocolate Manufacturers Association (CMA) and its public relations firm, Fleishman-Hillard. The CMA sponsored a chocolate-tasting program for food writers around the country. Participants received a "tasting kit" before the event and were encouraged to taste various chocolates as they viewed the webcast, which featured experts on chocolate. Thanks to the webcast, the organization doubled its attendance at the event from the previous year. Lynn Bragg, CMA president, told PRWeek, "It helped us connect with media and build relationships with them in a way that has increased awareness of CMA." The entire budget for the webcast was $19,500.

increase in visitors, and there were about 100,000 downloads of materials explaining the security features and other characteristics. In addition to the webcast, BEP and its public relations firm, Burson-Marsteller, conducted a satellite media tour with various media outlets and produced podcasts that were archived on the website.

In another application, Clarkson University uses webcasts to stream campus events in real time to its alumni and other supporters. One such event was a lecture by a Nobel Laureate, Dr. Paul Crutzen, who

was visiting the campus to talk about global warming; another was a "Night at the Opera." The audience for such events may not be very large, but Karen St. Hillaire, Director of University Communications for Clarkson University, thinks their promotional value makes the cost and effort worthwhile. She told *Interactive Public Relations*, "It is our belief that eventually this medium can be one of the most effective media to communicate with our alumni. It's a wonderful way to reach people who cannot be physically present for an event."

think

How can webcasts save an organization time and money?

THE RISE OF social media

The first generation of the Internet, often referred to Web 1.0, was primarily based on a model in which information was transmitted from supplier to receiver. Although websites still serve that function, the second generation of the Internet (Web 2.0) is a more interactive experience where users now have multiple tools available through which to talk to one another in real time. In the wake of Web 2.0, the term "social media" has entered the mainstream. Paul Rand, of Ketchum Communications, labels social media one of the most dramatic revolutions in history.

According to Wikipedia, "Social media describes the online technologies and practices that people use to share opinions, insights, experiences, and

think

In what ways can social media help a public relations organization conduct more effective research?

perspectives with each other." David Bowen, writing in the *Financial Times*, adds, "Social networks are all about a shift from vertical to horizontal communications on the Web." IDC, a technology consultancy, puts it in more pragmatic terms, stating that 70 percent of all the digital information in world is now created by consumers.

Several categories of social media exist. Blogs are now a mainstream application, and social networks such as MySpace, Facebook, and YouTube have become a major presence in today's world as more social network sites are created almost daily. The rise of Twitter, podcasts, and wikis have facilitated conversation among people around the world. This social media conversation is not organized, not controlled, and not on message. Instead, the conversation has the characteristics of being vibrant, emergent, fun, compelling, and full of chance insights. Some experts have called social networks the world's largest focus group. Markovsky Company puts it even more bluntly: "Collectively, the social media—including blogs, social networks, RSS feeds, podcasts, wikis, reviews, bulletin boards, and newsgroups—have the power to support or - destroy a brand or reputation. Transparency is the key; but it's risky business and required a new mindset and toolkit."

The growth of social networks, which exploded in 2007, has

> **"The direct, unfiltered, brutally honest nature of much online discussion is black gold—Texas tea to companies that want to spot trends or find out what customers really think."**
> *The Economist*

dramatically changed the landscape of public relations. Today public relations, more than ever before, needs to be focused on listening to facilitate conversations between organizations and their constituents.

Such conversations can't be controlled. That means organizations and their public relations staffs must get used to the idea that everything an organization does is more transparent and fair game for comment. David Pogue, technology columnist for *The New York Times*, thinks this is a good thing. He wrote, "When a company embraces the possibilities of Web 2.0, it makes contact with its public in a more casual, less sanitized way that, as a result, is accepted with much less cynicism. Web 2.0 offers a direct, more trusted line of communications than anything that came before it."

blogs: EVERYONE'S A JOURNALIST

Blogs, which first came on the scene in 1998, have now become mainstream media in terms of both their numbers and the scope of their influence. In the beginning, they were called weblogs, reflecting

their roots as websites maintained by individuals who wanted to post their commentary and opinions on various topics. Today, the abbreviated term "blog" is commonly used to identify these free-form sites.

Although the vast majority of blogs are still primarily the province

TO POST...
OR **NOT** TO POST.
THAT IS THE QUESTION.

BLOGGER'S DILEMMA

www.CoxAndForkum.com

of individuals who post their personal opinions, blogging is now widely recognized by public relations personnel as an extremely cost-effective way to reach large numbers of people.

Approximately 135 million blogs exist today. Of that number, however, Technorati says at any given time, only 7.4 million have been updated in the last 120 days. Even so, the *Wall Street Journal* has estimated that almost 500,000 Americans are now blogging as their primary source of income. Many of these bloggers have a large following because their postings have earned their creators a reputation for credibility and breaking major stories, which are subsequently picked up by the traditional media. Public relations writers are usually involved in three kinds of blogs: corporate or organizational blogs, employee blogs, and third-party blogs.

Corporate or Organizational Blogs

A corporate blog is usually written by an executive and represents the official voice of the organization. In many cases, someone in the public relations department actually writes the blog for the executive. Some corporate blogs are even outsourced to public relations firms, although some critics say this practice is a guaranteed way to ensure that the blog is artificial and full of "execu-babble."

Larry Genkin, publisher of *Blogger and Podcaster* magazine, offers a good description of what a corporate blog should be: "In its best incarnation, corporations will use blogs to become more transparent to their customers, partners, and internally. By encouraging employees to speak their minds, companies will be able to demonstrate their heart and character. Not an easy trick for a faceless entity. This will facilitate stronger relationships and act as 'grease in the gears' of a business operation."

Although all corporate blogs should provide an opportunity for the public to post comments, it's also important to provide useful and informative information that the audience can use. That was the aim of Ford & Harrison, a national labor and employment law firm, when it started a blog to address workplace issues from its uniquely legal perspective. The blog, called "That's What She Said," uses graphics and humor to explore workplace issues in terms of how much the behavior of the blog's main character would cost a company if the company were forced to defend his actions in a court of law. This tactic effectively showcases the firm's legal expertise in a user-friendly way. *PRWeek* noted, "This is pop culture meeting the conservative world of law in a way that sets the blogosphere on fire."

Employee Blogs

Many organizations encourage their employees to blog. Sun Microsystems, for example, has more than 4,000 employee blogs, representing

> **think**
>
> What are the potential upsides and downsides for individuals or organizations that blog?

Blog Advantages

The format and mechanics of blogs make them attractive for several reasons:

- Almost **anyone can create** a blog with open-source software. A blog is an ideal medium of communication for a small business as well as a large company.
- There are virtually **no start-up costs**.
- The format and writing are **informal**, which can give an organization a friendly, youthful human face.
- **Links** to other webpages and blogs can be embedded.
- Readers can **post comments** and responses directly on the blog.
- Material can be updated and **changed instantly**.
- Extensive use of syndication technologies allows for aggregation of information from hundreds of blogs at once. In this way, an organization **can immediately assess** what customers and various publics are saying about it.
- Blogs provide an outlet for **organizations to participate** in the online dialogue in progress on other blogs, using message boards.
- Blogs allow organizations to post their own points of view, **unfettered** by the editing process of the traditional media.

> ❝The exchange of links, comments, and trackbacks knits individual blogs into a dense network of **mutual reference and endorsement**, providing a giant boost in traffic for bloggers who get it right.❞
>
> Ben King, *The Financial Times*

about 15 percent of its workforce. More than half of them, according to the company, are "super-technical" and "project oriented," appealing only to fellow computer programmers and engineers. Others, such as those written by the CEO as well as by managers in human resources and marketing, are more general in subject matter. Even the company's legal counsel blogs; he opened a recent post with "I really dislike the word 'compliance'" and went on to explain why.

Many organizations are uncomfortable with employee blogs because of concerns about liability or the potential for proprietary information to be released. Other companies, which have more open systems of communication and management, believe employee blogs are great sources of feedback and ideas, and promote employee engagement.

Most companies typically establish at least some guidelines for employee

> **Web empowerment has made the consumer king, and it has also made long-standing corporate and individual reputations extremely vulnerable. With Web 2.0, reputations can be made or broken in a nanosecond.**
>
> Roy Vaughn, Chair of the PRSA Counselors Academy

blogs. Cisco, for example, tells employees, "If you comment on any aspect of the company's business . . . you must clearly identify yourself as a Cisco employee in your postings and include a disclaimer that the views are your own and not those of Cisco." Dell also expects its employees to identify themselves if they do any sort of blogging, social networking, Wikipedia entry-editing, or other online activities related to, or on behalf of, the company.

think *Which liability issues need to be addressed when corporation employees post messages on their blogs?*

Third-Party Blogs

In addition to operating their own blogs and providing guidelines for employee blogs, organizations today must monitor and respond to the postings on other blog sites. The products and services of organizations are particularly vulnerable to attack and criticism by bloggers,

and an unfavorable mention is often multiplied by links to other blogs and search engine indexing.

For example, Dell experienced the wrath of bloggers when it faced harsh criticism about its customer service, which ultimately caused the company's sales to decline. Today, according to *The New York Times*, "It's nearly impossible to find a story or blog entry about Dell that isn't accompanied by a comment from the company." Comcast, the cable giant, also gets its share of consumer complaints on blogs, but it, too, has stepped up its Internet monitoring, including having customer service representatives follow up with anyone who posts a complaint.

"You should also establish relationships with the most relevant and influential bloggers who are talking about your company," Rick Wion,

McDonald's started a blog called "Open for Discussion" about its corporate social responsibility (CSR) program. The company's Vice President of CSR, Bob Langert, gave his personal perspective on McDonald's programs, but also invited consumers to engage in dialogue about what the fast-food giant was doing right and wrong. According to Langert's post, "We want to hear from you because we are always learning and trying to improve. And you can't learn—or improve—without listening."

Words to Blog By

Steve Cody, Managing Director of the Peppercom public relations firm, brings up several important points for employee or client blogs:

1. Be **transparent** about any former, current, or prospective clients being mentioned in the blog.

2. Respond in a **timely** manner to individuals who post comments—pro, con, or indifferent.

3. Generate as much **original** material as possible instead of just commenting on current news events.

4. Only link to blog sites that are **relevant** to your post.

5. Make sure that readers know that the blog represents your **views** and not necessarily those of your employer or client.

Interactive Media Director of Golin Harris, told Susan Walton in *Public Relations Tactics*. "Treat them the same as you would any other journalist. In most cases, they will appreciate the recognition. By providing materials directly in a manner that is helpful to bloggers, you can build positive relationships quickly."

A good example of this tactic is Weber Shandwick's work with about twenty influential food bloggers on behalf of its food industry clients. The public relations firm regularly monitors posts to find out what bloggers are saying and which "hot button" issues are being discussed. This type of engagement al-

think How can bloggers be effectively included in the public relations relationship with the media?

lows the firm to build relationships with the bloggers and, in turn, offer information that they can use in their blogs. Janet Helm, Director of the Food and Nutrition Practice at Weber Shandwick, told *PRWeek*, "They are an influential source, and we can't leave them out of the marketing mix."

> **By engaging in online dialogue, companies are showing their customers that they care about their opinions, value their respect, and plan to rightfully earn their repeat business.**
>
> Darren Katz, *O'Dwyer's PR Report*

Today's Teens Tomorrow's Workers

ethics in ACTION

Almost 90 percent of U.S. teenagers use social networks every day, and approximately 70 percent say that they participate in social networking for an hour or more daily, according to the 2009 Junior Achievement/Deloitte Teen Ethics Survey, which surveyed 1,000 teens aged 12 to 17 years. Social networking has become so central to teens' lifestyle that 60 percent of teens surveyed said they would consider their ability to access networking sites during working hours when considering a job offer. According to the researchers, "This comes as many organizations have begun implementing policies that limit access to social networks during the workday due to concerns about unethical usage, such as time theft, spreading rumors about co-workers or managers, and leaking proprietary information, among other reasons."

Such policies, of course, raise some interesting issues when recent high school and college graduates enter the

workforce. One key issue is the matter of ethical sensitivity to the perceptions and expectations of others such as present and future employers. The Junior Achievement/Deloitte survey found that teenagers rarely consider the impact of their postings. Even adults fail to show much sensitivity. Another survey found that one-third of adults seldom consider what their employers, colleagues, or clients think when they post comments and photos online.

Ainar D. Aijala, Global Managing Partner of Deloitte Touche, says, "From an employer's perspective, it's clear that organizations need enhanced training and communication relative to social networking. This is particularly the case when more than half of the future talent pool feels so strongly about social networking that their ability to access those sites at work would play into their decision to take a job."

Do you think employers are justified in banning employees from social network-

ing while at work? Would you decline a job offer if the potential employer denied employee access to social networking sites during working hours? Should employers give employees training about the ethical use of social networking sites?

Consider the ten-day blogstorm that overtook Kryptonite Company, a prominent manufacturer of bike locks. A consumer complaint was posted to bike forums and blogs stating that a Bic pen could be used to open a Kryptonite lock. Two days later, videos were posted on blogs showing how to pick the lock. Three days later, the *New York Times* and AP reported the story, which was picked up by other mainstream media. Four days after that, the company was forced to announce a product exchange that cost $10 million.

making friends ON
MYSPACE AND FACEBOOK

althought multiple online social networking communities exist, including the business-oriented LinkedIn, MySpace and Facebook established early leads in popularity and have yet to relinquish their lofty perches. In 2010, Facebook eclipsed MySpace as the most popular site with 400 million users worldwide, 70 percent of whom reside outside the United States.

The popularity of social networking sites such as MySpace and Facebook has not gone unnoticed by advertising, marketing, and public relations professionals. They see such sites as excellent opportunities to make "friends" in several ways. A survey of executives by TNS Media Intelligence/Cymfony, for example, found that marketing and public relations personnel believed network-

ing sites were vital for gaining consumer insights, building brand awareness, and creating customer loyalty.

Accomplishing these objectives, however, takes a great deal of thought and creativity because you must shape messages that are relevant and interesting to your "friends." Achieving this goal often requires techniques such as humor,

short video clips, music, contests, and audience participation. Champion, an apparel manufacturer, established a Facebook group called Champion Fan Zone to generate interest among college students. Sarah Palin extensively used her Facebook page to promote her book *Going Rogue*, which described her experience as the Republican candidate for U.S. Vice President in

A survey by Student Monitor, a research firm, found that FACEBOOK AND BEER tied for the most popular "thing" among college students, after the iPod.

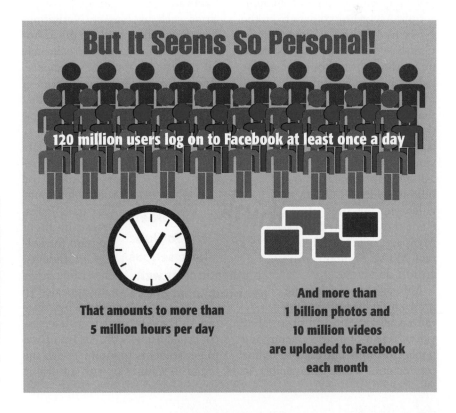

But It Seems So Personal!

120 million users log on to Facebook at least once a day

That amounts to more than 5 million hours per day

And more than 1 billion photos and 10 million videos are uploaded to Facebook each month

2008. More than 1 million people have "friended" her.

Coors has also expanded its traditional advertising and product publicity to embrace social networking sites. One initiative on Facebook enabled visitors (aged 21 and older, of course) to send friends a "Code Blue" alert inviting them to meet up for a Coors Light. They could even use Facebook maps to direct their buddies to the nearest bar. Aaron, one of Coors' almost 2,000 fans, gave the site five stars: "This app is epic. I used it to set up my birthday party and it was so easy to invite everyone."

Tim Sproul, a creative director for a Portland, Oregon, advertising agency, told *The New York Times*, "If you have anything to pitch in a social environment, it makes sense to pitch beer. We feel like we're not intrusive in the online experience; we're relevant, by giving people a chance to connect."

Even companies selling luxury goods have discovered the group and business pages of MySpace and Facebook. Cartier set up a MySpace profile to promote jewelry from its Love collection. Visitors to the site do more than gawk at the jewelry and the high price tags. According to Eric Pfanner, reporting in *The New York Times*, "[V]isitors can also sample music from artists like Lou Reed and Grand National, including several songs with the theme of love that were composed for Cartier. They can watch film clips with a romantic story line. And, of course, they can click on any of those friends' pictures to visit their profiles."

> **think** In light of the demographic it reaches, which other products might be good candidates for promotion on Facebook?

youtube:
VIDEO CLIPS AND CONTROVERSY

Video clips are an extremely popular medium of communication. According to data from the Nielsen Online VideoCensus, U.S.-based Internet viewers watch more than three hours of online videos in a typical month. In another study, Comscore reported that Google's YouTube ranked as the top U.S. video property; it contained 40 percent of all videos viewed during November 2008—approximately 5 billion videos. Other video-viewing sites include those operated by MySpace, Viacom Digital MTV, Yahoo!, Microsoft, and Hulu.

Although many videos are posted by individuals, organizations also create and post online videos as part of their marketing and public relations outreach to online communities. These communities, in general, are well educated and relatively affluent. In addition, research firms such as Nielsen/NetRatings have found that people in the 35-to-64 age group make up approximately 50 percent of YouTube's audience. Another large audience consists of college students; research shows that 95 percent of them regularly view videos online.

This kind of demographic data prompted AirTran Airways to use YouTube to publicize its X-Fares, a stand-by flight program for college students. The airline originally appealed to students by creating AirTran U complete with a mascot called Eunice, the AirTran Ewe, to get students to interact with the brand in a fun way with an online video contest. The airline, according to *PRWeek*, encouraged students to "Do a little (or big) dance, sing a fight song, chant, or whatever else comes to you." Students could post their videos at youtube.com/airtranu to compete for prizes. In addition, AirTran's public relations firm, CKPR, created profiles for Eunice on MySpace, Friendster, and Facebook that attracted more than 600 friends among the target audience. The EweTube contest attracted 24,000 unique visitors, and Eunice even appeared on NBC's *Today Show*. The campaign received *PRWeek*'s award for "Best Use of the Internet/New Media 2008." One judge commented, "This was really a nice approach to engage the jaded college audience in a brave, clever, and irreverent way."

A video parody made available on YouTube can also successfully increase awareness of a product and

> **think** Does YouTube have serious applications as well as entertaining ones?

Pizza Chain Responds to YouTube Video

IT WASN'T A VERY HAPPY EASTER WEEKEND for Domino's, the national chain of pizza and take-out restaurants. The delivery pizza giant suffered a major blow to its brand reputation when two employees at a Domino's restaurant in the small town of Conover, North Carolina, decided to entertain themselves on a boring Sunday night by shooting a short video of sandwich preparation that violated all health standards. The disgusting prank video was uploaded to YouTube. Within 24 hours, it had been viewed by 500,000 people. In 48 hours, more than a million had seen it. Inevitably, a number of blogs linked to the video, and ultimately the mainstream media picked up the story.

Domino's, alerted to the video, began to restore its reputation within 48 hours. First, it downloaded a two-minute video to YouTube that featured the company president, Patrick Doyle. Doyle apologized for the incident and went on to assure customers that Domino's had high standards of food quality and hygiene. He asserted, "Although the individuals in question claim it's a hoax, we are taking this incredibly seriously … The two team members have been dismissed, and there are felony warrants out for their arrest. The store has been shut down and sanitized from top to bottom. There is nothing more important or sacred to us than our customers' trust."

The public relations staff of Domino's initiated a number of tactics as well, including the following measures:

1. Starting a Twitter account to communicate with customers

2. Placing a "customer care" link about the incident on Domino's corporate webpage to answer consumer concerns

3. Communicating via e-mail to all franchises and employees to keep them informed

4. Conducting interviews with leading bloggers and mainstream media

5. Distributing news releases via electronic news services to media and social network sites

6. Using the company's Facebook profile to attract and gather "friends"

Online surveys indicated that their efforts were successful. Some time after the scandal, Domino's reputation and brand were once again in the favorable column.

1. Domino's chose to use the same medium that caused the problem, YouTube, to post its response to the prank. Was this a good strategy?

2. Did Domino's effectively use the full range of social media in its campaign to restore its reputation?

3. Do you think it was necessary to also contact the print and broadcast media about this incident, or would that tactic run the risk of simply make more people aware of the incident?

a brand. For example, Smirnoff launched a new iced-tea malt beverage on YouTube by creating a two-minute parody of a rap video titled "Tea Partay." It showed three blond men in polo-style shirts rapping lines such as "Straight outta Cape Cod, we are keepin' it real." It worked because croquet, yachting, and white men aren't typical rap-video imagery. The spoof was viewed more than 500,000 times and created a word-of-mouth buzz for Smirnoff as people e-mailed it to friends and colleagues.

Kevin Roddy, creative director of BBH Advertising, told the *Wall Street Journal* that the Smirnoff video cost about $200,000 to produce, but it was a good value. A traditional 30-second TV spot costs an average of $350,000 to make, plus the cost of air time—which can run into six figures. Roddy said, "The client bought into it. They understand that advertising is no longer about talking at someone; it's about engaging with the consumer. To do that, you have to play by different rules. It requires you to be more entertaining."

Not all YouTube videos have to be humorous and entertaining. The United Steelworkers, during a strike against Goodyear Tire & Rubber Company, posted a 30-second video spot on YouTube that showed a photo montage of auto accidents. As a sports utility vehicle flipped over, a

Humor was employed by H&R Block, a tax nationwide tax preparation company. Taxes and accounting are not exactly a "cool" subject, but the company wanted to reach younger audiences when it introduced such services as do-it-yourself online tax preparation. The campaign started in January, the beginning of tax season, with the arrival of Truman Greene on YouTube. According to *BrandWeek*, "In a dozen videos, the fictional oddball raves about the joys of online income tax preparation and spoofs popular YouTube shorts (like the precision treadmill routine dancers)." Truman Greene's YouTube videos received more than 556,000 views, and his MySpace page had about 3,300 friends. In all, *BrandWeek* reported that awareness of H&R Block's digital products increased 61 percent.

question appeared on the screen: "What tires do you plan to buy?" The union used the video to make the case against tires produced by replacement workers. The video ranked 24 on YouTube the day it was posted. Even if there aren't many immediate downloads of every video, organizations believe it's worth the effort to post videos because they may eventually be picked up by a blogger who will repost a video and give it new life. Ultimately, it may even attract the attention of traditional media outlets.

IT'S NICE TO SHARE

The popular site Flickr allows individuals to share photos of their vacations, their children's first steps, and even their twenty-first birthday parties with the rest of the world. The site is intended primarily for personal use, and organizations are strongly discouraged from trying to sell products or services. Public relations personnel, however, do find creative ways to use the social networking aspect of Flickr to build awareness of an organization or brand.

The Monterey Aquarium, for example, encourages visitors to post photos taken at the facility. To that end, it sponsored a photo contest in connection with World Ocean Day. The aquarium's public relations staff monitor blogs and, if someone posts a good photo of an exhibit, staff ask the individual to post it on the Flickr site. Ken Peterson, Communications Director for Monterey Aquarium, told Ragan.com, "We've let some people know that we're interested in using their photos on the aquarium Web site or in other vehicles. That creates great word of mouth, since the photographer will likely tell his or her friends to visit the aquarium Web site—or Flickr group—and see the photo on display."

The aquarium's example makes the point that social media sites such as Flickr can be used for public relations purposes only if the focus is on generating participation and involvement on the part of consumers and the general public. In these programs, the organization basically acts as a facilitator for people connecting to people.

texting: A WAY OF LIFE

Sending text messages via a mobile or cell phone is seemingly a pervasive and universal habit. In fact, Ragan.com reports that nearly 75 percent of mobile phone users worldwide send text messages on a daily basis. Text messaging is particularly popular among college students; almost 90 percent of them text on a daily basis, according to the 2009 Vingo Consumer Mobile Messaging Habits Report.

Texting is also used by organizations and public relations staffs to reach employees, customers, and key publics. Shel Holtz, a social media expert, told Ragan.com that there are three levels of texting for organizations. The first level is the broadcast text, which companies often use to send a brief message to all employees at the same time. Such a message may be as mundane as reminding people to sign up for the company picnic or it may play a more serious role in updating employees about a crisis situation. A second level of texting is subscription based, in which users sign up to receive text messages from groups or organizations in much the same way as they sign up for RSS feeds to their computers. A reporter, for example, may sign up to receive text messages from a company that he or she covers on a regular basis. The third method, says Holtz, is the "one-off," wherein a cell phone user sends a text message to a source to get an answer to a question. For example, an employee may text human resources personnel to get a short answer to a health benefits question.

The South Dakota Office of Tourism puts texting to good use as a communication tactic. Skiers visiting the state can sign up to receive daily text message alerts about snowfall and weather conditions. E-mail alerts to subscribers were already the norm for this organization, but sending messages directly to cell phones seemed to be more logical in terms of accessibility. Wanda Goodman, the public relations manager at the tourism office, told Ragan.com, "It adds a level of convenience for travelers and builds another level of connectivity with potential visitors to the state."

> **think** How is recent legislation focusing on the practice of "driving while texting" indicative of how important texting has become in our society?

wikis, tweets, AND PODCASTS, OH MY!

Another form of text messaging emerged with the introduction of Twitter, which became the fastest-growing web brand in 2009. Essentially, this social networking and micro-blogging service allows users (known as twits) to post messages of up to 140 characters in length on computers and other mobile devices. Messages are displayed on the user's profile page and delivered to other users (called followers) who have signed up to receive them. Twitter is web based, so its major advantage over texting is that posts are indexed by Google and readily available to anyone with Internet access.

The following examples illustrate how organizations and their public relations staffs employ Twitter:

- Qwest Communications, a telecommunications company, uses @TalkToQwest to handle customer questions, concerns, and complaints.
- Starbucks used Twitter messages to refute a rumor that it wasn't sending coffee to troops in Iraq in protest of the war.
- Barack Obama's presidential campaign used Twitter to keep volunteers and supporters up-to-date with motivational messages and late-breaking developments.
- Planned Parenthood has two Twitter accounts to answer queries and to provide basic information about contraception.

Interaction between individuals working a particular project is facilitated by wikis. Basically, wikis are a collection of webpages that enable anyone who accesses them to provide input and even modify the content. Ward Cunningham, co-author of *The Wiki Way: Quick Collaboration*

> **think** How do texts and tweets differ?

on the Web, sums up the essence of wikis in this way:

- They invite all users to edit any page within the website, using a basic web browser.
- They promote meaningful topic associations between different pages.
- They involve visitors in an ongoing process of creation and collaboration.

General Motors created a wiki site for its employees and customers as part of its centennial celebration. It encouraged individuals to contribute first-person experiences relating to the company's history via stories, images, video, and audio. The advantage of the wiki was that individuals could comment on other contributions, correct inaccurate information, and even add supplemental information regarding their experiences and viewpoints. GM originally considered publishing the standard "coffee table book" outlining the company's history. In the

end, as company spokesperson Scot Keller told *MediaPost*, "We felt that a more social, more inclusive approach was appropriate, and the story is best told not by the corporation or media but by men and women who were there." As a spin-off, GM also planned to package various stories and materials for distribution to other social networking communities and websites.

Wikis also are used by public relations departments and firms to keep employees and clients up-to-date on schedules and plans for executing campaigns.

A podcast is a digital media file, or a series of such files, distributed over the Internet for playback on portable media players and personal

computers. Most podcasts are audio only, but video podcasts are also finding a home on smart phones, websites, YouTube, and other social networking sites.

The three major advantages of podcasts for distributing messages are cost-effectiveness, the ability of users to access material on a 24/7 basis, and portability. A person can listen to an audio podcast while driving to work, walking down a mountain trail, or working in the garden. In fact, podcasts have many of the same advantages as traditional radio.

The equipment for producing a podcast is relatively simple. Podcasters just need (1) a computer; (2) a good microphone; (3) software

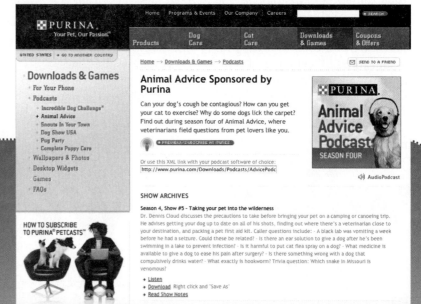

cover topics that are important to the life of the everyday consumer. It's an opportunity for us to connect our brand to her."

- Purina, the maker of pet food, has a podcast series that gives advice to pet owners. Its introduction of the series on its website shares the essence of the content: "Is it unusual for a cat to use the toilet? Is your dog bored out of its skull? Can cats and dogs suffer from heart attacks? Get answers to these questions and more in season two of Animal Advice, where veterinarians field questions from pet lovers like you." Titles in the series include

"Animal safety during the summer months" and "Itching dogs and cats."
- Disneyland used podcasts as part of its global campaign to generate interest in the park's fiftieth anniversary celebration. The content included interesting facts about Disneyland's history, current attractions, and in-depth interviews with employees about their work.
- The University of Pennsylvania's Wharton School produces podcasts that primarily feature insights from professors at the business school regarding current trends and issues.

such as Audacity to record, edit, and finish audio files; (4) a web server to store files in a folder; and (5) a website or a blog that users can access to download the podcast.

Creating a podcast that is interesting and relevant to the target audience can be more challenging, however. A podcast is not an infomercial or a disembodied speech reading the text of an executive's speech. Like radio programs, a podcast must be informal and conversational. Here are some other tips about podcast content:

1. Keep the program to less than 15 minutes.
2. Use several stories or segments.
3. Don't read from a script.
4. Create an RSS feed.
5. Create new podcasts on a weekly basis.

The evidence seems to indicate that podcasting will continue to grow as a major tool of communication for public relations professionals. The total U.S. podcast audience reached 18.5 million in 2007, but *eMarketer* predicts that it will expand to 65 million in 2012. Of those listeners, 25 million will be "active" users who tune in at least once a week. Two major factors are fueling the growth of podcasting and other social media: the continuing evolution of "smart" phones and the increasing affordability of mobile data plans.

THE NEXT GENERATION:
web 3.0

It's now widely predicted that "smart" phones and extensive mobile-enabled content will be the next major development in the evolution of the Internet. As the price of entry goes down, more users can afford to partake in the advanced technology of Web 3.0. Many consumers already use their phones to download videos, surf the Internet, receive e-mail and RSS feeds, post comments on blogs, and receive an extensive array of mobile-enabled content.

New applications ("apps") for the iPhone and other "smart" phones are introduced every day, and public relations professionals are getting better at using them to reach desirable audiences. Consider Quicken, the financial software firm. It introduced a budgeting "app" on iPhone to reach the 25- to 35-year-old age group that became the second-leading finance application in the iTunes application store within three days.

Indeed, the new generation of mobile phones has become the new portable computer—as powerful as today's notebooks and netbooks.

Handheld devices already have the ability to call up stored online videos, photos, and PowerPoint presentations. Other popular features include complete map navigation in 3-D format for any location on the planet, and interaction with social networks such as Facebook, allowing users to tell friends exactly where they are at any given moment. Access to a world of information and social interaction is as close as your pocket.

> **think**
> Why do so many people think that smart phones and mobile-enabled content will be the next big thing in the communications revolution?

APPLY YOUR KNOWLEDGE

WHAT WOULD YOU DO?

Happy Valley Yogurt distributes its products nationally and has approximately 25 percent of the market. The company makes a variety of flavors, and roughly 80 percent of its sales comes from eight-ounce, single-serving-size packages. The company has done the standard marketing, advertising, and public relations activities, but your public relations staff believes it could increase sales further by using social media—blogs, MySpace, Facebook, YouTube, Flickr, Twitter, and podcasts—to engage the teenagers, college students, and young professionals who actively frequent social networking sites. Prepare a proposal to management showing how Happy Valley Yogurt can tap into social media for fun and profit. As part of your plan, you need to consider the special characteristics of these media and determine which kind of content would be appropriate for dissemination via these channels.

Summary

How Has the Internet Caused a Communications Revolution? p. 228

- Embrace of the Internet and the World Wide Web has taken less time than the adoption of any other mass communication medium in history.

- The World Wide Web is the first medium that allows almost anyone to send messages to a mass audience without the message being filtered by journalists and editors. Prior to the advent of the Internet, mass media were costly to produce, were centralized, and featured primarily one-way communication with limited feedback.

- Thanks to mobile phones, more people than ever before are getting connected via the Internet.

Which Characteristics of the Internet Make It a Powerful Public Relations Tool? p. 229

- Public relations practitioners are heavy users of the Internet and the web. They disseminate information to a variety of audiences as well as use the Internet for research.

- The new media have unique characteristics, including easy updating of material, instant distribution of information, an infinite amount of space for information, and ready interaction with the audience.

- Public relations efforts on the Internet can be both interactive and cost-effective—two very appealing characteristics in today's business environment.

How Are Webcasts Used in Effective Public Relations? p. 232

- Webcasting—the streaming of audio and video in real time over a website—is now used by the majority of organizations for everything from news conferences to employee training.

Which Social Media Tactics Are Available to Public Relations Professionals? p. 233

- The second generation of the Internet, called Web 2.0, has given rise to "social media." These venues provide public relations professionals with the opportunity to participate in social networking sites to get feedback and to build relationships.

- Blogs have become mainstream sites in terms of both their numbers and their influence.

- MySpace and Facebook are the most popular social networking sites. Increasingly, organizations are establishing a presence on these sites. To successfully engage the audience in this venue, public relations materials need to be low-key and creative.

- YouTube is the premier social networking site for posting and viewing videos. Today's organizations are heavily involved in posting video clips. To garner attention, clips must be creative, interesting, and somewhat humorous.

- Flickr is the major photo sharing site; it is primarily used by individuals. In contrast, texting, Twitter, and wikis are extensively used in public relations work.

- Podcasts are gaining in popularity. These broadcasts can be either audio or video based, but must provide useful and relevant information in a conversational way if they are to capture and hold users' attention.

QUESTIONS
for *Review* and *Discussion*

1. In what way has the Internet completely revolutionized a media system that dates back to Gutenberg's printing press?

2. What are some characteristics of the Web that make it possible for public relations people to do a better job of distributing information?

3. Why is it important for an organization to have a website?

4. One aspect of web interactivity is the distinction made between "pull" versus "push." What is the difference between these two concepts?

5. How can a website generate revenue and save money for an organization?

6. What is the major difference between the first generation of the World Wide Web, known as Web 1.0, and the second generation, known as Web 2.0?

7. Which characteristics define "social media"?

8. In what ways does a corporate blog differ from the organization's website?

9. What are some typical guidelines imposed on employee blogs?

10. Which factors should an organization consider if it is thinking about producing a YouTube video?

11. How can organizations effectively use Facebook, texting, and wikis?

12. Which characteristics make for a good podcast?

the
THINK SPOT
www.thethinkspot.com

TACTICS

FINANCIAL TIMES

Tim Bradshaw and David Gelles, *Financial Times*, April 7, 2009

Social Media Puts Fizz into Coke

> Facebook is now the world's premier social networking site, with more than 400 million users worldwide.

When two Coca-Cola enthusiasts created a Facebook profile in honor of their favorite soft drink last year, they could not have known it would become one of the social network site's most popular profile pages—second only to Barack Obama's.

The page was created by Dusty Sorg, a Los Angeles–based actor who maintains it with his friend, Michael Jedzejewski, a writer. "I was already on Facebook a lot and I didn't see any Coke pages that seemed very official," says Mr. Sorg. So he started the page in August, invited his friends, and watched it grow.

And grow and grow and grow. By December, the page had 1.2 million fans, making it the most popular brand-related page on Facebook. It now has some 3.3 million members.

> High-quality visuals such as photos are a key component in attracting "friends" to a profile page. Regular updating with new and interesting information is another important tactic.

What spurred the enormous growth remains something of a mystery. There were already more than 200 Coke-related fan pages on Facebook. Michael Donnelly, Coca-Cola's group director of worldwide interactive marketing, who had been monitoring the page since October, believes it may have been as simple as a good visual cue. "They choose a great image," he says. "It was a high-resolution picture of a can of cold Coke, and it was just perfect."

> Company logos and slogans are trademarked; it's illegal to use a trademark on a regular basis in a blog or even a Facebook profile without permission from the owner of the trademark.

At any rate, the page is now an enormous asset for the company, which was forced by Facebook to jointly administer the page with Mr. Sorg to comply with the site's rules on trademarks. "It gives us an opportunity we didn't have in the past," says Mr. Donnelly. "It's a great way for us to expose a huge number of people to what we're doing at no cost."

> Public relations firms, like advertising agencies, are very active in the use of social media to inform the public about products and services, and to provide information about organizational policies. In many cases, social media are used to share information in a crisis situation.

While Coke's successful Facebook foray may have been inadvertent, more and more marketing departments and advertising agencies are trying to find ways to intentionally harness the power of the online social networks provided by the likes of Facebook, Twitter, YouTube, and MySpace.

A recent poll of members of the U.S.-based Chief Marketing Officer Council found that a third did not have the internal talent within their marketing departments to engage in new media programs. The same proportion have a limited understanding of social media, yet almost two-thirds are actively investing in it.

"That is a big opportunity for an (advertising) agency to come in," says Liz Miller, vice president of programs and operations at CMO Council. The opportunity has been widened by the economic downturn, which has forced many brands to reevaluate their expenditures on traditional forms of marketing, such as paid advertising.

While Carat, the media planning and buying agency, forecasts global advertising expenditures to fall by 5.8 percent this year, social media remain one of the few sectors where agencies are hiring rather than firing.

Indeed, in recent months, agencies have been falling over themselves to create dedicated social media divisions. MPG, the Havas-owned media agency; Creston, a British agency group; and LBi, a digital agency; all established social media units last month. Tribal DDB, the digital division of Omnicom's vast creative agency, DDB, in January brought its Canadian social media specialist, Radar DDB, to the United Kingdom, while Chime Communications Tolun Publicis' Vivaki media buying and trading business has created a set of media planning tools to help clients "engage consumers on the social web."

The first step when trying to harness social networks for marketing is to explore what consumers are saying about a brand by using "buzz-monitoring" services, such as Onalytics and Brandwatch. "The best way to get this stuff right is by listening and understanding before engaging," says Will Mcinnes, managing director and co-founder of NixonMcinnes, a specialist social media agency.

David Kenny, managing partner at Vivaki, says advertisers and marketers need to be aware of how digital media have changed the nature of marketing. "Now you don't start with the product, you start with human beings—where they are, how do they learn, how do they entertain themselves." But even if it becomes easier . . . to value the effectiveness of social media as a marketing tool, there is no easy way for agencies or their clients to emulate the kind of runaway success Coca-Cola has enjoyed on Facebook.

Mr. Sorg's fan page was a hit thanks to a combination of weak competition, good timing, and pretty pictures. It had a momentum of its own, and a community loyal to its quirky founders. Had Coke set up the page itself or taken it over, there is no guarantee it would still be thriving.

Indeed, the most effective thing Coca-Cola did—and perhaps the lesson for other companies—was not getting in the way.

The job market for college graduates with a good knowledge of social media is very promising.

Public relations professionals spend a lot of time analyzing the characteristics of the target audience, which helps them formulate appropriate messages and adopt the correct tone and context for the target audience.

In economic downturns, spending on public relations tends to increase because it is more cost-effective than paid advertising.

Major public relations firms, such as Edelman, Ketchum, and Burson-Marsteller, also have created social media practices and divisions to serve clients.

Organizations cannot control social media. The best approach is to collaborate, retain open communication, and engage in a dialogue with both "fans" and critics. What Coca-Cola did is a good example.

Google Alerts is one method that public relations practitioners use to monitor what is being said online about a company or its products and services. Some commercial services also monitor blogs, Twitter postings, YouTube, and chat groups for a fee.

12 PUBLIC RELATIONS

A Full Toolbox

While issuing news releases and media advisories is still extremely common in public relations, so is placing a spokesperson on *The Daily Show with Jon Stewart* or MSNBC's *Rachel Maddow Show* or taking advantage of Twitter to maintain contact with journalists. Opportunities for public relations professionals to influence key audiences with new tools are expanding all the time.

When Tiger Woods found himself in the midst of controversy following the revelation that he had several extramarital sexual liaisons, he didn't send out a press release—he posted a statement on his personal website.

When the Denny's restaurant chain was looking for a brand facelift, it turned to public and media relations. In an effort to show Americans that Denny's was on their side in tough economic times, the company offered free Grand Slam breakfasts to customers nationwide on "Fat Tuesday." Denny's let the public know about the offer in a number of ways—for example, tying the offer in to a Super Bowl ad campaign and taking full advantage of social media tools. Nelson Marchioli, CEO of Denny's, told PRSA's *The Public Relations Strategist*, "[On] that day, thanks to the PR coverage that we got, we changed the image of the brand, particularly with the media and the journalists here in America. I would have never thought one event could have

TACTICS

done that—but it did." Denny's media blitz got the word out; the restaurant served approximately 2 million free meals during the eight-hour event.

The Tiger Woods and Denny's examples are not unusual today. Digital and social media are playing an increasingly important role in public relations, marketing, and advertising, so much so that *PRWeek* reported that unless they stay current in their use of new tools, public relations pros are in danger of giving up important pieces of the digital pie to advertising and marketing. In *PRWeek,* Andy Lark, Vice President of Global Marketing, Communities, and Conversations at Dell, stated, "We have to find a way to change the perception of PR people as people who deal [only] with the media . . . . Owning digital is more about how people think of PR and whether [clients] think PR people have the skills to do things [that digital requires]."

1 Which public relations tactics are most effective in reaching you and your peers: Media relations? Social media? Events? Spokespersons on television?

2 Think of a recent celebrity or corporate crisis. How did the celebrity or corporation communicate with his or her audience? Was the strategy employed effective? Why or why not?

news releases

Public relations professionals rely on a toolbox full of varied tactics. News releases, public service announcements, media conferences, and special events are just some of the best-known and time-honored tactics. In this chapter, we introduce you to those tactics and others.

The news release, also called a media release, is the most commonly used public relations tactic. This simple document has as its primary purpose the dissemination of information to mass media such as newspapers, broadcast stations, and magazines. A great deal of the information in weekly and daily newspapers originates from news releases prepared by publicists and public relations practitioners on behalf of their clients and employers.

Newsrooms have had to cut staff dramatically in recent years, and this gives PR practitioners a tremendous opportunity to deliver worthwhile content to news media. As an editor of a major daily once said, public relations people are the newspaper's "unpaid reporters." It must be remembered, however, that a news release is not paid advertising. News reporters and editors have no obligation to use any of the information from a news release in a news story. News releases are judged solely on whether their content is newsworthy, timely, and potentially interesting to the readers.

think Why do some editors refer to public relations professionals as "unpaid reporters"?

Is It Time for a News Release?

Before writing a news release, a public relations professional should ask and answer a number of questions:

- *What is the key message?* This answer should be expressed in one sentence.
- *Who is the primary audience?* Is it consumers who may buy a product or service? Or is it purchasing agents in other companies? The answer to this question determines whether the release is sent to a daily community newspaper or to a trade magazine.
- *What does the target audience gain from the product or service?* What are the potential benefits and rewards?
- *What objective does the release serve?* Is it to increase product sales, to enhance the organization's reputation, or to increase attendance at an event?

A study by Bennett & Company (Orlando, Florida) found that **75%** of journalists surveyed said they used public relations sources for their stories.

Crafting a **NEWS RELEASE**

News releases adhere to a standard, traditional format. Consider the following tips when crafting your own news releases:

- Use standard 8.5- by 11-inch paper. The release should be printed on white paper or on the organization's letterhead.
- Identify the sender (contact) in the upper-left corner of the page and provide the sender's name, address, telephone number, fax number, and e-mail address.
- Leave 2 inches of space for editing convenience before starting the text. Leave at least a 1.5-inch margin. Double-space the copy to give editors room to edit the material.
- Provide a boldface headline that gives the key message of the release so the editor knows exactly what the release is about at a glance.
- Provide a dateline—for example, "Minneapolis, MN: January 21, 2010"—to indicate where the news release originated.
- Start the text with a clearly stated summary that contains the most important message you want to convey to the reader. Lead paragraphs should be a maximum of three to five lines.
- Use a 10- or 12-point standard type, such as Times Roman or Courier.
- Never split a paragraph from one page to the next. Place the word "more" at the bottom of each page of the news release (except the last page, of course).
- Place an identifying slug line (a short phrase or title used to indicate the story content) and page number at the top of each page after the first one.
- Use Associated Press (AP) style. The vast majority of newspapers and broadcast stations use this stylebook as a guide.
- Be concise. Edit the copy to remove excess words and "puff" words. Avoid clichés and over-used phrases. Few news releases need to be more than two pages long.
- Avoid technical jargon. Releases, for the most part, are written for general public consumption.
- Double-check all information. Be absolutely certain that every fact and title in the release is correct.
- Eliminate boldface and words in all capital letters.
- Include a short paragraph at the end of the news release that provides a thumbnail sketch of what the organization does, how many employees it has, and so on.
- Localize whenever possible. Most studies show that news releases with a local angle get published more often than generic news releases giving a regional or national perspective.

FOR IMMEDIATE RELEASE

Contacts:
Mike Duggan, Golden Valley Microwave Foods
952-832-3439
-OR-
Bernice Neumann, Morgan&Myers
612-825-0050

ACT II INTRODUCES FIRST AND ONLY KETTLE CORN MICROWAVE POPCORN

MINNEAPOLIS, Minn. – July   – Sweet and salty, two classic flavor combinations, have long been paired in all-time favorite foods. Now, Golden Valley Microwave Foods (GVMF) has made microwave popcorn – one of America's favorite snacks – available in delicious slightly sweet, slightly salty ACT II® Kettle Corn.

An American tradition introduced by settlers in the 1700-1800s, kettle corn was first made outdoors by popping corn in large cast-iron kettles with rendered lard and sweeteners, such as molasses, honey or sugar. In the past decade, this tasty snack started being served again at outdoor gatherings, such as fairs, concerts, carnivals and flea markets, primarily in the Midwestern states.

-more-

After the key public relations questions are addressed, the next step is to think like a journalist and write a well-crafted news story that includes the traditional five W's and H: who, what, when, where, why, and how.

The Content of a News Release

A news release is like a news story. The lead paragraph is an integral and important part of the text, because it forms the apex of the journalistic "inverted pyramid" approach to writing. With this approach, the first paragraph succinctly summarizes the most important part of the story and succeeding paragraphs fill in the details in descending order of importance. The inverted pyramid structure also applies to multimedia news releases. Unlike the humble news release that is primarily a word-based document, multimedia releases may include high-resolution photos/graphics, video, and audio components. Such releases, which are often distributed by major services such as *Business Wire, PR Newswire,* and *Marketwire,* are also tagged for distribution to social media such as digg and various blogs. Search engines such as Google and Yahoo! also index key words so the public can readily access news releases by conducting word or topic searches.

The news release is the workhorse of public relations. This is an example of a well-written and -formatted news release from Kettle Corn, prepared by the Morgan & Myers public relations firm.

Gary Putka, the Boston bureau chief of the *Wall Street Journal,* admits that "a good 50%" of the stories in the newspaper come from news releases.

THE INVERTED PYRAMID

Three reasons to use the inverted pyramid structure.

1. If the editor or reporter doesn't find anything interesting in the first three or four lines of the news release, it won't be used.

2. Editors cut stories from the bottom. *Business Wire News* estimates that more than 90 percent of news releases are rewritten in much shorter form than the original text. If the main details of the story appear at the beginning, the release will still be understandable and informative even if most of the original text has been deleted.

3. Readers don't always read the full story. Statistics show that the average reader spends less than 30 minutes per day reading a metropolitan daily newspaper. Readers look at a lot of headlines and first paragraphs—but not much else.

> **[T]hink of the electronic news release as a teaser to get a reporter or editor to your Web site for additional information.**
>
> B. L. Ochman, *The Strategist*

Publicity Photos

News releases are often accompanied by photos. Studies show that more people "read" photographs than read articles. The Advertising Research Foundation found that three to four times as many people notice the average one-column photograph as read the average news story. In another study, Wayne Wanta of Oklahoma State University found that articles accompanied by photographs are perceived as significantly more important than those without photographs.

Like news releases, publicity photos are not published unless they appeal to media gatekeepers. Although professional photographers should always be hired to take the photos, public relations practitioners should supervise their work and select which photos are best suited for media use.

A photo that looks gorgeous on the computer screen may not look as good in print.

Media kits often include photos of the product. This shot accompanied the media kit for Kettle Corn, Act II.

Six Tips for GREAT PHOTOS

1. Photos must have good contrast and sharp detail so that they can be reproduced in a variety of formats, including grainy newsprint.
2. The best photos are uncluttered. Use tight shots with minimum background and an emphasis on detail, not whole scenes, and limit wasted space by reducing gaps between individuals or objects.
3. Sometimes context may be important. Environmental portraits show the subject of the photo in his or her normal surroundings—for example, a research scientist in a lab.
4. Action gives a photo interest. It's better to show people doing something—talking, gesturing, laughing, running, or operating a machine.
5. Emphasize scale. Apple, for example, might illustrate its newest iPod by having a person hold the device while surrounded by a large stack of CDs, showing how much music could be stored on it.
6. Most websites use images at a resolution of 72 dpi (dots per inch) to ensure fast downloads, but newspapers and magazines need a minimum of 300 dpi for reproduction purposes. Consequently, organizations usually have an online newsroom that provides high-resolution JPEG-format photos for journalists.

media advisories, FACT SHEETS, MEDIA KITS, AND PITCH LETTERS

On occasion, public relations staff will send a memo to reporters and editors about a news conference or upcoming event. In public relations parlance, these memos are referred to as media advisories or media alerts. Advisories can also let the media know about an interview opportunity with a visiting expert or alert them that a local person will be featured on a network television program Alerts may be sent either alone or with an accompanying news release.

The most common format for media advisories is short, bulleted lists rather than long paragraphs.

A typical one-page advisory might contain the following elements: a one-line headline, a brief paragraph outlining the story idea, answers to some of journalism's five W's and H questions, and a short paragraph telling the reporter whom to contact for more information or to make arrangements.

Fact sheets are often distributed to the media as part of a media kit or with a news release to give additional background information about the product, person, service, or event. A variation on the fact sheet is the FAQ (frequently asked questions).

Fact sheets are usually one to two pages in length and serve as a "crib sheet" for journalists when they write a story. A fact sheet about an organization may use headings that provide the following items: (1) the organization's full name, (2) the products or services offered, (3) the company's annual revenues, (4) the number of employees, (5) the names and one-paragraph biographies of top executives, (6) the markets served, (7) the company's position in the industry, and (8) any other pertinent details.

A media kit, sometimes referred to as a media kit, is usually prepared for major events and new product

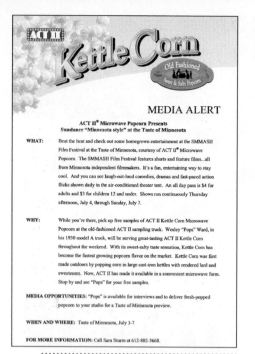

A media alert is a thumbnail sketch of a product and the special events surrounding its launch. As the name implies, it serves as an "alert" to the media in case they would like cover the announcement or event.

launches. It provides editors and reporters with a variety of information and resources to make it easier to report about the topic. The basic elements of a media kit are (1) the main news release; (2) a news feature about the development of the product or something similar; (3) fact sheets on the product, organization, or event; (4) background information; (5) photos and drawings with captions; (6) biographical material on the spokesperson or chief executives; and (7) basic contact information such as e-mail addresses, phone numbers, and website URLs.

Although organizations continue to prepare media kits in paper form, most such kits are now in digital form and are delivered to the media via the Internet or in CD format. This format not only saves trees, but also enables the organization to insert video clips showing the product being used or other relevant information.

Another public relations tactic is to write short letters or e-mails to editors that will grab their attention. In the public relations industry, this practice is called a *pitch*. In many cases, the letter will be accompanied by a sample of the product. Public relations people also use pitches—either mailed, e-mailed, phoned, or tweeted—to ask editors to assign a reporter to a particular event, to pursue a feature angle on an issue or trend, or even to book a spokesperson on a forthcoming show.

A pitch lets the editor know, in brief form, about the contents of the media kit. It also outlines why a periodical or broadcast outlet should consider the information as a news article, photograph, or video feature. Pitching is a fine art, which requires great skill. Before undertaking such an effort, public relations personnel must first do some basic research about the publication or broadcast show that they want to contact. It's important to be familiar with the kinds of stories that a publication usually publishes or the kinds of guests who typically appear on a particular talk show. Knowing a journalist's beat and the kinds of stories he or she has written in the past also is helpful. In addition, because the media tend to express great interest in trends, it's a good idea to relate a particular product or service to something that is already identified as part of a particular fashion or lifestyle.

think — What is a "pitch"?

Fact sheets are a useful public relations tool that focus on a product or service's strengths and capabilities. Some give ingredients; others discuss how to prepare the product.

btw...

The best pitch letters show a lot of creativity and are successful in grabbing an editor's attention. *Ragan's Media Relations Report* cites some opening lines from memorable pitches that generated media interest and resulting stories:

> "How many students does it take to change a light bulb?" (A pitch about a residence hall maintenance program operated by students on financial aid)

> "Would you like to replace your ex-husband with a plant?" (A pitch about a photographer who is expert at removing "exes" and other individuals out of old photos)

> "Our CEO ran 16 Boston Marathons . . . and now he thinks we can walk a mile around a river." (A pitch about a CEO leading employees on a daily walk instead of paying for expensive gym memberships or trainers)

Doing Good for the World and for the Balance Sheet

PR
CASEBOOK

CONSUMERS ARE INCREASINGLY conscious of corporate policies regarding environmental safety and sustainability. Companies that prove they are sincerely committed to addressing environmental issues earn customer loyalty. Beverage giant Coca-Cola addressed this issue with its "sustainability project." This initiative included both a theme—"Live Positively"—and a mission statement—"*Live Positively* is our commitment to make a positive difference in the world by redesigning the way we work and live so sustainability is part of everything we do."

In late 2009, Coke announced that its new PlantBottle beverage container was debuting in worldwide target markets. The company's goal was to produce 2 billion of the earth-friendly bottles by the end of 2010.

In a news release, Coca-Cola described the packaging: "PlantBottle PET plastic bottles are made partially from plants, which reduces the Company's dependence on a non-renewable resource—petroleum. It is 100 percent recyclable, and preliminary research indicates that from the growing of the plant materials through to the production of the resin, the carbon footprint for the PlantBottle packaging is smaller than for bottles made with traditional PET."

The release quoted Muhtar Kent, Chairman and CEO of Coca-Cola, "From Coke brands in Copenhagen to Dasani water in the western United States, we are starting to roll out the first generation of the bottle of the future."

In addition to a news release, Coca-Cola included high-resolution images of the bottles containing Coke and Dasani water as well as the recycle PlantBottle logo, an informative video about the bottle and video B-roll (background pictures, discussed later in this chapter), and an extensive online media kit. All of these promotional materials were made available at Coca-Cola's website media room.

Initiatives such as this one have positive spin-offs beyond increased customer loyalty and the immediate press attention that comes from the innovation. In 2009, Coca-Cola was listed on *Newsweek* magazine's first-ever "Green Rankings" of America's largest 500 companies, appeared on the Dow Jones Sustainability World Index, and received the World Environment Center's (WEC) Twenty-Fifth Annual Gold Medal for International Corporate Achievement in Sustainable Development "for implementing strategic business initiatives in the high-impact areas of water stewardship, sustainable packaging, energy management, and climate protection." This kind of positive press attracts the attention of consumers, investors, employees, members of the community and other opinion leaders.

1. List all of the public relations tactics you can find in this case study. Which do you think were most effective? Why?

2. Is "doing good" a valid public relations strategy and tactic? Why or why not?

3. Think of another company that has received media recognition—positive or negative—for its environmental policies. How did the company communicate about those policies? Which tactics did it use?

interviews
WITH JOURNALISTS AND
news CONFERENCES

Interviews

An interview with a newspaper reporter may last about an hour, perhaps taking place at lunch or over coffee in an informal setting. This person-to-person talk will typically result in a published story of perhaps 400 to 600 words, in which the interviewer weaves bits from the conversation together in direct and indirect quotation form, works in background material, and perhaps injects personal observations about the interviewee. The interview subject has no control over what is published, although he or she can exercise self-control in answering the questions.

News Conferences

At a news conference, communication is two-way. The person speaking for a company or a cause submits to questioning by reporters, usually after making a brief opening statement. A news conference makes possible quick, widespread dissemination of information and opinions through the news media. It avoids the time-consuming task of presenting the information to news outlets individually and ensures that the intensely competitive newspapers and electronic media hear the news simultaneously. From a public relations

point of view, these are the principal advantages of the news conference. These important pluses must be weighed against the fact that the

person holding the conference opens himself or herself up to direct and potentially antagonistic questioning.

In terms of public relations strategy, the news conference can be either an offensive measure or a defensive device, depending on the client's need. Most news conferences—or *media conferences*, as they frequently are called—are positive in intent; they are affirmative actions intended to project the host's plans or point of view. For example, a corporation may hold a news conference to unveil a new product whose manufacture will create many new jobs, or a civic leader may do so to reveal the goals and plans for a countywide charity fund drive she or he will head. Such news conferences should be carefully planned and scheduled well in advance.

If a business firm, an association, or a

Magazine interviews usually explore a subject in greater depth than interviews published in newspapers, because the writer may have more space available. Most magazine interviews have the same format as those in newspapers; others appear in question-and-answer form. These kinds of interviews require prolonged taped questioning of the interviewee by one or more writers and editors.

> **Neither the person being interviewed nor a public relations representative should ask to approve an interview story before it is published. Such requests are rebuffed automatically as a form of censorship.**

politician becomes embroiled in some kind of difficulty that is at best embarrassing, or at worst possibly incriminating, the media and public will demand an explanation. A bare-bones printed statement is not enough to satisfy the clamor and may draw greater media scrutiny if the organization appears to be stonewalling. A well-prepared spokesperson may be able to achieve a measure of understanding and sympathy by reading from a carefully composed statement when the news conference opens.

No matter how trying the circumstances, the person holding the news conference should create an atmosphere of cooperation and project a sincere intent to be helpful. The worst thing he or she can do is to appear angry or resentful of the questioning. A good posture is to admit that a situation is bad and that the organization is doing

everything in its power to correct it—an approach described by Professor Timothy Coombs at Eastern Illinois University as the "mortification" strategy.

There are two other types of news conferences of note. One occurs spontaneously, arising out of a news event: the winner of a Nobel Prize meets the media to explain the award-winning work or a runner who has just set a world's record breathlessly describes his or her feelings. The other type is the regularly scheduled conference held by a public official at stated times, even when there is nothing special to announce. Usually this type of event is called a *briefing*—the daily U.S. State Department briefing is one example of this type of news conference.

Planning and Conducting a News Conference

First comes the question, "Should we hold a news conference?" Frequently, the answer should be "No!" Reporters and camera crews should not be summoned to a media conference to hear propaganda instead of news

or information of minor interest to a limited group. When this happens, their valuable time has been wasted—and it *is* valuable. If the material involved fails to meet the criteria of significant news, a wise public relations representative will simply distribute it through a press release.

Every news outlet that might be interested in the material should be invited to a news conference. An ignored media outlet may become an enemy, like a person who isn't asked to a party. The invitation should describe the general nature of the material to be discussed so that an editor will know which type of reporter to assign to the event.

At a news conference, public relations representatives resemble producers of a movie or television show. They are responsible for briefing the spokesperson, making arrangements, and ensuring that the conference runs smoothly. They stay in the background during the actual event, however.

think

When is a printed statement enough? When is it necessary to hold a news conference?

THE media party
AND THE MEDIA TOUR

In the typical news conference, the purpose is to transmit information and opinions from the organization to the news media in a businesslike, time-efficient manner. Often, however, a corporation, an association, or a political figure wishes to deliver a message or build rapport with the media on

a more personal basis. In these circumstances, a social setting such as a media party or a media trip is desirable.

A press party may be a luncheon, a dinner, or a reception. Whatever form it takes, standard practice is for the host to rise at the end of the socializing period and make the

"pitch." This may be a hard-news announcement, a brief policy statement followed by a question-and-answer period, or merely a soft-sell thank-you to the guests for coming and giving the host an opportunity to get to know them better. Guests usually are provided with press packets of information, either when they arrive or as they leave. Parties may give the media an opportunity to preview an art exhibit or a new headquarters building, for example.

The host who expects that food and drink will buy favorable media coverage may receive an unpleasant surprise, however. Conscientious reporters and editors will not be swayed by this kind of "wining and dining." In their view, they have already given something to the host by setting aside a part of their day for the party. They accept invitations to media parties because they wish to develop potential news contacts within the host's organization and to learn more about its officials.

Three kinds of media tours may also be undertaken. The most common is a trip, often called a *junket*, during which editors and reporters are invited to inspect a company's manufacturing facilities in several cities, ride an inaugural flight of a new air route, or watch previews of the television network programs for the fall season in Hollywood or New York, for example. The host usually picks up the tab for transporting, feeding, and housing the reporters.

A second variation of the media tour is the *familiarization trip*. "Fam trips," as they are called, are offered to travel writers and editors by the tourism industry (see Chapter 16). Convention and visitors bureaus, as well as major resorts, pay all expenses in the hope that the writers will report favorably on their experiences. Travel articles in magazines and newspapers usually result from a reporter's fam trip.

In the third kind of media tour, the organization's executives travel to key cities to talk with selected editors. For example, Nokia executives might tour the East Coast to talk with key magazine editors and demonstrate the capabilities of the company's newest "smart" phone. Depending on editors' preferences, the executives may visit a publication and give a background briefing to key editors, or a hotel conference room may be set up so that the traveling executives can talk with editors from several publications at the same time.

think Why do reporters attend media parties?

Who Pays for What

In recent years, soul-searching by media members, as well as by professional public relations personnel who feel it is unethical to offer lavish travel and gifts, has led to increased self-regulation by both groups as to when a media tour or junket is appropriate and how much should be spent.

The policies of major dailies forbid employees from accepting any gifts, housing, or transportation; the newspapers pay all costs associated with a media tour on which a staff member is sent. In contrast, some smaller dailies, weeklies, and trade magazines accept offers for expense-paid trips. Their managers maintain that they lack the resources of large dailies to foot these expenses and claim that such trips are legitimate endeavors when reporters are covering a newsworthy activity.

Some newspapers with policies forbidding acceptance of travel and gifts don't extend the restrictions to all departments. Reporters in the hard-news area, for example, cannot accept gifts or travel, but such policies may not be enforced for reporters who write soft news for the sports, travel, and lifestyle sections. Few newspapers, for example, pay for the press box seats provided for reporters covering a professional football game, nor does the travel editor usually pay the full rate for rooms at beach resorts that are the focus of travel articles.

Given the mixed and often confusing policies of various media, public relations professionals must use common sense and discretion when offering "freebies" to reporters. First, they should not violate the PRSA code of ethics, which forbids

ethics in ACTION

handing out lavish gifts and free trips that have nothing to do with covering a legitimate news event. Second, public relations professionals should be sensitive to the policies of news outlets and should design events to stay within those parameters. A wise alternative is to offer reporters the option of reimbursing the company for travel and hotel expenses associated with a media tour.

THE REACH OF radio AND television

broadcasting and its various forms, including webcasting, are important because they reach the vast majority of the U.S. public on a daily basis. Each week, it is estimated that radio reaches 92 percent of Americans ages 12 and older, with a total audience of 234 million. With the average American now commuting nearly 50 minutes each workday, a large percentage of this audience is reached in their cars.

Television NEWS
Reaches a Mass Audience

23 million Americans **13%** watch **national** news on NBC, ABC, or CBS, according to Nielsen Media Research

158 million Americans **52%** watch the **local** news according to the Pew Research Center.

Writing and preparing materials for broadcast and digital media require a special perspective. Instead of writing for the eye, a practitioner has to shift gears and think about adding audio and visual elements to the story.

radio

think How does writing for radio differ from writing for television or print?

news releases prepared for radio differ in several ways from releases prepared for print media. Although the basic identifying information is the same (letter-head, contact, subject), the standard practice is to write a radio release using all uppercase letters in a double-spaced format.

The length of the printed radio news release should also be indicated. Radio announcements should take 30 or 60 seconds to read. The timing is vital, because broadcasters must fit their messages into a rigid time frame that is measured down to the second.

Radio news releases, like releases for print media, must be newsworthy and not too commercial. Unlike the case with regular news releases, however, radio demands that the story be told in 60 seconds (about 125 words).

A news release for a newspaper uses standard English grammar and punctuation. Sentences often contain dependent and independent clauses. In a radio release, a more conversational style is used, and the emphasis is on strong, short sentences. This format allows the announcer to breathe between thoughts and the listener to follow what is being said. An average sentence length of about 10 words is a good goal.

60-Second News Feature for Radio

The following is an example of a 30-second announcement distributed by the Field Museum in Chicago about one of its special exhibits:

Maps not only tell us where we are, but most importantly, who we are. The Field Museum's exhibition, "Maps: Finding Our Place in the World", allows visitors to take a look at some of the most rare and historically valuable maps ever created. Besides direction, maps can also give us clues on how a people, a nation, government, or organization viewed their worlds. Through contemporary, historical, flat or three-dimensional maps, this exhibition will explore a variety of themes, ranging from the history of maps to the mapmaker's political, cultural, or spiritual worldview. For more information, call (312) 922-9410 or visit www.fieldmuseum.org.

Audio News Releases

Although broadcast-style news releases can be sent to radio stations for announcers to read, the most common and effective approach is to send the radio station a recording of the news announcement.

An audio news release, commonly called an *ANR*, can take two forms. One simple approach is for someone with a good radio voice to read the entire announcement; the person doing the reading may not be identified by name. In the trade, this type of ANR is called an *actuality*. In a second approach, an announcer reads the release, but a quote called a *sound bite* is also included from a satisfied customer or a company spokesperson. This approach is better than a straight announcement because the message comes from a "real person" rather than a nameless announcer. This type of announcement is also more acceptable to stations, because the radio station's staff can elect either to use the whole recorded announcement or to use just the sound bite.

The preferred length for an ANR is one minute, although shorter ones can be used. The audio recording should also be accompanied by a pa-per copy of the script, which enables the news director to judge the value of the tape without having to listen to it.

Radio stations, like newspapers, have preferences about how they want to receive audio news releases. One survey by DWJ Television found that almost 75 percent of radio news directors prefer to receive actualities by phone. This is particularly true for late-breaking news events in the station's service area. When a forest fire threatened vineyards in California's Napa Valley, for example, a large winery contacted local stations and offered an ANR with a sound bite from the winery's president telling everyone that the grape harvest would not be affected. Approximately 50 stations were called, and 40 accepted the ANR for broadcast use.

Public Service Announcements

Public relations personnel working for nonprofit organizations often prepare public service announcements (PSAs) for radio stations. A PSA is an unpaid announcement that promotes the programs of government or voluntary agencies or that serves the public interest. As part of their responsibility to serve the public interest, radio and TV stations provide airtime to charitable and civic organizations to inform the public about such topics as heart disease, mental illness, and AIDS.

Radio PSAs, like radio news releases, are written in uppercase and double-spaced format. Their length can be 60, 30, 20, 15, or 10 seconds. Unlike radio news releases, the standard practice is to submit multiple PSAs on the same subject in various lengths, allowing the station flexibility in using a PSA of a particular length to fill a specific time slot. A PSA is usually delivered in CD format to stations along with a print out of the script.

Many national organizations, such as the American Cancer Society and the American Red Cross, make their nationally distributed PSAs more interesting by incorporating music, sound bites, and other sounds in the script. Major nonprofit organizations are also uploading their PSAs to the YouTube website.

Radio Media Tours

Another public relations tactic geared toward radio is the radio media tour (RMT). In an RMT, a spokesperson conducts a series of around-the-country, one-on-one interviews from a central location with radio announcers across the country or a region. A public relations practitioner (often called a publicist in such a situation) books telephone interviews with DJs, news directors, or talk show hosts at various stations, and the personality simply gives interviews over the phone that can be broadcast live or recorded for later use. A selling point for the RMT is its relatively low cost and the convenience of giving numerous short interviews from one central location.

> **Organizations sending ANRs for national distribution typically use satellite transmission or the World Wide Web.**

HOW LONG IS YOUR MESSAGE?

Most announcers read at a rate of 150 to 160 words per minute. Of course, word lengths vary, so it's not feasible to set the timing based on the number of words in a message. Instead, the general practice is to use an approximate line count.

With word processing software set for 60 spaces per line, the following standard can be applied:

2 lines = 10 seconds (about 25 words)

5 lines = 20 seconds (about 45 words)

8 lines = 30 seconds (about 65 words)

16 lines = 60 seconds (about 125 words)

> ❝It is such an easy, flexible medium. We can interview a star in bed at his hotel and broadcast it to the country. Radio is delicious.❞
>
> Laurence Mosowitz, President of Medialink

Is your cat *healthy*?

What pet owners should know about subtle signs of illness in cats.

1. :60 Radio PSA
2. :30 Radio PSA
3. :10 Radio PSA

American Veterinary Medical Association
1931 N. Meacham Road • Schaumburg, Illinois 60173
Phone (847) 925-8070 • www.avma.org

Almost any topic or issue can be the subject of a PSA, although stations seem to be more receptive to particular topics. A survey of radio station public affairs directors by WestGlen Communications, a producer of PSAs, found that local community issues and events were most likely to receive airtime, followed by children's issues. The respondents also expressed a preference for PSAs involving health and safety, service organizations, breast cancer, and other cancers.

television

there are four approaches for getting an organization's news and viewpoints on local television. The first approach is to simply send the same news release that the local print media receive. If the news director thinks the topic is newsworthy, the item may become a brief 10-second mention by the announcer on a news program. A news release may also prompt the assignment editor to consider visual treatment of the subject and assign the topic to a reporter and a camera crew for follow-up.

A second approach is a media alert or advisory (discussed earlier in the chapter) informing the assignment editor about a particular event or occasion that would lend itself to video coverage. The third approach is to phone or e-mail the assignment editor and make a pitch to have the station do a particular story. The secret to successfully pitching a television news editor is to emphasize the visual aspects of the story.

The fourth approach is to produce a video news release (VNR) that, like an ANR, is formatted for immediate use and requires a minimum effort on the part of station personnel. The VNR can be used by numerous stations on a regional, national, or even global basis.

Video News Releases

An estimated 5,000 VNRs are produced annually in the United States, primarily by large organizations seeking enhanced recognition for their names, products, services, and causes. The production of VNRs may be more easily justified if there is potential for national distribution and multiple pickups by television stations and cable systems.

A typical 90-second VNR may cost a minimum of $20,000 to

$50,000 for production and distribution. Costs vary, however, depending on the number of location shots, special effects, the use of celebrities, and the number of staff required to produce a high-quality tape that meets broadcast standards.

Public relations departments or firms must carefully analyze the news potential of the information and consider whether the topic lends itself to a fast-paced, action-oriented visual presentation. A VNR should not be produced if it contains nothing but "talking heads," charts, and graphs. Another aspect to consider is whether the topic will still be current by the time the video is produced. On average, it takes four to six weeks to script, produce, and distribute a high-quality VNR. In a crisis situation or for a fast-breaking news event, however, a VNR can be produced in a matter of hours or days.

Sankio Pharma, for example, learned at 11 A.M. that the FDA had approved its "wrist watch" device that consumers can use to monitor diabetes and glucose levels. By 3:30 P.M. the same day, WestGlen Communications had produced and distributed a VNR that was eventually aired 243 times on stations including the CNN and Fox News networks.

Because of the specialized knowledge that is required, public relations departments and firms usually outsource production to a firm specializing in scripting and producing VNRs. Public relations personnel, however, usually serve as liaison and give the producer an outline of what the VNR is supposed to accomplish. The public relations person also will work with the producer to line up location shots, props, and the individuals who will be featured.

The VNR package should also include two or three minutes of B-roll, or background pictures, for use by TV news producers in repackaging the story. Typical B-roll includes additional interviews, sound bites, and file footage. A Nielsen Media Research survey of 130 TV news directors, for example, found that 70 percent preferred VNRs with B-roll attached.

An advisory should accompany the VNR package or be sent to news directors before the actual satellite transmission of the video to the station. The advisory, which takes printed form, contains the key elements of the story, background and description of the visuals, editorial and technical contacts, satellite coordinates, and the date and time of the transmission. Many stations prefer to receive this advisory by fax instead of e-mail or wire service so it can be easily passed around the newsroom and many staffers can see it.

think What is B-roll and why is it important in a VNR?

Satellite transmission is the most cost-effective way to distribute VNRs nationally or even globally. In addition, it is the method of receiving these messages preferred by most news directors.

Today, VNRs often reach an even larger audience than is possible with local television through YouTube. Most organizations, with a few technical adjustments, regularly upload their VNRs to their YouTube channel and even their corporate websites.

Satellite Media Tours

The television equivalent of the radio media tour is the satellite media tour (SMT). An SMT is a series of prebooked, one-on-one interviews from a fixed location (usually a television studio) via satellite with a series of television journalists or talk show hosts. A survey by WestGlen Communications found that nearly 85 percent of all U.S. television stations participate in satellite tours.

The most efficient way to do an SMT is to make the organization's spokesperson available for an interview at a designated time. Celebrities are always popular, but an organization also can use articulate experts. In general, the spokesperson sits in a chair or at a desk in front of a television camera. Another popular approach to SMTs is to get out of the television studio and do the interviews on location. When the National Pork Producers Council wanted to promote outdoor winter grilling, its public relations staff hired a team from News Broadcast Network to fire up an outdoor grill in Aspen, Colorado, and have a celebrity chef in a parka give interviews, via satellite, while he cooked pork.

VNR Tips

Medialink, a major producer and distributor of VNRs, gives some tips about the production of VNRs that best meet the needs of TV news directors:

1. Allow TV news directors the ability to edit the VNR so they can use their own anchors and directors.

2. Make the VNR look like regular news footage and avoid commercial-like shots.

3. Don't use a stand-up reporter in the VNR; stations want to use their own reporters.

4. Provide a local angle if at all possible.

5. Good graphics and animation are a plus.

personal APPEARANCES

think — Which characteristics does a good talk show guest have?

adio and television stations increasingly operate on round-the-clock schedules, and they require vast amounts of programming to fill the time available. When your goal is to get spokespersons on talk and magazine shows, your contact is no longer the news department, but rather the directors and producers of such programs. The most valuable communication tools in reaching these people are the telephone and the persuasive pitch via e-mail or Twitter.

Before contacting directors and producers, however, it is necessary for the public relations staff to do their homework. They must be completely familiar with a show's format and content, as well as the type of audience that it reaches. A public relations professional should watch the program and study the format. This research will help determine whether a particular show is appropriate for your spokesperson and suggest how to tailor a pitch letter to achieve maximum results.

Talk Shows and Magazine Shows

Radio and television talk shows have been a broadcast staple for many years. KABC in Los Angeles started the trend in 1960, when it became the first radio station in the country to convert to an all-news-and-talk format. Since then more than 1,110 radio stations across the country have adopted this format. Stations that play music also may include talk shows as part of their programming. In fact, it is estimated that there are now more than 4,000 radio talk shows in the United States.

The same growth applies to television. Phil Donahue began his seminal talk show in 1967. Today, there are more than 20 nationally syndicated talk shows and a number of locally produced talk shows. For the past decade, the number one syndicated daytime talk show was the *Oprah Winfrey Show*, attracting about 8 million viewers on a daily basis. On the network level, three shows are the Holy Grail for publicists: NBC's *Today*, ABC's *Good Morning America*, and CBS's *Early Show*. Collectively, these three shows draw approximately 14 million viewers between 7 and 9 A.M. every weekday.

The advantage of talk shows is the opportunity to have viewers see and hear the organization's spokesperson without the filter of journalists and editors interpreting and deciding what is newsworthy. Another advantage is the opportunity to be on air longer than the traditional 30-second sound bite in a news program.

Booking a Guest

The contact for a talk show may be the executive producer or assistant producer of the show. If it is a network or nationally syndicated show, the contact person may have the title of talent coordinator or talent executive. Whatever the title, these people are known in the broadcasting industry as *bookers* because they are responsible for booking a constant supply of timely guests for the show.

One way to place a guest on a talk show is to phone the booker to briefly outline the qualifications of the proposed speaker and explain why this

person would be a timely guest. Publicists also can write a brief one-page letter or send an e-mail about the story angle, explaining why it is relevant to the show's audience and why the proposed speaker is qualified to talk on the subject. In many cases, the booker will ask for video clips of the spokesperson's appearances on previous TV shows or newspaper clips of media interviews. It's important to be honest about the experience and personality of the spokesperson, so the booker isn't disappointed and your credibility remains intact.

In general, talk shows book guests three to four weeks in advance. Unless a topic or a person is extremely timely or controversial, it is rare for a person to be booked on one or two days' notice. Public relations strategists must keep this time frame in mind as part of overall planning of a public relations campaign.

Broadcast Interviews

The current popularity of talk shows, both on local stations and syndicated satellite networks, provides many opportunities for on-air appearances. A successful radio or television broadcast interview appearance has three principal requirements:

1. *Preparation.* Guests should know what they want to say.
2. *Concise speech.* Guests should answer questions and make statements precisely and briefly without excessive detail or extraneous material. Responses should be kept to 30 seconds or less, because the interviewer must conduct the program under strict time restrictions.
3. *Relaxation.* "Mic fright" is a common ailment for which no automatic cure exists. It will diminish if the guest concentrates on talking to the interviewer in a casual person-to-person manner. Guests should speak up firmly; the control room can reduce volume, if necessary.

A public relations adviser can help an interview guest on these points. Answers to anticipated questions may be worked out and polished during a mock interview in which the practitioner plays the role of broadcaster.

All too often, talk show hosts know little about their guests for the day's broadcast. The public relations adviser can overcome this difficulty by sending the host in advance a fact sheet summarizing the important information and listing questions the broadcaster might wish to ask. On network shows and major metro stations, support staffs often do the preliminary work with guests. Interviewers on hundreds of smaller local television and radio stations, however, lack such staff resources. Hosts at these stations may go on the air almost "cold" unless public relations practitioners provide them with volunteered information.

product PLACEMENTS

television's drama and comedy shows, and theatrical films as well, are often good vehicles for promoting a company's products and services. It is not a coincidence that the hero of a detective series drives a Lexus or that the heroine is seen boarding a United Airlines flight.

Such product placements, sometimes called *plugs*, are often negotiated by product publicists and talent agencies. This practice is really nothing new. Product placements, however, truly came of age with the movie *ET* in the early 1980s. The story goes that M&M's Candies made a classic marketing mistake by

> "In the early 1900s, Henry Ford had an affinity for *Hollywood* and perhaps it is no coincidence that his Model T's were the predominant vehicle appearing in the first motion pictures of the era."
>
> IPRA *Frontline*

not allowing the film to use M&M's as the prominently displayed trail of candy that the young hero used to lure his big-eyed friend home. Instead, Hershey jumped at the chance to showcase Reese's Pieces in the blockbuster film, and the rest is history. Sales of Reese's Pieces skyrocketed. Even today, more than 20 years after the film's debut, the candy and the character remain forever linked in popular culture and the minds of a whole generation of *ET* fans.

Retailers are particularly active in seeking out product placements because studies show that today's youth gets many of their ideas about what products to buy from watching television shows. That's why Simon, Paula, and Randy had Coca-Cola glasses sitting in front of them on *American Idol*, Tom Cruise wore Ray-Bans in *Risky Business* and used an Apple computer in *Mission Impossible*, James Bond drives a BMW, the characters in *Swordfish* drank Heineken beer, and *Alias*'s Agent Bristow used a Nokia phone.

The *Wall Street Journal* explained how *American Idol* engages in product placement:

> The series launched in summer 2002 with a few sponsors, namely Coca-Cola Co., which paid to have a big Coke cup sitting in front of the three judges in every episode. . . . In the current season, Fox abandoned any pretense at subtlety. The Coke

cups are still there. . . , but now Coca-Cola's famous logo appears prominently onscreen for part of each show; fizzy bubbles fill a screen behind contestants as they describe what song they will sing each week. The contestants film a new commercial for Ford each week. And each episode is loaded with other hard sells for a truckload of other merchandise, ranging from Cingular phones and text-messaging services to Kenny Rogers' new CD.

Another opportunity for product exposure on television is on game shows. *The Price Is Right*, for example, uses a variety of products as prizes for contestants. In one episode, the prize was a tent, a camp table and chairs, and lanterns—a great, low-cost product placement for Coleman for less than $200.

think Why do film producers agree to product placements?

Summary

What Is the Role of News Releases in Public Relations? p. 250

- The news release is the most commonly used public relations tactic. These releases are key sources for a large percentage of newspaper articles.
- News releases must be accurate, informative, and written in journalistic style.
- Publicity photos often accompany news releases to make a story more appealing.

How Are Media Advisories, Fact Sheets, Media Kits, and Pitch Letters Used in Public Relations Campaigns? p. 253

- Advisories (also known as alerts) let journalists know about an upcoming event such as a news conference or photo or interview opportunities.
- Fact sheets provide the five W's and H of an event in outline form. They can also be used to provide background on an executive, a product, or an organization.
- A media kit (press kit) is typically a folder containing news releases, photos, fact sheets, and features about a new product, an event, or other newsworthy project undertaken by an organization.
- Public relations personnel pitches can take the form of letters, e-mails, or even telephone calls. A good pitch is based on research and a creative idea that will appeal to the editor.

Which Public Relations Tactics Are Best for Reaching Television and Radio Audiences? p. 259

- A news conference allows an organization to distribute information to multiple journalists at the same time. News conferences should be held only when there is news that requires elaboration and clarification.
- Radio news releases, unlike releases for print media, must be written for the ear. A popular format is the audio news release (ANR) that includes an announcer and a quote (sound bite) from a spokesperson. Radio news releases should be no longer than 60 seconds.
- Both radio and television stations accept public service announcements (PSAs) from nonprofit organizations that wish to inform and educate the public about health issues or upcoming civic events. Television PSAs require visual aids.
- Radio media tours (RMTs) and television satellite media tours (SMTs) involve an organization's spokesperson being interviewed from a central location by journalists across the country. Each journalist is able to conduct a one-on-one interview for several minutes.

- The video news release (VNR) is produced in a format that television stations can easily use or edit based on their needs. VNRs are relatively expensive to produce but have great potential for reaching large audiences.
- With a news feed, an organization arranges for coverage of a particular event, and television stations across the country can watch it in real time or receive an edited version of it for later use.

Which Steps Should Public Relations Practitioners Take to Arrange Personal Appearances on Talk and Magazine Shows? p. 263

- Public relations personnel often book spokespersons on radio and television talk shows. To be effective, the guest must have an appealing personality, be knowledgeable, and give short, concise answers.

How Can Product Placements Be Leveraged to Promote Products and Services? p. 264

- Producers are increasingly making deals with companies to feature their products on television shows or movies.

QUESTIONS
for *Review* and *Discussion*

1. How should a news release be formatted? Why is the inverted pyramid structure used in news releases?

2. List at least six guidelines for writing a news release.

3. Before pitching an item to a journalist or editor, why is it a good idea to first do some basic research on the individual, the publication, or the talk show?

4. Various methods can be used to deliver publicity materials to the media. Name the methods and compare their relative strengths and weaknesses. Some experts believe that e-mail is the ultimate distribution channel. Do you agree or disagree?

5. Radio news releases must be tightly written. What is the general guideline for the number of lines and words in a 30-second news release? Which other guidelines should be kept in mind when writing a radio news release?

6. How does an audio news release differ from a standard radio news release?

7. What are the advantages of a radio media tour (RMT) or a satellite media tour (SMT) for an organization and for journalists? Are there any disadvantages?

8. List four ways that an organization can get its news and viewpoints on local television.

9. Companies increasingly are working with television programs and film studios to get their products featured as part of a program or movie. What do you think of this trend?

the THINKSPOT

www.thethinkspot.com

13 EVENTS AND

Ask Yourself

> Which Planning and Logistical Steps Assure Successful Event Planning and Execution? p. 271

> Which Elements Must Be Taken into Consideration When Creating a Budget for an Event? p. 275

> Why Is the Investment in Events Justified for Most Organizations? p. 281

> How Can Public Relations Professionals Harness Creativity to Plan and Implement Memorable and Effective Events? p. 283

A Night to Remember

When the New York Women's Foundation hosted its first autumn benefit in midtown Manhattan, the organizers considered time, place, menu, centerpieces, entertainment, guest list, seating arrangements, and so much more, as reported in an article in the *New York Times* by Laura Lipton. "To produce the few hours of gaiety, five chairwomen and a brigade of behind-the-scenes workers had spent months vetting every detail, from the hors d'oeuvres to the guests of honor. Such considerations are crucial for a gala to succeed amid scores of other parties, all for organizations seeking benefactors for their good works."

The chairwomen set a budget of $175,000 and selected the theme of "Stepping Out and Stepping Up" for the event. They hired CMI Event Planning and Fundraising to handle the details of invitations and catering contracts, and to help the chairwomen keep on top of the details. Cathy McNamara, of CMI, told Lipton, "We're the professional nags."

One of the chairwomen described how she spent Labor Day writing personal notes in 70 to 100 invitations. " 'The New York Women's Foundation is extremely important to me. Please help support these extraordinary women,' " she said she wrote. "Then I might put, 'Say hey to your husband' or 'Hope you're well.' "

The foundation guaranteed 300 guests for the caterer. As the event drew nearer, the chairwomen met to test and select

PROMOTIONS

appetizers (mini-hamburgers), select floral arrangements (the coppery bowls were selected, but woven green reeds in one arrangement were rejected), and choose napkin colors (olive green was ultimately given the nod).

Lipton described the evening of the benefit: "At Gotham Hall, a grand, lofty space that was once the headquarters of a bank, guests sipped martinis and applauded the speeches. A mambo performance by a dozen school-age dancers momentarily transfixed the room." The competition among benefits is strong and the economy during this event was weak, so the organizers counted it as a great success that 280 guests contributed $675,000 to the foundation at the event.

❶ Which details did the event organizers focus on as they planned this gala event?

❷ Imagine planning an event for an organization—a sorority or fraternity or club. List all the things that you will have to take into account to make the event a success.

❸ Why are events an important part of an organization's public relations efforts? How can they help an organization meet its goals?

A WORLD FILLED WITH
meetings AND
events

meetings and events are vital public relations tools. One of the best things about meetings and events is that they provide an opportunity for an audience to gather face-to-face, in real time. In this era of digital communication and information overload, there is still a basic human need to convene, to socialize, and to participate in group activities.

Individuals attending a meeting or event use all five of their senses—hearing, sight, touch, smell, and taste—thereby becoming more emo-

> **"Events deliver face time between consumers and brands. They also introduce consumers to new products."**
> Yung Moon, associate publisher of *Self* magazine, as reported in *PRWeek*

tionally involved in the process. Marketing and public relations professionals can foster brand awareness and loyalty with these kinds of events.

Meetings and events come in all forms and sizes. A committee meeting of a civic club or an office staff meeting may include only 4 or 5 people. Corporate seminars may be presented to 50 to 250 people. At the other end of the scale are trade shows such as the Consumer Electronics Show (CES) in Las Vegas, which attracts 130,000 attendees over a three-day period.

Effective meetings and events don't just happen. Rather, detailed planning and logistics are essential to assure that defined objectives are achieved, whether the event is a committee meeting or a national conference. This chapter discusses various types of meetings and events and the steps public relations professionals take to plan and execute them effectively.

Macworld is held in San Francisco every year and typically has 50,000 attendees.

Macworld Conference & Expo®
January 5-9, 2009

The Las Vegas Convention and Visitors Authority reports that the meetings and convention industry spends more than **$8 BILLION** each year in that city. In 2008, Las Vegas hosted more than 22,000 conventions that attracted **6 MILLION ATTENDEES.**

think How does attending a meeting in person differ from participating in an online focus group or visiting a chat room?

group MEETINGS

the size and purpose of the meeting dictate the specifics of its plan. Even so, every plan must address some common questions: How many people will attend? Who will attend? When and where will the event be held? How long will it last? Who will speak? Which topics will be covered? Which facilities will be needed? Who will run the meeting? What is its purpose? How do we get people to attend?

Meeting Location

A meeting site must be the right size for the expected audience. If it is too large, the audience will feel that the meeting has failed to draw the expected attendance. If it is too small, the audience will be uncomfortable. Most hotels have a number of meeting rooms available, ranging in size from small to very large.

After selecting a room, a planner must make sure that the audience members can find it. The name of the meeting or group and the name of the room should be registered on the hotel or restaurant's schedule of events for a particular day.

Meeting Invitations

For clubs, an announcement in the newsletter, a flyer, or an e-mail should be an adequate invitation. For external groups—people who are not required to attend but whose

---

"TO DO" LIST
for Planning and Hosting a Successful Meeting

Here is a general "to do" list that should be the starting point for organizing an event—anything from a local weekly dinner meeting for a service club to the annual gathering of a professional association.

In Advance

- Determine the best date and time to ensure maximum attendance.
- Make a realistic estimate of how many people will attend.
- Select the restaurant or other facility at least four to six weeks in advance.
- Confirm in writing the following: date, time, menu, cocktails, seating plan, number of guaranteed reservations, and projected costs.
- Enlist one or more speakers four to six weeks in advance. If a speaker is in high demand, make the arrangements several months in advance. Discuss the nature of the talk, its length, and any audiovisual requirements.
- Publicize the meeting to the membership and other interested parties. This activity should be done a minimum of three weeks in advance.
- Organize a phone committee to call members 72 hours before the event if reservations are lagging.
- Prepare a timetable for the evening's events. Organizational leaders, as well as the serving staff, should be aware of this schedule.
- Decide on a seating plan for the head table, organize place cards, and tell VIPs as they arrive where they will be sitting.

On the Meeting Day

- Get a final count on reservations, and make an educated guess as to how many people might arrive at the door without a reservation.
- Check the speaker's travel plans and handle any last-minute questions or requirements.
- Give the catering manager a revised final count for meal service. In many instances, this might have to be done 24 to 72 hours in advance of the meeting day.
- Check the room arrangements one to two hours in advance of the meeting. Have enough tables been set up? Are tables arranged correctly for the meeting? Does the microphone system work?
- Set up a registration table just inside or outside the door.
- Designate three or four members of the organization to serve as a hospitality committee to meet and greet newcomers and guests.

After the Meeting

- Settle accounts with the restaurant, or indicate where an itemized bill should be mailed.
- Send thank-you notes to the speaker and any committee members who helped plan or host the meeting.
- Prepare a summary of the speaker's comments for the organization's newsletter and, if appropriate, send a news release to local media.

presence is desired—invitations must be sent in the mail or via e-mail. These invitations should go out early enough for people to fit the meeting into their schedules—three to six weeks is a typical lead time.

The invitation should list the time, day, date, place (including the name of the room), purpose, highlights of the program (including names of speakers), and a way for the person to accept or decline the invitation. The RSVP information may consist of a telephone number, an e-mail address, a reply card

mailed back to the event's organizers, or even an online registration service that handles everything from making the reservation to processing the credit card information to pay for the event. It is also a good idea to provide a map showing the location and parking facilities.

think How many weeks before a group meeting should invitations be sent?

MEETING FACILITIES

A small meeting may not need much in the way of facilities, whereas a large and formal gathering may require a considerable amount of equipment and furnishings. Items that should be considered—and supplied if needed—include the following:

- **MEETING IDENTIFICATION.** Is the name of the organization and meeting posted on the bulletin board near the building entrance?

- **LIGHTING.** Is it adequate? Can it be controlled? Where are the controls? Who will handle them?

- **CHARTS.** Are they readable? Is the easel adequate? Who will handle the charts?

- **SCREEN OR MONITORS.** Are they large enough for the size of the audience?

- **PROJECTORS AND VIDEO EQUIPMENT.** Are they hooked up and working? Who is the contact at the facility if you have technical difficulties?

- **SEATING AND TABLES.** Are there enough seats for the expected audience? Are they arranged properly?

- **SPEAKER'S PODIUM.** Is it positioned properly? What about a reading light? Is there a public address (PA) system? Is it working?

- **AUDIENCE AND SPEAKER AIDS.** Are there programs or agendas? Will there be notepaper, pencils, and handout materials?

Madame Butterfly
85th Anniversary Production
Hakone Estate and Gardens
Yes, I will attend

M _____ & M _____

Address: _____ City _____ Zip Code _____

Telephone: _____ Email: _____

My additional guests are _____

$150 per person

I am enclosing a check for $ _____

I am unable to attend but I wish to donate $ _____

Please Charge My Credit Card: Visa ___ Mastercard ___ Amex ___

Card Number _____ Expiration Date _____

Name on the Card _____ Signature _____

Kindly RSVP by August 29, 2008

408 741-4977 or www.hakone.us/event

Invitations to events require reply cards that include name, address, e-mail, and credit card information. This reply card, which was created by Hakone Gardens in Saratoga, California, is well organized and gives enough space for the invitee to provide the necessary details.

Getting the Meeting Started

If all of the attendees know one another, registration and identification can be highly informal. In contrast, if the group is large, it is customary to set up a registration desk or table at the entrance. A representative of the sponsoring organization should be available at the entrance of the room. If the number of people attending is not too large, a personal welcome is in order. If hundreds of people are expected, this kind of greeting isn't possible; in such a case, the chairperson should greet the audience in his or her opening remarks.

Name tags are a good idea at almost any meeting. Label-making software can prepare name tags for everyone with advance reservations. Names should be printed in bold, large block letters so they can be read from a distance of four feet. If attendee affiliation is included on the name tags, this information can be presented in smaller bold letters. For people showing up without advance registration, have felt-tip pens available to make on-the-spot name tags.

A Speaker NEEDS TO KNOW

Barbara Nichols, owner of a hospitality management firm in New York City, in conjunction with *Meeting News*, created this comprehensive checklist of things speakers need to know about a meeting:

- Information about the meeting sponsor and attendees
- Meeting purpose and objectives
- Presentation location, including meeting room, date, and hour
- Topic and length of presentation
- Anticipated size of the audience
- Session format, including length of time allowed for audience questions
- Names of those sharing the platform, if any, and their topics
- Name of person who will make the introductions

- Speaker fee or honorarium
- Travel and housing arrangements
- Meeting room setup and staging information
- A contact for audiovisual equipment requests
- Dress code (business attire, resort wear, black tie)
- Information about plans to tape or videotape the remarks (a release may be needed)
- Arrangements for spouse, if invited

Speakers

Speakers should be selected early—at least a month in advance, if possible. A speaker should be chosen because of his or her expertise, crowd-drawing capacity, and speaking ability. It is a good idea to listen to any prospective speaker before tendering an invitation, or at least to discuss the individual's speaking ability with an impartial person who has actually heard the speaker.

Meals

Club meetings and workshops often occur at a meal time. In fact, many meetings include breakfast, lunch, or dinner. Early-morning breakfast meetings have the advantage of attracting people who cannot take the time during the day to attend such functions.

Luncheons are either sit-down affairs with a fixed menu or a buffet. A 30- to 45-minute cocktail period may precede a luncheon, usually during registration as guests arrive. A good schedule for a typical luncheon is registration, 11:30; luncheon, noon; and adjournment, 1:30. In rare instances, the adjournment can be as late as 2 P.M., but it should never be later than that.

Dinner meetings are handled in much the same way as luncheons. A typical schedule is registration and cocktails, 6 P.M.; dinner, 7 P.M.; speaker, 8 P.M.; and adjournment, between 8:30 and 9 P.M. Speakers should talk for approximately 20 minutes.

An accurate count of people who will attend a meal function is essential. The hotel or restaurant facility will need a count at least 24 hours in advance to prepare the food and set up table service. The standard practice is for the organization to guarantee a certain number of meals, plus or minus 10 percent. If fewer people than expected show up, the organization still must pay for all the meals.

How GOOD Are Your Meetings?

Meetings are a way of life in all organizations, including all those committee meetings to brainstorm and plan a public relations campaign. Cliff Shaffran, writing in IABC's *Communication World*, suggests that the effectiveness of a meeting can be determined by asking attendees to rate the meeting from 1 (rarely) to 5 (always) on a number of criteria. How would you rate your last committee meeting on the following criteria?

- There is a clearly defined, results-focused theme and agenda.
- We make decisions and move forward; it isn't just a debating society.
- The meetings are friendly and don't generate conflict.

- Everyone contributes.
- No one dominates the discussion.
- Communication is open and positive.
- We generate many creative ideas.
- We challenge the status quo to explore alternative ideas and solutions.
- We fully maximize the knowledge and expertise of all participants.
- We keep on time.
- We always achieve our desired results.
- We have good return on time invested.
- Everyone enjoys the process.

banquets

banquets are fairly large and formal functions. They may be held to honor an individual, raise money for a charitable organization, or celebrate an event such as an organization's anniversary. A banquet or even a reception can have 100 or 1,000 people in attendance; for this reason, staging a successful one takes a great deal of planning. The budget, in particular, needs close attention.

Securing a well-known personality to speak at a banquet usually helps boost ticket sales, but is also a major expense item in a budget. Karen Kendig, president of the Speaker's Network, told *PR Tactics* that the going rate is $3,000 to $10,000 for "bread and butter" business-type talks, $15,000 or more for minor entertainment celebrities, and $50,000 or more for well-known politicians.

Because such fees cannot be fully absorbed in the cost of an individual ticket, in addition to sending out individual invitations, typically a committee is formed that solicits corporations and other businesses to sponsor the event

Al Gore, former Vice President and environmental movement guru, reportedly charges approximately $100,000 per speech, as do Sarah Palin and entertainment celebrities such as Jay Leno, Conan O'Brien, and Dana Carvey. For a mere $50,000, an organization may be able to book basketball player Charles Barkley, actor Angela Bassett, or tennis star Anna Kournikova.

BANQUET EXPENSES

Food

Room rental

Bartenders

Decorations and table centerpieces

Audio-visual requirements

Speaker fees

Entertainment

Photographers

Invitations

Tickets

Marketing and promotion

or "buy" tables for employees, clients, or friends. A corporate table for eight people, for example, may go for $25,000 or more, depending on the prestige and purpose of the event.

When organizing a banquet, contact the catering or banquet manager of the restaurant or hotel at least three or four months before your event. He or she will be prepared to discuss menus, room facili-

ties, availability of space, and a host of other items.

Organizing a banquet requires considerable logistics, timing, and teamwork. First, a timeline must be established for the entire process—from contacting catering managers to sending out invitations to lining up a speaker. Second, a detailed timeline must be drafted for the several days or day of the event to ensure that everything is in place.

Assorted expenses must be factored into the process of establishing the per-ticket cost of the event. Attendees are not just paying $100 or more for the traditional "rubber chicken" dinner, but are footing the bill for the total cost of staging the event. If the purpose is to raise money for a worthy charitable organization or a political candidate, tickets might go for $150 to $350. The actual price depends on how fancy the banquet is and how much the organization is paying for a speaker.

Third, a timeline for the event itself needs to be put in place, so that the event begins and ends at a reasonable time. In addition, organizers must work out the logistics to ensure that registration lines are kept to a minimum and everyone is assigned to a table.

think How can planning ahead and being flexible help an organization save money when planning an event?

This is the timeline for a typical banquet. A detailed schedule, shared with the scheduled speakers and the master of ceremonies, assures that the event stays on schedule and ends at the designated time.

CONSERVATION AWARDS BANQUET
JW MARRIOTT HOTEL
WASHINGTON, DC
WEDNESDAY, MAY 13

Crew Agenda

3:30 – 5:00 p.m.	Program agenda review – participants and staff only. Live run-through of C. Schwartz's remarks. (Grand Ballroom)
5:00 – 6:00	Private pre-reception for honorees, judges, staff. Honoree photo session including E. Tan and J. Morgan. (Suite 1231)
6:30 – 7:15	Greetings and reception, open bar. Photo opportunities available. (Grand Ballroom Foyer)
7:15 – 7:30	Close bar, enter Grand Ballroom.
7:30 – 7:35	C. Schwartz: Welcome and opening remarks.
7:30 – 8:20	Dinner served.
8:20 – 8:25	C. Schwartz: Introduces special guests at head table, introduces E. Tan.
8:25 – 8:30	E. Tan: Welcome, honoree toast, introduces judges, completes remarks.
8:30 – 8:35	C. Schwartz: Introduces J. Morgan.
8:35 – 8:45	J. Morgan: Remarks.
8:45 – 8:50	C. Schwartz: Introduces slide presentation.
8:50 – 9:25	Slide presentation. (C. Schwartz remains at podium) (a) Introduces/explains honoree category; (b) Comments on professionals. Introduces/explains honoree category. (c) Comments on citizens. Introduces/explains organizations' honoree category.
9:25 – 9:40	C. Schwartz: Comments on organizations. Invites J. Morgan and E. Tan for plaque presentation. Plaque presentation.

CONSERVATION AWARDS PROGRAM BANQUET

	Event Schedule	Staff Member
9:00 a.m.	Meet with hotel catering manager/staff Confirm event arrangements	Cal/Lauren/Deb
	5:00-6:00 VIP reception & photos 6:30-7:30 general reception 7:30-8:30 dinner (see attached schedule) 8:30-10:00 program-speaker & award presentation	
12:00-3:00	Coordinate ballroom set up Staging & A/V equipment	Deb/Zoe
12:00-3:00	Media interviews-award honorees	B.J.
1:00	Complete seating arrangements	Cal/Maria
2:00	Complete and organize nametags	Lauren/Gail
2:00-3:00	Rehearsal/AV run through	Cal/Deb/Zoe/Clair
4:00	Award booklets/program each place setting	Gail
4:30	Lobby signs	Gail
5:00-6:00	VIP reception-coordinate honoree photos (see attached)	Lauren/Gail
6:00	Brief hotel staff re reception table staffing	Gail

Banquets require coordination of logistics on the day of the event. This list identifies activities that had to be completed before the actual banquet scheduled in the evening.

Creating a BUDGET for a Special Event

All events have two entries on both sides of the ledger: costs and revenues. It is important to prepare a detailed budget so an organization knows exactly how much an event will cost. This process will enable an organization to determine how much it will need to charge. Here are some items to consider:

Facilities
• Rental of meeting or reception rooms
• Setup of podiums, microphones, and audio-visual equipment

Food Service
• Number of meals to be served
• Cost per person
• Gratuities
• Bartenders for cocktail hours
• Wine, liquor, and soft drinks

Decorations
• Table decorations
• Direction signs

Design and Printing
• Invitations
• Programs
• Tickets
• Name tags

Postage
• Postage for invitations or publicity
• Mailing house charges

Recognition Items
• Awards, plaques, and trophies

Miscellaneous
• VIP travel and expenses
• Speaker fees
• Security

Transportation
• Buses
• Vans
• Parking

Entertainment
• Fees

Publicity
• Advertising
• News releases
• Banners

Office Expenses
• Phones
• Supplies
• Complimentary tickets
• Staff travel and expenses
• Data processing

receptions AND COCKTAIL PARTIES

a short cocktail party can precede a club's luncheon or dinner. It can also be part of a reception. The goal with this type of event is to encourage people to relax and socialize, but it is also a cost-effective way to celebrate an organization's or an individual's achievement, to introduce a new chief executive to the employees and the community, or to allow groups, such as college alumni, to get together.

Whatever the party's purpose, the focus is on interaction, not speeches. If there is a ceremony or speech, it should last a maximum of 5 to 10 minutes.

A reception may last up to two hours, and the typical format is a large room where most people stand instead of sit. This arrangement facilitates social interaction and allows people to move freely around the room. Despite the informality, such gatherings, like any other event, require advance planning and logistics.

It is important, for example, that food be served in the form of appetizers, sandwiches, cheese trays, nuts, and chips. People get hungry, and food helps offset some effects of alcohol consumption. The bar is the centerpiece of any reception, but you should always make sure plenty of nonalcoholic beverages are offered, too. Such precautions will limit liability if someone drinks too much and has an accident on the way home. It can also limit liability to have a no-host bar, which means that guests buy their own drinks.

> **"Don't make a lengthy presentation part of an event. You'll lose the attendees' attention."**
>
> Erica Iacono, *PRWeek*

think Which special liability concerns should party planners take into account when planning a cocktail party?

Most receptions, however, have a hosted bar, meaning that drinks are free. This setup is generally favored when a corporation is hosting the cocktail party or reception for journalists, customers, or community leaders. In every case, it is important that bartenders be trained to spot individuals who appear to be under the influence of alcohol and politely suggest a nonalcoholic alternative.

As part of the planning process, the organizer of the cocktail party should find out how the facility will bill for beverages consumed. If the arrangement is by the bottle, it can lead to a problem with bartenders being very generous because more empty bottles mean higher profits for the caterer.

Starting a cocktail party is easy—just open the bar at the announced time. Stopping a party is not so easy, however. The only practical way to do so is to close the bar. The invitation may indicate a definite time for the reception to end, but don't rely on this method for shutting the party down. A vocal announcement typically does the job.

A reception, like a meal function, requires coordination with the catering manager to order finger foods and decide how many bartenders are needed. As a rule of thumb, there should be one bartender per 75 people. For large events, bars should be situated in several locations around the room, so as to disperse the crowd and shorten lines.

open houses
AND PLANT TOURS

Open houses and plant tours are conducted to develop favorable public opinion about an organization. Generally they are planned to show the facilities where the organization does its work and, in plant tours, how the work is done. For example, a factory might implement a plant tour to show how it turns raw materials into finished products, while a hospital open house could show its emergency facilities, diagnostic equipment, operating rooms, and patient rooms.

Open houses are customarily one-day affairs. If large numbers of people are likely to attend the event, however, it may be extended to more than one day. Attendance is usually by invitation, but in other instances, the event is announced in the general media, and anyone who chooses to attend may do so. If there is to be a community open

think Why do organizations welcome visitors to open house events?

house, think about entertainment and activities for the attendees.

Many plants offer tours daily and regularly while the plant is in operation. These tours are most common among producers of consumer goods such as beer, wine, food

Planning a SUCCESSFUL Open House
Things to Think About

Major factors to consider in planning an open house:

- Day and hour. The time must be convenient for both the organization and the guests.
- Guests. Invite families of employees, customers, representatives of the community, suppliers and competitors, reporters, or others whose goodwill is desirable.
- Publicity and invitations. Materials should be distributed at least a month before the event.

For any open house or plant tour, think of these points:

- Vehicles. Parking must be available, and the invitation should include a map showing how to get to the site and where to park.
- Reception. A representative of the organization should meet and greet all arriving guests
- Restrooms. If a large crowd is expected, arrangements need to be made for portable toilets to supplement the regular facilities.
- Safety. Hazards should be conspicuously marked and well lighted. Barricades should be placed so

as to prevent access to dangerous equipment.
- Routing. Routes should be well marked and logical (in a factory, the route should go from raw materials through production steps to the finished product).
- Guides. Tour leaders should be trained guides who have a thorough knowledge of the organization and can explain in detail what visitors are seeing on the tour.
- Explanation. Signs, charts, and diagrams may be necessary at any point

to supplement the words of the guides. The guides must be coached to say exactly what the public should be told. Many experts cannot explain what they do, so a prepared explanation is necessary.
- Housekeeping and attire. The premises should be as clean as possible. Attire should be clean and appropriate.
- Emergencies. Accidents or illness may occur. All employees should know what to do and how to request appropriate medical assistance.

products, clothing, and small appliances. These daily tours are geared to handle only a few people at any one time. By comparison, open houses generally have a large number of guests, so engaging in normal operations is not feasible during the tour.

Because the purpose of an open house or a plant tour is to create favorable opinion about the organization, it must be carefully planned, thoroughly explained, and smoothly conducted. Visitors need to understand what they are seeing. Achieving this goal requires careful routing, control to prevent congestion, signs, and guides. All employees should understand the purpose of the event and be thoroughly coached in their duties.

This flyer was distributed to community groups and schools to promote the opening of a new exhibit at the Martin Luther King, Jr. Library in San Jose, California. It uses color and a photo from the exhibit to promote the time and place of the new exhibit.

conventions

a convention is a series of meetings, usually spread over two or more days. People attend conventions to exchange information, meet other people with similar interests, discuss and act on common problems, and enjoy recreation and social interchange.

Most conventions are held by national membership groups and trade associations. Because membership is widespread, a convention is nearly always "out of town" for many attendees, so convention arrangements must give consideration to this factor.

Convention Planning

With conventions, it is essential to begin planning far in advance of the actual event. Planning for even the smallest convention should start months before the scheduled date; for large national conventions, it may begin several years ahead and require hundreds or thousands of

think — Why is location such an important factor when planning a convention?

hours of work. The main components covered in planning a convention are (1) timing, (2) location, (3) facilities, (4) exhibits, (5) program, (6) recreation, (7) attendance, and (8) administration.

In terms of timing, you should avoid peak work periods when deciding on the date of the convention. Summer vacation is an appropriate time for educators, and after the harvest is a suitable schedule for farmers. Preholiday periods are bad for retailers, and mid-win-

ter is a poor time in the northern states but may be very good in the South. Know the audience and plan for their convenience.

As real estate agents say, a critical consideration for conventions is location, location, location. A national convention can be held anywhere in the country, but Fairbanks, Alaska, is an unlikely venue, whereas Honolulu could be a great success because the glamour of the location might outweigh the cost and time of travel. Many organizations rotate their conventions from one part of the state, region, or country to another to equalize travel burdens.

btw...

Organizations attending conventions frequently want to show off their wares—which means that the convention manager must provide space suitable for that purpose. Most large convention centers have facilities that can accommodate anything from books to bulldozers. A charge is assessed for the use of these rooms, and the exhibitors pay for the space they use. The exhibit hall may be located in the hotel where the convention is being held, or it may reside in a separate building.

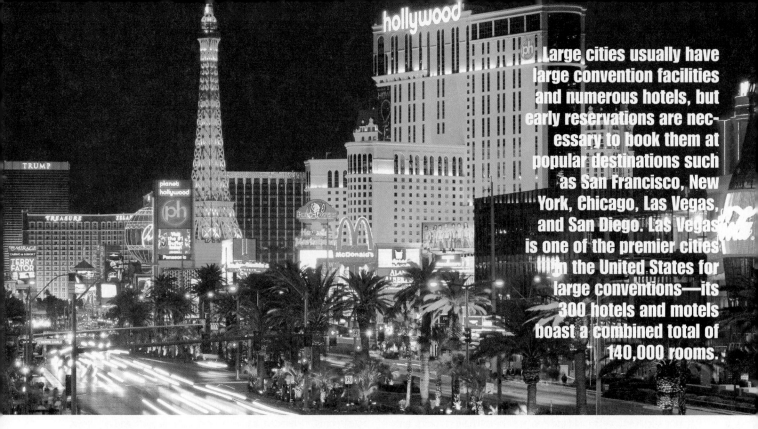

Large cities usually have large convention facilities and numerous hotels, but early reservations are necessary to book them at popular destinations such as San Francisco, New York, Chicago, Las Vegas, and San Diego. Las Vegas is one of the premier cities in the United States for large conventions—its 300 hotels and motels boast a combined total of 140,000 rooms.

Another factor in choosing a location is availability of accommodations. The site must have enough rooms to house the attendees and enough meeting rooms of the right size. Timing enters into this consideration, because many such accommodations are booked months or even years in advance. Once a tentative location has been selected, find out if the convention can be handled at the time chosen. Early action on this point can forestall later changes.

For every meeting to be held as part of the convention, it is necessary to have an appropriate room with necessary equipment. The convention might start with a general meeting in a large ballroom, where seating is theater fashion and the equipment consists of a public address system and a speaker's platform with large video monitors. After opening remarks, the convention might break into smaller groups that meet in different rooms with widely varying facilities. For example, one room may require a computer projector; another may need a whiteboard or an easel for charts; still another may need a VCR and monitor. To get everything right,

organizers need to know exactly what is to happen, who is going to participate, and when.

Convention Programs

A convention program usually has a basic theme. Aside from transacting the necessary organizational business, most of the speeches and other sessions will be devoted to various aspects of that theme. Themes can range from the specific ("New Developments in AIDS Research") to the more general ("Quality Management and Productivity"). Some groups use an even broader theme, such as "Connections" or "At the Crossroads."

With a theme chosen, the developer of the program looks for prominent speakers who have something significant to say on a particular topic. In addition, there may be a need for discussions, workshops, and other sessions focusing on particular aspects of the general theme.

Printing of the program should be delayed until the last possible moment. Last-minute changes and speaker defaults are common.

The printed program for the convention is a schedule. It identifies exactly when every session will take place, in which room it will be held, and who will speak on what subject. Large conventions often schedule different sessions at the same time, with attendees choosing which sessions they attend.

Recreation is a feature of practically all conventions; it can range from informal get-togethers to formal dances. Cocktail parties, golf tournaments, and sightseeing tours are among the many possibilities. Evening receptions and dinners at interesting venues such as an art gallery or museum are often planned for both attendees and their significant others.

Managing a convention is a strenuous job. The organization staff is likely to enjoy very little of the convention events and see, instead, a great many delegates with problems. Among the myriad tasks that must be handled are arranging for buses to convey delegates from the airport to the convention (if it is in a remote location) and to carry them on tours. Meeting speakers and getting them to the right place at the right time is another key task.

People arriving at the convention headquarters must be met, registered, and provided with all the essentials (name tags, programs, and any other needed materials). In addition, special arrangements should be made for the media. A small convention may interest only a few people from trade publications, whereas larger conventions

may draw attention from the major media. In this case, a newsroom should be set up with telephones, fax machines, and Internet-ready computers.

Getting people to attend a convention requires two basic things: (1) an appealing program and (2) a concerted effort to persuade members to attend. Announcements and invitations should go out several months in advance, to allow attendees to make their individual arrangements.

Making Reservations on the Web

The digital age has made event planning more precise. A number of companies now offer event planners the ability to send invitations via the Internet and to track the response rate to those offers.

E-mail invitations, according to cvent (www.cvent.com), a firm offering such services, should incorporate eye-catching graphics, an effective subject line, and relevant content such as the five W's and H.

Most individuals just concern themselves in generating a list of "yes," "no," and "maybe" answers in response to the online planning programs. Clubs and professional or trade groups, however, also need to bundle e-mail invitations with software that enables attendees to pay their registration fees online. Event planners can achieve up to three times the standard response rate by integrating e-mail, direct mail, and phone calling campaigns as part of their efforts to promote a meeting.

Software programs and online systems allow meeting planners the ability to manage an entire event. StarCite, and cvent, for example, offer a variety of services—from gathering hotel bids to sending electronic invitations and tracking registrations online. Software can even compile data on the reasons individuals provide for not coming to the

event, which may help in planning future meetings. Once an attendee does register, the site also allows him or her to book hotel, airline, and car reservations as needed.

Electronic tracking is helpful for figuring out exactly how many hotel rooms are needed; bad estimates, cancellations, and no-shows can add up to substantial hotel cancellation fees. Other management tools allow groups to track the flow of registrations. If registrations are lagging, another round of e-mails and direct mail can be sent out to bolster attendance. Session attendance can even be tracked once the meeting begins, with the data being used to inform decisions about future meetings. For example, if breakfast sessions aren't well attended, it might be wise to plan fewer early-morning meetings next year.

Although e-mail invitations are economical and efficient, they are most appropriate for business-related meetings and events. It's still considered tacky to send an e-mail invitation to a wedding or to a major fund-raising dinner for a community cause. In these instances, mailed invitations and replies remain the norm. However, if an invitation is mailed, an e-mail address or phone number can be provided for respondents in lieu of a reply card.

trade shows

trade shows are the ultimate marketing event. According to *Tradeshow Week* magazine, approximately 6,000 trade shows are held annually in the United States. They range in size from massive shows with more than 100,000 attendees to events geared toward very specialized industries that attract only several thousand people. It is estimated that nearly 65 million people attend trade shows on an annual basis.

The Consumer Electronics Show (CES), sponsored by the Consumer Electronics Association, illustrates the power and influence of a trade show. This show, which is only open to industry professionals, attracts 130,000 attendees to Las Vegas Convention Center every January. Almost 3,000 companies show their new consumer products, taking up approximately 2 million square feet of exhibit space. Bill Gates was the

keynote speaker in 2008 and gave his farewell address as CEO of Microsoft. Panasonic also introduced its new 150-inch plasma TV screen at CES, which caused considerable buzz in the industry and the media.

Exhibit Booths

Although food and entertainment costs are high at trade shows, the major expense at this kind of event is the exhibit booth. At national

Trade shows attract millions of people annually. They provide an opportunity to see new products from a number of companies, generate sales leads, and attract media coverage. For example, Samsung and Sony introduced their new 3D compatible HDTVs at the 2010 Consumer Electronics Show (CES) in Las Vegas, which attracted 120,000 professionals from the electronics industry. More than 2,500 companies hosted booths filling 3 million square feet of exhibit space. Over 5,000 media stories were written about the show.

trade shows, it is not unusual for the cost of a basic booth to start at $50,000, including design, construction, transportation,

think Why are organizations willing to spend so much and get so competitive when it comes to booth design?

and space rental fees. Larger, more elaborate booths can easily cost between $500,000 and $1 million.

Any booth or exhibit should be designed for maximum visibility. Experts say an organization has about 10 seconds to attract a visitor as he or she walks down an aisle of booths. Consequently, companies try to out-dazzle one another in booth designs.

Most organizations believe that the large investment required to operate a booth at a trade show is worthwhile for two reasons. First, a trade show facilitates one-on-one communication with potential customers and helps generate sales leads. It also attracts many journalists, so it is easier and more efficient to provide press materials, arrange one-on-one interviews, and demonstrate what makes the

product worth a story. Second, a booth allows an exhibitor to demonstrate how its products differ from the competition. This kind of hands-on demonstration for large numbers of people is more effective than just sending prospects a color brochure, and it is more cost-effective than making individual sales calls.

Press Rooms and Media Relations

Trade shows such as CES and Macworld attract many journalists. Nearly a thousand reporters, for example, descend on Macworld every year. Consequently, every trade show has a press room where the various exhibitors distribute media kits and other information to journalists. Press rooms typically have phone, fax, and Internet facilities that enable reporters to file stories with their employers.

Public relations professionals are often responsible for preparing an organization's media kit. Keep media kits short and relevant, and offer newsworthy information. A common complaint of reporters at a trade show is that "media kits" are too thick and just a compilation of sales brochures.

Trade Show Considerations

Here are some points to consider if your company is considering trade show participation:

- Select the appropriate trade shows that have the best potential for developing contacts and generating future sales.
- Start planning and developing an exhibit 6 to 12 months in advance. Exhibit designers and builders need time to create a booth.
- Make the display or booth visually attractive. Use bright colors, large signs, and working models of products.
- Think about putting action in the display. Have a video or slide presentation running all the time.
- Involve visitors. Have a contest or raffle in which visitors can win a prize. An exhibitor at one show even offered free foot massages. Give people an opportunity to operate equipment or do something.
- Have knowledgeable, personable representatives on duty to answer questions and collect visitor business cards for follow-up.
- Offer useful souvenirs. A key chain, a shopping bag, a luggage tag, or even a copy of a popular newspaper or magazine will attract traffic.
- Promote the exhibit in advance. Send announcements to potential customers and media kits to selected journalists 4 to 6 weeks before the trade show.

The competition for reporters' time is intense, so public relations professionals need to be creative in pitching ideas and showing why their company's products or services merit a journalist's time when multiple other companies are also pitching them. As many pre-show interviews and briefings should be arranged as possible.

A survey by Access Communications found that more than 90 percent of journalists assigned to a trade show want to hear about the company and product news before the show even starts. Michael Young, Senior Vice President of Access, told *PRWeek*, "Journalists have limited bandwidth at the show. They can only do so much, so they want to know what the news is before getting there." In other words, media relations work starts before the show; it continues through the show and requires follow-up with reporters to provide additional information.

Hospitality suites are an adjunct to the exhibit booth. Organizations use them to entertain key prospects, give more in-depth presentations, and talk about business deals. Serious customers will stay in a hospitality suite long enough to hear an entire presentation, whereas they are likely to stop at an exhibit hall booth for only a few minutes. Although goodwill can be gained from free concerts and cocktail parties, the primary purpose of a hospitality suite is to generate leads that ultimately result in product sales.

think

How can advance preparations help public relations professionals stand out in the crowd of the pressroom at a trade show?

WORKING WITH THE MEDIA at Trade Shows

Sarah Skerik, director of trade show markets for *PR Newswire*, provides some additional tips for working with the media during a trade show:

- Plan major product announcements to coincide with the show.
- Include the name of the trade show in news releases, so journalists searching databases can log on using the show as a keyword.
- Include the booth number in all releases and announcements.

- Make it easy for journalists to track down key spokespeople and experts connected with the product by including cell phone, pager, and e-mail addresses in press materials.
- Train spokespeople to make brief presentations and equip them with answers to the questions that are most likely to be asked.
- Consider using a looped videotape that runs in the booth, and make copies available to the media.

- Provide photos that show the product in use, in production, or in development.
- Provide online corporate logos, product photos, executive profiles, media kits, and PowerPoint presentations to those journalists who cannot attend or who prefer to lighten their suitcase by having everything in digital format.
- Make hard copies of news releases, fact sheets, and brochures available at the booth and in the press room.

promotional
EVENTS

Promotional events are planned to promote sales, increase organizational visibility, make friends, and raise money for a charitable cause. They also include the category of corporate event sponsorship.

The one essential skill for organizing promotional events is creativity. Multiple "ho hum" events compete for media attention and even attendance in every city, so it behooves a public relations professional to come up with something "different" that creates buzz and interest.

Grand openings of stores or hotels, for example, can be pretty dull and generate a collective yawn from almost every journalist in town, let alone all the chamber of commerce types who attend such functions. So how do you come up with something new and different for the same old thing? First, you throw out the old idea of having a ribbon cutting. Second, you start thinking about a theme or idea that fits the situation and is out of the ordinary. A new hotel in Texas, for example, used an exhibit of famous diamonds for its grand opening to signify that the facility was a "jewel" in terms of its outstanding service and accommodations. A bank in Arizona celebrated its grand opening by placing cash in blocks of ice that guests could chip at to retrieve the money. The theme revolved around the availability of "cold cash" at the bank.

Corporate Sponsorships: Another Kind of Event

Many corporations, in an attempt to cut through the media clutter and establish brand identity, sponsor any number of events that are covered by the media. In North America alone, $2 billion is spent by corporations on

> **"Events bring you face-to-face with your customer and can often serve as qualifying tools in reaching decision makers.** Most often, the individuals that attend events are there by choice."**
>
> Jennifer Collins, Event Planning Group, as quoted in *PRWeek*

sponsorship of various events. According to *The Economist*, almost two-thirds of this total consists of sponsorship fees for sporting events

The Olympics is one of the world's most prestigious corporate sponsorships. Companies such as Coca-Cola, General Electric, Visa, and Samsung are among the top 12 official sponsors of the Olympics. In fact, Coca-Cola has been an official sponsor since 1928 and marked its eightieth anniversary supporting this event at the Beijing Olympics in 2008. Between 2005 and 2008, the official sponsors provided almost $1 billion in financial support, goods, and services as part of their Olympic commitment. In addition, another $800 million was raised by the Beijing organizing committee from a number of other corporations operating in China.

If an employer or client is thinking about sponsoring an event, here are some questions to ask:

- Can the company afford to fulfill its obligation? The sponsorship fee is just the starting point. Count on doubling it so that the company can construct an adequate marketing and public relations campaign to publicize the event.
- Is the event or organization compatible with the company's values and mission statement?

Nonprofit organizations often use events to raise money. The Avon Walk for Breast Cancer, for example, is a major annual event held every spring in 9 American cities, which generates individual and corporate donations. The event attracted 21,000 participants in 2009 and raised $52 million for cancer research. Since its first occurrence, in 2003, more than 120,000 people have participated in the event, raising over $300 million.

- Does the event reach the organization's target audiences?
- Are the event organizers experienced and professional?
- Will the field representatives be able to use the event as a platform for increasing sales?

- Does the event give the organization a chance to develop new contracts and business opportunities?
- Can the organization make a multiple-year sponsorship contract that will reinforce its brand identity on a regular, consistent basis?
- Is there an opportunity to get employees involved in the event, thereby raising their morale?
- Is the event compatible with the personality of the organization or its products?
- Can trade-offs of products and in-kind services help defray the costs of the corporate sponsorship?

Celebrity Appearances

Attendance can be increased at a promotional event by the appearance of a television or film personality. A public relations professional can exercise creativity in determining which "personality" fits the particular product or situation. For example, a national conference on aging for policy makers, government officials, and healthcare experts attracted attendees because former senator and astronaut John Glenn was a major speaker. When Unilever wanted to reach a Hispanic audience through a series of events promoting its Suave and Caress brands, the company tapped famous stylists Leonardo Rocco and Fernando Navarro to give hair and beauty advice to women attending the events.

A celebrity—or "personality," as these individuals are called in the trade—is not exactly the most creative solution to every situation. Nevertheless, hiring one is a time-honored way to increase the odds that the media will cover an event, because "prominence" is considered a basic news value. A personality, however, can be a major budget item. Stars such as Oprah Winfrey, Jennifer Lopez, and John Daly typi-cally charge $100,000 for an appearance.

Promotional Event Logistics

Events that attract large crowds require the same planning as an open house. Planners must be concerned about traffic flow, adequate restroom facilities, signage, and security. Professionally trained security personnel should also be hired to handle crowd control, protect celebrities or gov-ernment officials from being hassled, and make sure no other disruptions occur that might mar the event.

Liability insurance is a necessity, too. Any public event sponsored by an organization should be insured, just in case an accident occurs and a subsequent lawsuit charges negligence. Charitable organizations also need liability insurance if they are running an event to raise money. This consideration is particularly relevant if an organization is sponsoring an event that requires physical exertion, such as a 10-K run, a bicycle race, or even a hot-air balloon race.

The logistics of arranging cleanup, providing basic services such as water and medical aid, registering craft and food vendors, and posting signs must be addressed as well. Promotion of an event can often be accomplished by having a radio station or local newspaper co-sponsor the event.

"Security at public events is a significant aspect that should get as much attention as lighting, sound, or signage."

Matt Glass, managing partner at Eventage, as reported in *PRWeek*

APPLY YOUR KNOWLEDGE

WHAT WOULD YOU DO?

The School of Business at your university has scheduled its annual awards banquet, which will be held six months from now. The event usually attracts about 500 alumni and members of the local business community. Traditionally, a speaker with a national reputation is asked to give the major address at the banquet. In addition, outstanding students will be recognized. Prepare a detailed outline of what must be done to plan the banquet, including a timeline or calendar stating what must be done by specific dates.

When Going to the Restroom Is an Event

TOILET TISSUE isn't exactly an item that generates a lot of consumer interest or inspires passionate brand loyalty. Procter & Gamble, however, organized a creative "event" that was a ringing success for its brand, Charmin. In an inspired bid to promote buzz about its product, the company installed 20 luxury restrooms for harried shoppers in New York's Times Square during the Christmas season.

And these facilities were not just a bunch of ordinary porta-potties. As visitors entered a room with plush carpeting and framed portraits of Charmin bears, hosts in attractive uniforms greeted them and directed them to a reception desk to sign in at the "Flush-O-Meter." In addition to residential-style restrooms, special New York–themed stalls were created, including a Broadway stall decorated like a theater dressing room.

Another stall had a Wall Street theme with an actual working stock ticker.

The restrooms were just part of the overall experience. More than 20 TV monitors played an instructional Potty Dance video and encouraged passers by to practice the dance on a convenient dance floor. Visitors could also get their pictures taken with a giant stuffed Charmin bear riding a toboggan or relax on white couches in a room with a working fireplace.

Between November 20 and December 31, more than 400,000 families from all 50 states and more than 100 nations visited the luxury Charmin bathrooms. The average family visit was 22 minutes, which *Corporate Event* magazine dubbed "an impressive amount of time for consumers to interact with any brand, but especially one whose product normally doesn't generate much thought." More than 400 visitors posted video clips of the restrooms on YouTube.

Procter & Gamble also enjoyed extensive coverage of its promotion in the traditional media. The "Disneyland of Bathrooms," as the *New York Times* dubbed it, generated roughly 200 million impressions (circulation and broadcast audience numbers) and garnered coverage on major morning television programs such as *Good Morning America* and *The Today Show*.

Adam Lisook, a brand manager for Charmin, makes the case for such attention-grabbing events: "We will always do advertising, but this kind of event can directly interface with hundreds of thousands of consumers, and bring an element of understanding as to what it is they need."

1 In your opinion, what were the main public relations benefits of this event: Publicity? Brand awareness? Why?

2 How did this event reach an audience beyond its geographic location in Times Square?

3 Was timing important to this event's success? Why or why not?

Which Planning and Logistical Steps Assure Successful Meeting and Event Planning and Execution? p. 271

- Before scheduling a staff or committee meeting, a public relations professional should ask, "Is this meeting really necessary?" Meetings are more effective if an agenda is distributed in advance, a schedule is adhered to, and people are kept from going off on tangents.

- Organizers must consider a number of factors: meeting or event time, location, seating, facilities, invitations, name tags, menu, speakers, registration, and costs.

- Banquets are elaborate affairs that require extensive advance planning. In addition to the factors necessary for a club meeting, banquet planners must consider decorations, entertainment, audiovisual facilities, speaker fees, and seating charts.

- Open houses and plant tours require meticulous planning and routing, careful handling of visitors, and thorough training of all personnel who will come in contact with the visitors.

- Conventions require the skills of professional managers who can juggle multiple events and meetings over a period of several days. A convention may include large meetings, cocktail parties, receptions, tours, and banquets.

Which Elements Must Be Taken into Consideration When Creating a Budget for a Meeting or an Event? p. 275

- Event planners must consider the characteristics of the audience to ensure that tickets are reasonably priced. Organizations need to consider whether the event will be subsidized by corporations or whether individual ticket sales are the primary income.

- The cost of facility rental, meals, speakers, invitations, programs, entertainment, and staffing must be considered.

Why Is the Investment in Meetings and Events Justified for Most Organizations? p. 281

- Meetings and events provide face-to-face social contact, which is better for building relationships instead of "virtual" communications.

- Exhibits at trade shows allow organizations to demonstrate their products and sales representatives to directly talk with potential purchasers.

- Attendance at events gets people involved and engaged through participation.

How Can Public Relations Professionals Harness Creativity to Plan and Implement Memorable and Effective Promotional Events? p. 283

- Planners should focus on those aspects or elements that make a product or service unique and determine how they can be highlighted through an event theme.

- Event organizers should brainstorm ideas and execute plans that are creative as well as realistic and practical.

QUESTIONS for *Review* and *Discussion*

1. Develop an agenda and outline for a meeting for an organization to which you belong or with which you are acquainted. How can you make the meeting most effective?

2. Describe an event you have attended, such as a fund-raising supper, a benefit walk/run, a festival, or a concert. Imagine yourself as an organizer of the event. Develop a list of items that you would have needed to handle to make the event successful.

3. There are several key things a banquet coordinator should consider. Identify five of them.

4. How can an open house serve as a public relations event?

5. How can journalists be encouraged to cover a trade show? How should they be accommodated at a trade show?

6. Why is "sponsorship" considered an event activity?

7. What key questions should be asked and answered when an employer or client is thinking about sponsoring a meeting or an event?

the THINK SPOT
www.thethinkspot.com

TACTICS

PRWeek

Craig McGuire, *PRWeek*, November 24, 2008

Dealing with Global Media Can Be Difficult, But if Done Correctly Brings Numerous Rewards

As this article makes very clear, media relations is now conducted on a global scale, and public relations professionals must use international news release distribution companies to effectively reach all audiences.

News releases should always be tailored to specific markets and individual countries.

In today's competitive global marketplace, multimedia news releases with photos, graphics, and video are most appropriate for major announcements and new product launches.

In many nations, news releases must be translated into several languages within a single country. In India, for example, news releases are often distributed in English, Hindi, and several regional languages such as Bengali.

The challenge of dealing with global media—mastering local markets, translating cultural sensitivities—are numerous but can be met with the right partner. The networks of offices, partners, and affiliates that newswire companies offer provide solid international distribution expertise.

It's important to make the news release specific to the local audience, according to Colleen Pizarev, VP of international distribution at PR Newswire, which has offices in 14 countries, servicing more than 170 countries, in more than 40 languages. "Sending a release about a major new client or product release in South Korea isn't necessarily news in South America," she says, "unless the release has been written to address the reasons why this product . . . could be equally important in the local market." New product releases, enhancements, and industry awards in one country usually only interest another country's trade media, though some papers do have tech and health sections, she says. Rather, local media are more interested in openings of offices, plants, deals with manufacturing reps—anything tied to employees and consumers in the target country.

In several markets, visuals are important. "Photos and multimedia video are increasingly popular in Europe, Asia, and Latin America," Pizarev says, noting that messaging supported by still images and short flash videos are in demand for online versions of general media and trade publications.

Business Wire touts a news distribution network spanning 150 countries and 45 languages, with 31 bureaus worldwide. Neil Hershberg, SVP of global media at BW, says translation remains one of the largest challenges for global campaigns. "Many folks have unrealistic expectations as to the amount of time it takes to do a proper translation," he says. "Professional translation services have a multistep, quality control work flow, and . . . attempts to compress the time frame will . . . be reflected in the translation quality."

PR pros need to be sensitive to time zones and holiday schedules, Hershberg says. He recommends sites such as timeanddate.com and bank-holidays.com. Rudi DeCeuster, BW's Brussels-based senior director of business development, says to be aware of local vocabulary and cultural nuances. These include switching to the euro or pound in Europe or signing messages by their European or Asian contacts, rather than U.S. ones. Marketwire provides its customers with new distribution throughout nine countries (including the United States) in 40 languages, through its 20 bureaus worldwide.

Thom Brodeur, SVP of global strategy and development at Marketwire, says new campaign technologies are particularly well suited to extend to overseas audiences because they know no geographical boundaries. "These tools have become a real leveler," he says. "No longer can you segregate social media and SEO enhancement of your news to just North America."

Brodeur expects that monitoring is dramatically shifting to a more real-time online media monitoring paradigm, where your reaction time can make or break outcomes for your brand. "Shotgun blanket approaches to news distribution overseas will render the same non-optimal result as they do here in North America," he says.

Above all, it is important to have a single point of oversight for your global communication efforts. "If you have too many individuals or groups coordinating on-the-ground efforts around the world . . . without a single point of oversight, you are likely missing out on important synergies or opportunities for streamlining, efficiency, and maximum return on invested efforts," Brodeur says.

Technique Tips

Do:
- Tailor your message to appeal to audiences in the local market.
- Focus first on core messages, then think about global distribution.
- Assign a single point of oversight.

Don't:
- Try to go it alone, even if you have a local presence.
- Expect the same story to play well in different countries.
- Forget visuals that support messaging.

In China, the Lunar New Year celebration goes on for several weeks and many offices are closed during all or some of that time. In Europe, August is a major vacation month when little commercial activity occurs. In addition, Asia is always one day ahead of U.S. time zones because of the International Dateline.

The meaning of words can vary in different cultures. For example, in the United Kingdom, the word "scheme" has no negative connotation; it simply means a business plan.

Blogs, Facebook, YouTube, and Twitter are now accessible around the globe.

Monitoring what the media in other nations are saying about your organization is now just as important as monitoring mentions in the U.S. media.

Senior-level public relations executives in organizations with global operations are responsible for ensuring that core messages remain consistent around the world.

14 GLOBAL PUBLIC

"Invest in a girl and she will do the rest."

The home page of the Girl Effect website (www.girleffect.org) boasts a stark design with an intriguing, puzzling declaration in large type: "The World Is a Mess. AGREE or DISAGREE."

This unusual approach draws the visitor into the world of a remarkable movement that might, without the arresting home page, easily be dismissed as yet another organization making a too-familiar request for donations to a good cause. A global effort, the Girl Effect organization was founded by Nike in 2008 as a fresh approach to making the world less of a mess. It employs "difference feminism," taking the position that not only should the rights of women be safeguarded as a simple matter of justice, but also that the rights of females should be viewed as especially important because healthy women have an exponentially positive impact on society. One statistic cited in support of this position is that when women and girls have the opportunity to earn income, they reinvest 90 percent of that income in their families. For males, this figure is closer to 30 to 40 percent.

The Girl Effect organization epitomizes the best of development public relations—a specialty that spans borders, cultures, religions, and jurisdictions to improve human conditions in developing economies. By combining appeals to major donors with a grassroots effort to engage individuals from developed countries, thousands of large and small contributions are solicited to fund the education of underprivileged girls and

RELATIONS

support small enterprises run by females in developing countries.

Girl Effect maintains a vibrant Facebook community, where individuals share their efforts and enthusiasm for protecting girls from dangers such as HIV infection, forced arranged marriages, and exclusion from educational opportunities. The movement employs many of the strategies and tactics covered in this chapter, from creative special event planning and fundraising efforts, to celebrity publicity featuring individuals such as Oprah Winfrey, George Clooney, and Hillary Clinton, as well as social media efforts on Twitter, YouTube, and Facebook.

1 Do you think that Girl Effect has any detractors? How might you manage potential conflict or crisis for this organization?

2 Which special strategies does Girl Effect need to consider in light of the cultural values of the countries it operates in? Should the values of other cultures or religions be honored even if they are detrimental to one segment of a population?

3 Would you prefer to work for a multinational, nonprofit organization such as Girl Effect or for a for-profit corporation?

WHAT IS global PUBLIC RELATIONS?

think

Why is public relations practice more likely to flourish in areas where there is an established industrial base and a large urban population?

global public relations, also called international public relations, comprises the planned and organized efforts of a company, institution, or government to establish and build relationships with the publics of other nations. These publics are the various groups of people who are affected by, or who can affect, the operations of a particular firm, institution, or government.

International public relations can also be viewed from the standpoint of its practice in individual countries. Although public relations is commonly regarded as a concept developed in the United States at the beginning of the twentieth century, some of its elements, such as countering unfavorable public attitudes through publicity and annual reports, were practiced by railroad companies in Germany as far back as the mid-nineteenth century, to cite just one example.

Even so, it is largely U.S. public relations techniques that have been adopted throughout the world, including in many totalitarian regimes. Today, although some languages lack a term comparable to *public relations*, PR practice has spread to most countries, especially those with industrial bases and large urban populations. This broadening of the scope of public relations is primarily the result of worldwide technological, social, economic, and political changes and the growing understanding that public relations is an essential component of advertising, marketing, and public diplomacy.

Public relations activity in China has grown tremendously in the past decade, beginning with the buildup to, and realization of, the world's largest special event, the 2008 Summer Olympics. The country's public relations efforts continues with the modern version of the World's Fair—Expo 2010 in Shanghai, which an estimated 70 million guests were expected to attend.

PUBLIC RELATIONS DEVELOPMENT IN other nations

Public relations as an occupation and a career has achieved its highest development in the industrialized nations of the world—the United States, Canada, the European Union (EU), and parts of Asia. It emerges more readily in nations that have multiparty political systems, considerable private ownership of business and industry, large-scale urbanization, and relatively high per capita income levels, which also affect literacy and educational opportunities.

China has experienced explosive growth in public relations as it has become industrialized and embraced a relatively free-market economy. Public relations revenues in that country have experienced double-digit gains over the past several years, and China is now the second largest market for public relations in Asia after Japan.

The United States and other European nations began exporting their public relations expertise to the People's Republic of China in the mid-1980s. Hill & Knowlton, which has been active in Asia for more than 30 years, began its Beijing operation in a hotel room with three U.S. professionals and a locally hired employee. Today, almost every global public relations firm has a Beijing office to represent U.S. and European companies in the Chinese market.

In addition, global public relations firms and advertising agencies are now buying stakes in, or affiliating themselves with, successful Chinese firms. Porter Novelli, for example, is affiliated with Blue Focus, one of the largest Chinese-owned firms with about 200 employees. Fleishman Hillard has an affiliation with Pegasus, another large Chinese agency. Gyroscope, a public relations consultancy firm, estimates that there are approximately 2,000 public relations firms in China, although most are simple one- or two-person operations primarily dealing with publicity and media relations.

> **There is at least one agency in China that offers whatever any one client might happen to be looking for. The problem for the client is determining what can actually be delivered, and what is merely promised.**
>
> **Gyroscope consultancy**

Homegrown Chinese firms in advertising, public relations, and marketing have now developed to the point that they have lured business away from large international firms. The Chinese firms offer low cost and an extended reach. The more sophisticated Chinese public relations firms have advanced beyond product publicity and have begun to offer services in analysis, government, community relations, and even sports marketing.

Other nations and regions, to varying degrees, have also developed larger and more sophisticated public relations industries within the past decade. Here are some

Public relations is now an international enterprise, and every country has its own industry. This ad is for a Japanese public relations firm.

thumbnail sketches from around the globe:

- **_Thailand._** Thailand receives a great deal of foreign investment and has established itself as an assembly center for automobiles. It's the primary hub in Southeast Asia for international tourism, and a number of public relations firms, advertising firms, and corporations have well-qualified staffs that are capable of handling media relations, product publicity, and special event promotion. Despite their presence, Thailand lacks a cohesive national organization of public relations practitioners to promote professional development. The country experienced image problems abroad as the result of a military coup in late 2006, but has somewhat recovered its reputation as a consequence of an aggressive tourism marketing and public relations campaign to promote the nation's beauty and attractions. The return of civilian rule in 2008 also helped improve Thailand's international reputation.
- **_Japan._** Business and industry are still at the stage of perceiving public relations as primarily media relations in Japan. Public relations firms and corporate communications departments work very closely with the more than 400-plus reporters' clubs that filter and process all information for more than 150 news-gathering organizations in Japan.
- **_Australia, Singapore, and Hong Kong._** In these relatively mature public relations markets, practitioners offer a variety of services ranging from financial relations to media relations and special event promotion. More attention is given to strategic planning and integrating communications for overall corporate objectives. A major growth area in Singapore is in the hospitality and service industry, as this island nation adds new resorts and casinos.
- **_Mexico._** Traditionally, small public relations firms dominated the Mexican market and provided primarily product publicity. Following adoption of the North American Free Trade Agreement (NAFTA), international firms established operations with more sophisticated approaches to strategic communications in Mexico.
- **_India._** India, with more than 1 billion people, is a major market for products, services, and public relations expertise. At least 1,000 large and small public relations firms serve the subcontinent, but training and educating qualified practitioners continues to be a major problem.
- **_Brazil._** As the largest economy in South America, Brazil is home to approximately 1,000 public relations firms, located primarily in the São Paulo area. To date, few global public relations firms have established a presence in this country, but this situation is changing rapidly, because the nation's booming economy has made it a major player in the world economy. Brazil will also host the 2016 Olympic Games, which will undoubtedly spur further development of its public relations industry. To date, issues management, public affairs, internal communications, and marketing communications remain somewhat underdeveloped fields in the Brazilian public relations market. The public relations industries in Brazil's South American neighbor countries, Argentina and Chile, also are well developed.
- **_The Russian Federation and former Soviet Republics._** The rise of a market economy and private enterprise has spurred the development of public relations activity in Russia, but the continuing stagnation of the Russian economy has stunted its development. The press and journalists are still very dependent on supplemental income, and news articles can be "bought" without much effort. In a more recent development, Russia's giant oil and energy company Gazprom signed a multimillion-dollar contract with a consortium of several global public relations firms

(including Moscow-based PBN) to improve the image of the state-controlled gas monopoly after it was scarred by "gas wars" with the former Soviet Republics. In 2009, the Russian government paid Ketchum $2.9 million for a six-month media relations campaign to promote its national leadership and policies. The contract included media relations for Prime Minister Vladimir Putin's talk at the Davos World Economic Forum. Ukraine, once part of the Soviet Union, now has a growing public relations industry, though it suffers from some of the same problems as Russian firms in terms of development.

- *Middle East.* The Middle East comprises 22 nations and more than 300 million people. In general, the public relations industry here is relatively immature and unstructured, and lacks trained personnel. In general, government-censored media and fear of transparent communications have hindered development of public relations in this region. Dubai, which is located in the United Arab Emirates, in recent years has positioned itself as a major business center and has attracted many international companies. Public relations services will likely continue to expand in Dubai as the world's economy recovers from a major recession.

- *Africa.* South Africa is a relatively mature market with a long tradition of public relations education, professional development for practitioners, and large corporations with international outreach. Nigeria, the most populous nation in Africa, has made strides in developing its public relations industry, in conjunction with its booming oil industry. Although Kenya has a relatively developed public relations industry owing to its tourism base, other nations in Africa are still relatively underserved in terms of public relations.

INTERNATIONAL corporate PUBLIC RELATIONS

for decades, hundreds of corporations based in the United States have been engaged in international business operations, including marketing, advertising, and public relations. All of these activities reached unprecedented heights during the 1990s, largely because of new communications technologies, development of 24-hour financial markets almost worldwide, the lowering of trade barriers, the growth of sophisticated foreign competition in traditionally "American" markets, and shrinking cultural differences. All of these forces have served to bring the "global village," as Marshall McLuhan once described it, ever closer to reality.

Today, almost one-third of all U.S. corporate profits are generated through international business. At the same time, overseas investors are moving into U.S. industries. It is not uncommon for 15 to 20 percent of a U.S. company's stock to be held abroad. The United Kingdom, for example, has a direct foreign investment in the United States exceeding $454 billion, according to the U.S. Department of State.

Fueling the new age of global public relations and marketing are advanced communication technologies—satellite television, computer networks, electronic mail, fax, fiber optics, cellular telephone systems, and technologies such as the integrated services digital network (ISDN), which enables users to send voice, data, graphics, and video over existing copper cables. For example, Hill & Knowlton has its own satellite transmission facilities. General Electric Company has formed its own international telecommunications network, enabling its employees to communicate worldwide using voice, video, and computer data simply by

AN INTERNATIONAL SUCCESS

In the case of Coca-Cola, probably the best-known brand name in the world, international sales account for 70 percent of the company's revenues. In addition, large U.S.-based public relations firms such as Burson-Marstellar and Edelman are now generating between 30 and 40 percent of their fees serving foreign clients.

dialing seven digits on a telephone. Using three satellite systems, Cable News Network (CNN) is viewed by more than 200 million people in more than 140 countries. The United

Trade is now a global enterprise, but not everyone is happy about it. Here, protestors in Rome demonstrate about the failure of the world's governments and largest corporations to agree on steps to take to address global warming. Today, as never before, international organizations and corporations must pay attention to international public opinion.

Kingdom's BBC World Service also reaches an impressive number of nations, including the 40-plus member nations of the British Commonwealth. A number of newspapers and magazines are also reaching millions through their international editions.

Much of the jousting for new business is taking place on the terrain of Western Europe, where the expansion of markets wrought by the formation of the European Union (EU) has attracted enormous interest. Although hampered by recession in recent years, public relations expenditures in this region have increased significantly. This increase has been generated in part by expansion of commercial television resulting from widespread privatization, the desire of viewers for more varied programming, satellite technology, and slowly developing EU business connections. Satellite TV now reaches more than 30 million people in the EU, mostly through direct transmission of programming to homes that bypasses conventional networks, local stations,

think How do recent technological innovations help to make the "global village" a reality?

and cable systems. On the print side, the European business press has been growing approximately 20 percent every year, and there are about 15,000 trade publications in Western Europe.

Although the EU has emphasized the phrase "a single Europe" to explain the benefits of its formation, corporations and public relations firms operating in this region still face the complex task of communicating effectively to 400 million people in 27 countries speaking multiple languages. Differences in language, laws, and cultural mores among countries pose a continuing challenge to culturally sensitive public

Five Cultural Dimensions

Geert Hofstede, a company psychologist for global giant IBM, studied national/cultural differences among employees around the world in the 1970s and came up with five basic cultural dimensions. Today, students still rely on his typology to understand various national cultures. Professors David Guth and Charles Marsh of the University of Kansas summarized Hofstede's cultural dimensions in their book, *Adventures in Public Relations: Case Studies and Critical Thinking*:

1 POWER DISTANCE measures how tolerant a society is about unequally distributed decision- making power. Countries with a high acceptance of power distance include Mexico and France. Countries with a low accep-

tance include Austria and the United States.

2 INDIVIDUALISM, as contrasted with collectivism, pits loyalty to oneself against loyalty to a larger group. Countries in Asia and Latin America gravitate toward collectivism, while the United States, Canada, and most European countries gravitate toward individualism.

3 MASCULINITY/FEMININITY contrasts competitiveness (traditionally considered masculine qualities) against compassion and nurturing (traditionally feminine). Masculine nations include Australia, Germany, and Japan. Feminine nations include Sweden and Spain.

4 UNCERTAINTY AVOIDANCE measures how well a society tolerates ambiguity. Nations that have difficulty functioning in climates characterized by uncertainty include Japan, Belgium, Greece, and China. Nations that tolerate ambiguity include Great Britain, the United States, and Sweden.

5 LONG-TERM VERSUS SHORT-TERM ORIENTATION measures a society's willingness to consider the traditions of the past and carry them into the future. China and other East Asian nations tend to have long-term orientations. The United States has a short-term orientation.

relations practice. There also is a need for both managers and employees to learn to think and act in global terms as quickly as possible. To meet this need, Burson-Marsteller, which has offices in many countries, is spending more than $1 million per year on training tapes and traveling teams of trainers to foster a uniform approach to client projects.

Language and Cultural Differences

Companies operating in nations outside the United States are confronted with essentially the same public relations challenges as those serving the U.S. market. Their objectives are to compete successfully and to manage conflict effectively—but the task is more complex on an international and intercultural level.

Public relations practitioners need to recognize cultural differences, adapt to local customs, and understand the finer points of verbal and nonverbal communication in individual nations. Experts in intercultural communication point out that many cultures, particularly non-Western ones, are "high-context" communication societies. In other words, the

meaning of the spoken word is often implicit and based on the environmental context and personal relationships rather than on explicit, categorical statements. The communication styles of Asian and Arab nations, for example, are high context.

In contrast, European and American communication styles are considered low context. Great emphasis is placed on exact words, and receivers are expected to derive meaning primarily from the written or verbal statements, not from nonverbal behavior cues. Legal documents produced in the West are the ultimate in explicit wording.

Americans and others not only must learn the customs of the country in which they are working, but also should rely on native professionals to guide them. Media materials and advertising must be translated, and the best approach is to employ native speakers who have extensive experience in translating ad copy and public relations materials.

think How is cultural insensitivity best overcome?

International public relations requires the translation of ad copy, news releases, and other public relations materials into several languages. The company that FedEx launched in China in 2007 is growing well, and its key selling point is a high level of reliability.

btw...

Cultural differences abound, no matter which country you may visit, as shown by the following examples:

> In China, tables at a banquet are never numbered. The Chinese think such table arrangements appear to rank guests and that certain numbers are unlucky. It's better to direct a guest to the "primrose" or "hollyhock" table.

> Americans are fond of using first names, but it's not proper business etiquette in Europe and Asia unless permission has been given.

> Early-morning breakfast meetings are not common in Latin America; by the same token, a dinner meeting might not start until 9 or 10 P.M.

> In Thailand, patting a child on the head is seen as a grave offense because the head is considered sacred. Also, it's a crime to make disrespectful remarks about the royal family, particularly the king.

> In Latin America, greetings may include physical contact such as hugging individuals or grabbing them by the arm. Men and women commonly greet each other with a kiss on the cheek in Argentina and Chile.

> News releases in Malaysia are distributed in four languages to avoid alienating any segment of the press.

> Gift giving is common in Asian cultures. Executives, upon meeting for the first time, will exchange gifts as a way of building a social relationship.

> In Muslim nations, particularly the Middle East, men traditionally are encouraged not to stand near, touch, or stare at women.

Foreign Corporations in the United States

Corporations and industries in other countries frequently employ public relations and lobbying firms to advance their products, services, and political interests in the United States. The Center for Public Integrity (CPI) reported that in a six-year span, 700 companies with headquarters in about 100 nations spent $520 million lobbying the U.S.

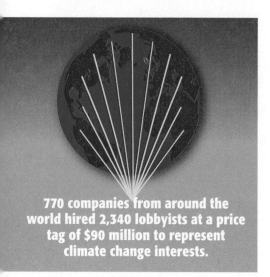

770 companies from around the world hired 2,340 lobbyists at a price tag of $90 million to represent climate change interests.

government. The center's analysis continued, "Over that time, those companies employed 550 lobbying firms and teams of 3,800 lobbyists, more than 100 of whom were former members of Congress." Investigative journalists at *ProPublica* found that in 2008, the top ten countries alone spent more than $43 million on lobbying in the United States. Top-spending countries range from oil-rich Dubai to impoverished Ethiopia.

Even companies that don't operate in the United States may engage in lobbying. For example, with the increased politicization of global policies surrounding climate change, new players have entered the U.S. lobbying arena. Countries and foreign corporations continually jockey for favorable positions on issues ranging from environmental regulation to new market opportunities for carbon-reducing technologies.

On the Payroll of a Foreign Government

Public relations firms that work for foreign governments often confront some tough problems:

- Deciding whether to represent a country whose human rights violations may reflect adversely on the agency itself
- Persuading the governments of such nations to alter some of their practices so that the favorable public image sought may reflect reality
- Convincing officials of a client country, which may totally control the flow of news internally, that the American press is independent from government control and that they should never expect coverage that is 100 percent favorable
- Deciding whether to represent a nation whose government openly criticizes American policies

Why do some firms choose to work for other governments, including those that are unpopular? Says Burson-Marsteller's Carl Levin, "I do not think it is overreaching to state that in helping friendly foreign clients we also advance our national interests. And we help in ways that our government cannot."

One nation that often seems to loom large in the fears of Americans is China, which has ramped up its public relations and lobbying efforts in recent years to counter criticisms in the United States about its growing economic and military power. China hired the Patton Boggs firm to lobby on its behalf on a wide range of issues before Congress, including trade tariffs, intellectual property, currency exchange rates, and Taiwan.

Foreign companies in the defense industry are particularly active in lobbying, according to watchdog groups. In the six-year period covered by a CPI analysis, 16 foreign companies lobbied the U.S. Department of Defense and received $16.4 billion in Pentagon contracts, $5.6 billion of which were awarded without competition.

Romania Rehabilitates Its Image "Virtually"

PR CASEBOOK

DISSATISFIED WITH A SERIES OF STUFFY governmental campaigns that were supposed to generate travel and tourism to Romania, a local entrepreneur commissioned Rogalski Grigoriu Public Relations to engage younger people around the world, by offering a virtual experience of Romania. The goal was to generate favorable media coverage of Romania and to effect a positive shift in perceptions of Romania among the under-30 population in other European countries.

The centerpiece of the campaign was the creation of Virtual Bucharest using Second Life, the virtual reality space where users register, create an avatar, and experience virtual locations and social interactions. When the Romanian campaign began, Second Life had an established following: Several characters from the popular television series *The Office* spend time in Second Life, for example.

The campaign planners began their work with sound formative research, such as content analysis of media coverage of Romania. In addition, they incorporated more innovative research techniques, such as hosting social media debates on Facebook and blogs to learn more about common perceptions of Romania. The campaign also hosted "cross-reality events"—a number of the events that took place in Virtual Bucharest were also carried out in the real world. For example, the "free hugs" event in the virtual world was mirrored by free hugs rallies in 26 Romanian cities.

The Internet was used initially to reach out or "push" messages to youth about features such as the "free hugs" campaign. Once a critical mass of participants was reached online, the campaign switched to "pull" mode by soliciting insights from participants. Ongoing campaign sustainability was ensured by offering space for rent in the Virtual Bucharest marketplace. Seventy-five percent of the virtual commercial space in the marketplace was eventually rented to local entrepreneurs.

The events and the virtual world generated a great deal of media buzz in Romania and garnered extensive positive media coverage in countries such as Spain, Italy, and the United Kingdom. The news coverage reached millions of readers and viewers, and a loyal community of 40,000 people joined the population of Virtual Bucharest.

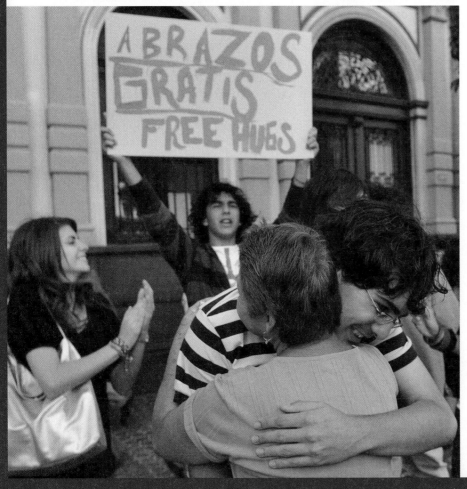

1 Do you think that virtual worlds such as Second Life have staying power? Will they someday be considered a quaint oddity of the early decades of the Internet or a pioneering settlement in a virtual world of the future?

2 Based on what you have learned about reliability and validity in research studies, as well as sampling techniques for conducting studies, how would you assess the use of debates on Facebook as a data source for country image and reputation?

Source: International Public Relations Association 2009 Golden World Award Winners, e-PR/Use of Internet category. www.ipra.org

representing
U.S. CORPORATIONS
IN OTHER NATIONS

many U.S. corporations are global in scope, with employees, products, manufacturing plants, and distribution centers around the world. The top six giant corporations, as well as hundreds of other U.S. companies, engage in extensive public relations and lobbying activities in other nations for virtually the same reasons that foreign countries lobby in the United States.

U.S.-Based GLOBAL GIANTS

ExxonMobil
$477 billion

Wal-Mart
$375 billion

Chevron
$214 billion

ConocoPhillips
$187 billion

Ford Motor Company
$173 billion

General Electric
$163.3 billion

The total amount expended on public relations and lobbying abroad is not known because the U.S. companies don't have to report such expenditures to the U.S. government.

Public relations professionals who work for these giants, as well as for a host of other American companies, are considered to be participants in the field of international public relations, because their work involves many nations. Many multinational corporations also retain global public relations firms such as Burson-Marsteller and Hill & Knowlton to provide services from offices in major cities around the world.

At the start of the twenty-first century and in the aftermath of the terrorist attacks on September 11, 2001, American companies face a number of challenges abroad: competing with other large corporations headquartered in other nations; dealing with sustainable development; being boycotted by nations that disagree with U.S. foreign policy; and striving to act as good corporate citizens at the local and national levels. David Drobis, a former senior partner and chair of Ketchum, outlined some of these challenges in a speech before the International Communications Consultancy Organization (ICCO). Drobis declared that one major challenge is to better communicate the economic advantages of global-

think With which three key audiences do public relations professionals need to communicate about the benefits of globalization?

ization to the world's people. *The Economist,* for example, has called globalization a massive communications failure because the public and private sectors have done such a poor job in communicating globalization's benefits, being transparent about their activities, and building important alliances.

Drobis believes that public relations professionals are best suited to explain the benefits of globalization, which must be communicated to three key groups. The first group comprises the companies themselves. Companies must realize that international capitalism has a negative connotation in many parts of the world. According to Drobis, most multinational firms have done little to correct this view, despite the efforts of a few highly responsible companies that have outstanding programs in this area. He asserts:

> Companies must take into consideration a broad group of stakeholders as they pursue their business goals globally. And by doing so, there are tangible and intangible business benefits. In this way, good corporate citizenship is not a cost of doing business, but rather a driver of business success. What's good for the soul is also good for business.

The second group that must be informed of the benefits of

> **Companies that pursue initiatives—be they related to the environment, labor standards, or human rights—are rewarded with improved business success in a number of areas, including shareholder value, revenue, operational efficiencies, higher employee morale and productivity, and corporate reputation.**
>
> David Drobis, former senior partner and chair of Ketchum

globalization consists of nongovernmental organizations (NGOs). Although many NGOs are outright hostile to all private enterprise, U.S. companies must realize that NGOs can become an important seal of approval and branding. Indeed, major mainstream NGOs such as the World Wildlife Federation and Greenpeace are working with corporations on sustainable development programs. *The Financial Times* notes, "A new type of relationship is emerging between companies and NGOs, where NGOs act as certification bodies, verifying and, in many cases, permitting the use of their logos, showing that products and services are being produced in a socially responsible and environmentally friendly ways."

The third group includes international institutions such as the World Trade Organization (WTO), the World Bank, the International Monetary Fund (IMF), and even the United Nations. Drobis says these organizations are unfairly criticized as being undemocratic, but fairly criticized for being nontransparent. An article in *Foreign Affairs* puts it this way: "To outsiders, even within the same government, these institutions can look like closed and secretive clubs. Increased transparency is essential. International organizations can provide more access to their deliberations, even after the fact."

Drobis, in giving advice to U.S. companies doing business abroad, states that the era of "relationship building" is over. Instead, he claims, the twenty-first century should be a time of "confidence building" in the international arena so that various publics not only trust corporations to do the right thing, but also believe globalization will benefit hundreds of millions of poor people around the globe.

PUBLIC diplomacy

the U.S. government is the major disseminator of information around the world. The process of information dissemination is called *public diplomacy*. This open communication process is primarily intended to present American society in all its complexity so citizens and governments of other nations can understand the context of U.S. actions and policies. Another function is to promote American concepts of democracy, free trade, and open communication around the world.

The United States Information Agency (USIA) was created in 1953 by President Dwight Eisenhower to be the primary agency involved in shaping America's image abroad. USIA, in many ways, was the direct descendant of George Creel's Committee on Public Information (CPI), which was active during World War I, and Elmer Davis's Office of War Information, which was active during World War II. After World War II, a new threat was perceived—namely, the outbreak of the Cold War with the Soviet Union and the Communist bloc nations in Eastern Europe. The Cold War was a war of words on both sides to win the "hearts and minds" of governments and their citizens around the world.

At the height of the Cold War, USIA had a budget of approximately $900 million and 12,000 employees. When the Soviet Union imploded in the early 1990s, the fortunes of the USIA began to fall

think Why is there typically an increased focus on public diplomacy in times of war?

as Congress and other critics decided that the United States didn't need such a large public profile in the world. As a result, the agency was abolished in 1999 and most of its functions were transferred to the U.S. Department of State under an

USIA Activities in the Cold War

In the past, USIA activities included (1) the stationing of public affairs officers (PAOs) at every American embassy to work with local media, (2) publication of books and magazines, (3) distribution of American films and TV programs, (4) sponsorship of tours by American dance and musical groups, (5) art shows, (6) student and faculty exchange programs such as the Fulbright Program, and (7) sponsorship of lecture tours by American authors and intellectuals.

undersecretary of state for public affairs and diplomacy. The staff was cut 40 percent and funding for projects decreased sharply.

The September 11 terrorist attacks on the United States created a new impetus to "sell" America and the U.S. decisions to invade Afghanistan and Iraq. Once again, the cry was to "win the hearts and minds" of the world's people and to gain public—as well as international—support for U.S. actions. This effort, however, was somewhat diffused and confused because the Department of Defense and the White House spearheaded public diplomacy efforts rather than the State Department.

The 9/11 Commission, in its 2004 final report, called for centralization of U.S. diplomacy efforts, creation of a more robust and targeted program, and a drastic increase in funding of diplomatic exchanges and campaigns. Under the Obama administration, increased emphasis has been placed on public diplomacy and cultural exchange. Today, the State Department particularly stresses the importance of youth exchanges and networking with exchange alumni to maintain long-term ties. As part of its $1.2 billion budget in 2010, the funding for the State Department included $520 million for worldwide public diplomacy and $633 million for educational and cultural exchange programs. Communication is clearly a crucial component in the mission and operations of the State Department.

Foreign Public Diplomacy Efforts

Virtually every country has one or more governmental departments devoted to communication with other nations. Much effort and millions of dollars are spent on the tourism industry, with the goal of attracting visitors whose expenditures will boost local economies. Even larger sums are devoted to lobbying efforts to obtain favorable legislation for a country's products; for example, Costa Rica urged the U.S. Congress to let its sugar be imported into the United States at favorable rates. Conflict and war also lead to public relations efforts.

What do countries that woo the US audience seek to accomplish? Burson-Marsteller's Carl Levin says that they pursue several goals:

- To advance political objectives
- To be counseled on the probable U.S. reaction to the client government's projected action
- To advance the country's commercial interests—for example, sales in the United States, increased U.S. private investment, and tourism
- To assist in communications in English
- To counsel and help win understanding and support on a specific issue undermining the client's standing in the United States and the world community
- To help modify laws and regulations inhibiting the client's activities in the United States

THE VOICE OF AMERICA

The Voice of America (VOA), created in 1942, was part of USIA for several decades. Its core work has traditionally been broadcasting news, sports, and entertainment around the world via shortwave radio. This is still the case to a large extent, but VOA has also established AM and FM radio transmitters throughout the world. In addition, the agency supplies many radio and television stations throughout the world with various news, music, and talk programs free of charge. More recently, the VOA has offered audio streaming of programs via the World Wide Web. The worldwide audience for VOA is difficult to judge, given the many different distribution methods, but estimates are that several hundred million listeners tune into the various VOA programs.

VOA is the major voice of the United States abroad, but the government isn't always happy with its strict adherence to journalistic standards and objectivity. Consequently, the government also operates radio and television services that are more proactive in advancing U.S. interests and foreign policy. Radio Free Europe was started in 1949 to reach the nations of Eastern Europe under the thumb of the Soviet Union. Radio Liberty was started, with CIA funding, to broadcast directly to the citizens of the Soviet Union. The Soviet response during the Cold War was to jam these broadcasts because they were American "propaganda." Although both services still exist, they have significantly fewer staff and do less broadcasting today than in their prime.

More recently, Congress has authorized radio and television services focusing on Iraq and the Middle East. Radio Sawa injects news tidbits written from an American perspective into a heavy rotation of American and Middle Eastern pop music. A similar radio service aimed at Iranian youth is known as Radio Farda. On the television side, the U.S. government started Al Hurra. According to the *New York Times*, Al Hurra is "a slickly produced Arab-language news and entertainment network that [is] beamed by satellite from a Washington suburb to the Middle East." It is the American government's answer to Al Jazeera, the popular pan-Arab television service.

It is worth repeating that VOA, and services such as Radio Sawa, are not directed at U.S. citizens. Under the United States Information and Educational Exchange Act of 1948, Congress prohibited the government from directing its public diplomacy efforts toward its own citizens, because of fears that the government would propagandize its own citizens.

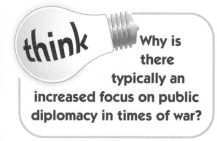

think Why is there typically an increased focus on public diplomacy in times of war?

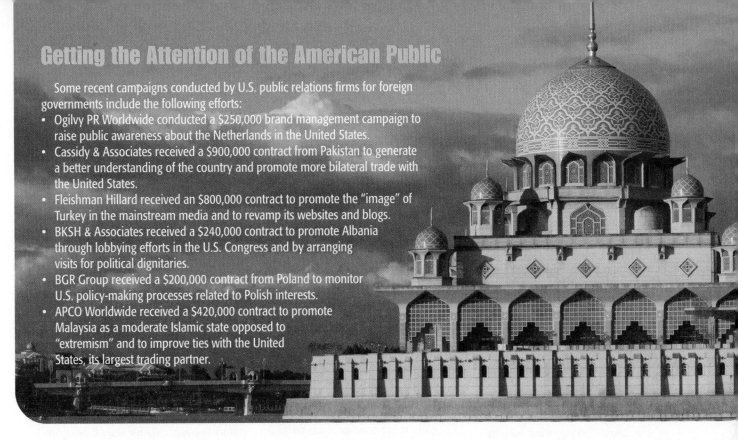

Getting the Attention of the American Public

Some recent campaigns conducted by U.S. public relations firms for foreign governments include the following efforts:

- Ogilvy PR Worldwide conducted a $250,000 brand management campaign to raise public awareness about the Netherlands in the United States.
- Cassidy & Associates received a $900,000 contract from Pakistan to generate a better understanding of the country and promote more bilateral trade with the United States.
- Fleishman Hillard received an $800,000 contract to promote the "image" of Turkey in the mainstream media and to revamp its websites and blogs.
- BKSH & Associates received a $240,000 contract to promote Albania through lobbying efforts in the U.S. Congress and by arranging visits for political dignitaries.
- BGR Group received a $200,000 contract from Poland to monitor U.S. policy-making processes related to Polish interests.
- APCO Worldwide received a $420,000 contract to promote Malaysia as a moderate Islamic state opposed to "extremism" and to improve ties with the United States, its largest trading partner.

Under the Foreign Agents Registration Act (FARA) of 1938, all legal, political, fundraising, public relations, and lobbying consultants hired by foreign governments to work in the United States must register with the Department of Justice. They are required to file reports with the U.S. Attorney General listing all activities on behalf of a foreign principal, compensation received, and expenses incurred.

Normally hired by an embassy after open bidding for the account, public relations firms that act on behalf of non-U.S. governments first gather detailed information about the client country, including past media coverage. Attitudes toward the country are ascertained both informally and through surveys.

The action program decided on will likely include the establishment of an information bureau to provide facts and published statements of favorable opinion about the

think How can public relations help a foreign country improve its image in the United States?

country. In many cases, a nation may also use paid issue advertising in publications such as the *New York Times*, *Washington Post*, *Wall Street Journal*, and *The Financial Times* that reach a high percentage of opinion leaders and elected officials. The Republic of Kazakhstan, for example, placed full-page ads in major U.S. newspapers after its national elections to reinforce the public perception that it was a democracy. The ad's headline: "Today, Kazakhstan has another asset besides oil, gas and minerals. Democracy."

Appointments also are secured with key media people and other influential individuals, including educators, business executives, and leaders of various public policy groups. In many cases, the primary audiences are key members of congressional committees, heads of various governmental agencies, and even the White House staff. These people are often invited to visit the

client country on expense-paid trips, although some news media people decline these invitations on ethical grounds.

Gradually, through expert and persistent methods of persuasion (including lobbying), public opinion about the client country may be changed, favorable trade legislation may be passed, foreign aid may be increased, or an influx of American tourists may visit the country.

Other countries that have experienced image problems in the United States have also hired professionals in attempts to address them. C/R International was criticized by members of Congress and human rights groups for having a $530,000 contract with Sudan, which has been accused of committing genocide in the Darfur region. In this case, the relationship between Sudan and the firm eventually led to real trouble for C/R. The U.S. Justice Department ended up indicting of C/R veteran Robert Cabelly for violating U.S. sanctions on Sudan, money laundering, passport fraud, and making false statements, and for acting as an unregistered agent of a foreign power.

THE RISE OF NGOs

> **The next five to ten years will be challenging for companies that operate on a world stage with the rise of technologically enabled activism.**
>
> Public Affairs Council president Doug Pinkham in *PRWeek*

hundreds of nongovernmental organizations (NGOs) depend on international support for their programs and causes. Organizations such as Greenpeace, Amnesty International, Doctors Without Borders, Oxfam, and a large number of groups opposed to globalization have been effective in getting their messages out via the World Wide Web, e-mail, and demonstrations.

One study by StrategyOne, the research arm of Edelman Worldwide, showed that media coverage of such organizations more than doubled over a four-year period, and NGOs were perceived by the public to be more credible than the news media or corporations when it came to issues such as labor, health, and the environment. Thought leaders, for example, indicate that they trust NGOs more than government or corporations because they consider the NGOs' motivation to be based on "morals" rather than "profit." Public Affairs Council president Doug Pinkham has said the StrategyOne report should be taken as a "wake-up call" by large corporations that have failed to embrace greater social responsibility and transparency.

There is increasing evidence that giant corporations are adopting a more accommodative stance by cooperating with activist NGOs to form more socially responsible policies. Citigroup, for example, adopted new policies to reduce habitat loss and climate change after the Rainforest Action Network (RAN) urged customers to cut up their Citicards and plastered the Internet with nasty jibes against executives.

think Why do some people find NGOs to be more credible than governments or corporations?

opportunities
IN INTERNATIONAL WORK

the 1990s, according to many experts, represented a new golden age of global marketing and public relations. The opening of the European market, coupled with economic and social reforms in the former Soviet Union, hastened the reality of a global economy.

 **think** In addition to studying a foreign language, what can an American student do to prepare for a job in global public relations?

These developments led Jerry Dalton, past president of the PRSA, to say, "I think more and more American firms are going to become part of those overseas markets, and I expect a lot of Americans in public relations will be living overseas." Indeed, Dalton believes that the fastest-growing career field for practitioners is international public relations. He adds. "Students who can communicate well and are fluent in a foreign language may be able to write their own ticket."

Gavin Anderson, chairman of Gavin Anderson & Company, a pioneer in international public relations, penned the following observations some years ago—but his message remains relevant today:

The field needs practitioners with an interest in and knowledge of foreign cultures on top of top-notch public relations skills. They need a good sense of working environments, and while they may not have answers for every country, they should know what questions to ask and where to get the information needed.

The decision to seek a career in international public relations should be made during the early academic years, so that a student can take multiple courses in international relations, global marketing techniques, the basics of strategic public relations planning, foreign languages, social and economic geography, and cross-cultural communication. Graduate study is an asset. Students should also study abroad for a semester or serve an internship with a company or organization in another nation as a desirable

starting point. Students may want to apply to the Fulbright Program, which funds travel and study abroad. Rotary International offers a student foreign study scholarship as well.

American students should not assume they have an "inside" track on working for a U.S.-based global corporation. Increasingly, global corporations are looking at a worldwide pool of young talent—including some excellent candidates who know several languages and are more accustomed to intercultural communications. Hewlett-Packard is one example of an organization that casts a global net; it prefers to hire European- or American-trained Russians for its corporate communications efforts in Moscow and the Russian Federation.

Taking the U.S. Foreign Service Officers' examination is the first requirement for persons seeking international government careers. Foreign service work with the innumerable federal agencies often requires a substantial period of government, mass media, or public relations service in the United States before foreign assignments are made, however.

APPLY YOUR KNOWLEDGE

WHAT WOULD YOU DO?

Turkey has a problem. The country was on track to becoming the fastest-growing tourist destination for Americans prior to September 11, 2001. That projection was derailed by the terrorist attacks and the subsequent invasions of Afghanistan and Iraq, which caused many Americans to think twice about visiting a Muslim nation—even one like Turkey with a secular government and a strong European orientation. The concerns about the stability and safety of Turkey are compounded by the country's ongoing tension with the Kurdish region of Iraq, a semi-autonomous state that makes claims to parts of Turkey where Kurds predominate.

At the same time, Turkey is a virtual treasure house of art, culture, and cuisine that would appeal to seasoned travelers looking for a new experience and destination. To this end, the Turkish Culture and Tourism Office has retained your public relations firm to conduct a media relations program in the American press (and to some extent the European media) to increase awareness of Turkey as a desirable tourist destination.

Research and interviews with Turkish tourism authorities indicate that segmentation of various audiences would be more fruitful than a general campaign. Travelers interested in food and wine, for example, might be reached through articles about the cuisine of Turkey. Music lovers might be interested in the new jazz sounds coming from Turkish musicians. In addition, shoppers looking for vintage jewelry and exotic products such as carpets in the famous bazaars of Istanbul would be a good, specialized public. Then, of course, there are the history buffs who would be interested in visiting the sites of ancient civilizations.

Now that you know the possible interests of several target audiences, develop a public relations plan that will include appropriate media and events for these various audiences. Your plan should outline possible feature stories for print and broadcast media, as well as the venues for special events.

How Is Public Relations Practice Developing Around the World? p. 289

- Public relations is a well-developed industry in many nations around the world. China, in particular, has a rapidly expanding industry that is becoming more sophisticated every year.

How Is the Practice of Public Relations Changing in the New Age of Global Marketing? p. 291

- In the new age of global marketing, public relations firms represent foreign interests in the United States as well as the interests of American corporations around the world.
- The international public relations practitioner must deal with issues related to language and cultural differences, including subtle differences in customs and etiquette and even ethical dilemmas involving bribery.

What Is Public Diplomacy? p. 297

- Most governments seek to influence the international policies of other countries as well as the opinions and actions of their publics. These communications can range from campaigns promoting tourism to attempts to influence trade policies.
- The U.S. government refers to its international information efforts as "public diplomacy," meaning the attempt to enhance understanding of U.S. culture and promote U.S. foreign policy objectives. The Voice of America radio broadcasts are part of this program.
- Many U.S. public relations firms work for foreign governments, helping them advance their political objectives and commercial interests in America, counseling them on probable U.S. reactions to their proposed actions, and assisting in communications in English.

How Has the Role of NGOs in the Global Marketplace Evolved? p. 300

- Nongovernmental organizations (which depend on international support for their causes) are widely believed to be more credible by the news media and the public on such issues as labor, health, and the environment, partly because they are perceived to lack the self-interest ascribed to governments and corporations.
- There is increasing evidence that giant corporations are adopting an accommodative stance by cooperating with activist NGOs to form more socially responsible policies.

Which Career Opportunities Are Available in Global Public Relations? p. 300

- As global marketing and communications have expanded in recent years, so, too, have opportunities for international public relations work.
- Fluency in foreign language is a valued skill but not a prerequisite for global public relations. Also important is a background in international relations, global marketing techniques, social and economic geography, and cross-cultural communication.

QUESTIONS for *Review* and *Discussion*

1. What is international public relations? What are some of the reasons for its growth in recent decades?

2. How does public relations fit into the mix of global marketing operations?

3. What are some of the difficulties that a corporation is likely to encounter when it conducts business in another country?

4. Which objectives do foreign nations seek to accomplish by hiring U.S. public relations firms to represent them in America?

5. International surveys indicate that citizens of other nations have low approval ratings of the United States and its policies. Which "public diplomacy" efforts might the United States undertake to change these negative perceptions?

6. The U.S. government conducted an extensive program of "public diplomacy" as part of the "War on Terrorism." Do you think it was effective? Why or why not?

7. The successful practice of international public relations requires knowledge of a nation's history and political sensitivities. It also requires knowledge of proper manners and cultural sensitivity. Which guidelines should business executives who travel abroad keep in mind?

8. Which kinds of ethical dilemmas do public relations firms face when they are asked to do work for a particular nation?

9. What is an NGO? How has new information technology enabled NGOs to expand their influence?

the **THINK** SPOT
www.**thethink**spot.com

15 CORPORATE

Ask Yourself

> What Role Can Public Relations Play in Rebuilding Public Trust in Business? p. 311

> How Do Media Relations, Customer Relations, Employee Relations, and Investor Relations Contribute to Corporate Health? p. 312

> What Is Integrated Marketing Communications? p. 318

> How Do Environmental Relations and Corporate Philanthropy Have a Positive Impact on the Public Image of a Corporation? p. 323

Smart, Greedy, Dangerous

Goldman Sachs, the renowned global investment banking and securities firm, received billions of U.S. taxpayers' dollars from the Troubled Assets Relief Program (TARP) in 2008. It paid the government back quickly and taxpayers made a tidy profit in the transaction. So why did Goldman Sachs still have a public relations problem? Maybe because when much of the U.S. economy was suffering from a recession in 2009, Goldman Sachs had a record-setting year in terms of profits, and the average pay for its 30,000 employees was $595,000 according to the *New York Times*. Lloyd Blankfein, Goldman Sachs CEO, told *The Times of London* that he was aware that "people are pissed off, mad, and bent out of shape" about the banking mess. He added, "I know I could slit my wrists and people would cheer."

In January 2010, *Vanity Fair* summarized its investigative piece on Goldman Sachs with this sentence: "One of the biggest disconnects on Wall Street today is between the way Goldman Sachs sees itself (they're the smartest) and the way everyone else sees Goldman (they're the smartest, greediest, and most dangerous)."

Goldman Sachs responded to the public critiques in a variety of ways. In October 2009, the firm announced it would donate $200 million to its charitable foundation, nearly doubling the philanthropical organization's size. It also announced a $500 million program, dubbed 10,000 Small Businesses, intended to "unlock the growth and job-creation potential of 10,000 small-businesses . . . through greater access to business education,

PUBLIC RELATIONS

mentors and networks, and financial capital." Further, the company made plans to expand an existing program that requires executives and top managers to give a percentage of their earnings to charity. Public relations executive David Langness told *PRWeek*, "We understand that [Goldman Sachs] has been through a very tough year with negative press. The bottom line is, they had to do something. In this environment where there's such declining trust in major corporations, CSR [corporate social responsibility] campaigns have risen to the top of the list as far as importance level. It used to be CSR campaigns were unusual, now they're common practice. They're a part of the PR toolbox."

The investment corporation also announced changes in compensation for its top 30 executives and used its website as a forum to respond to the media criticism. In February of 2010, *BusinessWeek* reported, "Goldman Sachs, the most profitable securities firm in Wall Street history, this year cut the percentage of revenue earmarked for pay to the lowest in a decade as a public company. The New York-based firm aimed to allay anger about banks whose profits and pay rebounded within a year of taking government bailouts while the U.S. jobless rate was about 10 percent."

Although the Dow Jones Media Lab noted that most media mentions of Goldman Sachs in October 2009 were negative, by mid-November more positive coverage was on the rise. Martin Murtland of Dow Jones, told *PRWeek*, "The data indicates that on a percentage basis, positive coverage of Goldman has increased by four percentage points, moving the needle from 14% to 18% positive coverage. This is a significant achievement; however this example is also evidence that an organization's reputation cannot be rebuilt over night."

❶ Were Blankfein's acknowledgments of public outrage just pithy sound bites or were his statements strategic?

❷ Which public relations tactics do you see at work in the Goldman Sachs story?

❸ Which strategies could financial institutions employ to engender more public trust in the aftermath of the government bailout?

modern
CORPORATIONS

today, giant corporations have operations and customers around the world. These companies deal with governments at local, regional, national, and international levels. Their operations affect the environment, control the employment of thousands of people, and influence the financial and social well-being of millions of individuals.

The large size of corporations can distance them from stakeholders. A corporation has a "face"—its products, logo, and brand are often readily visible in advertising and billboards from Azerbaijan to Zimbabwe. Even so, the average consumer can't really comprehend the sheer size of organizations such as Wal-Mart, the world's largest retailer with $401 billion in worldwide sales, or ExxonMobil, with $459 billion in global sales. These figures boggle the mind; in fact, they represent more than the com-

bined gross national product (GNP) of many nations.

The public is often distrustful of the power, influence, and credibility of such giant corporations and business in general. When U.S. gasoline prices rise rapidly, for example, rumors often spread that the oil companies have conspired to gouge the public—rumors that the oil companies never fully allay. Major corporate financial scandals and the misdeeds of corporate executives also take their toll on corporate reputations.

Public perceptions of greed and corporate misdeeds are reinforced by news stories. Hundreds of stories were written about the various misdeeds on Wall Street as companies accepted federal bailout dollars and then made news when they held lavish executive retreats and paid their own executives healthy bonuses.

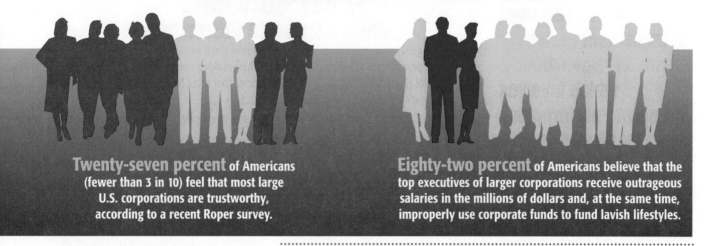

American Opinions About Business Leaders

Twenty-seven percent of Americans (fewer than 3 in 10) feel that most large U.S. corporations are trustworthy, according to a recent Roper survey.

Eighty-two percent of Americans believe that the top executives of larger corporations receive outrageous salaries in the millions of dollars and, at the same time, improperly use corporate funds to fund lavish lifestyles.

A Gallup poll revealed that business leaders and stockbrokers have joined used car dealers as the "least trusted" individuals in American society.

> **"People all over this country feel an incredible frustration that they are seeing their neighbors lose their jobs and the government is helping companies like A.I.G. and Goldman Sachs and then the next thing they are reporting huge profits and huge compensation. I think people are INCREDULOUS that this system is working this way."**
>
> Senator Sherrod Brown, Democrat of Ohio and a member of the banking committee, in the *New York Times*

The Role of Public Relations

The extensive negative publicity about specific corporations and business in general over the past several years has made it imperative that companies regain their credibility and public trust. The concept of corporate social responsibility ranks high on the priority list of executives and public relations staffs that are charged with improving the reputation of their employers.

To that end, the public relations profession has taken steps to outline a plan of action for rebuilding public trust in business. A coalition of 19 U.S.-based organizations—including the Council of Public Relations Firms, the International Association of Business Communicators, and the National Investor Relations Institute—published a white paper titled *Restoring Trust in Business: Models for Action* that described this plan.

The 10-page white paper asked American businesses and their leaders to (1) adopt ethical principles, (2) pursue transparency and disclosure, and (3) make trust a fundamental precept of corporate governance. The coalition sent copies of the report to *Fortune* 500 CEOs and the 50,000 public relations professionals represented by member groups in the coalition.

The importance of public relations in corporate social responsibility was succinctly explained by

think What reasons does the public have to be mistrustful of large corporations?

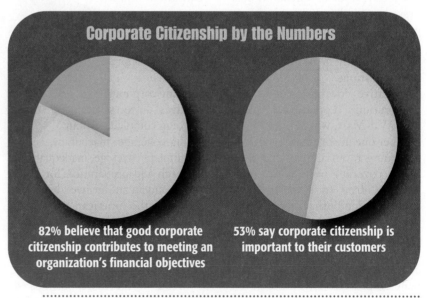

Corporate Citizenship by the Numbers

82% believe that good corporate citizenship contributes to meeting an organization's financial objectives

53% say corporate citizenship is important to their customers

Findings from a survey of executive attitudes conducted by the Center for Corporate Citizenship with the Hitachi Foundation.

4 KEY QUESTIONS
About Corporate Citizenship

Being a good corporate citizen is an admirable goal, but corporations also face a number of pressures and counter-pressures when making decisions and forming policies. General Electric once outlined four key factors that must be considered at all times when making a decision:

1. **POLITICAL:** How do government regulations and other pressures affect the decision?
2. **TECHNOLOGICAL:** Do we have the engineering knowledge to accomplish the goal?
3. **SOCIAL:** What is our responsibility to society?
4. **ECONOMIC:** Will we make a profit?

Jack Bergen, senior vice president of marketing and communications for Siemens Corporation. He told *PRWeek*, "We are the eyes and ears of an organization. The best way to be socially responsible is to have your eyes and ears trained on all the stakeholders, to know what they want and need from the company. These are classic public affairs issues and the idea that they should be handled by anyone else would show a lack of understanding."

Corporations may seek to achieve a better reputation for a variety of reasons. First, responsible business practices ward off increased government regulation. Demonstrating what can happen when companies fail to police themselves, as a result of major financial scandals during the first decade of the century, the U.S. Congress passed new laws regarding accounting practices and disclosure. Second, there is the matter of employee morale: Companies with good policies and good reputations tend to have less employee turnover. Corporate reputation also affects the bottom line.

media
RELATIONS

t he media are major sources of public information about business in general and individual companies. In recent years, the news appearing in media outlets hasn't been especially favorable in regard to corporations.

Negative coverage can cause a corporation's reputation to plummet. Wal-Mart, which once ranked number one in corporate reputation according to an annual analysis of media coverage by Cision, saw its position drop to seventh in the space of six months after coverage described its hiring of illegal immigrants and the filing of a class-action suit that claimed the company discriminated against female employees. Given the potential for such a backlash, corporate executives are somewhat defensive about how journalists cover business; they often believe that too much emphasis is given to corporate misdeeds.

Many corporate executives have several ongoing complaints about media coverage: inaccuracy, incomplete coverage, inadequate research and preparation for interviews, and an antibusiness bias. One survey by the American Press Institute found one-third of the CEOs polled were dissatisfied with the business news they found in their local newspapers.

In their own defense, business editors and reporters state that often they cannot publish or broadcast

thorough, evenhanded stories about business because many company executives, uncooperative and wary, erect barriers against them. Writers complain about their lack of direct access to decision-making executives and the proliferation of news releases that don't contain the information they need. Journalists assert,

What CEOS Think About the Media

> Almost half of corporate executive respondents agreed with the statement that a "CEO must view the media as an enemy."

> 60% said an executive can best avoid controversy by "limiting exposure to the media" and through "secrecy and tighter control of information."

Corporate executive attitudes about the media, according to a survey by Jericho Communications.

dle of this tug-of-war. They must interpret their companies and clients to the media, while showing chief executives and other high officials how open, friendly media relations can serve their interests. Savvy public relations professionals understand that business reporters often don't have adequate business preparation. For this reason, they spend a great deal of time and energy providing background and briefing reporters on the business operations of their clients and employers. It's one way of ensuring that coverage will be more accurate and thorough.

too, that some business leaders don't understand the concept of objectivity and assume that any story involving unfavorable news about their company is negatively biased.

A survey of journalists conducted by Middleberg Euro RSCG, a public relations firm, and the Columbia University Graduate School of Journalism, found that journalists believe corporations should focus on delivering more fact-driven messages.

Public relations practitioners serving businesses stand in the mid-

think What kinds of complaints do corporations have about the coverage they receive in the media?

> **"You (executives) should communicate factually, frequently, and consistently. Use this time wisely, say the journalists, to position yourself."**
>
> Don Middleberg, *PRWeek*

btw...

One survey by Hill & Knowlton found that Canadian CEOs believe that print and broadcast media criticism is the biggest threat to their company's reputation, even ranking ahead of such potential problems as disasters and allegations by the government about employee or product safety. At the same time, surveys show that the media coverage is probably the most effective way for an organization to get its message across to its publics and to achieve business goals. In one *PRWeek* survey of CEOs, more than 80 percent of the respondents said media interviews were the most effective way for the company to spread its message, followed by attending or speaking at industry conferences and trade shows. In third place was meeting with key industry and financial analysts; fourth place was "authoring op-eds, bylined articles, or letters to the editor."

customer RELATIONS

In today's society, sellers are expected to deliver goods and services of safe, acceptable quality on honest terms. Consumer rights are protected by the federal government, and federal and state agencies enforce those rights. In the United States, the Federal Trade Commission (FTC) regulates truth in advertising, the National Highway Traffic Safety Administration sets standards for automakers, and the Consumer Product Safety Commission examines the safety of other manufactured goods.

Customer service, in many respects, is the front line of public relations. A single incident, or a series

Word of Mouth

Customer satisfaction has always been considered important because of the power of "word of mouth" advertising. A person who has a bad experience, surveys indicate, shares his or her story with an average of 17 people. By comparison, a person with a good experience tells an average of 11 people.

of incidents, can severely damage a company's reputation and erode public trust in its products and services. Thanks to the rapid growth of the Internet and blogs, a dissatisfied customer is now capable of informing thousands, or even millions, of people of his or her unhappiness in just one posting. One somewhat embarrassing example happened to Comcast: A customer videotaped a Comcast repairman sound asleep on the customer's couch and posted it on www.snakesonablog.com. The clip was then picked up by a technology blog and eventually was shown on an MSNBC program. In a very short time, approximately 200,000 people saw the video. News of the incident reached an even greater audience when a story about the video in the *New York Times* noted that the repairman had fallen asleep while trying to get through to the cable company's repair office on the phone.

> **"Our reputation is probably based more on how we serve our customers than any other single thing. If we don't have a reputation for great service, we don't have travelers."**
>
> Rande Swann, director of public relations for the Regional Airport Authority of Louisville, Kentucky

Further illustrating this problem, *Pittsburgh Post-Gazette* reporter Teresa Lindeman wrote:

"[C]ompanies that consider ignoring tales of dissatisfied customers might want to take a look at a study released by the Wharton School of the University of Pennsylvania. Researchers there found that more than 50 percent of Americans said they wouldn't go to a store if a friend had a bad shopping experience there. Even worse, when someone has a problem, it gets embellished with every retelling, and pretty soon that store has a really, really big problem."

Traditionally, customer service has been kept separate from the communications or public relations function in a company. Bob Seltzer, a leader in Ruder Finn's marketing practice, told *PRWeek*, "I defy anyone to explain the wisdom of this. How a company talks to its customers is among, if not the, most critical communications it has."

Increasingly, however, corporations are realizing that customer relations serves as a telltale public relations barometer. Many public relations departments now regularly monitor customer feedback in a variety of ways to determine which policies and communications strategies need to be revised. One common method of doing so is to monitor customer queries on the organization's website. Another method comprises content analysis of phone calls to a company's customer service center.

It is important for public relations professionals to be involved in active listening to customer feedback so they can strategize the steps companies should take to ensure their good reputations. As Andy Hopson, CEO of Burson-Marsteller's northeast region, told *PRWeek*, "Ignoring complaints can ultimately damage a company's reputation."

think How has the Internet changed the role that a company's customer service reputation plays in its success or failure?

What Matters MORE Than Low Prices?

Public relations professionals also pay attention to consumer surveys. In particular, the American Customer Satisfaction Index is the definitive benchmark of how buyers feel about business practices. The index, which has been tracking customer satisfaction for 200 companies in 40 industries for more than a decade, has found that offering the lowest prices may not necessarily get a company the highest satisfaction rating. Wal-Mart, for example, scores only 70 out of a possible 100 points, compared with the national average of 75.2 for all retail companies.

Small companies can easily monitor the nature of customer comments and respond to them in a timely manner. This kind of real-time communication is more difficult for a large company, however. Ford Motor Company, for example, receives some 7,500 phone calls to its national customer service center every day.

DOS and DON'TS of Working with Consumer Groups

At the strategic level, a company weighs the potential impact of the allegations on customers and the expected effect on sales before deciding on a course of action. Activist consumer groups are a major challenge to the public relations staff of an organization. Is it best to accommodate their demands? Is it better to stonewall them? Should the company change its policy? Douglas Quenqua, writing in *PRWeek*, offered some general guidelines on how to take a proactive stance with working with consumer groups.

DO:

• Work with groups who are more interested in finding solutions than attracting publicity.

• Offer transparency. Activists who believe you are not being open with them are unlikely to keep dealing with you.

• Turn their suggestions into action. Activists want results.

DON'T:

• Get emotional when dealing with advocacy groups.

• Agree to work with anyone making threats.

• Expect immediate results. Working with adversaries takes patience—establishing trust takes time.

Consumer Activism

Dissatisfied customers can often be mollified by prompt and courteous attention to their complaints or even an offer by a company to replace an item or provide discount coupons toward future purchases. Consumer activists who demand changes in corporate policies pose a more serious and complex threat to corporate reputation, and their efforts can ultimately affect sales.

Tyson Foods, a major American producer of meat and poultry products, was accused of inhumane treatment of animals by various animal rights groups, including People for the Ethical Treatment of Animals (PETA). The corporate response was to establish an office of animal well-being to assure retailers and consumers that Tyson takes humane animal handling seriously.

KFC also has been targeted by PETA and other animal rights groups. The efforts of these groups have received extensive media publicity. Their charges of inhumane animal treatment affect consumer buying decisions, especially when activists stand outside franchises wearing T-shirts that say "KFC Tortures Animals." In such a situation, the public relations staff has the difficult job of defending the company against what it believes are unfounded allegations and, at the same time, assuring the public that KFC's policies do provide for the humane slaughter of its chickens.

Consequently, when it came to light that a KFC subcontractor was mistreating chickens, with the mistreatment being documented on videotape, the company immediately made a statement. It branded the abuse appalling and told the subcontractor to clean up its act—or lose its contract. In this instance, because of the quick corporate response, the media was able to include KFC's reactions in the story about the abuses.

Consumer Boycotts

The boycott—a refusal to buy the products or services of an offending company—has a long history and is a widely used consumer publicity tool. PETA, for example, announced that consumers should boycott Safeway until the company improved conditions for the farm animals raised by its meat suppliers. A key theater for this protest was Safeway's annual stockholders meeting, at which activists would unfurl a banner saying, "Safeway means animal cruelty." It was, as *PRWeek* reported, "a PR person's worst nightmare."

think

How can a boycott be used as an effective negotiating tactic for a consumer group?

Safeway headed off the nightmare by negotiating with the group. Just days before its annual meeting, the company's public affairs staff began working with PETA and quickly announced new standards for monitoring conditions with meat suppliers. Instead of a protest, PETA supporters showed up at the annual meeting with a large "Thank You" sign for entering stockholders. In addition, PETA ended its 20-state boycott of the chain. The director of public affairs for Safeway said the boycott didn't have any effect on sales, but PETA took a different tact. Its director told *PRWeek*, "It's just a truism that you don't want your corporation targeted by activists. My hunch is the timing of the call [from Safeway public affairs] was not purely coincidental."

The efficacy of consumer boycotts is mixed. For example, a variety of activist groups have boycotted Procter & Gamble for years without making much headway because the company manufactures so many products un-der a variety of brand names that consumers can't keep track of the complete P&G product line.

A single product name can sometimes be more vulnerable to a boycott than a large company that markets its goods and services under multiple brand names. When the iPhone was introduced in Canada, Rogers Communication had the only network on which the technology would work. Rogers offered monthly data plans ranging from $60 to $115—much more than the $30 plans offered in the United States by AT&T. Canadian consumers threatened a boycott of Rogers Communication; 56,000 people signed an online petition against the company at ruinediphone.com. Ultimately, Rogers Communication responded by offering a $30 monthly data package for a limited time, and the boycott was averted.

Activists point out that a boycott doesn't have to be 100 percent effective to change corporate policies. Even a 5 percent drop in sales will often cause corporations to rethink their policies and modes of operation.

employee
RELATIONS

Customers are a primary public for any profit-making organization, as are employees. In many ways, employees are the front line of any effective public relations program. A company's reputation is often enhanced or damaged by how rank-and-file employees feel about their employer. One Internet survey of consumers by GolinHarris found that 70 percent of respondents believed that the number one criterion for good corporate citizenship was good treatment of employees.

Employees have been called an organization's "ambassadors" because they represent the company within a large circle of family, relatives, and friends. On the one hand, if morale is low or if employees believe the company is not treating them fairly, that unhappiness will likely be reflected in their comments to others. On the other hand, enthusiastic employees can do

> **"Regardless of the topic, an organization(s) will find it difficult to motivate, engage, and retain their most talented employees if their messages are not believed."**
>
> Mark Schumann of Towers Perrin, in *Public Relations Tactics*

much to enhance an organization's reputation within a community as a good place to work. This factor, in turn, generates more job applicants and enhances employee-retention rates.

Consequently, the wise public relations department, often working with the human resources

think

How can public relations departments work with human resources to ensure an organization has positive employee relations?

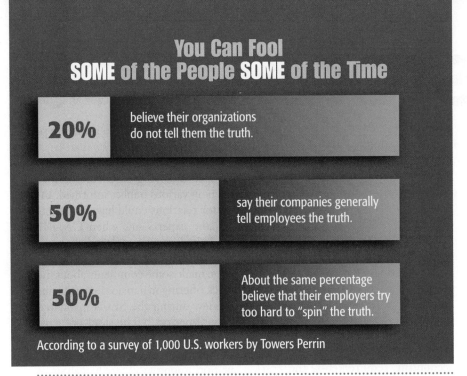

You Can Fool
SOME of the People SOME of the Time

20% believe their organizations do not tell them the truth.

50% say their companies generally tell employees the truth.

50% About the same percentage believe that their employers try too hard to "spin" the truth.

According to a survey of 1,000 U.S. workers by Towers Perrin

Surveys indicate that the success of communication efforts varies widely among organizations. In one survey, half of all employees claimed that they get more reliable information from their direct supervisors than they do from senior executives. The value of credible and trustworthy communication with employees cannot be underestimated. Seasoned public relations professionals know that effective employee relations is more than just a string of well-written and informative messages.

department, concentrates on communicating with employees just as vigorously as it does on delivering the corporate story to an external audience. Employees who respect management, have pride in their products, and believe they are being treated fairly are a key factor in corporate success.

One important workplace issue that affects both employees and management for legal and ethical reasons is sexual harassment. The U.S. Supreme Court ruled in *Meritor Savings Bank v. Vinson* (1986) that a company may be held liable in sexual harassment suits even if management is unaware of the problem and has a general policy condemning any form of verbal or nonverbal behavior that causes employees to feel "uncomfortable" or consider the workplace a "hostile environment." To protect themselves from liability and the unfavorable publicity associated with a lawsuit, organizations not only need

to establish a policy on sexual harassment, but must also clearly communicate that policy to employees and conduct workshops to ensure that everyone thoroughly understands what might be considered sexual harassment.

Layoffs present a major public relations challenge to an organization. In the case of widespread layoffs, the expertise of the public relations department should be harnessed to ensure employee understanding and support. One cardinal rule is that layoffs should never be announced to the media before employees are informed. Another rule is that an employee should be informed of the furlough or termination in person by his or her immediate supervisor. Employees who are being retained should also be called in by their immediate supervisors to be informed of their status.

The rumor mill works overtime when there is uncertainty among employees about job security, so it's also

important for the company to publicly announce layoffs and discuss their effects as quickly as possible. Companies should be forthright about layoffs; this is not the time to issue vague statements and "maybes."

Companies that are interested in their reputations and employee trust should make every effort to cushion the blows of a layoff by implementing various programs. Merrill Lynch, for example, laid off 6,000 employees by giving them the option of "voluntary separation" in exchange for one year's pay and a percentage of their annual bonuses. Other companies offer outplacement services, the use of office space, and other support programs. Such programs do much to retain employee goodwill even as workers are being laid off.

A contentious issue, and one that has become an emotional and political football in recent years, is the matter of outsourcing white-collar jobs. This practice is commonly called *offshoring*. Today, many American companies are employing lower-paid professionals in India and other Asian nations to handle everything from customer service to software engineering and accounting. The trend toward increased use of offshoring presents major internal communication challenges for public relations departments.

> **The way in which a company handles job reductions can have a significant impact on its reputation, its share price, and its ongoing ability to recruit and maintain good staff. And that presents a major challenge for communication departments.**
>
> Julia Hood, editor-in-chief of *PRWeek*

investor RELATIONS

another major indicator of corporate health and wealth is good communication with current shareholders and prospective investors. Investor relations (IR) is at the center of that process. Effective investor relations combines the disciplines of communications and finance to accurately portray a company's prospects from an investment standpoint. Some key audiences for these efforts are financial analysts, individual and institutional investors, shareholders, prospective

shareholders, and the financial media. Increasingly, employees are an important public, too, because they have stock options and 401K plans.

Individuals who specialize in investor or financial relations, according to salary surveys, are the highest-paid professionals in the public relations field. One reason for their high salaries is that they must be very knowledgeable about finance and the myriad regulations set down by the U.S. Securities and Exchange Commission (SEC) on initial public offerings (IPOs) of stock, mergers, accounting requirements, the contents of quarterly financial reports, and public disclosure of information. Government financial regulations are highly complex, and it is critical that they are followed to the letter. A company going public for the first time, for example, is required by the SEC to observe a "quiet time" when company executives are not allowed to talk about the offering to analysts

or the financial press to avoid "hyping" the stock.

Investor relations expertise is key both to satisfying SEC rules and to keeping various publics informed. Investor relations could have been better, the experts say, when Google's IPO had to be delayed because cofounders Sergey Brin and Larry Page made some comments about the stock offering in a major magazine interview during the SEC's mandated "quiet period." The foul-up gave Google a rocky start in terms of positioning the stock and building its reputation among Wall Street analysts.

Investor relations staff primarily communicate with institutional investors, individual investors, stockbrokers, and financial analysts. They also serve as sources of information for the financial press such as the *Wall Street Journal*, *Barron's*, and *The Financial Times*. In their jobs, investor relations professionals make numerous presentations, conduct field trips for analysts and portfolio managers, analyze stockholder demographics, oversee corporate annual reports, and prepare materials for potential investors.

think Why are public relations professionals who specialize in investor relations so well compensated?

marketing COMMUNICATIONS

many companies use the tools and tactics of public relations to support the marketing and sales objectives of their business. This type of activity is called *marketing communications* or *marketing public relations*. Thomas L. Harris, author of *The Marketer's Guide to Public Relations*, defines marketing public relations (MPR) as the "process of planning, executing, and evaluating programs that encourage purchase and consumer satisfaction through credible

communication of information and impressions that identify companies and their products with the needs, wants, concerns, and interests of consumers."

In many cases, marketing public relations is coordinated with a company's messages in advertising, marketing, direct mail, and promotion. In *integrated marketing communications (IMC)*, companies manage all the sources of information about a product or service so as to ensure maximum message penetration. IMC

was first discussed in Chapter 1 as an important concept in modern public relations practice.

In an integrated program, public relations activities attempt to garner early awareness and credibility for a product. Publicity in the form of news stories is leveraged to secure credibility, excitement in the marketplace, and consumer anticipation. The early messages make audiences more receptive to advertising and promotions about the product in the later phases of the campaign. Indeed,

Coors Brews a Community Relations Problem

IN LATE 2003, A YEAR AFTER COORS BREWERS LTD., a sub-sidiary of Molson Coors, had purchased the local company Bass Brewery in Burton-upon-Trent (Burton), England, it changed the name of the town's main tourist attraction from the Bass Museum to the Coors Visitors Centre. Public reaction was mixed.

Community leaders in the hometown of the 230-plus-year-old British beer were supportive. They said that Coors' promised investment of £500,000 (approximately $840,000) represented a strong commitment to the museum and the town. One Burton native gave voice to another predominant perspective: "it seems that Coors have tried their best to eradicate all traces of the existence of Bass in the town . . . Bass is a name which is identified with the town as well as the brewing industry and its traditions, and as such the Museum has always been seen as a place in which you can explore this heritage."

When Coors announced in early 2008 that it would close the museum because of its $2 million annual budget, both past supporters and detractors responded angrily. The local newspaper, the *Burton Daily Mail,* launched a campaign to reverse the decision. Burton Member of Parliament (MP) Janet Dean organized a trip to meet with the U.K. Minister of Culture and Tourism. A petition drive garnered 20,000 signatures against the decision. A "Save the Bass Museum" fan page appeared on Facebook. Community members and brewery workers organized a march in defense of the museum. According to London's *Guardian* newspaper, "Coors' executives in Colorado were horrified by this adverse publicity. The company . . . started to backtrack." Coors promised to let the museum remain in its home for a modest annual rent and promised an annual grant if Dean and her steering committee could find a buyer for the museum. Supporters continued to push Coors for a better solution.

In November 2009, Planning Solutions, which runs other U.K. attractions, was hired to run the museum for the duration of a 25-year lease. The museum was renamed the National Brewery Centre and scheduled to open in spring 2010. In a press release, John Lowther, CEO of Planning Solutions, stated, "Burton has a proud position in not only the United Kingdom's brewing industry, but throughout the world. We are delighted to be opening the National Brewery Centre here in Burton and celebrating the vital contribution that the town has made to our brewing industry and heritage."

John Polglass, of Molson Coors, said, "Molson Coors has always been committed to finding an organization that can provide a long-term future for a Brewing Museum in Burton. Planning Solutions has a great track record in running visitor attractions and we are delighted to support their exciting plans to put Burton on the U.K. tourist map."

1. Did Coors find a satisfactory solution to its public relations problem? Did the company give in to the community?

2. What could Coors have done to get a better understanding of the importance of Bass and the museum to the community?

3. Identify the Burton community activists' tactics and explain the role each may have played in pushing the various parties in the dispute toward a solution.

a growing body of research asserts that public relations is the cornerstone of branding and positioning a product or service. The objectives of marketing communications, often called *marcom* in industry jargon, are accomplished in several ways, such as product publicity, cause-related marketing, viral marketing, and corporate sponsorship.

Product Publicity

As the cost and clutter of advertising have mounted dramatically, companies have found that creative product publicity is a cost-effective way to reach potential customers. Even mundane household products, if presented properly, can be newsworthy and capture media attention.

Clorox, for example, generated numerous news articles and broadcast mentions for its Combat cockroach killer by sponsoring a contest to find America's five worst cockroach-infested homes. Dove Deodorant sponsored a Most Beautiful Underarms pageant at Grand Central Station in New York City, where Miss Florida won the crown. The contest received airtime on *Today* and *Fox & Friends*, and was mentioned on the news shows of 400 television networks.

A company also can generate product publicity by sponsoring a poll, even though the survey might be somewhat frivolous and the methodology unscientific. For example, *Food & Wine* magazine, in conjunction with AOL, conducted a survey and announced to the world that the supermarket checkout line is the most popular place to meet a mate. It also found that whipped

Special events can include publicity stunts. Hershey's celebrated the one-hundredth anniversary of its Kisses chocolate brand at a gala event in which it unveiled the world's largest piece of chocolate. The 12-foot-high structure weighed 30,540 pounds. Hershey's Kissmobile also traveled the country to generate publicity for its anniversary.

cream is the sexiest food, but that chocolate mousse was considered "better than sex" by respondents.

Product publicity can be generated in other ways. Old Bay Seasoning sponsors shrimp-eating contests; Briggs & Stratton, which makes lawnmowers, compiles an annual top ten list of beautiful lawns; Hershey Foods set a Guinness Record by producing the world's largest Kiss—a chocolate candy that weighed several tons.

Product placement (which was discussed in greater detail in Chapter 12) refers to the appearance of a product as part of a movie or television program, thereby helping to promote the brand. The Mercedes-Benz that the characters in a movie drive to the airport, the United Airlines flight that takes them to a destination, the Hilton where they stay, and the Grey Goose vodka martinis they drink in the bar are all examples of product placement.

Increasingly, product placements are the result of fees paid to film studios and television producers. Sometime, there is a trade-off. For example, when the Gap volunteers to provide the entire wardrobe for a

television show, such a deal reduces the cost of production for the producer and at the same time gives the clothing firm high visibility.

btw...

According to Stuart Elliott and Julie Bosman, writing in the *New York Times*, opportunities to promote products inside television shows "come in the form of what is called branded entertainment or product integration. They include mentioning brands in lines of dialogue, placing products in scenes so they are visible to viewers, and giving advertisers roles in plots of shows, whether it is a desperate housewife showing off a Buick at a shopping mall or a would-be apprentice trying to sell a new flavor of Crest toothpaste . . . . The goal of branded entertainment is to expose ads to viewers in ways that are more difficult to zip through or zap than traditional commercials. Devices like digital video recorders and iPods are making it easier than ever to avoid or ignore conventional sales pitches."

Cause-Related Marketing

Companies in highly competitive fields, where there is little differentiation between products or services, often strive to stand out and enhance their reputation for corporate social responsibility (CSR) by engaging in cause-related marketing. In this type of marketing, a profit-making company collaborates with a nonprofit organization to advance its cause and, at the same time, increase sales. Yoplait yogurt brand, for example, informs customers that 10 cents will be donated to support breast cancer research for each pink Yoplait lid they send in.

American Express was not the first company to engage in cause-related marketing, but its success in raising money to restore the aging Statue of Liberty and Ellis Island in 1984 set a new benchmark for effectiveness. The company spent $6 million publicizing the fact that one penny of every dollar spent on its credit cards would be donated to restoration efforts. American Express raised $1.7 million for the cause. It also saw the use of its cards jump 28 percent, and applications for new cards increased 17 percent. In addition, the marketing campaign proved to be an excellent branding strategy—promoting an automatic association in the public's mind between American Express and an American icon.

think

How is cause-related marketing a win-win situation for both a corporation and its community?

Corporate Sponsorships

One form of cause-related marketing is corporate sponsorship of activities and events such as concerts, art exhibits, races, and scientific expeditions. Companies spend approximately $10 billion annually in the United States sponsoring activities ranging from the Indianapolis 500 and the Kentucky Derby to the Grammy Awards, PGA golf tournaments, and even the concert tours of Christina Aguilera or Kelly Clarkson. Many of these events, unlike causes, are money-making operations in their own right. Even so, a large part of the underwriting often comes from corporate sponsorship.

Corporate-sponsored events serve four purposes:

1. They enhance the reputation and image of the sponsoring company through association.
2. They give product brands high visibility among key purchasing publics.
3. They provide a focal point for marketing efforts and sales campaigns.
4. They generate publicity and media coverage.

Sponsorships can be more cost-effective than advertising. Visa International, for example, spends roughly $200,000 each year (approximately the price of a 30-second prime-time TV commercial) sponsoring the USA-Visa Decathlon Team. Speedo, the swimwear manufacturer, sponsors the U.S. Olympic swim team, getting its name before millions of television viewers. At the Beijing games, nearly 90 percent of the Olympic swimmers wore Speedo gear—which in turn translated into brand dominance in terms of sales.

Local stadiums and concert halls almost everywhere now have corporate names. Bank of America agreed to pay $7 million per year to put its

GOOD DEEDS Are Rewarded

79% of Americans believe companies have a responsibility to support causes as part of their corporate citizenship.

81% of Americans say they are likely to switch brands, when price and quality are equal, to support a worthy cause.

Companies supporting worthy causes often elicit positive customer support, according to a study by Cone/Roper.

Cause-Related Marketing Tips

Selecting a charity or a cause to support involves strategic thinking. Here are some tips for conducting cause-related marketing:

- Look for a cause that is closely related to your products or services or one that exemplifies a product quality.
- Consider a cause that appeals to your primary customers.
- Choose a charity that doesn't already have multiple sponsors.
- Choose a local organization if the purpose is to build brand awareness for local franchises.
- Don't use cause-related efforts as a tactic to salvage your organization's image after a major scandal; such an attempt usually backfires.
- Understand that association with a cause or nonprofit organization is a long-term commitment.
- Realize that additional funds must be allocated to create public awareness and build brand recognition with the cause.

Warnaco CEO Joe Gromek presented Michael Phelps with a $1 million bonus check from Speedo at a broadcast of 'The Today Show' in New York City after Phelps won a record eight gold medals in swimming in the Beijing Olympics. Phelps used the $1 million bonus he earned for his record medal haul to start the Michael Phelps Foundation. As part of Phelps' most recent Speedo deal, which extends through 2013, the brand will donate $10,000 to the Michael Phelps Foundation for every World Record Phelps sets.

name on the Carolina Panthers' home stadium in Charlotte, North Carolina, until 2024. Federal Express pays $7.6 million each year (and will through 2025) for naming rights to FedEx Field, home of the Washington Redskins. Additionally, the shipping company has put its name on FedEx Forum in Memphis, home of the Memphis Grizzlies, at a cost of $4.5 million per year up until 2023. In Philadelphia, Lincoln Financial Group—not exactly a household name—snapped up naming rights for the new stadium for the Eagles pro football team. The company's reasoning: Its name will become recognized as a major brand by those attending Eagle games and the 10 million television fans who watch NFL games at home on television.

Viral Marketing

Long before the rise of the Internet, professional communicators recognized the value of favorable recommendations and "buzz" about a product or service. For public relations programs, the primary objective has always been to enhance or maintain the reputation of a company or celebrity. Today, thanks to technology, "word of mouth" can be used to generate greater traffic to a website, where both marketing and public relations objectives can be met. The primary purpose of viral marketing is to stimulate impulse purchases or downloads, but increasingly pass-it-on techniques on the web are also intended to help public relations professionals meet goals for reputation management and message dissemination. Generating excitement about the release of a musician's latest CD and touting the opening of a movie are two common ways viral marketing is employed in the entertainment business.

Viral marketing has adopted a new terminology and some special techniques that take advantage of new technology to stimulate the natural inclination of people to tell others about a good deal, a good service, or a good group. One classic example of viral marketing is Burger King's subservient chicken website (www.subservientchicken.com), which was launched in 2004.

btw...

On occasion, a company will sponsor an event for the primary purpose of enhancing its reputation among opinion leaders and influential decision makers. Atofina Chemicals, for example, usually sponsors events that advance science education. Nevertheless, it did agree to sponsor an exhibit of ballet-themed works by Degas at the Philadelphia Art Museum to highlight the company's history as a Paris-based corporation. One objective of this sponsorship was to increase employee pride. The company's 1,200 employees in Philadelphia and their families were invited to an exclusive showing at the museum before the exhibit was opened to the public. In addition, the company used the exhibit and museum as a centerpiece for entertaining customers and their significant others. It also organized events for and donations of products to the Philadelphia High School for the Creative and Performing Arts.

think Is viral marketing a new concept in public relations?

btw...

To explore viral marketing and to consider how to adapt the techniques to your own public relations activities on campus, visit the websites of the following viral marketing companies:

> Caffeine Online Marketing Solutions: www.getcaffeinated.com
> Mindcomet: www.mindcomet.com
> Oddcast: www.oddcast.com

The site features a human in a chicken suit who responds to whatever command the web viewer types in. If a viewer tells the chicken to dance, it dances. If a viewer instructs it to jump, it jumps. The connection to Burger King is twofold: (1) It plays on the restaurant's long-time slogan "Have it your way" and (2) it promotes the hamburger giant's chicken sandwich offerings.

"The intent here is to speak specifically to young adults in their 20s and 30s," Burger King spokesperson Blake Lewis told *The Wall Street Journal*. "These are people that are very Internet savvy. They are very active. They may not mirror a lot of the traditional TV, newspaper, or radio consumption patterns that older adults have come to adopt." When the site was launched, only 20 people—friends of employees in the agency that created the campaign—were told about the website. From those 20 people, use of the site exploded exponentially, to the point that the site garnered 46 million hits in its first week of operation. The popularity of the subservient chicken spawned an Xbox game in 2006 and a Halloween costume in 2007. The chicken is still taking orders and spreading virally through a "Tell a Friend" feature on the company's website.

Some viral marketing firms devise ways to stimulate the natural spread of recommendations through financial incentives called *cohort communication*. Going beyond the relatively organic spread of information via tactics such as Burger King's "Tell a Friend" feature, viral marketing specialists use more calculated tactics such as careful dissemination of favorable reviews. Software systems track referrals to a website or recommendations sent to friends, with senders chalking up cash or merchandise credits. Recommending a CD to friends might earn the recommender credit or free downloads of music tracks, for example.

Detractors worry that viral marketing is too easily recognizable as commercial manipulation, except among hard-core enthusiasts. Others say that it is deceptive and unethical to facilitate or reward what should be a natural process of trusted friends exchanging tips and links about great deals or great websites. When the music industry, for example, recruits fans to log on to chat rooms and fan websites to hype a band's new album, some liken the process to the questionable practice of "payola" in the radio industry, in which disk jockeys are paid to play certain tracks.

Viral marketing companies argue that the technique will work only when the idea, the movement, or the product earns genuine support from the marketplace. Public relations professionals need to make careful and ethical decisions to decide how best to use the web to spread messages.

environmental RELATIONS

another aspect of corporate responsibility that is gaining momentum is corporate concern for the environment and sustainable resources. The end of the twentieth century was witness to major clashes and confrontations between corporations and activist nongovernmental organizations (NGOs) about a host of environmental and human rights issues. The current trend, however, favors cooperation and partnerships among these former adversaries. Many companies, such as Shell, now issue annual corporate responsibility reports and work with environmental groups to clean up the environment, preserve wilderness areas, and restore exploited natural resources.

Take American Apparel, a clothing company founded by Dov Charney, which has long been known for its activism. Both the company and Charney have been plagued by negative press surrounding sexual harassment lawsuits

Made in Downtown LA—Vertically Integrated Manufacturing

American Apparel

its exemplary social and environmental policies.

In 2009, *Apparel* magazine named American Apparel as one of its first Sustainability All-Star Award winners. Among the environmentally friendly steps taken by the company is the development of a product line made entirely from the scraps of material that are a by-product of manufacturing. These scraps are made into headbands and belts rather than being sent to the landfill. The scraps are also made into underwear. This program recycles approximately 30,000 pounds of cotton per week.

According to American Apparel spokesperson Ryan Holiday, "We weren't thinking: 'How do we save the environment?' We were thinking: 'How can we do something fashionable with all these scraps?' It's not an act of charity, because the belts make money."

American Apparel offers a Sustainable Edition of its clothing as well. The sustainable line is made of 100 percent organic and certified pesticide-free cotton. And the company does not stop there: It generates 20 to 30 percent of its energy from solar panels, and it recycles cardboard boxes and cell phones. Timers and motion sensors save electricity in unused rooms. Employees are encouraged to use company bicycles to pedal back and forth to work. They are also supplied with bus passes to limit their driving.

against the company. In addition, American Apparel's public image has been forged through controversial, edgy advertising campaigns that some critics believe to be in questionable taste. Offsetting the sometimes negative press that has dogged the company, however, is the positive publicity generated by

corporate PHILANTHROPY

think — What is strategic corporate philanthropy?

another manifestation of organizational social responsibility is corporate philanthropy. This activity, in essence, consists of the donation of funds, products, and services to various causes, ranging from providing uniforms and equipment to a local Little League team to endowing a university with a multimillion-dollar gift to upgrade its science and engineering programs. In many cases, an organization's public relations department handles corporate charitable giving.

Corporations, of course, have long used philanthropy to demonstrate community goodwill and to polish

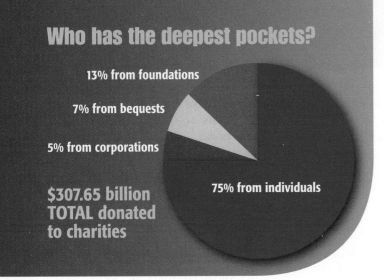

Who has the deepest pockets?

13% from foundations

7% from bequests

5% from corporations

75% from individuals

$307.65 billion TOTAL donated to charities

In 2008, U.S. corporations gave $15.4 billion to a variety of causes. Although there is a common perception that corporate philanthropy provides the lion's share of all donations, the actual percentage of charitable donations accounted for by corporations is very small. Of the $308 billion total given in 2008, only 5 percent came from corporations. The largest percentage of money given, 75 percent, was given by individuals.

> ❝Never do it for publicity. Do it for building your business, your brand equity, and your stakeholder relations.❞
>
> **Cone/Roper, a research firm**

their reputations as good citizens. There's also evidence that corporate giving is good for gaining and retaining customers. In the previously noted Hill & Knowlton survey, 79 percent of Americans claim to take corporate citizenship into consideration when purchasing products. At the same time, 76 percent of the respondents believe that companies participate in philanthropic activities to get favorable publicity, whereas only 24 percent believe corporations are truly committed to the causes they support.

Getting good publicity, no doubt, is a factor in philanthropy, but it should not be a company's ultimate objective. Cone/Roper, a survey organization, says companies should be very careful about touting their good deeds so the public does not become skeptical about their motivation. Companies should concentrate on the people they help, and the programs they showcase should be more than "window dressing."

A series of small grants to a wide variety of causes can dilute the impact of the contributions; sometimes a concentrated effort is more effective. HomeBanc Mortgage Corporation, for example, used to give $300,000 annually in small grants to a variety of causes, but it decided that the available funds could have more impact (and visibility) if they were directed to just one or two causes. Consequently, the company now directs most of its charitable funds to Habitat for Humanity, a nonprofit that builds homes for low-income families.

In HomeBanc's case, funding Habitat for Humanity is a strategic decision to funnel contributions to a cause directly related to home ownership, which is the business of the mortgage company.

APPLY YOUR KNOWLEDGE

WHAT WOULD YOU DO?

You've just begun work with a global corporation. Its home offices are located in Chicago, but because of your Spanish-language major and your two internships with Latin American companies, you've been hired to do public relations in the Mexico City office. How will you prepare for this assignment? What do you need to know about the company and about its operations and relationship with key stakeholders in Mexico? Who are the key stakeholders? Make a to-do list for yourself to help you effectively prepare for your new job and hit the ground running when you relocate to Mexico.

What Role Can Public Relations Play in Rebuilding Public Trust in Business? p. 311

- Corporations must make special efforts to win public credibility and trust, and the concept of corporate social responsibility (CSR) should rank high on the list of priorities.

- Public relations professionals are on the front line in this effort, counseling companies to be more transparent in their operations, to adopt ethical standards of conduct, and to improve corporate governance.

How Do Media Relations, Customer Relations, Employee Relations, and Investor Relations Contribute to Corporate Health? p. 312

- The public's perception of business comes primarily from the mass media. Consequently, it is important for organizations to effectively tell their stories and establish rapport with business editors and reporters by being accessible, open, and honest about company operations and policies.

- Customer satisfaction is important for building loyalty, generating positive word of mouth for products, and maintaining the reputation of a company. Public relations professionals solicit customer feedback as often as possible and act to satisfy customers' needs for communication and service.

- In today's society, any number of special-interest groups are likely to exert pressure on a corporation to be socially responsible. Often-

times, public relations staff serve as mediators in this tug-of-war.

- Employees are the "ambassadors" of a company and serve as the primary source of information about the company for friends and relatives. Employee morale is important for this reason, and a good communications program—coupled with enlightened company policies—does much to maintain high productivity and employee retention.

- Public relations professionals who work in investor relations must be knowledgeable about communications and finance.

What Is Integrated Marketing Communications? p. 318

- Increasingly, companies are taking an integrated approach to campaigns. With this approach, public relations, marketing, and advertising staffs work together to complement one another's expertise.

- Product publicity and product placement are often part of marketing communications. Cause-related marketing involves partnerships with nonprofit organizations to promote a particular cause.

How Do Environmental Relations and Corporate Philanthropy Have a Positive Impact on the Public Image of a Corporation? p. 323

- A new trend is for corporations and activist organizations to engage in dialogue and collaborative efforts to change situations that damage the environment or violate human rights.

- In general, corporate philanthropy is part of an organization's commitment to social responsibility. Companies give approximately $15 billion per year to worthy causes in the United States. When engaging in philanthropy, it is important that a company select a charity that is complementary to the organization's business and customer profile.

QUESTIONS for *Review* and *Discussion*

1. What are the characteristics of today's modern corporation? Why is there so much public suspicion and distrust of these business entities?

2. What is the concept of corporate social responsibility (CSR), and why is it important to today's corporations? What is the role of public relations professionals in CSR?

3. Traditionally, customer relations and public relations have been separate corporate functions. Do you think the two functions should be merged? Why or why not?

4. Consumer activists are often very vocal about the misdeeds of corporations. How should a company react to charges and allegations from activist groups such as PETA? As a public relations professional, which factors would go into your decision making if faced with this situation?

5. Why are employee relations efforts so important to a company's image and reputation?

6. Many companies give workers time off with pay to volunteer on local charitable projects. Would you be more inclined to work for such a company? Why or why not?

7. Give some examples of product publicity and product placement.

8. Why is corporate sponsorship of concerts, festivals, and even the Olympics considered a good marketing and public relations strategy?

9. Corporate philanthropy is now very strategic; companies support organizations and causes that have direct relationships to their businesses. Do you think this kind of linkage makes corporate philanthropy too self-serving? Why or why not?

the THINKSPOT
www.thethinkspot.com

TACTICS

New York Times
TV Sports Section

January 12, 2010

The How-To of an Admission in the Steroid Era

Richard Sandomir

The strategy that Mark McGwire used Monday to lay out his admission to using steroids demonstrated that lessons were learned from other baseball stars who preceded him in making mea culpa about their drug use.

He did it all in one afternoon, starting with a statement that was distributed widely to the news media, and that came across the Associated Press wire at 3 P.M. The A.P. followed quickly with a story that featured an interview with McGwire, who subsequently spoke to numerous other news media outlets—including *USA Today* and *The St. Louis Post-Dispatch*; Tim Kurkjian and John Kruk of ESPN (both by telephone, not on the air); KTRS Radio in St. Louis; and *The New York Times*, before talking to Bob Costas live at 7 P.M. Eastern on MLB Network.

The one-day plan—coordinated over the past month by Ari Fleischer, a former White House press secretary who runs a crisis-communications company, and the St. Louis Cardinals, who recently hired McGwire as their batting coach—contrasts with last year's roll-out of Alex Rodriguez's steroid admission.

Last February, Rodriguez's steroid use was first reported by Selena Roberts on SI.com; three days later, he confessed to ESPN in an interview with Peter Gammons that lacked adequate follow-up questions; eight days later, Rodriguez responded to questions at a news conference at the Yankees' spring training camp as his teammates looked on.

That all came more than a year after Rodriguez denied using steroids to Katie Couric of CBS News.

Rodriguez lacked any arrogance in his confession, unlike Roger Clemens, whose drug-use denials have been defiant and angry. The genial Andy Pettitte took two months to speak about his use of human growth hormone after it was revealed in late 2007 in the Mitchell report that investigated drug use in baseball.

The classic crisis communication strategy is "Tell it all and tell it fast."

The impressive breadth of these interviews shows that a personality campaign and a media strategy were clearly in place for McGwire.

The problem with a drawn-out confession in the media for a celebrity client is that it runs over several news cycles and keeps the bad news coming and coming and coming . . .

McGwire had been silent since his embarrassing refusal to discuss his steroid use during a Congressional hearing nearly five years ago. His strategy back then, concocted with avoiding prosecution on his mind, made him appear hapless and as guilty as if he had confessed. This time, McGwire and his handlers surely knew his credibility would be enhanced if he confessed before spring training and made himself widely available, not only on Monday but Tuesday. An interview with ESPN is to be scheduled, but because it's not exclusive, its thunder will be muted.

McGwire's personality has usually been low key, and he has not always been comfortable with the news media.

In his repeated confessions Monday, he had no defiance or anger, just sadness and tears.

"I like the door-to-door strategy, in that he is telling his story in long form and in less confrontational settings," said Kevin Sullivan, a former White House communications director who runs a strategic-communications company. "He needed to rip the Band-Aid off before heading to spring training."

Sullivan added: "I suspect McGwire will soon have some form of a press availability where he takes questions. He won't be able to completely turn the page until he satisfies the pent-up demand and takes some questions."

The McGwire interview was a coup for the year-old MLB Network and justifies what the channel is paying Costas. It provided McGwire with a stage for acceptance on a channel that is majority-owned by the league that has, after a long goodbye, welcomed him back to his old team. MLB has a little more than half the subscribers ESPN has. But MLB had an edge in Costas if, indeed, McGwire wanted to be interviewed at length by a smart interrogator.

(A corporate connection should be noted: Costas is represented by IMG, which owns half of Fleischer's company.)

Before he sat down to talk to McGwire, Costas said in a telephone interview, "Yes, they decided this was the place for Mark to tell the story, but not because it was the place where they'd get the easiest ride."

Costas said he talked to Cardinals Manager Tony La Russa last year about interviewing McGwire.

"I said to Tony that if Mark hopes to be able to proceed from opening day on, he has to address this forthrightly, to answer all legitimate questions and all secondary ones," Costas said.

Tony Petitti, the president of the MLB Network, said that although talks with McGwire's camp made it clear that McGwire was going to say something significant, he and Costas did not know until the release of McGwire's statement exactly what it would be.

"We didn't see the release ahead of time and we had to react to what he was going to say," Petitti said.

Whatever it was, the channel was guaranteed the exclusive interview.

Often public relations professionals will choose to give exclusive stories to reporters they believe will be friendly and go easy on their client. Costas argued that was not the case in this instance.

Journalists love an exclusive!

"Ripping the Band-Aid off" is a good and memorable analogy for crisis communication. The idea here is that the more quickly you address the situation, the less it will hurt. McGwire had let his problem fester for years as people speculated about his steroid use, but when he decided to "come clean," he did so all in one fell swoop.

Why would an exclusive have more "thunder"? Because it will be more widely anticipated by both sports fans and other media, and although other media will subsequently cover the exclusive interview the message will be diluted over several sources.

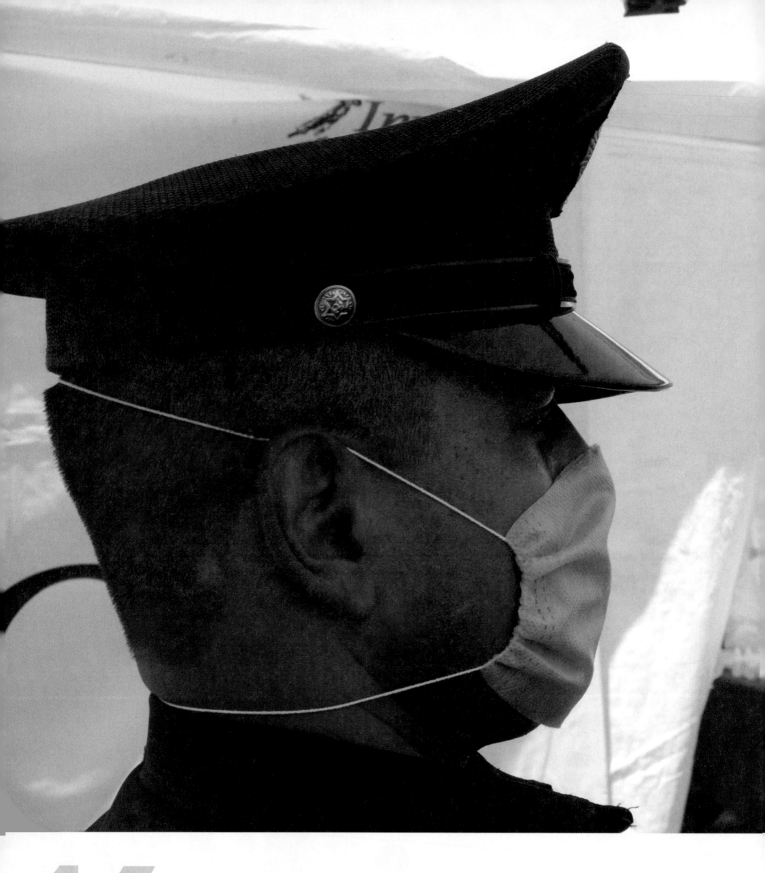

16 ENTERTAINMENT,

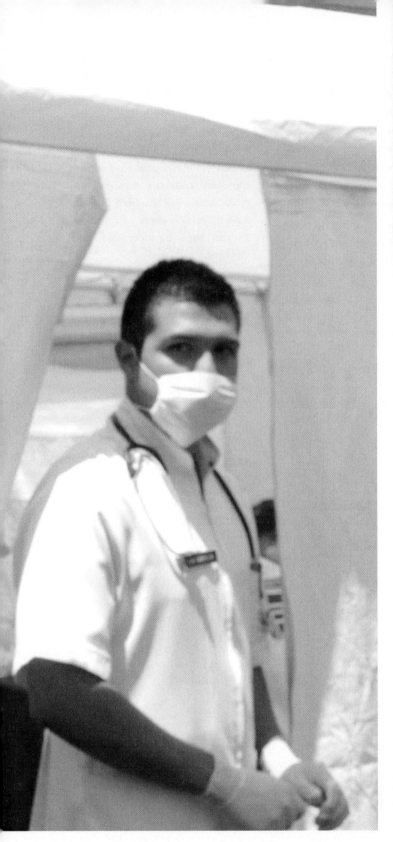

Ask Yourself

> **Which Elements Are Essential for an Effective Personality Campaign? p. 330**

> **How Can a Publicity Campaign Increase Event Attendance? p. 332**

> **What Role Does Public Relations Play in the Sports Mania Flourishing Around the World? p. 334**

> **What Role Does Public Relations Play in Attracting Visitors to Destinations and Keeping Them Happy Once They Arrive? p. 338**

A Costly Pandemic

When the H1N1 virus hit Mexico in late April 2009, it wreaked havoc on Mexico's $13 billion tourist industry, directly affecting the 2 million Mexicans who work in that industry. Just two weeks into the crisis, Mexico's finance secretary estimated the outbreak had cost the Mexican economy $2.2 billion.

Mexico City, the country's capital, was the epicenter of what became a pandemic. City officials immediately shut down nightclubs, movie theaters, museums, restaurants, and other places where people normally gather. Hotel occupancy rates plummeted 85 percent. The president of the city's Chamber of Trade, Services, and Tourism estimated that the shutdowns were costing the city $57 million per day.

Other Mexican tourist destinations were suffering as well. Cruise ships were rerouted to bypass Cancun and other port cities. In the initial days of the outbreak, 64 port calls were canceled by cruise companies, resulting in the absence of nearly 134,000 tourists. In May, visitors on cruise ships declined by 95 percent. In Cancun, hotel occupancy rates were down 40 percent; the Gulf Coast city lost $2.4 million in tourism-related revenues in the week following the initial flu outbreak. On the Pacific side of the country, resort town Huatulco experienced a hotel occupancy rate drop of 46 percent and Acapulco's mayor was forced to ask tourists from Mexico City to stay home and keep the virus to themselves. Around the country, T-shirts were printed that proclaimed, "I went to Mexico and all I got was the swine flu."

"We've never been hit so hard," Eduardo Chaillo, U.S. regional director at the Mexico Tourism Board, told United

SPORTS, AND TOURISM

Press International (UPI). "It's worse than September 11 or hurricanes."

To reignite Mexico's tourism industry, officials took several steps. Businesses offered cut-rate prices for rooms, meals, drinks, and souvenirs. Federal tourism officials queried their counterparts in China and Canada to see how those countries revived their tourist industries after the bird flu outbreak. A $90 million federally funded ad campaign showed celebrities on Mexico's beaches touting the country as a destination. Mexico City hired global PR agency Weber Shandwick to develop a $1.4 million campaign to enhance the city's reputation as a tourist destination for Americans and Canadians. Time and PR campaigns helped heal Mexico's tourism woes, as cruise ships, winter refugees, conventioneers, and spring breakers slowly returned.

❶ **Consider your favorite tourist destination. How did you learn about it? How is it promoted?**

❷ **Imagine you work for a Cancun hotel. How would you persuade tourists that it is safe to return following the pandemic?**

❸ **How could public relations professionals find out more about how Canada and China handled tourism public relations following the bird flu outbreak? Which sorts of research should they be doing as they devise campaigns?**

PUBLIC RELATIONS IN
entertainment, sports, AND tourism

Public relations in the for-profit realm is typically thought of as corporate work. Although a large percentage of public relations practitioners in for-profit organizations certainly do work for corporations, other significant for-profit segments of the public relations industry exist as well. In this chapter, we delve more deeply into some of the day-to-day issues that public relations practitioners face in the specialties of entertainment, sports, and tourism public relations. Increasingly, public relations students are expressing interest in careers in sports, entertainment, and hospitality. With the proliferation of major and minor league sports teams, university teams that rival for-profit clubs in terms of personnel, a growing cult of celebrity, and a strong convention and tourism sector, careers in these areas are viable options to persistent new graduates.

THE entertainment INDUSTRY

think How is our current public mania about celebrities manifested?

entertainment is big business. Public relations in the entertainment business can involve serving as a publicist for a celebrity or sports figure or working for an athletic team or a sports or entertainment venue. The field of entertainment public relations includes the travel industry, specific site or destination promotion, and specific

In some cases, celebrity results from natural public curiosity about an individual's achievements or position in life. Frequently, however, it is carefully nurtured by publicists for commercial gain.

DAMAGE CONTROL & Personal Publicity

Handling publicity for an individual involves special responsibilities. Clients may even turn to their publicists for personal advice, especially when trouble arises. A practitioner handling an individual client is responsible for both protecting the client from bad publicity and generating positive news. When the client appears in a bad light because of misbehavior or an irresponsible public statement, the publicist must try to minimize the harm done to the client's public image. The objective in such a case is damage control.

Personal misconduct by a client, or the appearance of misconduct, can strain a practitioner's ingenuity and at times his or her ethical principles. Some practitioners will lie outright to protect a client—a dishonest practice that looks even worse if the media show the statement to be a lie. On occasion, a practitioner acting in good faith may be victimized if his or her client has lied.

Issuing a prepared statement to explain the client's conduct, even though it may leave reporters and editors partially dissatisfied, is regarded as safer than having the client call a news conference, unless the client is a victim of circumstances and is best served by talking fully and openly. The decision about holding a news conference also is influenced by how articulate and self-controlled the client is. Under questioning, some individuals may say something that compounds an existing problem.

travel businesses such as a cruise line. These are just a few examples of public relations intersecting with the entertainment business.

A dominant aspect of today's mass media is the cult of celebrity. Sports heroes and television and movie personalities, in particular, along with radio talk-show hosts, members of the British royal family, high-profile criminals, and even some politicians, are written about, photographed, and discussed almost incessantly. The number and circulation of celebrity magazines continue to increase every year. *People*, the industry leader, has a circulation of almost 4 million copies per week.

The publicity buildup used to promote individuals lies outside the mainstream of public relations work, and some professional practitioners are embarrassed by the exaggerations and tactics employed by publicists for so-called beautiful people. Nevertheless, all students of public relations should know how the personal publicity trade operates.

the personality
CAMPAIGN

although a scandal often generates unwanted and unfavorable publicity for a celebrity, most public relations campaigns are initiated to generate public awareness of an individual who is intentionally seeking publicity. Such a campaign should be planned just as meticulously as any other public relations project. Practitioners conducting such campaigns follow a standard step-by-step process.

First, the client should answer a detailed personal questionnaire. The practitioner should be a dogged, probing interviewer, digging for interesting and possibly newsworthy facts about the person's life, activities, and beliefs. When talking about themselves, individuals frequently fail to realize that certain elements of their experiences have publicity value under the right circumstances. It is the job of the PR professional to identify those elements. Perhaps, for example, the client is an actress playing the role of a Midwestern farmer's young wife in a film. During her get-acquainted talks with the publicist,

she mentions that while growing up in a small town, she belonged to the 4-H Club. In this case, the publicist has struck gold by unearthing the fact that while she was a member of the youth organization, the actress participated in the actual farm activities portrayed in the film.

Not only must practitioners draw out such details from their clients, but they must also have the ingenuity to develop these facts as story angles. When the actress is a guest on a television talk show, the publicist should prompt her to recall incidents from her 4-H experience. Two or three humorous anecdotes about mishaps with pigs and chickens, tossed into the interview, give it energy and provide a sense of veracity.

In addition, the public relations professional should prepare a basic four-page (or even shorter) biography of the client. News and feature angles should be placed high in this "bio," so an editor or producer can find them quickly. The biography, photographs of the client, and, if possible, additional personal background items should be assembled in a media kit designed for extensive distribution via

printed folders, CD disks, and posting on websites.

As part of the publicity campaign's development, the public relations practitioner should determine precisely what is to be sold. Is the purpose solely to increase public awareness of the individual, or is it to publicize the client's product, such as a new television series, motion picture, or book? The practitioner should also decide which audiences are the most important to reach.

Conducting the Campaign

In most cases, the best course is to place the client on multiple media simultaneously. Radio and television appearances create public awareness and often make newspaper feature stories easier to obtain. The process works in reverse as well. Using telephone calls and e-mailed pitches to editors and program directors, the publicist should propose print and on-air interviews with the client. Every pitch should include a news or feature angle for the interviewer to develop. Because magazine articles take longer to reach readers, the publicist should begin efforts to obtain them as early as feasible.

An interview in an important magazine—a rising movie star in

> **think** How can a probing interview with a client help a publicist promote the client more effectively and creatively?

A politician trying to project herself as a representative of the woman's perspective should be scheduled to speak before female audiences and interviewed on radio and television programs that attract female listeners.

Cosmopolitan or *In Style*, for example—has major impact among readers. Backstage maneuvering often takes place before such an interview appears. Agents for entertainers on their way up eagerly seek to obtain interviews. When a personality is "hot," however, magazine editors compete for the privilege of publishing the interview. The star's agent plays them against one another, perhaps offering exclusivity but demanding such rewards as a cover picture of the star, the right to choose the interviewer (friendly, of course), and even final approval of the article. Some magazines yield to publicists' demands; other publications refuse to do so.

Photographs of the client should be submitted to the print media as often as justifiable. Media kits usually include the standard head-and-shoulders portrait, often called a "mug shot." Photographs of the client doing something interesting or appearing in a newsworthy group may be published with just a caption, without an accompanying story. The practitioner and the photographer should be inventive, putting the client into unusual situations. If the client seeks national attention, such pictures should be submitted to the news services so that, if newsworthy, they will be distributed to hundreds of newspapers and posted to online news sites.

Another way to intensify awareness of clients is to arrange for individuals to appear frequently in public places. Commercial organizations sometimes invite celebrities of various types or pay them fees to dress up dinner meetings, conventions, and even store openings. A major savings and loan association employed a group of early-day television performers to appear at

News releases are an important publicity tool, but the practitioner should avoid too much puffery.

The entertainment business generates immense amounts of publicity for individuals and shows with the Oscar, Golden Globe, and Emmy awards. Winning a Golden Globe, an Emmy, or an Academy Award bolsters a performer's career.

openings of branch offices. Each day for a week, an entertainer stood in a guest booth for two hours, signing autographs and chatting with visitors, who received a paperback book of pictures recalling television's pioneer period. Refreshments were served. A company photographer took pictures of the celebrity talking to guests. Visitors who appeared in the pictures received copies as souvenirs. These appearances benefited the sponsor by attracting crowds and helped the entertainers stay in the public eye.

A much-used device, and a successful one, is to have a client receive an award. The practitioner should be alert for news of awards to be given and nominate the client for appropriate ones. Follow-up communications with persuasive material from the practitioner may convince the sponsor to bestow the award on the client. In some instances, the idea of an award is proposed to an organization by a practitioner, whose client then conveniently is declared the first recipient.

Clients who employ practitioners want tangible results in return for their fees. To prove their worth, practitioners need to compile and analyze the results of personality campaigns to determine the effectiveness of the various methods used. Tear sheets, photographs, copies of news releases, and, when possible, video clips of their public appearances should be provided to clients. Clipping se`rvices can help

practitioners assemble this material. At the end of campaigns, or at intervals in long-term programs, summaries of what has been accomplished should be submitted to clients.

PROMOTING AN
entertainment
event

attracting attendance at an event—anything from a theatrical performance to a fund-raising fashion show or a street carnival—requires a well-planned publicity campaign.

The primary goal of any campaign for an entertainment event is to sell tickets. An advance publicity buildup informs listeners, readers, and viewers that an event will occur and stimulates their desire to attend. Except in the case of community events publicized in smaller cities, newspaper stories and broadcasts seldom include detailed information on ticket prices and availability. Those facts are typically deemed too commercial by editors. Performance dates, however, are typically included in publicity stories.

Stories about a forthcoming theatrical event, motion picture, rock concert, book signing, or similar commercial activity should focus on the personalities, styles, and popularity of the activities or products. Every time a product or show is mentioned, public awareness grows. Astute practitioners search for fresh news angles to generate as many stories as possible.

The "Drip-Drip-Drip" Technique

Motion picture studios, television production firms, and networks operate according to the principle of "drip-drip-drip" publicity when a show is being shot. In other words, a steady output of information is produced. For instance, a public relations specialist, called a unit man or woman, will be assigned to a film during production. That person turns out a series of stories for the general and trade press and plays host to media visitors to the set. In addition, television networks mail out daily news bulletins about their shows to media television editors. They assemble the editors annually to preview new programs and interview their stars. The heaviest barrage of publicity is released shortly before the show openings.

A much-hailed publicity tactic is to have a star unveil his or her star on the Hollywood

think *Why is this technique referred to as "drip-drip-drip" publicity?*

Walk of Fame, just before the star's new film or show appears. The late Beatle George Harrison received a star in 2009 after his death. The *Liverpool Daily Post* reported, "Harrison's honour comes as Capitol and EMI announce plans for the release of a new posthumous album by the guitarist." Harrison's former bandmate, Ringo Starr, received his star on February 8, 2010, the fiftieth anniversary of the beginning of construction of the famous Hollywood walkway. Starr also released a new album, titled *Y Not*, shortly before he received his star. Was the timing of the star ceremonies and the new albums a co-incidence, or was it part of a drip-drip-drip campaign aimed at selling more music?

One danger of excessive promotion of a celebrity is that audience expectations may become too high, so that the performance proves to be a disappointment. A skilled practitioner will stay away from "hype" that can lead to a sense of anticlimax.

Television is a high-stakes business characterized by a great deal of uncertainty. The national television networks—ABC, CBS, NBC, Fox, and CW—offer dozens of pilot programs, most of which prove to lack staying power. Some pilots survive, but many others fail. The 1990s prime-time steamy soap opera *Melrose Place* showed its staying power when it was resurrected by CW for its fall 2009 lineup, but a *Gossip Girl* spin-off that was piloted never took off.

The Movie Industry

Motion picture public relations departments use market research, demographics, and psychographics to define their target audiences. Most motion picture publicity is predominantly aimed at 12- to 24-year-olds, who make up the largest movie-going audience.

Professional entertainment publicity work is concentrated in New York and Los Angeles, the former as the nation's theatrical center and the latter as the motion picture center. American television production is also divided primarily between these two cities, with the larger portion occurring in Los Angeles.

A typical Los Angeles–area public relations firm specializing in personalities and entertainment has two staffs: "planters," who deliver to media offices publicity stories about individual clients and projects, and "bookers," whose job is to place clients on talk shows and set up other public appearances. Some publicity stories are intended for general release; others are prepared specifically for a single media outlet such as a syndicated Hollywood columnist or a major newspaper. The latter type is marked "exclusive," permitting the publication, station, or website that reports the

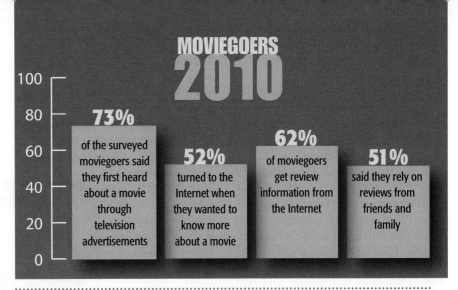

MOVIEGOERS 2010

73% of the surveyed moviegoers said they first heard about a movie through television advertisements

52% turned to the Internet when they wanted to know more about a movie

62% of moviegoers get review information from the Internet

51% said they rely on reviews from friends and family

A study titled "Moviegoers: 2010," sponsored by a consortium of diverse interested parties such as Microsoft, MovieTickets.com, and Facebook, among others, cites trends in information gathering that should shape public relations tactics for the promotion of both films and the celebrities who star in them.

item to claim credit for "breaking" the story.

Firms may provide tickets for a new movie or show to radio stations, where disc jockeys award them to listeners as prizes in on-the-air contests. In the process, these announcers mention the name of the show dozens of times. Occasionally firms invite media guests to glamorous premieres at distant locales, leveraging the luxury vacation to entice guests to speak highly of

the show they attend. For such services to individual or corporate entertainment clients, major Hollywood publicists charge a minimum of $3,000 per month, with a three-month minimum contract. The major studios and networks have their own public relations staffs.

Entertainment firms also may specialize in arranging product placements in movies and television programs. Usually movie or television producers trade visible

placement of a product in a show or film in exchange for free use of the item.

The fast-food industry provides excellent opportunities for market-based public relations, involving giveaways of character figures with meals. Movies such as 2009's *Star Trek* have received huge boosts in visibility and ticket sales from their relationships with fast-food purveyors. *Star Trek*, for example, was a highly anticipated movie with more than 1.8 million downloads of its trailer within the first 24 hours of the trailer's release. Burger King had both adult and kid tie-ins to the movie. It offered collector's cups for adults and *Trek*-themed toys in children's meals. Characters from the film also appeared with the Burger King mascot in ads on YouTube. For the fast-food chain, the appeal of the campaign was obvious: Movie-themed promotions can provide a key incentive to young customers in the highly competitive takeout business, providing a large but transitory advantage in the so-called burger wars. But, according to *Brandweek*, *Star Trek*'s integrated marketing effort moved well beyond the collector's cups and

children's toys at Burger King. Kellogg's Tony the Tiger flashed the "live long and prosper" hand sign in advertising. "Beam up badges" were found in boxes of Apple Jacks and Froot Loops. Lenovo computers tied in with the movie through a *Star Trek* sweepstakes and price promotion.

sports
PUBLICITY

The sports mania flourishing in the United States and around the world is stimulated by intense public relations efforts. Publicity programs at both the college and professional levels seek to arouse public interest in teams and players, sell tickets to games, and promote the corporate sponsors that subsidize events. Sports publicists also work with marketing specialists to drive sales of booster souvenirs and clothing, a lucrative sideline for many teams.

Sports publicists use the normal tools of public relations—media kits, statistics, interviews, television

think — Which tactics do sports publicists employ to stir audience emotions?

appearances, and the like—to distribute information about their clients. But conveying stats and facts is only part of their role—they also try to stir emotions. For college publicists, this goal means creating enthusiasm among alumni and making schools seem glamorous and exciting so that they can successfully recruit high school students to matriculate. Publicists for professional teams work to make them appear to be hometown representatives of civic pride, not merely athletes playing for high salaries.

Sometimes efforts succeed spectacularly, if a team wins. When a team is losing, however, the sports publicist's life turns grim. He or she must find ways to soothe public displeasure through methods such as having players conduct clinics at playgrounds and make sympathetic visits to hospitals.

Emerging sports are increasingly competing for prominence and fan loyalty with more established sports. Soccer is widely popular among youth in America, leading to hopes among its promoters that the professional game will make inroads in the U.S. sports market.

While some sports franchises have clamped down on athletes' tweeting habits, the Professional Golf Association (PGA) has embraced the social medium. In 2010, the PGA had a pgatour Twitter account with nearly 20,000 followers. Pro golfers Stewart Cink (1.2 million followers), Paul Casey (18,240 followers), and Chris DeMarco (11,170 followers) were among the leaders in the individual Twitter-follower race.

In America, sports is big business, garnering $410 billion in gross annual revenues. Unfortunately, an unseemly side sometimes crops up in sports coverage. Public relations plays a critical role in these situations in sports, going far beyond the mere promotion of celebrities to provide sports crisis management. According to John Eckel of Hill & Knowlton Sports, professional communicators must deal with the media focus on negatively charged issues ranging from player strikes to high ticket and concession costs to boorish athletes who deny that they are role models, even while they benefit from their visibility.

Sponsorship management is another key aspect of public relations in the sports world. The advertising agency DDB Worldwide studied the effectiveness of a very high-profile sponsorship—the Summer Olympics. The agency found that, for a company to benefit in terms of sales and goodwill, the Olympic Games require a huge commitment of $100 million per sponsor, plus extensive costs in marketing that sponsorship.

Despite the estimated $8.9 billion annually spent on sponsoring sports events, tallying the benefits of these relationships is still a less than scientific endeavor. With that point in mind, Publicis Groupe developed an optical-resolution technology to scan sports broadcasts for brand names and images. According to *The Wall Street Journal*, "The scan tracks the percentage of the TV screen that is taken up by an individual corporate logo, as well as the logo's location on the screen and whether there are other brands on the screen at the same time. The data are then used to calculate the financial value of the screen time, based on a formula loosely tied to the cost of TV ad time." The Publicis Groupe program, for example, found that Honda was the highest-scoring brand in terms of exposure during the Indy 500 race broadcast on ABC. The data show that Honda received 1,400 seconds of broadcast exposure, estimated to be worth $1.33 million.

Sponsorships may also have an effect on a company's stock price. When Professor Lance Kinney at the University of Alabama studied 61 sports

Because the public yearns for heroes, publicists focus on building up the images of star players, sometimes to excess.

event sponsorships, he found a significant increase in the stock prices of companies sponsoring Olympic events and baseball. Although no direct causal link can be proven, the relationship between sports sponsorships and corporate net worth is an interesting area of continuing research.

btw...

Soccer is the world's most popular sport, and the World Cup is the most costly of all sports sponsorships. The 2010 World Cup, to be held in South Africa, has a 48-game schedule. The previous World Cup, which took place in Germany in 2006, was seen by billions of viewers around the world.

Adidas has produced the official soccer balls for the last 11 World Cups. Soccer fans in 2006 saw the Adidas three-stripe logo on match balls, referee uniforms, outfits worn by volunteers, and billboards in and around the stadiums where the matches took place. In 2010, the logo on the Adidas ball had 11 colors, representing both the 11 players on each team and South Africa's 11 official languages. Adidas also had exclusive rights to air advertisements during broadcasts of games in the United States by ABC and ESPN.

The shoe and sports apparel manufacturer paid $351 million to the World Cup's governing body, the Federation Internationale de Football (FIFA), for these sponsorship rights, which extend through 2014. In addition, the Adidas partnership gives it prominent marketing placement on FIFA's World Cup website, which organizers estimated would attract 4 billion visitors during the tournament alone. Nike, the archrival of Adidas, paid an estimated $144 million to be the official sponsor of the Brazilian team, which has won more World Cup championships than any other nation, until 2018.

APPLY YOUR KNOWLEDGE

WHAT WOULD YOU DO?

Imagine that you are the public relations representative for a high-profile, major league athlete. You admire your client, perhaps even lionize him. You've been helping him fight charges that he used performance-enhancing drugs. One day, as you visit with him in the stadium locker room, you see a needle and drug bottle incompletely covered by some dirty socks. You begin to ask about it, but then decide to wait and think it over.

Now that you've thought about it, what should you do? If you don't ask your client for more details, then you can continue to state that you know nothing about his drug use. Perhaps it was just a pain reliever, after all. If you do ask and find out that what you saw was, indeed, some form of performance-enhancing substance, do you continue your campaign to defend your client, do you quit representing him, or do you take some other step? If you continue representing him, do you talk to him about what you saw? Why or why not?

Write a short essay on how you would handle this situation. Be clear on why you would make your choices and how public relations should be used in the situation.

Jay Rosenstein of Cohn & Wolfe attributes much of sports crisis public relations to the "human factor in the sports world, where egos are otherworldly, behavior is reminiscent of the entertainment world, and media focus is unrelenting."

In 2010, Mark McGwire came forward and tearfully admitted that he had used performance-enhancing drugs during the late 1990s. That included the 1998 season, when baseball fans—and most of the rest of America—watched breathlessly as McGwire and Sammy Sosa held a home-run hitting battle, which McGwire ultimately won.

A Tiger in Trouble

SPORTS, ENTERTAINMENT, and celebrity are intertwined. Never was that more obvious than when golf god Tiger Woods fell from grace, thanks to an odd 2:25 A.M. automobile accident.

Following the accident, in which Woods' wife Elin Nodegren was reported to have used a golf club to break a window in his Cadillac Escalade to rescue an unconscious Woods, rumors quickly circulated. Investigators said alcohol was not involved. Instead, a marital dispute was posited as the possible cause of the accident. Wood initially refused to talk with Florida Highway Patrol investigators, but later relented.

Three days after the "Escalade escapade," as the *Christian Science Monitor* dubbed it, Woods dropped out of a tournament that benefited his Tiger Woods Foundation—and news reports of his infidelity began to surface. By early 2010, the number of "alleged paramours" had reached 14, and *Vanity Fair* predicted that it was "a figure bound to multiply." A *USA Today*/Gallup poll showed that Woods' 87 percent approval rating in 2005 had dropped to 33 percent following the accident and allegations of infidelity. Tiger's once-golden reputation was in a tailspin.

Woods' initial public relations strategy was to lay low. On his website he wrote, "This situation is my fault, and it's obviously embarrassing to my family and me . . . This is a private matter and I want to keep it that way."

Less than a week into the growing scandal, with celebrity magazines and sports commentators scouring every corner for new and potentially salacious information, Woods apologized on his website to his family and fans. His move came in the wake of allegations that he had engaged in multiple affairs, published in a cover story of *US Weekly*.

Woods wrote, "I have let my family down and I regret those transgressions with all of my heart. I have not been true to my values and the behavior my family deserves. I am not without faults and I am far short of perfect. I am dealing with my behavior and personal failings behind closed doors with my family. Those feelings should be shared by us alone." The *New York Times* reported, "He spent much of his 317-word statement pleading for privacy, saying in part, 'Personal sins should not require press releases and problems within a family shouldn't have to mean public confessions.'"

Later, reports came that his wife was planning to file for divorce and that Woods was having trouble coping with the situation. Some of Woods' sponsors jumped ship—dumping Tiger like a hot potato—while others came to his aid. Eventually, Woods announced that he was taking a hiatus from the pro golf circuit.

In a *New York Times* opinion piece, Sam Tanenhaus quoted historian Daniel Boorstin, who in 1961 wrote, "The very agency which first makes the celebrity in the long run inevitably destroys him. He will be destroyed, as he was made, by publicity. The newspapers make him, and they unmake him."

1 Should Tiger Woods have made more forthright public statements earlier? Why or why not?

2 What would you advise Woods to do if you were his public relations counsel?

3 Do you think that the cult of celebrity automatically comes with a responsibility to share your personal life with your fans? Why or why not?

4 What do you think of Boorstin's quote? Does publicity both make and destroy celebrities? If so, as a public relations professional, how would you help a client avoid the downside of publicity?

5 Assess the reputation of Tiger Woods today. Do you think he has recovered from the scandal that engulfed him in late 2009? Several experts have predicted he would do so if he continues to win golf tournaments. Has that been the case?

travel PROMOTION

think **How do public relations professionals stimulate tourist interest in new locations?**

as soon as people collect a bit of money in their pockets, they tend to want to go places and see things. Stimulating that desire and turning it into the purchase of tickets is the goal of the travel industry. Public relations plays an essential role in this process—not only in attracting visitors to destinations, but also in keeping them happy once they arrive.

Traditionally, the practice of travel public relations has involved three steps:

1. Stimulating the public's desire to visit a place
2. Arranging for the travelers to reach it
3. Making certain that visitors are comfortable, well treated, and entertained when they get there

Interest in travel can be stimulated through articles in magazines and newspapers, alluring brochures distributed by travel agents and by direct mail, travel films and videos, and presentations on the World Wide Web. Locations also solicit associations and companies, en-couraging them to hold conventions in particular locations to encourage group travel.

Some publications have their own travel writing staff; others hire freelance writers and photographers. Well-done articles by public relations practitioners about travel destinations often are published, too, as long as they are written in an informational manner without resorting to blatant salesmanship and purple prose. Sensitive to public resistance to exaggeration, *Condé Nast Traveler* magazine carries the slogan "Truth in Travel" on its cover. But public relations practitioners beware: *O'Dwyer's PR Services Report* warns that "PR overkill" results from indiscriminate distribution of news releases, nagging follow-up calls to editors about releases, ignorance about the publication being pitched with a story, and excessive handling of writers on arranged trips so that they find it difficult to get a complete picture of the travel destination.

Treating travelers well is critical in the travel and tourist industry. If a person spends a large sum on a trip, but then encounters poor accommodations, rude hotel clerks, misplaced luggage, and inferior sightseeing arrangements, he or she comes home angry. Even more ominously for the destination, unhappy travelers readily tell their friends how bad the trip was.

Fear of terrorism has focused emphasis on a crucial new element of travel public relations—ensuring travelers' safety.

btw...

To promote sales, the 38,000 U.S. travel agencies distribute literature, sponsor travel fairs, and encourage group travel by showing destination films at invitational meetings. Cities and states operate convention and travel departments to encourage tourism. A widely used method of promoting travel is the familiarization trip, commonly referred to as a "fam trip," in which travel writers and/or travel salespeople are invited to a resort, theme park, or other destination for an inspection visit. In the past, fam trips often were loosely structured mass junkets. Today they are smaller and more narrowly focused.

Royal Caribbean's Oasis of the Seas is the largest cruise ship ever built. The massive ship cost $1.4 billion; it is 18 decks high, and 1,187 feet long. It features 2,706 rooms and requires a 2,100-person staff.

That said, even the best arrangements go awry at times. Planes are late, tour members miss the bus, and bad weather riles tempers. This is where the personal touch means so much. An attentive, cheerful tour director or hotel manager can soothe guests, and a "make-good" gesture such as a free drink or meal does wonders. Careful training of travel personnel is essential. Many travelers, especially in foreign countries, are uneasy in strange surroundings and depend more on others than they would at home.

Appeals to Target Audiences

Travel promoters identify target audiences, creating special appeals and trips for them. Great Britain's publicity in the United States is an example of a successful effort. It's an appealing invitation to visit the country's historic places and pageants. Promoters also highlight London theatrical tours, golf expeditions to famous courses in Scotland, genealogical research parties for those seeking family roots, and tours of famous cathedrals.

Packaging is a key word in travel public relations. Cruises for family reunions or school groups, family skiing vacations, university alumni study groups, archaeological expeditions, and even trips to remote Tibet are just a few of the so-called niche travel packages that are offered. A package usually consists of prepaid arrangements for transportation, housing, most meals, and entertainment, with a professional escort to handle the details. Supplementary side trips often are offered for extra fees.

The largest special travel audience is people older than age 40, and the 60-plus age cohort makes up a large percentage of cruise ship passengers. Many retired persons have time to travel, and some have ample money to do so. Hotels, motels, and airlines frequently offer discounts to attract this audience. As a means of keeping old-school loyalties alive, many colleges conduct alumni tours, which are heavily attended by senior citizens. A large percentage of cruise passengers, especially on longer voyages, are retirees. Alert travel promoters design trips with them in mind, including such niceties as

How Many "Freebies" to Accept?

ethics in ACTION

Newspaper and magazine stories about travel destinations, which are essential in tourism promotion, can pose a problem for writers and public relations people. Who should pay for the writers' expenses in researching these stories?

Some large newspapers forbid their travel writers to accept free or discounted hotel rooms, meals, and travel tickets. They believe that such subsidies may cause writers to slant their articles too favorably, perhaps subconsciously.

Many smaller publications and most freelance writers cannot afford such a rule, however, and following it would prevent them from preparing travel articles. Freelance travel writer Jeff Miller took the publishing industry to task in *Editor & Publisher* magazine for paying just $150 per newspaper story and $500 to $1,000 per magazine story while banning writers from taking subsidized trips. Travel writers claim the hypocritical policy makes the publications look good, but that it is regularly ignored by travel writers who simply cannot make a living without subsidized trips. The writers contend that pride in their professional objectivity keeps them from being influenced by their hosts' "freebies." Some point to critical articles they have written regarding subsidized trip destinations.

For the public relations director of a resort, cruise, or other travel attraction, the situation presents two problems: (1) How much hospitality can be given to the press before the "freebies" become a form of bribery? and (2) How does the director screen requests from self-described travel writers who request free housing or travel?

The Society of American Travel Writers (SATW) sets the following guideline:

Free or reduced-rate transportation and other travel expenses must be offered and accepted only with the mutual understanding that reportorial research is involved and any resultant story will be reported with the same standards of journalistic accuracy as that of comparable coverage and criticism in theater, business and finance, music, sports, and other news sections that provide the public with objective and helpful information.

What do you think of the SATW guidelines? What about the "no sponsored trips" policy at some newspapers and magazines?

Who Cruises?

The 40-59 year-old group takes approximately **36%** of all cruises.

The 25-39 year-old group takes approximately **29%** of all cruises.

The 60-year and older group takes approximately **35%** of cruises.

Shipboard entertainment and recreational activities with appeal to older persons—nostalgic music for dancing rather than current hits, for example—are important components of the cruise experience.

pairing compatible widows to share cabins and arranging shore trips that require little walking.

Tourism in Times of Crisis

Crisis management is an important part of public relations in the travel industry, just as it is in corporate work. Crises come in many forms, from dangerous political crises to small but embarrassing blips.

Aruba, for example, is a popular destination for U.S. tourists; nearly 1 million visit the Caribbean island annually. But its tranquil image of clear water, beautiful beaches, and swaying palm trees was considerably shaken when Natalee Holloway, an 18-year-old from Alabama on a class graduation trip, disappeared from one of Aruba's resorts. The disappearance—and the strong inference of foul play—became a major story in the print and broadcast media. At one point, 60 foreign reporters were on the Dutch-colony island covering the case. Howard Kutz, media critic for *The Washington Post*, noted, "Cable TV is treating this as the crime of the century, or at least, the obsession of the moment." He told the *Christian Science Monitor* that Aruba had garnered more media coverage over Holloway than it had received in the last 20 years.

The Holloway story was a major crisis for the Aruba tourism industry. Other Caribbean islands were also concerned that it would have a spill-over effect, with their tourism declining because of the negative coverage. The story continued to garner headlines as Holloway's mother gave extensive interviews and loudly complained about the lack of progress the Aruba police were making in finding her daughter. The Alabama legislature even got into the act and threatened a boycott of the island until the case was solved.

A "NOVEL" Approach to Getting Attention

When a Caribbean resort wanted to garner some media attention, its public relations agency, Nike Communications, suggested a "novel" approach.

The Little Dix Bay luxury resort arranged with some of the leading publishing houses in the United States to make advance copies of novels available exclusively to the guests of Little Dix Bay and affiliated properties. In a press release, the resort announced:

Ladies and gentlemen, you read it here first: The final word in intellectual one-upmanship is at Little Dix Bay, a Rosewood Resort that has forged an exclusive relationship with America's top publishing houses entitling its pampered, privileged guests bragging rights to the latest wave of best-sellers before they're even on sale.

The program, called "Hot Type," puts an end to the high-class ennui of "been there, read that." Little Dix Bay in the stunning British Virgin Islands makes available advance copies of new fiction and nonfiction works by the world's most prominent authors, including Candace Bushnell, John Updike, Steve Martin, Stephen King, Annie Proulx, and many more. New titles will arrive monthly to the "Hot Type" library.

Little Dix Bay's guests—who have always been avid readers—have more than just new titles to inspire their reading pleasure. The resort's breathtaking, free-form pool entices with a misting waterfall—the perfect accompaniment to a special "book menu" from which guests may choose an advance book copy to devour during their stay.

The campaign garnered coverage in *Fortune,* the *New York Times, The Wall Street Journal, Travel & Leisure, Condé Nast Traveller,* and *USA Today,* according to a report in *PRWeek.*

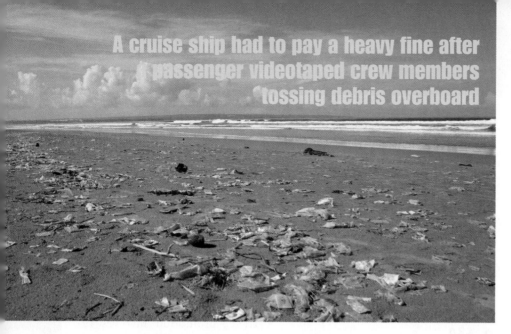

A cruise ship had to pay a heavy fine after a passenger videotaped crew members tossing debris overboard

found and no one had been charged with her alleged murder. The story has since faded from the headlines and the media moved on. In Aruba, tourism is nearly back to normal.

Travel public relations professionals need to be prepared to deal with all sorts of crises. In 2009, a Royal Princess Cruise in the fifth day of a 12-day Holy Land cruise had an engine fire that disrupted the cruise. The cruise ship was taken out of service and spokespeople were left to explain: "We will be providing the affected passengers . . . a full refund of their fare, plus a future cruise credit equal to 25 percent of the cruise fare paid for these sailings. We are currently securing flights home for all passengers currently onboard Royal Princess, and they will be returning home over the weekend."

Among numerous areas of concern, travel firms need to make certain that they provide equal facilities and service to all. They also need to ensure that their facilities and practices are environmentally sound or risk negative publicity.

Aruba's public relations firm, Quinn & Co. in New York, was originally retained to promote the island's beaches and resorts, but had to immediately switch gears and do crisis management. One tactic was to centralize information about the police investigation and to give regular updates on progress in the case. The firm also worked with cruise lines, travel agents, and airlines to assure them that the Aruba was safe and still an attractive destination. The government also issued a statement saying, "This comes as a shock to Aruba where crime against tourists is almost nonexistent," noting the island's repeat visitor rate of 40 percent, the highest in the Caribbean.

When Lifetime Movie Network premiered its made-for-TV film *Natalee Holloway* to an audience of 3.2 million viewers in 2009, no trace of Natalee Holloway had been

Luxury Cruise Ship Stumbles Ashore in Haiti

ethics in ACTION

Should a luxury liner continue to use a private beach in Haiti to entertain its passengers while, a mere 50 miles away, 275,000 Haitians died and several million lost their homes in the devastating January 12, 2010 earthquake?

That was the ethical dilemma faced by Royal Caribbean Cruise Lines, which has been frequenting the heavily-guarded private resort of Labadee for several years. One week after the earthquake that practically leveled the entire capital city of Port-au-Prince, the 4,370 berth Independence of the Seas visited the resort where passengers enjoyed swimming, parasailing, and rum cocktails delivered to their hammocks.

The public image of tourists enjoying the "good life" while astounding num-

bers of Haitians were without water or food caused many critics to complain that Royal Caribbean Lines was being insensitive and putting profit before human suffering. Even some of the cruise line's customers had misgivings. One passenger, for example, posted a note on the Cruise Critic Internet forum saying, "It was hard enough to sit and eat a picnic lunch at Labadee before the quake, knowing how many Haitians are starving; I can't imagine having to choke down a burger there now."

Whether to continue visiting Haiti was also a subject of debate within the company, but the decision was eventually made that the cruise line would help more Haitians by continuing to include Labadee in its scheduled stops. The

rationale was that the resort employed 230 Haitians and an additional 300 benefitted from their employment. The ships could also be employed to deliver food to the island. Ultimately, the company pledged to donate all profits from the visit to help the Haitian people. Royal Caribbean also pledged $1 million to the relief effort, diverting part of that amount as assistance to its 200 Haitian crew members.

Do you think Royal Caribbean Lines made the right decision to continue its visits to Labadee despite the massive devastation caused by the earthquake? What, if anything, should the cruise line have done about public perceptions?

Summary

Which Elements Are Essential for an Effective Personality Campaign? p. 330

- A big challenge for public relations practitioners who handle personalities is damage control when misbehaviors occur or irresponsible public statements are made.

- A public relations practitioner planning a campaign to generate public awareness of an individual must interview the client, prepare a biography, plan a marketing strategy, and conduct the campaign through news releases, photographs, and public appearances.

How Can a Publicity Campaign Increase Event Attendance? p. 332

- Publicity campaigns include publicity to stimulate ticket sales. The "drip-drip-drip" technique involves a steady output of information as the event is being planned.

- The entertainment industry defines target audiences to promote motion pictures and television shows.

What Role Does Public Relations Play in the Sports Mania Flourishing Around the World? p. 334

- Sports publicists promote both college and professional teams. This effort becomes more difficult when a team isn't winning.

- Emerging sports must compete for prominence and fan loyalty with more established sports. Some publicity focuses on building images of star players.

- Publicity efforts in the sports world also include both crisis management and sponsorship management.

What Role Does Public Relations Play in Attracting Visitors to Destinations and Keeping Them Happy Once They Arrive? p. 338

- Travel promotion involves increasing the public's desire to visit a place, arranging for travelers to reach it, making sure they enjoy their trips, and ensuring their safety.

- Campaigns sometimes include familiarization trips to increase travel agents' awareness of destinations

QUESTIONS for *Review* and *Discussion*

1. What is the first step in preparing a campaign to increase the public's awareness of an individual client?

2. Why do practitioners put emphasis on certain players on sports teams?

3. What are the basic phases of travel promotion?

4. What is the drip-drip-drip technique, and why is it often employed in the entertainment industry?

5. What do demographic and technology changes mean for the future of promotion in the movie industry?

6. How are sports sponsorships leveraged by companies?

7. Why do you think Adidas pays such a premium for its sponsorship of the World Cup?

8. Which demographic trends are affecting the cruise industry?

9. This chapter covered two major tourism crises—Natalie Holloway's disappearance in Aruba and the swine flu problem in Mexico. Which crisis do you think has had a more lasting impact? Why?

the THINKSPOT

www.thethinkspot.com

17 GOVERNMENT

Ask Yourself

> What Are the Basic Purposes and Functions of Public Relations in Government Organizations? p. 350

> Which Public Relations Activities Do Government Organizations Engage in at the Federal, State, and Local Levels? p. 352

> What Are Public Affairs, Governmental Relations, and Lobbying? p. 360

> What Role Does Public Relations Play in Election Campaigns? p. 363

Almost Ready for 2.0: Social Media and the 2008 Election

The Internet and social media sites such as Facebook, MySpace, and Meetup.org took a more prominent role during the 2008 presidential election than ever before. Barack Obama, John McCain, and Hillary Clinton all employed social media to raise funds and mobilize support. However, while all major candidates used social media somewhat effectively in 2007 and 2008, none of them consistently integrated social media into their campaign strategy. "Many [candidate] sites are poorly structured, are built without regard to best practices or search strategy, and don't seem to be part of a cohesive unit," asserts J. Barbush of independent public relations agency RPA. Also, social media initiatives have typically been geared toward younger demographics, limiting their appeal to 20- and 30-somethings. Given this fact, the failure to exploit social media for political purposes may reflect not so much that candidates have not fully exploited the potential of new media, but rather that the number of voters capable of, or interested in, receiving messages via social media has not reached a critical mass.

Despite these issues, there were some encouraging developments in the 2008 election. Obama was particularly effective in raising millions of dollars by soliciting small donations on sites such as Facebook. Libertarian fringe candidate Ron Paul (Republican–Texas) raised $4 million in a single day. This astounding figure was eclipsed by former governor of Massachusetts, Mitt Romney, who raised $ 6.5 million. And McCainblogett.com, a blog operated by

AND POLITICS

John McCain's daughter, Meghan, was well conceived, according to Barbush. He notes that it helped to "reframe perceptions and infuse humanity into the otherwise confusing area of campaign-based rhetoric." Barbush even adds this, about reading the blog: "I was relating to McCain as a father."

In the future, it is likely that there will be a gradual evolution in campaign strategies, as candidates and political parties become more sophisticated in their use of new media and move closer toward realizing the full potential of social media.

1 If you were in charge of the new media initiatives for a political candidate, what are some of the strategies and tactics that you might use to gain advantage over competitors?

2 Which social media–focused public relations activities would be appropriate for government organizations to use at the federal, state, and local levels?

3 What are the potential risks of using social media in corporate government relations or lobbying, and how can they be avoided?

GOVERNMENT organizations

federal, state, and local governments and agencies share a common bond—they all engage in the same types of public relations tasks to succeed and thrive. Government agencies and administrations share characteristics such as tax exemption and an intent to serve the public good, and all operate within the framework of regulations

that address social issues, and help develop long-range plans and visions. Aspiring public relations professionals will not want to overlook opportunities for employment in government.

Corporations and other nonprofit organizations also have specialized functions in regard to government organizations that are generally tied to lobbying. This lobbying activity serves to counterbalance the actions of governmental bodies at the local, state, and federal levels, which influence the business environment for both for-profit and nonprofit organizations. These functions typically involve gathering, analyzing, and disseminating information, in line with the individual organization's interests.

think Which tactics do governments use to communicate with their publics?

Nevertheless, the shortcomings of some government officials and employees should not blind citizens to the tangible benefits of the democratic system. For federal, state, and local governments to function efficiently, each branch needs to communicate effectively with its constituents. From election campaigns to military recruitment to floating a bond issue, the circulation of information—the core function of public relations—is an essential aspect of government administration. Skilled public relations professionals are required at every level of our government to ensure that information is disseminated clearly, efficiently, and to the largest number of people.

> **For students and young professionals who have an interest in public affairs and public service, the city [Washington, D.C.] can provide an amazing opportunity for learning both.**
>
> Tom Martin, former Vice President of Corporate Communications at FedEx Corporation

regarding the external distribution of funds to individuals or entities. The public relations functions of government agencies consist primarily of disseminating information. In particular, government agencies often promote the policies of the current administration and seek support from citizens. Such public relations efforts are also associated with reelection campaigns.

Government entities employ public relations specialists to promote their services, orchestrate fund-raising, spread news of their successes or crises, assist with smooth daily operations or crisis management, implement campaigns

Basic Purposes of Government Public Relations

Ideally, the mission of government is public service; no one makes private profit directly from the operation of governments, and governments are noncommercial. In practice, there is widespread perception that government falls far short of these ideals.

> **A nation of well-informed men who have been taught to know and prize the rights which God has given them cannot be enslaved. It is in the region of ignorance that tyranny begins.**
>
> Benjamin Franklin

public INFORMATION AND PUBLIC AFFAIRS

Since the ancient Egyptians established the first unified state more than 5,000 years ago, governments have engaged in what is now known as public information and public affairs. There has always been a need for government communications, if for no other reason than to inform citizens of the services available and the manner in which they may be used. In a democracy, public information is crucial if citizens are to make intelligent judgments about policies and the activities of their elected representatives. Governments provide information in the hope that citizens will absorb the necessary background to participate fully in the formation of government policies.

Many people, including journalists, often criticize public information activities for simply producing reams of useless news releases promoting individual legislators or justifying questionable policies. Such abuse, coupled with snide news stories about the cost of maintaining government "public relations" experts, rankle dedicated public information officers (PIOs) at the various state and federal agencies who work very hard to keep the public informed with a daily diet of announcements and news stories. One PIO for a California agency said, "I'd like to see the press find out what's going on in state government without us."

Indeed, a major source of media hostility seems to stem from the fact that reporters are heavily dependent

> think
>
> **How does public relations help citizens make more informed choices at the ballot box?**

It is not an exaggeration to say that human history is, to a large degree, rooted in the history of public relations.

on news subsidies. One study found that almost 90 percent of one state government's news releases were used by daily and weekly newspapers.

Public information efforts can be justified in terms of cost-efficiency. The U.S. Department of Agriculture public affairs office, for example, receives thousands of inquiries each year. Two-thirds of the requests can be answered with a simple pamphlet, a brochure, or a link on its website—all produced under the umbrella of public information.

Preventive public relations also saves money. The taxpayers of California spend approximately $7 billion annually to deal with the associated costs of teenage pregnancy. Consequently, $5.7 million spent on a successful education campaign potentially could save the state a great deal of money in the

form of reduced welfare costs. Michigan's $100,000 expenditure to educate citizens about recycling aerosol cans does much to limit the costs of opening more landfills.

One Associated Press reporter acknowledged in a story that government information does have value. He wrote:

> While some of the money and manpower goes for self-promotion, by far the greater amount is committed to an indispensable function of a democratic government—informing the people. What good would it serve for the Consumer Product Safety Commission to recall a faulty kerosene heater and not go to the expense of alerting the public to its action? An informed citizenry needs the government to distribute its economic statistics, announce its antitrust suits, tell about the health of the president, give crop forecasts.

According to William Ragan, former director of public affairs for the U.S. Civil Service Commission, government information efforts have the following objectives:

- Inform the public about the public's business. Communicate the work of government agencies.
- Improve the effectiveness of agency operations through appropriate public information techniques. Explain agency programs so that citizens understand and can take actions necessary to benefit from them.
- Provide feedback to government administrators so that programs and policies can be modified, amended, or continued.
- Advise management on how best to communicate a decision or a program to the largest number of citizens.
- Serve as an ombudsman. Represent the public and listen to its representatives. Make sure that individual problems of taxpayers are satisfactorily solved.
- Educate administrators and bureaucrats about the role of the mass media and ways to work with media representatives.

THE federal GOVERNMENT

t he U.S. government may well be both the world's premier collector of information and one of its greatest disseminators of information. Advertising is a key governmental activity. Federal agencies spend several hundred million dollars each year on public service advertising, primarily to promote military recruitment, government health services, and the U.S. Postal Service.

The White House

At the apex of government public relations efforts is the White House—that is, the president and his staff. The president receives more media attention than Congress and all the federal agencies combined. It is duly reported when the president visits a neighborhood school, tours a housing development, meets a head of state, or even takes his wife to New York City on a date.

All presidents have taken advantage of the intense media interest to implement public relations strategies to improve their popularity, generate support for programs, and explain embarrassing policy decisions. And each president has his own communication style.

Ronald Reagan was considered by many to be a master communicator. A former actor, he was extremely effective on television and could make his remarks seem spontaneous even when he was reading a teleprompter. He understood the importance of using symbolism and giving simple, down-to-earth speeches with memorable, personal appeal. Reagan's approach focused on the effective use of carefully packaged sound bites and staged events.

George H. W. Bush (senior) was no Ronald Reagan as a public speaker, but he did project enthusiasm for his job and had a friendly, but formal, working relationship with the White House press corps. Bill Clinton, by comparison, was more populist in his communication style. He was at home with information technology and made effective use of television talk shows. Clinton was most effective when he talked one-on-one with an interviewer or a member of the audience.

President George W. Bush adopted Reagan's approach to stagecraft and symbolism. A team of television and video experts made sure every Bush appearance was masterfully choreographed for maximum visual effect. The Bush administration's concept of stagecraft manifested itself in tight control over information and limited media access. Bush, for example, gave substantially fewer press conferences, interviews, and other media events than either Bill Clinton or his father in their first two years in office.

Barack Obama has also proved to be a master of the media. His campaign rallies were frequently compared to rock concerts. However, Obama has been criticized for

Terrance Hunt, an Associated Press reporter who covered the Reagan administration, says the former president's funeral in 2004 recalled the high style and stagecraft of his presidency. "Presidential appearances were arranged like movie scenes with Reagan in the starring role. There was a heavy emphasis on staging and lighting," says Hunt.

emphasizing style and rhetorical flourish over gravity and substance. Others have worried that his presentation, not unlike that of Vice President Joe Biden or Senator John Kerry (Democrat–Massachusetts), sometimes tends to be a little too verbose and intellectual. Nevertheless, Obama is a skilled orator with a riveting presence in the tradition of John F. Kennedy, Ronald Reagan, and Martin Luther King, Jr.

Congress

The House of Representatives and the Senate are major disseminators of information. Members regularly produce a barrage of news releases, newsletters, recordings, brochures, taped radio interviews, e-mails, electronic newsletters, and videos (often uploaded to YouTube)— all designed to inform voters back home about Congress as well as to keep the congressperson in the minds of voters. In fact, in a recent nine-month period, members of Congress spent approximately $3.5 million on electronic outreach.

Critics complain that most of these materials are self-promotional and have little value. In particular, the franking privilege (free postage) is singled out for the most criticism. The late Senator John Heinz, a Republican from Pennsylvania, once distributed 15 million pieces of mail, financed by taxpayers, during a single election year. Obviously, the franking privilege represents a real advantage for an incumbent during election season.

> **Capitol Hill's press secretaries play a significant role in the shaping of America's messages and consequent public policies. In their role as proxy for individual members, the press secretaries act as gatekeepers, determining what information to share with, and hold from, the media; thus, they have command over news shared with the citizenry.**
>
> Edward Downes, Boston University

Each member of Congress also employs a press secretary.

Federal Agencies

Public affairs officers (PAOs) and public information specialists engage in tasks that would be familiar to any member of the public relations department of a corporation. Specifically, they answer press and public inquiries, write news releases, work on newsletters, prepare speeches for top officials, oversee the production of brochures, and

Pay for Play: U.S. Government Plants Favorable Stories in the Iraqi Press

ethics in ACTION

It is a classic question: What constitutes public information versus propaganda? In November 2005, the *Los Angeles Times* reported that the Pentagon and the U.S. military had contracted with Washington, D.C.–based Lincoln Group to plant more than 1,000 "good-news" stories in several Iraqi Arab language papers. The contract specified that Lincoln would inform the Iraqi people of American goals and the progress being made in an attempt to gain public support for the new Iraqi government. At issue was how the company accomplished this goal. Lincoln paid the editors at papers such as *Azzaman* and *al Sabah* between $40 and $2,000 to publish articles that were supposedly written by local journalists. In reality, many of the stories were prepared by Lincoln staffers, soldiers at

"Camp Victory," and military public relations officers.

According to *New York Times* reporters Jeff Gerth and Scott Shane, the source of the articles and opinion pieces was concealed. Lt Col. Steven A. Boylan defended the practice, arguing that such "pay for play" was necessary because Iraqi papers "normally don't have access to those kinds of stories." Michael Rubin, formerly of the Coalition Provisional Authority, stressed the need for "an even playing field," implying that because the insurgents use deceptive messages, Lincoln's tactics were justified. In contrast, Gen. Peter Pace found the practice to "be detrimental to the proper growth of democracy" and then-President George W. Bush was reportedly "very troubled" by the disclosure. A Pentagon review found the pro-

gram basically "appropriate," although it recommended adhering to guidelines about attribution of authorship. The contract with Lincoln continued with some modifications. In September 2008, Lincoln was one of four firms awarded a $300 million contact for "information operations" in Iraq.

Journalists have widely denounced the practice of "pay for play." "Ethically, it's indefensible," said Patrick Butler, Vice President of the International Center of Journalists in Washington. Likewise, the Public Relations Society of America has issued a condemnation of the practice. Pamela Keaton, Director of Public Affairs for the Congressionally-funded Institute for Peace, worries about the long-term effects of what she labels a propaganda campaign: "It will get to the point where the news media won't trust anybody, and the people won't trust what's being quoted in news articles."

America's Image Overseas

THE YEARS FROM 2001 TO 2009 were not kind to the image of America abroad. A survey of twenty-four nations conducted in 2008 by the Pew Charitable Trusts indicated that 42 percent of French citizens had a favorable view of the United States. And that was the good news—only 31 percent of Germans, 22 percent of Egyptians, and 12 percent of Turks had a positive view of the country. As a result, U.S.-bound tourism declined sharply, foreign investment in the United States was threatened, and allies openly expressed hostility toward American political decisions. *The Guardian*, a liberal newspaper in the United Kingdom, predicted "the end of the era of American Dominance."

But as Mark Twain famously said, "The reports of my death are greatly exaggerated." In one fell swoop, the election of President Barack Obama in November 2008 heralded a new era of good feelings abroad about America and its prospects. As evidenced by Obama's rousing slogan, "Yes, we can," the election capitalized on the public desire for changes, not only at home but overseas as well. "Most French people saw Obama's election as a breath of fresh air and a reaffirmation of American values," said Seth Goldschlager, a U.S. public relations professional working in France. Germans held banners reading "Obama for Chancellor" when he visited during the campaign.

For many non-Americans, President Obama *is* the new face of America. Recognized as the personification of renewed optimism about international cooperation, Obama was awarded the Nobel Peace Prize in late 2009. And although the president's poll numbers had declined somewhat at home by late 2009, surveys abroad continued to suggest that he—and by extension the United States as a whole—remained popular abroad.

Lou Capozzi, PRSA fellow and senior counselor at MS&L, argued in an 2009 article in *The Public Relations Strategist* that public relations professionals can build on the good feelings abroad and play an important role in repairing connections between the United States and the rest of the world. He argues for a foundational approach—marshalling communication skills with cultural sensitivity, publicizing the good things that are being done by industry and organizations, and advocating for the United States.

1. What can we learn about the roles and outcome of government public relations from the election of Barack Obama?

2. If you worked for a firm with a contract to restore the image of George W. Bush's administration, which strategies and tactics would you consider?

3. As a public affairs or information specialist, which steps would you take if public opinion overseas were to turn against President Barack Obama?

plan special events. Senior-level public affairs specialists counsel top management about communications strategies and recommend how the agency should respond to crisis situations.

One of the largest public affairs operations in the federal government is conducted by the U.S. Department of Defense (DOD)—the cabinet-level agency that oversees the armed forces. Its operations vary from the mundane to the exotic.

A particularly exotic assignment for a military public affairs officer is

giving background briefings and escorting the journalists who cover battlefield military operations. When the military initiated the policy of "embedding" journalists within military units during the 2003 invasion and occupation of Iraq, it assigned a large number of PAOs as escorts. The policy of "embedded" journal-

ists has also been used with U.S. forces in Afghanistan. Journalists sometimes complain about restrictions on their freedom, however. For example, there has been criticism of the military's recent decision to forbid embedded journalists from photographing troops killed in action in Afghanistan.

The Pentagon (a nickname for the U.S. Department of Defense, derived from architecture of the agency's headquarters) also engages in recruitment drives. One tactic, used to bolster recruitment goals, was the payment of $36,000 to United Airlines to run a 13-minute video news release entitled "Today's Military" as part of the in-flight entertainment package. The campaign, which described exciting military jobs such as an Air Force language instructor and animal care specialist based in Hawaii, was designed to appeal to parents or other adult role models who might recommend the military to children or relatives.

Another major operation of the Pentagon is assisting Hollywood with the production of movies. More than twenty public information specialists work as liaisons with the film and television industries. They review scripts and proposals, advise producers on military procedures, and decide how much assistance, if any, a film or TV show

portraying the military should receive. Movies portraying the military in a positive light, such as *Transformers: Revenge of the Fallen* (2009), *Iron Man* (2008), *Pearl Harbor* (2001), and *Saving Private*

think — How do corporate public relations and government public relations differ?

Ryan (1998), are more likely to receive assistance from the military than those with less flattering or ambiguous messages, such as *Stop Loss* (2008), *Redacted* (2007), *Jarhead* (2005), and *Broken Arrow* (1996). The military military also denied requests for assistance from Oliver Stone for *Platoon* (1986) and *Born on the Fourth of July* (1989), presumably because these films often raise questions about government actions and motives.

Other federal agencies also conduct campaigns to inform citizens. In many cases, the agency selects a public relations firm through a bidding process. Ogilvy Public Relations Worldwide was awarded six government contracts in October 2009. Its clients include the Centers for Disease Control and Prevention, the U.S. Department of Health and Human Services, and the Department of Veteran Affairs. The Reardon Group, a public relations firm based in Washington, D.C., received a $1.5 million contract from the Pentagon to assess the "perspective, style and tone" of journalists reporting on military subjects. The contract was canceled in August 2009 because of pressure from advocacy groups such as the First Amendment Center, which questioned "the line between government review of the press and censorship."

Politicians often capitalize on their

Public relations in the line of fire.

Promoting No Child Left Behind

Does the government have the right to promote its programs with taxpayer money, even when partisan issues are involved? Should government agencies acknowledge their role in public relations campaigns? Promotion of the No Child Left Behind (NCLB) Act during the George W. Bush administration raised ethical questions that will face politicians and public relations professionals working for them in the coming years.

Signed into law by President Bush in 2001, the NCLB legislation required that every school provide adequate educational opportunities for all students. From the outset, the Bush administration used public relations strategies to gain support for NCLB from communities and families. For example, the Department of Education paid the Ketchum public relations firm $1 million to produce and distribute video news releases that promoted the programs.

In 2004 investigative journalists discovered that part of the contract with

Ketchum included paying conservative commentator Armstrong Williams $240,000 to promote the NCLB Act in his television and radio appearances. Representative George Miller (Democrat–California) was among many who questioned what appeared to be an illegal promotion of the Bush administration's initiative to gain political advantage.

At the heart of the issue was the use of video news releases (VNRs), which are often run by TV stations without attribution, a common broadcasting practice.

Federal law specifically prohibits the government from using public funds to actively promote or support a partisan issue. The Government Accounting Office ruled in September 2005 that Ketchum failed to openly acknowledge the government's role in the production of the NCLB VNRs and that, as such, the VNRs were covert propaganda.

Although Ketchum no longer promotes the NCLB Act, the firm was awarded a $1.7 million contract by the Federal Communications Commission to publicize the transition from analog to digital television. The "Drop-In Article/Matt Releases" that Ketchum issued about the television format transition often appeared in newspapers without attribution. Known as news subsidies, the practice of distributing information in this way, is embraced widely by PR firms and publishers as a means to communicate their messages to the public BUT it is considered ethical only as long as the source is clearly attributed.

---

connections after they leave office, by going to work for lobbying or public relations companies. For example, former Senator Jim Talent (Republican–Missouri) joined the Public Affairs division of Fleishman-Hilliard in 2007.

Information campaigns are fairly common undertakings in most federal agencies. Sometimes, however, public affairs staffs may find themselves on the front lines of a crisis or in the midst of a controversy that requires handling hundreds of press calls in a single day. The Department of Homeland Security (DHS), which became operational on Janu-

ary 26, 2003, was formed by merging 22 different agencies. As was to be expected in light of such a major reorganization, DHS experienced a variety of growing pains. One problem was cohesion; it took time to get public affairs staffs from so many agencies to operate as a cohesive unit. There were also problems in message formulation. Dennis Murphy, Director of Public Affairs for Border and Transportation Security, told *PRWeek*, "We want to get the word out quickly . . . but operations folks want to make sure we're not saying too much." Another example of communication

breakdowns between government agencies and the public was the dissemination of information to the public about the "Cash for Clunkers" program in 2009. Started on July 27 and ended abruptly on August 24, the program provided cash incentives for consumers to trade their older vehicles in for newer, more fuel efficient models. Lack of clear information about how long the program would last, which cars qualified for trade-in, and how dealers would be reimbursed with rebates led to widespread confusion and created frustration for both consumers and car dealers.

Mexican Government Moves Aggressively to Contain SWINE FLU OUTBREAK

Health officials announced the outbreak of the H1N1 virus, better known as swine flu, in Mexico on March 18, 2009. By late April, news of 80 deaths and approximately 3,600 confirmed cases had been disseminated to the American public. Swine flu was declared a public emergency and the World Health Organization (WHO) announced a pandemic alert level of 5—the second to highest level. In the United States, the Centers for Disease Control and Prevention (CDC) in Atlanta served as a clearinghouse for information about the progress of the disease.

Although the U.S. response in general, and the CDC's efforts in particular, have been widely praised by health officials, politicians, and journalists, comparatively little credit has been given to Mexican health and public information officials. Their swift action and the sacrifices made by the Mexican people appear to have stemmed the tide of what could have been an international pandemic.

In the mid-1980s, Mexico established a network of 11,000 disease surveillance units. Mexico was among the first counties to implement this program, which was originally designed by the CDC. Upon first identifying the disease, Mexican health officials worked closely with the CDC and Canadian geneticists, who mapped the genome within three weeks. On April 29, recognizing the threat posed by the H1N1 infection, the Mexican government suspended nonessential public and private activities for five days.

Effective communication ensured that residents complied with the order—the streets of Mexico City, normally jammed with traffic, were all but empty. Messages were disseminated over a variety of channels. Public communications stressed, for example, that anyone exhibiting symptoms should see a physician for immediate treatment. Most importantly, health officials and government agencies for the most part followed the rules of effective public relations. They delivered messages that were factual, consistent, and repeated. Thus panic did not ensue. Most importantly, closing the country probably averted a pandemic at least through the summer of 2009. It did, however, wreak havoc on the tourism industry and probably cost the country as much as 0.5 percent of its annual GDP.

state GOVERNMENTS

Like the federal government, the government of each of the fifty states disseminates information about its programs to various constituents. States also compete to develop campaigns to encourage tourism, to attract new residents, and to advance the interest of the state. State public information officers are often tasked with encouraging business and economic development. Often, this work is subcontracted to private public relations firms.

For example, Delaware, a small state with fewer than 800,000 people, awarded a public relations firm a $600,000 contract to create a campaign to attract business investment to the state. The public relations firm used the slogan "It's good being first," referring to Delaware's role as the first colonial state to ratify the U.S. Constitution. The public relations firm admitted it was a difficult assignment. But the slogan does

seem to have been a success, allowing a number of tie-ins to promote tourism. Playing on the theme of "first," the state ran a promotion in 2009 offering a free first night when visitors booked at least two nights' lodging at participating hotels.

Publicizing quality of life issues has emerged as a highly competitive arena, drawing on the resources of public relations professionals across many divisions or branches of state government. North Carolina, for

The public relations firm's president told *PRWeek*, "As opposed to having a bad image, Delaware simply has no image at all."

think — Why do states work so hard to attract tourists?

example, saw a 2.2 percent decline in its aggregate crime rate from 2007 to 2008. Public affairs officers from the State Bureau of Investigation, the Attorney General, and Department of Justice publicized the decline. A particular point of pride was that the city of Carey was named the fourth safest city in the United States, according to "City Crime Rankings 2008–2009: Crime in Metropolitan America."

Every state provides an array of public information services. In California, the most populous state, approximately 175 public information officers (PIOs) work in about 70 state agencies. On a daily basis, these PIOs provide routine information to the public and the press on the policies, programs, and activities of the various state agencies.

State agencies conduct a variety of public information and education campaigns, often with the assistance of public relations firms that have been selected via a bidding process. In a typical bidding process, a state agency will issue a request for proposal (RFP) and award a contract on the basis of presentations from competing firms.

One area that is often targeted by public relations campaigns is health and safety. In recent years, most states have spent considerable money convincing people not to smoke. The funds, which typically come from the national tobacco settlement and state-imposed cigarette taxes, have provided somewhat of a windfall for public relations efforts. For instance, California generates approximately $120 million annually from tobacco taxes, 10 percent of which is devoted to antismoking advertising and public relations. In a somewhat ironic twist, as smoking decreases, the amount of taxes collected also decreases, leaving less money to support the campaigns.

The California Department of Health Services runs campaigns on a variety of health issues, such as childhood immunizations, breast cancer screening, and teen pregnancy prevention. The California Highway Patrol also conducts safety campaigns. One recent campaign sought to increase seat belt use and decrease drunk driving accidents among African Americans; this audience was targeted because statistical data indicated that African Americans was less likely to use seat belts and more likely to die in an alcohol-rated crash than members of other demographic groups.

States also promote tourism through advertising and public relations campaigns. Tourism and conventions are the second largest industry in Wisconsin, so the Department of Tourism concentrates on branding Wisconsin as a destination for cheese lovers (350 types of cheese are produced there) and beer drinkers ("Beer Capital of the U.S."). The Illinois Department of Commerce and Economic Opportunity recently awarded a $6.5 million contract to Edelman Worldwide to develop a tourism campaign. Tourism is also big business in Texas. Approximately 500,000 people are employed in the Lone Star State's tourism industry, which generates nearly $57 billion in spending on an annual basis. In 2009, for example, the state spent almost $2 million on public relations and advertising in an effort to lure European travelers to Texas.

In 2006, the Arizona Office of Tourism received the Mercury Award from the Travel Industry of America for its Grand Canyon IMAX Road Show campaign, which was screened in six cities in the United Kingdom. In conjunction with the screenings, British Airways donated six 12-day travel packages to sweepstakes winners. The initiative generated an estimated $555,000 worth of free publicity about Arizona.

local GOVERNMENTS

Cities employ information specialists to disseminate news and information from numerous municipal departments. Agencies include the airport, transit district, redevelopment office, parks and recreation department, convention and visitors bureau, police and fire departments, city council, and the mayor's office.

The information flow occurs in many ways, but the objectives are always to inform citizens about, and help them take full advantage of, government services. The city council holds neighborhood meetings; the airport commission sets up an exhibit showing the growth needs of the airport; the recreation

department promotes summer swimming lessons; and the city's human rights commission sponsors a festival promoting multiculturalism.

Cities also promote themselves to attract new business. According to *PRWeek*, "The competition for cities and wider regions to attract businesses is as intense as ever, experts say, with an estimated 12,000 economic development organizations vying for the roughly 500 annual corporate moves/expansions that involve 250 or more jobs each." Many cities pump millions of dollars into efforts to attract new business through a variety of communication tools, including elaborate brochures,

placement of favorable "success" stories in the nation's press, direct mail, telemarketing, trade fairs, special events, and meetings with business executives.

Cities may promote themselves in an effort to increase tourism. As an example, consider the campaign by the Panama City (Florida) Convention and Visitors Bureau to position itself as a prime destination for college students during spring break. According to *PRWeek*, the bureau spent roughly $300,000 promoting the city through posters, news releases, brochures, advertising, and special events to let students know that they were welcome.

Cities often promote tourism by publicizing their cultural attractions and special events. Initiatives range from traditional tactics, such as issuing press releases, to more ambitious efforts at outreach, such as creating interactive media sites. The city of Little Rock, Arkansas, for example, took an active role in promoting the

"Spring breakers," attracted by public relations efforts of the local government, pump about $135 million into the local economy of Panama City, Florida, annually.

exhibition "World of the Pharaohs: Treasures of Ancient Egypt Revealed" at the Arkansas Arts Center in 2009 by issuing press releases and providing other news subsidies. The city of Boston operates a social media center (http:// www.cityofboston. gov/news/socialmedia.asp) with links to the Facebook, Twitter, YouTube, and LinkedIn sites.

btw...

The nuclear ambitions of North Korea, also known as the Democratic People's Republic of Korea (DPRK), has sparked several recent international crises. Despite assurances that he would cease the country's nuclear weapons programs, dictator Kim Jong-Il has continued to authorize such weapons since at least 1994. International sanctions, embargos, and name calling (George W. Bush labeled Korea as part of the "Axis of Evil") have done little to curb Kim's nuclear aspirations.

More recently, the DPRK has made some rather unexpected overtures to the United States, suggesting that a warmer relationship may eventually be possible. First, the North Koreans welcomed the New York Philharmonic Symphony, which gave a concert at the East Pyongyang Grand Theatre on February 26, 2008. The concert was warmly received. As White House press secretary Dana Perino noted, however, "We consider this to be a concert . . . it's not a diplomatic coup." Second, Kim issued a "special pardon" for Laura Ling and Euna Lee, two American journalists arrested in 2009 for entering North Korea illegally. President Bill Clinton, acting on a "solely private mission," negotiated the release.

These events raise the obvious question of whether Kim and other North Korean leaders are attempting to manage their image through strategic public relations moves. Seasoned diplomats (and public relations professionals) know how to make the most of such opportunities. Time will tell if the DPRK is genuinely interested in opening diplomatic channels, or whether the overtures are merely a smokescreen to draw attention away from larger issues.

It is not possible to learn much from the North Korean press. According to the country's constitution, journalists in the DPRK enjoy freedom of the press. In actuality, any story critical of the government is swiftly censored. Disobedient journalists are routinely jailed—or worse. For citizens, even listening to a foreign broadcast may be considered a serious crime. Businesses or organizations that engage in public relations must ensure that their messages align with the government's position—in other words, those messages must serve as propaganda. According to a report issued by the Committee to Protect Journalists, "When the state controls all media, opposition voices don't get heard, [and] critical analysis of the government's performance is hidden from the public."

WHAT WOULD YOU DO?

Disaster response in Louisiana has improved vastly since hurricanes Katrina and Rita devastated the coast and flooded New Orleans in 2005. Katrina and Rita had horrific impacts, in terms of both physical and emotional damage. And as they attacked the state, it became immediately clear that they represented communication disasters as well, revealing a lack of comprehensive risk management.

One of the dilemmas faced by local, state, and federal governments when a hurricane looms is how and when to warn residents of the danger. If government officials issue warnings too often or too early, or if they raise the alarm in cases where a major hurricane does not hit, there is a risk that residents will become desensitized and learn to disregard warnings. Conversely, officials face criticism and loss of public trust if they fail to warn citizens in a timely manner.

Consider a scenario where another Category V storm looms off the coast of Louisiana. National Oceanographic and Atmospheric Administration (NOAA) meteorologists predict that there is a 65 percent chance that the storm will hit the city in four days—but there is also a chance that it will miss entirely. If you were a public affairs specialist for the mayor of New Orleans, which steps would you take immediately to inform the public? Which channels of communication would you use? How would you structure your message? Which steps would you recommend taking regarding communication with the public if the wrong decisions were made and the situation became a catastrophic disaster? Working with a small group, quickly brainstorm a communication plan.

> **If a newspaper were to quit relying on news releases, but continued covering the news it now covers, it would need at least two or three times more reporters.**
>
> Peter Sandman, David Rubin, and David Sachsman, in *Media: An Introductory Analysis of American Mass Communications*

government
RELATIONS BY
CORPORATIONS

government relations is a specialized component of corporate communications, closely related to lobbying. This activity is so important that many companies, particularly in highly regulated industries, have separate departments of government relations. The reason is simple: The actions of governmental bodies at the local, state, and federal levels have a major influence on how businesses operate. Government relations specialists, often called public affairs specialists, have a number of functions: They gather information, disseminate management's views, cooperate with government on projects of mutual benefit, and motivate employees to participate in the political process.

As the eyes and ears of a business or industry, practitioners in government relations positions spend considerable time gathering and processing information. They monitor the activities of many legislative bodies and regulatory agencies to keep track of issues coming up for debate and possible vote. This intelligence gathering enables a corporation or an industry to plan ahead

think How do the actions of government agencies affect how businesses operate?

and, if necessary, adjust its policies or provide information that may influence the nature of government decision making.

Businesses monitor government in many ways. Probably the most active parties in Washington, D.C., and many state capitals are the trade associations that represent various industries. A Boston University survey showed that 67 percent of the responding companies monitored government activity in Washington, D.C., through their trade associations. The second monitoring effort cited on the list was frequent trips to the city by senior public affairs officers and corporate executives; 58 percent of the respondents said they engaged in this activity. Almost 45 percent of the responding firms reported that they had a company office in the nation's capital.

Government relations specialists also spend a great deal of time disseminating information about their company's position to a variety of key publics. The tactics employed may include informal office visits to government officials or testimony at public hearings. In addition, public affairs people are often required to give speeches or to write speeches for senior executives. They may write letters and op-ed articles, prepare position papers, produce newsletters, and place advocacy advertising.

Although legislators are the primary audience for government relations efforts, the Foundation for Public Affairs reports that 9 out of 10 companies also communicate with employees on public policy issues. Another 40 percent communicate with retirees, customers, and other publics such as taxpayers and government employees.

lobbying

the term *lobbyist* may have been coined by President Ulysses S. Grant, who often sought refuge from the White House by having a cigar and brandy in the Hotel Willard's lobby in Washington, D.C. Grant is said to have used the term to describe the people who sought favors from him when he was engaged in this kind of relaxation.

Today, lobbying is more formal and closely aligned with governmental relations or public affairs; in fact, the distinction between the two often blurs. In part, this overlap occurs because most campaigns to influence impending legislation have multiple levels. One level is informing and convincing the public about the correctness of an organization's viewpoint, which the public affairs specialist does. Lobbyist efforts are aimed at the defeat, passage, or amendment of legislation and regulatory agency policies.

Lobbyists work at the local, state, and federal levels of government. California has approximately 900 registered lobbyists who represent more than 1,600 special-interest groups. The interests represented in the state capital of Sacramento include large corporations, business and trade groups, unions, environmental groups, local governments, nonprofit groups, school districts, and members of various professional groups.

The number and variety of special interests increase exponentially at the federal level. James A. Thurber, a professor of government at American University and a lobbying expert, estimates that Washington, D.C., now has about 260,000 lobbyists, including supporting staffs. This number, says Thurber, doubled during the eight years of the George W. Bush administration. According to him, lobbying is now a $2 billion industry.

Lobbyists represent the interests of virtually the entire spectrum of U.S. business, educational, religious, local, national, and international pursuits. Lobbying is also conducted on behalf of foreign governments and interests. The American–Israel Public Affairs Committee (AIPAC), for example, is a major player in Washington, D.C., because of its impressive resources. According to *The Economist*, "AIPAC has an annual budget of around $60 million, more than 275 employees, an endowment of over $130 million, and a new $80 million building on Capitol Hill.

The diversity of lobbying groups at the federal level is apparent when we consider the continuing debate about health care. Initially opposing new regulations were (1) insurance companies, (2) health maintenance

Many of the "tea parties" held to oppose health care reform in 2009 were organized by a conservative activist group, Americans for Prosperity (AFP).

organization (HMO) trade groups, (3) the U.S. Chamber of Commerce, (4) the National Federation of Independent Business, and (5) the American Association of Health Plans, among others. Groups supporting patient rights included (1) a broad coalition of consumer groups, (2) the American Medical Association, and (3) the Trial Lawyers of America. The pharmaceutical and biotechnology industry, for example, spent approximately $110 million in the first nine months of 2009 to influence health care legislation, which translates to a burn rate of nearly $600,000 per day. According to *Time* magazine, "The drug industry's legion of registered lobbyists numbers 1,228, or about 3.3 lobbyists for every member of Congress." As the debate and legislation evolved, many organizations shifted positions.

Competing lobbying efforts often cancel each other out, which leaves legislators and regulatory personnel with the daunting chore of weighing the pros and cons of an issue before voting. Indeed, *Time* magazine notes that competition among lobbyists representing different sides of an issue does "serve a useful purpose by showing busy legislators the virtues and pitfalls of complex legislation."

A perennial conflict that lobbyists weigh in on is the debate between saving jobs and improving the environment. A coalition of environmental groups constantly lobbies Congress for tougher legislation to clean up industrial pollution or protect endangered species. Simultaneously, local communities and unions may counter that the proposed legislation would result in the loss of jobs and economic chaos.

Most groups claim to be lobbying in the "public interest."

Pitfalls of Lobbying

Although a case can be made for lobbying as a legitimate activity, deep public suspicion exists about the motivations of former legislators and officials who capitalize on their connections and charge large fees for doing what is commonly described as "influence peddling." Indeed, the roster of registered lobbyists in Washington, D.C., includes a virtual who's who of former legislators and government officials. According to the watchdog group Center for Public Integrity, more than 12 percent of current lobbyists are former executives and legislative branch employees. This group includes more than 200 former members of Congress and 42 former agency heads.

The Ethics in Government Act forbids government officials from actively lobbying their former agencies for one year after leaving office. According to critics, this law has had little or no impact. A good case study is the U.S. Department of Homeland Security. Tom Ridge became the first head of the agency when it was established in 2002. He has since left his government position to become a lobbyist with a long list of clients from the security industry that seek contracts with DHS, which has a budget of more than $40 billion to spend. Ridge is not alone. A *New York Times* article written during the George W. Bush administration reported that at least 90 officials at DHS or in the White House Homeland Security office—two-thirds of the most senior executives—have become lobbyists.

Unlike federal agency personnel, members of Congress can become lobbyists immediately after leaving office. Consider former Representative J. C. Watts (Republican–Oklahoma), who announced the formation of a group of lobbying and public affairs firms

Why is it necessary to regulate lobbyists?

exactly one day after leaving office. High-ranking members of Watts' congressional staff moved with him to his new offices to begin their careers as lobbyists of their former colleagues.

Instances of people "cashing in" on connections give the press and public the uneasy feeling that influence peddling is alive and well in the nation's capitol. This practice also gives credence to the cliché, "It's not *what* you know, but *who* you know." The scandal involving lobbyist Jack Abramoff, for example, revealed just how closely tied legislators are to lobbyists. Abramoff's financial mismanagement and willingness to dispense illegal perks to legislators earned him a lengthy prison sentence. House Majority Leader Tom Delay (Republican–Texas) had to resign his leadership post and Ohio Congressman Bob Ney pleaded guilty to two counts of conspiracy and making false statements in the Abramoff scandal. And other legislators and dozens of congressional aides and government officials still remain under scrutiny.

Grassroots Lobbying

Politicians in both parties have regularly decried the influence of lobbyists, but reform has taken a half-century. At least ten times since the first loophole-riddled lobbying regulations were passed in 1946, efforts to update the law failed to get past the legislative obstacles. In 1995, Congress did pass a measure designed to reform lobbying, and President Clinton signed it. Part of the impetus behind this legislation was undoubtedly the impact of polls indicating that the public believed lobbyists had runaway influence over Congress.

One key provision was an expanded definition of who is considered to be a "lobbyist." The 1995 law defines a lobbyist as "someone hired to influence lawmakers, government officials or their aides, and who spends at least 20 percent of his or her time representing any client

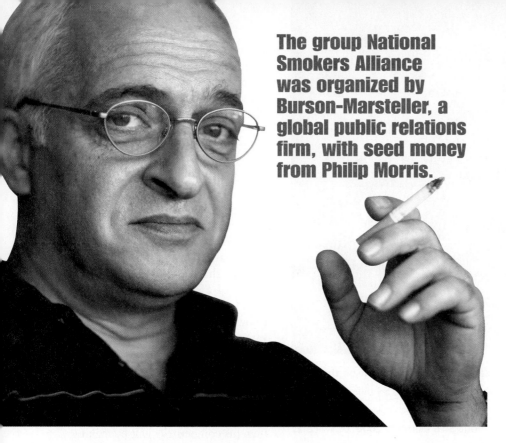

The group National Smokers Alliance was organized by Burson-Marsteller, a global public relations firm, with seed money from Philip Morris.

in a six-month period." Another key provision requires lobbyists to register with Congress and disclose their clients, the issue areas in which lobbying is being done, and roughly the amount they are paid for their services. Violators face civil fines of as much as $50,000.

One area exempted from the lobby reform bill was financial disclosures for so-called grassroots lobbying—the fastest-growing area in the political persuasion business. Grassroots lobbying is now an $800 million industry, according to *Campaigns and Elections*, a bimonthly

magazine for "political professionals." What makes this area so attractive to various groups is that the lack of rules or regulations governing it. The tools of this sort of lobbying include advocacy advertising, toll-free phone lines, bulk faxing, websites, and computerized direct mail aimed at generating phone calls and letters from the public to Congress, the White House, and governmental regulatory agencies.

Grassroots lobbying also involves coalition building. The basic idea is to get individuals and groups with no financial interest in an issue to speak on the sponsor's behalf. The underlying premise is that letters and phone calls from private citizens are more influential than arguments from vested interests. Such campaigns make public interest groups wonder if they really shouldn't be called "Astroturf" campaigns, because the "grass" is often artificial. Michael Pertschuk, codirector of the Advocacy Institute in Washington, D.C., told *O'Dwyer's PR Services Report*, "Astroturf groups are usually founded with corporate seed money that is funneled through PR firms."

election CAMPAIGNS

Public affairs activities and lobbying, either in the halls of Congress or at the grassroots level, are year-round activities. During election years, either congressional or presidential, an army of fund-raisers, political strategists, speechwriters, and communications consultants mobilize to help candidates win elections.

The high cost of running for office in the United States has made fund-raising virtually a full-time,

year-round job for every incumbent and aspirant to office. In fact, American-style campaigning is the most expensive in the world.

Candidates retain professionals to organize fund-raising activities. A standard activity in Washington, D.C., and other major cities across the country is the luncheon, reception, or dinner on behalf of a candidate. *The Wall Street Journal*, for example, reported that 14 such events were held on a single day,

raising $650,000 for Congressional incumbents. Individual donors and lobbyists for various organizations regularly attend these events. Although a chicken dinner or a cheese platter with crackers and champagne are not exactly worth $2,000 per person in literal terms, the event shows support for the candidate and allows donors to have contact with him or her. No business is actually discussed, but the occasion gives both individuals and lobbyists

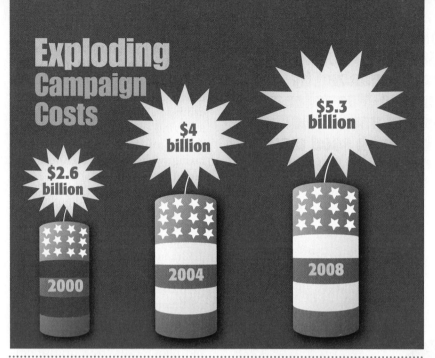

Exploding Campaign Costs

$2.6 billion — 2000

$4 billion — 2004

$5.3 billion — 2008

According to *The Economist,* a colossal $5.3 billion was spent on the 2008 Congressional elections, which topped the unprecedented $4 billion spent on the 2004 campaigns. In 2000, spending was just two-thirds of that spent in 2004. The White House race alone cost about $1.6 billion in 2008, or twice as much as the 2004 presidential race. Just the paid advertising by the two major presidential candidates in 2004 topped $600 million.

for special interests an opportunity to show the "flag" and perhaps indirectly influence legislation or open the door for personnel appointments at a later date after the election, if the candidate wins.

Some consultants specialize in direct mail and telemarketing. They are assisted by firms that have developed computer databases and mailing lists. Aristotle Publishers, for example, claims to have records on 128 million registered voters. A candidate can obtain a list of prospects tailored using any number of demographic variables, including party affiliation, voting record, contribution record, age, geographic location, and opinions on various issues.

Other firms handle mass mailings on behalf of candidates. Kiplinger Computer and Mailing Services is capable of running 10,000 envelopes per hour and printing personalized letters at a rate of 120 pages per minute.

The latest tool for fund-raising and reaching supporters is the Internet. One use of the Internet is for research. *The Wall Street Journal,* for example, reported that an organization supporting the presidential candidacy of Senator John Kerry (Democrat–Massachusetts) in Concord, New Hampshire, was able to track down Democratic women voters, aged 18 to 30, who were interested in abortion rights. Within

seconds, the computer was able to generate the names of 812 local women and provide a street map marking their addresses. Members of Planned Parenthood and other Kerry supporters followed up on this information by making a door-to-door visits on behalf of the candidate.

Although the Internet was used to some extent for campaign fund-raising and building grassroots support during the 2000 presidential election, its effectiveness was not fully realized until the 2004 election. In that year, former Vermont governor Howard Dean (a Democrat) took advantage of the Internet to build a grassroots network, motivate potential voters, and—perhaps most importantly—raise funds. Dean also used social networks such as Meetup.com to interact with constituents. Dean's campaign initially had fewer financial resources than his competitors, but by making efficient use of the Internet, he soon leveled the playing field by raising a large amount of money thanks to thousands of small web-generated donations.

Candidates during the 2008 campaign wisely followed Dean's strategy of using the Internet to mobilize their supporters and obtain donations. Although some have argued that no one candidate exploited its full potential (see the chapter-opening box), Barack Obama achieved notable success by leveraging technology to build core support among college students, young professionals, and independents. Effective use of social media was one crucial factor that allowed the relatively unknown candidate to outmaneuver more experienced and better financed contenders to secure the Democratic Party nomination and eventually defeat Republican candidate John McCain.

Like Dean in 2004, Obama raised an enormous sum of money online by soliciting small donations. In March 2008, for example, he raised $40 million—90 percent of which came in the form of donations of $100 or less. Advisors helped

Lobbyist's To-Do List

Professional fund-raisers recruit lobbyists to handle the following tasks:

- *Hock tickets*
- *Decide whom to invite*
- *Design and mail invitations*
- *Employ people to make follow-up calls*
- *Rent the room and hire the caterer*
- *Make name tags*
- *Tell the candidate who came—and who didn't*
- *Hound attendees to make good on their pledges*

> **"The Obama campaign has come closest to achieving the Holy Grail of politics on the Internet—converting online enthusiasm to offline action."**
>
> Andrew Rasiej, a leading analyst of online politics

Obama crafted a strategy to interact with supporters online, encouraging them to submit content via sites such as Facebook, YouTube, and Twitter. YouTube videos by Obama Girl were particularly memorable examples of his grassroots online support. Obama interacted with wired voters by post regularly on his Facebook site and sending a constant stream of tweets. A recap of each campaign stop was shared, along with news of upcoming rallies and events. By contrast, Republican candidate John McCain made what was perhaps a fatal error that disconnected him from younger voters—he admitted he knew almost nothing about computers or the Internet.

Of course, there is a downside to reliance on the Internet and social media. Candidates must surrender some measure of control over the message and discussion. Any gaffes are instantly amplified through retweets and message boards. Constant vigilance is needed to rebut gossip and misinformation. Also, the opposition can create rogue websites that spoof or mimic the candidate's official site. Despite these caveats, the Internet and social media have proven to be effective as both a public relations tactic and strategy. As Kate Kenski of the National Annenberg Election Survey notes, "Considering that over half of young adults are using the Internet for obtaining political information, the Internet will continue to capture a larger share of where people get their political information with each passing election cycle." Candidates in the future will ignore it at their peril.

Candidates in election campaigns also employ groups of consultants and other technicians such as position paper writers, speechwriters, graphic artists, computer experts, webmasters, media strategists, advertising experts, radio and television producers, public affairs experts, pollsters, and public relations specialists. A highly visible and critical job is done by advance people, who spend many hours organizing events, arranging every detail, and making sure a cheering crowd, armed with enthusiastic signs, is on hand when the candidate arrives. On a single day, for example, a presidential candidate may give five to seven talks at rallies in multiple states. As is the case with most of the public relations activities and events described in this chapter, a cadre of individuals often work behind the scenes to orchestrate these events and initiatives. To ensure that the candidate's speech is received under the best possible circumstances, public relations professionals mobilize the audience and the media, manage potential risks, avert or handle any crises that arise, and provide assessment of the results with polls and reports after each speech.

THE GENERATIONAL GAP:
Social Media and the 2008 Campaign

BARACK OBAMA
- In his 40s
- Internet savvy
- Uses a BlackBerry
- Advanced degree (Harvard Law School)
- Young campaign team well-versed in social media
- He "gets it."

JOHN McCAIN
- In his 70s
- Notable lack of knowledge about new media
- Doesn't "do" e-mail
- B.A. degree
- Old-style campaigner
- Older campaign team recruited from George W. Bush years
- He doesn't "get it."

Summary

What Are the Basic Purposes and Functions of Public Relations in Government Organizations? p. 350

- Governments have always engaged in campaigns to educate, inform, motivate, and even persuade the public.
- In the United States, Congress forbids federal agencies from "persuading" the public, so the emphasis is on "public information" efforts.

Which Public Relations Activities Do Government Organizations Engage in at the Federal, State, and Local Levels? p. 352

- The U.S. federal government is the largest disseminator of information in the world.
- The apex of all government information and public relations efforts is the White House; the president's every move and action are chronicled by the mass media. Presidents throughout history have used this media attention to lead the nation, convince the public to support administration policies, and get reelected.
- All agencies of the federal government employ public affairs officers and public information specialists. Members of Congress also engage in extensive information-focused efforts to reach their constituents.
- Various states employ public information officers to tell the public about the activities and policies of various agencies. In addition, state agencies conduct a number of campaigns to inform the public about health and safety issues and to promote the state as a tourist destination.
- All major cities employ public information specialists to tell citizens about city services and promote economic development.

What Are Public Affairs, Governmental Relations, and Lobbying? p. 360

- A major component of corporate communications is public affairs, which primarily deals with governmental relations at the local, state, national, and even international levels.
- Public affairs specialists build relationships with civil servants and elected officials; they also monitor governmental actions that may affect their employer or client.
- Trade groups, which are typically based in state capitals or in Washington, D.C., have public affairs specialists representing various professions and industries who engage in governmental relations.
- A public affairs specialist primarily provides information about an organization's viewpoint to the public and government entities. A lobbyist has a more specialized function—he or she directly works for the defeat, passage, or amendment of legislation and regulatory agency policies.
- In recent years, public concern has been heightened about "influence peddling" in terms of former legislators and other officials becoming lobbyists and "cashing in" on their knowledge and connections. To curb abuse, several laws have been passed to regulate lobbyists.

What Role Does Public Relations Play in Election Campaigns? p. 363

- An army of specialists, including public relations experts, are retained by major candidates to organize and raise money for election campaigns.
- In recent years, the Internet has played an important role in raising money, generating high visibility for candidates, and increasing the number of registered voters.

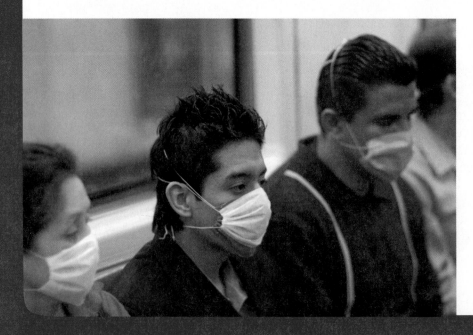

QUESTIONS for *Review* and *Discussion*

1. What are the basic purposes and functions of government relations?

2. What is the difference between someone who works in corporate public affairs (government relations) and a lobbyist?

3. Many lobbyists are former legislators and government officials. Do you think they exercise undue influence in the shaping of legislation? Why or why not?

4. Fund-raisers play a crucial role in elections. Would you like to be a political fund-raiser? Why or why not?

5. Why do government agencies engage in "public information" efforts instead of "public relations" activities? Are there any laws involved? If so, what are they?

6. Federal agencies engage in any number of public information campaigns. What is your opinion on this practice? Are these campaigns just a waste of taxpayer dollars, or are they legitimate and necessary?

7. List some examples of public relations campaigns run by state or local governments.

8. How does public relations at the local level differ from public relations efforts at the state and federal levels? Which channels are typically used by federal and local officials to disseminate messages to the public?

9. How do grassroots groups use technology to disseminate their message? What are the benefits and risks of using social media to promote an agenda within the political arena?

the
THINKSPOT
www.thethinkspot.com

TACTICS

PRWeek

Laura Gross, *PRWeek*, April 15, 2009

First 100 Days of the Obama Administration: PR Review

President Obama's effective use of social media in his campaign marked a watershed in political communication. Obama is quite tech savvy, and has even insisted on keeping his personal BlackBerry—an unprecedented move.

When a problem arises, it is often necessary to express a shared sense of outrage with an audience to win in the court of public opinion. Accepting responsibility is also often a wise public relations move for a politician—so long as he or she does not appear weak or defeatist. This tactic of Barack Obama contrasts sharply with that his predecessor, George W. Bush. When asked which mistakes he made during the 2004 presidential campaign, Bush stated that he could not recall any.

Obama's communication style creates the impression of an intimate relationship between communicator and the audience. As a result, his message may be more likely to be discussed by the public and easily spread by word of mouth.

Washington has definitely seen change since President Obama has come to town—not just with policy, but with a public relations strategy, too. President Obama has kept his promise of governing in a more transparent and open way—there have been press conferences, numerous media interviews, and frequent online communication. The Obama–Biden team is showing leadership when this country is hungry for direction.

The first 100 days have not been perfect, but when faced with adversity—this administration knows how to respond. When Sen. Daschle withdrew his nomination for [Health and Human Services] secretary, Obama took full responsibility for the vetting problem. When people were outraged over the AIG bonuses, President Obama admitted he was angry and upset, too. He did not place the blame on another elected official or another political party; he said he would do whatever it took to fix this problem.

Obama has personally stepped up to the plate. When the stimulus package was in jeopardy, he empowered grassroots supporters to call their congressperson to say they support the bill. Obama communicated this message through e-mail campaigns, town hall meetings, and media interviews. He has constantly repeated the same message by saying that the economy will not be fixed overnight. This seems to be working; according to a recent *Washington Post*–ABC News poll, Americans do not blame Obama for the downfall in the economy.

It is always good to keep campaign promises—not only for PR purposes, but more importantly because it is the reason candidates get elected. And Obama has done just that—Guantanamo will be closing, restrictions on federal funding for stem cell research have been reversed, and troops will come home from Iraq. The rollout of announcements like this has been strategic and well planned. Whether it is at a well-timed signing ceremony, media interviews, and press conferences or through an online component, this administration has successfully spoken about why its decisions are the right ones.

Press conferences have been more than just an opportunity for national media outlets to ask questions—Obama and his team are savvy enough to know that the media landscape is changing and they must adjust. At his first news conference, he called on a blogger from *The Huffington Post*. And at his other press conference, reporters from *Ebony*, Univision, and *Stars and Stripes* asked questions, too. Smart move—this enabled him to get specific messages out. For example, the Univision reporter asked about his Mexico border policy, while the *Stars and Stripes* reporter asked about benefits for veterans—two things Obama has been touting.

It is also important to realize that White House Press Secretary Robert Gibbs is not just a mouthpiece for the administration—he is a part of the inner circle of advisors. Reporters know that he has the ear of the president and is part of important meetings, which makes him trustworthy and extremely reliable. He is serious when he needs to be, yet has proven he has witty sense of humor, too.

And Michelle Obama's PR strategy has also been successful—visiting government agencies to boost morale, appearing on the cover of *Vogue*, *People*, and *O* and talking about life at the White House. Her brutal honesty is refreshing. She has spoken about her family's home life, which makes the Obamas seem like your next-door neighbors. While she has kept her promise to be "mom-in-chief," she is also using her celebrity status to also talk about issues she and her husband care about.

Not everything has been PR perfect for the Obama administration. I personally love a good sarcastic, funny comment, but President Obama needs to realize that the world's stage is not an episode of *30 Rock*. He still needs to be more careful with his off-the-cuff remarks (i.e., Special Olympics) and flashing a smile at the wrong time.

Overall, I believe that Obama and his communications team are extremely focused. They have responded quickly to problems and have been successful in managing their daily message. They answer questions directly, 'fess up when they have made a mistake, and are remaining cool under a lot of pressure. The first 100 days of the Obama administration have been a definite PR success.

Former President George W. Bush also had this characteristic—perhaps even more so than Obama. His demeanor suggested both familiarity and friendliness. But it is possible to go too far in this regard: One risks losing the sense of gravitas that befits a leader.

Humor appeals to the audience, humanizes a leader, and can even help break through an impasse. Bill Clinton, George W. Bush, and even Richard Nixon could, on occasion, deliver a good one-liner. Again, it is possible to go too far: The public is not likely to appreciate a comedian-in-chief.

In today's highly contentious political landscape, it is important to reinforce messages through a variety of channels. Effective politicians understand the power of repetition. Obama's addresses on YouTube can be easily shared by his audience.

Presidents, to a greater or lesser degree, understand that the Press Secretary wields enormous power in the formation of public opinion. Robert Gibbs, who has become an important member of President Obama's inner circle, demurs, saying, "I'm just the messenger."

Concise, incisive, and repeated messages delivered on a regular basis can help persuade a target audience. This is one reason why the combination of social media and micro-targeting has emerged recently as a successful PR tactic.

18 NONPROFIT,

Apple Splits with U.S. Chamber of Commerce over Climate Change

In the fall of 2009, Apple Corporation resigned from the U.S. Chamber of Commerce, the country's largest industry advocacy group, citing a difference of opinion over proposed climate change legislation. The letter sent to Chamber president Thomas Donahue by Apple's vice president of worldwide government affairs, Catherine A. Novelli, indicated that "we strongly object to the Chamber's recent comments opposing the EPA's efforts to limit greenhouse gases" and noted that the "Chamber's position differs so sharply from Apple." Other companies had already resigned from the Chamber citing the same reason—Exelon, PNM Resources, and Pacific Gas & Electric. Even so, Apple was, according to *Business Week,* "the first highly visible consumer brand" to split with the Chamber on the issue.

The Chamber has long opposed (through lobbying) many of the provisions of the Clean Air Act as well as initiatives to reduce carbon emissions through cap-and-trade programs. Apple, in contrast, has gradually emerged as a leading "green" company, recently advertising its efforts to reduce the carbon footprint associated with its products. By late 2009, the schism between Chamber and Apple had become an irreconcilable gulf.

At issue are two dissenting worldviews. According to polls, public opinion in the United States is split just about evenly on

HEALTH, AND EDUCATION

the issue of climate change. One view—represented by the U.S. Chamber of Commerce, and presumably most of its 3 million members—is that global warming has been exaggerated and that the steps needed to curb warming will hurt American competitiveness. The other position—adopted by Apple—suggests that the evidence for climate change is overwhelming and steps to reduce emissions are necessary. According to *Newsweek*, Apple has recognized that arguing against the existence of climate change or opposing carbon limits may be "bad for business."

❶ **What are some of the ways that the U.S. Chamber of Commerce could respond to Apple's resignation?**

❷ **What are the benefits and risks of the Chamber's position?**

❸ **Which strategies and tactics would you recommend as a public relations professional to reopen the dialogue?**

the role OF PUBLIC RELATIONS IN NONPROFIT, HEALTH, AND EDUCATION ORGANIZATIONS

nonprofit organizations, which are often referred to as *charities* or *not-for-profit organizations*, encompass a broad area of public relations work. In the United States, there are almost 2 million such groups, according to GuideStar, an organization that compiles information on nonprofits. Approximately 7 million people work in the nonprofit sector. The range of nonprofit institutions is astounding—from membership organizations, advocacy groups, and social service organizations, to educational organizations, hospitals and health agencies, small city historical societies, and global foundations that disperse multimillion-dollar grants.

Nonprofit organizations are noncommercial entities whose main purpose is to serve the public interest. By definition, they do not distribute monies to shareholders or owners. This is not to say that nonprofit organizations

cannot generate income or hold assets, but rather that a number of complicated restrictions regulate how their income may be generated and how their finances must be managed. From a public relations perspective, nonprofit organizations are often represented as fostering goodwill, and as beacons of social responsibility.

Nonprofits are tax exempt. The federal government grants them this status because these organizations enhance the well-being of their members, as is the case for trade associations, or enhance the human condition in some way, as is the case for environmental groups and medical research organizations. Many nonprofit organizations could not survive if they were taxed. Nonprofit organizations do

think What are the key characteristics of a nonprofit organization?

A crucial point about nonprofit organizations is that they are generally set up to serve the public good.

Traditionally, non-profit social agencies have been seen as the "good guys" in our society—high-minded, compassionate organizations whose members work to help people achieve better lives.

All nonprofit organizations create communication campaigns and programs, including special events, brochures, radio and television appearances, and websites to stimulate public interest in organizational goals and invite further public involvement. Recruiting volunteers and keeping them enthusiastic are essential ends. Most of these organizations also establish fund-raising goals and formulate plans to raise money, although government agencies are funded primarily through taxes.

Competition, Conflict, and Cooperation in Nonprofit, Health, and Education Organizations

For many nonprofit organizations, partnerships are mutually beneficial. The United Way is a good case in point—many business and nonprofit organizations, ranging from the National Football League to the Advertising Council to numerous

Philanthropic, cultural, and religious organizations are often funded by corporations or wealthy people who are motivated by altruism, seeking public recognition and improved reputation, or both.

local organizations, partner with the United Way. This relationship maximizes donations to the United Way, which are distributed to hundreds of associated charities. Unfortunately, the frustrating reality is that nonprofits, instead of partnering, often compete with one another for members, funds, and other resources. For example, universities or colleges within the same state compete for funding from their respective state governments, even as they enter into collaborative partnerships with one another to obtain federal funding. Hospitals compete for "customers," but need to work together to resolve shared concerns and issues. Government agencies struggle for budget allocations, but then must cooperate to serve the public.

Competition among nonprofit agencies for donations is intense. For many nonprofit groups, fund-raising, by necessity, is their most time-consuming activity. Without generous contributions from companies and individuals, nonprofit

not have shareholders who invest in the organizations and buy and sell stocks. As a result, they face the never-ending task of raising money to pay their expenses, finance their projects, and recruit both volunteer workers and paid employees.

At first glance, federal and state governments, state universities, and health and human services organizations or nonprofit hospitals might seem to have little in common with the Public Relations Society of America (PRSA), the National Academy of Songwriters, Mothers Against Drunk Driving (MADD) and the American Red Cross. Yet all engage in the same types of public relations tasks to succeed and thrive.

Because these organizations are not profit oriented, the practice of public relations on their behalf differs somewhat from public relations activities conducted in the business world.

think How do the public relations tactics of advocacy groups differ from those of cultural and religious organizations?

Nonprofit organizations have a willingness to cooperate but must also compete for limited or scarce resources. Sometimes nonprofit groups enter into partnerships based on common interests, such as the United Way. In general, however, when advocating their individual interests, they are no different from business organizations that must struggle for market share.

organizations could not exist. The scope of philanthropy in the United States and the amount of the money needed to keep voluntary service agencies operating are staggering. In 2008, American contributions to charity totaled $307 billion, according to the Giving Institute. Other funds are donated to specialized nonprofit organizations that do not fall under the "charity" mantle, and still more are contributed by federal, state, and local governments.

Activist groups that espouse certain causes may sometimes come into conflict with other organizations that embrace different values, leading to high-profile disputes. For example, in recent years, a number of religious organizations have tussled with groups that advocate for secular values. The American Civil Liberties Union (ACLU), a nonprofit organization founded in 1920 "to defend and preserve the individual rights and liberties guaranteed to every person in this country by the Constitution and laws of the United States," often clashes with the American Center for Law and Justice, a conservative group founded by Pat Robertson to preserve "religious liberty, the sanctity of human life, and the two-parent, marriage-bound family." Although both organizations state that they are committed to preserving "liberty," their respective views of what constitutes "liberty" are often diametrically opposed.

fund-raising

finding ways to pay the bills is a critical problem for virtually all nonprofit organizations, including those that receive government grants to finance part of their work. Fund-raising methods are highly developed, particularly for nonprofit organizations.

Although the largest, most publicized donations are made by corporations and foundations, individual contribution totals far exceed combined corporate and foundation giving. In fact, individual contributions account for approximately 75 percent of annual U.S. philanthropic donations, amounting to $223 billion.

Depending on their needs, voluntary organizations may try to catch minnows—hundreds of small contributions—or they may angle for the huge marlin—a large corporate gift. Some national organizations raise massive sums. In 2008, for example, the American Red Cross raised approximately $3.2 billion, followed by Food for the Poor ($1.5 billion), Feed the Children ($1.2 billion), World Vision ($1.1 billion), and the Brother's Brother Foundation ($1.1. billion). Charities often receive a flood of donations following well-publicized catastrophes, such as Hurricane Katrina in 2005 or the January 12, 2010, earthquake in Haiti.

Public relations professionals may participate directly in fund-raising by organizing and conducting solicitation programs; alternatively, they may serve as consultants to specialized development departments in their organizations. Organizations may employ professional firms to conduct their fund-raising campaigns on a fee basis. In those instances, the organizations' public relations professionals usually serve a liaison function.

Motivations for Giving
An understanding of what motivates individuals and companies to give money or volunteer their time is important to anyone involved in fund-raising. An intrinsic desire to share a portion of one's resources,

Charitable Contributions Decline in Response to Global Economic Woes

Charitable giving is a well-established U.S. institution. American contributions to charity totaled approximately $325 billion in 2007, according to the Giving Institute. The recession that began in 2008, however, took a toll on giving—sixty leading charities reported an average decline of 38 percent in that year. The following is a breakdown of the various categories by distribution of funds.

In 2008, charitable contributions totaled $307.7 billion in the United States.

U.S. Contributions to Charity by TYPE OF DONOR Organization, 2008

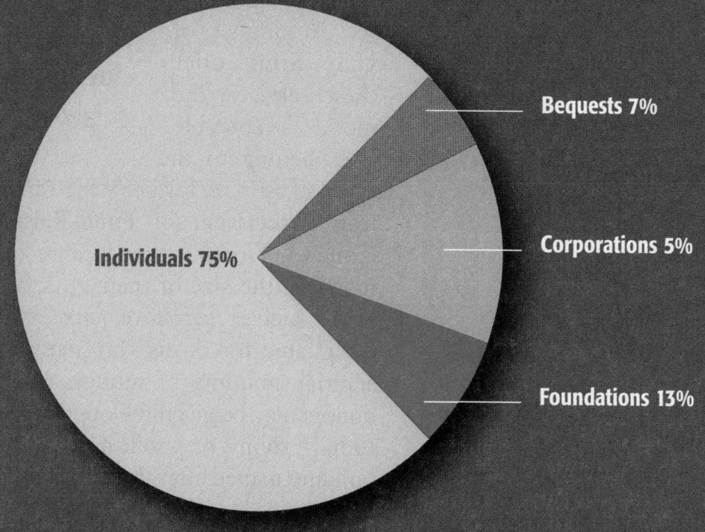

- Individuals 75%
- Bequests 7%
- Corporations 5%
- Foundations 13%

U.S. Contributions to Charity by TYPE OF RECIPIENT Organization, 2008

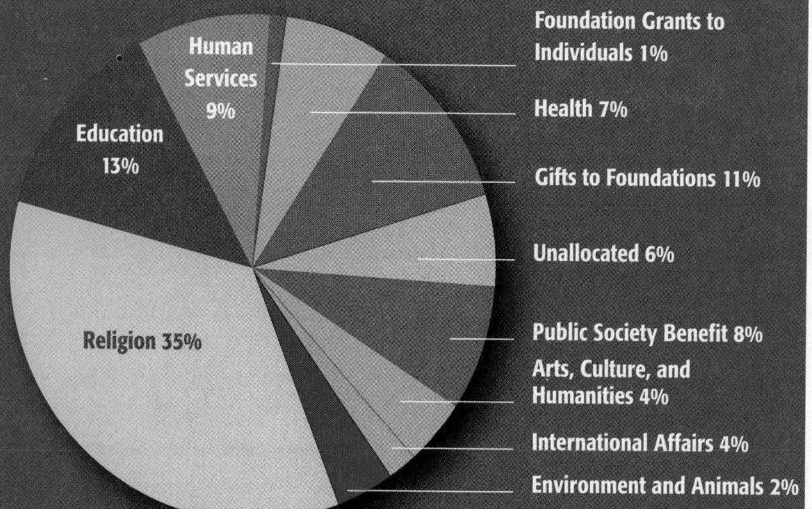

- Human Services 9%
- Education 13%
- Religion 35%
- Foundation Grants to Individuals 1%
- Health 7%
- Gifts to Foundations 11%
- Unallocated 6%
- Public Society Benefit 8%
- Arts, Culture, and Humanities 4%
- International Affairs 4%
- Environment and Animals 2%

however small, with others—an inherent generosity possessed in some degree by almost everyone—is a primary factor. Another urge—also very human, if less laudable—is ego satisfaction. The donor who makes a large contribution gets a building named for his or her family, and individuals get their names published in a list of contributors. Peer pressure—overt or subtle—is a third factor. Saying "no" to a direct request from a friend, neighbor, or coworker is difficult. Despite the recent downturn in the economy, a Gallup Poll found that while the number of people who donated to charitable causes declined slightly, volunteerism actually rose between 2008 and 2009.

Fund-raising involves risks as well as benefits. If an organization is to maintain public credibility, then both adherence to high ethical standards when soliciting contributions and close control of fund-raising costs, so that expenses constitute a reasonable percentage of the funds collected, are essential. Numerous groups have had their reputations severely damaged by disclosures that only a small portion of the money they raise is actually applied to the causes they advocate, with the rest being consumed by solicitation expenses and administrative overhead.

Fund-Raising Methods

Corporate and foundation donations. Public relations professionals generally implement different types of campaigns for fund-raising efforts that target corporations versus those that target individuals. Organizations seeking donations from major corporations normally do so through the local corporate offices or sales outlets. Some corporations give their local offices a free hand in making donations to local groups up to a certain amount. Even when the donation decisions are made at corporate headquarters, local recommendations are important. Requests to foundations generally should be

WHY and HOW We Give

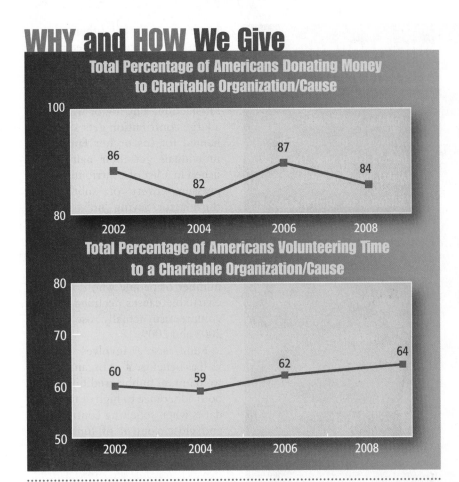

Total Percentage of Americans Donating Money to Charitable Organization/Cause

- 2002: 86
- 2004: 82
- 2006: 87
- 2008: 84

Total Percentage of Americans Volunteering Time to a Charitable Organization/Cause

- 2002: 60
- 2004: 59
- 2006: 62
- 2008: 64

In a Gallup Organization survey commissioned by Independent Sector, 53 percent of those responding cited "assisting those who are less fortunate" as their personal motive for volunteering and giving. The second most frequently cited reason was gaining a feeling of personal satisfaction; religion was third. Only 6 percent cited tax considerations as a major reason for giving.

made to the main office, which typically provide application forms.

Increasingly, corporations are establishing programs that match employee donations. Most commonly, matching is done on a dollar-for-dollar basis: If an employee gives $1 to a philanthropic cause, the employer does the same. Some corporations match donations at a two-to-one rate, or even higher. Corporations also make contributions to charities in less direct ways, some of which are quite self-serving. For example, Goldman Sachs announced that it would donate about $1 billion to charity in 2009. Pundits and many members of the public were skeptical of the corporation's motives, considering they were the recipients of billions of federal bailout dollars and were scheduled to pay more than $22 billion in bonuses to top executives the same year.

Structured capital campaigns. An effort to raise major amounts of money for a new wing of a hospital, for an engineering building on a campus, or for the reconstruction and renovation of San Francisco's famed cable car system is often called a *capital campaign*. In a capital campaign, emphasis is placed on obtaining substantial gifts from corporations and individuals.

Capital campaigns require considerable expertise and, for this reason, many organizations retain professional fund-raising counsel. A number of U.S. firms offer these services; the most reputable ones belong to the Giving Institute, formerly the American Association of Fund-Raising Counsel. Donors often are recognized by the size of their gifts, and terms such as *patron* or *founder* are designated for those who give substantial amounts of money. Major donors may be given the opportunity to have rooms or public areas in the building named after them.

Direct mail. Although direct mail can be an expensive form of solicitation because of the costs of developing or renting mailing lists, preparing the printed materials, and mailing them, this tactic has become increasingly competitive. An organization can reduce its costs by conducting an effective local, limited, direct mail campaign. Attractive, informative mailing pieces that motivate

think

Which strategies and tactics can public relations professionals use to incentivize giving?

btw...

Organizations must regularly analyze the competition they face from other fund-raising efforts. The public becomes resentful and uncooperative if approached too frequently for contributions. This rationale explains why the United Way of America exists: to consolidate solicitations of numerous important local service agencies into a single unified annual campaign. The voluntary United Way management in a community, with professional guidance, announces a campaign goal. The money collected in the drive is distributed among participating agencies according to a percentage formula determined by the United Way budget committee.

One key concept of a capital campaign is that 90 percent of the total amount raised will come from only 10 percent of the contributors. In a $10 million campaign to add a wing to an art museum, for example, it is not unusual that the lead gift will be $1 million or $2 million.

recipients to donate are keys to successful solicitation. The classic direct mail format consists of a mailing envelope, letter, brochure, and response device, often with a postage-paid return envelope.

Recently, however, *Chronicle of Philanthropy* has reported a sharp decline in direct mail contributions to several large national organizations, such as the Disabled American Veterans and Easter Seals. The publication asserts, "Americans have become increasingly fed up with direct-mail appeals from charities."

Event sponsorship. The range of events that a philanthropic organization can sponsor to raise funds is limited only by the imagination of its members. Participation contests are an especially popular method. Walkathons and jogathons appeal to the American desire to exercise more. Staging parties, charity balls, concerts, exhibitions, and similar events in which tickets are sold is another widely used fund-raising approach. Unfortunately, big parties often create more publicity than profit, with 25 to 50 percent of the money raised going to expenses. Other fund-raising methods include sponsorship of a motion picture premiere, a theater night, or a sporting event. In 2007 the GRAMMY Charity Online raised more than $500,000 in an online auction of

items, including a Mercedes-Benz donated by the Rolling Stones. On a more modest scale, in December 2009, the True Colors Foundation offered lunch and a tarot card reading with pop icon Cyndi Lauper as incentive for donors.

Telethons. A television station sometimes sets aside a block of airtime for a telethon sponsored by a philanthropic organization. The best known of the national telethons is the one conducted annually by comedian Jerry Lewis to raise funds to combat muscular dystrophy. Another high-profile event was the MTV's celebrity telethon to aid victims of the 2010 earthquake in Haiti.

Telephone solicitations. Solicitation of donations by telephone is a relatively inexpensive way to seek funds but is not always effective. Some people resent receiving telephone solicitations. If the recipient of the call is unfamiliar with the cause, it must be explained clearly and concisely—which is not always easy for a volunteer solicitor to do. In addition, there is now a national Do Not Call Registry that prevents fund-raisers from randomly calling people, although legitimate charities are exempt from the regulation. Converting verbal telephone promises into confirmed written pledges is also problematic.

A number of political candidates and political action committees made effective use of robocalls during the 2008 elections. Automated calls cost the candidate or organization only between 5 and 8 cents each. Even though messages are targeted to the potential voters most likely to support a candidate's message, many people have expressed objections to the impersonal nature of robocalls. Even so, the practice persists.

btw...

Rather than depending entirely on contributions, some nonprofit organizations go into business on their own or make tie-ins with commercial firms from which they earn a profit. This approach is increasingly popular, but, like any business venture, entails economic risks that must be carefully assessed. Three types of commercial money-raising are the most common:

> Licensing use of an organization's name to endorse a product and receiving payment for each item sold, such as American Heart Association's commission for its endorsement of Healthy Choice frozen dinners
> Sharing profits with a corporation from sales of a special product, such as Newman's Own salad dressing
> Operating a business that generates revenue for the organization, such as the Metropolitan Museum of Art's gift shop

Online and social media. Using the Internet to fund raise is cost-effective, compared with the cost of sending out thousands of pieces of mail. On the downside, most people are wary of online solicitations. This skepticism likely explains why organizations such as the Salvation Army and Greenpeace, which are highly visible and trusted, have been more successful in soliciting donations online than other, lesser-known organizations. Nevertheless, some smaller groups have used the Internet successfully to raise money. For example, charitywater.org, an initiative founded in 2006 with the goal of providing clean drinking water to impoverished areas, has a particularly well-designed online site that successfully solicits donation.

Since the late 1990s, a variety of advocacy groups have used the Internet to raise funds, generate support, and galvanize their constituents' attitudes. Social media such as blogs, Twitter, Facebook, LinkedIn, and YouTube are vital avenues that allow individuals to easily and interactively engage with causes that they support or oppose. A group of women in India developed the Pink Chaddi (underwear) campaign to oppose paternalistic views. Organizers regularly blog and maintain a Facebook page to chronicle their fight for women's rights.

membership
ORGANIZATIONS

Membership organizations are composed of people who share common business or social interests. Their purpose is mutual help and self-improvement. Membership organizations often use the strength of their common bond to promote the professionalism of their members, endorse legislation, and support socially valuable causes.

Professional Associations
Members of a profession or skilled craft organize for mutual benefit. Examples include the Royal Institute of British Architects, the National Association of Professional Organizers, or the seemingly anachronistic Society of Gilders. Some professional organizations, such as the American Medical Association, also function as advocacy and lobbying groups. In many ways, their goals resemble those of labor unions, in that they seek improved earning power, better working conditions, and public appreciation of their roles in society. Professional associations place their major emphasis on setting standards for professional performance, establishing codes of ethics, determining requirements for admission to a field, and encouraging members to upgrade their skills through continuing education. In some cases, they have quasi-legal power to license and censure members. In most cases, however, professional groups rely on peer pressure and persuasion to police their membership.

Public relations specialists for professional organizations use the same techniques as their colleagues in other branches of practice. Also like their counterparts in trade groups and labor unions, many professional associations maintain offices near the seat of government in Washington, D.C., and the various

think What benefits do member organizations gain from belonging to trade associations?

state capitals, and employ lobbyists to advocate for their positions.

Trade Associations
The membership of a trade association usually comprises manufacturers, wholesalers, retailers, or distributors in the same field. Memberships are held by corporate entities, not individuals. Examples of trade associations include the Electronic Industries Alliance, American Beverage Association, Property Casualty Insurers Association, and National Association of Home Builders. Approximately 6,000 trade and professional associations are active in the United States.

Because federal laws and regulations often can affect the fortunes of an entire industry, about one-third of these groups are based in the Washington, D.C. area. There, association staff members can best monitor Congressional activity, lobby for or against legislation, communicate late-breaking developments to the membership, and interact with government officials on a regular basis.

btw...
One of the most politically active and successful professional associations is the American Medical Association (AMA). With 240,000 physician members, the AMA has developed lobbying and grassroots efforts to influence medical liability, or "tort," reform to its members' advantage. The AMA argues that medical liability settlements are excessive. It provides Physician Action Kits and talking points for members to use when speaking about medical liability reform. In addition, this organization sponsors letter-writing campaigns and provides experts to testify before Congress.

When a news situation develops involving a particular field, reporters frequently turn to the spokesperson of its association for comment. To promote their industry, many trade organizations create video news releases (VNRs) for broadcast on local and national news outlets. Some controversy surrounds this practice, however, because VNRs are often presented by television stations as "straight news" without proper attribution and it is not always clear to the public that the material was underwritten or developed by a trade organization.

Labor Unions

Like trade associations, labor unions represent the interests of an entire industry. Whereas trade associations typically represent the interests of management, however, labor unions advocate on behalf of employees. As with other membership organizations, labor unions lobby for better working conditions, higher wages, increased safety regulations, better benefits, and education for their memberships. Since their apex in the late 1970s, labor unions have suffered serious membership losses in business and industry, but made gains in public employees, which now constitute more than half of America's union members.

Labor unions have been largely responsible for many positive things that Americans today take for granted: the end of child labor, the 40-hour workweek, laws against discrimination in hiring and firing, and the minimum wage. Unions are still are very much a part of the U.S. business scene, representing teachers, players in the National Basketball Association, UPS employees, and many other familiar groups.

Unions rely on public relations tools to assert their strength and influence. Unions employ public relations when communicating with their internal audiences in various companies or organizations. They must keep their memberships informed about the benefits that they receive in return for their dues, including recreational and social programs and representation in communication and negotiations

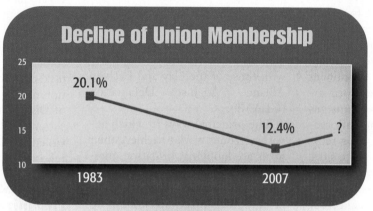

Decline of Union Membership

20.1%

12.4%

?

1983

2007

Union membership declined from 1983 to 2008, according to the U.S. Department of Labor's Bureau of Statistics. However, the number of union members rose by 428,000 between 2007 and 2008, perhaps reflecting workers' concerns about their job security during the economic recession. The percentage of union members is lowest in the private sector and highest in the public sector; 38 percent of all public sector workers belong to a union.

with company management. Labor unions may engage in conflict with management, which typically has the upper hand in negotiations in terms of both financial strength and political clout.

In every national political campaign, unions spend millions of dollars to support candidates they regard as friendly to their cause. Although some of this money goes directly to candidates, significant amounts are devoted to "issue ads" that do not explicitly endorse an individual. Despite rhetoric to the contrary, this practice represents only a fraction of the money spent on issue ads supporting pro-business interests—it enables unions to provide support for candidates beyond the limits imposed on individual campaign contributions. And union spending on political races may well be on the rise in the wake of the January 2010 Supreme Court decision that removed all limits on campaign contributions by businesses, unions, and professional organizations.

Chambers of Commerce

A chamber of commerce is an association of business professionals who work to improve their city's commercial climate and to publicize its attractions. Above all, chambers of commerce serve as boosters of local business growth. State chambers of commerce and, on a national scale, the U.S. Chamber of Commerce, help guide local chambers and speak for business interests before state and federal government. According to the Center for Public Integrity, the U.S. Chamber of Commerce, one of the most powerful lobbying organizations in Washington, D.C., spent almost $530 million on lobbying activities between 1998 and 2009. (The American Medical Association, the second most aggressive spender, invested less than half of that amount in lobbying efforts.) In 2008–2009, the U.S. Chamber of Commerce concentrated its lobbying efforts on opposing climate change legislation. It has also opposed healthcare legislation. According to a report in *The Financial Times*, the U.S. Chamber of Commerce spent $37 million in the first nine months of 2009 opposing healthcare reform.

advocacy
GROUPS

a number of pressing issues affect communities to varying degrees—from social issues such as poverty, abortion, and racism, to threats such as epidemic diseases and environmental degradation. Organizations that fight for social causes can have significant effects on those issues, both positive and negative. For example, climate change currently has a prominent place on the public agenda, primarily because of vigorous campaigns conducted by environmental organizations. By advocating for recycling, eliminating toxic waste sites, purifying the air and water, and preserving natural resources, such organizations strongly influence our collective conscience.

Advocacy groups include activist groups such as Greenpeace and People for the Ethical Treatment of Animals (PETA) and social issue organizations such as the National Rifle Association (NRA) and American Family Association (AFA). They advocate to promote their own causes, but may be perceived as lobbying for the good of the whole society. The positions such groups espouse often come in conflict with the views of other advocacy groups, however. For example, the AFA frequently expresses views that clash with those of the Gay and Lesbian Alliance Against Defamation (GLAAD).

The principal ways in which advocacy groups work to achieve their goals are lobbying, litigation, mass demonstrations, boycotts, reconciliation, and public education. Some of these organizations work relatively quietly through lobbying or reconciliation. Others are stridently confrontational, using more hardcore tactics such as litigation or mass demonstrations to advance their goals.

Activist Groups

Greenpeace, an organization that operates in 41 countries including the United States, is perhaps the best known of the confrontational groups. With 2.8 million members, Greenpeace is second in size to the much less flamboyant National Wildlife Foundation among environmental groups. Recently contributions to Greenpeace have declined; so has the group's political influence. However, the movement of which this group is a part remains vital. Television viewers are familiar with the daredevil efforts of some members in small boats to stop nuclear warships and whaling vessels. Christian activist groups also sometimes adopt a confrontational tack. The Southern Baptist Convention mounted an aggressive boycott of Disney corporation and all of its subsidiaries in protest of sex and violence in Disney entertainment releases.

Social Issue Organizations

Social issue organizations are similar to activist groups in structure, but often have more broadly defined social and behavioral goals. Mothers Against Drunk Driving (MADD) is one such group. Social issue organizations are often very visible and politically active. Right to Life, a very vocal opponent of abortion in the United States, spent slightly less than $500,000 on its lobbying efforts in 2009. This amount was down slightly from 2004, the year in which George W. Bush won his second election. Pro-choice groups such as Planned Parenthood spent a record $1.75 million on lobbying initiatives in 2008 during the run-up to the presidential election. Animal rights groups such

The Southern Baptist Convention's eight-year boycott of the Disney Corporation and all of its subsidiaries was mounted partially in response to "gay days" at the company's theme parks.

think Why do advocacy groups sometimes employ confrontational public relations tactics?

Advocacy Groups Face Off over Whole Foods CEO John Mackey's Position on Healthcare

IN AUGUST 2009, JOHN MACKEY, the CEO of Whole Foods, the largest retailer of organic and specialty foods in the United States, wrote an op-ed piece in the *Wall Street Journal* attacking proposed health reform legislation. Whole Foods customers, who tend toward the liberal or progressive end of the political spectrum as a group, were outraged. Mackey not only attacked the concept of a single-payer system by way of advocating unfettered free market principles, but also seemingly ridiculed the concept as "ObamaCare" and made light of social democracies by opening with a flippant line, a quote from noted conservative Margaret Thatcher.

their CEO's views, noting that they were his personal opinions based on faith in free market principles. Mackey himself tried to play the whole thing down, blogging about wanting to spark honest debate and civil discourse. To this end, Whole Foods did establish a forum on its website on which various constituents could express their views.

1 How did advocacy groups use this opportunity to further their own goals?

2 Which steps could Whole Foods take to defuse the controversy?

3 Are there risks to Whole Foods in aligning with conservative groups that have not been its traditional patrons? Do upside opportunities exist?

Advocacy groups such as the United Food and Commercial Union International (UFCW) and Single Payer Action called for an immediate boycott of Whole Foods. Within a week, the Facebook page "Boycott Whole Foods" had 13,000 fans. In response, conservative groups such as the National Tea Party Coalition organized "buycotts" in support of Mackey's position. Urged on by prominent right-wing commentators such as Glenn Beck, conservative activists gathered to support Mackey with their checkbooks.

According to commentary by Jaimy Lee in *PRWeek*, Jason Schechter of Burson-Marsteller questioned the wisdom of the Whole Foods executive publicizing an opinion that so "directly contradicts the viewpoint of its core customer base." Leslie Gaines-Ross of Weber Shandwick was equally puzzled as to why Mackey was "speaking up and speaking out and not really taking into consideration the views of his constituency." The Whole Foods board of directors and public relations department were slow to respond. Perhaps they were weighing their options very carefully. In the end, Whole Foods public relations staff and board of directors tried to distance the company from

as PETA at times resort to extremely confrontational tactics such as raiding animal research laboratories and splashing red paint symbolizing blood on people who wear fur. The group's campaign against the dairy industry takes a different tack, employing humor and parody on the website at www.milksucks.com.

Other groups, such as the American Family Association, press advertisers to drop sponsorship of television shows that they consider contrary to family values. They have been particularly active countering what they identify as "affirmation of homosexual behavior." An ongoing boycott of Pepsi-Cola was instigated

by the AFA when Pepsi denied the group's request that Pepsi "remain neutral in the culture war." As of November 2009, almost 400,000 supporters had signed an online petition in support of the boycott. The AFA continues to maintain a Facebook page entitled "Boycott Pepsi" with about 36,000 followers.

Advocacy Groups: STRATEGIES and TACTICS

Advocacy groups work in a variety of ways to achieve their goals.

LOBBYING. Much of this lobbying takes place at the state and local government levels. In just one example, approximately 150 organizations have campaigned for laws to forbid smoking in public places and to restrict the sale of tobacco around the country.

LITIGATION. Organizations may file suits seeking court rulings favorable to their projects or attempting to block unfavorable projects. The Sierra Club did so in a multiyear action that resulted in a decision by the U.S. Fish and Wildlife Service declaring the northern spotted owl an endangered species.

MASS DEMONSTRATIONS. Designed to showcase public support for a cause and in some cases to harass the operators of projects to which the groups object, mass demonstrations require elaborate public relations machinations. Organizers must obtain permits, inform the media, and arrange transportation, housing, programs, and crowd control.

BOYCOTTS. Some boycotts achieve easily identifiable results. Others stay in effect for years with little evident success. One success story occurred when the Rainforest Action Network boycotted Burger King for buying Central American beef raised in cleared rainforests. The fast-food chain agreed to stop such purchases.

RECONCILIATION. Some environmental organizations have achieved good results by cooperating with corporations to solve pollution problems. The Environmental Defense Fund joined a task force with McDonald's to deal with the fast-food chain's solid-waste problem, leading to a company decision to phase out its polystyrene packaging.

FUND-RAISING. With so many groups in the field, competition for donations is intense. Some professional fund-raisers believe that as a whole, nonprofit groups depend too much on direct mail and should place more emphasis on face-to-face contacts. Ironically, while some environmental groups advocate preservation of forests, they also create mountains of waste paper by sending out millions of solicitation letters to raise funds for their organization.

social service
ORGANIZATIONS

Social service organizations include social service, philanthropic, cultural, and religious groups that serve the public in various ways. These organizations require active and creative public relations programs.

Organizations frequently have dual roles—both service and advocacy—and serve the needs of individuals, families, and society in many ways. Prominent national organizations of this type are Goodwill Industries, the American Red Cross, the Boy Scouts and Girl Scouts of America, and the YMCA. Their advocacy is rooted in a sense of social purpose and the betterment of society as a whole. Local chapters carry out national programs. Service clubs such as the Rotary Club, Kiwanis Club, Lions Club, and Exchange Club raise significant amounts of money for charitable projects. The New York Philharmonic, Metropolitan Museum of Art, and Southern Baptist Convention, among many others, serve the interests of the community, while advocating for their own existence.

Philanthropic Foundations

Hundreds of tax-free foundations in the United States are collectively responsible for approximately 9 percent of all charitable giving in this country. Money to establish a foundation is typically provided by a wealthy individual or family, a group of contributors, an organization, or a corporation. The foundation's capital is invested, and earnings from the investments are distributed as grants to qualified applicants.

In addition to large, highly visible national foundations, which make grants to a variety of causes, smaller organizations such as the Susan G. Komen Breast Cancer Foundation, the Annenberg Foundation, and the Avon Foundation have become quite well known. Many smaller foundations—some of them extremely important in their specialized fields—distribute critical funds for research, education, public performances, displays, and similar purposes. Most of these organizations

> **"Seeing a problem resolved is extraordinarily gratifying."**
>
> Evelyn Lauder, founder of the Breast Cancer Research Foundation, which has raised more than $250 million since its inception in 1993

port ongoing fund-raising, present many opportunities for public relations campaigns.

Religious Organizations

The mission of organized religion, as perceived by many faiths today, includes much more than holding weekly worship services and underwriting parochial schools. Churches distribute charity, conduct personal guidance programs, provide leadership on moral and ethical issues in their communities, and operate social centers where diverse groups gather.

Public relations goals vary depending on the purposes of social service organizations. In general, nonprofit social service organizations design their public relations to achieve the following objectives:

- Develop public awareness of their missions and activities
- Encourage individuals to use their services
- Recruit and train volunteer workers
- Obtain operating funds

Most cultural institutions have in-house divisions of public relations and marketing, but others, such as the Getty Museum and the New York Philharmonic, employ outside agencies for these purposes.

not only dispense money, but also engage in numerous fund-raising activities to collect money for foundation efforts.

think — How is corporate giving a win/win situation for communities and corporations?

Cultural Organizations

Generating interest and participation in the cultural aspects of life often is the responsibility of nonprofit organizations in the United States. So, too, in many instances, is the operation of libraries; musical organizations, such as symphony orchestras; and museums of art, history, and natural sciences. Such institutions frequently receive at least part of their income from government sources; in fact, many are operated outright by the government. But even government-operated cultural institutions such as the Smithsonian Institution depend on private support to raise supplementary funds. Cuts to government programs that subsidize the arts at the state and federal levels have caused many affected organizations to turn to private supporters with increased urgency. Not surprisingly, then, cultural organizations have a great need for public relations professionals. Their constant efforts to publicize exhibitions, performances, and events, as well as to sup-

Social Service Organizations: STRATEGIES and TACTICS

PUBLICITY. The news media provide well-organized channels for stimulating public interest in nonprofit organizations and are receptive to newsworthy material from them. Public relations practitioners should look for unusual or appealing personal stories

CREATION OF EVENTS. Events make news and attract crowds and are another way to increase public awareness. Such activities might include an open house in a new hospital wing or a concert by members of the local symphony orchestra for an audience of blind children.

USE OF SERVICES. Closely tied to increasing overall public awareness are efforts to induce individuals and families to use an organization's services. Written and spoken material designed to attract should emphasize ease of participation and privacy of services in matters of health, financial aid, and family.

CREATION OF EDUCATIONAL MATERIALS. Because a brochure often provides a first impression of an organization, it should be visually appealing and simply written, and should contain basic information as well as answer the reader's obvious questions. Organizations also strive to design logos, or symbols, that help make their materials memorable to the public. Increasingly, an organization's website is its "front door."

NEWSLETTERS. Another basic piece of printed material is a news bulletin, usually generated monthly or quarterly, aimed at members, the news media, and a carefully composed list of other interested parties. In addition to the publication and distribution of brochures explaining an organization's objectives, periodic newsletters distributed to opinion leaders are a quiet but effective way to tell an organization's story. Today, an increasing number of organizations are choosing to distribute newsletters online via listservs or social networking sites.

health
ORGANIZATIONS

there are two types of organizations in the health sector. The first type is hospitals, some of which are nonprofit organizations and some of which are for-profit businesses. Because hospitals sell a product (improved health), parallels exist between their public relations objectives and those of other corporations. They focus on four major publics: patients and their families, physicians and medical staff, news media, and the community as a whole. Administrators and their public relations personnel involve themselves in public affairs and legislation because they operate under a maze of government regulations; and stress consumer relations, which involves keeping patients and their families satisfied, as well as seeking new clients. Hospitals produce publications and publicity for both external and internal audiences. They also have another need that other corporate public relations practitioners don't handle—the development and nurturing of volunteer networks.

The second type of organization comprises private and government health agencies, which serve the public interest by providing health care, funding for health initiatives, and oversight. The most familiar health agencies are administered at the federal and state levels, such as Medicare, Medicaid, and the Children's Health Insurance Program (CHIP). Nonprofit health agencies range from national organizations such as

the American Heart Association, the American Cancer Society, and the National Multiple Sclerosis Society to smaller groups such as the Conservation, Food & Health Foundation in Boston.

The Department of Health and Human Services (HHS) is the federal government's leading health agency. It provides more than 300 programs, including emergency preparedness, Head Start for preschoolers, maternity and infant programs, disease prevention and immunizations, and insurance programs such as Medicaid and Medicare. Divisions include major initiatives such as the Food and Drug Administration, Centers for Disease Control and Prevention (CDC), and the National Institutes for Health (NIH), as well as smaller services such as the Administration on Aging and the Agency for Healthcare Research and Quality.

In addition to federal health initiatives, each state has a statewide health agency. Within the states, many regions, counties, and cities provide taxpayer-supported health services as well.

HHS provides funds and guidance to state and local health agencies. With the assistance of private nonprofit foundations, they provide a coordinated network of free or low-cost health services.

> think — **Which publics make up the audience for hospital public relations efforts?**

> **Public relations professionals working for health agencies deal with an enormous amount of public information, and they need to be prepared to handle crisis situations.**

Public relations professionals should build working relationships with these agencies not only to secure funding but also to build coalitions for health campaigns or programs. Public relations professionals must understand both the technical aspects of a public health risk such as a chemical spill or disease outbreak and the needs of the community in order to facilitate effective dialogue between emergency responders, affected members of the public, and the media.

Public relations professionals who specialize in health communication have an impact on all Americans who are concerned about both their personal health risks and threats to their financial security from burdensome medical costs. Essentially, health communicators strive to convey health information, prevention measures, and emergency response information as a means of reducing health risks. Because personal health and the related costs are so important to Americans, health issues and related policies often are leading stories in the news. Medical breakthroughs, the introduction of high-profile drugs such as Viagra, the graying of 76 million baby boomers, and the ongoing controversies over health costs, medical malpractice reform, and claims of excessive profits for doctors and healthcare companies guarantee robust opportunities to practice sophisticated public relations.

Health Campaigns: Strategies and Tactics

Health campaigns to prevent and respond to diseases, and to promote health and quality of life, began applying social marketing practices in the late 1980s. A number of public relations strategies and techniques have been implemented for these initiatives, mainly by federal and state governments and private health agencies.

Campaigns to promote breast cancer awareness, the importance of diet and exercise, and encouraging screenings for colon cancer are examples of recent health promotion efforts sponsored by government and nonprofit health organizations. The American College of Emergency Physicians (ACEP), for instance, sponsors a Risky Drinking Campaign, an alcohol awareness program; Failure Is Not an Option, a project to alert the public to the symptoms of heart failure; and the Partnership for Anthrax Vaccine Education, a partnership with George Washington University to provide the latest information about vaccination initiatives. In addition to having altruistic motives, the ACEP sponsors these campaigns as a public relations tool to build goodwill and a positive public image.

Health information and advice on the Internet has grown exponentially over the past several years. For example, the National Cancer Institute has a single database with more than 650 articles on cancer risk. According to *O'Dwyer's PR Services Report*, 55 percent of the U.S. adult population has online access, and 86 percent of them use the Internet to find health-related information. Some experts estimate that nearly 25 percent of all web searches are health related. Public relations companies now produce video and audio programming on the web for their healthcare clients, providing doctors, medical reporters, investors, and patients with medical and pharmaceutical information.

Go RED for Women

There is something to be said for keeping the message simple and concentrating on excellent execution. This is true of the Go Red for Women campaign launched in 2007 by the American Heart Association. The goal—to educate women of all backgrounds about the dangers of heart disease—was clearly defined. All campaign messages were designed to combat misconceptions about the risk. By focusing on "untold stories" of women who have been affected by heart disease, the campaign was at once compelling, educational, and noncontroversial. The campaign, which won the Nonprofit Campaign of the Year award from *PRWeek* in 2009, continued into 2010.

Go Red for Women was based on research showing that women tend to respond to information presented by peers. Personal stories of loss and survival from "women like me" were disseminated in the hopes of encouraging participation. To complement personal narratives gleaned from ordinary women, Marie Osmond added her voice as celebrity spokesperson.

The campaign relied on a variety of media. Social media such as Twitter and Facebook were important components, as was the common website to which these sites linked. The site witnessed approximately 75,000 visitors per month. A compelling feature of the Go Red for Women campaign was a participatory-casting call for women who had suffered from heart disease to share their stories.

The result was a measurable change in perception. Whereas just 57 percent of women acknowledged the risk of heart disease at the onset of the campaign, 65 percent of women knew that it was a leading cause of death among women by 2009. By March 2009, Go Red for Women had reached 70 percent of its $200 mil-

lion fund-raising goal. The campaign was praised by a *PRWeek* judge as "an effective, integrated campaign that raised awareness." In the days of guerrilla marketing and viral campaigns, Go Red for Women was far from cutting edge. What it lacked in novelty, however, it more than made up for in efficacy.

educational
ORGANIZATIONS

educational institutions include programs that provide child-care, instruction for primary and secondary students, colleges, universities, trade schools, and schools for special-needs students. These organizations are often licensed or regulated by state and federal agencies, as in the case of primary and secondary schools, or by private accreditation bodies such as the Southern Association of Colleges and Schools. Most educational institutions have nonprofit status. Educational institutions demonstrate a staggering array of organizational structures and functions. Like other nonprofit organizations, educational institutions are often supported to some degree by government agencies, but also usually depend on donations from alumni or other donors for supplemental support.

Colleges and Universities

Higher education is big business in the United States. California, the most populous state with 36 million residents, spends $20 billion annually on four-year public colleges and universities. Another $6 billion is spent on two-year community colleges. Key publics for colleges and universities include faculty and staff, students, alumni and other donors, federal, state, and local governments, local community members, and prospective students.

Higher education is also a business that has millions of customers—namely, students. In the United States, almost 17.5 million students are enrolled at more than 4,000 colleges and universities. Almost every one of these institutions has personnel working in such activities as public relations, marketing communications, and fund-raising.

In large universities, the vice president for development and university relations (or a person with a similar title) supervises the office of development, which includes a division for alumni relations, and an office of public relations; these functions are often combined in smaller institutions. Development and alumni personnel seek to enhance the prestige and financial support of the institution. Among other activities, they conduct meetings and seminars, publish newsletters and magazines, and arrange tours of the campus. Their primary responsibilities are to

think When do universities and colleges compete outside their sporting arenas?

build alumni loyalty and generate funding from private sources.

The public relations director, generally aided by one or more chief assistants, supervises the information news service, publications, and special events. Depending on the size of the institution,

APPLY YOUR KNOWLEDGE

WHAT WOULD YOU DO?

Your university has a potential public relations problem. The campus is midway through a ten-year contract with Coca-Cola to be the exclusive soft drink provider of beverages in vending machines, at the student union, and in the residence halls. The contract is worth $1.4 million annually, and the university uses the revenue to pay for a variety of academic and campus life programs.

Coca-Cola, however, has been under attack by activist student groups at other universities for labor and human rights abuses at its bottling plants abroad. In addition, the global giant is accused of damaging the environment in India by exploiting and polluting scarce water resources around its bottling plants. Students have protested against the company's presence on some campuses, carrying signs and chanting slogans such as "Kick Coke off campus." Some institutions, such as Rutgers University and New York University, have, indeed, kicked Coke off campus.

Imagine that Coca-Cola has now offered to renegotiate the agreement with your university on slightly more favorable terms. In opposition to the student groups that are protesting, other groups are organizing a "buycott" to support the move and the revenue it would generate. Analyze the various public relations issues that arise. How should the contract be presented to students and to the public? How can public relations strategies be used to mediate disagreements?

> **"When I say I'm a lobbyist, some people look at me as if I need a shower. It's a new business with the universities, and some people think it's a dirty business. But nothing's dirtier than not having resources."**
>
> Robert Dickens, coordinator of government relations, University of Nevada–Reno

perhaps a dozen or more employees will carry out functions supporting these efforts, including writing, photography, graphic design, broadcasting, and computer networking. The most visible aspect of a university public relations program is its news bureau. An active bureau produces hundreds of news releases, photographs, and special columns and articles for the print and other media.

To carry out their complex functions, top development and public relations specialists must be a part of the management team of the college or university.

Fund-raising has increased dramatically at most public and private universities in recent years as costs have risen and allocations from state legislatures and federal agencies have shrunk dramatically. Total nongovernmental financial support for education was $40.9 billion in 2008, according to Giving USA, a unit of the Giving Institute, which publishes an annual tally of charitable contributions. This amount represents 13 percent of the total charitable giving in the United States, which was $307 billion in 2008. In addition to annual operating fund campaigns, universities are increasingly conducting long-range capital campaigns to raise large amounts of money.

Elementary and Secondary Schools

Competition among districts for students—particularly given new initiatives focused on charter schools development and voucher programs to subsidize private school education—has led many school systems to confront the need for strategic outreach plans to communicate with their constituents, which include students, parents, teachers, voters, and taxpayers. Adding to this pressure, various ballot initiatives in many states have made it necessary for individual schools to present a good case to the public about their achievements to justify additional funding, attract students, and maintain their reputations in the district. A handful of individual schools—mostly private— now have public information officers. Otherwise, public relations are the responsibility of principals, teachers, and guidance counselors, who are often advised regarding contentious issues by school district staff. Parent–Teacher Associations (PTA) frequently assume public relations duties as well, serving as boosters for the school by giving media interviews, generating news stories, and sponsoring events.

Individual elementary and secondary schools often publish newsletters heralding their achievements. Many schools in the country also have websites that provide updates about events, performance data, personnel, student accomplishments, team scores, and so forth. Websites are also a good way for schools to provide links to assignments and allow the school to interact with parents and students.

School Districts

Public relations initiatives that affect the entire district are typically administered at the district level. This is generally true of public schools, but similar coordination takes place among parochial schools that are part of a larger organizational body such as an archdiocese. Public information officers, and administrators who serve that function in smaller districts, are utilized by most school districts in the United States. This person is typically the face of the school district to the press and public, or the advisor to those who interact with the public. In the best cases, his or her work complements and coordinates public relations functions, and often builds on the work of individual schools.

School districts have also reached out to public relations firms for help. For example, the South Bay School district in Campbell, California, hired a public relations firm in late 2007. According to superintendent Rhoda Farber, the district hired Mackenzie Communications, a San Francisco–based public relations company, to "share the good things that are happening in our district, our facilities, our faculty, and enable us to recruit and retain the best possible teachers we can for our students." Mackenzie helped the district place "good news" stories in various media outlets. The move drew some criticism from the community, however, because taxpayer money was used to fund what was essentially a promotional campaign.

Crisis communications is another area of public relations undertaken by school districts. The most famous example of effective communications during a crisis came in the wake of the shooting death of twelve students at Columbine High School in Colorado. The district's skillful handling of media and community relations earned it a Silver Anvil Award from the PRSA.

What Are the Basic Purposes and Functions of Public Relations in Nonprofit, Health, and Education Organizations? p. 372

- Nonprofit organizations have been given tax-exempt status because their primary goal is to enhance the well-being of their members or the human condition.
- Although a broad range of nonprofit organizations exist, all nonprofit, health, and education organizations create communications campaigns and programs, require a staff (including volunteers) to handle their work, and are involved in fund-raising.

What Role Does Public Relations Play in the Fund-Raising Efforts of Nonprofit Organizations? p. 374

- Fund-raising is a major public relations task in these groups and is a critical issue for nonprofit organizations.
- Depending on their mission and strategy, nonprofits may seek major donations from large corporations or foundations and smaller contributions from individuals. Recruiting volunteer labor is often crucial to make up for lack of operating funds and involve the community to reach the nonprofit's goals.

Which Public Relations Goals Do Advocacy Groups, Social Service Organizations, and Health and Educational Organizations Pursue? p. 378

- Public relations goals for advocacy groups, service groups, and philanthropic, cultural, and religious organizations include developing public awareness, getting individuals to use their services, creating educational materials, recruiting volunteers, and fund-raising.
- In health organizations, public relations professionals help communicate information about medical advances, the availability of health services, and potential health risks. Public relations for hospitals focus on enhancing the public's perception of the institution and marketing its services.
- The audiences for education institution communications include alumni, students, prospective students, faculty and staff, government, and the general public.

Which Public Relations Tactics and Strategies Do Nonprofit, Health, and Education Organizations Rely on? p. 383

- Advocacy group efforts include lobbying, litigation, mass demonstrations, boycotts, reconciliation, and public education.
- Foundations, nontraditional schools, communities, and membership organizations frequently support existing educational institutions or initiate their own programs.
- Health campaigns to prevent and respond to diseases, and to promote health and quality of life, started to apply social marketing practices in the late 1980s.
- Public relations at colleges and universities involve both development/fund-raising and enhancing the prestige of the institution.

1. What are the differences and similarities among trade associations, labor unions, professional associations, and chambers of commerce?

2. Identify public relations strategies and tactics that advocacy groups use to further their causes.

3. Name and describe some types of social service agencies.

4. What motivates people to serve as volunteer workers?

5. Describe commonly used types of fund-raising.

6. What are the major roles of public relations professionals in health organizations?

7. List some components of successful health campaigns.

8. The non-profit sector has job opportunities in organizations ranging from membership groups to advocacy causes, healthcare, and even universities. What of these organizations do you think you might prefer to work in?

9. With which primary public does a sound university public relations program begin? What other constituents must be addressed when designing a higher education public relations campaign?

the
THINKSPOT
www.thethinkspot.com

>credits

Text Credits

Luckovich cartoon. By permission of Mike Luckovich and Creators Syndicate, Inc.

Cartoon—"Blogger's Dilemma"—"To post . . . or not to post. That is the question." © 2004 Cox & Forkum. www.coxandforkum.com. Reprinted with permission.

Hakone—Madame Butterfly image; Artwork by Kathy Toy. Reprinted with permission of Hakone Estate and Gardens, Saratoga, CA.

Martin Luther King, Jr. Library flyer © Dr. Martin Luther King, Jr. Library, San José State University. Reprinted with permission.

Two Gallup graphs—Why and How We Give; Source: From Dec. 19, 2008. "Despite Economy, Charitable Donors, Volunteers Keep Giving," by Lydia Saad, p. 1. Reprinted with permission of Gallup.

Photo Credits

Chapter 1
2–3: Klaus Tiedge/Blend/Photolibrary; **4–5:** Red Chopsticks/ Photolibrary; **5:** (tr)Tomislav Forgo/Used under license from Shutterstock.com; (c) Matt Trommer/Used under license from Shutterstock.com; **6:** John Terence Turner/Alamy; **7:** Mike Margol/ PhotoEdit; **9:** Ron Edmonds/AP Photo; **11:** Courtesy of the Charleston Animal Society; **12:** FRANCK FIFE/AFP/Getty Images; **13:** Harry Vorsteher/PhotoLibrary; **15:** (l) Hans Neleman/The Image Bank/Getty Images; (r) Rubberball/Jupiter Images; **16:** Used under license from Shutterstock.com; **17:** (bl) PARAMOUNT/THE KOBAL COLLECTION/Picture Desk; (tr) Stephen Coburn/Used under license on Shutterstock.com; **18:** (t) Vladimir Sretenovic/Used under license from Shutterstock.com; (b) Roberto Brosan/Time Life Pictures/Getty Images; **20:** Ron Edmonds/AP Photo.

Chapter 2
24–25: LajosRepasi/istockphoto.com; **26:** Stefan Kiefer/ imagebroker.net/PhotoLibrary; **27:** (t) Christopher Futcher/Used under license from Shutterstock.com; (b) tracy boulian/The Plain Dealer/Landov; **29:** LWA-Dann Tardif/Flirt Collection/ PhotoLibrary; **30:** Stephen Coburn/Used under license from Shutterstock.com; **31:** AP Photo/Dan Goodman; **32:** aldegonde/ Used under license from Shutterstock.com; **33:** Pakhnyushcha/Used under license from Shutterstock.com; **36:** (l) Joselito Briones/ Istockphoto; (r) webphotographeer/Istockphoto; **37:** Monkey Business Images/Used under license from Shutterstock.com; **39:** NetPics/Alamy; **40:** LWA-Dann Tardif/Flirt Collection/ PhotoLibrary.

Chapter 3
42–43: REUTERS/Korean Federation for Environmental Movement/ Handout; **44:** JOHN GRESS/Reuters/Corbis; **46:** Z.Legacy.Corporate Digital Archive/Pearson Education; **47:** (t) AP Photo/Jason Straziuso; (b) AP Photo/Tony Gutierrez; **49:** (tl) Alex Staroseltsev/Used under license from Shutterstock.com; (tr) Danylchenko Iaroslav/Used under license from Shutterstock.com; (b) Spiderstock/istockphoto.com; **51:** Gary Ombler/Dorling Kindersley; **52:** H-Gall/iStockphoto.com; **53:** AP Photo/Carolyn Kaster; **54:** Peter French/Pacific Stock/ PhotoLibrary; **55:** AP Photo/Steven Day; **56:** AP Photo/Gerald Herbert; **57:** Alex Staroseltsev/Used under license from Shutterstock .com; **59:** qingqing/Used under license from Shutterstock.com; **60:** AP Photo/Steven Day.

Chapter 4
64–65: Corbis; **66:** ©PHOTOPQR/L'EST REPUBLICAIN Alexandre MARCHI. ARCHEOLOGIE—EGYPTE—GRANDE BRETAGNE—BRITISH MUSEUM—LONDON/Newscom; **67:** Library of Congress Prints and Photographs Division Washington, D.C. [LC-USZC4-3170]; **68:** Bettmann/Corbis; **69:** (t) David J. & Janice L. Frent Collection/Historical/Corbis; (b) Getty Images; **70:** (t) National Museum of American History, Smithsonian Institution; (b) Bettmann/Corbis; **71:** © 2004 Metropolitan Transit Authority; **72:** Bettmann/Corbis; **73:** Carin Baer/AMC/Everett Collection; **75:** (t) AP Photo/File; (b) Richard Levine/Alamy; **77:** webphotographeer/ iStockphoto.com; **79:** mehmetcan/Used under license from Shutterstock.com; **84:** Corbis.

Chapter 5
86–87: FoodCollection/SuperStock; **88:** Bettmann/Corbis; **89:** g_studio/ istockphoto; **92:** AP Photo/Mark Lennihan; **93:** AP Photo/Paul Sakuma; **97:** (t) AP Photo/Pablo Martinez Monsivais; (cr) Barry Lewis/Alamy; **98:** Alexander Dashewsky/Used under license from Shutterstock.com; **99:** Dadang Tri/Reuters/Landov; **101:** Rahav Segev/WireImage/Getty Images; **104:** Barry Lewis/Alamy.

Chapter 6
108–109: Leanne Pedersen/Masterfile; **111:** Hill Street Studios/ Blend/Photolibrary; **113:** Marty Inc/age fotostock/PhotoLibrary; **114:** Copyright 2010 LexisNexis, a division of Reed Elsevier Inc. All Rights Reserved. LexisNexis and the Knowledge Burst logo are registered trademarks of Reed Elsevier Properties Inc. and are used with the permission of LexisNexis.; **116:** Jeff Greenberg/PhotoEdit; **117:** David Young-Wolff/PhotoEdit; **118:** (t) Nadia Borowski Scott/San Diego Union-Tribune/Zuma Press; (c) asiseeit/iStockphoto.com; (b) Beau Lark/Corbis; **123:** Bill Bachman/Alamy; **124:** AP Photo/Damian Dovarganes; **126:** J Lightfoot/Robert Harding Travel/Photolibrary; **129:** Stockbyte/Getty Images; **130:** Bill Bachman/Alamy.

Chapter 7
132–133: Christophe Testi/Used under license from Shutterstock.com; **134:** AP Photo/Jay LaPrete; **137:** (top to bottom) David Young-Wolff/ PhotoEdit; Chris Haston/NBC/Everett Collection; Nicholas Roberts/The New York Times/Redux Pictures; AP Photo/Chris O'Meara; **140:** (t) Transtock/Terra/Corbis; (b) STEPHEN SHAVER/ UPI/Landov; **142:** Robert Caplin/Bloomberg/Getty Images; **144:** acilo/ istockphoto.com; **146:** kmaassrock/istockphoto.com; **148:** Photo by Ken McKay/Rex USA, courtesy Everett Collection; **150:** LDF/ istockphoto.com; **154:** Christophe Testi/Used under license from Shutterstock.com.

Chapter 8
158–159: REUTERS/Danny Moloshok; **161:** Kathy deWitt/Alamy; **162:** Jim Young/Reuters/Landov; **163:** (Bono) Dimitrios Kambouris/ WireImage/Getty Images; (African-American female) Sandy Jones/istockphoto.com; (older, Caucasian male) DNF-Style Photography/Used under license from Shutterstock.com; (younger Caucasian male) PhotoInc/istockphoto.com; (older, African-American male) Rob Marmion/Used under licence from Shutterstock.com; **164:** AP Photo/Holloway Family; **165:** Ho/Reuters/Landov; **166:** Abbas/Magnum Photos; **167:** Mike Simons/Corbis News/Corbis; **169:** Daniel Morduchowicz, 2005, Provided courtesy of Brave New

>index

Social media (*Continued*)
to, 236; Facebook,
237–238; fundraising,
378–379; health care
reform, 160; MySpace,
237–238; Phoenix Suns
basketball team and,
227–228; podcasts,
241–243; rise of, 233;
texting, 241; Twitter,
241–243; web 3.0, 243;
wikis, 117, 241–243;
YouTube, 238–240
Social networking, 7, 31, 79;
See also Social media
Social science research skills, 29
Social service organizations,
383–384
Society for Professional
Journalists, 185
Society of American Travel
Writers (SATW), 343
Soft data, 113
Solid Relations, 98
Sony Entertainment, 219, 281
Sony Pictures, 197
Sorrell, Martin, 99
Sosa, Sammy, 340
Soul Food Recipes, 206
Sound bites, 207, 260
Source credibility, 173–174
Sources/questions, as step in
management by objectives,
123
South Africa, 295
South Bay School district, 388
South by Southwest music
festival, 101
South Carolina Department of
Parks, Recreations, and
Tourism, 215
"South Carolina Is so Gay!," 215
South Dakota Office of
Tourism, 241
Southern Baptist Convention, 381
Southern Christian Leadership
Conference (SCLC), 218
Speakers, at meetings, 273
Speaker's Network, 274
Special events, 11
Speedo, 321–322
Spokesperson, challenges of, 93
Sponsorship management, 339
Sports publicity, 338–340
Sproul, Tim, 238
SRI International, 171
St. Hillaire, Karen, 232
Stacks, Don, 116
Stafford, Ventphis, 215
Stand Up Speak Up
campaign, 205
Stanford, Allen, 207
Stansberry, Frank R., 151
Staples, 187
Star Trek, 338
Starbucks, 195, 230, 241

StarCite, 279
Starck, Ken, 168
Starr, Ringo, 336
State Department, 302
State governments, 357–358
*Statistical Abstract of the United
States*, 114, 115
Statistics, 175
Statue of Liberty, 321
Staycation trend, 16
"Stealing thunder," 47
Steele, Charles, 218
Stevenson, Veronis Suhler, 5
Stonecipher, Harry, 190
Stonewall riots, 215
Stop Huntingdon Animal
Cruelty, 207
Stop Loss, 355
Stowe, Harriet Beecher, 69
Strategic communication, 17–19
Strategic conflict management, 46
Strategic phase, of conflict
management, 50, 70
"Strategic Planning Model for
Public Relations," 122
Strategic positioning, 53–54
The Strategist, 18, 81
Strategy, 111–112, 127
Strategy options, in issues
management, 52
StrategyOne, 304
Structionalist perspective, 77
Structure, of messages, 175
Structured capital campaign, 377
Student Monitor, 237
Subaru, 213
Subservient chicken website,
322–323
The Subway Sun, 71
Success, measurement of, 112
Sudan, 303
Suggestions for action, 173
Super Bowl ads, 7
Supervisor level positions, 32
Surveys, 116, 175
"Sustainers and survivors," 172
Swine flu: *See* H1N1 infection
Symbols, 140
Symmetric communication
model, 137
Symptoms of Withdrawal
(Lawford), 173
Systematic tracking, 148–149

Tactics, 81, 199
Tactics, public relations, 127,
243, 248–265; interviews,
70, 116–117, 256, 264,
334–335; media advisories,
253–254; media party and
media tour, 257–258; news
conferences, 70, 256–257;
news releases, 250–253,
335; personal appearances,
263–264; product

placements, 264–265, 320,
337; radio, 259–261;
television, 261–262
Talent, Jim, 356
Talk shows, 263–264
Tanenhaus, Sam, 341
Tankard, James, 165
Tappening, 51
Target audience, 116, 124, 208,
343–344
Target stores, 44
Tatomkhulu-Xhosa, 374
Taylor, Maureen, 76
Taylor, William, 139
"Tea Partay" video, 240
"Tea parties," 361
"Technician mentality," 82
Technorati, 234
Teddy bears, 70
Telemundo, 216
Telephone solicitations, 378
Telephone surveys, 120
Telethons, 378
Television, 175, 216, 221,
261–262
Television industry, 336
"A Terrific Budget-Stretching
Meal," 172
Terrorism, 342
Testimonial propaganda, 171
Testimonials, 197
Texas, 358
Text mining, 149
Texting, 241
Thailand, 294, 297
"The People's Choice"
(Lazarsfeld et al), 162
"Think tanks," 82
Third-party blogs, 235
Thomson Financial, 232
Threat appraisal model, 48
Thumb, Tom, 68
Thurber, James A., 361
Tierney Communications, 99
Time magazine, 76, 170,
186–187, 219, 362
Timeline, for a banquet, 275
The Times of London, 309
Timetable, as element of PR
plan, 127–128
Timing, of messages, 175–176
TNS Media
Intelligence/Cymfony, 237
Today Show, 7, 127, 238, 263,
285, 320
"Today's Military," 355
The Tonight Show with Jay Leno, 7
Tony the Tiger, 338
Toth, Elizabeth, 37, 77
Tourism in times of crisis, 344
Tourism promotion, 358, 359
Trade associations, 379–380
Trade shows, 280–282

Trademark infringement,
194–195
Trademark law, 194–196
Tradeshow Week, 280
Traditional media, 7
Tranformers: Revenge of the Fallen,
355
Transfer propaganda, 171
TransMedia, 187
Transparency, 79, 186
Travel & Leisure, 344
Travel libel, 190
Travel packages, 343
Travel promotion, 342–345
Travel writers, and "freebies," 343
Travelocity, 125
Treasury Department, 218
Trialability, 143
Troubled Assets Relief Program
(TARP), 309
Trucost, 169
True Colors Foundation, 378
True Experience, 172
Turkey, 303
Turkish tourism campaign, 126,
129, 149
Tween market, 208
Twentieth Century Fox, 197
Twitter, 31, 79, 149, 241–243; as
a channel, 175; Domino's
Pizza, 239; health care
reform, 160; and Hispanic
audiences, 217; Phoenix
Suns basketball team and,
227; sports promotion,
339; women and, 212
Two-step flow theory, 162
Two-way asymmetric model,
74, 76
Two-way symmetric model,
74, 76
Tyco, 207
Tye, Larry, 72
Tylenol tampering crisis, 75, 92
Tyson Foods, 315

Ukraine, 295
Uncertainty avoidance, 296
Uncle Tom's Cabin (Stowe), 69
Unilever, 284, 324
United Airlines, 320, 355
United Arab Emirates, 295
United Food and Commercial
Union International
(UFCW), 382
United Health Foundation
(UHF), 146
United Mine Workers, 70
United National Educational,
Scientific, and Cultural
Organization
(UNESCO), 324
United Nations, 301
United Parcel Service (UPS),
26, 125